REPRESENTING

TEXAS

A COMPREHENSIVE HISTORY OF

U.S. AND CONFEDERATE

SENATORS AND REPRESENTATIVES FROM TEXAS

BEN R. GUTTERY

FIRST EDITION
Copyright © 2008
By Ben R. Guttery
Published in the United States of America
ALL RIGHTS RESERVED.
1 2 3 4 5 6 7 8 9
ISBN-10: 1-4196-7884-1
ISBN-13: 978-1-4196-7884-4

Visit www.booksurge.com to order additional copies.

Cover photo: 1960 Texas delegation. See page 24 for names.

Library of Congress Cataloging-in-Publication Data

Guttery, Ben R.
    Representing Texas : a comprehensive history of U.S. and Confederate
senators and representatives from Texas / Ben R. Guttery.—1st ed.

    Includes bibliographical references.
    ISBN 978-1-4196-7884-4
    1. Legislators—United States—Biography. 2. Texas—Politics
and government. 3. United States. Congress. Senate—Biography.
4. United States. Congress. House—Biography. 5. Texas—Biography. I.
Title
E176.G95 2008
328.73'092'2764–dc21   2001023278

CONTENTS

ACKNOWLEDGMENTS

This work would not have been possible without the generous contributions of a number of people. These include:

★ The Texas State Historical Association and their fine work *The New Handbook of Texas*, which generally provided a starting point for my research.
★ Michael Dubin for sharing his expertise on congressional elections.
★ Lynda Welch for sharing the photos of her late husband, June, had collected. June Welch wrote a number of popular books about Texas.
★ The sitting congressional delegation from Texas for their help in verifying information and supplying photos.
★ The former members of Congress from Texas for their work in verifying information and supplying photos. Thanks also to them for their role in creating this history.
★ The families of former members of Congress, including John V. Dowdy Jr., Helen Pickett Larsh, Earle Cabell Jr., Steve Grimes, Anne Thomas Lasater, Dan Sweeney, Molly Thornberry, and Mary Milford.
★ The *Texas Observer* for allowing me access to their files of photographs.
★ Ben Rogers, Edwin Cook, Maycie Mayfield, and Michael Holdridge of the Poage Library at Baylor University for updating the text, final editing, and publishing.

A number of others have helped in a variety of ways. Let me also thank Barry Brown, Senator Mike Moncrief, Larry Norris, Robert Platt, Chandler Robinson, Kirby Childress, D. B. Hardeman, Jerry Summers, and David Quintin.

Let me also thank the people at the Speaker Jim Wright Collection at Texas Christian University, the Center for American History at the University of Texas, the Special Collections at the University of Texas at Arlington, the Dallas and Local History Collection at the City of Dallas Public Library, the Genealogy and Local History Department of the Fort Worth Public Library, and the State Library and Archives.

A special thanks to my parents, who raised me to be interested in the world and shared so many of their beliefs with me.

A final thanks must go to my dear wife, Liz, who has accepted her husband's interest in history, writing, and everything else crazy.

INTRODUCTION

Politics in Texas has been called a contact sport. Texas has had a unique and colorful history of people representing the state in the United States Congress—the House and Senate—and in the Confederate Congresses. This book attempts to look into the lives of the men and women who have represented the state and the interests of the state on the national level. In almost every case, each individual is worthy of an entire publication, and indeed, some are represented by one, but the purpose here is simply to aid in the basic understanding of each individual.

This book details the professional career of each person who has served in the United States and Confederate Congress from Texas. Among the information provided are the congressman's full name, vital statistics such as birth date and place, death date and place, and burial location. Other information includes the offices held, either public or private. Those candidates whom the member of Congress defeated in the general election are also noted. All known political party affiliations and party changes are noted, as are educational, professional, and personal backgrounds. Photographs or drawings of each member are included, with four exceptions.

Following the bibliographical section are several important reference lists. This section includes a chronological list of U.S. senators by succession; U.S. representatives by district; representatives to the Confederate Congress, which includes delegates to the Confederate Provisional Congress, senators to the Confederate Congress, and representatives to the Confederate Congress; the composition of Confederate congressional districts by county; Confederate Congress session dates; U.S. Congress session dates; composition of U.S. congressional districts by county; legislative elections for U.S. senator; U.S. senator election returns; and U.S. representative election returns.

REPUBLIC OF TEXAS

Following the War for Independence with Mexico in 1836, Texas was a sovereign nation. During this time, the Republic formed a House and Senate and elected men to these posts. In the first election following Texas' independence, the citizens voted to join the United States. However, no treaty on annexation between Texas and the U.S. was negotiated during this time. The U.S. Congress did pass a resolution for the annexation of Texas into the United States of America. The state Constitutional Convention of 1845 agreed to accept annexation, and the ordinance was put up for a vote by the general population; it passed along with the new constitution. Both houses of the U.S. Congress accepted the state's constitution by resolution, and President Polk signed the resolution on December 29, 1845.

STATEHOOD

Following the signature by President Polk on the joint resolution from Congress regarding Texas' statehood, its powers as a state took effect on February 19, 1846. Texas would remain a state for just over fifteen years, until it seceded with the other southern states in 1861.

First Representatives

The first congressmen from Texas were elected during 1846. These four men, two senators and two representatives, would serve in the 29th Congress, which met from March 4, 1845, until March 3, 1847.

The two senators were chosen by the state legislature in early 1846. Texas' first U.S. senator was Thomas Rusk, who took office on March 26, 1846. He was followed four days later by Sam Houston. The length of their terms was set by a lottery. Houston received the shorter term, just under a year, which ended on March 3, 1847. Rusk received the longer term ending March 3, 1851.

The two representatives were chosen by popular election on March 30, 1846. The first U.S. representative was David Kaufman, who took office on June 1, 1846. Nine days later, he was followed by the second U.S. representative from Texas, Timothy Pilsbury. The men represented Texas' two congressional districts which were separated by the Trinity River. The 1st District was east of the Trinity River and the 2nd District was west of the river.

Secession

Following the election of Abraham Lincoln and the secession of North Carolina from the United States in 1861, numerous southern states vowed to take the same action. In Texas, the secession convention met and passed an ordinance of secession on February 1, 1861, and a declaration of causes the following day. The citizens voted and approved the ordinance. Prior to this, the provisional government of the Confederate States of America had accepted Texas as a state of the Confederacy on March 1, 1861. The secession convention in Austin accepted the Confederate statehood. Representatives were elected and sent to the Provisional Confederate Congress in Montgomery, Alabama. This congress would be followed by two others before the end of the war that met in Richmond, Virginia. There, they voted on the Confederate constitution and performed the same functions they had in Washington. Their efforts toward developing a new constitution were approved by the secession convention on March 23, 1861.

The U.S. senators from Texas at the time were Louis T. Wigfall and John Hemphill. They were both expelled from the U.S. Senate on July 11, 1861. The U.S. representatives at the time, John H. Reagan and Andrew Jackson Hamilton, had already left Washington. Reagan was appointed as postmaster general of the Confederacy and took an active role in government. Hamilton mostly sat out the war in New Orleans. He did not agree with secession and was made the U.S. military governor over Texas late in the war.

During the war, as before it, representatives were chosen by popular election, and senators were chosen by the legislature. The selection process mirrored that of the U.S. Constitution. Texas had a total of seven representatives at the Confederate Provisional Congress. For the following two congresses, Texas was allocated six congressional districts and therefore six representative seats in Congress. These districts generally ran in bands from the Rio Grande northward. Elections could be described as popularity contests between Democratic Party candidates. There were no provisions for soldiers from Texas to vote for their representatives.

The Texas delegation did not stand out in any way in the Confederate Congress. Members were generally interested in keeping the young men of the state from being drafted. In the second congress, Texas representatives were dismayed, tired of seeing the sons of the state killed in a war between easterners. To them, the state had simply become a source of troops, leather, and beef. (Oddly, none of the Texas delegation was born in the state.) About half of the Texas delegation began to break from President Davis. One called for Texas to secede from the Confederacy. The last meeting day of the last session was on March 18, 1865.

The Civil War ended in April 1865, although word was slow in reaching Texas. A state of peace with the southern states began on April 2, but the order was not issued for Texas until August 20.

Reconstruction

The period following the Civil War was especially difficult for the once rebellious southern states, including Texas. A military government was established in each state. Each state was required to ratify three amendments to the U.S. Constitution—the Thirteenth, Fourteenth, and Fifteenth—before they could be readmitted to the U.S. These amendments dealt with abolishing slavery (Thirteenth); limiting the powers of states and providing the Bill of Rights protection to citizens under state law, effectively creating a guarantee of "equal protection under the law" for all citizens of the United States (Fourteenth); and universal male suffrage (Fifteenth).

On November 30, 1869, an election was held for four of Texas' four congressional seats. Three of the four men elected were Republicans. Only one of these—William T. Clark—was a carpetbagger. The new state constitution was finalized, voted upon, and approved in November 1869. The three amendments to the U.S. Constitution were also ratified. During February 1870, the legislature selected two new U.S. senators, Morgan C. Hamilton and J.W. Flanagan. Both were Republicans. President Grant signed the act to readmit Texas to the Union on March 30, 1870. Nevertheless, some representatives and senators met with resistance upon trying to take their seats, as they had once been part of the Confederacy, but this would eventually subside. Military rule ended in Texas on April 16, 1870.

SOURCE OF POWER AND RESPONSIBILITIES

The House of Representatives and the Senate are the two equal branches of the Congress of the United States. Both were created by the Constitutional Convention in 1787, and both began work in 1789 after the Constitution was ratified by the states. The U.S. Constitution outlines the power and responsibilities of the Congress. Along with the Constitution, tradition has long ruled the powers of each branch. The Congress holds all the national legislative powers and is known as the legislative branch of the U.S. government. The House of Representatives originates all bills for "raising revenue" and has given itself the power to originate bills that appropriate money. The House can also elect a president if the electoral college fails to give a majority of votes to any single candidate. This has occurred just twice, in 1801 and 1825.

METHOD OF ELECTION AND TERMS OF OFFICE

Each state determines how and when to elect its senators and representatives. This ability is granted to the state by Article 1, Section 4 of the U.S. Constitution.

"The Times, Places and Manner of holding Elections for Senators and Representatives, shall be prescribed in each State by the Legislatures thereof;"

U.S. representatives are selected by direct election of the voting population of each congressional district every even-numbered year for a two-year term. A U.S. representative serves a two-year term. This is found in Article I, Section 2 of the U.S. Constitution.

"The House of Representatives shall be comprised of Members chosen every second Year by the People of the several States..."

U.S. senators are also selected by a direct vote of the people for a six-year term. Each election year (every even-numbered year), one-third of all the Senate seats are up for election or reelection. Their terms are staggered so that the two seats from each state are up for election in different years. A U.S. senator serves a six-year term. These requirements are found in Article I, Section 3 of the U.S. Constitution.

"The Senate of the United States shall be composed of two Senators from each State, chosen by the Legislatures thereof, for six Years..." (changed by the Seventeenth Amendment)

The direct election of senators by the voters has not always been the case. Until 1913 and the ratification of the Seventeenth Amendment to the U.S. Constitution, the state legislature and the state senate nominated, voted for, and selected the U.S. senators to represent the state. These legislative elections were responsible for choosing each U.S. senator from 1846 until 1913. The first direct election for a U.S. senator in Texas was in 1912.

The July 1912 Democratic primary election and the subsequent November general election were held to fill the seat of Joseph W. Bailey for the term beginning in March 1913. Bailey did not seek reelection in 1912 and eventually resigned, in January 1913. Governor Colquitt appointed Rienzi Johnston of Houston to the remainder of Bailey's term in the U.S. Senate. The legislature did not approve of Johnston, as he was a "wet" during the early stages of the prohibition movement. Morris Sheppard had already won the 1912 elections, so he and the legislature began a movement to encourage Johnston to resign. Johnston did eventually resign his Senate seat, on February 2, 1913, after only twenty-eight days in office. Sheppard took office on February 3, 1913, giving him about one month's seniority over every other new U.S. senator scheduled to take office in March.

The Seventeenth Amendment also provided the governor the power to appoint an U.S. senator in the event of a vacancy. The governor of Texas has appointed five U.S. senators. Oddly though, none of these men were able to retain their seats through election.

QUALIFICATIONS FOR THE OFFICE

To serve as a U.S. representative, one must be at least twenty-five years old, a U.S. citizen for at least seven years, and reside in the state one represents. These requirements are found in Article I, Section 2 of the U.S. Constitution. There is no requirement to reside in the congressional district one represents.

"No Person shall be a Representative who shall not have attained to the Age of twenty five Years, and been seven Years a Citizen of the United States, and who shall not, when elected, be an Inhabitant of that State in which he shall be chosen."

To serve as a U.S. senator, one must be at least thirty years old, a U.S. citizen for at least nine years, and reside in the state one represents. These requirements are found in Article I, Section 3 of the U.S. Constitution.

"No Person shall be a Senator who shall not have attained to the Age of thirty Years, and been nine Years a Citizen of the United States, and who shall not, when elected, be an Inhabitant of that State for which he shall be chosen."

OFFICIAL BENEFITS

Both representatives and senators are paid a salary set by Congress. They receive health insurance, life insurance, a retirement plan, and a tax-deferred savings plan. They also receive a sum for maintaining staffs in Washington and in their home state or district. Travel expenses and office supplies are provided but must remain within a budget also set by Congress. Representatives and senators receive franking privilege, whereby they can use the U.S. Postal Service for official mail. Both enjoy immunity from some types of arrest and are immune from legal action for statements made in an official capacity.

NUMBER OF REPRESENTATIVES

Article I, Section 2 of the U.S. Constitution originally set forth the equation for determining the number of U.S. representative from each state. This was changed by the Fourteenth Amendment of the Constitution, Section 2.

"Representatives shall be apportioned among the several States according to their respective numbers, counting the whole number of persons in each State, excluding Indians not taxed."

The House of Representatives originally had 65 members. Until the early 1900s, the House of Representatives simply added seats to each state's delegation as the state's population increased. However, by 1913 there were 435 members, and in 1929 the House agreed that there would be no more than 435 representatives. This was the number of representatives called for from the population statistics in the 1910 dicennial census.

The distribution of representative positions is based on population. In 1930 the first major redistricting occurred, and twenty-one states had their total number of U.S. representatives reduced. Following each dicennial census, Congress reapportions the number of districts or representatives among the states. The idea is to assign a fair number of representatives to each state based on its population. The method of doing this has changed over the years. Interestingly, the Constitution is silent on precisely how to assign a number of representatives to a state. It only notes that the number of representatives shall be based upon each state's population. Following each dicennial census of the U.S., Texas has gained seats in the U.S. House of Representatives. Texas initially had two seats, and its number has now grown to thirty-two. The following shows how the number of congressional seats in Texas has grown.

Census	Year	Number of Districts
7th	1850	2
8th	1860	4
9th	1870	6
10th	1880	11
11th	1890	13
12th	1900	16
13th	1910	18
14th	1920	18
15th	1930	21
16th	1940	21
17th	1950	22
18th	1960	23
19th	1970	24
20th	1980	27
21st	1990	30
22nd	2000	32

As mentioned earlier, Article I, Section 3 of the U.S. Constitution sets forth the allocation of two senators per state.

DISTRICTS

Once Congress determines the number of representatives a state is to have, it is up to the state legislature to determine the boundaries of each district. During the past decades, state legislators have been faced with the challenge of carving up existing districts to create new ones as Texas has gained representatives with each apportionment. To say that politics is involved in the creation of new congressional districts out of existing districts would be an incredible understatement.

Until 1842 there was no preference between having "at large" representatives from the state or representatives from districts within the state. However, just before Texas became a state, Congress passed a law that created the general concept of a single-member district. Congress left the task of dividing the state into districts to the state legislatures. The idea was to keep the districts as compact areas containing like numbers of people. If districts were drawn unfairly, federal courts could intervene to ensure fair distribution. All federal courts largely stayed out of redistricting issues until the 1960s because the issue was simply too political. However, in the 1960s the court said that the principle of one person, one vote was paramount (*Baker v. Carr*, 1962) and that congressional districts should be as closely equal in population "as is practicable" (*Wesberry v. Sanders*, 1964).

As recently as 1996, this was put to a test in Texas when a three-judge court of the U.S. District Court for the Southern District of Texas redrew the boundaries of Congressional Districts 18, 29, and 30, and redrew portions of the boundaries for Districts 3, 5, 6, 7, 8, 9, 22, 24, 25, and 26. This affected almost half of Texas' congressional districts. The court ordered that the candidates in these districts who had filed for reelection by August 30, 1996, and been certified by September 5, 1996, would compete in an open primary—a special election—on November 5, 1996. That was the same day as the 1996 general election.

In the court decision, the governor was ordered to canvass the results of the special election on November 12, 1996, and order a runoff election if necessary. That runoff was held on December 10, 1996.

The most interesting story regarding district creation involves John Nance Garner. He fought hard for a new congressional district—the 15th—and fought hard for it to be located around his home in Uvalde. He then resigned from the legislature, ran for the new congressional seat in 1902, won, and became a congressman in 1903.

When the state legislature fails to create a new district's boundaries, an at-large district may be created. The representative for this at-large "district" is voted on by the entire population of the state. Typically, this occurs only when the legislature is unable to agree upon the boundaries of the new district in time to meet an election filing deadline. These offices are temporary until the boundaries can be decided and an official is elected to the post. Interestingly, the ban on at-large congressional districts mentioned above has been largely ignored and unenforced.

Following extensive redistricting after the 2000 Census, two new districts were created and the boundaries of existing districts were changed. Some saw this as a way for the Republican Party to redraw the boundary lines to benefit their party. The 2004 elections saw a number of long-time Congressmen unseated and replaced with Republican newcomers.

ELECTIONS

Prior to 1900, Texas had only a handful of elections laws, and nominations for public office were made almost entirely at party conventions. These conventions operated by force and party rules and were completely open to back-room negotiations and deals. However, elected officials and the public forced the creation of election laws in an attempt to prevent illegal voting, false returns, and voter and election-judge bribery. Thus was born the primary election.

The system for primary elections in Texas was created in 1895 when the 24th Legislature passed a law requiring primary elections. The law established the general or first primary on the first Saturday in May of even-numbered years. If a runoff was necessary, it would be held in the runoff or second primary, held on the first Saturday in June. These laws and election dates have changed many times. The purpose of the primary election was and is to select a candidate for the general election.

The initial law governing primary elections expanded in 1903, repealed and replaced in 1905, and further amended in 1907, 1913, and 1918. Election laws have been amended to some extent in almost every legislative session. In 1905 the Terrell Election Law, sponsored by State Representative Alexander Terrell, created the direct primary for state, district, and county offices. The law also required primaries for parties that received more than 100,000 votes in the previous election. This applied only to the Democratic Party for many decades. This threshold was increased to 200,000 and then changed to 20 percent of the votes in the previous gubernatorial election. In primary elections, a candidate was required to receive plurality to be declared the nominee. However, this was changed in 1918 for all offices (1913 for senatorial elections) and created a second primary or runoff election.

For many decades following the Civil War, blacks were not allowed to vote in primary elections. Changes to election laws in 1903 allowed local party leaders to exclude black voters. This was expanded in 1923, when the legislature created a law that explicitly barred blacks from voting in Democratic Party primary elections. Primary elections were then called "White Primaries," and Texas was one of eleven southern states to carry on such a practice. This followed the 1921 U.S. Supreme Court decision *Newberry v. United States*, which said that a primary election was a function of a party and that party could do what it liked.

In March 1927, the U.S. Supreme Court declared White Primaries unconstitutional because they violated the equal protection clause of the Fourteenth Amendment. The Court was completely silent as to how the scheme of the White Primary violated the Fifteenth Amendment. The Court's decision was based on a suit by black El Paso physician, Lawrence Nixon. The victory was short, as the State Democratic Executive Committee moved to allow only whites to vote in the primaries. It was not until 1944, following another Court decision, this time in *Smith v. Allwright*, that it was ordered that blacks be allowed to vote in primary elections. The Court concluded that under state law, primary elections were an integral part of the general election process and that everyone should have a vote. This ended the legal attempts to exclude blacks from the political process in Texas.

Another impediment to voting was the poll tax. Texas had a poll tax from 1876 until 1966. The Twenty-fourth Amendment to the United States Constitution abolished the poll tax as a requirement for voting for the president, vice-president, presidential electors, and U.S. senators and representatives. However, the tax was still required for state elections through 1964. Two years later, the poll tax was eliminated completely by the courts and the voter registration system was begun. Absentee voting was allowed between 1925 and 1987. In 1987 "early voting" replaced "absentee voting" and the requirement to prove your expected whereabouts on election day was removed.

In 1918 women were allowed to vote in primary elections in Texas. However, it was two more years before they were allowed to vote in general elections. Women's suffrage came about by the passage of the Nineteenth Amendment to the United States Constitution, which stated that the right "to vote shall not be denied or abridged by the United States or by any State on account of sex." This was ratified on August 18, 1920.

From 1906 until 1960, the first primary was held on the fourth Saturday in July and the runoff or second primary was held on the fourth Saturday in August. In 1960 the first primary was moved to the first Saturday in May and the second primary to the first Saturday in June. The date was again changed in 1986, to allow the first primary election to coincide with "Super Tuesday"—the second Tuesday in March which was the day of many other primary elections in southern states. This first Super Tuesday vote in Texas occurred in 1988. The second primary or runoff election was moved to the second Tuesday in April.

On the first Tuesday in November of every even-numbered year, a general election is held to select the candidate for the given office. In general elections, nominees from each party compete in the final race for each office. A majority of votes is required. If no majority is received, a runoff election is scheduled. Elected members take office the following January. So, the year a candidate is elected is typically the year they were sworn in, less one.

SPECIAL ELECTIONS

Texas has a unique method of handling special elections for House and Senate candidates. Prior to 1961, all candidates from all parties ran in a race against one another and the candidate receiving the most votes was declared the winner. Candidates could get less than a majority (50 percent) of the votes and still win. In 1961 state election law was changed to the "open primary" system. Under an open primary, a candidate must receive a majority—50 percent or more—of the votes to be declared the winner. If a majority is not received, then a special election runoff is held between the top two candidates, regardless of party affiliation. In the 1961 special election to fill Lyndon Johnson's Senate seat, there were seventy-one candidates running in the first election. No candidate received a majority, so the top two candidates—John Tower and Bill Blakley—were put into a runoff election which Tower won.

In 1996 a unique special election was held. As a result of a lawsuit mentioned above (*Bush v. Vera* [Sup. Ct. Doc. No. 94-09805], and *Vera v. Bush* [Civil No. H-0994-090277, S.D. Tex.]), almost half of the Texas congressional district boundaries were redrawn. This affected the entire boundary of Districts 18, 29, and 30, and portions of the boundaries for Districts 3, 5, 6, 7, 8, 9, 22, 24, 25, and 26. The U.S. District Court further ordered that a special election be held the same day as the 1996 general election for these seats.

Prior to the 73rd Congress (1933–34), a session of Congress was held after the November general election, beginning in December. This was the second session of the sitting congress and was held prior to the arrival of the newly elected congress in January. Not surprisingly, this "lame duck" session of Congress was responsible for a number of unusual pieces of legislation. The state has seen a handful of candidates elected to both the lame duck session and to a full session of Congress beginning the following January. This has occurred when a congressman has died during the summer or fall of an election year and a special election to fill his seat for the December session is held coincidentally with the general election for the term beginning in January.

BUSINESS AND ORGANIZATION

The U.S. House of Representatives is large and handles a great volume of business. Because of this, a complex structure and method of operation has evolved. Most of the activities of the House are handled by committees and subcommittees by subject area. There are now twenty committees, with thirty to fifty-five members each, and eighty-six subcommittees. As needed, special or select committees may be formed to address a single problem or issue. Committees are each led by a chairman.

The party with the most members in the House is the majority. The majority also retains a majority of members on each committee and controls who is appointed to each committee. A representative may serve on several small committees or one major committee. The three major committees are Ways and Means, which has jurisdiction over tax measures; Appropriations, which has jurisdiction over all bills supplying funding to federal agencies; and Rules, which regulates the flow of bills to the House floor. Each committee develops its own rules for conducting business. Most of these have evolved over decades and reflect the nature of their business. Even the names of committees have changed over the years to reflect the business of the day.

The power of the committee chair may be very strong, to the point of dictating every action of the committee, or may be more evenly distributed among the members of the committee. Other leaders in the House include those of the majority party, namely the Speaker of the House, the majority leader, and the majority whip. The minority party also names a minority leader and minority whip. There are numerous assistant whips in each party. These leaders organize their parties, schedule business before the House, promote House attendance to meet their needs, distribute and collect information, persuade members to vote as needed, and provide a liaison with the president.

The Senate has also developed a similar and equally complex organization. It, like the House of Representatives, operates with committees and subcommittees. There are now twenty standing committees and approximately sixty-eight subcommittees, along with a handful of select and special committees. Party leaders in the Senate have only become significant in this century. Until the early decades of this century, no majority leader or minority leader was chosen in the Senate. Since then, they have become both leaders in the Senate and within their respective parties.

Most business in the Senate is handled by "unanimous consent," whereby agreements are worked out between the floor leaders of the two parties beforehand. This gives the casual observer the impression of a smoothly operating machine. However, the Senate has a tradition of allowing "unlimited debate," whereby a few senators can effectively prevent a vote on a bill for weeks or months.

In addition to the powers of the House of Representatives, the Senate enjoys three additional powers granted by the Constitution. The Senate sits as a court in cases of impeachment. A conviction by the Senate requires a two-thirds vote. Only about a dozen such cases have been heard, and only four convictions have resulted. The Senate has sat before impeachment of two presidents, Andrew Johnson and Bill Clinton. The Senate confirms presidential nominations by a majority vote. The Senate ratifies treaties the president makes with foreign governments by a two-thirds vote. The Senate has refused ratification eleven times. The most important, in 1920, was the rejection of the Treaty of Versailles, which contained the Covenant of the League of Nations.

PARTIES

The last decades of the 1800s saw a great increase in the importance of political parties in the House of Representatives. During this era, division along party lines virtually stopped the House from operating for the first time. Since then, there has always been one major party in power and another in the minority position. This has allowed powers to coalesce around the Speaker of the House who is supported by the majority in power.

With the exception of the rise of the Radical Republicans following the Civil War, Texas was a one-party state of Democrats through the 1950s. The party, however, began to split between liberal and conservative factions. The latter were in control of the party machine, and their candidates eventually ran as both Democrats and Republicans on the same ballot for statewide office. The Republican Party had fielded candidates since Reconstruction, but with little success. Almost 100 years later, with the election of John Tower as U.S. senator in 1961, the Republicans brought Texas into the world of two-party politics. The state, however, remained largely Democratic until the early 1980s, when the Reagan Revolution swept many Democrats from office. Republicans now sit in every statewide elected office, both senatorial seats, and twenty-two of thirty-two U.S. representative seats.

GOVERNORS AS REPRESENTATIVES

Texas has had a handful of governors who have also served as U.S. senators. Most served as governor prior to becoming a senator.

- ★ Sam Houston was U.S. senator from 1846 until 1859 and governor from 1859 until 1861.
- ★ David G. Burnet, who was ad-interim president of the Republic during 1836, was selected as a U.S. senator in 1866 but was never seated.
- ★ Oran Roberts was elected as U.S. senator in 1866 but was never seated, and he served as governor from 1879 until 1883.
- ★ Richard Coke was governor from 1874 until 1876 and U.S. senator from 1877 until 1895.
- ★ Charles A. Culberson was governor from 1895 until 1899 and U.S. senator from 1899 until 1923.
- ★ W. Lee O'Daniel was governor from 1939 until 1941 and U.S. senator from 1941 until 1949.
- ★ Price Daniel was a U.S. senator from 1953 until 1957 and governor from 1957 until 1963.

Four U.S. Representatives have also been governor.

- ★ Peter H. Bell was governor from 1849 until 1853 and U.S. representative from 1853 until 1857.
- ★ Samuel W. T. Lanham was a U.S. representative from 1883 until 1893 and governor from 1903 until 1907.
- ★ Joseph D. Sayers was a U.S. representative from 1885 until 1899 and governor from 1899 until 1903.
- ★ James W. Throckmorton was governor from 1866 until 1867 and U.S. representative from 1875 until 1879 and again from 1883 until 1887.

Numerous congressmen have run for governor, including Joseph W. Bailey, Chris Bell, Lemuel Evans, Bob Gammage, Henry B. Gonzalez, Andrew Jackson Hamilton, Kent Hance, Andrew Jackson Houston, Sam Houston, George Washington Jones, Jim Mattox, William Beck Ochiltree, Ewing Thomason, and James Young.

There has been only one individual who has been a U.S. representative, a U.S. senator, and Texas governor. However, that man was not a U.S. representative from Texas; he was from Tennessee. That man was Sam Houston.

DEATHS, RESIGNATIONS, AND APPOINTMENTS

The death of an elected official while in office is always a sad occasion. Elected officials have also resigned to pursue other interests. Both deaths and resignations create opportunities for others. These opportunities have been used to carry many on to higher office and launch the careers of a number of politicians. The governor of Texas has the ability to fill the position of senator in cases of death or resignation, but representative positions must be filled by special election.

Four U.S. senators from Texas have died in office: Thomas J. Rusk, J. Pinckney Henderson, Morris Sheppard, and Andrew Jackson Houston. On each of these occasions, the governor appointed a man to fill the remaining term of the late senator.

Five U.S. senators from Texas have resigned from office: John H. Reagan, Joseph Weldon Bailey, Price Daniel, Lyndon Johnson, and Phil Gramm. They resigned for a variety of reasons. Reagan resigned to take on the role of chairman of the newly created Texas Railroad Commission. Bailey resigned because he feared he could not win reelection. Price Daniel resigned following his election to the governorship. Lyndon Johnson resigned following his election as John Kennedy's vice-president. Gramm resigned to help his party create an incumbent with John Cornyn. Each time, the governor appointed a man to fill the remainder of the senator's terms.

Six men have been appointed by the governor to serve as U.S. senator: Horace Chilton, Rienzi Johnston, Andrew Jackson Houston, Bill Blakley, Bob Krueger, and John Cornyn. Andrew Jackson Houston was appointed by Governor O'Daniel to fill the remainder of the late Morris Sheppard's seat, but he, too, died in office. Not all these men were called to office by a death, as some have been called by a resignation. Chilton was called by Governor Hogg to serve the remainder of John H. Reagan's term. Rienzi Johnston was appointed by Governor Colquitt to serve the balance of Joseph Bailey's term. Blakley was appointed to serve following the resignations of Price Daniel and Lyndon Johnson. Bob Krueger was appointed by Governor Richards to fill the seat vacated by Lloyd Bentsen, who had resigned to become treasury secretary. John Cornyn was appointed by Governor Perry to fill the seat vacated by Phil Gramm after Cornyn had been elected to the post. By taking office a bit early, he gained a bit of seniority over other new senators.

Twenty-two representatives have died in office. These include: Clay Briggs, James Buchanan, Robert Burke, William Crain, John Cranford, Reese De Graffenreid, Daniel Garrett, David Kaufman, Robert Lee, Mickey Leland, Joseph Mansfield, Simpson Morgan, Lucian Parrish, Wright Patman, John M. Pinckney, Joe Pool, Sam Rayburn, Gustav Schleicher, Frank Tejeda, Albert Thomas, Milton West, and Harry Wurzbach. These vacancies have spurred the careers of men such as Lyndon Johnson, who ran for James Buchanan's seat following his death. Typically, a special election is called to fill the seat of a representative who has left office by death or a resignation. A number of U.S. representatives have resigned for a variety of reasons. Some have moved on to higher office, such as John Nance Garner, who resigned to become vice-president. Many have resigned to accept federal judgeships. Some have resigned to accept private-sector positions.

FORMER MEMBERS

Fewer than 300 men and women have served Texas in Congress. Many have continued productive careers following their time in office. Some have sought higher office, as mentioned above. Some take up careers of lobbying their old colleagues. Others accept federal judgeships. Some have been appointed to presidential cabinet posts, such as former secretary of the treasury, Lloyd Bentsen. Some have taken on other governmental positions, such as Ambassador Bob Krueger. Some simply retired to enjoy life, teach, or possibly write their memoirs, as Jim Wright did. However, several former members of Congress spent some time in jail following their stints in Congress, for wrongdoing while in office.

UPWARD MOBILITY

A number of men who have worked as aides or secretaries to a congressman have become congressmen themselves. Lyndon Johnson worked for Richard Kleberg; Wingate Lucas worked for Fritz Lanham; Burleson worked for Sam Russell; Marvin Leath worked for Bob Poage; Ken Bentsen worked for Ron Coleman; Albert Bustamante worked for Henry B. Gonzalez; Tom Loeffler worked for John Tower; Jim Mattox worked for Earle Cabell; Ray Roberts worked for Sam Rayburn; Pete Geren worked for Lloyd Bentsen; and Jeb Hensarling worked for Phil Gramm.

RECENT TRENDS

In the past thirty years, the ethnic and gender diversity of U.S. Representatives from Texas has come to more closely reflect the diversity of the state. Latinos, women, and African Americans have taken their place among the other representatives. Texas has had eleven Latino congressmen, including the first, Henry B. Gonzalez, in 1961. Others include Henry Bonilla, Albert Bustamante, Henry Cuellar, Charlie Gonzalez, Ruben Hinojosa, Abraham Kazen, Solomon Ortiz, Sylvestre Reyes, Ciro Rodriquez, and Frank Tejeda. Texas has had six congresswomen. The first was Lera Thomas, who succeeded her late husband, Albert, for the balance of his term. Others include Barbara Jordan (the first woman elected to a full term), Kay Granger, Eddie Bernice Johnson, and Sheila Jackson Lee. Kay Bailey Hutchison was the first woman to serve as U.S. senator from Texas. The first black to represent Texas in Congress was Barbara Jordan in 1973. The five other African Americans to serve are Eddie Bernice Johnson, Sheila Jackson Lee, Mickey Leland, Craig Washington, and Al Green.

OATH OF OFFICE

I, (name), do solemnly swear (or affirm) that I will support and defend the Constitution of the United States against all enemies, foreign and domestic; that I will bear true faith and allegiance to the same; that I take this obligation freely, without any mental reservation or purpose of evasion, and that I will well and faithfully discharge the duties of the office on which I am about to enter. So help me God.

FIRSTS AND FACTS FOR TEXAS

★ The first U.S. representative from Texas was David Spangler Kaufman in 1846. He was also the first representative to die in office, in 1851, and was the first and only representative of Jewish descent to serve, until the 1970s.

★ The first U.S. senator from Texas was Thomas Rusk in 1846. He was also the first senator to die in office and the first to die by his own hand.

★ The first female member of Congress from Texas was Lera Thomas—the widow of Albert Thomas—in 1966. She also holds the title of the oldest female representative, as she took office at sixty-six years of age.

★ The first black Texan elected to Congress was Barbara Jordan in 1973. She was also the first black female to serve in Congress.

★ The first black male congressman from Texas was Mickey Leland in 1979.

★ The first Republican female member of Congress from Texas was Kay Granger in 1997.

★ The first representative from Texas to receive more than 10,000 votes was George M. Smyth in 1853.

★ The first representative from Texas to receive more than 100,000 votes in a district race (not an at-large position) was Albert Thomas in 1948.

★ The first senator from Texas to receive more than 1,000,000 votes was Price Daniel, in 1952 when he ran as both a Democrat and a Republican.

★ The first Hispanic congressman from Texas was Henry B. Gonzalez in 1961.

★ The first Hispanic congressman in the U.S. to chair a House committee was Eligio "Kika" de la Garza in 1981.

★ The oldest person elected to serve as U.S. representative from Texas was Sterling Price Strong in 1932. He was seventy-one and just a few months older than George Terrell who took office the same year. Both served as at-large representatives.

★ The oldest person from Texas to serve as senator was Andrew Jackson Houston in 1941. He was eighty-seven and died less than two months after being sworn in.

- ★ The youngest person from Texas elected to serve as representative was Lindley Beckworth in 1938. He was twenty-five.
- ★ The youngest person from Texas elected to serve as senator was John Tower in 1961. He was thirty-five.
- ★ The person from Texas to serve the longest as representative was Sam Rayburn. He served from 1913 until 1961—forty-nine years. His longevity is followed closely by Wright Patman with forty-seven years and Eldon Mahon with forty-four years.
- ★ The person from Texas to serve the longest as senator was Morris Sheppard. He served twenty-eight years.
- ★ The first case of expulsion against a congressman from Texas was against Thomas Blanton in 1921. He was responsible for some foul language being printed in the *Congressional Record*. He was eventually censured by the Congress and was not expelled.
- ★ The first cases of expulsion against senators from Texas were against John Hemphill and Louis Wigfall in 1861 for their support of secession.
- ★ Texas had a congressman from South Texas named "West" and a congressman from West Texas named "South."
- ★ The first man to serve in both successions of U.S. senators from Texas was Horace Chilton in 1891 and 1895. Bill Blakley was the only other to do the same, in 1957 and 1961.
- ★ The first representative from Texas to be elected as Speaker of the House was John Nance Garner in 1931, for the 72nd Congress. He served for one term. The second was Sam Rayburn, and the third was Jim Wright.
- ★ Harry Wurzbach was the first Texas-born Republican to be elected to Congress.
- ★ The first congressman from Texas to serve as vice-president was John Nance Garner in 1933. The second was Lyndon Johnson, and the third was George H. W. Bush.
- ★ The first congressman from Texas to serve as president was Lyndon Johnson. The second was George H. W. Bush.

BIOGRAPHIES

JOSEPH O. "JO" ABBOTT

Jo Abbott

     Born on January 15, 1840, near Decatur, Alabama. Moved with family to Freestone County, Texas about 1853. Attended private schools and studied law both before and after serving in the Confederate State Army. Wounded in battle, but recovered and returned to his unit. Admitted to the state bar in 1866 and practiced with Lochlin J. Farrar in Springhill. Quit his legal practice, moved to Hill County, and taught school for five months. Began practicing law again in 1868. Democrat. Married Rowena Sturgis in 1868 and they had five children. Served one term as state representative, District 20, from 1870 until 1872. Appointed judge, 28th District, by Governor Roberts in 1879. Elected to this post in 1880 and served until 1884. Colleagues attempted to nominate him for the Supreme Court without success in 1886. Elected U.S. representative, 6th District, in 1886 by defeating Independent J.C. Kearby and Republican A. B. Norton. Succeeded Olin Wellborn on March 4, 1887. Reelected in 1888 by defeating Labor Party candidate Sam Evans, in 1890 by defeating Republicans Darter Isaac and H. W. Barclay, in 1892 by defeating People's and Republican candidate J.C. Kearby, and in 1894 by defeating now Populist candidate J. C. Kearby and Republican B. O. James. Did not seek reelection in 1896 and was succeeded by Robert E. Burke on March 3, 1897. Upon leaving Congress, he returned to Hillsboro and his law practice. Died in Hillsboro on February 11, 1908, and was buried there at Old Cemetery.

BRUCE REYNOLDS ALGER

     Born on June 12, 1918, in Dallas. Moved to Missouri in 1924. Lived and attended school in Webster Groves, Missouri. Graduated from high school in 1936 and Princeton University in 1940. Worked for RCA Victor in 1940 and 1941. Married Lucille "Lynn" Antoine in 1943 and they had three children: Linda Jill, David Bruce, and Steven Van. Served in the Army Air Force during World War II. Returned to Dallas. Owned Alger Development Company. Republican. Elected U.S. representative, 5th District in 1954 by defeating Democrat Wallace Savage. He succeeded J. Frank Wilson on January 3, 1955. Reelected in 1956 by defeating Democrat Henry Wade, in 1958 by defeating Democrat Barefoot Sanders, in 1960 by defeating Democrat Joe Pool, and in 1962 by defeating Democrat Bill Jones. Alger was an outcast among the Texas

Bruce Alger

Texas Delegation from about 1887.
Members pictured are: Charles Stewart, William H. Martin, C. B. Kilgore, David B. Culberson, Silas Hare, Jo Abbot, William H. Crain, Littleton W. Moore, John H. Reagan, Richard Coke, Roger Q. Mills, Joseph D. Sayers, and S.W.T. Lanham.

delegation at the time, as he was the only Republican for many years. For decades the Texas delegation was treated to a lunch every Wednesday with Speaker Sam Rayburn, but Alger was not welcome. This went back to Alger's initial meeting with Sam Rayburn as a new member of Congress. Rayburn, as Speaker of the House and dean of the Texas delegation, met with all new members of Congress to welcome them and to get to know them. Following his meeting with Rayburn, Alger was reported to say that Rayburn was more interested in the party than in the country, and that effectively ended any pleasant relationship with Rayburn. Divorced from his wife Lynn in 1961. His son David was killed in an automobile accident in 1964 on the newly constructed Washington Beltway. Unseated by Democrat Earle Cabell with a 15 percent margin in the November 1964 general election. Succeeded by Cabell on January 3, 1965. Moved to Boca Raton, Florida, but now splits his time between Dallas and New England.

My ignorance of politics couldn't be matched by anybody in politics.

—Bruce Alger, upon being elected to Congress

MICHAEL ALLEN "MIKE" ANDREWS

Mike Andrews

Born on February 7, 1944, in Houston. Attended Fort Worth public schools and graduated from Arlington Heights High School in 1962. Received a B.A. from the University of Texas in 1967 and a J.D. from Southern Methodist University in 1970. Admitted to the state bar in 1971 and practiced in Houston. Married Ann Bowman and they had two children: Emily and Caroline. Democrat. Served as clerk for the U.S. District Court in Houston from 1971 until 1972 and Harris County assistant district attorney from 1972 until 1976. In private legal practice from 1976 until 1983 with Baker, Brown, Sharman, Wise and Stephens. Served in U.S. Naval Reserves. Ran for U.S. representative, 22nd District in 1980 but was defeated by Ron Paul. Elected as the first U.S. representative for the newly created 25th District in 1982 by defeating Republican Mike Faubion, Libertarian Jeff Calvert, and Citizens Party candidate Barbara Coldiron. Took office on January 3, 1983. Served on the House Ways and Means Committee. Reelected in 1984 over Republican Jerry Patterson, ran unopposed in 1986, and in 1988 defeated Republican George H. Loeffler Jr. and Libertarian Kevin Southwick. In 1989 he was one of the "Gang of Six," a group of Democrats who broke with the party to join Republicans for a lower capital gains tax. Andrews ran unopposed in 1990, in 1992 defeated Republican Dolly Madison McKenna and Libertarian Richard Mauk, and in 1994 did not seek reelection to Congress and was succeeded by Ken Bentsen in January 1995. Unsuccessful candidate for U.S. Senate in 1994, but placed third in the Democratic primary election behind Jim Mattox and Richard Fisher. Went to work for the Vinson and Elkins law firm in Washington, D.C.

... there's a lot right with congress. As an institution, it is a place I'm proud to have served in. It is the most important deliberative body in the world, and it is the best microcosm of our democracy. It has everything: the best and the worst of America.

—Mike Andrews

EDWIN LEROY ANTONY

Born January 5, 1852, in Waynesboro, Georgia. Moved to Columbia, Texas, in 1859 with parents. Graduated from the University of Georgia in 1873. Admitted to the state bar in 1874 and practiced in Cameron. Democrat. Married Augusta Houghton in 1876 and they had two daughters: Beryl Pauline and Alice August. Served as prosecuting attorney in Milam County from 1876 until 1878. Appointed special judge in 1886 following an illness by the local district judge. Served as alderman in Cameron from 1890 until 1892. Elected as U.S. representative, 9th District, on June 14, 1892, by defeating People's Party candidate I. N. Barber in a special election to fill the seat of Roger Q. Mills, who resigned after being elected U.S. senator. Antony was unseated a few months later in November 1892, when he failed to be renominated for the office. He was succeeded by Joseph D. Sayers. Anthony served in Congress from June 14, 1892, until March 3, 1893. Returned to Cameron and his law practice. Died January 16, 1913, in Dallas and was buried there at Oakland Cemetery.

WILLIAM REYNOLDS "BILL" ARCHER, JR.

Bill Archer

Born on March 22, 1928, in Houston. Graduated salutatorian from St. Thomas High School in Houston in 1945. Attended Rice University from 1945 until 1946 and received a B.B.A. and L.L.B. from the University of Texas in 1951. Served in U.S. Air Force from 1951 until 1953, but continued serving in the U.S.A.F. Reserves. Married Patricia Moore in 1953 and they had five children: Reyn, Rick, Sharon, Lisa, and Barbara. Attorney and businessman. President of Uncle Johnny Mills—a family business—from 1953 until 1961 and was a director with Heights State Bank in Houston. First elected office was to Hunters Creek Village Council and mayor pro tempore and served from 1955 until 1962. Served as state representative, District 22-5, from 1967 until 1971. In 1967 changed from the Democratic to the Republican Party. Elected to the U.S. House, 7th District in 1970 by defeating Democrat Jim Greenwood, succeeding George Bush on January 3, 1971. Served on the House Banking and Currency Committee. Reelected in 1972 and 1974 by defeating Democrat Jim Brady, ran unopposed in 1976, in 1978 defeated Democrat Robert L. Hutchins, in 1980 defeated Democrat Hutchins and Libertarian William Ware, and in 1982 defeated Democrat Dennis Scoggins and Libertarian William Ware. Divorced from his first wife, Patricia, in 1981. Married Sharon Sawyer in 1983 and she brought two children into the union from her previous marriage: Scott and Shannon. Reelected in 1984 by defeating Democrat Billy Willibey, in 1986 by defeating Democrat Harry Kniffen and Libertarian Roger Plail, in 1988 by defeating Democrat Diane Richards, and ran unopposed in 1990, 1992, and 1994. The U.S. District Court redrew part of the boundary for Archer's district, requiring him to run in an open primary or special election in November 1996. This election coincided with the general election, in which he was reelected by defeating Independents Gene Hsiao and Robert R. "Randy" Sims Jr., and Democrat Al J. K. Siegmund. Reelected in 1998 by defeating Libertarian Drew Parks and Independent John R. Skone-Palmer. Served on the House Banking Committee, then Ways and Means, and the Joint Taxation Committee; eventually served as chairman of the House Ways and Means Committee. Retired from Congress and did not seek reelection in 2000. Succeeded by fellow Republican John Culberson in January 2001.

> *The militants expound the rights of free speech and expression, and then they boo moderate speakers off the platform. They talk about their constitutional rights, and then they conspire to trample the rights of hundreds of thousands of citizens here in Washington.*
>
> —Bill Archer

RICHARD KEITH "DICK" ARMEY

Born July 7, 1940, in Cando, North Dakota. Graduated from Cando High School in 1958. Received B.A. from Jamestown College in Jamestown, North Dakota, in 1963, M.A. from the University of North Dakota in 1964, and a Ph.D. from the University of Oklahoma in 1969. Married and the father of three children: Scott, Kathy, and David. Served on economics faculty at University of Montana from 1964 to 1965, assistant professor at West Texas State University from 1967 to 1968, assistant professor at Austin College from 1968 to 1972, associate professor at North Texas State University from 1972 until

1977, and chair of the Department of Economics, North Texas State University, from 1977 to 1983. Divorced from his first wife about this time. Republican. Economics professor and consultant. Married Susan Marlene Byrd Oxentine—a former student—in 1981 and she brought two children from a previous marriage: Scott and Chip Oxentine. Elected U.S. representative, 26th District, in 1984 by unseating incumbent Democrat Tom Vandergriff. He succeeded Vandergriff in January 1985. Reelected in 1986 by defeating Democrat George Richardson, in 1988 by defeating Democrat Jo Ann Reyes, in 1990 and 1992 by defeating Democrat John Wayne Caton and write-in candidate Steve Love, and in 1994 by defeating Democrat Le Earl Ann Bryant and Libertarian Alfred Adask. The U.S. District Court redrew part of the boundary for Armey's district, requiring him to run in an open primary or special election in November 1996. This election coincided with the general election. Armey was reelected by defeating Democrat Jerry Frankel and

Dick Armey

a handful of write-in candidates. Reelected in 1998 by defeating Libertarian Joe Turner and Independent William Kenneth Cheek. Reelected in 2000 by defeating Democrat Steve Love and Libertarian Fred E. Badagnani. Wrote *Price Theory: A Policy-Welfare Approach* (1977), *The Freedom Revolution* (1995), *The Flat Tax* (1996), and *Armey's Axioms* (2003). Did not seek re-election in 2002 and was succeeded by Republican Michael Burgess in 2003. Joined the Washington law office of DLA Piper Rudnick Gray Cary (formerly Piper Rudnick). Also became co-chair of Citizens for A Sound Economy, which merged with Empower America to become FreedomWorks. Joined the law firm DLA Piper as a policy advisor.

JOSEPH WELDON BAILEY

Joseph Weldon Bailey

Born October 6, 1863, near Crystal Springs, Mississippi. His middle name was originally Edgar, but he took the family name Weldon during the 1880s. Attended public schools and at least five colleges. Studied law in Lebanon, Tennessee. Returned to Mississippi in 1883 and was admitted to the state bar. Practiced in Hazelhurst. Democrat. Presidential elector from Mississippi in 1884 on the Cleveland-Hendricks ticket. Moved to Gainesville, Texas, in 1885 and began legal practice. Married Ellen Murray in 1886 and they had two sons: Weldon Murray and Joseph Weldon Jr. The latter was also a U.S. representative and U.S. Senate candidate. Presidential elector at-large in 1888. Elected U.S. representative, 5th District in 1890 by unseating incumbent Silas Hare in the Democratic primary election and by defeating Republican A. W. Atchison and Independent W. R. Lamb in the general election. Succeeded Hare on March 4, 1891. Reelected in 1892 by defeating Lily-White Republican Party candidate R. B. Bell and Republican John Grant, in 1894 by defeating Populist N. M. Browder and Republican W. S. Farmer, in 1896 by defeating Republican W. D. Gordon and Populist R. C. Foster, and again in 1898 by defeating Populist W. S. Hot, Republican A. W. Atchison, and Independent J. W. Thomas. Did not run for representative in 1890 and was succeeded by Choice B. Randell on March 3, 1901. Elected U.S. senator by the state legislature on January 23, 1901. Succeeded Horace Chilton in 1901 and took his place in the Houston succession of U.S. senators from Texas. Lost the respect of others after attacking Senator Albert Beveridge in 1902 following a debate. While a representative, he served on the House Rules and Ways and Means committees. Reelected in 1906. Did not seek re-election in 1912. He had served from March 4, 1901, until his resignation on January 3, 1913. Controversy over legal clients and supporters, namely the Waters-Pierce Oil Company, greatly reduced his popularity. While a senator, he served on the Senate Judiciary, Canadian Relations, Census, Finances, Fisheries, Irrigation, and Privileges and Elections committees. He was succeeded for about a month by appointee Rienzi Johnston in January 1913 and then by the elected Morris Sheppard in February 1913. Bailey remained in Washington to practice law but eventually returned to Texas and was a candidate for governor in 1920. Bailey won the primary but lost the runoff to Pat Neff. Bailey's platform opposing prohibition, suffrage for women, and just about every other progressive reform faded when compared to Neff's energetic campaign. Moved to Dallas and continued to practice law. First wife, Ellen, died in 1926 and Bailey married Prudence Rosengren the following year. He died April 13, 1929, in a courtroom in Sherman and was buried at Fairview Cemetery in Gainesville.

I have recently acquired a prejudice against the word "conservative" which I once valued as the best of adjectives with which to describe a Democrat. They have used and abused that word until a conservative now means a man who is unwilling to deprive men of unfair and special privileges because they have long been unmolested in the enjoyment of them. That is not my concept of conservatism; nor do I think that it is the least radical to abolish an ancient abuse—it is the essence of conservatism to correct wrong wherever we find it, because it is by correcting the wrongs which exist today that we can hope to prevent the greater wrongs which may be inflicted upon the country tomorrow.

—Joseph Weldon Bailey

JOSEPH WELDON BAILEY, JR.

Joseph Weldon Bailey Jr.

Born December 15, 1892, in Gainesville. Son of Joseph Weldon Bailey (1863–1929), also a U.S. representative and senator from Texas. Attended public schools in Gainesville and Washington, D.C. Made headlines when as a child he refused to sit on President William McKinley's knee because he was a Republican. Graduated from Princeton University in 1915 and received a law degree from the University of Virginia in 1919. Presbyterian and Democrat. Married Roberta Lewis in 1924 and they had one son, Joseph Weldon Bailey III. Served with U.S. Army during World War I. Admitted to the state bar in 1920 and practiced in Fort Worth. Moved to Dallas later in the year and practiced with Bailey and Shaeffer. Elected to place two of three at-large U.S. representative positions in 1932 by defeating Republican Enoch Fletcher, Socialist Ben Miller, Jacksonian Democrat John Andrews, and Libertarian H. G. Estridge. Served for one term, from March 3, 1933, to January 3, 1935, until three new congressional districts—the 19th through the 21st—were created in 1934. Instead of running again for Congress, he ran as a candidate for U.S. Senate in 1934, but lost the primary election to incumbent Tom Connally. Ran Texans-for-Willkie groups in 1940. Received the help of Tom Connally for a commission in the U.S. Marine Corps during World War II. Suffered fatal injuries in an auto crash and died at Camp Howze, near Gainesville, on July 17, 1943, and was buried at Fairview Cemetery in Gainesville, but in 1958 was reinterred at Sparkman Hillcrest Cemetery in Dallas.

THOMAS HENRY BALL

Born January 14, 1859, in Huntsville. Orphaned at the age of six and was sent to be raised by an uncle, Sidney Spivey, a Confederate Civil War veteran. Attended private schools and graduated from Austin College in 1871. Studied law at the University of Virginia. Admitted to the state bar in 1888 and practiced law in Huntsville until 1902. Served as mayor of Huntsville from 1887 until 1893. Democrat. Married Minnie Thompson in 1882; they had three children—Minnie, David, and Rebecca—and adopted three more. Delegate to the Democratic National Convention in 1892, 1924, and 1928. Elected U.S. representative, 1st District in 1896 by defeating Joe Eagle, who was running as a Populist and Republican, and Republican A.C. Tompkins. He succeeded Joseph Chappel Hutcheson on March 4, 1897. Reelected in 1898 by defeating Republican O. A. Blackwell and Populist Joe Eagle, and in 1900 by defeating Republican S.E. Tracy and Populist S.E. Traylor. Following some redistricting, Ball was elected to the 8th District

Thomas Henry Ball

seat in 1902 by defeating Republican Lock McDaniel, M. H. Kimpton, and Sam Bongio. He was succeeded in his old 1st District seat by Morris Sheppard. While in Congress, he earmarked the first federal funds for the Houston Ship Channel in 1899. Resigned from the House of Representatives on November 16, 1903, and was succeeded by John M. Pinckney the same year. Moved to Houston and continued his practice of law on the behalf of railroads and corporations with Andrews, Ball, and Streetman. Served as general counsel for the Port Commission of Houston. Elected to the Prohibition Statewide Executive Committee in 1911. Encouraged to run as the prohibition candidate for governor against Oscar Colquitt but did not. Candidate for governor in 1914 with "Play Ball" as his slogan, but was defeated in the July primary election by Jim Ferguson. Endorsements were received for Ball from President Wilson and William Jennings Bryan, but Ferguson used this against him, saying that national politicians should stay out of Texas affairs. Served as general counsel for the Houston Harbor and Ship Channel from 1922 until his retirement in 1931. Died May 7, 1944, in Houston and was buried there at Forest Park Cemetery. In 1907 the community of Peck, northwest of Houston, was renamed Tomball in his honor.

HARRY STEPHEN "STEVE" BARTLETT

Born on September 19, 1947, in Los Angeles, California. Moved to Lockhart, Texas in 1951 with his family. Attended Lockhart public schools until he moved to Dallas in 1963. Graduated from Kimball High School in 1966. While in high school, Bartlett was active in the Young Republicans and worked in campaigns for, among others, Jim Collins, whom he later succeeded in Congress. Received a B.A. from the University of Texas in 1971. Married Gail Coke in 1969 and they had three children: Allison, Courtney, and Brian. Businessman. Republican. Served on the Dallas City Council from 1977 until 1981. Elected U.S. Representative, 3rd District, in 1982 by defeating Democrat James L. McNees Jr. and Libertarian Jerry R. Williamson. Succeeded Jim Collins in January 1983. Reelected in 1984 by defeating Democrat Jim Westbrook, in 1986 by defeating Independent Brent Barnes and Libertarian Don Gough, in 1988 by defeating Democrat Blake Cowden, and in 1990 by defeating write-in candidate Noel Kopala. Resigned from Congress

Steve Bartlett

on March 11, 1991, to run for mayor of Dallas and was succeeded by Sam Johnson. Served as mayor of Dallas from 1991 until 1995. Currently serves on a number of boards, consults, and owns a plastics manufacturing business. Resides in Dallas.

JOE LINUS BARTON

Born on September 15, 1949, in Waco. Graduated from Waco High School in 1968. Received a B.S. from Texas A&M University in 1972 and an M.S. from Purdue University in 1973. Married Janet Sue Winslow and they had three children: Brad, Allison, and Kristin. Plant manager and executive with Ennis Business Forms from 1973 until 1981. Methodist and Republican. Served as White House Fellow from 1981 until 1982 and served as an aide to James B. Edwards, secretary, U.S. Department of Energy. Returned to Texas in 1982 as a natural gas consultant. Elected U.S. representative, 6th District in 1984, defeating Democrat Dan Kubiak. Succeeded Phil Gramm in January 1985. Reelected in 1986 by defeating Democrat Pete Geren, in 1988 by defeating Democrat N. P. "Pat" Kendrick, in 1990 by defeating Democrat John Welch and write-in candidate Michael Worsham, in 1992 by defeating Democrat John Dietrich, and in 1994 by defeating Democrat Terry Jesmore and Libertarian Bill Baird. The U.S. District

Joe Barton

Court redrew part of the boundary for Barton's district, requiring him to run in an open primary or special election in November 1996. This election coincided with the general election, in which he was reelected by defeating Janet Carroll Richardson, Independent Libertarian Catherine Anderson, and U.S. Taxpayers Party candidate Doug Williams. (Richardson was a Democrat, but due to an error had to be listed on the ballot as an Independent.) Reelected in 1998 by defeating Democrat Ben Boothe and Libertarian Richard Bandlow. Reelected in 2000 by defeating Libertarian Frank Brady, in 2002 by defeating Democrat Felix Alvarado, Libertarian Frank Brady, and Green Party candidate B. J. Armstrong, and in 2004 by defeating Democrat Morris Meyer and Libertarian Stephen Schrader. Divorced from wife Janet in 2002. In 1993 he sought the Senate seat vacated by Lloyd Bentsen, but came in third behind Hutchison and Krueger in the open election. Married Terri Barton in 2003 who brought two children to the union and they had one child: Jack Kevin. Reelected in 2004 by defeating Democrat David T. Harris and Libertarian Carl Nulsen, in 2006 by defeating Democrat Jim Henley and Libertarian Drew Parks. Serves on the House Science and Energy Committee and Commerce Committee.

I ran for Congress because I felt this country has been slipping away from the value system of our fathers and grandfathers.

—Joe Barton

JOHN ROBERT BAYLOR

Born on July 20, 1822, in Paris, Kentucky. Attended local schools. Moved in 1839 to Fort Gibson, Indian Territory, where his father served as a surgeon. Baylor's father died while he was attending school in Cincinnati. Returned to the community of Rocky Creek, near LaGrange, Texas, to live with an uncle. Joined the Texas Army in 1840. Returned to Fort Gibson in 1842 to teach school. Fled Texas after being convicted as an accessory after his brother-in-law killed an Indian trader. Married Emily Hanna in 1844 and they had seven sons and three daughters. Baylor settled to farm near Ross Prairie in Fayette County. Served one term as state representative, District 55, from 1853 until 1855. In 1853 he was admitted to the state bar. In 1855 he was appointed Indian agent to the Comanches but was fired from this position in 1857 and promoted hatred of Indians for the rest of his life. Edited an anti-Indian newspaper called *White Man* from 1860 until 1866. Delegate to Texas Secession Convention in 1861. Served in the Confederate States

John Baylor

Army. Appointed governor of the Territory of Arizona but was demoted to private when word got back to Confederate headquarters that he had issued a command to kill any Apaches. His commission was restored just before the end of the war. Elected representative, 5th District, to the Second Confederate Congress in August 1863, by defeating incumbent Malcolm D. Graham, and served from 1864 to 1865. Re-settled in San Antonio following the war. Attempted to challenge Richard Coke for governor in 1873 but failed. Practiced Greenback and Populist politics during the later part of his life. Moved to Montell in 1878 to farm. In the 1880s he was reported to have killed a man over a livestock issue, but was never prosecuted. Died on February 6, 1894, in Montell and was buried there at Ascension Episcopal Cemetery.

JAMES ANDREW "JACK" BEALL

Born October 25, 1866, in Mountain Peak in Ellis County. Attended public schools in Ellis County.

Taught school in 1884 and 1885. Attended the University of Texas from 1886 until 1889, received a law degree in 1890, and was admitted to the state bar in 1890. Methodist, Mason, and Democrat. Practiced law in Waxahachie. Served two terms as state representative, District 37 and 68, from 1891 until 1895, and two terms as state senator, District 10, from 1895 until 1899. Married Patricia Martin in 1898 and they had one child. Elected U.S. representative, 5th District, in 1902 by defeating Republican S.H. Lumpkin, Populist A. F. Dornblaser, and Socialist M. C. Scott. Succeeded Choice B. Randell in March 4, 1903. Reelected in 1904 by defeating Republican J. J. Cypert, in 1906 by defeating Republican A. M. Cochran, Reorganized Republican Party candidate Marion T. Connor, and Socialist Virgil Pittman, in 1908 by defeating Republican Marion T. Connor and Socialist John Kerrigan, in 1910 by defeating Socialist C. G. Schwartz, Republican Marion T. Connor, and Socialist-Labor candidate Z. Gilder, and in 1912 by defeating M. C. Scott. Served

Jack Beall

on the House Judiciary Committee. Retired and did not seek reelection in 1914 and was succeeded by Hatton W. Sumners on March 3, 1915. Re-settled in Dallas in 1915 and became a law partner with M. D. Templeton and Tony B. Williams. Served as president of the Texas Electric Railway in 1921. In 1923 he was made a senior partner of law practice Beall, Watson, Rollins, Burford, and Ryburn. In 1927 he became president of the Dallas Union Trust Company. Died February 12, 1929, of a heart attack and was buried at Oakland Cemetery in Dallas.

LINDLEY GARRISON "GARY" BECKWORTH, SR.

Gary Beckworth

Born June 30, 1913, in Kaufman County. Moved with his family to Huntsville in 1914 and on to Upshur County in 1916. Attended local schools and graduated from Gilmer High School in 1931. Baptist, Mason, Odd Fellow, and Democrat. Attended Abilene Christian College, East Texas State Teachers College, Sam Houston State Teachers College, and Southern Methodist University from 1931 until 1932. Taught school in Shady Grove from 1932 until 1933. During 1934 he was employed by the Civilian Work Corps and continued his education with correspondence studies from Abilene Christian College. He continued teaching school. Attended the law schools of the University of Texas and Baylor University. Admitted to the state bar in 1937. Served one term as state representative, District 4, from 1937 until 1938. Elected U.S. representative, 3rd District, in 1938 by unseating incumbent Morgan G. Sanders in the first primary and defeating Brady Gentry in the second primary. He ran unopposed in the 1938 general election. He was the youngest person, at age twenty-five, elected to the House of Representative during the century. He took office on January 3, 1939. Ran unopposed for reelection in 1940 and 1942. Married Eloise Carter in 1942 and they had five children: Mary Eloise, Linda Louise, Carter Otis, Lindley, Jr., and John Barney. Reelected in 1944 by defeating Republican O. P. Stephens, in 1946 ran unopposed, and in 1948 and 1950 defeated Republican R. E. Kennedy. Served on the House Interstate and Foreign Commerce Committee. Did not seek reelection to the House of Representatives in 1952 and was succeeded by Brady Gentry in 1953. Candidate for U.S. Senate seat of Tom Connally in 1952, but lost the primary election to Price Daniel. Ran again for U.S. representative, 3rd District, in 1954, but lost to Brady Gentry in the Democratic primary election. Reelected in 1956 over old-time opponent Republican R. E. Kennedy. Ran unopposed in 1958 and 1960. Served on the House Interstate and Foreign Commerce, Foreign Affairs, Post Office, and Civil Service committees. Reelected in 1962 by defeating Republican William Steger and 1964 by defeating Republican James Warren. The Reapportionment of Congressional Districts Act of 1965 eliminated Beckworth's 3rd District and placed it within Ray Roberts' 4th District.

Beckworth lost to Roberts in the 1966 Democratic primary. Succeeded by Joe Pool in the 3rd District seat on January 3, 1967. Appointed by President Johnson as U.S. Customs Court judge and served from 1967 until 1968 in New York. Practiced law in Longview with Whitehead and Whitehead. Served one term as state senator, District 2, from 1971 until 1973 and then returned to his law practice. Died on March 9, 1984, from cancer in Tyler and was buried there at Rose Hill Cemetery. (See also photo page 24)

It is important to every segment of American endeavor that our family-size farmers and ranchers in particular be prosperous and continue to progress.

—Gary Beckworth

CARLOS BEE

Born July 8, 1867, in Saltillo, Mexico. His parents were there temporarily waiting out the repercussions in Texas following the Civil War. Great-grandson of Thomas Bee (1725–1812), who was a delegate to the Continental Congress from South Carolina. Family returned to San Antonio in 1874. Attended San Antonio public schools and the Agricultural and Mechanical College, now Texas A&M University. Studied law and clerked at the Judge Advocates Office at Fort Sam Houston. Married Mary Kyle Burleson, sister of Albert S. Burleson. She died and he married Mary Elizabeth Bee. Admitted to the state bar in 1893 and practiced in San Antonio. Democrat. Appointed U.S. commissioner for the Western District of Texas in 1897. Served as district attorney, 37th District, from 1898 until 1905. Served on the San Antonio School Board from 1906 until 1908. Chaired the state Democratic convention in Houston in 1904 and was a delegate to the Democratic national conventions in 1904 and 1908. Presided over the Bexar County

Carlos Bee

School Board from 1912 until 1914. Served two terms as state senator, District 24, from 1915 to 1919. Elected U.S. representative, 14th District, in 1918 by defeating Republican John Hartman. Succeeded James L. Slayden on March 4, 1919. Unseated by Republican Harry M. Wurzbach in 1920 and was succeeded by him on March 3, 1921. Bee returned to his law practice in San Antonio. Died on April 20, 1932, in San Antonio and was buried there at the Confederate Cemetery.

Charles Bell

CHARLES KEITH BELL

Born April 18, 1853, in Chattanooga, Tennessee. Nephew of Reese Bowen Brabson (1817–63), a U.S. representative from Tennessee. Attended public schools and Sewanee College. Moved to Belton, Texas, in 1871, but returned briefly to Tennessee in 1873 to study law. Returned to Hamilton and lived there from 1874 until 1893. Admitted to Texas bar in 1874. Democrat. Practiced law in Hamilton. Served as Hamilton County prosecuting attorney from 1876 until 1880 and district attorney, 29th District, from 1880 until 1882. Delegate to the Democratic national convention in 1884. Served two terms as state senator, District 23, from 1885 until 1889, and district judge, 29th District, from 1888 until 1890. Elected U.S. representative, 8th District, in 1892 by defeating People's Party candidate Evan Jones and Republican C. C. Drake. Succeeded Littleton Wilde Moore on March 4, 1893. Reelected in 1894 by defeating Populist C. H. Jenkins. Did not seek reelection in 1896 and was succeeded by Samuel W. T. Lanham on March 3, 1897. Continued his legal practice in Fort Worth. Appointed attorney general by Governor Sayers in May 1901 and served until 1904. Returned to law practice. Candidate for governor in 1906, but was defeated by Thomas M. Campbell at the Democratic convention and retired from politics. Married

Florence Smith in 1906 and they had one son. Died on April 21, 1913, and was buried at East Oakwood Cemetery in Fort Worth.

JOHN JUNIOR BELL

Born on May 15, 1910, in Cuero. Attended public schools. Graduated from the University of Texas in 1932 and received a law degree from the same institution in 1936. Admitted to the state bar in 1936 and practiced in Cuero. Married Mabel Claire Breeden in 1948, but they had no children. Democrat. Lawyer and president of cotton compress company. Served seven terms as state representative, District 68, from 1937 until 1949 and three terms as state senator, District 18, from 1949 until he resigned in September 1954. While there, he was responsible for the Texas Veterans Land Act. Served in the U.S. Army during World War II. Delegate to the Democratic national convention in 1948 and 1952. Elected U.S. representative, 14th District, in 1954 by defeating Republican D. C. DeWitt. Succeeded John E. Lyle on January 3, 1955. Served one term and was unseated in the Democratic primary election by John Young in 1956 and was succeeded by him on January 3, 1957. Indicted on July 19, 1955, in Seguin for conspiracy in connection with a

John Bell

veterans land deal. The case was dismissed on a technicality on December 12, 1955, as it was found one of the grand jury members had not paid their poll tax. Bell returned to his farming and ranching business in Cuero. Died on January 24, 1963, of a heart attack and was buried at Hillside Cemetery in Cuero.

PETER HANSBOROUGH BELL

Born on May 18, 1812, in Culpepper, Spotsylvania County, Virginia. Educated in Virginia and Maryland Democrat. Served in Texas Army during War for Independence. Fought at San Jacinto. Served as assistant adjutant general in 1837 and was made inspector general in 1839. Joined the Texas Rangers in 1840. Joined the U.S. Army in 1845 to fight in the Mexican War. Elected governor in 1849 and 1851 and served until 1853. Following the death of David Kaufman, Bell resigned on November 25, 1853—a few months early—from the governor's post to take his seat in Congress. Elected U.S. representative, 2nd District, in 1853, by defeating Democrats William R. Scurry and G. K. Lewis, Whig Party candidate B. F. Carouthers, and Democrat F. M. Blake. Succeeded Volney Howard on March 4, 1853. Reelected in 1855 by defeating American Party candidate John Hancock. Did not seek reelection in 1856 and was succeeded by John H. Reagan in what was now the 1st District seat on March 3, 1857. Moved to North Carolina. Married widow Ella Reeves Eaton

Peter Hansborough Bell

Dickens in 1857 and settled at her home in Littleton, North Carolina. He was rumored to have accepted a Confederate commission, but spent much of the war on his wife's plantation. Voted a land donation and a pension from the State of Texas in 1891 for his service to the state. Died on March 8, 1898, in Littleton, North Carolina, and was buried at the City Cemetery, but he and his wife were reintered in 1930 at Texas State Cemetery in Austin. Bell County is named in his honor.

ROBERT CHRISTOPHER "CHRIS" BELL

Born November 23, 1959, in Abilene. Grew up in Dallas. Attended public schools. Received Bachelor of Journalism degree from the University of Texas at Austin in 1982 and law degree from South Texas College of Law in 1992. Admitted to the state bar. Television reporter and, after law school, served as an attorney with Beirne, Maynard and Parsons. Episcopal and Democrat. Married Alison Ayres in

Texas Delegation from about 1960 in the Speaker of the House's Dining Room.

Back row, left to right: Bob Casey, John Young, J. T. Rutherford, Jack Brooks, Frank Ikard, Homer Thornberry, Omar Burleson, Olin Teague, Clark Thompson, Walter Rogers, John Dowdy, Joe Kilgore, Jim Wright, and Gary Beckworth.

Front row, left to right: Paul Kilday, Bob Poage, Wright Patman, Senator Lyndon B. Johnson, Speaker of the House Sam Rayburn, Senator Ralph Yarborough, George Mahon, Albert Thomas, and O. C. Fisher. The only delegation member not present is Republican Bruce Alger.

1992 and they have two children: Atlee and Connally. Elected Houston City Council, At-Large Position 4 and served from 1998 through 2001. Unsuccessful candidate for Houston City Council At-Large Position 3, 1995. Sought Mayor's post in 2001, but lost to Lee Brown. Elected Representative, District 25, in 2002 by defeating Republican Tom Reiser, Libertarian Guy McLendon, and Green Party candidate George Reiter. Succeeded Ken Bentsen in January 2003. Served on the International Relations Committee and Financial Services Committees. Unseated in 2004, by Al Green in the Democratic Primary election and succeeded by him the following year. Democratic nominee for Governor in 2006, but was defeated by Republican incumbent Rick Perry.

Chris Bell

KENNETH F. "KEN" BENTSEN, JR.

Born on June 3, 1959, in Houston. Nephew of Lloyd Millard Bentsen Jr. (1921–2006), former U.S. congressman, senator, and secretary of the treasury. Presbyterian and Democrat. Graduated from Deerfield Academy in 1977. Received B.A. from the University of St. Thomas in Houston in 1982 and M.P.A. from American University in Washington, D.C., in 1985. Worked as legislative assistant to Representative Ron Coleman from 1983 until 1987. Served as associate staff to the House Appropriations Committee. Employed as investment banker from 1987 until 1994. Married Tamra Kiehn in 1990 and they had two children: Louise and Meredith. Chair of Harris County Democratic Party from 1990 until 1993. Elected U.S. representative, 25th District, in 1994 by defeating Republican Gene Fontenot, Libertarian Robert Lockhart, and Independent Sarah Klein-Tower. Succeeded Mike Andrews in January 1995. The U.S. District Court redrew part of the boundary for Bentsen's district, requiring him to run in an open primary or special election in November 1996. This election coincided with the general election. Bentsen was challenged by Democrat Beverley Clark, Republicans

Ken Bentsen

Dotty Collins, John Devine, Ken Mathis, Dolly McKenna, Ron Meinke, Lloyd Oliver, Brent Perry, and John Sanchez, and Socialist Worker's Party candidate Jerry Freiwirth. Receiving no clear majority, he defeated Republican Dolly McKenna in a December 1996 runoff election. Reelected in 1998 by defeating Republican John Sanchez and Libertarian Eric Atkisson. Reelected in 2000 by defeating Republican Phil Sudan and Libertarian Clifford Lee Messina. Served on the Budget and Banking Committee and Financial Services Committee. Did not seek re-election as U.S. Representative in 2002. Unsuccessful candidate for the Democratic Party nomination for U.S. Senate in 2002; placed third behind Kirk and Morales. Succeeded by Chris Bell in 2003. Joined the Austin firm, Public Strategies in their Washington and New York City offices and is now President of the Equipment Leasing Association.

LLOYD MILLARD BENTSEN, JR.

Born on February 11, 1921, in Mission. Attended public schools. Graduated from the University of Texas law school and was admitted to the state bar in 1942. Served as a bomber pilot during World War II. Returned to McAllen to practice law. Married Beryl Ann "B. A." Longino in 1943 and they had three children: Lloyd III, Lan Chase, and Tina Ann. Presbyterian and Democrat. Served as Hidalgo County judge from 1946 until 1948. Elected U.S. representative, 15th District, in November 1948 by running unopposed to succeed the late Milton West. He was also elected to fill the remainder of West's seat for the December session of Congress a few weeks later in a December 1948 special election that he won without opposition. He took office on December 4, 1948, and began his first full term as U.S. representative the following January. Reelected without opposition in 1950 and 1952. Did not seek reelection

Lloyd Bentsen

in 1954 and was succeeded by Joe Kilgore on January 3, 1955. During 1955, he founded the Consolidated American Life Insurance Company, which merged with the Lincoln Liberty Life Insurance Company three years later. Elected U.S. senator in 1970 by unseating incumbent Ralph Yarborough in the Democratic primary and defeating George H. W. Bush in the general election. Took place in the Rusk succession of U.S. senators from Texas. Unsuccessfully sought the Democratic nomination for president in 1976. Reelected in 1976 by defeating Republican Alan Steelman, in 1982 by defeating Republican Jim Collins, and in 1988 by defeating Republican Beau Boulter and Libertarian J. Daiell. Served on the Senate Finance Committee and served as its chairman from 1987 until he left the Senate. Also served on the Joint Committee on Taxation, and Economic and Commerce committees. Vice-presidential candidate with running mate Michael Dukakis in 1988. Served from January 3, 1971, until January 20, 1993, when he resigned from office to accept an appointment from President Clinton as secretary of the treasury. Served as secretary of the treasury from January 20, 1993, until December 22, 1994. Awarded the Presidential Medal of Freedom by President Clinton on August 11, 1999. Uncle of Kenneth E. "Ken" Bentsen Jr. (1959–), a former U.S. representative from Texas. Died on May 23, 2006, at his home in Houston and was buried in Forest Park Lawndale Cemetery in Houston.

I served with Jack Kennedy. I knew Jack Kennedy. Jack Kennedy was a friend of mine. Senator, you're no Jack Kennedy.

—Lloyd Bentsen to Dan Quayle

Eugene Black

EUGENE BLACK

Born on July 2, 1879, near Blossom. Attended public schools. Family moved to Clarksville in the 1890s. Taught school in Lamar County from 1890 until 1900 and worked for the local post office. Married Maimie Coleman in 1903 and they had six children: Margaret, Lyda Gene, Adelle, Rachael, Harold, and Barbara. Democrat. Received law degree from Cumberland University in Lebanon, Tennessee, in 1905. Admitted to the state bar in 1905 and practiced in Clarksville. He and his brother Ernest began what was to become a successful wholesale grocery company. They were also an early bottler of Coca-Cola. Elected U.S. representative, 1st District, in 1914, by defeating Socialist J. C. Thompson. Succeeded Horace W. Vaughan on March 4, 1915. Reelected in 1916 over Republican David H. Morris and Socialist J. C. Thompson, ran unopposed in 1918, defeated Republican G. T. Bartlett in 1920 and 1922, defeated Republican R. B. Johnson in 1924 and Republican O. F. Wimmer in 1926. Unseated by Wright Patman in the 1928 Democratic primary and was succeeded by him on March 3, 1929. He remained in Washington and was appointed U.S. Tax Court judge by President Hoover and served from 1929 until 1953, then served as needed until he retired completely in 1966. Died on May 22, 1975, in Washington, D.C., and was buried at Cedar Hill Cemetery in Suitland, Maryland. (See also photo page 29.)

WILLIAM ARVIS BLAKLEY

Born on November 17, 1898, in Miami Station, Missouri. Moved to Arapho, Oklahoma, with family while an infant. Graduated from Arapho High School in 1917. Attended a U.S. Army training program at the University of Oklahoma during World War I. Presbyterian and Democrat. Married Villa Darnell in

1922. They had no children. Moved to Dallas, Texas in 1925, became a CPA, and studied law. Admitted to the state bar in 1933. Was the largest shareholder in Braniff Airlines at one time and founded the Exchange National Bank. Appointed by Governor Shivers and served as U.S. senator from January 15 until April 28, 1957, following the January 14, 1957, resignation of Price Daniel, who had been elected governor. Governor Shivers refused to appoint an interim senator until the newly elected Governor Daniel resigned from his Senate seat. In the waning hours of his office, Shivers appointed Blakley as interim senator until the post could be filled by a special election. The appointment was quite important, as control of the U.S. Senate rested with the Democrats by just a slim margin (forty-nine to forty-seven). At the time, the Senate majority leader was Lyndon Johnson. With one more voting Republican in the Senate (and one less voting Democratic), a vote along party lines would end in a tie, thus requiring Vice-president Nixon to cast the tie-break-

Bill Blakely

ing vote. This would effectively have relieved the Democrats of control of the Senate. Blakley served in the Rusk Succession but did not run in the April 1957 special election to fill the post. There were more than twenty candidates for the office, which was won by Ralph W. Yarborough. In 1958 Blakley ran an unsuccessful campaign against Ralph Yarborough for the Democratic nomination for the post. In 1961 Blakley was again appointed U.S. senator in the Houston succession, upon the resignation of Lyndon B. Johnson, who left his senate seat to become vice-president. Blakley served from January 3 until June 14, 1961. Blakley placed second in a pack of seventy-one for the seat in the special election and was forced into a runoff election with Republican John Tower. In the runoff, Blakley was defeated by John Tower, who succeeded him on June 15, 1961. Donated $100 million to the Blakley-Braniff Foundation. Died on January 5, 1976, and was buried at Restland Memorial Park in Dallas.

THOMAS LINDSAY BLANTON

Born on October 25, 1872, in Houston. Attended public schools in Houston and LaGrange. Received law degree from the University of Texas in 1897 and was admitted to the state bar the same year. Married May Louise Matthews in 1899 and they had five children: Thomas Jr., John Matthew, Anne Louise, Joseph Edwin, and William Watkin. Presbyterian, Prohibitionist, and Democrat. First practiced law in Cleburne, but moved to Albany. Elected district judge, 42nd Judicial District, in 1908 and 1912 and served until he was elected to Congress. Elected as the first U.S. representative for the newly created 17th District in 1916 over Socialist T. B. Holiday and Republican C.O. Harris. Took office on March 4, 1917. Ran unopposed for reelection in 1918. Served on the House Education, Claims, Womans Suffrage, and Railways and Canals committees. Reelected in 1920 by defeating American Party candidate W. D. Cowan. Blanton was brought up on charges that could have resulted in his expulsion from

Thomas Blanton

Congress in 1921. Blanton grated on so many people, the Texas delegation thought that Congressman Buchanan would eventually lose his temper and shoot Blanton. The *New York Times* said in a February 1921 editorial, "He is universal, perpetual, persistent ... Mr. Blanton has succeeded in bothering everybody. The rest of the Texas delegation has long looked for the hour of reprisals." That day came when Blanton was found responsible, albeit inadvertently, for foul language printed in the *Congressional Record*. Although he didn't speak the words, he was responsible for them being printed. The language so outraged the public printer of the Government Printing Office, George H. Carter, that he had pages 7417 through 7425 removed from the October 22, 1921, *Congressional Record*. The daily issue of the Record had the pages removed by hand, and the cloth-bound, permanent editions do not include the remarks. Many called for Blanton's expulsion, but he wound up being censured instead. Blanton remains the only representative from Texas to receive such treatment. Reelected in 1922 by defeating Republican W. D. Girand, ran unopposed in 1924, and in 1926 defeated Republican H. B. Tanner. Did not seek reelection in 1928 and was succeeded for one term by Robert Q. Lee on March 3, 1929. Blanton ran instead for the U.S. Senate in 1928, but lost the primary election to Earle B. Mayfield. Blanton sought and was reelected to his former 17th District U.S. House seat in a May 20, 1930, special election to fill the seat of the man who had replaced him—Robert Lee. Lee had died while in office. Reelected in 1932 and 1934 without opposition. Unseated by Clyde Garrett in the 1936 Democratic primary and succeeded by him on January 3, 1937. Practiced law in Washington until 1938, when he returned to Albany. In 1954 he ran briefly for U.S. representative again but withdrew from the race. Died on August 11, 1957, and was buried at Albany Cemetery in Albany, Texas. While serving in Congress, Blanton opposed extravagance, communists, and strikers during wartime. (See also photo page 29.)

HENRY BONILLA

Henry Bonilla

Born on January 2, 1954, in San Antonio. Graduated from South San Antonio High School in 1972. Received bachelors degree from the University of Texas in Austin in 1976. Television-reported with KTVV in Austin from 1976 until 1978 and KENS in San Antonio from 1978 until 1980. Moved to Philadelphia in 1980 and worked sales at Saks Fifth Avenue. Served as press secretary to Pennsylvania governor Richard Thornburgh from 1980 until 1982. Married Deborah JoAnn Knapp in 1981 and they had two children: Alicia and Austin. Writer/producer for WABC in New York from 1982 until 1985, assistant news director at WTAF in Philadelphia from 1985 until 1986, executive producer at KENS in San Antonio from 1986 until 1990, and public affairs at KENS from 1990 until 1992. Republican. Elected U.S. representative, 23rd District, in 1992 by unseating incumbent Democrat Albert Bustamante and defeating Libertarian David Alter. Succeeded Bustamante in January 1993. He was the first Hispanic Republican elected to Congress from Texas. Reelected in 1994 by defeating Democrat Rolando Rios, in 1996 by defeating Democrat Charles Jones and Natural Law Party candidate Linda Caswell, in 1998 by defeating Democrat Charlie Urbina Jones and Libertarian Bill Stallknecht, and in 2000 by defeating Democrat Isidro Garza Jr. and Libertarian Jeffrey C. Blunt, in 2002 by defeating Democrat Henry Cuellar, Libertarian Jeffrey C. Blunt, and Green Party candidate Ed Scharf, and in 2004 by defeating Democrat Joe Sullivan and Libertarian Nazirite "Comrade" Perez. Served on the House Appropriations Committee. On June 28, 2006, the United States Supreme Court ruled that the Texas Legislature had violated the rights of Hispanic voters when it moved most of Laredo out of the neighboring 23rd District and replaced it with several heavily Republican San Antonio suburbs. It also ruled that the 25th District was not compact enough to be a replacement. The 25th District was nicknamed "the fajita strip" because of its shape. The ruling forced the redrawing of five districts between El Paso and San Antonio including the 23rd and a special election to select their representatives. This election coincided with the November general election. In the November 7, 2006, Special Election, Bonilla faced Democrats August G. "Augie" Beltran, Ciro D. Rodriguez, Rick Bolanos, Adrian DeLeon, Lukin Gilliland, and Albert Uresti and Independent Craig T. Stephens. The raced was close enough between Bonilla and Rodriguez that a runoff was held on December 12, 2006. Ciro Rodriguez won the election and succeeded Bonilla.

Watching Nixon in China, I realized that all of the ideas I had about politics—a belief in free enterprise system, a strong defense, less government—didn't have a thing in common with the Democratic Party, so I became a Republican.

—Henry Bonilla

Texas Delegation from the late 1920s. Members pictured are: 1. Eugene Black, 2. John C. Box, 3. Morgan Sanders, 4. Sam Rayburn, 5. Hatton Sumners, 6. Luther Johnson, 7. Clay Stone Briggs, 8. Daniel Garrett, 9. Joe Mansfield, 10. Joseph P. Buchanan, 11. Tom Connally, 12. Fritz Lanham, 13. Guinn Williams, 14. Harry Wurzbach, 15. John N. Garner, 16. Claude Hudspeth, 17. Thomas Blanton, 18. Marvin Jones

ELDON BEAU BOULTER

Beau Boulter

Born on February 23, 1942, in El Paso. Graduated from Levelland High School in 1960. Graduated from the University of Texas in 1965 and received a law degree from Baylor University in 1968. Admitted to the state bar in 1968 and began practice in Amarillo. Married Rosemary Rutherford in 1963 and they had three children: Rebecca, Matthew, and Elizabeth. Republican. Served on the Amarillo City Commission from 1981 until 1983. Ran unsuccessfully for U.S. representative, 13th District, in 1982 and was defeated by Ron Slover in the Republican primary election. Elected U.S. representative, 13th District, in 1984 by unseating incumbent Democrat Jack Hightower. Succeeded Hightower in January 1985. Reelected in 1986 by defeating Democrat Doug Seal. Did not seek reelection to the Congress in 1988 and was succeeded by Democrat Bill Sarpalius in January 1989. Sought and received the Republican nomination for U.S. Senator in 1988 after defeating three contenders in the primary and Wes Gilbreath in the runoff, but lost to Lloyd Bentsen in the general election. Unsuccessfully sought his old 13th District seat in 1992 and was defeated by Bill Sarpalius. Currently a lobbyist in Washington, D.C.

JOHN CALVIN BOX

John Box

Born on March 28, 1871, near Crockett. Attended Henderson County schools. Was a practicing Methodist Episcopal minister. Studied law at the Alexander Institute in Kilgore. Admitted to the state bar in 1893 and practiced in Lufkin. Married El Mina Hill in 1893 and they had two children: Mary (Bish) and John Jr. Moved to Jacksonville in 1897. Mason and Democrat. Served as Cherokee County judge from 1898 until 1901 and mayor of Jacksonville from 1902 until 1905. Served on the State Democratic Executive Committee from 1902 until 1905. Served on the Board of Education. Elected U.S. Representative, 2nd District, in 1918, running unopposed. Succeeded Martin Dies on March 4, 1919. Reelected in 1920 by defeating American Party candidate G. E. Meyer, in 1922 by defeating Republican C. A. Lord, in 1924 by defeating Republican A. E. Sweatland, in 1926 by defeating Republican William C. Hall, and in 1928 ran unopposed. Unseated in the 1930 Democratic primary by Martin Dies—the son of the man he replaced—and was succeeded by him on March 3, 1931. Box returned to Jacksonville and his law practice. Died on May 17, 1941, and was buried at City Cemetery in Jacksonville. (See also photo page 29.)

I could have taken the money from lobbyists, come home driving a Cadillac, and I would have been known as "Congressman Box," but I didn't. I came home driving a Ford, and now everyone refers to me as "Old Man Box."'

—John C. Box

KEVIN PATRICK BRADY

Born on April 11, 1955, in Vermillion, South Dakota. Graduated from Rapid City Central High School in South Dakota. Moved to Beaumont, Texas in 1981. Graduated from the University of South Dakota in 1990. Catholic and a Republican. Married Cathy Patronella in 1991 and they have two sons: Will and Sean. President of the South Montgomery County-Woodlands Chamber of Commerce. Served as state representative, District 15, from 1991 until 1997. Elected U.S. representative, 8th District, in the 1996 special election by defeating Republican Gene Fontenot and Democrats Robert Musemeche and Cynthia J. Newman. This special election came about as a result of the U.S. District Court redrawing part of the boundary for the 8th District, which required Brady to run in an open primary or special election in November 1996. This election coincided with the general election. Receiving no clear majority, Brady was forced into a runoff and defeated Fontenot in a December special runoff election. Succeeded Jack Fields in January 1997. Reelected in 1998 by defeating Libertarian Don Richards and in 2000 by defeating Libertarian Gil Guillory, in 2002 by defeating Guillory again, and in 2004 by defeating Democrat James Wright and Libertarian Paul Hansen, and in 2006 by defeating Democrat Jim Wright. Served on the House International Relations and Science Committees, but now serves on Ways and Means.

ANTHONY MARTIN BRANCH

Kevin Brady

Anthony Branch

Born on July 16, 1823, in Buckingham County, Virginia. Graduated from Hampden-Sydney College in 1842. Moved to Huntsville, Texas in 1847. Formed law practice with Henderson Yoakum. Great friend of Sam Houston and served as the executor of Houston's estate upon his death. Married Amanda Smith in 1849. Elected district attorney, 7th Judicial District, in 1850. Served one term as state representative, District 38, from 1859 until 1861 and very briefly as state senator, District 17, beginning in 1861. One of ten state senators who resigned to join the Confederate States Army. Elected representative, 3rd District, to the Second Confederate Congress in 1863 by defeating incumbent Peter W. Gray. Served from 1864 until 1865. Elected U.S. representative, 3rd District, in 1866 by defeating Mills, Bassett, and Greeley. However, the four representatives elected in 1866 were denied their seats by the Radical Republicans. It was more than three years before the representatives from Texas were allowed to take their seats in the House following the Civil War. Co-founded the Central Transit Company. Died on October 3, 1867, of yellow fever, in Huntsville, and was buried there at Oakwood Cemetery.

CLAY STONE BRIGGS

Clay Briggs

Born on January 8, 1876, in Galveston. Attended public and private schools. Attended the University of Texas and Harvard University. Graduated from the Yale University law school in 1899. Admitted to the state bar in 1899 and practiced law in Galveston. Democrat. Served one term as state representative, District 23, from 1907 until 1909 and served as judge, 10th Judicial District, from 1909 until he resigned in 1919. He resigned from his judgeship as he was elected U.S. representative, 7th District, in 1918 with no opposition. He succeeded Alexander Gregg on March 4, 1919. Ran unopposed for reelection in 1920, in 1922 defeated Republican Frank Sneed Camper, in 1924 defeated Republican John T. Wheeler, in 1926 defeated Republican Sam Halstead, in 1928 defeated Republican Arthur J. Long, in 1930 ran unopposed, and in 1932 defeated Republican Arthur J. Long. Died from a heart attack while serving in office on April 29, 1933, in Washington and was buried at Oakwood Cemetery in Syracuse, New York. His office was filled briefly by Clark Thompson until 1935. Married twice; he was survived by his second wife, Lois Slayton Woodworth. (See also photo page 29.)

MOSES LYCURGUS BROOCKS

Born on November 1, 1864, near San Augustine, Texas. Attended local schools. Received law degree from the University of Texas in 1891. Practiced law in San Augustine. Democrat. Served one term as state representative, District 34, from 1893 until 1895. Moved to Beaumont, Texas. Elected district attorney, 1st District, in 1896 and served one term. Elected U.S. representative, 2nd District, in 1904 by defeating Republican Andrew Jackson Houston. Succeeded Samuel Cooper on March 4, 1905. Served just one term and did not seek reelection in 1906. Succeeded by the man he replaced—Samuel Cooper—on March 3, 1907. Returned to his law practice in San Augustine and died a short time later on May 27, 1908, in San Antonio and was buried at Old Broocks Cemetery east of San Augustine.

Moses Broocks

JACK BASCOM BROOKS

Born on December 12, 1922, in Crowley, Louisiana. Moved to Beaumont, Texas in 1927. Graduated from Beaumont High School in 1939. Attended Lamar Junior College from 1939 until 1941 and received a journalism degree from the University of Texas in 1942. Served in the U.S. Marine Corps during World War II and stayed in the Marine Corps Reserves until he retired as a colonel. Received a law degree from the University of Texas and was admitted to the state bar in 1949. Married Charlotte Collins in 1960 and they had three children: Jeb, Katherine, and Kimberly. Democrat. Served two terms as state representative, District 16-1, from 1947 until 1951. Elected U.S. representative in 1952, 2nd District, by defeating Republican Randolph Reed. Succeeded Jesse Combs on January 3, 1953. Ran unopposed for reelection in 1954, 1956, and 1958. Reelected in 1960 by defeating Republican F. S. Naumann and Constitution Party candidate Robert Allen, in 1962 by defeating Republican Roy James Jr., and in 1964 by defeating Republican John Greco. Redistricting occurred in 1966 and the 2nd District became the 9th District. Brooks was succeeded in the 2nd District seat by John Dowdy and succeeded Clark Thompson in the 9th District. Elected U.S. representative, 9th District, in 1966 after running unopposed. Reelected in 1968 and 1970 by defeating Republican Henry Pressler, in 1972 by defeating Republican Randolph Reed, in 1974 by defeating Republican Coleman Ferguson. In 1976 he ran unopposed, in 1978 defeated Republican Randy Evans, in 1980 defeated Independent Dean Allen, in 1982 defeated Republican John W. Lewis and now Libertarian Dean Allen, in 1984 defeated Republican Jim Mahan, in 1986 defeated Republican Lisa Duperier, in 1988 ran unopposed, in 1990 defeated Republican Maury Meyers, and in 1992 defeated Republican Steve Stockman and Libertarian Billy Joe Crawford, but was unseated in 1994 by Republican Steve Stockman and was succeeded by him in January 1995. Served on numerous committees including Government Operations and eventually chaired the Judiciary Committee. Retired to his home in Beaumont. In 2001, NASA Administrator Daniel Goldin presented the agency's highest honor, the Distinguished Service Medal to Brooks for long-standing support of the U.S. space program and praised his role in "strengthening the agency during its formative years". Jack Brooks Park in Galveston County was named in his honor along with the Federal Building in Beaumont. (See also photo page 24.)

> *Constructive change doesn't come just because you think something isn't right ... it is tough, tedious work ... I've tried to change a thousand things in government and only managed a few.*
>
> —Jack Brooks

Jack Brooks

GUY MORRISON BRYAN

Born on January 12, 1821, in Herculaneum, Missouri. Nephew of Stephen F. Austin. His father died when he was young and his mother remarried. The family moved to San Felipe and Pleasant Bayou in the Mexican state of Texas in 1831, and then finally to Peach Point, Brazoria County, in 1832. Attended private schools. Served briefly in Republic of Texas after Battle of San Jacinto. Graduated from Kenyon College in 1842. Served in U.S. Army during the Mexican War. Lawyer. Served three terms as state representative from Brazoria County (later Districts 27 and 35), from 1847 until 1853, and two terms as state senator, District 24, from 1853 until 1857. Delegate to the Democratic national convention in 1856 and chaired the Texas delegation to the convention in 1860. Married Laura Harrison Jack in 1858 and they had four children: William Jack, Laura Parker, Halley Ballinger, and Guy Morrison Jr. Nominated at the first regular state Democratic convention in 1857 in Waco. Elected U.S. representative, 2nd District, in 1857 by defeating American Party

Guy Morrison Bryan

candidate William Howth. Succeeded Peter Hansborough Bell on March 4, 1857. Served one term and did not seek reelection to Congress in 1858. He was encouraged by his wife to return home to Texas and was succeeded by Andrew Jackson Hamilton on March 3, 1859. Moved to Galveston in 1860. Served in Confederate States Army. His wife, Laura, died in 1872 following the birth of Guy, Jr. Served three more non-congruent terms as state representative, District 12, from 1874 until 1875; District 35, from 1879 until 1881; and finally District 64, from 1889 until 1891. Elected Speaker of the House and served from 1874 until 1875. Moved to Quintana in 1890 and Austin in 1898. Served as president of the Texas Veterans Association from 1892 until his death. Died on June 4, 1901, in Austin and was buried there at the Texas State Cemetery.

JOHN WILEY BRYANT

John Bryant

Born on February 22, 1947, in Velasco, but was raised in Lake Jackson. Attended Lake Jackson Elementary School and graduated from Brazosport High School in Freeport in 1965. Received a B.A. from Southern Methodist University in 1969 and a J.D. in 1972. Admitted to the state bar in 1972 and began practice in Dallas. Served as special counsel to the Consumer Protection Committee in the Texas Senate in 1973. Methodist and Democrat. Married Janet Watts in 1968 and they had three children: Amy, John, Jr., and Jordan. Served most of five terms as state representative, District 33-L, from 1974 until 1983. Elected in a January 24, 1974, special election to fill the seat of the late Joseph P. Hawn. Delegate to the Democratic national convention in 1976, 1980, 1984, 1988, 1992, and 1998. Elected U.S. representative, 5th District, in 1982 by defeating Republican Joe Devany, Citizens Party candidate John Bridges, and Libertarian Richard Squire. Succeeded Jim Mattox in January 1983. Served on the House Energy and Commerce, Judiciary, Budget, and Veterans Affairs committees. Reelected in 1984 by running unopposed, in 1986 by defeating Republican Tom Carter and Libertarian Robert Brewer, in 1988 by defeating Republican Lon Williams and Libertarian Kenneth Ashby, in 1990 by defeating Republican Jerry Rucker and Libertarian Kenneth Ashby, in 1992 by defeating Republican Richard Stokley and Libertarian William H. Walker, and in 1994 by defeating Republican Pete Sessions, Independents Barbara Morgan and Regina Arashvand, and Libertarian Noel Kopala. Did not seek reelection to Congress in 1996 and was succeeded by Pete Sessions in January 1997. Authored the Texas Wilderness Bill and in 1995 wrote the Lobby Disclosure Act, which required lobbyists to identify their clients, the legislators they lobbied, and the amount they spent. Campaigned briefly for the state attorney general's post in 1989, but withdrew before the end of the year. Bryant announced a run for Phil Gramm's U.S. Senate seat in December 1995. Finished second in the close March 1996 Democratic primary behind Victor Morales, but lost the runoff to Morales the following month. Since leaving Congress, Bryant served as U.S. ambassador in charge of U.S. negotiations on International Telecommunications and Satellite Treaty at the International Telecommunications Union and World Radiocommunications Conference in Geneva, Switzerland, in 1997. In 1998 he returned to the practice of law in Dallas with Glass, Phillips, and Murray.

JOSEPH PAUL BUCHANAN

Born April 30, 1867, in Midway, South Carolina. Cousin of Edward William Pou (1863–1934), a U.S. representative from North Carolina. Moved to Chapel Hill in Washington County, Texas as a child in 1875. Attended local schools. Graduated from the University of Texas in 1889. Admitted to the state bar and practiced in Brenham. Democrat. Married Emma Nicholson and they had one son: James Paul Jr. Served as Washington County justice of the peace from 1889 until 1892. Served as the county's prosecuting attorney from 1892 until 1899 and district attorney, 21st Judicial District, from 1899 until 1906. In private legal practice with Mathis and Buchanan from 1906 until 1913. Served three terms as state representative, District 47, and finally 69, from 1909 until his resignation in 1913 to run for Congress. Elected U.S. representative, 10th District, in 1913 by defeating fellow Democrat George Calhoun in the April 5 special election to fill the vacancy created by the resignation of Albert Sidney Burleson. Burleson had left to become U.S. Post

Joseph Buchanan

Master General. Buchanan was reelected in 1914 running unopposed, in 1916 by defeating Republican Robert A. Brooks, in 1918 by running unopposed, in 1920 by defeating American Party candidate B. G. Neighbors, in 1922 by defeating Republican W. J. Kveton, in 1924 by defeating Republican Otto Stolley, in 1926 by defeating Republican W. H. Matthai, in 1928 by defeating Republican David H. Morris, and in 1930, 1932, 1934, and 1936 by defeating David Lyons and two write-in candidates. Served on the House Appropriations Committee and served as its chairman beginning in 1933. Died while serving in office on February 22, 1937, in Washington, D. C., of a heart attack and was buried at Prairie Lea Cemetery in Brenham. Succeeded by Lyndon B. Johnson the same year. Buchanan Dam on the Highland Lakes in the Hill Country was named in his honor. (See also photo page 29.)

GEORGE FARMER BURGESS

Born on September 21, 1861, in Wharton County. Attended local schools. Moved to Fayette County, Texas in 1880. Farmed, clerked, and studied law. Admitted to the state bar in 1882. Practiced law in La Grange, but moved to Gonzales in 1884. Democrat. Served as prosecuting attorney from 1886 until 1889. Married to Marie Louise Sims in 1888. Served as presidential elector in 1892. Elected U.S. representative, 10th District, in 1900 by defeating Republican Walter Jones and People's Party candidate C. K. Walter. He succeeded Robert Hawley on March 4, 1901. Following some redistricting, the 10th District of Texas became the 9th District. Reelected to the 9th District seat over Republican B. R. Burrow in 1902. Succeeded by Albert Sidney Burleson in the 10th District while succeeding him in the 9th District. Reelected in 1904 over Republican B. L. Osgood, in 1906 over Republican A. M. Waugh and Socialist J. B. Gay, in 1908 over Republican O. S. York and Socialist Frank Hubbel, in 1910 over Republican E. C. Webster, now Independent Frank Hubbel, and Socialist G. W. Dunn, ran unopposed in 1912, and in 1914 defeated Socialist B. F. Wright and Irvin

George Burgess

Kibbe. Did not seek reelection to Congress in 1916 and was succeeded by Joseph Mansfield on March 3, 1917. Instead, Burgess was a candidate for U.S. Senator in 1916 but was defeated by Charles Culberson in the Democratic primary election. Resumed law practice in Gonzales. Died on December 31, 1919, in Gonzales and was buried there at the Masonic Cemetery.

MICHAEL CLIFTON BURGESS

Michael Burgess

Born on December 23, 1950, in Rochester, Minnesota. Grew up in Denton County. Received Bachelor and Masters degrees in Physiology from North Texas State University (now the University of North Texas) in 1972 and 1976. Received M.D. from the University of Texas Medical School in Houston in 1977 and completed residency programs at Parkland Hospital in Dallas. Received Masters Degree in Medical Management from the University of Texas, Dallas, in 2000. Practicing physician and Republican. Married Laura Burgess in 1974 and they had three children. Founder of Private Practice Specialty Group for Obstetrics and Gynecology, former Chief of Staff for Lewisville Medical Center, and the current Chief of Obstetrics at Lewisville Medical Center. He is the past president of the Denton County Medical Society, a Denton County delegate to the Texas Medical Association, and has recently been elected as an alternate delegate to the American Medical association. Elected Representative, 26th District, in 2002 by defeating Democrat Paul William LeBon, Libertarian David Wallace Croft, and Green Party candidate Gary R. Page. Succeeded Dick Armey on January 3, 2003. Reelected in 2004 by defeating Democrat Lico Reyes and Libertarian James Gholston and in 2006 by defeating Democrat Tim Barnwell and Libertarian Rich Haas. Served on the House Transportation and Infrastructure, Government Reform and Science Committees during his first term. In 2004, joined the House Energy and Commerce Committee.

ROBERT EMMET BURKE

Robert Burke

Born August 1, 1847, near Dadeville, Alabama. Attended public schools. Served in the Confederate State Army. Moved to Jefferson, Texas in 1866. Taught school, clerked, and studied law. Admitted to the state bar in 1870. Married Mary L. Henderson in 1870 and they had three children: Robert E., Albert C., and Lucille. Practiced law in Dallas. Baptist and Democrat. Served on Dallas City Council from 1874 until 1875, as Dallas County judge from 1878 until 1888, and judge, 14th Judicial District, from 1888 until 1896. Elected U.S. representative, 6th District, in 1896 by defeating Populist Barnett Gibbs. Succeeded Jo Abbott on March 4, 1897. Reelected in 1898 by defeating Populist T. B. Goren and Republican Andrew Jackson Houston and in 1900 by defeating Populist S. H. Lumpkin, Republican O. F. Dombhager, and A. N. Cochran. Died while serving in Congress on June 5, 1901, in Dallas, and was buried there at Greenwood Cemetery. Succeeded in Congress by Dudley Wooten.

ALBERT SIDNEY BURLESON

Born on June 7, 1863, in San Marcos. Attended the Coronal Institute in San Marcos and the Agricultural and Mechanical College of Texas (now Texas A&M University). Received B.A. from Baylor University in 1881 and B.L. from the University of Texas in 1884. Admitted to the state bar in 1884. Democrat and Mason. Member of the Texas Volunteer Guard. Practiced law in Austin. Served as assistant city attorney from 1885 until 1890. Appointed attorney, 26th Judicial District, in 1891 and was elected to the post the following year. Married Adele Lubbock Steiner in 1889 and they had three daughters: Lucy

Albert Burleson

Kyle, Adele Sidney, and Laura. Elected U.S. representative, 9th District, in 1898 over Populist and former congressman and Populist candidate George Washington Jones of Bastrop. Succeeded Joseph Sayers on March 4, 1899. Reelected in 1900 over Republican Nat Q. Henderson. Following some redistricting, the 9th District of Texas became the 10th District. Reelected to the 10th District seat in 1902 by defeating Republican Charles Schenken, in 1904 ran unopposed, in 1906 defeated Republican Carl Beck, in 1908 defeated Republican Joseph W. Burke, in 1910 ran unopposed, and in 1912 ran unopposed. During his time in Congress, important issues were oleomargarine, cotton, and mistletoe. Served on the House Agriculture, Appropriations, and Banking and Currency committees. Resigned from Congress upon his appointment by President Wilson as postmaster general in 1913. Succeeded in Congress by James P. Buchanan on March 6, 1913. Served as postmaster general from March 7, 1913, until March 5, 1921. During his time as postmaster, airmail service was begun. In 1918 he was also made the chairman of the U.S. Telephone and Telegraph Administration. Died of a heart attack on November 24, 1937, at his home in Austin and was buried there at Oakwood Cemetery.

OMAR TRUMAN BURLESON

Omar Burleson

Born on March 19, 1906, in Anson. Attended public schools. Attended Abilene Christian College and Hardin-Simmons University. Graduated from Cumberland University in 1929. Attended the University of Texas law school. Admitted to the state bar in 1929 and began practice in Gorman. Married Ruth DeWeese in 1929; they had no children. Member of the Church of Christ, a Mason, and a Democrat. Served as Jones County attorney from 1931 until 1934 and county judge from 1934 until 1940. Employed by the Federal Bureau of Investigation from 1940 until 1941. Secretary to Congressman Sam Russell from 1941 until 1942 and general counsel for the District of Columbia Housing Authority in 1942. Served in the U.S. Navy during World War II. Elected U.S. Representative, 17th District, in 1946, running unopposed. Succeeded Sam Russell on January 3, 1947. Reelected in 1948, 1950, 1952, 1954, 1956, 1958, running unopposed, in 1960 defeated Constitutional Party candidate Max Mossholder, in 1962 ran unopposed, in 1964 defeated Republican Phil M. Bridges, and ran unopposed in 1966, 1968, 1970, 1972, 1974, and 1976. During the 1960s, Burleson was chairman of the Boll Weevils Club—a group of Democratic and Republican conservatives from the South. Served on the House Ways and Means, Administration, Foreign Affairs, Library, Printing, and Administration committees. He eventually chaired the Administration Committee. Did not run in 1978, resigned from the House on December 31, 1978, and was succeeded by Charles Stenholm in 1979. His wife, Ruth, died in 1983. Burleson died on May 14, 1991, in Abilene and was buried in Mt. Hope Cemetery in Anson. (See also photo page 24.)

There can be no perpetual prosperity through perpetual budget deficits.

—Omar Burleson

DAVID GOUVERNEUR BURNET

Born on April 4, 1788, in Newark, New Jersey. Orphaned and raised by an older half-brother in Cincinnati. Received empresario grant in 1826 from Mexico to settle 300 families near Nacogdoches in exchange for land. Having no success in recruiting settlers, he sold the rights in 1830 to the Galveston Bay and Texas Land Company. Married Hannah Este in 1830 and they had four children: Sarah,

David Burnet

William, Jacob, and Gertrude. He and Hannah had moved to Texas in 1830 and established a sawmill. The venture lost money, and he sold the mill in 1835. Represented the Liberty area in the convention at San Felipe in 1833. Appointed to head Brazos District Court. Elected president of Republic of Texas at the convention of 1836 and served from March 17 until October 22, 1836. His time as president was very turbulent, as he disagreed with most everyone and everything around him. He was elected vice-president in 1838, but was defeated by Sam Houston in the race for president in 1841. After Texas became a state, he sought a federal district judge's position in 1846 but was instead appointed secretary of state by Governor Henderson. Unsuccessfully sought a U.S. Customs collector position in 1849. His wife, Hannah, died in 1858. Burnet was selected as U.S. senator by the state legislature in 1866—it was essentially an honorary position but was never seated due to the radical Republican climate in Washington. Succeeded Confederate-era senator Williamson Oldham. Succeeded by Morgan Calvin Hamilton, who took office on February 22, 1870. Burnet was a Mason, Presbyterian, and Whig Party member. He died on December 5, 1870, and was buried in the Episcopal Cemetery in Galveston, but was later moved to Magnolia Cemetery and then to Lakeview Cemetery. The town and county of Burnet were named in his honor in 1852.

Do you suppose that Texas who has fought and won its right to govern itself, is going to tolerate the dictation of strangers, whether officers or soldiers, just landed on our shores? I for one, assure you here and now that we do not intend to let you become the dictator of this country.

—David Burnet

George Herbert Walker Bush

Born on June 12, 1924, in Milton, Massachusetts. Son of Prescott Sheldon Bush (1895–1972), a U.S. senator from Connecticut. Graduated from Phillips Academy in 1942. Served as an aviator in the U.S. Navy during World War II. Married Barbara Pierce in 1946 and they had six children: George Walker; Robin, who died in 1953; John (Jeb); Neil; Marvin; and Dorothy. Their sons George W. and Jeb would eventually be the governors of Texas and Florida, respectively. George W. Bush was elected president of the United States in 2000. Graduated from Yale University in 1948. Republican. Moved to Texas and went to work for Dresser Industries. Co-founded Bush-Overbey Oil Development Company in 1951. Co-founded Zapata Petroleum Corporation in 1953. Co-founder and president, Zapata Off-Shore, in 1954. Chairman of Harris County Republican Party in 1963. Delegate to the Republican national conventions in 1964 and 1968. Republican candidate for U.S. senator in 1964, but was defeated by Democrat

George Bush

Ralph Yarborough. Resigned from Zapata in 1966. Elected U.S. representative, 7th District, in 1966 by defeating Democrat Frank Briscoe and Constitution Party candidate Bob Gray. Succeeded John Dowdy on January 3, 1967. Reelected in 1968 by running unopposed. Did not seek reelection to his congressional seat and instead ran again for U.S. senator in 1970, but was defeated by Democrat Lloyd Bentsen. Succeeded by Bill Archer in the Congress in January 1971. Appointed U.S. representative to the United Nations by President Richard Nixon and served from 1971 until 1973. Served as chairman of the Republican National Committee from 1973 until 1974. Served as chief of the U.S. Liaison Office during reopening of relations with China from 1974 until 1975. Served as director of the Central Intelligence

Agency from January 1976 until January 1977. Ran for U.S. president in 1980, but was chosen as vice presidential candidate by Ronald Reagan. Elected and served as vice-president from 1981 to 1989. Succeeded Ronald Reagan as the 41st president of the United States in 1988 by defeating Democrat Michael Dukakis and served from 1989 to 1993. Defeated by Bill Clinton in 1992. Retired to Houston.

We can't solve today's problems with yesterday's programs.

—George Bush

Albert Bustamante

ALBERT GARZA BUSTAMANTE

Born on April 8, 1935, in Asherton. Attended public schools. Served in the U.S. Army from 1954 until 1955. Attended San Antonio College from 1956 until 1958 and graduated from Sul Ross State University in 1961. Teacher and coach from 1961 until 1968. Married Rebecca Pounders in 1971 and they had three children: Albert Anthony, John Marcus, and Celina Elizabeth. Aide to Congressman Henry B. Gonzalez from 1968 until 1971. Served as Bexar County commissioner from 1973 until 1978 and county judge from 1979 until 1984. Elected U.S. representative, 23rd District, in 1984 by unseating incumbent Abraham Kazen in the Democratic primary and running unopposed in the general election. Succeeded Kazen in January 1985. Reelected in 1986 by defeating Libertarian Ken Hendrix, in 1988 by defeating Republican Jerome L. Gonzales and Libertarian Tony R. Garza, and in 1990 by defeating Republican Gonzales again. Served on the House Armed Services and Government Operations committees. Redistricting in 1990 altered his 23rd District seat by giving much of it to the new 28th District and giving him a large portion of the 21st Congressional District. Bustamante was unseated in the 1992 general election by Republican Henry Bonilla and was succeeded by him in January 1993. He was unseated partly because of an investigation into his participation in racketeering and accepting an illegal gift while in office. He was indicted on ten counts and convicted in July 1993 of two counts—racketeering and influence peddling—of accepting a $35,000 bribe. His conviction was based on the sale and repurchase of a real estate note and the acceptance of a loan guaranty. His wife, Rebecca, was also indicted on seven counts, but following a three-week trial, she was found not guilty on all counts. Bustamante was sentenced to three and a half years in federal prison. He maintains his innocence.

Earle Cabell

EARLE CABELL

Born October 27, 1906, in Dallas County. Attended Dallas public schools and graduated from North Dallas High School in 1925. Attended Texas A&M University and Southern Methodist University. Episcopal and Democrat. Married Elizabeth "Dearie" Holder in 1932 and they had two children: Earle Jr. and Elizabeth Lee (Pulley). Salesman for Morning Glory Creameries of Houston. Returned to Dallas and co-founded Cabell's, Inc., a dairy-product and food-retailing business, with his two brothers, Ben and Charles. Served as mayor of Dallas from 1961 until 1964. Rode with Congressman Ray Roberts in the vehicle procession where President Kennedy was killed. Resigned as mayor in 1964 to run for Congress. Elected U.S. representative, 5th District, in 1964 by defeating incumbent Republican Bruce Alger. Succeeded Alger on January 3, 1965. Reelected in 1966 by defeating Republican Duke Burgess, in 1968 by defeating Republican Roy Wagoner, and in 1970 by defeating Republican Frank Crowley. Served on the House Science and Astronautics, District of Columbia, and Fiscal Affairs committees. Unseated by Republican Alan Steelman in the 1972 general election and was succeeded by him on January 3, 1973.

Retired to Dallas. The Dallas Federal Building was named in his honor in 1974. Died on September 24, 1975, of emphysema in Dallas and was buried there at Restland Memorial Park.

To be mayor of Dallas was my only political ambition.

—Earle Cabell

Francis Oscar Callaway

Oscar Callaway

Born October 2, 1872, in Harmony Hill, Rusk County, but moved with his family to Mercers Gap, Comanche County, in 1876. Attended public schools. Graduated from Comanche High School in 1894. Taught school from 1894 until 1897. Received a law degree from the University of Texas and was admitted to the state bar in 1900. Began law practice in Comanche. Democrat. Served as prosecuting attorney in Comanche County from 1900 until 1902. Married Stella Couch in 1904; they had no children. Elected U.S. representative, 12th District, in 1910 by unseating incumbent Oscar Gillespie in the Democratic primary and by defeating Socialist Robert G. Martin, Republican C.C. Littleton, and Prohibition Party candidate N. C. Pile in the general election. Succeeded Gillespie on March 4, 1911. Served on the House Insular Affairs, Patents, Treasury Expenditures, and Naval Affairs committees. Reelected in 1912 by defeating Socialist Clarence Nugent, and in 1914 by defeating Republican S. J. Browson. Unseated by James C. Wilson in the 1916 Democratic primary and was succeeded by him on March 3, 1917. Returned to Comanche to practice law and ranch. Died on January 31, 1947, and was buried at Oakwood Cemetery in Comanche.

When a representative abandons necessity and justice in the expenditure of the public money he has weighed anchor, reefed sail, torn out his rudder, thrown away his chart and compass, and battened down the hatches. He is on the high seas, subject to the press of the winds.

—Oscar Callaway

John Rice Carter

John Carter

Born in Houston on November 6, 1941. Graduated from Houston's Bellaire High School in 1960. Received degree in history from Texas Tech University in 1964 and graduated from the University of Texas Law School in 1969. Admitted to the state bar in 1969. Married Erika Carter in 1968 and they had four children: Gilianne, John, Theodore, and Danielle. Lawyer. Lutheran and Republican. Served on the Williamson County Juvenile Board from 1984 until 2001. City of Round Rock Planning and Zoning Commission. Municipal Judge in Round Rock until 1980. Appointed Judge, 277th District Court, on May 19, 1981. Elected to this position in 1982. Reelected four times. Retired November 30, 2001. Elected as the first Representative for the newly created 31st District in 2002 by defeating Democrat David Bagley, Libertarian Clark Simmons, Green Party candidate John S. Petersen, and Independent R.C. Crawford. Reelected in 2004 by defeating Democrat Jon Porter and Libertarian Celeste Adams and in 2006 by defeating Democrat Mary Beth Harrell and Libertarian Matt McAdoo. Serves on Border Security & Immigration and Appropriations Committees.

ROBERT RANDOLPH "BOB" CASEY

Bob Casey

Born on July 27, 1915, in Joplin, Missouri. Moved with his parents to Houston, Texas in 1930. Attended local schools and graduated from San Jacinto High School in 1930. Married Hazel Marion Brann in 1935 and they had ten children: Hazel Mary, Robert Jr., Catherine, Bonnie, Mike, Shawn, Bridget, Eileen, Timmy, and Kevin. Attended the University of Houston and graduated from the South Texas School of Law in 1940. Admitted to the state bar in 1940. Began his legal practiced in Alvin in 1941. Democrat. Served as Alvin city attorney from 1942 until 1943 and was also a member of the Alvin Independent School District Board. Moved to Houston in 1943. Employed as assistant district attorney from 1943 until 1947. In private legal practice with Casey and Spiller from 1947 until 1948. Served as state representative, District 19-1, from 1948 until 1949. Served as Harris County judge from 1950 until 1958. Elected as the first U.S. representative from the newly created 22nd District, in 1958, by defeating Republican T. Everton Kennerly and Constitution Party candidate Jack Gardner. Took office on January 3, 1959. Served on the House Merchant Marine and Fisheries, Appropriations, Administration, and Science and Astronautics committees. Reelected in 1960 by defeating Republican J. C. Noonan and Constitution Party candidate D. F. Vancleve, in 1962 by defeating Republican Ross Baker, in 1964 by defeating Republican Desmond Barry, in 1966 by running unopposed, in 1968 by defeating Republican Walter Blaney, in 1970 by defeating Republican A. W. Busch, in 1972 by defeating Republican James Griffin and Independent Frank Peto, and in 1974 by defeating Republican Ron Paul, Socialist Workers Party candidate Jill Fein, and American Party candidate James T. Smith. Resigned on January 22, 1976, to accept an appointment by President Ford as a federal maritime commissioner, and was succeeded in Congress by Ron Paul in 1976. Died on April 17, 1986, in Houston and was buried there at Memorial Oaks Cemetery. (See also photo page 24.)

The people in my district are pretty independent characters.

—Bob Casey

JAMES LOUIS "JIM" CHAPMAN

Jim Chapman

Born on March 8, 1945, in Washington, D.C. Attended public schools in Sulphur Springs, Texas. Received a B.B.A. from the University of Texas in 1968 and a J.D. from Southern Methodist University in 1970. Admitted to the state bar in 1970 and began practicing in Sulphur Springs. Democrat. Married Betty Brice in 1971 and they have two children: Jennifer and Trey. Served as a district attorney, 8th Judicial District, from 1977 until 1985. Elected U.S. representative, 1st District, in a 1985 special election and runoff to fill the seat of Sam Hall, who had resigned to accept a federal judgeship. In the June 29 special election, Chapman was defeated by Republican Edd Hargett. However, Hargett failed to receive a majority and a runoff between the top two candidates—Hargett and Chapman—was required. In the August 3 runoff, Chapman defeated Hargett. Reelected in 1986 by running unopposed, in 1988 by defeating Republican Horace McQueen, in 1990 by defeating Republican Hamp Hodges, in 1992 by running unopposed, and in 1994 by defeating Republican Mike Blankenship and Independent Thomas "Jefferson" Mosser. Served on the House Appropriations Committee. Retired from the House in December 1996. Ran for the U.S. Senate the same year, but came in third in the Democratic primary election behind Victor Morales and John Bryant. Succeeded in Congress by Max Sandlin. In 1998 Cooper

Lake in Northeast Texas was renamed Jim Chapman Lake in his honor. Chapman has practiced law with Arter & Hadden in Washington, D.C., and later with Bracewell & Giuliani. .

We need to stop searching for scape-goats, roll up our sleeves and work together to fix what is wrong in America today.

—Jim Chapman

GEORGE WASHINGTON CHILTON

George Chilton

Born on June 4, 1828, in Elizabethtown, Kentucky. Son of Thomas Chilton (1798–1854), a U.S. representative from Kentucky who allegedly helped Davy Crockett write his autobiography. Attended Howard College in Alabama. Served in the U.S. Army during the Mexican War. Returned to Alabama following the war. Studied law and was admitted to the Alabama state bar in 1848. Began legal practice in Talladega. Moved to Tyler, Texas, in 1851. Married Ella Goodman in 1852 and they had two children, one of whom was Horace Chilton, a U.S. senator from Texas. Democrat, Knights of the Golden Circle, slave owner, and proponent of the slave trade. Served as a delegate to the 1861 Secession Convention. Served in the Confederate States Army. Elected U.S. representative, 1st District, in 1866 by defeating I. M. Burroughs, I. M. Camp, A. B. Norton, A. T. Rainey, Y. G. Word, and William B. Ochiltree. However, the four representatives elected in 1866 were denied their seats by the Radical Republicans. It was more than three years before the representatives from Texas were allowed to take their seats in the House following the Civil War. Presidential elector for Tilden in 1876. Died in 1883 and was buried in Oakwood Cemetery in Tyler.

HORACE CHILTON

Horace Chilton

Born on December 29, 1853, near Tyler. Son of George Chilton (1828–83) and grandson of Thomas Chilton (1798–1854), a U.S. representative from Kentucky who, as legend has it, helped Davy Crockett write his autobiography. Received public and private schooling. Attended the Lynnland Institute in Kentucky. Began a newspaper—the *Tyler Sun*—in 1871. Episcopalian and Democrat. Studied law and was admitted to the state bar in 1872. Wedded Mary W. Grinnan in 1877 and they had five children. Served as assistant attorney general from 1881 until 1883 and as delegate to the Democratic national convention in 1888 and 1896. Appointed by Governor Hogg, a boyhood friend, to serve the remainder of John H. Reagan's term as U.S. senator and took his place in the Rusk succession of senators from Texas. Reagan had resigned to take on role as chair of the newly formed Railroad Commission. Served from March 4, 1887, to June 10, 1891, and was the first native Texan to serve. Such a political storm grew over Chilton's appointment over Roger Mills that Chilton considered withdrawing his name for reelection to help his friend Governor Hogg. However, Mills defeated Chilton and succeeded him on March 29, 1892. Chilton was elected in his own right in 1894 by the legislature and this time served in the Houston succession of U.S. senators from Texas. He succeeded Richard Coke and served from March 4, 1895, until March 3, 1901. Chilton dropped out of the race for reelection and was succeeded by Joseph W. Bailey on March 4, 1901. He returned to Tyler and continued to practice law. He moved to Beaumont in 1901 and worked for ex-governor Hogg representing his oil interests. Returned to Tyler in 1906 and eventually moved to Dallas to continue the practice of law. Died on June 12, 1932, in Dallas and was buried at Oakwood Cemetery in Tyler.

WILLIAM THOMAS CLARK

Born on June 29, 1831, in Norwalk, Connecticut. Self-educated. Taught school in 1846. Moved to New York in 1854. Studied law and was admitted to the state bar in 1855. Married Laura Clark in 1856 and moved to Iowa. Served in the Union Army during the Civil War. Moved to Galveston, Texas in 1866 and became a banker. Republican and carpetbagger. Elected as the first U.S. representative from the 3rd District in 1869 by defeating Democrat Jacob Elliot. He was one of the first four Texas congressmen seated following the Civil War. Three of these were Republicans, and Clark was the only one considered a carpetbagger. Took office on March 31, 1870. Unseated by DeWitt Clinton Giddings in 1871 and was succeeded by him on March 3, 1871. Governor Davis did everything he could to keep Giddings out. Clark even returned to Washington to take his old seat but was expelled by a unanimous vote of the House. He remained in Washington and held several government jobs. Served as postmaster of Galveston from 1872 to 1874, until taking

William Clark

a position with the Bureau of Internal Revenue in New York. Moved to Fargo, North Dakota, in 1883 and practiced law. Edited the *Fargo Daily Argus*. Moved to Denver in 1890 and practiced law. Moved to Washington, D.C., in 1898 and was employed by the Internal Revenue Service. He worked there until his death. Died on October 12, 1905, in New York and was buried at Arlington National Cemetery in Arlington, Virginia.

Jeremiah Cockrell

JEREMIAH VARDAMAN COCKRELL

Born on May 7, 1832, near Warrensburg, Missouri. Brother of Francis Marion Cockrell (1834–1915), a U.S. senator from Missouri in the late 1800s. Attended local schools and Chapel Hill College. Traveled through New Mexico to California during the late 1840s. Returned to Missouri in 1852 and married Maranda J. Douglas. Served in Confederate States Army. Following severe wounds, he moved to Sherman before the end of the war. Democrat. Farmed while he studied law and was admitted to the state bar in 1874. Served as judge, 39th Judicial District, from 1885 until 1893 following a move to Jones County. Elected as the first U.S. representative from the newly created 13th District in 1892 by defeating People's Party candidate W. J. Maltby and Republican A. G. Malloy. Took office on March 4, 1893. Reelected in 1894 by defeating Populist D. B. Gilliland, Independent Democrat J. M. Dean, and Republican B. B. Kenyon. He did not seek reelection and was succeeded by John H. Stephens on March 3, 1897. He returned to farm in Jones County. Died on March 15, 1915, in Abilene and was buried there at the Masonic Cemetery.

RICHARD COKE

Born on March 18, 1829, near Williamsburg, Virginia. Nephew of Richard Coke, Jr. (1790–1851), a U.S. representative from Virginia. Attended local schools. Received law diploma from William and Mary College in 1849. Admitted to the bar in 1850, moved to Waco, Texas, and practiced law. Wedded Mary Evans Horne in 1852 and they had four children: two girls who died while infants, and two sons, Jack and Richard Jr. (both died while young adults). Baptist and Democrat. Appointed by Governor Runnels to a commission to decide the fate of Comanche Indians on the Brazos Reservation. They decided that the Comanches should leave the state. Served in the Secession Convention in 1861 and as an officer in Confederate States Army. Served briefly as judge, 19th Judicial District, in 1865 following an appointment by Governor Hamilton. Served as justice of Texas Supreme Court beginning in 1866, but was removed the following year by military governor Sheridan. Returned to Waco to practice law. Elected governor in 1873 and served from 1874 until 1876. Upon election as U.S. senator by the legislature in May 1876, he resigned the governorship. Served as senator from March 4, 1877, until March 3, 1895. He succeeded Morgan C. Hamilton in the Houston succession of senators from Texas. Nicknamed "Old Brains." Reelected by the legislature in 1883 and 1889. Did not seek reelection in 1894. Succeeded by Horace Chilton in 1895. Died on May 14, 1897, in Waco and was buried there at Oakwood Cemetery. Coke County is named in his honor. (See also photo page 14.)

Richard Coke

RONALD D'EMORY COLEMAN

Born on November 29, 1941, in El Paso. Attended public schools of El Paso and graduated from Austin High School in El Paso in 1959. Received B.A. from the University of Texas at El Paso in 1963 and a J.D. from the University of Texas in 1967. Teacher at the Texas School for the Deaf from 1963 until 1964. El Paso public school teacher in 1967. Served in the U.S. Army from 1967 until 1969. Admitted to the state bar in 1969. Democrat. Served as El Paso assistant county attorney in 1969 and first assistant county attorney in 1971. Served five terms as state representative, District 72-3 and 72-B, from 1973 until 1982. Attended the University of Kent in Canterbury, England, in 1981. Elected U.S. representative, 16th District, in 1982 by defeating Republican Pat Haggerty and Libertarian Catherine McDivitt. Succeeded Richard White in January 1983. Reelected in 1984 by defeating Republican Jack Hammond, in 1986 by defeating Republican Roy Gillia, by running unopposed in 1988, in 1990 by defeating Independent William Burgett, in 1992 by defeating Republican Chip Taberski, and in 1994 by defeating Republican Bobby Ortiz. Married Amy Crandus in 1989 and they have three children: Kimberly, Michael, and Travis. Served on the House Armed Services, Government Operations, Appropriations, and Intelligence Committees. Did not seek reelection in 1996 and was succeeded by Silvestre Reyes in January 1997. Remained in Washington and co-founded Advantage Associates, Inc., a consulting and lobbying firm, where he is senior vice-president. A park and trail were named in his honor in El Paso.

Ron Coleman

JAMES MITCHELL "JIM" COLLINS

Born April 29, 1916, in Hallsville. Attended William Lipscomb and Woodrow Wilson High School in Dallas. Received B.S. from Southern Methodist University in 1937, M.B.A. from Northwestern University in 1938, and M.B.A. from Harvard University in 1943. Served in the U.S. Army during World War II. Baptist, and Democrat until September 1940, when he resigned as state vice-president of the Young Democrats, became a Republican, and supported Willkie for president. Married Dorothy "Dee" Dann in 1942 and they had three children: James Michael, Dorothy Colville, and Nancy Miles. Businessman. Served as regional chairman of the White House Conference on Youth in 1955. President of Consolidated Industries from 1954 until 1968, Internal Industries from 1961 until 1968, All Products from 1965 until 1968, Fidelity Union Life Insurance from 1954 until 1965, and Pacific Industries from 1983 to present. Fidelity Union Life Insurance Company was founded by the congressman's father, political activist Carr P. Collins. Candidate for U.S. representative, 3rd District, in 1966, but was defeated by Democrat Joe Pool. Delegate to the Republican national convention in 1968. Elected U.S. representative, 3rd District, in the August 24, 1968, special election to fill the seat of the late Joe Pool by defeating

Jim Collins

Democrat Elizabeth Pool, widow of the late congressman. Reelected a few months later in November 1968 for his first full term by defeating Democrat Robert H. Hughes, in 1970 by defeating Democrat John Mead, in 1972 by defeating Democrat George A. Hughes, in 1974 by defeating Democrat Harold Collum, in 1976 by defeating Democrat Les Shackleford, in 1978 by running unopposed, and in 1980 by defeating Democrat Earle Porter and Libertarian William Stephen Briggs. In April 1970 two of Collins' aides were fired in a scandal broken by Washington journalist Jack Anderson. Collins himself was also investigated but was never indicted. In September 1976, following the bicentennial celebrations, Collins introduced a bill to change the national anthem because the "Star Spangled Banner" was too difficult to sing. He did not seek reelection to Congress in 1982 and was succeeded by Republican Steve Bartlett in January 1983. Candidate for U.S. senator in 1982; defeated Walter H. Mengden and Don L. Richardson in the Republican primary, thus becoming the candidate to oppose Lloyd Bentsen, but was defeated by Bentsen in the general election. Collins made one last try at political office when he ran as a candidate for mayor of Dallas in 1987. He placed third in a field of nine candidates led by Annette Strauss. Died July 21, 1989, in Dallas and was buried there at Restland Memorial Park.

Square describes a person who is honest, straightforward, and a straight arrow. I like squares.

—Jim Collins

LARRY ED COMBEST

Born on March 20, 1945, in Memphis, Texas. Graduated from Panhandle High School in 1963. Received B.B.A. from West Texas State University in 1969. Married Sharon McCurry and they had two children: Tonya and Haydn. Farmer. Republican. Employed by the Agriculture Stabilization and Conservation Service, U.S. Department of Agriculture, in 1971. Legislative assistant to U.S. Senator John Tower from 1971 until 1978. Owner, Combest Distributing Company, from 1978 until 1984. Elected U.S. representative, 19th District, in 1984 by defeating Democrat Don R. Richards. Succeeded Kent Hance in January 1985. Reelected in 1986 and 1988 by defeating Democrat Gerald McCathern, in 1990 by running unopposed, in 1992 by defeating Democrat Terry Lee Moser, in 1994 by running unopposed, in 1996 by defeating Democrat John W. Sawyer, in 1998 by defeating Democrat Sidney Blankenship, and in 2000 by defeating Libertarian Dr. John A. Turnbow, and in 2002 by defeating Libertarian Larry Johnson. Combest's daughter Tonya died in 1999 and

Larry Combest

his father in 2002. Resigned on May 31, 2003. Succeeded by Randy Neugebauer who was elected to fill the remainder of his term in a special election runoff held in June 2003. Served on the House Select Committee on Intelligence (chairman) and the Committee on Agriculture (chairman).

JESSE MARTIN COMBS

Born on July 7, 1889, in Center. Orphaned and raised by maternal grandparents. Graduated from Center High School. Married Katherine Alford in 1911 and they had two sons. Graduated from Southwest Texas State Teachers College (now Southwest Texas State University) in 1912. Baptist and Democrat. Taught school and became the Hardin County agent in 1914. Admitted to the state bar in 1918 and was elected Hardin County Judge and served in 1919 and 1920. Served as judge, 75th Judicial District, from 1923 until 1925. Moved to Beaumont and was judge, 9th District Court of Appeals, from 1933 until

1943. South Park School Board trustee from 1926 until 1940. Served as president of the board of trustees for Lamar Junior College (now Lamar University) from 1940 until 1944. Elected as U.S. representative, 2nd District, in 1944 by defeating Republican Lamar Cecil. Succeeded Martin Dies on January 3, 1945. Reelected in 1946 by running unopposed, in 1948 by defeating Republican Don Parker, and in his last race in 1950 by running unopposed. Served on the House Post Office and Civil Service and Ways and Means Committees. Due to failing health, he did not seek reelection in 1952. Succeeded by Jack Brooks on January 3, 1953. Retired to Beaumont. Died on August 21, 1953, of lung cancer in Beaumont and was buried there at Magnolia Cemetery.

Jesse Combs

K. MICHAEL CONAWAY

Born in Borger on June 11, 1948. Grew up in Odessa and graduated from Permian High School in 1966. Received BBA in Accounting from Texas A & M University-Commerce in 1970. Served in U.S. Army from 1970 to 1972. Employed by Price Waterhouse. Employed by George W. Bush as Chief Financial Officer for Bush Exploration. In 1995, appointed to Texas State Board of Public Accountancy. Baptist and Republican. Married to Julie Flannagan and they had two children: Brian and Erin. Julie died from leukemia. Married Suzanne Conaway and together they they had four children: Kara, Stephanie, Brian and Erin. Ran unsuccessfully in the 2003 special election to fill the seat of Larry Combest. Elected U.S. Representative, 11th District, in 2004 by defeating Democrat Wayne Raasch and Libertarian Jeffrey Blunt. Ran unopposed for re-election in 2006. Serves as Assistant Whip for the 109th Congress. Serves on the House Committees on Armed Services, Agriculture and Budget.

Michael Conaway

THOMAS TERRY "TOM" CONNALLY

Born on August 19, 1877, on his family farm in McLennan County. Step-grandfather of Connie Mack (1940–), U.S. representative and senator from Florida. Moved to Falls County in 1882. Attended public schools. Graduated from Baylor University in 1896. Served briefly in the U.S. Army during the Spanish-American War. Received law degree from the University of Texas in 1898, *in absentia* because of his military service. Admitted to the state bar in 1898. Practiced law in Waco. Moved to Marlin in 1899. Democrat. Served as state representative, District 72 (and later 69), from 1901 until 1905. Married Louise Clarkson in 1904 and had one son, Ben, about 1910. Served as Falls County attorney from 1906 until 1910. Elected U.S. representative, 11th District, in 1916 by defeating Republican John L. Vaughn and Socialist T. M. De Loach. On March 4, 1917, succeeded Robert L. Henry, who retired from Congress.

Tom Connally

Connally was commissioned a captain in the U.S. Army during World War I. He remarked, "I have been in more wars and fought less than any living man." Reelected in 1918 by running unopposed, in 1920 by defeating American Party candidate W. D. Lewis, in 1922 by defeating Republican R. A. Hanrick, in 1924 by defeating Republican C. C. Baker, and in 1926 by defeating Republican W. H. Black. Delegate to the Democratic national conventions of 1920, 1932, 1936, 1940, and 1948. Did not seek reelection to his congressional seat in 1928 and instead ran for U.S. senator. Succeeded by Oliver H. Cross on March 3, 1929. Elected U.S. senator in 1928 by unseating incumbent Earle Mayfield in the Democratic primary runoff and defeating Republican T. M. Kennerly, Socialist David Curran, and Communist John Rust in the general election. Succeeded Mayfield the following year, taking his place in the Rusk Succession of U.S. senators from Texas. Took office on March 4, 1929. Reelected in 1934 by defeating Joe Bailey, Jr. in the Democratic primary election and Republican U. S. Goen, Socialist W. B. Starr, and Communist L. C. Keel in the general election, in 1940 by defeating Republican George Shannon and Communist Homer Brooks, and in 1946 by defeating Republican Murray C. Sells. Signed United Nations Charter on behalf of the U.S. in 1945 and worked toward ratification of the treaty in the Senate. Dim prospects for reelection in 1952 caused him not to seek office. Succeeded by Price Daniel on January 3, 1953. First wife, Louise, died in 1935, and he married Lucille Sanderson Sheppard, widow of former senator Morris Sheppard, in 1942. Practiced law in Washington following his retirement from the Senate. Died on October 23, 1963, in Washington and was buried at Calvary Cemetery in Marlin. In 1992 the Veteran's Administration Medical Center in Marlin was renamed in his honor. (See also photo page 29.)

It was gratifying to me, as it doubtless was to others, that in fighting primarily for American rights we could also fight the battles of the world and civilization, and that having triumphed we can impose conditions of peace that will liberate peoples long oppressed and misruled by our enemies and their allies.

—Tom Connally

John Conner

JOHN COGGSWELL CONNER

Born on October 14, 1842, in Noblesville, Indiana. Attended local schools and Wabash College. Received an appointment to the U.S. Naval Academy at Annapolis, but stayed only briefly. Joined the U.S. Army and served during the Civil War. He sought a seat in the Indiana House of Representatives, but was defeated. Re-joined the U.S. Army, served in Texas, and eventually settled in Sherman during the late 1860s. Democrat. Elected as U.S. representative, 2nd District, in 1869 by defeating Republican B. F. Grafton, Independent Democrat J. F. Johnson, and Independent R. H. Taylor. Succeeded Andrew Jackson Hamilton, who was the last pre–Civil War Congressmen and who had left office in 1861. He was one of the first four Texas congressmen seated following the Civil War. Three of these were Republicans; Conner was the only Democrat. He took office on March 31, 1870. He did face some opposition to taking his seat in the House, but was eventually seated. He was described as a "Democratic carpetbagger from Indiana" by the *New York Times*, and oddly it was a representative from Indiana who fought his being seated. Reelected in 1871 by defeating Republican Anthony M. Bryant. Due to poor health, he did not seek reelection in 1872 and was succeeded by William Pinckney McLean on March 3, 1873. Died on December 10, 1873, in Washington, and was buried at Old Cemetery in Noblesville, Indiana.

SAMUEL BRONSON COOPER

Samuel B. Cooper

Born on May 30, 1850, in Caldwell County, Kentucky, and moved to Texas with his family the same year. His father died three years later, and he was raised on a farm by an uncle. Mason, Odd Fellow, Elk, Knight of Pythias, and Democrat. Attended local schools and studied law. Admitted to the state bar in 1872. Practiced in Woodville. Married Phoebe Young in 1873 and they had five children. Phoebe died in 1911. His daughter William, nicknamed "Willie," eventually married William P. Hobby. Served as Tyler County prosecuting attorney from 1876 until 1880. Served as state senator, District 1, from 1881 until 1885. Appointed Collector of Internal

Revenue in Galveston by President Cleveland and served from 1885 until 1888. Made a run for district judge in 1888 but was defeated. Elected U.S. Representative, 2nd District, in 1892 by unseating incumbent John Long and defeating People's Party candidate T. A. Wilson, and Republicans T. A. Skillern and W. C. Averill. Succeeded Long on March 4, 1893. Reelected in 1894 by defeating Populist B. A. Calhoun, in 1896 by defeating Populist Calhoun again and Republican J. M. Claiborne, in 1898 by defeating Populist T. J. Russell, Republican John McAyeal, and Robert B. Hawley, in 1900 by defeating Republican J. B. Wallace, and in 1902 by defeating Republican Warren McDaniel. Unseated by Moses Brooks in the 1904 election and was succeeded by him on March 3, 1905, for one term. Cooper was returned to his seat in 1906 by ousting Brooks in the primary and defeating Republican J. H. Kurth and Charles E. Second in the general election. He returned to office on March 4, 1907, served one more term, and was unseated by Martin Dies in the 1908 Democratic Primary. Succeeded by Dies on March 3, 1909. Appointed by President Taft to the Board of General Appraisers in New York in 1910. Died on August 21, 1918, in New York and was buried at Magnolia Cemetery in Beaumont.

JOHN CORNYN III

Born February 2, 1952 in Houston, Texas. Attended public schools. Attended Oliver Wendell Holmes High School in San Antonio, but graduated from high school in Japan as his father was serving in the military. Graduated from Trinity University in 1973 and St. Mary's School of Law in 1977. Admitted to the state bar in 1977. Married Sandy Hansen in 1979 and they had two daughters: Danley and Haley. Republican. Lawyer with Groce, Locke, and Hebdon in San Antonio. Received Masters of Law from University of Virginia Law School in 1995. Elected and served as Judge, District Court, 1984-1990. Appointed by Governor Bill Clements as Presiding Judge for the Fourth Administrative Judicial Region in 1989. Elected Justice, Texas Supreme Court, 1990 and served from 1991 until he resigned in 1997 to run for Attorney General. Named St. Mary's Distinguished Law School Graduate in 1994 and Trinity University Distinguished Alumnus in 2001. State Attorney General, 1999-2002. Elected Senator in 2002 by defeat-

John Cornyn

ing Democrat Ron Kirk, Libertarian Scott Lanier Jameson, Green Party candidate Roy H. Williams, and Independent James W. "Jim" Wright. Succeeded retiring Senator Phil Gramm who resigned from the senate on November 30, 2002. Cornyn was actually appointed by Governor Perry to fill the remainder of Gramm's term – about one month -- and therefore took his oath of office on December 2, 2002, thus gaining valuable seniority over other new incoming senators. Serves on Committees for Armed Services, Budget, Judiciary, Small Business and Entrepreneurship, and the Joint Economic Committee.

WILLIAM HENRY CRAIN

Born on November 25, 1848, in Galveston. His father died six years later and he was sent to live in New York. Attended the Christian Brothers' School. Received an A.B. and M.A. from St. Francis Xavier College in New York. Returned to Texas. Studied law at Indianola while working at the law firm Stockdale and Proctor. Admitted to the state bar in 1871. Catholic and Democrat. Married Angelina G. Mitchell in 1873 and they had seven children: Frank, Viva, William Henry, James Kerr, Newton Mitchell, Mary, and an infant who died at an early age. Crain's wife Angelina died in 1880s. Elected district attorney, 23rd Judicial District, and served from 1872 until 1876. Served as state senator, District 28, from 1876 until 1878. Moved to Halletsville and practiced law with S. C. Patten for four years. Presidential elector in 1880 for

William Crain

Democrat Winfield Hancock. Moved to Cuero by 1882 and practiced law with Rudolph Kleberg. Elected as the first U.S. representative for the newly created 7th District in 1884 by defeating Republicans R. B. Renfro and Richard Nelson. Took office on March 4, 1885. Reelected in 1886 by defeating Republicans J. L. Haynes and N. W. Cuney, in 1888 by defeating Republican Calvin Brewster, and in 1890 by defeating Republican J. V. Spohn. Following some redistricting, the 7th District became the 11th District. Crain was succeeded by George Cassety Pendleton for the 7th District seat in 1893. Crain was elected to represent the 11th District in 1892 by defeating Republican Calvin Brewster and People's Party candidate Ben Terrell. Succeeded S. W. T. Lanham in 1893. Reelected in 1894 by defeating Populist V. Weldon, but lived only a short period longer. Did not plan to seek reelection, but died while serving in Congress on February 10, 1896, of pneumonia and was buried at Hillside Cemetery in Cuero. Succeeded in Congress by his law partner, Rudolph Kleberg, in 1896. (See also photo page 14.)

The people of the North and West want to find a more congenial climate than they now enjoy in their present homes. They are well aware that no such climate and soil can be found in the world as are found within the confines of the State of Texas. Deep water in itself would not build up and develop this country. We had a Northern Invasion many years ago, and our fathers, sons, and brothers bared their breasts to repel the invaders. But that era has happily passed, and times have changed. We want another Northern invasion, and we will receive the invaders with open arms and shouts of joy. We want them to come with wives, families, and kinfolk. We want them to come and stay with us—be one of us—and help develop the resources of the country.

—William Henry Crain

John Cranford

JOHN WALTER CRANFORD

Born on July 28, 1862, near Grove Hill, Alabama. Moved to Hopkins County, Texas with family in 1865, but both his parents died within seven years. Studied law in Fort Worth and Sulphur Springs and was admitted to the state bar in 1880. Married Medora Ennis in 1880 and they had four children. Practiced in Sulphur Springs with Hunter, Putman, and Cranford, then Cranford and Garrison, and then Cranford, Garrison, and Keasler. Democrat. Served three sessions as state senator, District 5 (and in his last session, District 2), from 1889 until 1895. Elected U.S. representative, 4th District, in 1896 by defeating Populist James H. "Cyclone" Davis and National Democrat M. W. Johnson. Succeeded David Culberson on March 4, 1897. His wife died in 1898, and he also suffered from very poor health. He did not seek reelection in 1898 and died on his last day in office on March 3, 1899, in Washington, D.C. He was buried at City Cemetery in Sulphur Springs and was succeeded in Congress by John Sheppard on March 4, 1899.

OLIVER HARLAN CROSS

Born on July 13, 1868, in Eutaw, Alabama. Attended local schools. Received a B.A. from the University of Alabama in 1891. Taught school in Union Springs, Alabama, from 1891 until 1892 and studied law. Moved to Deming, New Mexico, and worked on a newspaper owned by Governor Ross. Admitted to the New Mexico state bar in 1893 and practiced law briefly before moving to McGregor, Texas, in 1894. Presbyterian, Odd Fellow, and Democrat. Served as McGregor city attorney from 1895 until 1896, when he moved to Waco. Appointed and served as McLennan County assistant attorney from 1898 until 1902. Served as state representative, District 66, from 1899 until 1901.

Oliver Cross

Served as McLennan County district attorney from 1902 until 1906. Wedded Mary Watt in 1907 and they had two children: Harlan Watt and Mary Augusta. Retired from the field of law in 1917. Elected U.S. representative, 11th District, in 1928 by defeating Republican R. C. Bush. Succeeded Tom Connally on March 4, 1929. Reelected in 1930 without opposition, in 1932 by defeating Republican C. C. Baker. In 1934 defeated W. R. Poage in the primary and ran unopposed in the general election. Served on the House Committee for Banking and Commerce. Did not seek reelection in 1936. Returned to Texas and continued his farming and real estate pursuits. Succeeded by W. R. Poage on January 3, 1937. Wrote *Congressional, After Dinner, and Other Speeches* (1937). Tried to reclaim his seat in 1940 but was defeated by Poage this time in the primary. Died on April 24, 1960, and was buried at Hearne Cemetery.

> *I was up making a speech one time, and when I was through a man came up and asked if I was kin to the Crosses in Arkansas. I said no, I certainly was not kin to them. The man said, "By God, brother, I can tell you they are some of the best people there," and he went off mad, and I saw I had lost his vote. I decided that if anybody else asked me if I was related to a certain man by the name of Cross in Arkansas, I would tell him I was. So later when a man asked me if I was related to a certain man by the name of Cross in Arkansas, I said yes, and he was one of the finest men there. The man who asked looked sort of embarrassed. I asked him what about that Cross in Arkansas. He said, "They just hung him the other day.*

—Oliver H. Cross

MILES CROWLEY

Born on February 22, 1859, in Boston, Massachusetts. Attended public schools. Worked as a longshoreman. Moved to Galveston, Texas during the 1870s. Served as assistant chief, Galveston Fire Department. Studied law and was admitted to the state bar in 1892. Democrat. Served one term as a state representative, District 65, from 1891 until 1893, and two-terms as state senator, District 17, from 1893 until 1894, when he resigned early to run for Congress. Elected U.S. representative, 10th District, in 1894 by defeating Republican A. J. Rosenthal and Populist J. C. McBride. Succeeded Walter Gresham on March 4, 1895. Served one term, did not run for reelection in 1926, and was succeeded by Robert B. Hawley on March 3, 1897. Returned to Galveston to practice law. Served as Galveston County attorney from 1909 until 1912 and county judge from 1920 until his death. Died on September 22, 1921, and was buried at Calvary Cemetery in Galveston.

Miles Crowley

ENRIQUE ROBERTO "HENRY" CUELLAR

Born in Laredo on September 19, 1955. Attended Nixon High School. Received Associate's degree from Laredo Community College in 1976. Received B.S. from Georgetown University in 1978 and J.D. from the University of Texas in 1981. Also received M.A. From Texas A&M University Laredo in 1982 and Ph.D. from the University of Texas in 1998. Studied at the Universidad Pan Americana in Mexico City. Married Imelda Rios and they have two daughters: Christina Alexandra and Catherine Ann. Customs broker and lawyer in private practice. Catholic and Democrat. Served as State Representative, District 43, 1987-2001. Unsuccessful candidate for U.S. Representative, 23rd District, in 2002. Served as Texas Secretary of State in 2001. Elected U.S. Representative, 28th District, in 2004, by unseating incumbent Ciro Rodriguez in the Democratic primary and defeating Republican Jim Hopson and Libertarian Ken Ashby in the general election. Began

Henry Cuellar

service on January 3, 2005. On June 28, 2006, the United States Supreme Court ruled that the Texas Legislature had violated the rights of Hispanic voters when it moved most of Laredo out of the neighboring 23rd District and replaced it with several heavily Republican San Antonio suburbs. It also ruled that the 25th District was not compact enough to be a replacement. The 25th District was nicknamed "the fajita strip" because of its shape. The ruling forced the redrawing of five districts between El Paso and San Antonio including the 28th and a special election to select their representatives. In the 2006 Special Election, Cueller was reelected by defeating Conservative Ron Avery and Democrat Frank Enriquez. This election coincided with the November general election. Serves on the House Budget and Agriculture Committees.

CHARLES ALLEN CULBERSON

Born on June 10, 1855, in Dadeville, Alabama. Son of David Browning Culberson (1830–1900), who was also a U.S. congressman. Moved to Gilmer, Texas with his family in 1856. Attended public schools. Graduated from the Virginia Military Institute in 1874 and studied law at the University of Virginia. Admitted to the state bar in 1877 and practiced law in Daingerfield, Texas. Served as Marion County attorney for a brief time beginning in 1880. Married Sally Harrison in 1882 and they had one daughter, Mary. They moved to Dallas in 1887 and began a law partnership known as Bookhout & Culberson. Offered a seat on the Interstate Commerce Commission by President Harrison. Elected attorney general in 1890 and served from 1891 until 1895. Elected governor in 1894 and served from January 15, 1895, until January 17, 1899, succeeding Jim Hogg. He was elected U.S. senator by the legislature on January 25, 1899, succeeding Roger Q. Mills, and was sworn in on March 4, 1899, taking his place in the Rusk succession of

Charles Culberson

U.S. senators from Texas. Reelected in 1904 and 1910 by the legislature. Served on the Senate Judiciary Committee. Served as Democratic leader in the Senate in 1907 and 1909. Delegate to the Democratic national conventions of 1896, 1900, 1904, 1908, 1912, and 1916. Following the Seventeenth Amendment to the U.S. Constitution, he was elected by the people of Texas in 1916 by defeating Republican Alex W. Atcheson, Socialist F. A. Hickey, and Prohibition Party candidate F. H. Combeau. He was never in the state to campaign but was supported by his friends who covered for his poor health due to Bright's disease and alcoholism. He placed third in the 1922 Democratic primary for Senator behind Earle B. Mayfield and Jim Ferguson and thus failed to make the runoff and was unseated. He was succeeded by Mayfield in March 1923. Remained in Washington during his brief retirement. Died on March 19, 1925, of pneumonia in Washington, D.C., and was buried at East Oakwood Cemetery in Fort Worth.

> *If not curbed, it will usurp the functions of the State and be destructive of government itself. It will indeed overthrow our Anglo-Saxon civilization in its relation to government.*
> —Charles A. Culberson on the Ku Klux Klan, who helped unseat him

DAVID BROWNING CULBERSON

Born on September 29, 1830, Troup County, Georgia. Father of Charles Allen Culberson (1855–1925), who was governor and U.S. senator from Texas. Studied at the Brownwood Institute in La Grange, Georgia, and studied law at Tuskegee, Alabama. While there, he was schooled by William B. Chilton, chief justice of the state. Admitted to the Alabama state bar in 1850 and practiced in Dadeville, Alabama. Married Eugenia Kimball and they had two sons. Moved to Upshur County, Texas, in 1856. Mason, Odd Fellow, and Democrat. Practiced law with Hinche P. Mabry. Moved to Jefferson in 1861. Served as state representative from 1859 until 1860 and resigned due to his opposition to secession. He eventually went along with the masses and served briefly in Confederate State Army. Returned to Austin to serve as adjutant general following a bout of poor health. Returned to the legislature in 1864 following his election and resigned from the military to serve again as state representative. Served as state senator from 1873 until his election to Congress the following year. Elected U.S. representative, 2nd District, in 1874, running unopposed. Succeeded William P. McLean on March 4, 1875. Reelected in 1876 by defeating Republican Stilwell H. Russell, in 1878 by defeating Greenback Party candidate Henry F. O'Neal and Democrat R. H. Taylor, and in 1880 by defeating Greenback candidate O'Neal. Following some redistricting, Culberson left the 2nd District seat and ran for the 4th District seat about 1882. Succeeded by John H. Reagan in the 2nd District seat in 1883. Elected U.S. representative, 4th District, in 1882 by defeating Greenbacker E. L. Dehoney. Succeeded Roger Q. Mills in 1883. Reelected in 1884 by running unopposed, in 1886 by defeating Opposition Party candidate James T. Fleming, in 1888 by running unopposed, in 1890 by defeating

David Culberson

Republican J. C. Gibbons and Independent Patrick B. Clark, in 1892 by defeating now People's Party candidate Patrick B. Clark and Republican J. A. Hurley, and in 1894 by defeating Populist James H. "Cyclone" Davis and Republican H. S. Sanderson. Did not seek reelection in 1896 and was succeeded by John W. Cranford on March 3, 1897. He was appointed by President McKinley in 1897 to assist in codifying the laws of the United States. He served on this committee until he died on May 7, 1900, in Jefferson and was buried there at Oaklawn Cemetery. Culberson County was named in his honor. (See also photo page 14.)

JOHN ABNEY CULBERSON

Born on August 24, 1956, in Houston, Texas. Received a B.A. from Southern Methodist University and a J.D. from South Texas College of Law in 1981 and 1990, respectively. Married Belinda Burney in 1989 and they have one child: Caroline Virginia. Methodist and Republican. Civil defense attorney with Lorance and Thompson. Elected and served as state representative, District 125, 1987–2000. Elected U.S. representative, 7th District, in the 2000 general election. Culberson placed first in a field of eight Republican candidates (Mark Brewer, Wallace Henley, Gene Hsiao, Ron Kapche, Susan Malfer, Catherine McConn, and Peter Wareing) in the March 14 primary election and was forced into a runoff election with Wareing on April 11. He won the November 2000 general election by beating Democrats Jeff Sell and John Richard Skone-Palmer, and Libertarian Drew Parks. Succeeded the retiring Bill Archer in January 2001. Reelected in 2002 by defeating Libertarian Drew Parks and Independent John R. Skone-Palmer and in 2004 by defeating Democrat

John Culberson

John Martinez, Libertarian Drew Parks, and Independent Paul Staton and in 2006 by defeating Democrat Jim Henley and Libertarian Drew Parks. Serves on the House Appropriations Committee, but has served on Steering, Budget, Education & Workforce, and Transportation and Infrastructure Committees.

PRICE MARION DANIEL

Born on October 10, 1910, in Dayton, Texas. Graduated from Fort Worth High School in 1927. Worked as newspaper reporter for *Fort Worth Star-Telegram* and *Waco News-Tribune* between 1926 and 1931. Graduated from Baylor University with a journalism degree in 1931 and in 1932 with a law degree. Practiced law in Liberty. Co-publisher of *Liberty Vindicator* and *Anahuac Progress*. Married Jean Houston Baldwin in 1940 and they had four children: Price Daniel, Jr., Jean Houston, Houston Lee, and John. Baptist and Democrat. Served three two-year terms as state representative, District 14, from 1939 until

Price Daniel

1943. Elected Speaker of the House and served from 1940 until 1943. Served in U.S. Army during World War II. Elected attorney general and served from 1947 until 1953. Elected U.S. senator in 1952 by running unopposed, as he was running as both a Democrat and a Republican. Took office on January 3, 1953, succeeding retiring senator Tom Connally and took his place in the Rusk succession of U.S. senators from Texas. Served only one term. Resigned from the Senate in January 1957 after being elected Governor. Succeeded in the Senate by William A. Blakley. In the 1956 race for governor, he defeated Ralph Yarborough in the Democratic primary election and Republican William R. Bryant and write-in candidate W. Lee O'Daniel in the general election. Served three terms as governor and was succeeded by John Connally in 1963. Practiced law in Liberty from 1963 until 1967. Appointed by President Johnson as Assistant for Federal-State Relations and director of the Office of Emergency Preparedness and served from 1967 until 1969. Served as a special assistant to the attorney general from 1969 until 1970. Appointed and later elected to the Texas Supreme Court and served from 1971 until 1979. Died on August 25, 1988, of a stroke in Liberty and was buried there on his family ranch.

STEPHEN HEARD DARDEN

Stephen Darden

Born on November 19, 1816, in Lafayette County, Mississippi. Moved to Texas in 1836 to fight in the Texas Revolution. Returned briefly to Mississippi, but settled in Gonzales County in 1841. Served two terms as state representative, Districts 62 and 54, from 1853 until 1857 and state senator, District 25, from 1861 until 1863. Served in the Confederate States Army. Married Catherine Mays, his second wife, in 1862 and they had two children. Elected as a representative, 1st District, to the Second Confederate Congress in an August 1864 special election to fill the seat of the late John A. Wilcox. Took his seat on November 21, 1864, and served until 1865. Following the war, he served as comptroller of public accounts from 1873 until 1879 and in various state jobs (superintendent of public buildings and grounds, chief clerk of the comptrollers office, and secretary of the Texas Veterans Association) through the 1880s. Died on May 16, 1902, in Wharton and was buried at the Texas State Cemetery in Austin.

JAMES HARVEY "CYCLONE" DAVIS

Born on December 24, 1853, near Walhalla, South Carolina. Moved to near Winnsboro, Texas, with his family in 1857. His mother died two years later. Attended public schools. Taught school from 1875 until 1878. Married Belle Barton in 1878 and they had five children: Ira (a girl who died at eighteen months of age), Arlon Barton, Valton Gerston, Landon Vardo, and Henry Leroy. They also adopted an orphan girl. Served as Franklin County judge from 1878 until 1883. Admitted to the state bar in 1879. Acquired the *Franklin Herald* newspaper in 1882. Campaigned for and spoke in behalf of John D. Templeton in the 1882 governor's race, for John Ireland in 1884, and James Hogg in 1890. Delegate to the Democratic national convention in 1884. Became famous for his speechmaking skills and acquired the nickname "Methodist Jim." Democrat until 1888, when he became a Populist. Davis was one of

Cyclone Davis

the founders of and presided over the Texas Press Association from 1886 until 1888. Began the *Sulphur Springs Alliance Vindicator* newspaper in 1889. Became an ardent populist and prohibitionist just before the turn of the century. Ran unsuccessfully for attorney general in 1892. The nickname "Cyclone" was acquired in 1894 in Kentucky following a debate with that state's attorney general, Wat Hardin, which was so one-sided, the media compared Davis to a "Texas Cyclone." Ran unsuccessfully for U.S. representative, 4th District, in 1894, defeated by John Cranford. As the Populist movement waned, he worked to join the Populists with the Democrats and re-joined the Party himself in 1906. During that year, he returned to making speeches on behalf of candidates, and one of the first was gubernatorial candidate Thomas Campbell. Appointed as superintendent of agriculture for the Philippine Islands in 1914, but declined. Elected U.S. representative along with Atkins McLemore for one of two at-large seats in 1914. Together, the pair defeated Socialists Nat B. Hunt and Reddin Andrews, Republicans Charles A. Warnken and E. E. Diggs, and Progressives J. E. Williams and H. L. McCulston. They succeeded Daniel Garrett and Hatton Sumners on March 4, 1915. McLemore ran again in 1916, but Davis was unseated in the Democratic primary election by Daniel Garrett. He was succeeded by one of the men he had replaced, Daniel Garrett, on March 3, 1917. He worked on efforts supporting the Chautauqua movement, Farmers Alliance, prohibition, and the Ku Klux Klan. He returned to Sulphur Springs. He had mostly retired from politics, but reemerged in 1932 to run unsuccessfully for another at-large congressional seat against Joseph Weldon Bailey. During that year, his nickname became part of his legal name when he changed it to James Harvey Cyclone Davis. Following the death of his first wife, Belle, in 1934, he remarried in 1935 and moved to Kaufman. He published *Memoir* about this time with his son Arlon. Died on January 31, 1940, and was buried at City Cemetery in Sulphur Springs.

We have the grandest pattern of a government written in the language of men, but for sixty years, have refused to cut the cloth according to the pattern.

—Cyclone Davis

EDWARD DEGENER

Born on October 20, 1809, in Brunswick, Germany. Educated in Germany and England. Served in the Anhalt-Dessay council and the German National Assembly in the 1840s before immigrating to the U.S. and Sisterdale, Texas, in 1850. Farmer. As with a number of German immigrants, he was prosecuted during the Civil War for supporting Union causes. Republican. Began a grocery business in San Antonio following the war. Served as delegate to the Constitutional Convention in 1866 and from 1868 until 1869. Elected as the first U.S. representative from the 4th District in 1869 by defeating Democrat J. L. Haynes. He was one of the first four Texas congressmen seated following the Civil War. Three of these were Republicans. Served for one day less than a year from March 4, 1870, until he was unseated by Democrat John Hancock. Succeeded by Hancock on March 3, 1871. Served on San Antonio City Council from 1872 until 1878. Died on September 11, 1890, in San Antonio and was buried there at City Cemetery.

Edward Degener

REESE CALHOUN DE GRAFFENREID

Born on May 7, 1859, in Franklin, Tennessee. Attended local schools. Graduated from the University of Tennessee in 1878 and the Cumberland School of Law in Lebanon. Admitted to the state bar of Tennessee in 1879 and practiced in Knoxville and Chattanooga. Moved to Texas in 1880 and on to Longview in 1882. Went to work for the Texas & Pacific Railroad. Democrat. Served as Gregg County judge for two months in 1882 and then returned to private practice. Married Annie Berry in 1883. Ran unsuccessfully for U.S. representative, 3rd District, in 1890 and was defeated by Constantine B. Kilgore in the primary election. Elected U.S. representative, 3rd District, in 1896 by defeating Populist W. E. Farmer. Succeeded Charles Henderson Yoakum on March 4, 1897. Reelected in 1898 by defeating Populist H. D. Wood and in 1900 by defeating Republican C. G. White. Had the nickname "De." Died while serving in office on August 29, 1902, in Washington, D. C., and was buried at Greenwood Cemetery in Longview. His was succeeded in Congress in a special election by Gordon J. Russell.

Whether it is ours to command or obey; to walk in the gilded halls and marble palaces of wealth, or to dwell in the peasant's humble cottage, we should ever be ready to lend an ear to that still, small voice which says, "Let your light shine and let not that light be darkness."

—Reese De Graffenreid

Reese De Graffenreid

THOMAS DALE "TOM" DELAY

Tom DeLay

Born on April 8, 1947, in Laredo. Spent much of his youth in Venezuela as his father was in the oil business. Graduated Calallen High School in Corpus Christi in 1965. Attended Baylor University in 1967 and graduated from the University of Houston in 1970. Began pest control business in 1973. Baptist and Republican. Married Christine Ann Furrh and they had one child: Danielle. Served three terms as state representative, District 21 and 26, from 1979 until 1984. Elected U.S. representative, 22nd District, in 1984 by defeating Doug Williams. Succeeded Ron Paul in January 1985. Reelected in 1986 by defeating Democrat Susan Director, in 1988 by defeating Democrat Wayne Walker and Libertarian George Harper, in 1990 by defeating Democrat Bruce Director, in 1992 by defeating Democrat Richard Konrad, and in 1994 by defeating Democrat Scott Cunningham and Independent Gregory D. Pepper. The U.S. District Court redrew part of the boundary for DeLay's district, requiring him to run in an open primary or special election in November 1996. This election coincided with the general election. DeLay was reelected by defeating Cunningham again. Reelected in 1998 by defeating Democrat Hill Kemp and Libertarian Steve Grupe and in 2000 by defeating Democrat Jo Ann Matranga, Independent Robert A. Schneider, and Libertarian Kent J. Probst, in 2002 by defeating Libertarian Gerald W. "Jerry" LaFleur, Democrat Tom Riley, and Green Party candidate Joel West, and in 2004 by defeating Democrat Richard R. Morrison, Libertarian Thomas Morrison,and Independent Michael Fjetland. Elected House Majority Leader in 2002. Indicted in 2005 of conspiring to violate Texas political fundraising laws and was forced to step aside as majority leader. Served on the House Appropriations Committee. Resigned from House of Representative on June 9, 2006. Wrote with Stephen Mansfield *No Retreat, No Surrender: One American's Fight* (2007).

ELIGIO "KIKA" DE LA GARZA II

Born on September 22, 1927, in Mercedes, Texas. Attended Our Lady of Guadalupe Catholic School and Mission High School. His nickname came from his uncle Enrique, who was called "Kika." They both lived with the future congressman's grandparents and were seen everywhere together. So, they were called "Big Kika" and "Little Kika" and eventually just "Kika." Served in U.S. Navy during World War II and in the U.S. Army during the Korean conflict. Attended Edinburg Junior College and St. Mary's University. Received L.L.B. and J.D. from St. Mary's law school in 1952. Admitted to the state bar in 1952. Catholic and Democrat. Employed as attorney from 1950 until 1952 with Rakin, Kern, and Martines. Married Lucille Alamia and they had three children: Jorge, Michael, and Angela. Served six terms as state representative, District 38-3, from 1953 until 1964. Elected U.S. representative, 15th District, in 1964 by

Kika de la Garza

defeating Republican Joe Coulter. Succeeded Joe Kilgore on January 3, 1965. Ran unopposed and was reelected in 1966 and 1968, in 1970 defeated Republican Ben A. Martinez, ran unopposed in 1972 and 1974, in 1976, 1978, and 1980 defeated Republican R. L. "Lendy" McDonald, in 1982 defeated Libertarian Frank L. Jones, III, ran unopposed in 1984 and 1986, in 1988 defeated Libertarian Gloria Joyce Hendrix, ran unopposed in 1990, in 1992 defeated Republican Tom Haughey, and in 1994 defeated Republican Tom Haughey and Independent John C. C. Hamilton. Served on the House Agriculture Committee and chaired this committee from 1981 until 1997. He was the first Hispanic to chair any House committee. He was considered for U.S. Agriculture Secretary in 1994. Did not run for reelection in 1996 and was succeeded by Rubén Hinojosa in January 1997. The U.S. Border Crossing Station in Pharr was named in his honor.

No one wants to work together anymore. Everyone just wants to blast everyone else. That's no way to get anything done.

—Kika de la Garza

MARTIN DIES

Martin Dies

Born on March 13, 1870, in Jackson Parish, Louisiana. Moved to Fairfield, Texas, with his family in 1876; they later moved to Woodville. Attended public schools. Worked on the local newspaper with his father. Worked a variety of jobs. Some sources say he received a law degree from the University of Texas. Methodist and Democrat, although he had been a Populist in his younger days. Admitted to the state bar in 1892. Practiced law in Woodville and was a Freestone County marshall. Married Olive Cline Blackshear in 1892. This was her second marriage. They had two daughters, Hazel and Eren, and one son, Martin Dies (1900–1972), who was also a U.S. representative from Texas. Martin Dies served as Tyler County judge from 1894 until 1896. Served briefly in the local militia during the Spanish-American War. Served as district attorney, 1st Judicial District, from 1898 until 1900. Because of debts and his health, he moved to Colorado City in 1899 and Beaumont in 1902. Elected U.S. representative, 2nd District, in 1908 by unseating incumbent Samuel B. Cooper in the Democratic primary and defeating Republican C. E. Smith and Socialist John Johnson in the general election. He succeeded Cooper on March 4, 1909. Divorced from his first wife Olive in 1910. She had been institutionalized by this time. Dies married his stenographer a few months later. He served on the House Immigration and Naturalization, Weights and Measures, and Rules committees. Reelected in 1910 by defeating Republicans W. J. Collier and George W. Eason, in 1912 by defeating Socialist J. A. Freeland, Republican Howard M. Smith, and Progressive Party candidate E. G. Christian, in 1914 by defeating Socialist A. Lingan and Progressive Charles A. Chaison, in 1916 by defeating Socialist J. B. Truitt and Republican A. E. Sweatland. Did not seek reelection in 1918 and was succeeded by John Box on March 3, 1919. Retired to Tyler County and then moved to Kerrville in 1921. Died on July 13, 1922, in Kerrville and was buried at Glenwood Cemetery in Houston.

What we need in this country is for the laboring man, the farmer, the banker, the people of the United States to return to the old-time religion of Lincoln, of Jefferson, of Grover Cleveland, and the democracy of the country. Why do we not tell the people honestly and fairly that ... it is the business of the individual to depend upon himself?

—Martin Dies

MARTIN DIES

Born on November 5, 1900, in Colorado City, Texas. Son of Martin Dies (1870–1922) also a U.S. representative from Texas. Grew up in Beaumont and Greenville. Attended public schools, Wesley College in Greenville, and the Cluster Spring Academy in Virginia. Graduated from Beaumont High School in 1918. Graduated from the University of Texas in 1919. Received law degree from National University in Washington, D.C., in 1920. Practiced law with his father. Married Myrtle M. Adams in 1920 and they had three sons: Martin, Jr., Robert, and Jack. Admitted to the state bar in 1920. Began practice in Marshall, but soon moved to Orange. Practiced law with his father in Orange. Served on the faculty at East Texas law school in Jasper. Served briefly as district judge. Democrat. Elected U.S. Representative, 2nd District, in 1930 and succeeded John Box, the man who succeeded his father, on March 4, 1931. Served on the House Rules Committee. Reelected in 1932 by defeating Republican J. H. Buchanan and Liberty party candidate John W. Conner.

Martin Dies

In 1934 he ran unopposed, in 1936 he defeated two write-ins (A. E. Sweatland and Sam Lipscomb who garnered three votes between them), and in 1938, 1940, and 1942, ran unopposed. Served as the first chairman of the Special House Un-American Activities Committee (HUAC) in 1938. The committee was charged with investigating potentially subversive groups but concentrated on communists and the Soviet threat. Did not seek reelection in 1944 due to enormous opposition and health concerns and was succeeded on January 3, 1945, by Jesse Combs. Practiced law in Lufkin with Collins, Dies, Garrison, and Renfro. Ran for U.S. senator in the 1941 special election to fill Morris Sheppard's seat but was defeated by W. Lee O'Daniel. Reelected as U.S. representative at-large in 1952 by running as both a Democrat and a Republican. He was not allowed to return to his old committee as it was thought his publicity had damaged the anti-communist effort. Took office on January 3, 1953. Reelected in 1955 by defeating Republican Tom Nolan and in 1956 ran unopposed. Did not seek reelection in 1958 as the at-large positions were eliminated with the creation of the 22nd Congressional District. His term ended on January 3, 1959. Ran for U.S. senator again in the 1957 special election but was defeated by Ralph Yarborough. Authored *The Trojan Horse* (1940) and *The Martin Dies Story* (1963). The former was actually ghostwritten by J. B. Matthews. Dies also contributed articles to *American Opinion* magazine. Died on November 14, 1972, of a heart attack in Lufkin and was interred at the Garden of Memories Mausoleum in Lufkin.

Hell yes, I've made mistakes. Who could get hold of a bearcat like this without making mistakes?

—Martin Dies

LLOYD ALTON DOGGETT, JR.

Born on October 6, 1946, in Austin. Graduated from Austin High School in 1964. Received B.B.A. from the University of Texas in 1967 and a J.D. in 1970. Married Libby Belk in 1969 and they had two daughters: Lisa and Cathy. Admitted to the state bar in 1971. Served six terms in the Texas Senate, District 14, from 1973 until 1985. Elected to the Senate on August 14, 1973, in a special election to fill the seat of Charles F. Herring. He was one of "the Killer Bees" who evaded capture to keep the State Senate from reaching a quorum. Served as president *pro tempore* during the 68th Legislature, 1983–85, and was governor for a day on September 21, 1983. He was the Democratic nominee for the 1984 U.S. Senate race for the seat vacated by John Tower but was defeated in the general election by Phil Gramm. Served in Texas Supreme Court from 1989 until 1994. Elected U.S. representative, 10th District, in 1994, defeating John Longsworth in the Democratic primary and Republican A. Jo Baylor, Libertarian Jeff Hill, Independent Michael L. Brandes, and Independent Jeff Davis in the general election. Succeeded retiring congressman Jake Pickle in January 1995. Reelected in 1996 by defeating Republican Jo Baylor, in 1998 by defeating

Libertarian Vincent May, and in 2000 by defeating Libertarian Michael Davis, in 2002 by defeating Libertarian Michele Messina, and in 2004 by defeating Republican Becky Armendariz Klein and Libertarian James Werner. Following redistricting, 2004 found Doggett representing the 25th District. On June 28, 2006, the United States Supreme Court ruled that the Texas Legislature had violated the rights of Hispanic voters when it moved most of Laredo out of the neighboring 23rd District and replaced it with several heavily Republican San Antonio suburbs. It also ruled that the 25th District was not compact enough to be a replacement. The 25th District was nicknamed "the fajita strip" because of its shape. The ruling forced the redrawing of five districts between El Paso and San Antonio including the 25th and a special election to select their representatives. In 2006, Doggett was reelected by defeating Libertarian Barbara Cunningham, Independent Brian Parrett, and Republican Grant Rostig. He had regained most of his old Austin base. This election coincided with the November general election. Serves on the House Ways & Means Committee, but has also served on Budget and Resources Committees.

Lloyd Doggett

... pointing up contradictions in an opponent's position is legitimate debate and that perhaps here, there is a little too much of the 'Honorable this and that' and not enough getting down to what really makes a difference.

—Lloyd Doggett

John Vernard Dowdy

Born on February 11, 1912, in Waco. Lived in Rusk and graduated from Henderson High School in 1928. Attended a Waco business college and moved to Marshall for work. Attended College of Marshall (now East Texas Baptist University) from 1929 until 1931. Clerked in law office in Center beginning in 1932. Wedded Mary Ellen "Sunshine" Fite in 1932 and they had two children: Carol Sue Roberts and John V., Jr., nicknamed "Skipper." Baptist and Democrat. In August 1932 he became a court reporter for the 123rd Judicial District. Served in the same position in the 3rd District in Athens from 1937 until 1945. Admitted to the state bar and began practicing in 1940. His wife Sunshine died in 1943 from pregnancy complications, along with an infant son. Elected district attorney, 3rd District, in 1944 and served from 1945 until 1952. Dowdy married Johnnie Dena "J. D." Riley in 1946. She was the district clerk of Henderson County. Elected U.S. representative, 7th District, in a September 1952 special election to fill the seat of Tom Pickett by

John Dowdy

defeating Jack Weisener and Jim Norton. Pickett had resigned from Congress, and Dowdy took his place on September 23, 1952. Reelected to his first full term a few months later in the 1952 general election, running unopposed. Served on the House Post Office and Civil Service, Administration, Judiciary, and District of Columbia committees. Reelected in 1954 and 1956 running unopposed, in 1958 by defeating Republican Joseph E. A. Ross, and in 1960 by running unopposed. Reelected in 1962 by defeating Republican Raymond Ramage and in 1964 by defeating Republican James W. Orr. Following some redistricting, Texas' 7th Congressional District became its 2nd District. Therefore, Dowdy found himself running for Jack Brooks' old 7th District seat. Elected to the 2nd District seat in 1966, running unopposed. Ran unopposed for reelection in 1968. Reelected in 1970 over write-in candidates Eugene Hoyt and Joe Runnels. Did not seek reelection in 1972 due to legal problems and was succeeded in January 1973 by

Charles Wilson. Dowdy had been indicted by a federal grand jury in 1970 for conspiracy, perjury, and promoting bribery following charges of accepting a $25,000 bribe. He was convicted on eight counts, but two counts were overturned on appeal. Served six months in prison during 1974. Retired to Athens. His second wife "J. D." died in 1992. He died on April 12, 1995, in Athens and was buried in the Athens cemetery. (See also photo page 24.)

> *I am afraid both parties will practice unprincipled, vicious, political persecution in the future. If you are on the wrong side, you get it in the neck*
>
> —John Dowdy

JOE HENRY EAGLE

Joe Henry Eagle

Born on January 23, 1870, in Tompkinsville, Kentucky. Graduated from high school in 1883. Taught school. Graduated from Burritt College of Tennessee in 1887 and moved to Vernon, Texas. Democrat. Taught school and studied law in Vernon from 1887 until 1893. Served as acting school superintendent until 1891. Admitted to the state bar in 1893. Practiced in Wichita Falls. Served as Wichita Falls city attorney from 1894 until 1895. Moved to Houston in 1895. Ran unsuccessfully for U.S. Representative, 1st District, in 1896 and 1898 as a Populist, defeated by Thomas Ball on both occasions. Wedded Mary Hamman in 1900 and they had two children: Virginia (Mrs. Walter E. Boyd) and John Henry. Elected U.S. representative, 8th District, in 1912 by defeating Republican Jeff N. Miller and J. E. Curd. Succeeded John M. Moore on March 4, 1913. Reelected in 1914 by defeating Socialist E. B. Miller and Republican S. L. Hain, in 1916 by defeating Republican Ira P. Jones and Socialist John W. Connor, and in 1918 by defeating M. H. Broyles. Did not seek reelection in 1920 and was succeeded by Daniel Garrett on March 3, 1921. Elected again to the 8th District seat in the January 1933 special election by running well ahead of more than 30 candidates in the race to fill the seat of the late Daniel Garrett. Garrett died in December 1932, having just won reelection to a term beginning in January 1933. There were actually two special elections held simultaneously to fill Garrett's seat. The first was to fill the balance of Garrett's unexpired term in the standing congress and the second was for Garrett's full term. Eagle took office on January 28, 1933. Reelected in 1934 by defeating Republican P. Loreng Petersen and E. J. Hicks. Eagle did not seek reelection in 1936 and was succeeded by Albert Thomas on January 28, 1937. Ran unsuccessfully for U.S. senator in 1936 and was defeated by Morris Sheppard in the primary election. Practiced law in Houston. Ran unsuccessfully for reelection to the U.S. Congress in 1940 and was defeated by Albert Thomas in the Democratic primary election. His wife Mary preceded him in death. Died on January 10, 1963, and was buried at Forest Park Lawndale Cemetery in Houston.

ROBERT CHRISTIAN "BOB" ECKHARDT

Born July 16, 1913, in Austin. Grandnephew of Rudolph Kleberg (1847-1924), nephew of Harry Wurzbach (1874-1931), and cousin of Richard Mifflin Kleberg, Sr., (1887-1955) all U.S. Representatives from Texas. Graduated from Austin High School in 1931. Graduated from the University of Texas in 1935 and the University of Texas Law School in 1939. Edited the *Texas Ranger*, the University's magazine, from 1937 until 1938. Served in the U.S. Army Air Corps during World War Two. Married Orissa Stevenson in 1942 and they had two children: Orissa and Rosalind. Served as Southwestern Director of the Office of Coordinator of Inter-American Affairs from 1944 until 1945. Democrat. Published cartoons in the *State Observer*, the *Texas Spectator*, and the *Texas Observer*. Served four terms as State Representative, District 22-2, from 1959 until 1966. Labor law attorney representing the Texas Congress of Industry Organizations (CIO) and the Communications Workers of America (CWA). Divorced from his first wife Orissa in 1960. Married Nadine Ellen Cannon in 1962. She brought three children into the marriage: Sidney, Shelby, and William and together they had Sarah. Elected U.S. Representative, 8th District, and in 1966 by defeating Constitution Party candidate W. D. Spayne. Succeeded Lera Thomas, the first woman to serve in Congress from Texas, on January 3, 1967. Served on the House Interstate and Foreign Commerce Committee. Reelected in 1968 by defeating Republican Joe Stevens, in 1970 ran unopposed, in 1972 by defeating Republican Lewis Emerich and Socialist Workers candidate Susan Ellis, in 1974 by defeating Republican Donald D. Whitefield, in 1976 by defeating Republican Nick Gearhart and Socialist Workers candidate Gene Lantz, and in 1978 by defeating Republican Gearhart again. Co-authored *The Tides of Power* (1976) with childhood friend and Yale Professor Charles L. Black, Jr. Divorced from his second wife Nadine in 1976 and married Celia Buchan in 1977. Celia had one grown son, David. In 1980, Eckhardt

Bob Eckhardt

was unseated by Republican Jack Fields and was succeeded by him in January 1981. The efforts to remove him from Congress by the Republicans were tremendous. Guy Vander Jagt, who was chairman of the National Republican Congressional Committee said that they were "throwing every dollar the law will allow" against Eckhardt. John Connally noted, "I don't know of any more worthwhile endeavor that anyone can undertake than to unseat Bob Eckhardt." Eckhardt remained in Washington, D.C. and worked as a lobbyist through the 1980's. He was divorced from Celia in 1987. Retired to Austin in 1990 to lecture, lobby, write, and draw political cartoons. Died in Austin on November 13, 2001, and was buried there at Austin Memorial Park.

I won't stand still for the rape of the environment. I won't let the greedy get the biggest slice of the pie. I won't kill a bill just to get campaign money.

—Bob Eckhardt

THOMAS CHESTER "CHET" EDWARDS

Born November 24, 1951, in Corpus Christi. Graduated from Memorial High School in Houston, 1970. Received B.A. degree from Texas A&M University, 1974. Received M.B.A. from Harvard Business School, 1981. Democrat. Served as legislative assistant to Olin Teague from 1974 until 1977. Marketing representative for Trammell Crow Company from 1981 until 1985. President of Edwards Communications. Sought Democratic nomination to fill Teague's congressional seat in 1978, but lost to Phil Gramm. Served two terms as state senator, District 9, from 1983 until 1991. Began campaigning for lieutenant governor in 1989, but when Marvin Leath announced his retirement, Edwards then focused on that race. Elected U.S. representative, 11th District, in 1990 by defeating Republican Hugh D. Shine. Succeeded Marvin Leath in January 1991. Married Lea Ann Wood in 1992 and they have two sons: John Thomas and Garrison. Reelected in 1992 and 1994 by defeating Republican James W. Broyles, in 1996 by defeating

Chet Edwards

Republican Jay Mathis and Natural Law Party candidate Ken Hardin, in 1998 by defeating Libertarian Vince Hanke, and in 2000 by defeating Republican Ramsey Farley and Libertarian Mark Swanstrom, in 2002 by defeating Republican Ramsey Farley and Libertarian Andrew Paul Farris, and in 2004 by defeating Republican Arlene Wohlgemuth and Libertarian Clyde L. Garland. Following redistricting, 2004 found Edwards representing the 17th District. Reelected in 2006 by defeating Republican Van

Taylor and Libertarian Guillermo Acosta. Currently serves on the House Budget and Appropriations Committeees.

If I ever find a woman willing to marry an Aggie politician, I don't want to give her a chance to change her mind.

—Chet Edwards in opposition to a state senate bill requiring more time between marriage license purchase and the wedding

Ben Epperson

BENJAMIN HOLLAND EPPERSON

Born on November 3, 1826, in Amite County, Mississippi. Moved to Shelby County, Tennessee. Attended Bingham Brothers' School in North Carolina and Princeton University. Moved to Clarksville, Texas, in 1848. Studied law and was admitted to the state bar in the 1850s. Served as Red River County commissioner and state representative from 1847 until 1849. Married Harriet Amanda Shields in 1848 and they had five children: Caro (who died while young), Shields, Eugenia, Robert Benjamin, and Louis (who died while young). Originally a Whig Party member, but would eventually belong to a number of political parties. Texas gubernatorial candidate in 1851, but was defeated by Peter H. Bell. Joined the American or Know-Nothing Party. Delegate to the American Party convention in 1856. Continued his legal practice and entered into a number of business ventures. Returned as a state representative, District 2, and served from 1859 until 1861. He did not support secession and worked to keep Texas part of the United States and encouraged Sam Houston to accept President Lincoln's offer of U.S. troops to keep Texas in the Union. Joined the Constitutional Union Party, was a delegate to their 1860 national convention, and served as a presidential elector for the Bell-Everett ticket. Following secession, Epperson, along with the majority, supported the Confederacy. Candidate for representative to the Confederate Congress, District 6, in the fall of 1861, but was defeated by William B. Wright. He was physically unable to serve in the Confederate States Army, but probably provided more support through his donations of money and materiel. Served as president of the Memphis, El Paso and Pacific Railroad following the war. Candidate for U.S. Senate, but was finally defeated by Oran M. Roberts on the twenty-fourth ballot of the legislature in 1866. Elected later in the year as U.S. representative, 2nd District, by defeating Amzi Bradshaw and others. However, the four Representatives elected in 1866 were denied their seats by the Radical Republicans. It was more than three years before the Representatives from Texas were allowed to take their seats in the House following the Civil War. Moved to Jefferson in 1871. There, in 1872, he had built the House of the Seasons which is now a museum and an official Texas Historic Landmark and is listed on the National Register of Historic Places. His first wife Harriet died in 1873. Epperson served one last time as a state representative, District 7, from 1874 until 1876. He married Nancy Reed and they had one son, Benjamin Holland, and one daughter, Jeannie. Died on September 7, 1878, in Jefferson and was buried there in Oakwood Cemetery.

Resist secession.

—Ben Epperson to Sam Houston

LEMUEL DALE EVANS

Born on January 8, 1810, in Tennessee. Educated in Tennessee and was admitted to the bar there in 1840. Moved to Fannin County in 1843. Served as delegate to the Annexation Convention of 1845. Moved to Harrison County. Practiced law and was elected district judge. Served as Democratic Presidential elector in 1852. In 1853 he ran unsuccessfully for governor, finishing fourth behind Elisa Pease. Elected

U.S. representative, 1st District, in 1855 by defeating Democrat Matthias Ward. Succeeded Peter H. Bell on March 4, 1855. He was a member of the American or Know-Nothing Party. Unseated by Democrat John H. Reagan in 1857 and was succeeded by him on March 3, 1857. Left Texas because of his support of the Union. Advised Secretary of State Seward and was given a commission by Seward in Mexico to report on the movement of material across the border. He resigned in March 1862. Served as delegate to the Constitutional Union Party in 1866. Attended the State Constitutional Convention of 1868–69. Appointed by General Sheridan as presiding judge of the state Supreme Court, or the "Semicolon Court," as it was nicknamed, and served from 1870 until 1872. Again ran for governor unsuccessfully in 1872, this time as a Republican, and was defeated by Edmund J. Davis, who received their party's nomination. Appointed U.S. marshall, Eastern Judicial District of Texas, in 1875. Died on July 1, 1877, and was buried at the Congressional Cemetery in Washington, D.C.

Lemuel Dale Evans

SCOTT FIELD

Born on January 26, 1847, in Canton, Mississippi. Attended the McKee School. Served in the Confederate States Army. Graduated from the University of Virginia in 1868. Returned to Mississippi. Taught school and studied law. Admitted to the Mississippi state bar in 1871. Moved to Calvert, Texas, in 1872 and began private practice. Democrat. Served as Robertson County attorney from 1878 until 1882 and served two terms as state senator, District 14, from 1887 until 1891. Delegate to Democratic national convention in 1892. Elected U.S. representative, 6th District, in 1902 by running unopposed and succeeded Dudley Wooten on March 4, 1903. Unopposed for reelection in 1904. Did not seek reelection in 1906. Succeeded by Rufus Hardy on March 3, 1907. Returned to his law practice and farmed. Married three times: first to Victoria Lucky, then to Lucy Randolph—they had three sons: Thomas, Scott, and Eugene—and finally to Maude Green. Died on December 20, 1931, and was buried at Calvert Cemetery.

Scott Field

JACK MILTON FIELDS, JR.

Born on February 3, 1952, in Humble. Attended public schools. Received a B.A. from Baylor University in 1974 and a J.D. from Baylor in 1977. Admitted to the state bar in 1977 and began practicing in Humble. Married Roni Sue Haddock in 1979; they had no children and were eventually divorced. Baptist and Republican. Employed in the family business—Rosewood Memorial Park—from 1977 until 1980. Elected to the U.S. House, 8th District, in 1980 by unseating incumbent Democrat Bob Eckhardt whom he succeeded in January 1981. Reelected in 1982 by defeating Democrat Henry E. Alee and Libertarian Mike Angwin, in 1984 by defeating Democrat Don Buford, in 1986 by defeating Democrat Blaine Mann, in 1988 and 1990 by running unopposed, in 1992 by defeating Democrat Charles Robinson, and in 1994 by defeating Democrat Russ Klecka. In 1996 he did not run for reelection and was succeeded by Kevin Brady in January 1997. Served on the House Commerce Committee. Married Lynn Hughes in 1988 and they had two

Jack Fields

children: Jordan and Lexi. Fields sought the departing Lloyd Bentsen's U.S. Senate seat in the May 1993 special election. He placed fourth in the race of twenty-four candidates but failed to make the runoff. Resides in Humble, but maintains Washington ties through a government-affairs practice specializing in telecommunications and energy. Sits on several company boards. Investor, rancher, and is a lobbyist.

Term limits will remind officeholders why they were elected in the first place: to be public servants committed to getting the job done.

—Jack Fields

O. C. Fisher

OVIE CLARK FISHER

Born on November 22, 1903, near Junction. Attended Junction public schools, University of Colorado, the University of Texas, and Baylor University. Democrat. Received law degree from Baylor in 1929 and was admitted to the state bar. Began law practice under Carter Dalton in San Angelo. Married Marion De Walsh in 1926 and they had one daughter: Rhoda (Grimes). Ranched in Menard and Kimble counties. Served as Tom Green County attorney from 1931 until 1935. Served one term as state representative, District 91, from 1935 until 1937 and district attorney, 51st Judicial District, from 1937 until 1943. Elected U.S. representative, 21st District, in 1942, by unseating incumbent Charles L. South in the Democratic primary. Actually, South and Fisher both qualified for a runoff election, but South withdrew, thus making Fisher the party's nominee for the general election. Fisher ran unopposed in the 1942 general election and succeeded South on January 3, 1943. Reelected in 1944 by defeating Republican Maurice J. Lehman, ran unopposed from 1948 through 1960, in 1962 by defeating Republican E. S. Mayer Jr., in 1964 defeated Republican Harry Claypool, in 1966 ran unopposed, in 1968 defeated Republican W. J. Alexander, in 1970 defeated Republican Richardson B. Gill, and in 1972 defeated Republican Douglas S. Harlan. Served on numerous House committees, including Labor, Armed Services, and Elections. Did not run for reelection, and retired on December 31, 1974. Succeeded by Robert Krueger in January 1975. Author of *It Occurred in Kimble* (1937), *The Texas Heritage of the Fishers and Clarks* (1963), *King Fisher: His Life and Times* (1966), *Cactus Jack* (1978), *From New Deal to Watergate* (1980), *The Speaker of Nubbin Ridge* (1985), and his last book, an autobiographical work entitled *My Early Life—and Later*. Died on December 9, 1994, in Junction and was buried there at Junction City Cemetery. The San Angelo Federal Building was renamed in his honor, along with O. C. Fisher Reservoir and Dam. (See also photo page 24.)

Lop-sided majorities in the Congress have always been the bane of good government.

—O. C. Fisher

James Flanagan

JAMES WINRIGHT FLANAGAN

Born on September 5, 1805, in Gordonsville, Virginia. Received a public and private education. Moved to Kentucky in 1814. Horsetrader and freight merchant. Admitted to the Kentucky state bar in 1825 and served locally as justice of the peace. Married Polly Miller Morgan in 1826 and they had five children. Served as Justice of the Peace of Cloverport, Mississippi, from 1833 until 1834. Moved to far East Texas in 1843 and settled in Henderson the following year. His wife died in 1844. Operated Henderson's first store, practiced law, farmed, and owned a newspaper, *The Star-Spangled Banner*. A Whig Party member until the 1840s, when he became a Republican. Baptist and Odd Fellow.

Married Elizabeth Ware in the 1850s. Served one term as state representative, District 10, from 1851 until 1853; one term as state senator, District 9, from 1855 until 1858; presidential elector in 1856; and attended Sam Houston's Peace Conference in 1860. Was generally opposed to secession, but after much of the town of Henderson was burned by a reported Unionist, Flanagan went along. He spent the war producing leather for the Confederates. He became a moderate Republican among the Hamilton faction. Served in 1866 and 1868 state constitutional conventions. Elected, but was never inaugurated as lieutenant governor. He instead was elected by the legislature as U.S. senator in 1870 and served from March 30, 1870, until March 3, 1875. He was one of the first Texas senators seated following the Civil War along with Morgan C. Hamilton. Both were Republicans, and Flanagan received the shorter of the two staggered terms. While in the Senate, he served on the Education and Labor, Mines, and Post Office committees. Succeeded Oran M. Roberts in the Rusk succession of U.S. senators from Texas and was succeeded by Samuel B. Maxey in March 1875. Delegate to the Republican national convention in 1872, 1876, and 1880. Retired to Longview after leaving the Senate. Married three times: first to Polly Moorman, then to Elizabeth Ware, and then to Elizabeth Moore. In total, he had eleven children. Died on September 19, 1887, in Longview and was buried in Henderson.

EDGAR FRANKLIN "ED" FOREMAN

Born on December 22, 1933, in Portales, New Mexico. Attended Portales public schools and Eastern New Mexico State University. Received civil engineering degree from New Mexico State University in 1955. Served in the U.S. Navy from 1956 until 1957 and followed this with time in the Naval Reserves and the Air Force Reserves. Married Barbara Lynn Southard in 1955 and they had two children: Kirk and Rebecca. President of Valley Transit Mix, Atlas Land, and Foreman Oil. Republican. Elected U.S. representative, 16th District, in 1962 by defeating incumbent Democrat J. T. Rutherford. Succeeded Rutherford on January 3, 1963, served one term, and was in turn unseated by Democrat Richard C. White in 1964. Succeeded by White in January 1965. Delegate to the Republican national conventions in 1964 and 1968. Later elected U.S. representative from New Mexico and served in that position for one term beginning in 1969. Resided in Las Cruces. Moved to Dallas. Appointed as assistant at the U.S. Department of Agriculture in 1971

Ed Foreman

and assistant secretary, U.S. Department of Transportation, serving from 1972 until 1976. Now an entrepreneur and motivational speaker in Dallas.

JONAS MARTIN FROST, III

Born on January 1, 1942, in Glendale, California. Graduated from R. L. Paschal High School in Fort Worth in 1960. Received B.A. and B.J. from the University of Missouri in 1964 and a J.D. from Georgetown Law Center in Washington in 1970 and was admitted to the state bar the same year. Writer for *Congressional Quarterly Weekly* from 1965 until 1967. Served in the U.S. Army Reserves from 1966 until 1972. Democrat. Practicing lawyer in Dallas. Law clerk for Federal Judge Sarah T. Hughes from 1970 until 1971. Married Valerie Hall in 1976 and they had three daughters: Alanna, Mariel, and Camille. Elected U.S. representative, 24th District, in 1978 by unseating incumbent Dale Milford in the Democratic primary and Republican Leo Berman in the general election. Succeeded Milford in January 1979. Reelected in 1980 by defeating Republican Clay Smothers, in 1982 by defeating Republican Lucy P. Patterson and Libertarian David Guier, in 1984 and 1986 by defeat-

Martin Frost

ing Republican Bob Burk, in 1988 by defeating Libertarian Leo Sadovy, in 1990 by running unopposed, in 1992 by defeating Republican Steve Masterson, and in 1994 by defeating Republican Ed Harrison. Divorced in 1998. The U.S. District Court redrew part of the boundary for Frost's district, requiring him to run in an open primary or special election in November 1996. This election coincided with the general election. Frost was reelected by defeating Republican Ed Harrison, Democrat Marion Jacob and Independent Dale Mouton. Reelected in 1998 by defeating Republican Shawn Terry, Libertarian David Stover, and Independent George Arias and in 2000 by defeating Republican James "Bryndan" Wright and Libertarian Robert "Bob" Worthington, and in 2002 by defeating Republican Mike Rivera Ortega and Libertarian Ken Ashby. Delegate to the Democratic national conventions of 1976, 1984, 1988, 1992, 1996, 1998, and 2000. Married former U.S. Army general Kathy Carlson in 1998. Following significant redistricting in 2004, Frost was forced to run in the new 32nd District. He was defeated by Republican Pete Sessions. His wife Kathy died in 2006.

I always remember Texas is my home.

—Martin Frost

ROBERT ALTON "BOB" GAMMAGE

Born March 13, 1938, in Houston. Attended public schools. Served in the U.S. Army in 1959 and 1960 and in the Naval Reserves. Received an A.A. from Del Mar College in 1958, a B.S. from the University of Corpus Christi, an M.A. from Sam Houston State University in 1965, a J.D. from the University of Texas in 1969, and an L.L.M. from the University of Virginia in 1986. Taught at Sam Houston State University from 1963 until 1965. Dean at the University of Corpus Christi from 1965 until 1966. Instructor at San Jacinto College from 1969 until 1970. Admitted to the state bar in 1969 and practiced law in Houston until 1973. Adjunct professor at South Texas School of Law from 1971 until 1973. Democrat. Served one term as state representative, District 24-3, from 1971 until 1973. Served just under two terms in the State Senate, District 7, from 1973 until he resigned on January 23, 1976. Candidate for U.S. representative, 22nd District, in the April 1976 special election to fill the seat of Bob Casey but was defeated by Republican Ron Paul.

Bob Gammage

Elected U.S. representative, 22nd District, a few months later in the November 1976 general election by unseating Republican Ron Paul. Paul had served about nine months before turning the office over to Gammage in January 1977. Gammage, in turn, was unseated by his rival Ron Paul in 1978 and was succeeded by him in January 1979. Served as assistant state attorney general from 1979 until 1980. Consultant to U.S. Department of Agriculture during 1980. Practiced law in Austin from 1980 until 1982. Elected to and served on the Texas Court of Appeals. Unsuccessful candidate for the gubernatorial nomination in the 2006 Democratic Party primary election. Lives in Austin.

Justice is best served when the law serves all the people.

—Bob Gammage

JOHN NANCE GARNER, IV

Born on November 22, 1868, near Detroit, Texas, and was the fourth Garner to carry this name. Attended school at Bogata and Blossom Park. Attended Vanderbilt University one semester but because of limited educational opportunities could not succeed. Moved to Clarksville. Worked, studied law with Captain M. L. Simms and was admitted to the state bar in 1890. Democrat. Ran unsuccessfully for Clarksville city attorney. Moved to Uvalde and practiced law with Clark and Fuller. In lieu of a legal fee, he acquired the local newspaper *The Uvalde Leader*. His exposure editing this newspaper led to his appointment as county judge. When he was later elected to this office, his opponent was Mariette "Ettie" Rheiner, whom he later married in 1895. They had one son: Tully. Garner served from 1893 until 1896 as county judge. Served two terms as state representative, District 91, from 1899 until 1903. It was while he was in the legislature that he received the nickname "Cactus Jack" because of a failed attempt to have the cactus declared the state flower of Texas. In 1901 he headed a caucus of Joseph Bailey supporters in the legislature. They were the first to investigate the Waters Pierce issue that effectively brought about Bailey's downfall. He chaired the redistricting committee that helped create the 15th Congressional District. He was elected as the first U.S. representative from that new district in 1902 by defeating Republican John C. Scott. Took office on March 4, 1903. Reelected in 1904 by defeating Republican J. S. Morin, in 1906 and 1908 by defeating

John Garner

Republican T. W. Moore, in 1910 by defeating Republican Noah Allen. In 1912 and 1914 he ran unopposed, in 1916 he defeated Republican H. M. Wingback, in 1918, 1920, 1922, and 1924 he ran unopposed, in 1926 he defeated Republican Hardie M. Jeffries, in 1928 he ran unopposed, in 1930 and 1932 he defeated Republican Carlos G. Watson. Served as minority floor leader from 1929 until 1931 and as Speaker of the House from 1931 until 1933. Later nicknames included "the wise old man of Congress" and "the conniver-in-chief" for his ability to get things done. He would "Strike a blow for liberty" by inviting colleagues to his office for drinks. Initially, he was a candidate for president in 1932, but eventually became a running mate with Franklin Roosevelt. Elected vice-president in 1932 and was also returned to Congress by his district. Resigned from the House of Representatives on March 3, 1933, and was succeeded in Congress by Milton H. West. Served as vice-president until January 20, 1941. Strong supporter of the New Deal, but became disenchanted with its ideals and eventually split with Roosevelt following the efforts to pack the Supreme Court. Briefly a candidate for president in 1940, but withdrew after a few primaries. Retired to his home in Uvalde in 1941. On his eighty-ninth birthday in 1957, he reportedly gave up drinking whiskey and smoking cigars and became a vegetarian. One year later, more than 5,000 people attended his birthday party. Died on November 7, 1967, and was buried at Uvalde Cemetery in Uvalde. (See also photo page 29.)

I wish there was less government to talk about.

—John Nance Garner

CLYDE LEONARD GARRETT

Born on December 16, 1885, near Gorman. Attended local public schools and Hankins' Normal College. Taught school in Sweetwater from 1906 until 1907. Served as Nolan County assistant tax collector from 1907 until 1912. Baptist, Knight of Pythias, Odd Fellow, Woodman, Yeoman, Mason, and Democrat. Employed for three years as cashier at the City National Bank in Eastland and served two years as Eastland County deputy county clerk. Married Sallie Day in 1912 and they had five children: Carl, Clyde, Mary Katherine, Virginia Nell, and Sarah. Elected Eastland County clerk and served from 1913 until 1919. Worked in the burgeoning oil business. Vice-president of First State Bank in Eastland. Appointed as Eastland city manager and served from 1922 until 1924. Ran unsuccessfully for county court of law judge in 1924. Entered the insurance business. Served briefly as Eastland County sheriff's deputy in 1928 and county judge from 1929 until 1936.

Clyde Garrett

Elected U.S. representative, 17th District, in 1936 by defeating W. F. Nelson. Succeeded Thomas Blanton in January 1937. Reelected in 1938 by running unopposed. Unseated by Sam Russell in the August 24, 1940, Democratic primary runoff election and was succeeded by him on January 3, 1941. Served as an administrative officer for the U.S. Secretary of Commerce from 1941 until 1942 and was then a staff specialist for the Office of War Information until 1943. Sought the Democratic nomination for his old 17th District congressional seat in 1944 but was defeated by Sam Russell in the primary election. Worked public relations issues for the Secretary of Commerce following his departure from Congress. Employed by the Veteran's Administration in Washington, Dallas, and Waco from 1949 until 1956. Returned to Eastland. Unsuccessfully sought the Eastland County judgeship in 1958. Died on December 18, 1959, and was buried at Eastland Cemetery in Eastland.

It is my feeling that Communism can best be fought by bringing out its evils, rather than by precluding the evils being shown.

—Clyde L. Garrett

DANIEL EDWARD GARRETT

Daniel Garrett

Born on April 28, 1869, near Springfield, Tennessee. Attended local schools. Taught school and studied law. Admitted to the Tennessee state bar in 1893 and began private practice in Springfield. Married Ida Jones the same year. Baptist, Mason, and Democrat. Served as Tennessee state representative from 1892 until 1896 and Tennessee state senator from 1902 until 1906. Moved to Houston, Texas in 1906 and continued to practice law. Elected U.S. representative at-large in 1912 with Hatton Sumners by defeating Socialists D. D. Richardson and J. M. Haggard, Republicans R. B. Harrison and J. E. Elgin, Progressives Z. T. White and F. M. Etheridge, and Prohibition Party candidate E. H. Coniber. Took office on March 4, 1913. Served one term. Was not renominated to one of the at-large positions in 1914 Democratic primary and left office on March 3, 1915. Unseated Cyclone Davis in the 1916 Democratic primary election and ran again for one of the two at-large U.S. representative posts in 1917 and won along with Atkins Jeff McLemore. Together, the pair defeated Republicans Charles A. Warnken and M. A. Taylor, Socialists Arch Lingan and W. D. Simpson, and Prohibition candidates I. E. Teague and E. G. Cook. Took office on March 4, 1917. Did not seek reelection in 1918 as his at-large seat was eliminated by the creation of the 17th and 18th Congressional Districts. Garrett left office on March 3, 1919. In 1920 he was elected U.S. representative, 8th District, by defeating Republican E. B. Barden, Black and Tan Republican candidate M. H. Broyles, and American Party candidate J. M. Gibson. He succeeded Joe Eagle on March 4, 1921. He was reelected in 1922 by defeating Republican E. B. Barden, in 1924 by defeating Republican Clarence A. Miller, in 1926 by defeating Republican J. M. Gibson, in 1928 by defeating Republican George E. Kepple, in 1930 by running unopposed, and in 1932 by defeating Republican W. E. Long and Liberty Party candidate J. W. McDonald. Garret died, however, shortly after his final election on December 13, 1932, in Washington, D.C. He was buried at Forest Park Cemetery in Houston. Succeeded in the 8th District seat in 1933 by the man he had replaced, Joe Eagle. (See also photo page 29.)

BRADY PRESTON GENTRY

Born on March 25, 1896, in Colfax. Attended public schools and East Texas State College. Attended Cumberland University and Tyler Commercial College. Democrat. Admitted to the state bar in 1917. Practiced briefly in Tyler before serving in the U.S. Army during World War I. Served as a clerk in Van Zandt County tax office. Served as assistant city tax collector and Smith County attorney. Served as Smith County judge from 1931 until 1939. Appointed by Governor O'Daniel as chair of Texas Highway Commission and served from May 1939 until March 1945. Served as president of the American

Association of State Highway Officials (AASHO). Continued law practice in Tyler. Elected U.S. representative, 3rd District, in 1952, running unopposed. Succeeded Lindley Beckworth on January 3, 1953. Reelected in 1954 without opposition. Did not seek reelection in 1956 and was succeeded by Beckworth on January 3, 1957. Returned to his law practice and was appointed again to the Highway Commission in 1957, but did not accept. Gentry never married. Died on November 9, 1966, in Houston and was buried at Rose Hill Cemetery in Tyler.

Brady Gentry

PRESTON MURDOCH "PETE" GEREN, III

Born on January 29, 1952, in Fort Worth. Graduated from Arlington Heights High School in 1970. Attended Georgia Tech from 1970 until 1973. Received a B.A. and a J.D. from the University of Texas in 1974 and 1978, respectively. Admitted to the state bar in 1978. Practiced law in Houston from 1978 until 1979, then in Fort Worth from 1979 until 1982. Served as an aide to Lloyd Bentsen from 1983 until 1985. Resumed his law practice until 1989. Married Rebecca Ray in 1986 and they have three daughters: Tracy Elizabeth, Sarah Anne, and Mary Caroline. Baptist and Democrat. Unsuccessful candidate for U.S. representative, 6th District, in 1986, defeated by Republican Joe Barton. Elected U.S. representative, 12th District, in a special election held on September 20, 1989, to fill the seat vacated by the resignation of Jim Wright. Reelected in 1990 by defeating Republican Mike McGinn, in 1992 by defeating Republican David Hobbs, and in 1994 by defeating Republican Ernest J. Anderson Jr. Served on the House Armed Services, Public Works and Transportation, Science, and Space and Technology committees. Did not seek reelection in 1996 and was succeeded by Kay Granger in January 1997. Employed as an attorney and lives in Fort Worth. Served as Secretary of the Army, Acting Secretary of the Air Force, and other Department of Defense posts during the George W. Bush administrations.

Pete Geren

> *Only when our defense is strong will our words invite moderation in others.*
>
> —Pete Geren

DEWITT CLINTON GIDDINGS

Born on July 18, 1827, in Susquehanna County, Pennsylvania. Taught school and was trained as an engineer. Studied law. Moved to Brenham, Texas in 1852 and was admitted to the state bar the following year. Practiced with his brother Jabez. Married Malinda C. Lusk in 1860 and they had five children, three surviving: DeWitt, May Belle (Cooke), and Lillian. Served in the Confederate States Army. Delegate

DeWitt Clinton Giddings

to state constitutional convention in 1866. Co-founded the Giddings and Giddings Bank in Brenham in 1866. Elected U.S. representative, 3rd District, in 1871, unseating incumbent Republican William Clark. However, Governor Davis believed that incumbent Clark had actually won and was cheated in the election. Clark was seated on January 10, 1872, but Giddings appealed to the House of Representatives. The House agreed with Giddings and seated him on May 13, 1872. He was reported to be the first Southern Democrat to take a congressional seat during Reconstruction. He was reelected in 1872 by defeating Republican A. J. Evans. Succeeded by James W. Throckmorton in 1875 in the 3rd District seat on March 3,

1875. Again elected U.S. representative, but for the 5th District, in 1876 by defeating Republican George Washington Jones. Succeeded John Hancock on March 4, 1877. Served one term and was succeeded by now Greenback Democratic candidate George W. Jones on March 3, 1879. Served as presidential elector in 1876 and as a delegate to the Democratic national conventions in 1884, 1888, and 1892. Ran unsuccessfully for governor in 1886, defeated by Sul Ross. Died on August 19, 1903, in Brenham and was buried there at Prairie Lea Cemetery.

Oscar Gillespie

OSCAR WILLIAM GILLESPIE

Born on June 20, 1858, near Quitman, Mississippi. Attended private schools. Moved to Texas and graduated from Mansfield College in 1858. Married Ada Kate Hodges in 1884 and they had five children: Frances Elma, Mary Guinn, Hannah Schrock, Oscar Hodges, and Sallie. Studied law, was admitted to the state bar in 1886, and practiced in Fort Worth. Democrat, Mason, and Odd Fellow. Served as Tarrant County assistant attorney from 1886 until 1888 and prosecuting attorney from 1890 until 1894. Elected U.S. representative, 12th District, in 1902 by defeating Republican S. A. Greenwell. Succeeded James L. Slayden on March 4, 1903. Served on the House Banking and Commerce Committee. Reelected in 1904 by defeating Republican Frank M. Stanley and People's Party candidate Republican J. M. Mallett, in 1906 by defeating Laura B. Payne, and in 1908 by defeating Republican W. A. Dodge and Socialist G. V. Stratton. He backed the Gillespie-Tillman Resolution, which called for an Interstate Commerce Commission review of railroads hauling coal for potential trust violations. Gillespie was unseated by Oscar Callaway in the 1910 Democratic primary and was succeeded by him on March 3, 1911. Died on August 23, 1927, in Fort Worth and was buried at Mansfield Cemetery in Mansfield.

Louie Gohmert

LOUIS BULLER "LOUIE" GOHMERT, JR.

Born in Pittsburg, August 18, 1953. Grew up in Mount Pleasant. Received BA from Texas A&M University in 1975 and J.D. from Baylor University in 1977. Served in the U.S. Army from 1978 until 1982. Baptist, Republican and lawyer in private practice. Married Kathy Gohmert and have three daughters: Katy, Caroline, and Sarah. Served as District Judge, Smith County from 1992 until 2002 and Judge, 12th Circuit Court, from 2002 until 2003. Elected U.S. Representative, District 1, in 2004 by defeating incumbent Democrat Max Sandlin. Reelected in 2006 by defeating Democrat Roger L. Owen and Libertarian Donald Perkison. Serves on House Committees on Judiciary, Resources and Small Business.

Charlie Gonzalez

CHARLES AUGUSTINE "CHARLIE" GONZALEZ

Born on May 5, 1945, in San Antonio. Son of Henry B. Gonzalez (1916–2000), whom he succeeded in Congress. Attended public schools in San Antonio and graduated from Thomas Edison High School in San Antonio. Received a B.A. from the University of Texas in 1969 and a J.D. from St. Mary's law school in 1972. Served in the Texas Air National Guard from 1969 until 1975. Employed as an elementary school teacher from 1969 until 1972. Admitted to the state bar in 1972 and was in private practice in San Antonio from 1972 until 1982. Married Becky

Whetstone in 1998 who brought two children into the marriage: Benjamin and Casey. The couple later had a son, Leo. Catholic and Democrat. Elected and served as Bexar County Court judge from 1982 until 1987. Elected and served as judge, district judge, 57th Judicial District, from 1989 until 1997. Elected U.S. representative, 20th District, in 1998 by defeating Republican James Walker, Libertarian Alejandro DePeña, and Independent Steve Mendoza. Succeeded his father, Henry B. Gonzalez, on January 6, 1999. Reelected in 2000 by defeating Libertarian Alejandro de Pena, in 2002 ran unopposed, in 2004 by defeating Republican Roger Scott, Libertarian Jessie Bouley, and Independent Michael Idrogo, and in 2006 by defeating Libertarian Michael Idrogo. Divorced in 2003. Serves on the Energy & Commerce, Small Business, and House Administration committees and had served on House Banking and Financial Services committees.

HENRY BARBOSA GONZALEZ

Born on May 3, 1916, in San Antonio. Attended San Antonio College and the University of Texas, and received J.D. and L.L.B. from St. Mary's University School of Law. Married Bertha Cuellar in 1940 and they had eight children: Henry, Rose Mary, Charles, Bertha, Stephen, Genevieve, Francis, and Anna Maria. Language and business consultant from 1947 until 1950. Bexar County chief probation officer from 1947 until 1951. Democrat. Elected to San Antonio City Council beginning in 1953. Served three terms as state senator, District 26, from 1957 until 1961, when he resigned following his congressional victory. Ran unsuccessfully for the Democratic nomination for governor in 1958 but was defeated by Price Daniel. Ran unsuccessfully for U.S. senator in the April 1961 special election to fill Lyndon Johnson's seat. Elected U.S. representative, 20th District, on November 4, 1961, by defeating Republican John Goode, Ernest Cude, G. H. Allen,

Henry B. Gonzalez

and Norman Brock in a special election to fill the unexpired term of Paul Kilday. Kilday had resigned in September 1961. Gonzalez was reelected in 1962, running unopposed, in 1964 by defeating Republican John O'Connell, in 1966 by defeating Conservative Party candidate Robert Moore and Constitution Party candidate Bert Ellis, in 1968 by defeating Republican Robert Schneider, in 1970 by running unopposed, and in 1972 by defeating Socialist Workers Party candidate Steve Wattenmaker. In 1974, 1976, and 1978 he ran unopposed, in 1980 he defeated Republican Merle Nash and Libertarian Tom Burnham, in 1982 he defeated Libertarian Roger Gary and Independent Benedict LaRosa, in 1984 and 1986 he ran unopposed, in 1988 he defeated Republican Lee Trevino and Libertarian Theresa Doyle, in 1990 and 1992 he ran unopposed, in 1994 he defeated Republican Carl Colyer, and in 1996 he defeated Republican James Walker, Libertarian Alejandro de Pena, and Natural Law Party candidate Lyndon Felps. Nicknamed "Gabby" for his lengthy speeches. Retired from Congress and did not seek reelection in 1998. Succeeded by his son Charlie Gonzalez in January 1999. An elementary school in San Antonio was named in his honor, as was San Antonio's convention center. Died on November 28, 2000, in San Antonio and was buried there at San Fernando Cemetery No. 2.

> *We must have more representation for the plain, common, ordinary run-of-the-mill citizen. The rich and powerful can afford the services of able, competent, and highly paid lobbyists. But what about the plain ordinary citizen? He tends to get lost in the shuffle.*

> —Henry B. Gonzalez

ED LEE GOSSETT

Born on January 27, 1902, near Many, Louisiana. Moved with his parents, who settled near Henrietta, Texas, in 1908. Grew up and attended school in Clay and Garza counties. Received A.B. in 1924 and

L.L.B. in 1927 from the University of Texas. Admitted to the state bar and began legal practice in Vernon with Berry, Stokes, Warlick, and Gossett. Presbyterian and Democrat. Served as district attorney, 46th Judicial District, from 1933 until 1937. Moved to Wichita Falls in 1937. Elected U.S. representative, 13th District, in 1938 by unseating incumbent W. D. McFarlane in the Democratic primary and runoff and by defeating Republican Adolph Lohman in the November general election. Succeeded McFarlane on January 3, 1939. Married Mary Helen Mosely in 1939 and they had six children: Glenn, Stephen, Murray, Judy, Jane, and Melissa. Reelected in 1940 and 1942 by defeating Republican Louis Gould. Served on the House Judiciary and Expenditures in the Executive Department committees. Reelected in 1944 by defeating Republican L. C. Harper and then ran unopposed in 1946, 1948, and 1950. Resigned from Congress on July 31, 1951, to accept job as general counsel for Southwestern Bell Telephone Company. Succeeded by Frank

Ed Gossett

Ikard in 1953. Served on the Texas Women's University board of regents. Criminal district court judge in Dallas from 1968 until 1976, when he reached the mandatory retirement age of 75. He is reported to have tried more felony cases than any other criminal judge in the country. He served occasionally as a visiting judge, as needed. Died on November 6, 1990, of a heart attack in Dallas and was buried there at Restland Memorial Park.

MALCOLM DANIEL GRAHAM

Malcolm Graham

Born on July 6, 1827, in Autauga County, Alabama. His middle name can also be found as Duncan. Attended Transylvania University in Kentucky. Studied law and practiced in Wetumpka, Alabama. Appointed clerk of the Alabama House of Representatives in 1853. Democrat. Moved to Henderson, Texas, in 1854. Married Amelia Cunningham Ready and they had two sons. Served one term as state senator, District 9, from 1857 until 1859. Elected attorney general and served from 1858 until 1860. Presidential elector for Breckenridge in 1860. Served in the Confederate States Army. Elected as representative, 5th District, to the Confederate Congress in November 1861 by defeating R. B. Hubbard. Unseated by John R. Baylor in the 1863 general election. Appointed by President Davis as judge advocate, but was captured and imprisoned. He was eventually traded in a prisoner swap in 1865. Moved to Montgomery, Alabama, in late 1860s. Returned to legal practice. Served as chair of the executive committee of the Conservative Democrats Party. A year later, he considered but declined a run for the Alabama governor's office. Died on October 8, 1878, in Montgomery and was buried there at Oakwood Cemetery.

WILLIAM PHILIP "PHIL" GRAMM

Born on July 8, 1942, in Fort Benning, Georgia. Moved to College Station, Texas, in 1967. Received B.B.A. and Ph.D. in economics from the University of Georgia in 1961 and 1967. Professor of economics at Texas A&M University from 1967 until 1978. Married Dr. Wendy Lee in 1970 and they had two sons: Marshall and Jeff. Democrat, but became a Republican in 1983. Ran unsuccessfully for Lloyd Bentsen's U.S. Senate seat in 1976. Elected U.S. representative, 6th District, in 1978 by defeating Republican Wesley H. Mowery. Succeeded Olin Teague in January 1979. Reelected in 1980 by defeating Dave "Buster" Haskins and in 1982 by defeating Libertarian Ron Hard. Resigned his seat on January 5, 1983, upon being denied a seat on the House Budget Committee and joined the Republican Party. On February 12, 1983, a special election was held to fill the seat. He defeated Democrat Dan Kubiak. Did not run for reelection in 1984 and was succeeded by Joe Barton in January 1985. Elected U.S. senator in 1984 in the Houston succession of U.S. senators from Texas. The seat had been vacated by John Tower and was won by defeating Democratic nominee Lloyd Doggett. Reelected in 1990 by defeating Democrat Hugh Parmer and in 1996 by defeating Democrat Victor Morales. Candidate for the Republican Party's nomination for U.S. president in 1996. He was not successful in the early primaries and withdrew from the race in February 1996. Author of *The Economics of Mineral Extraction* (1979), *Role of Government in a Free Society* (1982).. Did not seek re-election in 2002. Resigned from the senate on November 30, 2002. Succeeded by fellow Republican John Cornyn on December 2, 2002. Serves as vice-chairman of UBS Investment Bank.

Phil Gramm

> *I didn't come to Washington to be loved, and I haven't been disappointed.*
>
> —Phil Gramm

KAY MULLENDORE GRANGER

Born on January 18, 1943, in Greenville. Attended Fort Worth public schools and graduated from Eastern Hills High School in 1961. Married John Dean Granger in 1964 and they had three children: John Dean Jr., Brandon Keith, and Chelsea Elizabeth. Received B.S. from Texas Wesleyan University in 1965. Taught school and owns Kay Granger Insurance Agency. Divorced from John Granger in 1978. Served on the Fort Worth Zoning Commission from 1981 until 1987, city council from 1989 until 1991, and as mayor from 1991 until 1995. Methodist and Republican. Elected U.S. representative, 12th District, in 1996 by defeating Democrat Hugh Parmer and Natural Law Party candidate Heather Proffer. Succeeded Pete Geren in January 1997. Became first Republican woman to represent Texas in the U.S. House. Reelected in 1998 by defeating Democrat Tom Hall and Libertarian Paul Barthel, and in 2000 by defeating Democrat Mark Greene and Libertarian Rick Clay, in 2002 by defeating Libertarian Edward A. Hanson, and in 2004

Kay Granger

by defeating Democrat Felix Alvarado, and in 2006 by defeating Democrat John R. Morris and Libertarian Gardner Osborne. Serves on the House Appropriations Committee, but has served on National Security, Transportation, Budget and Oversight Committees. *Wrote What's Right About America, Celebrating Our Nation's Values* (2006).

> *America is the greatest nation in the world because our land is filled with ordinary people who achieve extraordinary things.*
>
> —Kay Granger

PETER W. GRAY

Born on December 12, 1819, in Fredericksburg, Virginia. Adopted the middle initial "W" because he had no middle name. Moved to Houston, Texas with his family in 1838. Worked and studied law in his father's office. Served in the Army of the Republic. Episcopalian, member of Church of Christ, Mason, and Democrat. Ran unsuccessfully for city secretary in 1840. Elected as alderman in 1841. Appointed district attorney for Houston and served from 1841 until 1845. Married Abby Jane Avery in 1843. Appointed to city's board of health in 1844. Served one term as state representative, in the first legislature, from 1846 until 1847. One of the founders of the Houston Lyceum in 1848. Served as state senator, District

17, from 1851 until 1853. Served as judge for the Houston District from 1854 to 1861. Served as delegate to state Secession Convention. Elected representative, 3rd District, to the Confederate Congress in November 1861 and served from 1862 until 1864. Unseated by Anthony Martin Branch in the 1863 general election. Co-founded the law firm of Gray, Botts, and Baker. Elected first president of Houston Bar Association in 1870. Appointed by Governor Coke as justice of State Supreme Court in 1874 but resigned shortly thereafter due to his health. Died on October 3, 1874, in Houston of tuberculosis and was buried there at Glenwood Cemetery. He financed Henderson Yoakum's *History of Texas* (1855), the first comprehensive history of Texas. Gray County was named in his honor in 1876.

Peter W. Gray

ALEXANDER N. "AL" GREEN

Al Green

Born in New Orleans, Louisiana, on September 1, 1947. Raised in Florida. Attended Florida A&M University from 1966 through 1971 and Tuskegee University. Received J. D. from Texas Southern University in 1974. Baptist, Lawyer, and Democrat. Co-founded law firm of Green, Wilson, Dewberry and Fitch. Served as Justice of the Peace, Precinct 7, Position 2, from 1977 until 2004. Elected U.S. Representative, 9th District, in 2004 by defeating Republican Arlette Molina and Libertarian Stacey Bourland. Ran unopposed for re-election in 2006. Serves on Financial Services and Science Committee.

RAYMOND EUGENE "GENE" GREEN

Born on October 17, 1947, in Houston. Married Helen Albers in 1970 and they had two children: Angela and Christopher. Methodist and Democrat. Received B.A. from University of Houston in 1971. Attended the Bates College of Law at the University of Houston and was admitted to the state bar in 1977. Business manager and attorney. Served seven terms as state representative, District 95 and 140, from 1973 until May 27, 1985, when he resigned from the House and was sworn in and began serving three terms as state senator, District 6, from 1985 until 1992. Served as majority whip and eventually as Democratic majority leader. Elected as the first U.S. representative from the newly created 29th District in 1992 by defeating Republican Clark Kent Ervin. Took office in January 1993. Reelected in 1994 by defeating Harold "Oilman" Eide. The U.S. District Court redrew the boundary for Green's district, requiring him to run in an open primary or special election in November 1996. This election coincided with the general election, and Green was reelected by defeating U.S. Taxpayers Party candidate Jack W. Klinger and Republican Jack Rodriguez. Reelected in 1998 by defeating Libertarian James Chudleigh and Independent Lee Sherman and in 2000 by defeating Republican and former congressman Joe Vu and Libertarian Ray Dittmar, in 2002 by defeating Libertarian Paul Hansen and in 2004 by defeating Libertarian Clifford L. Messina, and in 2006 by defeating Republican Eric Story and Libertarian Clifford Lee Messina. Serves on the House Energy & Commerce Committee.

Gene Green

ALEXANDER WHITE GREGG

Born on January 31, 1855, in Centerville. Attended local schools. Graduated from Kings College in Bristol, Tennessee, in 1874. Studied law at the University of Virginia. Admitted to the state bar in 1878.

Democrat. Began law practice in Palestine. Wedded Mary Bridges and they had one child. Mary died in 1885, and he wedded Mary Brooks; they had three children. Served one term as state senator, District 7, from 1887 until 1889. Elected U.S. representative, 7th District, in 1902, running unopposed. Succeeded Robert L. Henry on March 4, 1903. Ran unopposed for reelection in 1904 and 1906. Reelected in 1908 by defeating Republican J. W. Boynton, and in 1910 by defeating Republican Willis Kendall. Ran unopposed in 1912 and 1914. Reelected in 1916 by defeating Republicans Theodore Heiger and W. C. Kendall, and Socialist T. E. Foster. Did not run for reelection in 1918 and was succeeded by Clay S. Briggs on March 3, 1919. Died on April 30, 1919, and was buried at East Hill Cemetery in Palestine.

Alexander Gregg

JOHN GREGG

Born on September 28, 1828, in Lawrence County, Alabama. Attended Tutwiller's School in La Grange, Georgia. Taught following graduation in 1847 until 1851. Studied law. Moved to Fairfield, Texas, in 1852. Married Mollie Winston in 1855. Widowed and married Mary Frances Garth and they had two children. Practiced law and began *Freestone County Pioneer* newspaper. Served as district judge from 1856 until 1860. Served as delegate to Texas Secession Convention in 1861 and as delegate to Confederate Provisional Congress from 1861 through 1862. Resigned to take up a Confederate gray uniform. Served as general in Confederate States Army and was killed in action along New Market Road below Richmond on October 7, 1864. He was buried at Odd Fellows Cemetery in Aberdeen, Mississippi. His open seat in the Confederate Congress was not filled. Gregg County was named in his honor in 1876.

John Gregg

WALTER GRESHAM

Born on July 22, 1841, near Newton, Virginia. Attended Stevensville and Edge Hill academies. Served in the Confederate States Army. While recovering from a wound, he studied law and was graduated from the University of Virginia law school in 1863 with a B.L. Moved to Galveston in 1866 and practiced law. Married Josephine Cory Mann in 1868 and they had nine children: Henry and Edward (who died while infants), Walter, Jr., Esther (Lockhart), Josephine (Armstrong), Beulah (Oakes), Thomas Dew, Frank Spencer, and Philip. Democrat. In private legal practice with Walter L. Mann from 1867 until Mann's death in 1875, Samuel W. Jones from 1878 until 1897, and his son, Walter, Jr. in Gresham and Gresham from 1897 until his son's death in 1905. Elected district attorney for the area which included Galveston and Brazoria counties and served from 1887 until 1892. Served as an official with the Gulf, Colorado, and Santa Fe Railroad. This line was later sold to

Walter Gresham

the Atchison, Topeka, and Santa Fe Railroads. Served two terms as state representative, District 65, from 1887 until 1891, when he resigned. He chaired the Deep Water Conventions in Fort Worth, Denver, and Topeka. He lobbied western states to pressure Washington into appropriating funds for Galveston Bay, as they, too, could use the railroads and the bay to ship goods. Through his efforts, Galveston Bay was deepened from twelve to thirty-two feet in depth, thus allowing deeper draft ships to use the bay. Served on the board of the Cotton Exchange. Manager and then president of the Galveston Western Railway and the Senorita Valley Land and Colonization Company. Gresham worked to rebuild Galveston following the devastating hurricane of 1900. Elected U.S. representative, 10th District, in 1892 by defeating Republican A. J. Rosenthal and People's Party candidate E. O. Meitzn. Succeeded Joseph D. Sayers on March 4, 1893. He was unseated by Miles Crowley at the 1894 Democratic convention and was succeeded by him on March 3, 1895. Following his time in Congress, Gresham spent his time in Galveston and Washington. He served on the Inter-Coastal Canal Commission and, as president of the Trans-Mississippi Commercial Congress in 1901 and 1902. Died on November 6, 1920, in Washington, D.C., and was buried at Lakeview Cemetery in Galveston. Gresham's family home in Galveston is a historical site known as the Bishop's Palace.

BEN HUGH GUILL

Ben Guill

Born on September 8, 1909, in Elmyrna, Tennessee. Moved to El Paso, Texas with his parents in 1918. Graduated from Canyon High School. Graduated from West Texas State College in 1933. Taught school in Amarillo, Pampa, Panhandle, and Hopkins from 1929 until 1936. Married Marjorie Buckler; they had one son: Hugh. President of Royal Crown Bottling Company of Amarillo from 1939 until 1942. Served in the U.S. Navy during World War II. Switched parties after Roosevelt's second term as president. This caused a bit of a stir in his family, and his mother remarked, "What will our relatives back in Tennessee think of you—being a Republican." Returned to Pampa following the war. Episcopalian. Businessman in real estate and insurance. Elected U.S. representative, 18th District, in a May 1950 special election of eleven candidates to fill the seat of Eugene Worley. Worley had resigned to accept a U.S. Court of Customs and Patents Appeals judgeship. So many Democrats competed against one another in the 1950 election, that they spread the vote out too thin and Guill, with all the Republican votes, won. Guill was the first Republican elected from the South since 1930. Unseated by his Pampa neighbor Walter Rogers in the 1950 general election and was succeeded by him January 3, 1951. Guill served as President Eisenhower's campaign manager in Texas and the Panhandle. Delegate to the Republican national convention of 1952. Guill was appointed and served as an administrative assistant to U.S. Postmaster General Summerfield from 1953 until 1955 and was appointed to the Federal Maritime Board on which he served from January 1955 until December 1959. He was made vice chair in April 1956. Worked as a public relations consultant in Washington, D.C. Died on January 15, 1994, in Pampa and was buried there in Fairview Cemetery.

I am no intellectual giant, and I didn't have any ideas about going to the capital and changing up the government. But if I go up there as one small protest, maybe the powers that be won't think they have the whole country in the bag. Maybe some of those big shots will take a look at a little segment of Texas and take warning.

—Ben Guill

RALPH MOODY HALL

Born on May 3, 1923, in Fate. Graduated from Rockwall High School in 1941. Served as a U.S. Naval aviator during World War II. Married Mary Ellen Murphy in 1944 and they had three sons: Hampton, Brett, and Blakley. Attended Texas Christian University and the University of Texas. Received L.L.B. from Southern Methodist University in 1951. Democrat. Lawyer and was admitted to the state bar in 1951. Practiced in Rockwall. Former president and chief executive officer of Texas Aluminum Corporation. Served as Rockwall County judge from 1950 until 1962. Served five terms as state senator, District 9, from 1963 until 1973. Sought Democratic nomination for lieutenant governor in 1972, but was defeated in the Democratic primary by Bill Hobby. Elected U.S. representative, 4th District, in

1980 by defeating Republican John H. Wright. Succeeded Ray Roberts in January 1981. Reelected in 1982 by defeating Republican Peter J. Collumb and Libertarian Jerry Williamson, in 1984 and 1986 by defeating Republican Thomas Blow, in 1988 by defeating Republican Randy Sutton and Libertarian M. Dunn, in 1990 by defeating write-in candidate Tim J. McCord, in 1992 and 1994 by defeating Republican David L. Bridges and Libertarian Steven Rothacker, in 1996 by defeating Natural Law Party candidate Enos M. Denham, Jr., Republican Jerry R. Hall, and Libertarian Steven Rothacker, in 1998 by defeating Republican Jim Lohmeyer and Libertarian Jim Simon, and in 2000 by defeating Republican Jon Newton and Libertarian Joe Turner, in 2002 by defeating Republican John Graves and Libertarian Barbara Robinson. Became a Republican and was successfully reelected in 2004 by defeating Democrat Jim Nickerson and Libertarian Kevin D. Anderson. Reelected in 2006 by defeating Democrat Glenn Melancon and Libertarian Kurt G. Helm. Serves on the House Energy & Commerce and Science committees, but has also served on Health and the Environment committee.

Ralph Hall

SAMUEL BLAKELEY HALL, JR.

Born on January 11, 1924, in Marshall. Graduated from Marshall High School in 1940. Received A.A. from Marshall College (later East Texas Baptist University) in 1942. Attended University of Texas law school from 1942 until 1943. Served in U.S. Army Air Forces during World War II. Married Mary Madeline Segal i 1946 and had three daughters: Becky Palmer, Amanda Wynn, and Sandra Bodenhamer. Received law degree from Baylor University in 1948. Practiced law in Marshall from 1948 until 1976. Democrat. Candidate for U.S. representative, 1st District, in 1962, but was defeated by Wright Patman in the Democratic primary election. Elected U.S. representative, 1st District, in June 1976 special election by defeating Democrats Glen Jones and Fred Hudson and Republican James Hogan to fill seat of the late Wright Patman. Took office on June 19, 1976. Reelected a few months later in the November 1976 general election by defeating Republican James Hogan, in 1978 by defeating Republican Fred Hudson, in 1980 by running unopposed, in 1982 by defeating Libertarian John Traylor, and in 1984 by running unopposed. Appointed by President Reagan in 1985 as a federal judge and resigned from the House of Representatives on May 27, 1985. Succeeded by Jim Chapman in 1987. In 1993 a professorship was endowed in his honor at East Texas Baptist University in Marshall. Died April 10, 1994 and was buried at Grover Cemetery in Marshall. Later in the year, the Federal Building and U.S. Courthouse in Marshall was renamed in his honor.

Sam Hall

Andrew Hamilton

ANDREW JACKSON HAMILTON

Born on January 28, 1815, in Huntsville, Alabama. Educated, studied law, and was admitted to the bar in his home state. Brother of Morgan Calvin Hamilton (1809–93), who was a Republic of Texas official and a U.S. senator during Reconstruction. Andrew Hamilton moved to Texas in 1846 to join his brother. Independent Democrat. Married Mary Bowen and they had two sons and four daughters. Appointed acting attorney general by Governor Bell and served from January 1850 until August 1850. Served one term as state representative, District 42, from 1851 until 1853. Elected U.S. representative, 2nd District, in

1859 by defeating Democrat Thomas N. Waul. Succeeded Guy M. Bryan on March 4, 1859. Served one term and left office on March 3, 1861. He opposed secession and most of the other southern trends of the day and worked to calm the secessionists' efforts. Following the war, his seat in Congress was filled by John Cogswell Conner in 1869. Hamilton served as state senator from 1861 until 1862. He escaped to Mexico following threats against his life. Appointed military governor of Texas by President Lincoln and served from 1862 until 1865. He spent most of the war in New Orleans. He also served as provisional governor from June 17, 1865, until August 9, 1866. Served briefly as a bankruptcy judge in New Orleans, but returned to Texas and served as a justice on the state supreme court from 1866 until 1870. Nicknamed "Colossal Jack." In 1870 he ran unsuccessfully for governor. Died on April 11, 1875, and was buried at Oakwood Cemetery in Austin.

MORGAN CALVIN HAMILTON

Morgan Calvin Hamilton

Born on February 25, 1809, near Huntsville, Alabama. Brother of Andrew Jackson Hamilton (1815–75), who was a congressman and was military and provisional governor of Texas during and following the Civil War. Attended public schools. Moved to Texas in 1830 and moved to Austin seven years later. Moved to Washington-on-the-Brazos in 1842 and lived there for three years before returning to Austin. Served as secretary of war in the Republic from 1844 until 1845. Owned a mercantile business in Austin until 1852. A Republican; he was opposed to secession. He was appointed state comptroller in 1867 and served until 1870. Served as a delegate to Texas state constitutional convention in 1868. Elected U.S. senator and served from March 30, 1870, until March 3, 1877. Succeeded David G. Burnet in the Houston succession of U.S. senators from Texas. He was one of the two senators seated following the Civil War. Both were Republicans, and Hamilton received the longer of the two staggered terms. Although a part of the Radical Republicans, he moderated some of their strong-armed efforts. Because of this, the state legislature tried to replace him with General J. J. Reynolds. However, the U.S. Senate would not seat Reynolds and in March 1871 declared that Hamilton would serve his full term. Succeeded by Richard Coke in 1877. After leaving, the senate he lived primarily in New York and traveled. Hamilton never married and died on November 21, 1893, in San Diego, California, and was buried at Oakwood Cemetery in Austin.

KENT RONALD HANCE, SR.

Kent Hance

Born on November 14, 1942, in Dimmitt. Graduated from Dimmitt High School in 1961. Received a B.B.A. from Texas Tech University in 1965 and an L.L.B. from the University of Texas in 1968. Admitted to the state bar in 1968 and practiced in Lubbock. Taught law at Texas Tech University. Married Carol Hays and they had two children: Kent Ronald "Ron," Jr. and Susan. Professor at Texas Tech from 1968 until 1973. Served two terms as state senator, District 28, from 1975 until 1978. Elected U.S. representative, 19th District, in 1978 by defeating Republican George W. Bush. Succeeded George Mahon in January 1979. Reelected in 1980 by defeating Libertarian J. D. Webster and in 1982 by defeating Republican E. L. Hicks and Libertarian Mike Read. Did not seek reelection in 1984 and was succeeded by Republican Larry Combest in January 1985. Candidate for U.S. senator in 1984. He received the most votes in the Democratic primary runoff, but lost the recount to Lloyd Doggett, who eventually lost to Phil Gramm in the 1984 general election. Baptist and Democrat until 1985, when he joined the Republican Party. Candidate for governor in 1986, but was defeated by Bill Clements in the Republican primary.

Appointed to the Railroad Commission in 1987 by Governor Clements and was the first Republican to serve on the Commission. Elected to the Railroad Commission in 1988 and served until 1990. Candidate for governor in 1990 but was defeated by Clayton Williams in the Republican primary. In private legal practice with Hance, Scarborough, and Wright in Austin until elected chancelor of Texas Tech University in 2006.

> *Deliver the mail and keep the Communists out.*
>
> —Kent Hance on the two rules of government as learned from his father

JOHN HANCOCK

John Hancock

Born on October 24, 1824, near Bellefonte, Alabama. Attended the University of East Tennessee in Knoxville. Farmed and studied law. Admitted to the state bar of Alabama in 1846. Democrat. Moved to Austin, Texas in 1847. Practiced law. Elected district judge, 2nd Judicial District, and served from 1851 until 1855 when he resigned to return to private practice. Married Susan Richardson in 1855. Episcopalian. Served briefly as state representative, District 57, from 1860 until he resigned. He was a Unionist, and although did not flaunt it, he was expelled from the legislature for failing to take an oath to the Confederacy. Spent a number of months of Civil War in Mexico, along with a number of other Texas Unionists. Returned to Texas following the war. He served as a delegate to the state constitutional convention in 1866. Reportedly declined a nomination to Congress in 1870, but this must have piqued his interest, as he was elected U.S. representative, 4th District, in 1871 by defeating incumbent Republican Edward Degener. Succeeded Degener on March 4, 1871. Reelected in 1872 by defeating Republican W. O. Hutchinson. Was succeeded in the 4th District seat by Roger Q. Mills in 1875. Ran instead for the newly created 5th District seat in 1874 and won without competition. Hancock was not renominated in 1876 by the Democratic Party and was succeeded by DeWitt C. Giddings on March 3, 1877. Elected U.S. representative for the newly created 10th District in 1882 by defeating Republican Edmund J. Davis. Took office on March 4, 1883. Did not seek reelection in 1884 and was succeeded by Joseph Sayers on March 3, 1885. Returned to Austin and his law practice. Died on July 19, 1893, and was buried at Oakwood Cemetery in Austin.

RUFUS HARDY

Born on December 16, 1855, near Aberdeen, Mississippi. Moved with family to near Millican, Texas in 1861. Educated at the Somerville Institute in Mississippi and received a law degree from the University of Georgia in 1875. Episcopalian, Elk, Knight of Pythias, and (Jeffersonian) Democrat. Admitted to the state bar in 1875. Practiced law in Navasota beginning in 1876, but moved to Corsicana two years later. Served as Navarro county attorney from 1880 until 1884; district attorney, 13th Judicial District, from 1884 until 1888; and district judge from 1888 until 1896. Married Felicia E. Peck in 1881 and they had seven children: Fay, Paukline, Nanerl, Ilva, Helen, Mildred, and Rufus, Jr. Practiced law in Corsicana. Elected U.S. representative, 6th District, in 1906 by defeating Prohibition Party candidate T. S. Henderson, Jonathan T. Atkisson, and Richard Mays. Succeeded Scott Field on March 4, 1907. Reelected in 1908 by defeating Republican C. L. McCoy, in 1910 and 1912 by defeating Socialist W. H. Wilson, in 1914 by defeating now Republican W. H. Wilson, in 1916 by again defeating Socialist W. H. Wilson, in 1918 by defeating Republican Charles Beck, and in 1920 by defeating American Party candidate Clyde Essex and Republican D. H. Merrill. Served on the House Reform in Civil Service, Merchant Marine and Fisheries, Territories, Expenditures in the Navy Department, and State of the Union committees. He eventually chaired the latter two committees. Did not seek reelection in 1922 and was succeeded by Luther A.

Johnson on March 3, 1923. Returned to Corsicana to practice law. Died on March 13, 1943, in Corsicana and was buried there at Oakwood Cemetery.

Rufus Hardy

> *We want a new Thomas Jefferson, who will revive the principles of the Democratic Party and bring back government by law in this country. Who will right the ship of state and, with the Constitution for chart and statutory laws for compass, save her from the rocks of empire and centralization and guide her back into the calm waters of sovereign States and sovereign United States, each supreme in its sphere, and who will not seek for fame or grasp for power, but only labor for his people's freedom and happiness and only ask for their love.*

—Rufus Hardy

SILAS HARE

Silas Hare

Born on November 13, 1827, in Ross County, Ohio. Raised mostly by his grandfather, but rejoined his mother and family in 1835. Moved to Indiana in 1840. Attended public and private schools. Democrat. Served in U.S. Army during Mexican War. Studied law. Married Octavia Elizabeth Rector in 1849 and they had six surviving children:Luther, Silas, Jr., Winnie, Henry, George, and Eula. Hare traveled widely. Admitted to the state bar in 1850 and practiced law in Noblesville, Indiana. Moved to Belton, Texas in 1853. Participated in the Hardeman Expedition in 1858. Occupied Fort Stanton, near Mesilla, New Mexico, following the withdrawal of Union troops at the beginning of the Civil War and claimed it for the Confederates. Served in the Confederate States Army. Presided as the Confederate chief justice in New Mexico in 1862. Settled in Sherman after the war and co-founded the *Sherman Courier* newspaper in 1866. Served as criminal court district judge from 1873 until 1876. Returned to private practice. Delegate to the Democratic national convention in 1884. Elected U.S. representative, 5th District, in 1886 by defeating Independent Democrat G. B. Pickett and Independent H. C. Mack. Succeeded James Throckmorton on March 4, 1887. Reelected in 1888 by defeating Republican J. W. Thomas. Unseated by Joseph Weldon Bailey in 1891 and was succeeded by him on March 3, 1891. Hare remained in Washington to practice law. He married a second time to Mary Louise (Canniff) Kenaday. He died on November 26, 1907, in Washington, D.C. and was buried at West Hill Cemetery in Sherman. (See also photo page 14.)

ROBERT BRADLEY HAWLEY

Born on October 25, 1849, in Memphis, Tennessee. Attended public schools and the Christian Brothers' College in Memphis. Moved in 1875 to Galveston, Texas where he was a merchant. Hawley's wife apparently died while very young. They had one daughter, Sue (Oakes), who also died young and left Hawley to raise her two sons. Republican. Served as president of the Board of Education in Galveston from 1889 until 1893. Delegate to several Republican national conventions. Elected U.S. representative, 10th District, in 1896 by defeating Democrat J. H. Shelburne and Populist Noah Allen. Succeeded Democrat Miles Crowley on March 4, 1897. Reelected in 1898 by defeating Democrat W. S. Robson, Populist J. W. Baird, and Frank Gary. Served on the House Ways and Means, Rivers and Harbors, Coast Defense, Construction of the Nicaragua Canal, International Exposition, Military Affairs (eventu-

Robert Hawley

ally chaired), Inter-oceanic Canal, Coastal and Insular Surveys, Railroads, and Philippines Commission committees. Did not seek reelection in 1900 and was succeeded by George F. Burgess on March 3, 1901. Founded and served as President of the Cuban-American Sugar Company from 1900 until his death. Died on November 28, 1921, in New York and was buried at Lakeview Cemetery in Galveston.

No one man or any set of men can say they dominate the Republican Party of Texas.

—Robert Hawley

JOHN HEMPHILL

Born on December 18, 1803, in Blackstock, Chester County, South Carolina. Uncle of John James Hemphill (1849–1912), a U.S. Representative from South Carolina in the late 1800s and great-grand-uncle of Robert Witherspoon Hemphill (1915–83), also a U.S. representative from South Carolina, from 1957 until 1964. Attended local schools in the Hopewell area. Graduated from Jefferson College (now Washington & Jefferson) in 1825. Taught school, studied law, and was admitted to South Carolina bar in 1829. Practiced law and edited the *Sumpter Gazette*. Served in the army during the Seminole War in 1836 until he was discharged for medical reasons. Continued to practice law. Moved to Washington-on-the-Brazos, Texas in 1838. President Lamar offered Hemphill the position of secretary of the treasury, but he declined. He moved to Bastrop in 1839. Served as judge, 4th Judicial District, in the Republic from 1840 until 1842. Participated in the Council House Fight on March 19, 1840. Became chief justice of the Supreme Court that

John Hemphill

December. Hemphill was responsible for forming much of the early Texas legal system. Served as adjutant to the Mier Expedition in 1842 and went on several campaigns against the Comanches. Represented Washington County in the Annexation Convention in 1845. Served as chief justice from 1840 until 1858. He was appointed to the post by Governor Henderson in 1846, but was also elected to the post in 1851. He resigned from the post to accept his position as U.S. Senator. A States Rights Democrat, he served as U.S. senator from March 4, 1859, until July 11, 1861, when he was expelled following a recommendation for secession on January 8, 1861. He had succeeded Sam Houston and was succeeded by Williamson Oldham on November 16, 1861. Served as delegate to the Confederate Provisional Congress from 1861 until 1862 and was a candidate for senator in the Confederate Congress in 1861, but lost a close race to Oldham. Died on January 7, 1862, in Richmond, Virginia, but he was buried in the State Cemetery in Austin. He had never married. Hemphill County was named in his honor in 1876.

JAMES PINCKNEY HENDERSON

Born on March 31, 1808, in Lincolnton, North Carolina. Attended Lincolnton Academy and studied law at the University of North Carolina. Served in militia in 1830. Admitted to North Carolina bar in 1835 and practiced in Lincolnton. Moved to Canton, Mississippi, in 1835, but was recruited to come to Texas to fight in the revolution in 1836. Commissioned as a brigadier general by David Burnet and returned to the U.S. to recruit more volunteers. Appointed attorney general of the Texas Republic in November 1836 and was secretary of state on December 29, 1836, upon the death of Stephen F. Austin. Served as a diplomat to England and France in 1838 to establish trade relations and gain recognition for Texas as a sovereign nation. While in France, he met Frances Cox. They were married in October 1839 and they had five children: Martha, Julia, Frances, and two who died while

James Henderson

very young. Returned to practice of law in 1840. Worked with Isaac Van Zandt in preparing the treaty of annexation with the U.S. Represented San Augustine at the state constitutional convention in 1845. Elected first governor of the state and served from 1846 until 1847. He did not seek reelection. During his term, the war with Mexico began and he took command of the Texas troops. Served temporarily as a major general in the U.S. Army from July until October 1846. Following his single term as the first governor of the state, he returned to the private practice of law. Succeeded as Governor by George T. Wood. Elected by the legislature to serve as U.S. senator upon the death of Senator Rusk and served from November 9, 1857, until his death on June 4, 1858. Politically, he was a States Rights Democrat. He was buried at the Congressional Cemetery in Washington, D.C., but was reinterred in 1930 at the Texas State Cemetery in Austin. He was succeeded in the U.S. Senate by Matthias Ward in 1858. Henderson County was named in his honor in 1846.

ROBERT LEE HENRY

Robert Lee Henry

Born on May 12, 1864, in Linden, and was the great-great-great-grandson of Patrick Henry (1736–99), U.S. Revolutionary War hero. Attended local schools. Moved to Bowie County in 1878 with his family. Graduated Georgetown University in 1885, was admitted to the state bar in 1886, and received a law degree from the University of Texas the following year. Democrat. Served as mayor of Texarkana from 1890 until 1891. He resigned to work for the attorney general. Served as assistant attorney general from 1893 until 1896. He moved to McLennan County about this time. Elected U.S. representative, 7th District, in 1896 by defeating Republican T. A. Pope and Populist W. F. Douthitt. Succeeded George Pendleton on March 4, 1897. Reelected in 1898 by defeating Populist A. W. Cunningham and Republican Russell Kingsbury, and in 1900 by defeating Populist W. L. Harrison and Republican J. E. Boynton. Following some redistricting in the state, the 7th Congressional District became the 11th District in 1902. Henry was succeeded in the 7th District seat by Alexander W. Gregg in 1903. Elected to the 11th District seat in 1902 by defeating Republican A. Wurts, G. B. Harris, and G. A. Boynton. Reelected in 1904 by defeating Republican Joe E. Williams, in 1906 and 1908 by running unopposed, in 1910 by defeating Republican E. J. Vesey, in 1912 by defeating Socialist C. G. Davidson, and in 1914 by defeating Republican Duncan Carrick. He eventually was the chairman of the Committee on Rules. Chose not to run for reelection to the U.S. House in 1916 and was succeeded by Tom Connally on March 3, 1917. Ran unsuccessfully for the Democratic nomination for U.S. senator in 1916. Tried unsuccessfully again for the nomination in 1922 and was defeated in the primary by Earle B. Mayfield. Tried one last time in 1930 and was defeated by Morris Sheppard in the Democratic primary. Just after his second try for the Senate, he moved to Houston and continued the practice of law. Died on July 9, 1931, at home in Houston from a gunshot wound and was buried at Rose Hill Cemetery in Texarkana. He was married to Lourine Tyler and they had two sons and one daughter.

The cost may be considerable, but there come times in the history of states and republics when men who are commissioned to serve the people should evince proper courage, no matter what may be the expense.

—Robert L. Henry

T. JEB HENSARLING

Born May 29, 1957, in Stephenville. Raised in Naples, Slayton, and College Station. Received B.A. in economics from Texas A&M University in 1979 and law degree from University of Texas School of Law in 1982. Admitted to the state bar in 1982. Lawyer in private practice in San Antonio from 1982 to 1984. Republican and Episcopal. Moved to Dallas in 1984. State Director for U.S. Senator Phil Gramm from 1985 through 1989. Married Melissa Fore and they have two children: Claire and Travis. Campaign manager for Gramm's re-election campaign in 1990. Executive director, National Republican Senatorial Committee in Washington, D.C., 1991 through 1993. Vice-president, Maverick Capital, 1993 to 1996. Owner, San Jacinto Ventures, 1996-present. Vice-president, Green Mountain Energy Company, 1999 through 2001. Chief executive officer, Family Support Assurance Corp., 2001 to date. Elected Representative, 5th District, in 2002 by defeating Democrat Ron Chapman, Libertarian Dan Michalski, and Green Party candidate Thomas J. Kemper. Reelected in 2004 by defeating Democrat Bill Bernstein and Libertarian John Gonzalez and in 2006 by defeating Democrat Charlie Thompson and Libertarian Mike Nelson. Serves on the House Committees for Budget and Financial Services.

Jeb Hensarling

CALEB CLAIBORNE HERBERT

Born about 1814 in Goochland County, Virginia. Details of his family life are unclear, although it is known that his wife was Mary and they had a number of sons. Moved to Colorado County, Texas about 1846. Served as two terms state senator, District 32, from 1857 until 1861. Encouraged secession and served in the Confederate States Army. Elected representative, 2nd District, to the Confederate Congress in November 1861 by defeating Fred Tate, A. M. Lewis, and F. W. Chandler. Reelected in 1863 by defeating Eggleston D. Townes and served from 1862 until 1865. He opposed the conscription of Texans and eventually desired to secede from the Confederacy. Elected U.S. representative, 4th District, in 1866 by defeating Henderson, Finley, and Darden. However, the four representatives elected in 1866 were denied their seats by the Radical Republicans. It was more than three years before the representatives from Texas were allowed to take their seats in the House following the Civil War. Died on July 5, 1867, from a gunshot wound received outside a saloon in Columbus and was buried at the family cemetery at Reel's Bend in Colorado County.

C. C. Herbert

WILLIAM SMITH HERNDON

Born on November 27, 1835, in Rome, Georgia. Moved to Wood County, Texas, with his family in 1852. Graduated from McKenzie College near Clarksville in 1859. Read law and was admitted to the state bar in 1860. Married Louise Kellar the same year, and they had eight children. Democrat. Served in the Confederate States Army along the Texas coast. Returned to the practice of law in Tyler following the war. Specialized in railroad law and served many lines in Texas during that period. Elected U.S. representative, 1st District, in 1871 by unseating incumbent Republican George W. Whitmore in the general election. Succeeded Whitmore on March 4, 1871. Reelected in 1872 by defeating

W. S. Herdon

Republican R. K. Smith and Liberal Republican William Chambers. Apparently unseated in 1874 by John H. Reagan and was succeeded by him on March 3, 1875. Continued practicing law and was connected with railroad industry. Served as a delegate to many state and national Democratic conventions. Died on October 11, 1903, in Albuquerque and was buried at Oakwood Cemetery in Tyler.

JACK ENGLISH HIGHTOWER

Born on September 6, 1926, in Memphis, Texas. Graduated from Memphis High School in 1944.

Jack Hightower

Baptist, Mason, and Democrat. Served in U.S. Navy during World War II. Received B.A. in 1949 and L.L.B. in 1951 from Baylor University. Admitted to the state bar in 1951. Married Colleen Ward in 1950 and they had three daughters: Ann, Amy, and Alison. Practiced law with Storey, Storey, and Donaghey in Vernon. Served one term as state representative, District 82, from 1953 until 1955. Appointed by Governor Shivers as district attorney, 46th Judicial District, in Vernon from 1955 until 1961. Ran unsuccessfully for U.S. representative, 13th District, in the December 1961 special election to fill the seat of Frank Ikard and was defeated by Graham Purcell in this open primary. Served five terms as state senator, District 23, 30, from 1965 until 1975. Delegate to the Democratic national convention in 1968. Served as president pro tempore of the Senate during the 62nd Legislature and was governor for a day on April 3, 1971. Elected U.S. representative, 13th District, in 1974 by unseating incumbent Republican Bob Price. Succeeded Price in January 1975. Reelected in 1976 by defeating former congressman Price again and American Party candidate William Hathcock, in 1978 by defeating Republican Clifford A. Jones, in 1980 by defeating Republican Ron Slover, in 1982 by defeating Republican Slover again and Libertarian Rod Collier, but in 1984 was unseated by Republican Beau Boulter who succeeded him in January 1985. While in Congress, served on the House Agriculture, Appropriations, and Government Operations Committees. Appointed as first assistant attorney general by Attorney General Mattox and served from 1985 until 1987. Resigned from the attorney general's office and was elected to the State Supreme Court in 1988. Received an L.L.M. from the University of Virginia in 1992. Reelected in 1992, but resigned in 1996 to accept a position with Hilgers and Watkins. Lives in Austin.

Regardless of who occupies the White House in the future, I will continue to serve with, and help, the President of the United States—whatever his name or his party—in order that America may remain strong and free.

—Jack Hightower

Rubén Hinojosa

RUBÉN HINOJOSA

Born on August 20, 1940, in Mercedes. Received B.B.A. from the University of Texas in 1962 and an M.B.A. from the same institution in 1980. Married Martha L. Hinojosa and they had five children: Ruben, Jr., Laura, Iliana, Kaitlin, and Karen. President and chief financial officer for H&H Foods. Democrat. Served on Texas State Board of Education from 1975 until 1984. Served on board of directors, National Livestock and Meat Board and Texas Beef Industry Council from 1989 until 1993. Past president and chairman of the board, Southwestern Meat Packers Association. Chairman and member of board of trustees, South Texas Community College, from 1993 until 1996. Elected U.S. representative, 15th District, in 1996 by defeating Republican Tom Haughey and Natural Law Party candidate Rob Wofford. Succeeded Kika de la Garza in January 1997. Reelected in 1998 by defeating Republican Tom Haughey and in 2000 by defeating Libertarian Frank Jones, III and write-in Israel Cantu, in 2002 was unopposed, and in 2004 by defeating Republican Michael D. Thamm and Libertarian William R. Cady. On June 28, 2006, the United States Supreme Court ruled that the Texas Legislature had violated the rights of Hispanic voters when it moved most of Laredo out of the neighboring 23rd District and replaced it with several heavily Republican San Antonio suburbs. It also ruled that the 25th District was not compact enough to be a replacement. The 25th District was nicknamed "the fajita strip" because of its shape. The ruling forced the redrawing of five districts between El Paso and San Antonio including the 15th and a special election to select their representatives. This election was concurrent with the November general election. In 2006, Hinojosa was reelected by defeating Republicans Paul B. Haring and Eddie Zamora. Serves on the House Education and the Workforce, Financial Services, and Resources Committees, but has also served on the Small Business Committee.

ANDREW JACKSON HOUSTON

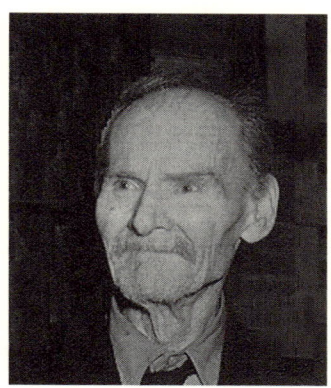

Andrew Jackson Houston

Born on June 21, 1854, in Independence. Son of Texas Revolutionary War hero Sam Houston (1793–1863). Attended Texas Military Institute in Austin, the Military Institute in Bastrop, and Baylor College. Clerk for a number of state agencies in Austin. Studied law and was admitted to the state bar in 1876. Served as U.S. District Court clerk in Dallas from 1879 until 1889. During this time, his first wife—Carrie Glenn Purnell—died in 1884. Served in the Texas National Guard from 1884 until 1893. Attorney in Dallas from 1889 until 1901. Republican nominee for governor in 1892, but lost the election to Jim Hogg. Was not a member, but recruited Rough Riders for Teddy Roosevelt in 1898. Candidate for U.S. representative, 6th District, in 1898, but was defeated by Democrat Robert Burke. Practiced law in Beaumont in 1901 and 1902. Appointed by President Roosevelt as U.S. marshall, Eastern District of Texas, and served from 1902 until 1910. Candidate for U.S. representative, 2nd District, in 1904, but was defeated by Democrat Moses L. Broocks. During this time, his second wife—Elizabeth Hart Good—died in 1907. Unsuccessful candidate for governor in 1910 and 1912 as Prohibition Party candidate. Professor of military science and tactics at St. Mary's University from 1917 until 1918. Retired to near La Porte. Appointed by Governor Neff as the superintendent of the new state park at the San Jacinto Battleground in 1924. Wrote *Texas Independence* (1938). Catholic. Appointed a major general (honorary) in the Texas National Guard in 1939. Appointed U.S. senator by Governor O'Daniel following the death of Morris Sheppard in 1941. O'Daniel wanted the job but could not appoint himself to the position, so chose someone who would not run against him for the seat. Houston was elderly and in poor health when he took the job and died after attending one committee meeting. He did, however, introduce two bills. The first was for $250,000 in funding for the San Jacinto Monument Building, and the second was for recognizing the work by the Sam Houston Museum of History Association. He served from April 21, 1941, until his death June 26, 1941, and was in the Houston succession of senators from Texas. He remains the oldest man to enter the U.S. Senate and continues to hold the record for the shortest time served. Died in Baltimore, Maryland, was interred briefly at the Abbey Mausoleum in Arlington, Virginia, and was later buried at the San Jacinto Battlefield. He was succeeded by the man who appointed him, former governor W. Lee O'Daniel, on August 4, 1941. Houston had three daughters: Ariadne, Marguerite, and Mrs. A. D. Paulus.

SAMUEL "SAM" HOUSTON

Born on March 2, 1793, near Lexington, Virginia. Moved with family to eastern Tennessee in 1807 following the death of his father. Ran away from home in 1809 and lived with nearby Cherokee Indians who took him in. Served in the U.S. Army from 1813 until 1818 and served under Andrew Jackson. This began his identification with the Jacksonian Democrats. Studied law in Nashville, was admitted to the Tennessee state bar, and practiced in Lebanon. Appointed adjutant general of the Tennessee militia by Governor McMinn. Elected Davidson County district attorney in 1818, but returned to private practice in Nashville in 1821. He was an active Mason. Served as U.S. representative, 9th District, from Tennessee from 1823 until 1827 and governor of Tennessee from 1827 until 1829. Married Eliza Allen in 1829. The marriage lasted only a few months, and Eliza returned home. Houston resigned as governor and moved to the Cherokee territory, now Oklahoma. Married Diana Rogers Gentry and established a trading post

Sam Houston

near Fort Gibson. He left Diana and moved to Texas in 1832. Served as delegate from Nacogdoches at constitutional convention in 1833 and later represented Refugio in 1835 and 1836. Appointed commander in chief of the Texas armies in 1836. Defeated Santa Anna at the Battle of San Jacinto a few months later. Signer of the Texas Declaration of Independence in 1836. President of the Republic of Texas—the first regularly elected—and served from 1836 until 1838 and again from 1841 until 1844, as the Republic's constitution prevented a president from succeeding himself. The city, then a town, of Houston was named in his honor in 1836. He was divorced from Diana in 1837. Between his terms as president of the Republic, he served in the Texas House of Representatives from 1839 until 1841. He was married for a third time to Margaret Moffette Lea in 1840 and they had eight children. He was elected one of the first U.S. senators from Texas along with Thomas Rusk in 1846. Joined the Baptist Church in 1854. Served from February 21, 1846, until his support of northern anti-slavery issues brought about the end of his Senate career on March 4, 1859. He had run for governor again in 1857, but was defeated by Hardin Runnels, who became the Democratic nominee and eventually the governor. The legislature chose not to return Houston to the Senate and effectively replaced him with John Hemphill. He became a follower of the American or Know-Nothing Party. He challenged Runnels for the job of governor in 1859 and won. Houston served as governor from December 21, 1859, until March 16, 1861. During this time, he was nominated as the U.S. presidential candidate by the Union Party at their convention in May 1860, but was defeated by John Bell, who was later defeated by Lincoln. Following Lincoln's election, Texas joined a number of southern states in holding a secession convention. Houston opposed this vehemently and he was eventually deposed as governor in 1861 by the convention for failing to take a loyalty pledge to the Confederacy. Lincoln had offered him troops to stay in office, but Houston refused. He was replaced by Lieutenant Governor Edward Clark. He moved his family to Huntsville where he died of pneumonia on July 26, 1863. He was buried at Oakwood Cemetery. Houston counties in Minnesota, Tennessee, and Texas are named in his honor along with the city of Houston in Texas. Cousin of David Hubbard (1792–1874), a U.S. representative from Alabama and father of Andrew Jackson Houston (1854–1941), who was also a senator from Texas in the 1940s.

VOLNEY ERSKINE HOWARD

Volney Howard

Born on October 22, 1809, in Norridgewock, Maine. Studied at Bloomfield Academy and Waterville College. In 1832 he moved to Mississippi to live with an uncle. The uncle, however, died before Howard arrived. He studied law, was admitted to the Mississippi state bar, and began a private practice in Brandon. Democrat. Served in Mississippi House of Representatives beginning in 1836. Married Catherine Elizabeth Gooch the same year. Appointed in 1837 as a court reporter. Owned and edited the largest newspaper—The *Mississippian*—in Vicksburg. Candidate for Congress in 1840 from Mississippi but lost a close election. Involved in an argument with Hiram Runnels, who was then president of the Union Bank which controlled much of Mississippi politics. In a duel between the two, Howard was wounded in the chest, but recovered. Published *A Digest of the Laws of Mississippi and Mississippi Law Reports* from 1834 until 1844. Moved to New Orleans and continued his law practice. Moved to San Antonio, Texas in 1844. Served as delegate to Texas state constitutional convention in 1845 representing Bexar County. Elected to the 10th session of the House of Representatives of the Republic, but the session was never held since Texas had become a state. Served as state representative in the first state legislature from 1846 until 1847. Nominated by Governor Henderson to be attorney general in 1846 but was rejected by the Texas State Senate on an eleven-to-ten vote. Elected U.S. representative, 2nd District, in 1849 by unseating Calhoun Democrat Timothy Pilsbury and defeating Judge Robert M. "Three-legged Willie" Williamson and Democrat Hugh McLeod. Succeeded Timothy Pilsbury on March 4, 1849. Reelected in 1851 by defeating Gideon K. Lewis, Hugh McLeod, Henry N. Potter, and William Menifee. Unseated by Peter H. Bell in 1853 and was succeeded by him later that year. Appointed by President Pierce as a U.S. attorney in California, but resigned after serving only a brief period. Remained in San Francisco and practiced law until 1858 before moving to Sacramento. He then moved to Los Angeles and served as district attorney there from 1861 until 1870. Served as California Superior Court judge from 1878 to 1884 and as a delegate to state constitutional convention from 1878 until 1879. Offered a nomination to the U.S. Supreme Court, but as he had done earlier with another appointment, declined. Died on May 14, 1889, in Santa Monica and was buried at Fort Hill Cemetery in Los Angeles, California. Howard County, Texas, was named in his honor in 1876.

CLAUDE BENTON HUDSPETH

Born on May 12, 1877, in Medina. Democrat. Little formal education. Worked and owned ranches. In 1893 he moved to Ozona and edited the local newpaper—the *Ozona Kicker*—with his brother. Moved to El Paso and married Marie Cliborne in 1902, and they had a son and a daughter. Served two terms as state representative, District 102, from 1903 until 1907 and six terms as state senator, District 25, from 1907 until 1919. He resigned during the 33rd State Legislature but returned to office in 1915. Admitted to the state bar in 1909 and was a partner with Nealon, Hudspeth, and McGill in El Paso. Director of Texas Oil and Land Company. Elected U.S. representative, 16th District, in 1918, running unopposed. Succeeded Thomas Blanton on March 4, 1919. Reelected in 1920 by defeating Republican William Easterling, in 1922 by defeating Republican John A. Simpson, in 1924 by defeating Republican Vernon L. Sullivan, in 1926 by defeating Republican A. W. Norcop, and in 1928 by running unopposed. When he was almost fifty,

Claude Hudspeth

he drove 1,400 cattle from Crockett to Brewster County. He wrote of this epic event in the March 1927 edition of *Cattleman*. He did not seek reelection in 1930 and was succeeded by R. Ewing Thomason on March 3, 1931. Retired to San Antonio. Died on March 19, 1941, and was buried at Mission Burial Park in San Antonio. Hudspeth County was named in his honor. (See also photo page 29.)

JOSEPH CHAPPELL HUTCHESON

Born on May 18, 1842, near Boydton, Virginia. Attended local schools. Graduated from Randolph-Macon College in 1861. Served in the Confederate States Army. Received law degree from the University of Virginia in 1866 and was admitted to the state bar the same year. Married Mildred Carrington in 1867 and they had eight children. Moved to Anderson, Texas, about this time and moved on to Houston in 1874. Democrat. Served one term as state representative, District 33, from 1881 until 1883. His first wife Mildred died in 1882. He married Betty Palmer Milby in 1886 and they had two sons. Served as state Democratic chairman in 1890. Elected U.S. representative, 1st District, in 1892 by defeating People's Party candidate J. B. Stephenson and Republican Daniel Taylor. Succeeded Charles Stewart on March 4, 1893. Reelected in 1894 by defeating Populist J. J. Burroughs and Republican L. E. Dunn. Did not seek reelection in 1896 and was succeeded by Thomas Ball on

Joseph Hutcheson

March 3, 1897. Returned to Houston to practice law. Died on May 25, 1924, at his summer home in Tennessee, and was buried at Glenwood Cemetery in Houston.

KATHYRN ANN "KAY" BAILEY HUTCHISON

Kay Bailey Hutchison

Born on July 22, 1943, in Galveston. Grew up in LaMarque and graduated from LaMarque High School in 1961. Received a L.L.B. from the University of Texas in 1967 and completed her bachelor's degree there in 1992. Admitted to the state bar in 1967. Employed as an attorney in Galveston. Married John P. Parks on April 8, 1967, but they were eventually divorced. Served as secretary to then Co-Chair of the Republican National Committee, Anne Armstrong, in 1971. Served two terms as State Representative, District 90, from 1973 until 1977 and was the first Republican woman elected to the Texas Legislature and was one of only three women serving in the House at the time. Served as a member of the State Republican Executive Committee from 1978 until 1981 and was a delegate to state and local conventions from 1972 until 1980. Precinct chair from 1972 until 1978. Served on the Advisory Council of the Texas Federation of Republican Women. Employed as television reporter in Houston. Following a move to Dallas, she became an executive with RepublicBank. Co-founded Fidelity National Bank in Dallas. Acquired and then operated McCraw Candies of Dallas. Served on the Dallas County Hospital Board. Appointed by President Ford as Vice-Chair of the National Transportation Safety Board and served from 1976 until she resigned in 1978. Continued her banking positions and was counsel with Hutchison, Boyce, Brooks, and Fisher. Married Ray Hutchison in 1978; he had two daughters, Brenda and Julie. Chairwoman of the Texas Women Leaders for Reagan-Bush campaign in 1980. Ran for U.S. Representative, 3rd District in 1982, but was defeated by Steve Bartlett in the Republican primary. Elected State Treasurer in 1990 and served there until 1993, succeeding Ann Richards. Served as temporary Co-Chair of the Republican National Convention in 1992. Lloyd Bentsen resigned his U.S. Senate seat in 1993 to take a place in the Clinton administration. Bob Krueger was appointed by Governor Richards to fill his seat for a few months before the special election to replace him could be held. Hutchison and Krueger were the top two candidates in the May 1993 special election, but neither received a majority and a runoff election was called. Hutchison defeated Krueger in the June 1993 special election runoff. She succeeded Krueger in the Rusk succession of U.S. Senators from Texas and was sworn-in on June 14, 1993. She was the first female U.S. Senator from Texas. Hutchison was indicted on four felony counts on September 27, 1993, along with two former aides for wrongdoing while she was State Treasurer. The charges were dropped a month later. She was reelected in 1994 by defeating Democrat Richard Fisher. Serves on the Committees for Appropriations, Commerce, Science, and Transportation, Rules and Administration, and Veterans' Affairs. Had served on Environment and Public Works. Reelected in 2000 by defeating Democrat Gene Kelly, Libertarian Mary J. Ruwart, and Green Party candidate Douglas S. Sandage and in 2006 by defeating Democrat Barbara Ann Radnofsky and Libertarian Scott Lanier Jameson. Adopted two children: daughter, Kathryn Bailey, and son, Houston Taylor, in 2001.

Tomorrow's new era is one of inclusion, of empowerment for all Texans, of restoring hometown values, facing issues directly, making hard choices, restoring confidence in our public institutions and releasing the energy of hope in America so that others, too, can achieve their impossible dreams.

—Kay Bailey Hutchison

FRANK NEVILLE IKARD

Born on January 30, 1914, in Henrietta. Attended school in Henrietta and at Schreiner College. Received an A.B. from the University of Texas in 1936 and an L.L.B. in 1936. Episcopalian and Democrat. Served as deputy sergeant-at-arms of the state legislature. Admitted to the state bar in 1936. Moved to

Wichita Falls in 1937 and practiced law. Married Jean Hunter in 1940 and they had two sons: Frank, Jr. and William. Served in the U.S. Army in World War II, but was captured and was a prisoner of war in Germany from 1944 through 1945. Following the war, he continued his law practice and became active in politics. Chaired the Texas Veterans Affairs Commission from 1947 until 1948 and served as judge, 30th Judicial District, following an appointment by Governor Jester. Elected U.S. representative, 13th District, in the September 1951 special election by defeating Democrat Walter Jenkins, Republican Joe Jackson, Democrats Wayne W. Wagonseller, William D. McFarlane, Mr. Crouch, Edith E. Wilmans, and James A. Stephens to fill the seat of Ed Gossett, who had resigned. Took office on September 8, 1951. Reelected in 1952, 1954, 1956, 1958, and 1960 by running unopposed each time. Served on the House Merchant Marine and Fisheries and Ways and Means committees.

Frank Ikard

Resigned on December 15, 1961, and was succeeded by Graham Purcell in 1963. Chaired the state Democratic convention in 1960 and was a delegate to the Democratic national conventions in 1956, 1960, and 1968. His wife, Jean, died in 1970, and Ikard married Jayne Brumley two years later. Brumley has a son, Bryan, from her previous marriage. During this time, served as executive vice-president of the American Petroleum Institute in New York and later served as its president until 1978. Retired the following year. Practiced law and lobbied in Washington. Served as chair of the Industrial Communications Company. Died on May 1, 1991, in Washington, D.C. (See also photo page 24.)

EDDIE BERNICE JOHNSON

Eddie Bernice Johnson

Born December 3, 1935, in Waco. Received nursing diploma from St. Mary's at Notre Dame in 1955 and B.S. in nursing from Texas Christian University in 1967, and M.P.A. from Southern Methodist University in 1976. Married Lacy Kirk Johnson in 1957; they had one son, Dawrence Kirk. Divorced in 1971. Baptist and Democrat. Proprietor of Eddie Bernice Johnson and Associates Consulting and Airport Concession Management. Served most of three terms as state representative, District 33-0, from 1973 until 1977. Resigned from the Texas House on September 30, 1977, to accept an appointment from President Carter as regional director of the Department of Health, Education, and Welfare and served from 1977 until 1981. Served three terms as state senator, District 23, from 1987 until 1992. Elected as the first U.S. representative for the newly created 30th District in 1992 by defeating Republican Lucy Cain. Took office in January 1993. Reelected in 1994 by defeating Cain again along with Libertarian Kenneth Ashby. The U.S. District Court redrew the boundary for Johnson's district that required her to run in an open primary or special election in November 1996. This election coincided with the general election and Johnson was reelected by defeating Republicans John Hendry and Lisa Kitterman, Democrat Marvin E. Crenshaw, and Independents Lisa Hembry, Ada Granado, and Stevan A. Hammond. Reelected in 1998 by defeating Republican Carrie Kelleher and Libertarian Barbara Robinson and in 2000 by defeating Libertarian Kelly Rush, in 2002 by defeating Republican Ron Bush and Libertarian Lance Flores, and in 2004 by defeating Libertarian James Davis, and in 2006 by defeating Republican Wilson Aurbach and Libertarian Ken Ashby. Serves on the House Transportation and Infrastructure and Science committees.

To sacrifice education today is to sacrifice one's whole being. It would relegate us to a great sea of ignorance.

—Eddie Bernice Johnson

LUTHER ALEXANDER JOHNSON

Luther Johnson

Born October 29, 1875, in Corsicana. Attended public schools. Received law degree from Cumberland University in 1896 and was admitted to the Texas state bar the same year. Practiced in Corsicana. Democrat and Presbyterian. Married Turner Read in 1899 and they had three children: Mary Frances (McGee), Luther, Jr., and Turner Read. Served as Navarro County attorney from 1898 until 1902 and district attorney, 13th Judicial District, from 1904 until 1910. He returned to his private practice with Callicutt and Johnson and remained there from 1910 until 1923. Delegate to the Democratic national convention in 1916 and chair of the state Democratic convention in 1920. Elected U.S. representative, 6th District, in 1922 by defeating Republican D. H. Merrill. Succeeded Rufus Hardy in March 4, 1923. Reelected in 1924 by defeating Republican Tyler Haswell, in 1926 by defeating John A. Newsom, in 1928 by defeating H. Lee Monroe, in 1930, 1932, and 1934 by running unopposed, in 1936 by defeating C. David Thompson, in 1938, 1940, and 1942 by running unopposed, and in 1944 by defeating Republican Charles Beck. Served on the House Foreign Relations Committee. Resigned on July 17, 1946, to accept a federal judgeship and was succeeded by Olin Teague later that year. Appointed Federal Tax-Court judge by President Truman and served from 1946 until his retirement in 1956. Died on June 6, 1965, in Corsicana and was buried there at Oakwood Cemetery. (See also photo page 29.)

LYNDON BAINES JOHNSON

Born on August 27, 1908, near Stonewall. Moved to Johnson City in 1913. Attended public schools and graduated from Johnson City High School in 1924. Worked at a variety of jobs until entering Southwest Texas State Teachers College in 1927. Taught school and acted as a school principal in Cotulla in 1928 and 1929. Returned to college and received a B.A. in 1930. Taught school in Houston in 1930 and 1931. Served as secretary to Congressman Richard M. Kleberg from 1931 until 1935. While in Washington, during 1934 he attended Georgetown University law school. Married Claudia Alta "Lady Bird" Taylor in 1934 and they had two daughters: Luci and Lynda. Served as state director of the National Youth Administration (NYA) from 1935 until 1937. Elected U.S. representative, 10th District, in an April 1937 special election to fill seat left by death of James Buchanan. Defeated Morton Harris, Polk Shelton, Sam V. Stone, C. N. Avery, Houghton Brownell, and Ayers K. Ross. Reelected in 1938, 1940, and 1942 running unopposed, in 1944

Lyndon Johnson

defeated Republican Arthur Bartelt, in 1946 ran unopposed, and did not seek reelection in 1948. Served as chairman of Democratic Congressional Campaign Committee in 1940. Ran for U.S. senator in a 1941 special election to fill the seat created by the death of Andrew Houston, but lost the close election to W. Lee O'Daniel. Served on the House Armed Services Committee. Served in the U.S. Navy briefly during late 1941 and 1942 prior to President Roosevelt ordering all congressmen back to their offices. Delegate to the Democratic national conventions of 1940, 1956, and 1960. Elected U.S. senator in 1948 by defeating former governor Coke Stevenson in the Democratic primary runoff by 87 votes, and Republican Jack Porter in the general election. Succeeded by Homer Thornberry in Congress on January 3, 1949, and succeeded W. Lee O'Daniel in the Houston succession of U.S. senators from Texas. Served from January 3, 1949, until January 3, 1961. Elected majority whip in 1951 and served until 1953, became minority leader in 1953 and served until 1955, and was majority leader in 1955 and served until 1961. Reelected in 1954 by defeating Republican Carlos G. Watson and Constitution Party candidate Fred T. Spangler and in 1960 by defeating Republican John Tower and Constitution Party candidate Bard Logan. Sought Democratic nomination for president in 1960, but John Kennedy received the nomination. He joined Kennedy and ran as his vice-president. They defeated Republicans Nixon and Lodge. He resigned from the Senate upon swearing in as vice-president in 1961. Succeeded in the Senate briefly by William A. Blakley, who was appointed by the governor and was eventually replaced by Republican John Tower. Sworn in as U.S. president in Dallas upon death of John Kennedy on November 22, 1963. Served as U.S. president from 1963 until 1969. Defeated Republican Senator Barry Goldwater for U.S. presidency in 1964 by a large margin. Designer of the Great Society and signer of the Civil Rights Act of 1964 and the Voting Rights Act of 1965. Did not seek reelection in 1968 and upon his retirement from the presidency in 1969 he wrote his memoirs, *The Vantage Point: Perspective of the Presidency, 1963–1969* (1971). Died on January 22, 1973, and was buried on the LBJ Ranch in Stonewall. The Lyndon B. Johnson Space Center, in Houston, was named in his honor. (See also photo page 24.)

The greatest strength of free people… is their unique ability and their traditional willingness to change, to adapt themselves to varying circumstances, to find new answers to old problems.

—Lyndon B. Johnson

SAMUEL ROBERT "SAM" JOHNSON

Born October 11, 1930, in San Antonio. Grew up in Dallas and graduated from Woodrow Wilson High School in 1947. Received a B.S. from Southern Methodist University in 1951 and an M.A. from George Washington University in 1974. Married Shirley L. Melton in 1950 and they had three children: Bob, Gini, and Beverly. Served in U.S. Air Force for twenty-nine years during both Korean and Vietnam wars. Held as Prisoner of War in Vietnam for six years, ten months, beginning in 1966. Director of U.S. Air Force Fighter Weapons School. Flew with U.S. Air Force Thunderbirds Precision Flying Demonstration Team. Graduate of Armed Services Staff College and National War College. Received two Silver Stars, two Legions of Merit, the Distinguished Flying Cross, the Bronze Star with Valor, two Purple Hearts, four Air Medals, and three Outstanding Unit awards. Retired at rank of colonel in 1979. Began home-building company in 1979. Serves on Smithsonian board of regents and U.S./Russian Joint Commission on POW/MIAs.

Sam Johnson

Republican. Served three terms as state representative, District 60, from 1985 until he resigned on May 21, 1991, to accept his congressional seat. Chaired predecessor Steve Bartlett's campaigns in 1988 and 1990. Elected U.S. representative, 3rd District, on May 18, 1991, in a special election to fill the seat held by Steve Bartlett. Tom Pauken actually received the most votes in the special election, but failed to receive a majority, so the top two candidates were forced into a runoff. Johnson won the runoff. Reelected in 1992 by defeating Libertarian Noel Kopala and in 1994 by defeating Libertarian Tom Donahue in the general election. The U.S. District Court redrew part of the boundary for Johnson's district requiring him to run in an open primary or special election in November 1996. This election coincided with the general election, and Johnson was reelected by defeating Democrat Lee Cole and Libertarian John Davis. Reelected in 1998 by defeating Libertarian Ken Ashby and in 2000 by defeating Democrat Billy Wayne Zachary and Libertarian Lance Flores, in 2002 by defeating Democrat Manny Molera and Libertarian John Davis, and in 2004 by defeating Independent Paul Jenkins and Libertarian James Vessels, in 2006 by defeating Democrat Dan Dodd and Libertarian Christopher J. Claytor. Wrote *Captive Warriors* (1992) about his almost seven years as a prisoner of war in Vietnam. Serves on the House Ways & Means and Social Security Committees, but has also served on Education and the Workforce.

RIENZI MELVILLE JOHNSTON

Born on September 9, 1849, in Sandersville, Georgia. Cousin of Benjamin Edward Russell (1845–

Rienzi Johnston

1909), who was a congressman from Georgia. Attended public schools. Served in the Confederate States Army. Wedded Mary E. Parsons in 1875 and they had three children. Worked as a newspaper editor for the *Savannah Morning News* and moved to Crockett, Texas in 1878 to edit to the *Crockett Patron*. In 1879 he became the editor of the *Corsicana Observer*. Shortly thereafter, he began his own newspaper, the *Independent*. Moved to Austin in 1880 and worked for the *American Statesman*, then moved to Houston in 1883 to work for the *Houston Post*. Elected journal clerk for the Texas House of Representatives and served at this post during the 19th Legislature in early 1885. He moved to Houston and became editor-in-chief of the *Post*. Served in a number of positions related to the newspaper and printing industry. Nominated for lieutenant governor in 1898, but declined the nomination. Served on the Democratic National Committee from 1900 until 1912. Appointed U.S. senator in 1913 by Governor Colquitt to fill the unexpired term of Joseph W. Bailey, who had resigned. He served briefly from January 4 until February 2. The legislature did not approve of Johnston, as he was a "wet" during the early stages of the groundswell for the prohibition movement. Morris Sheppard had already won the November 1912 general election a few months earlier for the seat, his term to begin in March 1913. Sheppard and the legislature began a movement to encourage Johnston to resign. Johnston did resign his senate seat on February 2, 1913, after only twenty-eight days in office. Returned to Houston and resumed duties as editor and president of the *Houston Post*. He retired from this post in 1919. Served two terms as state senator, District 16, from 1917 until 1920. He resigned from the State Senate upon his appointment by Governor Hobby as chairman of the State Prison Commission. Died on February 28, 1926, in Houston and was buried there at Glenwood Cemetery.

GEORGE WASHINGTON JONES

George Washington Jones

Born on September 5, 1828, in Marion County, Alabama, but grew up in Tipton County, Tennessee. Moved to near Bastrop, Texas in 1848. Attended local schools. Farmed and taught school. Democrat and later a Greenbacker. Studied law and was admitted to the state bar in 1851. Ran unsuccessfully for state representative in 1853. Elected Bastrop County attorney and served from 1858 until about 1860. Ran unsuccessfully for State Senate. Reported to have shot and killed another attorney named Rose in Bastrop. He opposed secession, but served in the Confederate States Army. Following the war, practiced law with Joseph Sayers in Bastrop. Served as delegate to State Constitutional Convention in 1866. As a result, was elected lieutenant governor, defeating Livingston Lindsay, and served from August 1866 until July 1867. Jones and Governor Throckmorton were removed by General Sheridan, who believed that they were hindering the reconstruction efforts. This was only part of the story, as the so-called Radical Republicans had taken power in March and were looking to remove any former Confederate from office. In July 1867, a law was passed whereby military officials could remove civilian officeholders who were slowing reconstruction efforts. The office was vacant for seven years following Jones' ouster. He left the Democratic Party in 1870s. Ran for U.S. representative, 5th District, as an Independent and Republican in 1876 but was defeated by Democrat DeWitt C. Giddings. Elected U.S. representative, 5th District, in 1878 as a Greenback Democrat by defeating Democrat John Hancock, and succeeded Giddings on March 4, 1879. Reelected as a Greenback in 1880 by defeating Democrat Seth Sheppard. Did not seek reelection in 1882 and instead sought higher office. Succeeded by James W. Throckmorton in Congress on March 3, 1883. Unsuccessful Republican-Greenback-Fusion gubernatorial candidate in 1882 and 1884, but lost both races to John Ireland. Jones ran again for U.S. representative, 9th District, in 1898 as a Populist, but was defeated by Democrat Albert Sidney Burleson. Died on July 11, 1903, in Bastrop and was buried there at Fairview Cemetery. It is unclear if he was ever married or had a family.

JAMES HENRY JONES

Born on September 13, 1830, in Shelby County, Alabama. Educated at public schools. Studied law, was admitted to the bar in 1851, and settled in Henderson, Texas. Democrat. Served as colonel in Confederate States Army and commanded a brigade of Walker's Texas Division. Served as a delegate to the Democratic national convention in Cincinnati in 1880. Elected U.S. representative, 3rd District, in 1882 by defeating Republican S. H. Russell and Independent H. W. Wade. Succeeded Olin Wellborn on March 4, 1883. Served on the House Post Offices and Post Roads and Mines and Mining committees. Reelected in 1884 by defeating Republican G. F. Conley and John O'Brien. He was not a candidate for reelection in 1886 and was succeeded by Constantine Kilgore on March 3, 1887. Returned to Henderson and his law practice. Died on March 22, 1904, in Henderson and was buried there at New Cemetery. It is unclear if he was ever married or had a family.

James Henry Jones

JOHN MARVIN JONES

Born on February 26, 1886, near Valley View in Cooke County. Attended local schools in Elm Grove and Valley View. Attended Clarenden College for one year. Taught school for one year in Elm Grove. Received a B.A. from Southwestern University in 1905 and an L.L.B. from the University of Texas in 1908. Methodist and Democrat. Admitted to the state bar in 1908 and began his practice in Amarillo. Served on the Board of Legal Examiners from 1913 until 1916. Elected U.S. representative, 13th District, in 1916 by unseating John Hall Stephens in the Democratic primary and defeating Republican J. L. Vannatto and Socialist J. A. Pressly in the general election. Succeeded Stephens on March 4, 1917. Because of redistricting, Jones did not run for reelection for the 13th District and was succeeded by Lucian Parrish. Instead, he was elected U.S. representative from the newly created 18th District in 1918 by defeating Hugh E. Exum. He served very briefly in the U.S. Army during 1918 following a trip to Europe to see the war. Reelected in 1920 by defeating Republican L. P. Loomis, in 1922 by defeating Republican H. O. Ward, in 1924 by defeating Republican A. B. Spencer, in 1926 by defeating Republican S. E. Fish, in 1928 by defeating Republican V. C. Nelson, in 1930 and 1932 by defeating Fish again, in 1934 by defeating Republican James M. Kernan and R. D. Tomlinson, in 1936 by defeating Republican Fish again along with Union Party candidate Theodore Conrad, and by running unopposed in 1938. His sister Metze was married to fellow Texan and Congressman Sam Rayburn briefly in 1927. The failure of this marriage did not affect the brotherly relationship between Marvin Jones and Rayburn. Jones was very active in aiding legislation during President Roosevelt's first 100 days. Served on the House Insular Affairs, Reform in Civil Service, Industrial Arts, Expositions and Roads, and Agriculture committees. Did not seek reelection in 1940 and instead sought a federal judgeship. Resigned from Congress on November 20, 1940, and was succeeded by Eugene Worley in January 1941. Supported agriculture like few before him. Helped found the Farm Credit Administration and the Federal Farm Mortgage Corporation. While chair of the House Agriculture Committee, he supported a tremendous amount of legislation that aided farmers, including the Agricultural Adjustment Act of 1933, the Farm Credit Administration Act, the Jones-Connally Cattle Act, the Soil Conservation and Domestic Allotment Act, the Bankhead-Jones Farm Tenancy Act, the Jones-Costigan Sugar Act, and the Agricultural

Marvin Jones

Adjustment Act of 1938. Appointed and served as judge of U.S. Court of Claims from 1940 until 1943 and again from 1945 until 1964. During the intervening two years, he led and reformed the War Food Administration following an appointment by President Roosevelt. He was made chief judge in 1947 and was made Senior Judge in 1964 upon his retirement, and was called to work as needed. Wrote *How War Food Saved American Lives* (no date), *Marvin Jones Memoirs* (1973), *Report of the Special Master: State of Louisiana v. State of Mississippi* (1965), *Should Uncle Sam Pay: When and Why?* (1963), *The Tariff Bill* (1921), and *Vocational Retraining of Disabled Soldiers* (1918). Appointed by President Johnson to the Commission on Food Marketing. Retired to Amarillo. Died on March 4, 1976, and was buried at Llano Cemetery in Amarillo. Jones was never married. (See also photo page 29.)

> *The tiller of the soil is the most important citizen in this country and has always been. He is the foundation and groundwork of this country's surpassing prosperity. On his primary efforts rests the magnificent commercial superstructure that has been reared in our land. If he fails, all is lost.*
>
> —Marvin Jones

Barbara Jordan

BARBARA CHARLINE JORDAN

Born on February 21, 1936, in Houston. Graduated from Phillis Wheatley High School in 1952. Received B.A. from Texas Southern University in 1956 and an L.L.B. from Boston University in 1959. Admitted to the state bars of Massachusetts and Texas in 1959. Democrat. Taught at the Tuskegee Institute for one year. Practiced law in Houston. Ran for state representative, District 22-10, in 1962 and 1964, but was defeated by Willis J. Whatley. Employed as an assistant to Harris County Judge Bill Elliott from 1965 until 1966. Served most of three terms as state senator, District 11, from 1967 until 1973. She was also the first black to serve in the state senate since 1883 and was the first black woman. Served as president pro tempore of the Senate during the 62nd Legislature, 1971–73, and served as governor for a day on June 10, 1972. This made her the first black female to serve as a governor of any state in the U.S. Like John Nance Garner, Jordan served on the state redistricting panel following the 1970 reallocation of congressional districts. Lieutenant Governor Ben Barnes told her to set the lines of her district within central Houston. Charles N. Wilson, who was also in the state senate with Jordan, also created a district for himself. Jordan was very close to Lyndon Johnson. He guided and advised her and sought nothing in return. Elected U.S. representative, 18th District, in 1972 by defeating Republican Paul Merritt and Socialist Workers candidate Emmanuel "Tank" Barrera. Succeeded Bob Price, who was running for the 13th District seat in January 1973. She was the second black woman elected to Congress and the first black woman ever elected to Congress from the South. She and Andrew Young of Georgia were the first blacks to serve in Congress from the "modern" South. Served on the House Government Operations and Judiciary Committees. While serving on the Judiciary committee during Watergate hearings in 1974, she became known for the statement, "My faith in the Constitution is whole, it is complete, it is total. I am not going to sit here and be an idle spectator to the diminution, the subversion, the destruction of the Constitution." Reelected in 1974 by defeating Republican Robbins Mitchell and Socialist Workers candidate Kris Vasquez, and in 1976 by defeating Republican Sam H. Wright and Socialist Workers candidate Sylvia Zapata. Gave the first keynote address by a woman at the Democratic national convention in 1976. Did not seek reelection in 1978 and was succeeded by Mickey Leland in January 1979. Wrote autobiography *Barbara Jordan: A Self Portrait* (1979). Professor at University of Texas, Lyndon B. Johnson School of Public Affairs, from 1979 until her death. Inducted into the National Women's Hall of Fame in 1990. Gave her second keynote address at the 1992 Democratic national convention. Received the first Nelson Mandela Award for Health and Human Rights in 1993. Founder and board member of the People for the American Way. Appointed by President Clinton as chair of the U.S. Commission on Immigration

Reform in 1994 and received the Presidential Medal of Freedom the same year. Served on the boards of Mead, Texas Commerce Bank, Public Broadcasting Service, Burlington Northern Sante Fe, Federal Home Mortgage Loan Corporation, and Northrup-Grumman. Inducted in the African American Hall of Fame (1993), the National Woman's Hall of Fame (1990), and Texas Woman's Hall of Fame (1994). Died of leukemia and multiple sclerosis on January 17, 1996, and was buried at the Texas State Cemetery in Austin. She was the first black person buried there. Jordan never married. The Houston federal building and post office were named in her honor. The passenger terminal at Austin-Bergstrom International Airport was also named in her honor.

> *The human condition must be improved and government must help to improve it ... Government is here not to just build roads and bridges ... Government is our appointed mediator, prosecutor, defender—our means of guaranteeing our freedom and protecting our frailties.*

> —Barbara Jordan

David Spangler Kaufman

Born on December 18, 1813, in Boiling Springs, Pennsylvania. Graduated from Princeton in 1833. Studied law in Natchez, Mississippi, under John A. Quitman and was admitted to the Mississippi state bar. Practiced in Natchitoches, Louisiana. Moved to Nacogdoches, Texas in 1837. Democrat and Mason. Served as aide to General Thomas J. Rusk in the Cherokee War during 1839. Served as representative from Nacogdoches to Texas Republic House of Representatives from 1838 until 1841. Served as Speaker of the House in the last two sessions. Married Jane Baxter Richardson in 1841 and they had one daughter and three sons: Anna, Daniel, David Spangler, Jr., and Sam Houston. Served as senator in Texas Republic Senate from 1843 until 1845. Appointed Chargé d'Affaires to the United States in February 1845 by President Jones. In this role, he worked on the details of statehood and was effectively an ambassador from Texas to the United States. Elected as the first U.S. representative from Texas, 1st District, in a March 1846 special

David Kaufman

election by defeating William R. Scurry and William B. Ochiltree. Reelected a few months later in the November 1846 general election by running unopposed and in 1849 by defeating candidate Fitzpatrick. Served until his death on January 31, 1851, of a heart attack in Washington, D.C., and was buried at the Congressional Cemetery in Washington, but was reburied at the Texas State Cemetery in Austin in 1932. He was the first and only Jewish Texan to serve in Congress until the 1970s. Kaufman County was named in his honor in 1848, along with the town of Kaufman.

> *It is generally admitted that there is no government on earth where rational liberty and the rights of man, combined with the protection that all men hold dear, are enjoyed to so great an extent as in the United States. Can it be possible that we would madly refuse to enjoy the privileges afforded by the most free and greatest nation of the earth?*

> —David Kaufman, as chairman of the Senate Committee on Foreign Relations preceding Texas statehood

Abraham "Chick" Kazen Jr.

Born January 17, 1919, in Laredo of Lebanese immigrants. Graduated from Laredo High School in 1937. Attended the University of Texas from 1937 until 1940 and Cumberland University in 1941. Attended the law school at the University of Texas. Admitted to the state bar in 1942. Married Consuelo "Connie" Raymond in 1943 and they had five children: Abraham III, Norma Ann, Christine, Catherline,

Chick Kazen

and Jo Betsy. Practiced law in Laredo. Served in the U.S. Army Air Forces during World War II. Catholic and Democrat. Served three terms as state representative, District 75, from 1947 until 1953. Served seven terms as state senator, District 21, from 1953 until 1967. He and Henry B. Gonzalez waged a thirty-two-hour filibuster in the state senate against segregation legislation. Elected president pro tempore of the Senate and served as governor for a day on August 4, 1959. Delegate to the Democratic national convention in 1960 and 1964. Elected as the first U.S. representative from the newly created 23rd District in 1966 by defeating Constitution Party candidate Richard K. Troxell. Took office in January 1967. Served on the House Interior and Armed Services committees. Ran unopposed for reelection in 1968, 1970, 1972, 1974, and 1976. Reelected in 1978 by defeating La Raza Unida candidate Augustin Mata, in 1980 by defeating Republican Bobby Locke, and in 1982 by defeating Republican Jeff Wentworth and Libertarian Parker Abell. Unseated by Albert G. Bustamante in the 1984 Democratic primary and succeeded by him in January 1985. Died on November 29, 1987, of a heart attack in Austin and was buried at Catholic Cemetery in Laredo. A middle school in Laredo was named in his honor.

I'd be the happiest man on earth if I could just find jobs for my people.

—Chick Kazen

PAUL JOSEPH KILDAY

Paul Kilday

Born on March 29, 1900, in Sabinal. Moved to San Antonio in 1904. Attended public and private schools. Graduated from Old Main Avenue High School in San Antonio. Attended St. Mary's College. Employed as a clerk with the U.S. Army Air Service Headquarters and the U.S. Shipping Board in Washington, D.C., while attending law school. His appointments to these civil service jobs were acquired by predecessor Harry Wurzbach. Graduated from Georgetown University in 1922. Admitted to the state bar in 1922 and began practicing law in San Antonio. Married Cecile Newton in 1932 and they had two daughters: Mary Catherine and Betty Ann. Catholic and Democrat. Served as Bexar County assistant district attorney from 1935 until 1938. Elected U.S. representative, 20th District, in 1938 by unseating incumbent Maury Maverick in the Democratic primary and ran unopposed in the general election. Succeeded Maverick on January 3, 1939. Reelected in 1940 by defeating Republican Harry Hotchkin and Communist Emma Tenoyuca, in 1942 by defeating Republican William Turner, by running unopposed in 1944 and 1946, in 1948 by defeating Republican J. P. Ledvina, by running unopposed in 1950, 1952, 1954, 1956, 1958, and 1960. Served on the House Military Affairs and Armed Services committees. Upon appointment as a federal judge in 1961, resigned from Congress on September 24, 1961. Succeeded by Henry B. Gonzalez in a November 4, 1961, special election. Served as a judge on the Military Court of Appeals from 1961 until his death. Died on October 12, 1968, at home in Chevy Chase, Maryland, and was buried at Arlington National Cemetery in Arlington, Virginia. (See also photo page 24.)

CONSTANTINE BUCKLEY "BUCK" KILGORE

Born on February 20, 1835, in Newnan, Georgia. Attended local schools. Moved to Rusk County with his parents in 1846. Attended the Fowler Institute. Worked as a law clerk for Timothy Pilsbury and was admitted to the state bar shortly thereafter. Married Frances Barnett in 1858 and they had several children. Served in the Confederate States Army and was wounded at Chickamauga and captured. He was imprisoned at Fort Delaware from 1864 until March 1865. Following the war, he returned to his law practice. Democrat, Presbyterian, and Mason. Served as state judge beginning in 1869. Delegate to the Constitutional Convention of 1875. Served part of one term as state senator, District 7, from 1885 until 1886. Resigned from the State Senate and was elected U.S. Representative, 3rd District, in 1886 by defeating Opposition Party candidate W. E. Farmer. Succeeded James Henry Jones on March 4, 1887. Reelected in 1888 by defeating now Labor-Republican candidate W. E. Farmer, in 1890 by defeating Republican L. B. Fish and Prohibition Party candidate John O. Byrne, and in 1892 by defeating People's Party candidate J. M. Perdue. He appears not to have run for reelection in 1894, although it is more likely he was not renominated by the state convention in Dallas. Succeeded by Charles Henderson Yoakum on March 3, 1895. Appointed federal judge in 1895 in the Indian Territory (now Oklahoma) by President Cleveland. Served until his death on September

Buck Kilgore

23, 1897, in Ardmore and was buried at White Rose Cemetery in Wills Point. The town of Kilgore was named in his honor. (See also photo page 14.)

JOE MADISON KILGORE

Born on December 10, 1918, near Brownwood. Attended local schools. Moved to Mission in 1929 and attended local schools there. Graduated from Mission High School in 1935. Attended Westmoreland College (now Trinity University) in 1935 and 1936. Attended the University of Texas briefly before serving in the U.S. Army Air Corps during World War II. Remained in the air force reserve and eventually retired as a major general. Married Jane Redman in 1945 and they had four children: Mark, Dean, William, and Shannon. Attended the University of Texas law school and was admitted to the state bar in 1946. Began practice in Edinburg. Methodist and Democrat. Served four terms as state representative, District 73 (and later 38-1), from 1947 until 1954. While there, he served on the Judiciary Committee. Elected U.S. representative, 15th District, in 1954 by running unopposed. Succeeded Lloyd M. Bentsen, Jr. on January 3, 1955. Served on the House Government Operations, Post Office and Civil Service,

Joe Kilgore

International and Foreign Commerce, and Public Works committees. Unopposed for reelection in 1956, 1958, 1960, and 1962. Did not seek reelection in 1964 and was succeeded by Eligio "Kika" de la Garza on January 3, 1965. Moved to Austin and joined the law firm of McGinnis, Lochridge & Kilgore in 1965. Delegate to the Democratic national convention in 1956, 1960, and 1968. Encouraged to run against incumbent Ralph Yarborough for U.S. Senator in 1964, but refused. Appointed by Governor Connally to the Texas Water Commission in 1964. Served as regent for the University of Texas system from 1967 until 1973. Co-owned Rio Airlines. Served as chairman of the board of Texas State Bank (later Republic Bank Austin) and was a director of First Republic Bank. Served on the board of directors of Texas Regional Bancshares, Texas State Bank in McAllen, Reno Air, and Photo Control. Trustee of the Scott & White Memorial Hospital and Scott, Sherwood and Brindley Foundation. Died on February 10, 1999, in Austin and was buried there at the State Cemetery. (See also photo page 24.)

RICHARD MIFFLIN KLEBERG, SR.

Born on November 18, 1887, near Kingsville. Nephew of Rudolph Kleberg (1847–1924) and cousin of Robert Eckhardt (1913–2001), both U.S. representatives from Texas. Attended public schools in Corpus Christi and graduated from Corpus Christi High School in 1906. Graduated from the University

Richard Kleberg

of Texas in 1911. Studied law and was admitted to the state bar shortly after leaving law school. Mason, Rotarian, and Democrat. Married Mamie Searcy in 1911 and they had four children: Mary Etta, Richard Mifflin, Jr., Katherine Searcy, and Alice Gertrudis King. Played a division management role at King Ranch from 1913 until 1924 and was a banker. Received a special commission from the Texas Rangers for his work toward intelligence along the U.S.-Mexican border in 1918. President of the board of Texas College of Arts and Industries, now Texas A&M University, Kingsville, from 1930 until 1931. Along with Mark Francis, the first dean of Texas A&M University's Veterinary College, invented the submersible dipping vat to eradicate the ticks that carried Texas cattle fever. Elected U.S. representative, 14th District, in the November 24, 1931, special election by defeating Carl W. Johnson, Charles W. Anderson, and Republican Tom B. Smiley to fill the seat of Harry M. Wurzbach, who had died in office. Known as the "Cowboy Congressman" because of his family's affiliation with King Ranch. Reelected in 1932 by defeating Republican Frank B. Vaughn, by running unopposed in 1934, in 1936 by defeating Republican Howell Ward, Adolph Seideman, and Ed Lyons, and in 1940 and 1942 by running unopposed. Initially a strong supporter of the New Deal, but grew to oppose it. Sat on the House Agriculture Committee during his entire tenure in Congress, sponsored Farm Credit Administration Establishment bill, authored the Duck Stamp Act, sponsored the Migratory Bird Conservation Act, and worked for laws to combat the boll weevil. Unseated by John E. Lyle in the 1944 Democratic primary election and was succeeded by him on January 3, 1945. Employed Lyndon Johnson as secretary until Johnson accepted the post as state director of the National Youth Administration in 1935. Following his time in Congress, he returned to serve as chairman of the board of directors of King Ranch. Served as director of the State National Bank in Corpus Christi, vice-president of the Gulf and West Texas Railroad, and worked with many agriculture-related associations. Served on the Texas Game and Fish Commission from 1951 until 1955. Died on May 8, 1955, in Hot Springs, Arkansas, and was interred at Chamberlain Burial Park in Kingsville.

If we can blast open a new channel for this dammed-up river and at the same time benefit all other classes, then we in Congress would be signally remiss in not blasting.

—Richard M. Kleberg

RUDOLPH KLEBERG

Born on June 26, 1847, in Cat Spring. Great uncle of Bob Eckhardt (1913–2001) and uncle of Richard Kleberg Sr. (1887–1955) both U.S. representatives from Texas. Moved to DeWitt County with his family in 1848. Privately schooled. Democrat. Served in Confederate State Army. Graduated from Concrete College in 1868. Taught school in Yorktown. Served as district clerk. Studied law in San Antonio and was admitted to the state bar in 1872. Married Mathilde Elise Eckhardt in 1872 and they had five children: Caesar, August Joseph, Alfred Leon ("Al"), Louise Indiana ("Lula"), and Mathilde Violet ("Tillie"). Practiced law in Cuero. Co-founded the *Cuero Star*, a weekly newspaper he edited for four years. Served as DeWitt County attorney from 1876 until 1880. Law partner of Congressman William Henry Crain. Served one term as state senator, District 26, from 1883 until he resigned in 1885. While a senator, he served on the Senate Finance Committee that approved the first general appropriation for the University of Texas and the purchase of the Alamo. Served as U.S. Attorney, Western District, from 1885 until 1889 following an appointment

Rudolph Kleberg

by President Cleveland. Elected U.S. representative, 11th District, in the April 7, 1896, special election by defeating Republican Calvin G. Brewster and Populist Luther Lawhon to fill the seat of his old law partner, the late William Crain. Elected to his first full term a few months later in November 1896 by defeating Republican H. Gras and Populist J. M. Smith. Reelected in 1898 and 1900 by defeating Republican B. L. Crouch. Did not seek reelection in 1902 and was succeeded by Robert L. Henry on March 3, 1903. Moved to Austin in 1905. Served as court reporter for the Court of Criminal Appeals from 1905 until his death in 1924. Wrote song entitled "Texas Shine on Forever." Died on December 28, 1924, in Austin and was buried there at Oakwood Cemetery.

ROBERT CHARLES KRUEGER

Bob Krueger

Born on September 19, 1935, in New Braunfels. Attended New Braunfels public schools and graduated from New Braunfels High School in 1953. Received a B.A. from Southern Methodist University in 1957, an M.A. from Duke University in 1958, an M.Litt. from Oxford University in 1961, and a D.Phil. from Oxford in 1964. Married Kathleen Tobin in 1983 and they had three children: Mariana Faye, Sarah Eileen, and Christian Freeman. Democrat. Professor of English Literature, vice provost, and dean of Arts and Sciences at Duke University. Elected U.S. representative, 21st District, in 1974 by defeating Republican Douglas S. Harlan and American Party candidate Ed Gallion. Succeeded O. C. Fisher on January 3, 1975. Reelected in 1976 by defeating Republican Bobby A. Locke, La Raza Unida candidate Ramon E. Carrillo, and, for a second time, American Party candidate Gallion. Did not seek reelection to the House in 1978 and was succeeded by Republican Tom Loeffler on January 3, 1979. Ran instead for U.S. senator in 1978 but was defeated by Republican John Tower in a very close general election. Appointed U.S. Ambassador-at-Large and coordinator of Mexican affairs in 1979 by President Carter and served from July 1979 until January 1981. In this role, Krueger was responsible for "any and all matters concerning U.S.-Mexico relations." President of Krueger and Associates in New Braunfels. Candidate for U.S. senator in 1984, but failed to make the Democratic Primary runoff. Professor at the University of Texas, LBJ School of Public Affairs, in Austin from 1985 until 1986. Public affairs professor at Rice University from 1986 to 1988. Appointed U.S. Senator by Governor Ann Richards to fill the seat vacated by Lloyd Bentsen, who had resigned to become U.S. secretary of the treasury. Ran for the office in the June 1993 special election, but was defeated by Republican Kay Bailey Hutchison. Served from January 21, 1993, until June 14, 1993. Appointed by President Clinton and served as U.S. Ambassador to Burundi from 1994 until 1996 and then as Ambassador to Botswana from 1996 until 2000. Wrote *Cry from the Heart of Africa* (2006).

The greatest theft in Washington has not been of documents or dollars, but of hope and trust.

—Bob Krueger

Nick Lampson

NICHOLAS VALENTINO LAMPSON

Born on February 14, 1945, in Beaumont. Graduated from South Park High School in 1964. Received B.S. in biology from Lamar University in 1968 and M.Ed. from Lamar University in 1971. Married Susan Floyd in 1976 and they had two children: Hillary and Stephanie. Teacher. Democrat. Served as Jefferson County Tax Assessor-Collector from 1977 until 1995. Elected U.S. representative, 9th District, in 1996 by unseating incumbent Republican Steve Stockman in a runoff election. Succeeded Stockman on January 3, 1997. Reelected in 1998 by defeating Republican Tom Cottar and Libertarian Ken Eckel Jr., and in 2000 by defeating Republican Paul Williams and Libertarian Chuck Knipp, and in 2002 by defeating Republican Paul Williams and Libertarian Dean L. Tucker. Served on the House Science and Resources Committees. Following significant redistricting, Lampson ran unsuccessfully for the 2nd District Seat in 2004. He was succeeded by Republican Ted Poe the following year. Elected U.S. Representative, 22nd District, in 2006 by defeating Libertarian Bob Smither, and write-ins Joe Reasbeck, Don Richardson, and Shelley Sekula Gibbs. Succeeded Shelly Sekula-Gibbs who had replaced Tom Delay briefly. Serves on the House Transportation and Infrastructure, Science and Technology, and Agriculture Committees.

FREDERICK GARLAND "FRITZ" LANHAM

Fritz Lanham

Born January 3, 1880, in Weatherford. Son of Samuel Willis Tucker Lanham (1846–1908), former congressman and governor. Attended public schools in Washington, D.C., and received B.A. from Weatherford College in 1897 and from the University of Texas in 1900. During this time he also attended Vanderbilt University (1897–1898). First student editor of UT's newspaper *The Texan* and served from 1900 to 1901. Methodist, Mason, Odd Fellow, and Democrat. Served as secretary to his father who was a U.S. representative at the time. Worked in a bank briefly in 1902 and then went to work for his father, who was by then governor. Worked for the Deaf and Dumb Institute and the *Dallas Morning News* while attending law school in Austin from 1903 to 1907. Married Beulah Rowe in 1908. He did not receive a law degree, but eventually qualified and was admitted to the state bar in 1909. Practiced in Weatherford.

Edited the *Alcalde* from 1913 until 1917. Wrote *Putting Troy in a Sack: A Candid and Chronological Account of the Events of the Trojan War in the Light of Modern Discovery* (1916). It was a humorous treatment in verse of the epics of Homer and Virgil relating to Troy. Ran but lost seat for Parker County Attorney in 1916. Moved east to Fort Worth to work in the Tarrant County Attorney's office. Lanham, also a magician, and his brother Frank toured and entertained troops during 1917. Elected U.S. representative, 12th District, in an April 1919 special election by running unopposed to fill the seat of James Wilson. Wilson had resigned to accept a federal judgeship. Elected to his first full term in the November 1920 general election by defeating Republicans Sam Davidson and S. T. Green. Reelected 1922 by defeating Republican Joe Kingsberry Jr., in 1924 ran unopposed, in 1926 and 1928 defeated Republican David Sutton, ran unopposed in 1930, in 1932 defeated Republican George Calvert, in 1934 defeated Republican Joe Ingraham, in 1936 defeated Republican Arnold Davis, and ran unopposed in 1938, 1940, 1942, and 1944. Did not seek reelection to Congress in 1946 and was succeeded by Wingate Lucas on January 3, 1947. Served on the House District of Columbia, Patents, Public Lands, and Public Buildings and Grounds committees. He chaired the latter from 1932 until 1947. He was noted for the National Housing for Defense Act of 1940 and the Lanham Community Facilities Act of 1941. His wife Beulah died in 1930 of Hodgkin's disease, and he remarried in 1931 to Hazel Walker Head. She had two sons—Jack D. and C. Walker—from a previous marriage. Following his time in Congress, Lanham was employed by the National Patent Council, the American Fair Trade Council, and the Trinity Improvement Association as a lobbyist in Washington. Moved to Austin in 1961. Died on July 31, 1965, in Austin of a heart attack and was buried at Greenwood Cemetery in Weatherford. The new federal office building in Fort Worth was named in his honor in 1966. (See also photo page 29.)

If Congressmen voted the way someone said every time we might as well not have a Congress.

—Fritz Lanham

SAMUEL WILLIS TUCKER LANHAM

Born on July 4, 1846, near Woodruff, South Carolina. Attended school at Glenn Springs. Democrat and Mason. Served in Confederate States Army. Married Sarah Beona Meng in 1866, and they moved to Red River County, Texas. They had eight children, including Grace and Fritz (1880–1965), who was also a congressman from Texas. Lanham taught school near Clarksville and at Old Boston. They moved in 1868 to Weatherford where he taught school and studied law. Admitted to the state bar in 1869. Served as district attorney from 1871 until 1876 following an appointment by Governor Davis. Prosecuted Chief Satanta and Big Treeq, both Kiowas, for infamous Warren Wagon Raid. Served as presidential elector in 1880. Elected as the first U.S. representative from the newly created 11th District in 1882 by defeating Greenbacker candidate J. W. Barnett and Independent Democrats J. H. Davenport and S. C. Buck. This was very likely the largest congressional district in U.S. history, as it consisted of ninety-eight counties. Took office in March 4, 1883. Reelected in 1884 by defeating Republican W. A. Saylor, in 1886 by defeating Independent J. W. Barnett, in 1888 by defeating Independent D. M. Rumph and Republican David Redfield, and in 1890 by defeating Republican C. W. Johnson. Did not seek reelection in 1892 and was succeeded by William H. Crain on March 3, 1893. Sought the Democratic nomination for governor in 1894, but was defeated by Culberson. Returned to Congress upon his election again as U.S. representative, 8th District, in 1896 by defeating Populist C. H. Jenkins and Republican J. P. Smith. Succeeded Charles K. Bell on March 4, 1897. Reelected in 1898 by defeating Populist W. J. Shands and Republican Arthur Springer and in 1900 by defeating Populist J. S. Daley and Republican N. A. Dodge. Served on the House Judiciary, Territories, Military Affairs, Claims, and Irrigation of Arid Lands committees. He eventually chaired Claims and Irrigation of Arid Lands committees. Did not run for reelection to Congress in 1902, resigned from Congress on January 15, 1903 and was succeeded by Thomas Ball a few weeks later. Instead, Lanham was the Democratic nominee for governor, and he defeated the Republican candidate

Samuel Lanham

George W. Burkett in the November 1902 general election. Reelected governor in 1904 by defeating Republican J. G. Lowden. Served as governor from January 20, 1903, until January 15, 1907, and was the last Confederate soldier to serve as Texas governor. The Terrell Election Law was enacted during his term as governor. This created the system for primary elections. Thus, he was also the last gubernatorial candidate to be chosen via a party convention. Appointed regent of the University of Texas in 1907 by Governor Campbell, but he did not serve, as his health was declining rapidly. He was preceded in death by his wife by less than a month. He died on July 29, 1908, in Weatherford and was buried there at Greenwood Cemetery. (See also photo page 14.)

I was very happy for years and years seeing the people in my district as their congressional representative. Then I became governor. Office-seekers, pardon-seekers, and concession-seekers overwhelmed me. They broke my health and when a man finds his health gone, his spirit is broken.

—S. W. T. Lanham

Greg Laughlin

GREGORY H. "GREG" LAUGHLIN

Born on January 21, 1942, in Bay City. Graduated West Columbia High School in 1960. Received a B.A. from Texas A&M University in 1964 and an L.L.B. from the University of Texas law school in 1967. Served in the U.S. Army from 1968 to 1970 and the U.S. Army Reserves in 1970. Was the only member of Congress to serve on active duty during Operation Desert Storm. Married Ginger Jones and they had two children: Mary and Brad. Attorney. Admitted to the state bar in 1967. Democrat until June 26, 1995, when he became a Republican. Served as Harris County assistant district attorney from 1970 until 1974. Practiced law with Griggs, Griggs and Laughlin from 1986 until 1989. Ran unsuccessfully for U.S. representative, 14th District, in 1986. Elected U.S. representative, 14th District, in 1988 by defeating incumbent Republican Mac Sweeney and Libertarian Don Kelly. Succeeded Sweeney on January 3, 1989. Reelected in 1990 by defeating Republican Joe Dial, in 1992 by defeating Republican Humberto J. Garza and Independent Vic Vreeland, and in 1994 by defeating Republican Jim Deats. Served on the House Ways and Means, Transportation and Infrastructure, and Merchant Marine and Fisheries committees. His last year to run as a Democrat was 1994. In 1996 he was unseated by Republican Ron Paul in the Republican primary runoff and was succeeded by him on January 3, 1995. Remained in Washington and was with the Patton Boggs law firm and is now with Pillsbury, Winthrop, Shaw, Pittman.

JAMES MARVIN LEATH

Marvin Leath

Born on May 6, 1931, in Henderson. Attended public schools in Rusk County. Graduated from Henderson High School in 1949 and attended Kilgore Junior College. Received a B.B.A. from the University of Texas in 1954. Married Alta Neill in 1954 and they had two sons: Thomas and Jim. Jim died in 1970 from leukemia. Served in the U.S. Army from 1954 until 1956. Teacher and coach at Henderson High School from 1957 to 1959. Salesman and banker in Marlin, Bremond, Clifton, and Rosse from 1962 to 1977, director of Marlin Mills from 1966 to 1977, and director of the Clifton Corporation from 1977 to 1978. Special assistant to Congressman W. R. Poage from 1972 until 1974. Founded Central National Bank in Waco in 1975. Elected U.S. Representative, 11th District, in 1978 by defeating Republican Jack Burgess. Succeeded W. R. Poage on January 1, 1979. Served on the House Armed Services and Budget committees. Reelected in 1980 by running unopposed, in 1982 by defeating Libertarian Thomas B. Kilbride, in 1984 and 1986 by running unopposed, and in 1988 by defeating Libertarian Frederick M. King. Did not seek reelection in 1990 and was succeeded by Chet Edwards on January 3, 1991. Following the end of his congressional career, became a lobbyist in Washington, D.C., with Leath and Associates. Divorced in 1992. Died on December 8, 2000, in Arlington, Virginia, and was buried at Memorial Gardens in Henderson.

I am convinced that I did make a difference the first eight years, but the last four have been the most frustrating of my life as I saw our government totally break down and begin to spin out of control. Partisan and personal politics reigned supreme perhaps more so than any time in history, creating an impasse.

—Marvin Leath

ROBERT QUINCY LEE

Born on January 12, 1869, near Coldwater, Mississippi. Family moved to Fort Worth, Texas in 1886. Attended public schools and Fort Worth High School. Moved to Caddo in 1891. Salesman and general store owner, and served briefly as postmaster. Moved to Cisco in 1913. Farmed and ranched. Became a banker and was president of the Cisco Banking Company from 1915 to 1930. Founded the Cisco and Northeastern Railroad Lines in 1919 and was the company's president until 1927. Baptist and Democrat. Married Ada Cook and they had three children. Ada later died and Lee married Clara E. Lee. They had two children. Served as president of West Texas Chamber of Commerce from 1926 to 1927 and was a member of the Cisco School Board. Elected U.S. representative, 17th District, in 1928, running unopposed. He succeeded Thomas Blanton on March 4, 1929. Died while serving in office on April 18, 1930, in Washington, D.C. and was buried at

Robert Q. Lee

Oakwood Cemetery in Cisco. His wife Clara lost a special election to the man Lee had succeeded, Thomas L. Blanton. Blanton succeeded Lee in Congress in 1931.

SHEILA JACKSON LEE

Born on January 12, 1950, in Queens, New York. Graduated from Jamaica High School. Received B.A. from Yale University in 1972 and J.D. from University of Virginia law school in 1975. Married Dr. Elwyn Cornelius Lee in 1973 and they had two children: Erica Shelwyn and Jason Cornelius Bennett. Admitted to the state bar in 1975. Practicing attorney. Democrat. Served as staff counsel, U.S. House Select Committee on Assassinations, from 1977 until 1978. Served as City of Houston Associate Municipal Court Judge from 1987 until 1990 and was on the Houston City Council from 1990 to 1994. Elected U.S. representative, 18th District, in 1994 by defeating Republican Jerry Burley, Libertarian George Hollenbeck, and Independent J. Larry Snellings. Succeeded Craig Washington on January 3, 1995. The U.S. District Court redrew the boundary for Jackson Lee's district, requiring her to run in an open primary or special election in November 1996. This election coincided with the general election. Jackson Lee was reelected by defeating Republican

Sheila Jackson-Lee

Jerry Burley, Democrat Mike Lamson, Republican Larry White, and Republican George A. Young. Reelected in 1998 by defeating Libertarian James Galvan and in 2000 by defeating Republican Bob Levy and Libertarian Colin E. Nankervis, in 2002 by defeating Republican Phillip J. Abbott and Libertarian Brent Sullivan, and in 2004 by defeating Libertarian Brent Sullivan and Independent Tom Bazán, and in 2006 by defeating Republican Ahmad Hassan and Libertarian Patrick Warren. Serves on the House Judiciary, Homeland Security, and Foreign Affairs Committees.

GEORGE THOMAS "MICKEY" LELAND, III

Born on November 27, 1944, in Lubbock. While he was an infant, his father abandoned the family and his mother moved them to Houston. Graduated from Phyllis Wheatley High School in Houston. Democrat and Roman Catholic. Received B.S. in pharmacy from Texas Southern University. Instructor at Texas Southern University from 1970 until 1971. Served as director of special development projects with Hermann Hospital from 1971 to 1978. Served as vice-president of King State Bank in 1977. Served three terms as state representative, District 88, from 1973 until 1979. Delegate to state constitutional convention in 1974. Delegate to the Democratic national convention from 1976 until 1985. Elected U.S. representative, 18th District, in 1978 by defeating Socialist Workers candidate Deborah Vernier. Succeeded Barbara Jordan on January 3, 1979. Reelected in 1980 by defeating Republican C. L. Kennedy and Libertarian William Fraser, in 1982 by defeating Republican C. Leon Pickett and Libertarian Thomas P. Bernhardt, in

Mickey Leland

1984 by defeating Republican Glen E. Beaman and Independent Jose Alvarado, in 1986 by defeating Independent Joanne Kuniansky, and in 1988 by defeating Libertarian J. Alejandro Snead. Chaired the Congressional Black Caucus and served on the House Energy and Commerce committees and the Select Committee on Hunger. Married Alison Clark Walton in 1983 and they had three sons: Jarrett David, and twins that were born after Leland's death: Austin Mickey and Cameron George. Served as freshman majority whip in the 96th Congress, at-large majority whip in the 97th and 100th congresses, first chairman of the Postal Personnel Subcommittee, chairman of the Subcommittee on Postal Operations and Service, chairman of the House Select Committee on Hunger (1984–89), chairman of DNC Black

Caucus from 1981 until 1985. Died on August 7, 1989, in a plane crash near Gambela, Ethiopia, while visiting refugee camps and was buried in Houston at Golden Gate Cemetery.

So long as people keep addressing me as a black member of Congress, I have to respond and see that black people are able to achieve in this society their equal place.

—Mickey Leland

ROBERT MACLIN LIVELY

Born on January 6, 1855, in Fayetteville, Arkansas. When he was nine, his family moved to Smith County, Texas. Attended private schools, read law in Kaufman beginning 1875, and was admitted to the state bar the following year. Practiced law in Wills Point and later Canton. Methodist and Democrat. Married Julia Cannon in 1878 and they had four children: A. G., J. C., Estelle, and Ethel. Served as Van Zandt County Prosecuting Attorney from 1882 until 1884. Served briefly as Van Zandt County Judge before being elected to Congress. Elected U.S. representative, 3rd District, in a July 1910 special election to fill the seat of James Russell who had resigned to accept a federal judgeship. Served from July 23, 1910 until March 3, 1911. He did not seek reelection and was succeeded by James Young in 1911. Served again as Van Zandt County Judge from 1916 until 1918. Died January 16, 1929, in Canton and was buried in Canton Cemetery.

Robert Lively

THOMAS GILBERT "TOM" LOEFFLER

Born on August 1, 1946, in Mason. Attended Mason County public schools and graduated from Mason High School in 1964. Received a B.B.A. from the University of Texas in 1968 and a J.D. in 1971. Admitted to the state bar of Texas in 1971 and the District of Columbia bar in 1981. Married Kathy Crawford in 1970 and they had three children: Lance, Cullen, and Lauren Kathryn. Republican. Served as counsel at the U.S. Department of Commerce from 1971 until 1972. Legislative aide to Senator John Tower from 1972 to 1974. Deputy for Congressional Affairs for the Federal Energy Administration from 1974 to 1975. Special assistant for legislative affairs for President Ford from 1975 until 1977. Private legal practice in Kerrville from 1977 until 1978. Elected U.S. representative, 21st District, in 1978 by defeating Democrat Nelson Wolff. Succeeded Bob Krueger on January 3, 1979. Reelected in 1980 by defeating Democrat Joe Sullivan and Libertarian William Rice, in 1982 by defeating Democrat Charles S. Stough and Libertarian Jeffrey J.

Tom Loeffler

Brown, and in 1984 by defeating Democrat Sullivan again. Served on the House Energy and Commerce, Appropriations, and Budget committees, and as Republican chief deputy whip from 1981 until 1987. Divorced in 1986. Did not seek reelection to Congress in 1986 and was succeeded by Lamar Smith on January 3, 1987. Unsuccessful candidate for governor in 1986 and was defeated by Bill Clements in the Republican primary. Practiced law in San Antonio, Austin, and Washington, D.C., with McCamish, Martin, Brown, & Loeffler. Principal Central American coordinator for the Office of Legislative Affairs at the White House in 1987. Married Nancy Brown in 1987. Appointed University of Texas regent by Governor Clements in 1989 and was reappointed by Governor Bush in 1995. Texas co-chairman of the Bush for President campaign in 1988. Texas co-chairman of the Gramm for Senate campaign in 1990. National Advisor to the Bush-Quayle campaign in 1992. Texas finance co-chairman of the George W. Bush for Governor campaign in 1994. National finance chairman for the Gramm for President campaign in 1996.

National deputy finance chairman of the Dole for President campaign in 1996. National co-chairman for the Republican National Committee's Team 100 in 1997 and 1998. National finance co-chairman for the George W. Bush for President campaign in 2000. Texas delegate to the Republican national conventions in 1984, 1988, and 1992. Co-chairman of Comptroller Rylander's E-Texas Citizens State Government Review Commission. A senior partner in Arter & Hadden, a national law firm, then an administrator at the University of Texas. Retired to Mason in 2001.

Texas today has too much government by photo opportunity, too much leadership by public opinion poll. Texans demand a governor of substance, not of imagery.

—Tom Loeffler

JOHN BENJAMIN LONG

John B. Long

Born on September 8, 1843, in Douglass. Family settled near Rusk in 1846. Privately educated. Presbyterian, Mason, Democrat, and prohibitionist. Served in the Confederate States Army. Studied law, was admitted to the state bar, but never practiced law. Married Emma Wiggins in 1869 and they had seven children. Delegate to National Cotton Planters Association convention in 1883. Acquired the *Standard Herald* in Rusk in 1886 and edited the paper himself as time allowed. Elected U.S. representative, 2nd District, in 1890, running unopposed. Succeeded William Harrison Martin on March 4, 1891. Served one term and was unseated by Samuel Bronson Cooper in 1892. Succeeded by Cooper on March 3, 1893. Involved in the Texas Grange movement. Headed the Agricultural and Mechanical College (now Texas A&M University) beginning in 1895. Operated the local newspaper in Rusk from 1886 until 1905. Served one term as state representative, District 26, from 1913 to 1915. Died on April 27, 1924, in Rusk and was buried there at Cedar Hill Cemetery.

WINGATE HEZEKIAH LUCAS

Wingate Lucas

Born on May 1, 1908, in Grapevine. Attended public schools and graduated from Grapevine High School. Attended North Texas State Teachers College, Oklahoma Agricultural and Mechanical College, and the University of Texas, but was too poor to continue his studies. Went to work for Representative Fritz Lanham in Washington, D.C. While there, he finished law school at American University in the mid-1930s. Admitted to the state bar in 1938. Methodist and Democrat. Married Jerry Clark in 1936 and they had two sons and three daughters: Mary Dell, Joy Christian, Ellen, Wingate, Jr. (also known as "Wink"), and William Clark. Moved to Fort Worth in 1939. Served as assistant district attorney in Tarrant County during 1941 and 1942. Served in the U.S. Army during World War II, from 1943 until he received a medical discharge in 1945. Served as Assistant U.S. Attorney in 1945. Elected U.S. representative, 12th District, in 1946 by defeating Republican Elton M. Hyder. Succeeded Fritz Lanham on January 3, 1947. Reelected in 1948 by defeating Hyder again, in 1950 by defeating Republican H. G. Neely, and in 1952 by running unopposed. Served on the House Education and Labor committees. He was the author of the Lucas Minimum Wage Law which was an amendment to the Fair Labor Standards Act. Unseated in the 1954 Democratic primary by Jim Wright and was succeeded by him on January 3, 1955. Following his departure from Congress, Lucas joined the law firm of Poole, Shroyer, and Denbo. Employed by General Electric in New York from 1958 until 1966. His wife, Jerry, was killed in an automobile accident in Connecticut in 1966.

He moved to Bristol, Tennessee, where he served as executive director of Mid-Appalachia College from 1966 to 1986. Died on May 26, 1989, in Bristol, Tennessee.

JOHN EMMETT LYLE JR.

John Lyle

Born on September 4, 1910, in Boyd. Attended public schools and graduated from Wichita Falls High School in the 1920s. Attended a junior college in Wichita Falls, the University of Texas, and the Houston School of Law. Admitted to the state bar in 1934 and practiced in Corpus Christi. Episcopal, Lawyer, and Democrat. Married Gertrude Swanner in 1937; they had no children. Served two terms as state representative, District 71, from 1941 until 1945. Technically, he resigned from the State House in 1942, and served in the U.S. Army during World War II. Elected U.S. representative, 14th District, in 1944 by unseating incumbent Richard Kleberg in the Democratic primary election and by running unopposed in the general election. Strongly supported by the Parr family of Duval County. Succeeded Kleberg on January 3, 1945. Reelected in 1946, in 1948 by defeating Republican James M. Swafford and Progressive Tom Neal, and in 1950 and 1952 by running unopposed. Served on the House Post Office and Civil Service Committee. Did not seek reelection in 1954 and was succeeded by John J. Bell on January 3, 1955. Returned to Corpus Christi to practice law. Married Nadine Lyle. They had no children. Lived in Houston and was director of several companies, including Falcon Seaboard. Died November 11, 2003, and was buried in the Texas State Cemetery in Austin.

GEORGE HERMAN MAHON

George Mahon

Born on September 22, 1900, in Mahon, Louisiana. Moved with parents to Loraine, Mitchell County, Texas, in 1908. Attended public schools and graduated from high school in Loraine in 1918. Attended Tyler Commercial College. Taught at the Brownlee School in Nolan County. Received B.A. from Simmons College (now Hardin-Simmons University) in Abilene in 1924 and L.L.B. from the University of Texas in 1925. Married Helen Stevenson in 1923 and they had one daughter: Daphne. Served as the school superintendent in Liberty Hill. Moved to Minnesota to attend the University of Minnesota in 1925. Returned to Colorado City, Texas. Methodist, Mason, and Democrat. Admitted to the state bar in 1925. Practiced in Colorado City with Charlie Thompson. Served as Mitchell County Attorney in 1926 and appointed district attorney, 32nd Judicial District, by Governor Moody and served from 1927 until 1933. Elected as the first U.S. representative from the newly created 19th District in 1934 by running in a field of eight candidates in the Democratic primary, by defeating Clark Mullican in the primary runoff, and by running unopposed in the general election. Took office on January 3, 1935. Reelected without opposition from 1936 to 1944, in 1946 defeated Republican Mohler D. Temple, in 1948 defeated Mike Phipps, in 1950 defeated Republican Mohler Temple, ran unopposed from 1952 to 1958, in 1960 defeated Republican Constitutional Party candidate John Anderson, in 1962 defeated Republican Dennis Taylor, in 1964 defeated Republican Joe Phillips, ran unopposed from 1966 to 1974, and in 1976 defeated Republican Jim Reese. Did not seek reelection in 1978. Mahon's forty-four years in Congress made him its most senior member. Served on the House Appropriations Committee beginning in 1939 and became its chairman in 1964. Succeeded by Kent Hance on January 3, 1979. Served as a delegate to the Democratic national convention from 1936 until 1964. Regent for the Smithsonian Institution from 1964 until 1978. Chairman of House Appropriations Committee (1964–79) and the Joint Committee on the Reduction of Federal Expenditures (90th through 95th congresses). Also served on the House Census,

Civil Service, Elections, and Insular Affairs committee, the Joint Study Committee on Budget Control, and the President's Commission on Budget Concepts. Died on November 19, 1985, in San Angelo and was buried at Loraine City Cemetery in Loraine. The federal building and U.S. Courthouse in Lubbock were renamed in his honor in 1993. (See also photo page 24.)

Except for time of war or deep emergency, why not restrict public spending to the reserves on hand or in sight? Pay for it or put it off until we are willing or able to do so.

—George Mahon

Joseph Mansfield

JOSEPH JEFFERSON MANSFIELD

Born on February 9, 1861, in Wayne, Virginia (now West Virginia). Attended public schools. Moved to Alleytown, Texas, in 1881. Farmed and worked on the railroad. Episcopalian, Mason, and Democrat. Worked a variety of jobs until he was admitted to the state bar in 1886 and practiced law in Eagle Lake. Served as city attorney and eventually as mayor, from 1889 until 1892. Married Annie Scott Bruce in 1888 and they had three children: Bruce Jefferson, Margaret Byrd (Dorsey), and Jaquelin Amanda (Schmidt). Mansfield also edited the local newspaper. Served as Colorado County Attorney from 1892 until 1896 and County Judge from 1896 until 1916. Served in the volunteer guard. Elected U.S. representative, 9th District, in 1916 by defeating Republican C. M. Hughes and Socialist B. F. Wright. Succeeded George F. Burgess on March 4, 1917. Reelected in 1918 by running unopposed, in 1920 by defeating Republican James R. Rugeley, in 1922 by defeating Republican Willett Wilson, in 1924 by defeating Republican Ed Franz, in 1926 by defeating Republican E. F. Glaze, in 1928 by defeating Republican Louis B. Allen, in 1930 by defeating Republican George Seydler Sr., in 1932 by defeating Republican Lewis Allen, in 1934 by running unopposed, in 1936 by defeating Republican F. W. Dusek and Lewis Allen, in 1938, 1940, and 1942 by running unopposed, in 1944 by defeating Republican Lewis Allen, and in 1946 by running unopposed. Served on the House Merchant Marine, Public Works, and River and Harbors committees. He eventually chaired the latter. Paralyzed and confined to a wheelchair following surgery in 1920. His wife, Annie, died about 1940. Mansfield died while serving in office on July 12, 1947, at the Naval Hospital in Bethesda, Maryland, and was buried at the Masonic Cemetery in Eagle Lake. Succeeded by Clark W. Thompson in 1949. Marshall Ford Dam on Lake Travis and the port at Red Fish Bay were renamed Mansfield Dam and Port Mansfield in his honor. (See also photo page 29.)

I must keep working constantly, I find it easier that way.

—Joe Mansfield on living with his debilitating pain

Ken Marchant

KENNY EWELL MARCHANT

Born February 23, 1951, in Bonham. Attended public schools and graduated from R. L. Turner High School in Carrollton. Received B.A. from Southern Nazarene University in 1974. Attended Nazarene Theological Seminary in Kansas City, Missouri, from 1975 to 1976. Real estate developer Church of Nazarene, and Republican. Married Donna Marchant and they have four children (three sons and one daughter): Matthew, Luke, Kenny, Jr., and Dallas. Served on Carrollton city council from 1980 until 1984 and Mayor from 1984 until 1987. Served as State Representative, District 99, from 1987 until 2004. Elected US Representative, District 24, in 2004 by defeating Democrat Gary R.

Page and Libertarian James H. Lawrence. Reelected in 2006 by defeating Democrat Gary R. Page and Libertarian Mark Frohman. Serves on the committees on Education and the Workforce, Government Reform, and Transportation and Infrastructure.

WILLIAM HARRISON "HOWDY" MARTIN

Howdy Martin

Born on September 2, 1823, in Uphala, Alabama. Studied law in Troy, Alabama, and was admitted to the Alabama state bar. Moved to Athens, Texas, in 1850. Married Martha E. Gallimore in 1867 and they had six children. Democrat. Served three terms as state representative, District 22, from 1853 until 1858. Served in the Confederate States Army. legend has it that in the war he earned his nickname during a battle. He caught sight of General Lee, stood up in his stirrups, and yelled, "Howdy!" More likely, he gained this nickname from his standard greeting. Served as Henderson County District Attorney from 1872 until the 1880s. Served as the president of the Hood's Texas Brigade Association from 1883 to 1885. Elected U.S. representative, 2nd District, on April 5, 1887, running unopposed in a special election to fill the seat of John H. Reagan. Reelected in 1888 by defeating Union Labor Party candidate R. M. Humphries. Succeeded John H. Reagan in 1889. Served one term and did not seek reelection in 1890. Succeeded by John B. Long on March 3, 1891. Removed to a farm near Hillsboro. Died on February 3, 1898, and was buried at Hillsboro Cemetery in Hillsboro. (See also photo page 14.)

JAMES ALBON MATTOX

Jim Mattox

Born on August 29, 1943, in Dallas. Graduated from Woodrow Wilson High School in Dallas in 1961. Received B.B.A. from Baylor University in 1965 and J.D. from Southern Methodist University in 1968. Baptist and Democrat. Aide to Congressman Earle Cabell in 1967. Served as Dallas County Assistant District Attorney from 1968 to 1970. Partner and lawyer with Crowder and Mattox in Dallas beginning in 1970. Served two terms as state representative, District 33-K, from 1973 until 1976. Elected U.S. representative, 5th District, in 1976 by defeating Republican Nancy Judy and American Party candidate Sam McDonnell. Succeeded Republican Alan Steelman on January 3, 1977. Served on the House Budget, Banking and Currency, and Housing committees. Reelected in 1978 by defeating Republican Tom Pauken and Socialist Workers candidate James Michael White and in 1980 by defeating Republican Tom Pauken and a handful of write-in candidates. Did not seek reelection to Congress in 1982 and was succeeded by Democrat John Bryant on January 3, 1983. Elected state attorney general in 1982 and served from 1983 to 1990. Sought Democratic Party nomination for Governor in 1990, but was defeated by Ann Richards. Partner and lawyer with Mattox Lawyers in Austin beginning in 1991. Candidate for U.S. senator in 1994. Defeated Richard Fisher in the primary, but lost to him in the runoff election. Candidate for attorney general in 1998, but was defeated by Republican John Cornyn. Married Marta Jane Karpan in 1990 and they had two children: James Sterling ("Jimmer") and Janet Mary Kathryn ("Sissy").

FONTAINE MAURY MAVERICK

Born on October 23, 1895, in San Antonio. Cousin of Abram Poindexter Maury (1801–48), a U.S. representative from Tennessee and John Wood Fishburne (1868–37), a U.S. representative from Virginia, and nephew of James Luther Slayden (1853–1924), a U.S. representative from Texas. Attended public schools and the Virginia Military Institute. Attended the University of Texas and their law school. Worked for the *Amarillo Daily News* in 1915. Admitted to the state bar in 1916 and practiced in San Antonio. Served in the U.S. Army during World War I. Democrat. Married Terrell Louise Dobbs in 1920 and they had two children: Maury Maverick, Jr., and Terrilita. Worked in the lumber, building materials, and mortgage business from 1925 until 1930. Served as Bexar County Tax Collector from 1930 until 1934. Delegate to the Democratic national conventions in 1928 and 1940. Elected as the first U.S. representative for the newly created 20th District in 1934 by defeating Republican H. M. Shelton. Served on the House Military Affairs Committee. Took office on January 3, 1935. Reelected in 1936 by defeating Republican Ernest W. Clements and Independent James O. Rail. Unseated in the 1938 Democratic Primary by Paul Kilday by less than 500 votes. Succeeded by Kilday on January 3, 1939. Coined the term for bureaucratic terminology "gobbledygook." Wrote *A Maverick American* (1937) and *In Blood and Ink: The Life and Documents of American Democracy*

Maury Maverick

(1939). Served as mayor of San Antonio from 1939 to 1941. Oversaw the reconstruction of La Villita. Served with the Office of Production Management, the War Production Board, was chief of the Bureau of Government Requirements, and chaired the Smaller War Plants Corporation from 1941 until 1946. He was a voracious collector of books, stamps, autographs, and any other items that caught his interest. Died on June 7, 1954, and was buried at San Jose Burial Park in San Antonio. Alistair Cooke said of him, "In the beginning and the end, he was nothing but a maverick." His wife later married Walter Prescott Webb, the noted Texas author.

> *Everything you do that is new or that inconveniences anybody will bring self-righteous criticism, pious warnings. Often when you act as a true statesman you will be ridiculed and thought a fool.*
>
> —Maury Maverick

SAMUEL BELL MAXEY

Born on March 30, 1825, in Tompkinsville, Kentucky. Moved to Albany, Kentucky, in 1834. Appointed to U.S. Military Academy at West Point and graduated 58th in a class of 59 in 1846. While there, roomed with Stonewall Jackson. Served in the Mexican War. Resigned his commission in 1849. Studied, then practiced, law and served as Clinton County (Kentucky) Clerk from 1852 until 1856. Married Marilda Cass Denton in 1853. They never had children, but adopted a girl—Dora Rowell—in 1863 and helped raise a nephew. Democrat. Moved to Paris, Texas, in 1857. Maxey and his father again practiced law together. Served as Lamar County District Attorney from 1858 until 1859. Served briefly as state senator, District 9, beginning in 1861, but resigned, and his term was filled by his father, Rice. Maxey formed a regiment of Texas infantry for the Civil War at Camp Benjamin. By the end of the war, he had attained the rank of major general. He was forbidden to practice law by the occupation forces working toward reconstruction, but with

Samuel Bell Maxey

help from a classmate from West Point—U.lysses Grant—he was pardoned in 1867. Following the war, he returned to his law practice in Paris. Ran for U.S. representative in 1872, but did not receive his party's nomination. Appointed as judge, 8th Judicial District, 1873, but declined the position. Elected U.S. senator by the legislature and served from March 4, 1875, until March 3, 1887. Succeeded James W. Flanagan in the Rusk succession of U.S. senators from Texas. Reelected in 1881. Defeated by John H. Reagan in the legislative balloting for the job in 1887 and was succeeded by him. Died on August 16, 1895, at Eureka

Springs, Arkansas, and was buried at Evergreen Cemetery in Paris. During World War II, an army camp built near Paris was named Camp Maxey in his honor.

In this country, thanks to free government, we have no hereditary nobility, but we have a nobility far above any that earthly title can give—the nobility God impresses on an honest man.

—Sam Maxey

EARLE BRADFORD MAYFIELD

Earle B. Mayfield

Born on April 12, 1881, in Overton. Attended public schools. Graduated from Overton High School in Timpson in 1895. Received diploma from Tyler Business College. Graduated from Southwestern University in 1900 and attended the University of Texas law school. Democrat. Worked in father's grocery business. Married Ora Lumpkin in 1902 and they had three sons: Earle, Jr., John S., and Horace M. Admitted to the state bar in 1907 and practiced in Meridian. Ran a Meridian flour mill until he began to practice law in Meridian. Served three terms as state senator, District 27, from 1907 until his resignation in 1913. Served on the Railroad Commission from 1913 until 1923. Elected U.S. senator in 1922 by defeating incumbent Charles A. Culberson in the Democratic primary, Jim Ferguson in an ugly runoff, and Independent George E. B. Peddy in the general election. He was called the "klan candidate" because he was supported by the blossoming Ku Klux Klan. He succeeded Charles A. Culberson in the Rusk succession of U.S. senators from Texas. Due to protests by Peddy and an investigation by the Senate, it was two years before Mayfield was allowed to take his seat. Served from March 4, 1923, to March 3, 1929. He served on the Senate Agriculture and Forestry, Interstate Commerce, Banking and Commerce, Public Buildings and Grounds, Claims, and Inter-oceanic Canals committees. Unseated by Congressman Tom Connally in the 1928 Democratic primary although he had the endorsement of Jim Ferguson. He was succeeded by Connally the following year. Delegate to the Democratic national conventions in 1924, 1928, and 1932. Candidate for governor in 1930, but placed behind most of the candidates in the Democratic primary, which was won by Miriam Ferguson. Continued to practice law, and owned the Mayfield Wholesale Grocery Company until he retired in 1952. Died on June 23, 1964, in Tyler and was buried there at Oakwood Cemetery.

MICHAEL T. McCAUL

Mike McCaul

Born on January 14, 1962, in Dallas. Received B.S. from Trinity University and J.D. from St. Mary's University in 1987. Catholic and Republican. Professional lawyer in private practice. Married Linda Mays and they had five children: Caroline, Jewell, and triplets Lauren, Michael, and Avery. Served as the Chief of Terrorism and National Security in the United States Department of Justice for the Western Judicial District of Texas. Served as State Deputy Attorney General during the 1990s. Elected U.S. Representative, District 10, in 2004 by defeating write-in candidate Lorenzo Sadun and Libertarian Robert Fritctie. Lloyd Doggett had served this district prior to redistricting. Reelected in 2006 by defeating Democrat Ted Ankrum and Libertarian Michael Badnarik. Serves on Committees for Homeland Security, Foreign Affairs, Science and Technology, and Standards of Official Conduct.

AUGUSTUS McCLOSKEY

Born on September 23, 1878, in San Antonio. Attended Atascosa School, St. Joseph's Academy, and

St. Mary's College. Studied law and worked as a stenographer from 1903 to 1907. Admitted to the state bar in 1907 and practiced in San Antonio. Democrat. Married Kathryn Salter in 1908 and they had four children: James A., Anthony, Mary Kathryn, and Thomas Q. Served as Bexar County Judge from 1920 to 1928. Presided over the Highway Club of Texas in 1927 and 1928. Delegate to the Democratic national convention in Houston in 1928. Elected U.S. representative, 14th District, in 1928 by unseating incumbent Republican Harry M. Wurzbach. However, the election was contested by Wurzbach, and Wurzbach eventually regained his seat. McCloskey served from March 4, 1929, to February 10, 1930. He returned to private law practice and served as judge of a Corporation Court from January 1943 until July 1947. Died on July 21, 1950, and was buried at San Fernando Cemetery in San Antonio.

Augustus McCloskey

WILLIAM DODDRIDGE MCFARLANE

Born on July 17, 1894, in Greenwood, Arkansas. Attended public schools. Merchant in Greenwood from 1914 to 1918. Served in the U.S. Army during World War I. Received a B.A. from the University of Arkansas in 1919, an L.L.B. from Kent law school in Chicago in 1921, and a J.D. from Kent in 1969. Admitted to the state bar in 1921 and practiced in Graham, Texas with his father at McFarlane and McFarlane. Married Alma Carl in 1923 and they had five children: Mary, Betty, Barbara, William, Jr., and Robert. Methodist, Legionnaire, Mason, and Democrat. Served two terms as state representative, District 109, from 1923 to 1927 and two terms as state senator, District 23, from 1927 to 1931. Elected U.S. representative, 13th District, in 1932 by running unopposed. Succeeded Guinn Williams on March 4, 1933. Served on the House Appropriations and Naval Affairs committees. Reelected in 1934 by running unopposed and in 1936 by defeating Republican R. L. Ratliff. Unseated in the 1938 Democratic primary and lost the run-off to Ed Gossett. His first wife, Alma Carl, died in 1938. Succeeded by Gossett on January 3, 1939. Served as special assistant to the U.S. Attorney General in Texarkana from 1941 until 1944. Director of the Surplus Property Smaller War Plants Corporation from 1944 to 1946. Married Inez Bishop, his second wife, in 1945. Served again as Special Assistant to the U.S. Attorney General in Washington, D.C., from 1946 until 1951. Sought the office of U.S. representative, 13th District, in the 1951 special election to fill the seat of Ed Gossett, but was defeated by Frank Ikard. Served with the U.S. Department of Justice from 1951 to 1966. Retired in Washington, D.C. Died on February 18, 1980, in Graham of cancer and was buried there at Oak Grove Cemetery.

William D. McFarlane

WILLIAM PINCKNEY MCLEAN

Born on August 9, 1836, in Copiah County, Mississippi. Moved to Marshall, Texas, with his mother in 1839 following the death of his father. Attended private schools. Graduated from University of North Carolina with a bachelor's degree in 1857 and with a law degree in 1858. Admitted to the state bar in 1858 and began practice in Jefferson. Married Margaret Batte in 1859 and they had eight children, four of whom survived: Margaret, W. P. Jr., John H., and Bessie. Episcopalian, Mason, and Democrat. Lived and practiced law in Marshall and Jefferson before moving to Victoria. Served the first of two terms as state representative, District 62, from 1861 to 1863, but resigned to

William Pinckney McLean

serve in Confederate States Army. Returned to Titus County following the war. Served his second term as state representative, District 9, from 1870 to 1873. Served as presidential elector in 1872 and was himself elected U.S. representative, 2nd District, in 1872 by defeating Republican F. W. Minor. Succeeded John Cogswell Conner on March 4, 1873. Served one term and did not seek reelection in 1874. Succeeded by David Browning Culberson on March 3, 1875, and returned to private law practice in Mount Pleasant in 1875. Served in 1875 State Constitutional Convention. Served one term as judge, 5th Judicial District, from 1884 until 1888. Appointed by Governor Hogg as one of the first Railroad Commission members and began serving in 1891. He was reappointed in 1893, but resigned in 1894 and moved to Fort Worth. Continued his law practice. Chaired the Democratic state convention in 1902. Died on March 12, 1925, and was buried in Fort Worth at Mount Olivet Cemetery.

ATKINS JEFFERSON "JEFF" MCLEMORE

Jeff McLemore

Born on March 13, 1857, in Maury County, Tennessee. Moved to Texas in 1878. Worked in a variety of jobs and even searched for gold in neighboring western states. Moved to San Antonio in 1883 and worked for a newspaper. Published a weekly newspaper in Kyle from 1883 until 1886. Moved to Corpus Christi in 1889 and published the *Gulf News*. Democrat. Served two terms as state representative, District 87, from 1893 until 1897. Moved to Austin in 1895. Served on the town council from 1896 until 1898 and was secretary of the Democratic Executive Committee from 1900 until 1904. Co-founded *State Topics* in 1903. Published *Indianola and Other Poems* (1904). Moved to Houston in 1911. Elected U.S. representative along with James H. "Cyclone" Davis for one of two at-large districts in 1914. Together, the pair defeated Socialists Nat B. Hunt and Reddin Andrews, Republicans Charles A. Warnken and E. E. Diggs, and Progressives J. E. Williams and H. L. McCulston. They succeeded Daniel Garrett and Hatton Sumners on March 4, 1915. McLemore was reelected along with Daniel Garrett for one of the two posts in 1916. Together, they defeated Republicans Charles A. Warnken and M. A. Taylor, Socialists Arch Lingan and W. D. Simpson, and Prosperity Party candidates I. E. Teague and E. G. Cook. The at-large positions were eliminated with the creation of the 17th and 18th congressional districts in 1918. McLemore left office on March 3, 1919, and returned to Hebronville to work on a newspaper. McLemore married May Clark in 1916 and they had one daughter, also named May Clark. Ran for U.S. senator in 1928, but placed near the back of the group seeking the Democratic nomination. Died on March 4, 1929, in Laredo and was buried at Oakwood Cemetery in Austin.

HOMER DEALE "DALE" MILFORD

Born on February 18, 1926, in Bug Tussle. Attended public schools and graduated from Commerce High School in 1942. Attended a communications trade school and then served in the U.S. Army during World War II. Married Barbara Cockrell in 1948 and they had two children: Shari and Stephan. Employed as an aircraft communicator in the Civil Aeronautics Administration and as an air controller in the army. Attended Baylor University from 1944 to 1953. Democrat. Owned and operated Dale Milford Flight Service in Waco until 1958. Television weather forecaster for KWTX in Central Texas from 1953 to 1958 and WFAA in Dallas from 1958 to 1971. Divorced in 1965 and was married to Mary Michaelle Shattuck later that year. Elected as the first U.S. representative for the newly created 24th District in 1972 by defeating Republican Courtney Roberts. Delegate to the Democratic national convention in 1972. Took office on January 3, 1973. Served on the House

Dale Milford

Science and Astronautics and Public Works committees. Reelected in 1974 by defeating Joseph Beaman, Jr. and American Party candidate Earl W. Armstrong, and in 1976 by defeating Berman and Armstrong again. Unseated by Martin Frost in 1978 Democratic primary election and was succeeded by him on January 3, 1979. Served on the board of the Dallas County Department of Public Welfare. Appointed regional director of the Federal Emergency Management Agency by President Carter and served in that post from 1978 until 1980. Died on December 26, 1997, at his home in Howe and was buried at Dial Cemetery near Honey Grove.

The No. 1 priority in the 24th District is for us to survive and progress economically.

—Dale Milford

JAMES FRANCIS MILLER

James F. Miller

Born on August 1, 1830, in South Carolina. Came to Texas with family in the 1840s. Attended Rutersville College and taught school in Gonzales while studying law. Admitted to the state bar in 1857. Practiced in Gonzales. Married Elmyra (Almira) Matthews in 1860, but she died two years later. Their infant son died the following year. Served in the Confederate States Army. Returned to Gonzales after the war to practice law. Married Julia Turner Batchelor in 1868. Co-founded a bank, farmed, and raised cattle. Became the first president of Texas Live Stock Association. Presbyterian, Mason, and Democrat. Elected as the first U.S. representative from the newly created 8th District in 1882 by defeating Greenbacker Robert Zapp and Independent Joseph O'Connor. Took office on March 4, 1883. Served on the House Banking and Currency Committee, which he chaired in his second term, along with the Mines and Mining, and Education committees. Reelected in 1884 by defeating Republican W. P. Burns. Served as the first president of the Texas Bankers Association beginning in 1885. Did not seek reelection to House in 1886. Succeeded by Littleton Moore on March 3, 1887. Died on July 3, 1902, in Gonzales and was buried there at the Masonic Cemetery.

ROGER QUARLES MILLS

Born on March 30, 1832, in Todd County, Kentucky. Moved to Jefferson, Texas, in 1849 and to Palestine in 1850. Methodist, Mason, and Prohibitionist, and belonged to the Whig Party, then the American or "Know Nothing" Party, but finally ended up a Democrat. Elected by the state legislature as engrossing clerk during the 4th Legislature, 1851 until 1853, after he had traveled with his friend State Representative W. G. W. Jowers. Studied law and, following a special act of the legislature, was admitted to the state bar in 1852 before he was twenty-one. Ran unsuccessfully for judge, 13th District, in 1853. Appointed road overseer by the Navarro County Commissioners. Married Carolyn R. "Carrie" Jones in 1858 and they had one son, Charles Henry, and three daughters, including Nannie and Carrie. Practiced law with his brother-in-law Reuben Reeves in Corsicana. Served one term as state representative, District 43, from 1859 to 1861. Wounded twice while serving in the Confederate States Army during the Civil War. Elected U.S. represen-

Roger Mills

tative for one of two at-large districts along with Asa H. Willie in 1872 by defeating Republicans I. D. Evans and A. B. Norton. Took office on March 4, 1873. The two at-large districts ceased to exist in 1875 when the 5th and 6th Congressional Districts were formed. Mills ran for and was elected U.S. representative from the 4th District in 1874 by defeating Republican Pleasant M. Yell. Succeeded John Hancock in this seat in March 1975. Reelected in 1876 by defeating Republican J. P. Osterhaut, in 1878 by defeating Greenback A. N. Smith and James Mitchell, and in 1880 by defeating Greenback candidate John T. Brady. Succeeded by David Browning Culberson in the 4th District in 1883. Elected the first U.S. representative from the newly created 9th District in 1882 by defeating Greenback candidate J. D. Rankin. Reelected in 1884 by defeating Republican J. P. Osterhaut, in 1886 by defeating now Population-Labor candidate J. D. Rankin, in 1888 by defeating Independent Democratic Republican Prohibition candidate E. A. Jones, and in 1890 by defeating Republican D. W. Roberts. Served on the House Ways and Means Committee, which he eventually chaired. Ran unsuccessfully for Speaker of the House in 1891. Did not run for reelection to Congress in 1892 and was succeeded by Edwin LeRoy Antony in March 1893. Instead, Mills was elected U.S. senator by the state legislature in 1892 and served from March 29, 1892, to March 3, 1899. He succeeded Horace Chilton, who retired from his brief tenure in the Rusk succession of U.S. senators from Texas. Mills was elected to a full term in the Senate by the legislature in 1893. He announced for reelection in 1898, but, seeing his chances of success as poor, he withdrew from the race and was succeeded by Charles Culberson in 1899. Died on September 2, 1911, and was buried at Oakwood Cemetery in Corsicana. Roger Mills County, Oklahoma, was named in his honor. (See also photo page 14.)

I am but one congressman in the house, and represent my constituents, to whom and not the newspapers or anybody else I am responsible.

—Roger Q. Mills

John Moore

Littleton Moore

John Matthew "Jaybird" Moore

Born on November 18, 1862, near Richmond, Texas. Attended local schools. Attended the Agricultural and Mechanical College (now Texas A&M University). Married Lottie Dyer in 1883 and they had four sons and two daughters: Maxwell (who died as an infant), Raymond Emmett, John Matthew, Jr., J. Foster Dyer, Ivy, and Henrietta Catheron. Dabbled in business and raised cattle. Democrat. From 1888 to 1892, presided over the Fort Bend County Jaybird Democratic Association, which became notorious for the Jaybird-Woodpecker War. Served as state representative, District 41, from 1897 to 1899. Delegate to the Democratic national convention in 1900 and 1916. Elected U.S. representative, 8th District, in the June 1905 special election by defeating Republican Max Urwitz to fill the seat of the late John M. Pinckney. Reelected in 1906 by defeating Republican W. A. Matthai, in 1908 by defeating Republican T. M. Kennerly and Socialist Laura B. Payne, and in 1910 by defeating Republicans A. M. Lawson and James M. Lairson. Served on the House Immigration and Naturalization Committees. Did not seek reelection in 1912. Succeeded by Joe Eagle on March 3, 1913. Returned to Richmond to raise cattle and to follow business interests. Died on February 3, 1940, and was buried at Morton Cemetery in Richmond.

Littleton Wilde Moore

Born on March 25, 1835, in Marion County, Alabama. Moved to Mississippi in 1836. Graduated from the University of Mississippi in 1855. Studied law and was admitted to the Mississippi state bar in 1857 and moved to Texas. Practiced in Bastrop. Married Anna Dunn Wright in 1857 and they had six children: Mrs. W. H. Thomas, Lytie, Lottie, twins Wright and Walter, and Clay. They moved to Bastrop County, Texas. Served in the Confederate States Army. Moved to LaGrange following the war. Democrat. Delegate to the Constitutional Convention of 1875. Served as district judge from 1876 until 1885. Elected U.S. representative, 8th District, in 1886 by defeating Republican W. O. Hutchinson. Succeeded James F. Miller on March 4, 1887. Reelected in 1888 by defeating Republican T. C. Cook and Union Labor Party candidate R. G. Sledge, and in 1890 by defeating Republican William Greene. Did not seek reelection in 1892 and was succeeded by C. K. Bell on March 3, 1893. Appointed by Governor Sayers as judge, 22nd Judicial District, in 1901. Served until his death on October 29, 1911, and was buried in City Cemetery in LaGrange. (See also photo page 14.)

SIMPSON HARRIS MORGAN

Born about 1821 in Rutherford County, Tennessee. Moved to Red River County, Texas, in 1844. Lived in Paris and Clarksville. Admitted to the state bar. Married a Miss Garland in 1852, but she died the following March. Morgan married Laura Morgan in 1859 and they had one daughter. President of the Memphis, El Paso, and Pacific Railroad. Elected representative, 6th District, to the Second Confederate Congress in November 1863 by unseating incumbent William B. Wright. While en route to the second session of this congress, he died of pneumonia on December 15, 1864, at Monticello, Arkansas. He had attended only one session. Buried at Simpson H. Morgan Memorial Park in Clarksville. Father-in-law of Albert Bacon Fall (1861–1944), who was U.S. senator from New Mexico.

GEORGE HENRY NOONAN

George Noonan

Born on August 20, 1828, in Newark, New Jersey. Studied law and was admitted to the bar. Married Cornelia Bowen and they had several children, including R. J. and George B. Catholic and Republican. Moved to Castroville, Texas in 1852 and opened his law practice. Elected judge, 18th Judicial District, and served from 1862 until 1894, when he resigned to run for Congress. Elected U.S. representative, 12th District, in 1894 by unseating incumbent Democrat Thomas Paschal and defeating Democrat A. W. Houston and Populist A. V. Gates. Succeeded Paschal on March 4, 1895. Served one term and was unseated by Democrat James L. Slayden in 1896. Succeeded by Slayden on March 3, 1897. Returned to law practice in San Antonio. Noonan sought reelection to his old seat in 1898, but was again defeated in the general election by Slayden. Died on August 17, 1907, in San Antonio and was buried there at St. Mary's Cemetery.

RANDY NEUGEBAUER

Born on December 24, 1949, in St. Louis, Missouri. Graduated from Coronado High School in Lubbock, Texas. Received degree from Texas Tech University in 1972. Married Dana Neugebauer in 1971 and they had two sons: Toby and Todd. Republican and Baptist. Served as Lubbock City Councilman from 1992 until 1998. Banker and Land Developer. Elected U.S. Representative, 19th District, in a May 2003 special election receiving the most votes, but not enough to secure a victory and a special runoff election was called for the top two candidates. Neugebauer defeated Mike Conaway in this June 2003 election. Succeeded the retiring Larry Combest on June 5, 2003. Redistricting found Neugebauer running against incumbent Democrat Charlie Stenholm in 2004. Neugebauer defeated Stenholm and Libertarian Richard "Chip" Peterson in the general election. Reelected in 2006 by defeating Democrat Robert Ricketts, Libertarian Fred C. Jones, and write-in Mike Sadler. Serves on the Committees for Agriculture and Financial Services.

Randy Neugebauer

THOMAS PECK OCHILTREE

Thomas P. Ochiltree

Born in Livingston, Alabama, on October 26, 1837. Son of William Beck Ochiltree (1811–67), a Republic of Texas–era leader. Served in the Texas Rangers from 1854 to 1855. Served as 1st Assistant Chief Clerk of the Texas House of Representatives for Adjourned Session of the 6th and the regular 7th legislatures from 1856 until 1857. Admitted to the state bar in 1857. Practiced law with his father in Marshall and Jefferson. Served as secretary of the state democratic convention in 1859 and as a delegate to the Democratic national convention in 1860. Edited the *Star State Jeffersonian* from 1860 to 1861. Served as major in the Confederate States Army. Following the war, he found work writing for the *New York News* and the *New York Sportsman* and editing for the *Houston Daily Telegraph* from 1866 until 1867. His support of Ulysses Grant for president earned him appointments as commissioner of emigration in Galveston from 1870 until 1873 and as U.S. marshal in 1874. As an Independent, he was elected as the first U.S. representative for the newly created 7th District in 1882 by defeating Democrat George P. Finlay. Took office on March 4, 1883. Served one term and did not seek reelection in 1884, and was succeeded by William Henry Crain on March 3, 1885. Moved to New York. He worked and lobbied for U.S. businesses abroad. Died on November 25, 1902, in Hot Springs, Virginia, and was buried at Greenwood Cemetery in Brooklyn, New York, but was reburied at Mount Hope Cemetery in Mount Hope, New York, in 1903.

WILLIAM BECK OCHILTREE

William Beck Ochiltree

Born on October 18, 1811, in Fayetteville, North Carolina. Moved to Florida, then Alabama. Studied and practiced law in Alabama. Moved to Nacogdoches, Texas in 1839 and practiced law. Married and had a number of children, including Thomas Peck Ochiltree (1837–1902), who was also a Texas congressman. Appointed judge of 5th Judicial District of Texas Republic in 1842. Appointed by President Anson Jones as secretary of the treasury in 1844, but was sent to the adjutant general's post in 1845. Served as delegate from Nacogdoches to Texas state constitutional convention in 1845. Appointed to earlier post of judge, but held the office only briefly before returning to private practice. Served as state representative from 1855 until 1861. Served as delegate from Harrison County to Texas Secession Convention in 1861. Delegate to the Confederate Provisional Congress from 1861 to 1862. Resigned and returned home to recruit an infantry regiment for Walker's Division to fight in the war. Resigned his military commission in 1863 due to his health and returned home to Jefferson, where he died on December 27, 1867. He was buried there at Oakwood Cemetery. Ochiltree County was named in his honor.

WILBERT LEE "PAPPY" O'DANIEL

Born on March 11, 1890, in Malta, Ohio. His father died while he was young, his mother remarried, and they moved to Kansas. Attended public schools. Received business diploma from the Salt City Business College in 1908. Began working in the business office of a flour mill in Anthony, Kansas. Married Merle Estella Butcher in 1916 and they had three children: Pat, Mike, and Molly. Lived in Kansas City and New Orleans, but settled in Fort Worth, Texas in 1925 after landing a job as sales manager for the Burrus Flour Mills. There he hired a country band and named them the Light Crust Doughboys to promote the mill. Presided over the Fort Worth Chamber of Commerce from 1933 until 1934. The contacts he made there gave him the initial capital to begin his own company, Hillbilly Flour, in 1935. His statewide advertising with another band—the Hillbilly Boys—endeared him to a wide, mostly rural audience. Mason and Democrat. He ran for governor in 1938 and defeated Ernest O. Thompson, William McCraw, and Tom F. Hunter in the Democratic primary and ran unopposed in the general election. He was reelected in 1940 by defeating Ernest O. Thompson, Harry Hines, former governor Miriam Ferguson, and Jerry Sadler in the Democratic primary and Republican G. C. Hopkins in the general election. He served as governor from January 1, 1939, until August 4, 1941. His administration is remembered for little more than its ineptness. As governor, he appointed Andrew Jackson Houston to fill the post of U.S. senator vacated by the death of Morris Sheppard. O'Daniel wanted the job himself, but could not appoint himself, so he appointed a man who would not oppose him in the subsequent election. Houston died shortly after his appointment, and O'Daniel ran for the post in a 1941 special election and was elected by defeating Lyndon B. Johnson, Gerald

Pappy O'Daniel

C. Mann, Martin Dies, Sam Morris, and twenty-four other candidates. He took office on August 4, 1941, and took his place in the Houston succession of U.S. senators from Texas. He was reelected in the 1942 regular election by defeating former governors James Allred and Dan Moody in the Democratic primary, Allred in a runoff, and Republican Dudley Lawson and People's Party candidate Charles Sommerville in the general election. Served on the Senate Commerce, Claims, District of Columbia, Public Works, and Irrigation committees. O'Daniel was very much a part of the Texas Regulars and their effort to collect conservative southern Democratic votes for the Republicans in the 1944 presidential race. He did not seek reelection to the Senate in 1948 and served until January 3, 1949. Succeeded by Lyndon B. Johnson. Retired to Fort Worth and was involved in a variety of business ventures, including life insurance. Ran for governor again in the 1956 and 1958 Democratic primaries but was defeated by Price Daniel on both occasions. Died on May 11, 1969, in Dallas and was buried there at Sparkman Hillcrest Cemetery.

I do not feel that the United States senate is under any obligation whatever to accept my version of what should be done or what should not be done.

—W. Lee. O'Daniel

WILLIAMSON SIMPSON OLDHAM

Born on July 19, 1813, in Franklin County, Tennessee. Received little formal education, but started his own school in 1831. Employed at the District Clerk's office in Franklin County. Studied law and was admitted to the Tennessee state bar in 1836. Moved to Fayetteville, Arkansas, in 1836 and began law practice, and eventually entered politics. Married Mary Vance McKissick in 1837 and they had five children, including Williamson Simpson, Jr. Episcopal and State Rights Democrat. Served the first of two terms as Arkansas state representative beginning in 1838. He was not reelected in 1840, but was reelected in 1842 for his second term. Upon his return to the legislature, he was elected Speaker of the House at the age of twenty-nine. Served as a presidential elector for James Polk in 1844. Also served as justice of Arkansas Supreme Court from 1844 until 1848. Unsuccessful candidate for U.S. representative from Arkansas in 1846 and unsuccessful candidate for U.S. senator from Arkansas in 1848. Moved to Austin, Texas in 1849 to escape the

Williamson Oldham

political embarrassment of his loss, and for his health. Oldham's first wife died while en route to Austin, and he married Anne S. Kirk in 1850. She lived only a few years, and Oldham married Agnes Harper in 1857. Presided over the Austin Railroad Association in 1852 and edited the *Austin State Gazette* from 1854 to 1857. Oldham faced a series of political defeats about this time. He ran again for state representatives in 1853 and was defeated. He was nominated to replace Sam Houston in the U.S. Senate in 1857, but John Hemphill won. He ran for U.S. representative, 2nd District, in 1859, but Thomas Waul received the Democratic Party's nomination. Oldham moved to Brenham in 1859. Served as delegate from Washington County to the Texas Secession Convention in 1861 and as a delegate to Confederate Provisional Congress from 1861 to 1862. Elected senator by the state legislature to the Confederate Congress on November 16, 1861. Oldham drew a six-year term and served from 1862 until the fall of the Confederacy in 1865. Served on the Post Offices, Commerce, Indian Affairs, Naval Affairs, Finance, and Judiciary committees. He eventually chaired the Post Office Committee. He lived in Mexico and Canada following the war. Began writing a book about the war which was turned into a series of articles that appeared in *De Bow's Monthly Review* and was entitled "Last Days of the Confederacy." Moved to Houston in 1866. Died on May 8, 1868, of typhoid in Houston and was buried there at Episcopal Cemetery. Reinterred in 1938 at Brookside Memorial Park, also in Houston. Oldham County is named in his honor.

The road to the peace I covet is enfiladed by hostile armies, hedged by glittering bayonets, and slippery with blood, but it leads to the temple where Liberty sits enthroned.

—Williamson Oldham

SOLOMON PORFIRIO ORTIZ

Born on June 3, 1938, in Robstown. Democrat. Attended Robstown High School. Served in U.S. Army from 1960 to 1962. Attended Del Mar College. Received law officer's certificate from Institute of Applied Science in Chicago in 1962 and officer's certificate from National Sheriffs Training Institute in Los Angeles in 1977. Served as Nueces County Constable from 1965 until 1968, Nueces County Commissioner from 1969 until 1976, and Nueces County Sheriff from 1977 until 1982. Elected as first U.S. representative for the newly created 27th District in 1982 by defeating Republican Jason Luby and Libertarian Steven R. Roberts. Took office on January 3, 1983. Reelected in 1984 by defeating Republican Richard Moore, ran unopposed for reelection in 1986, 1988, and 1990, in 1992 defeated Republican Jay Kimbrough and Libertarian Charles Schoonover, in 1994 defeated Republican Erol A. Stone, in 1996 defeated Republican Joe Gardner and Natural Law Party candidate Kevin G. Richardson, in 1998 defeated Republican Erol Stone and Libertarian Mark Pretz, and in 2000 by defeating Republican Pat Ahumada and Libertarian William Bunch, in 2002 by defeating Republican Pat Ahumada and Libertarian Christopher J. Claytor, and in 2004 by defeating Republican William "Willie" Vaden and Libertarian Christopher J. Claytor, and in 2006 by defeating Republican William "Willie" Vaden and Libertarian Robert Powell. Married and the father of two children: Yvette and Solomon, Jr. Serves on the House Merchant Marine and Fisheries and Armed Services committees.

Solomon Ortiz

LUCIAN WALTON PARRISH

Born on January 10, 1878, in Sister Grove. Moved with family to Clay County in 1887. Attended public schools in Joy and Bowie. Attended North Texas Normal School (now the University of North Texas) and returned home to teach school for two years. Graduated from the University of Texas in 1906 and received an M.A. and law degree in 1909. He was admitted to the state bar the same year.

Lucian Parrish

Democrat. Returned home and began a practice in Henrietta. Married Gladys Edwards in 1912 and they had two children: Mary and Lucian, Jr. Elected U.S. representative, 13th District, in 1918 by running unopposed. Succeeded Marvin Jones on March 4, 1919. Served on the House Accounts, Mines and Mining, Post Office and Post Roads committees. Reelected in 1920 by defeating Republican C. W. Johnson. He was killed in a traffic accident while serving in office on March 27, 1922, in Wichita Falls and was buried at Hope Cemetery in Henrietta. Succeeded by Guinn Williams in 1923. Inducted into the University of Texas Men's Athletics Hall Of Honor in 1970 for his role in the 1903 through 1906 football and track teams.

Let us do common justice to all, and no matter what the disturbances of the moment may be, our country will survive the tests of time, and will realize the expectation of those who laid so well its foundation.

—Lucian Parrish

THOMAS MOORE PASCHAL

Born on December 15, 1845, in Alexandria, Louisiana. Moved along with his parents to San Antonio, Texas the following year. Attended private schools. Presbyterian, Mason, and Democrat. Attended St. Mary's College, but graduated from Centre College in Danville, Kentucky, in 1886. Studied law and was admitted to the state bar in 1867. Served as the United States Commissioner for the Western District from 1867 until 1869 San Antonio City Attorney during the late 1860s, and was appointed by Governor Davis as district attorney, 24th Judicial District, and served in that post from 1870 until 1871. Moved to Castroville in 1870 and to Brackettville in 1873. Married Florida A. Mays in 1871 and they had five children: Harold A., Mrs. S. E. Hampton, Florence Lenore, Thomas Elmo, and Mrs. C. H. Benson. Served as judge, 38th Judicial District and served from 1876 until 1892. Appointed by Governor Coke in 1876 as an extradition agent to Mexico. Re-appointed by Governor Roberts in 1880. Returned to Castroville in 1885. Elected as the first

Thomas M. Paschal

U.S. representative for the newly created 12th District in 1892 by defeating Republican Henry Terrell and People's Party candidate T. J. McMinn. Took office on March 4, 1893. Paschal was not renominated in 1894 and was succeeded by George Noonan on March 3, 1895. Returned to his law practice in San Antonio. Delegate to the Democratic national convention in 1896. Died of pneumonia in New York City on January 28, 1919, and was interred at Mission Burial Park in San Antonio.

WILLIAM NEFF PATMAN

Born on March 26, 1927, in Texarkana. Son of Wright Patman (1893–1976), also a U.S. congressman from Texas. Went to public schools in Texarkana, Washington, D.C., and attended Kemper Military School. Served in the U.S. Marine Corps from 1945 to 1946. Received a B.B.A. and an L.L.B. from the University of Texas. Served as a courier in the U.S. Foreign Service from 1949 to 1950. Admitted to the state bar in 1953. Employed by the Texas Railroad Commission from 1953 until 1955. In private legal practice during 1955. Served as Ganado City Attorney from 1955 to 1960. Served in the U.S. Air Force Reserve from 1953 to 1966. Married Carrin Mauritz in 1953 and they had one daughter: Carrin. Democrat. Served one term as state representative, District 18, from 1961 to 1963 and ten terms as state senator, District 18, from 1963 to 1980. Served as president pro tempore of the Senate during the 60th Legislature, 1967–69, and served as governor for a day on March

Bill Patman

28, 1967. Elected U.S. representative, 14th District, in 1980 by defeating Republican Charles L. Concklin. Succeeded Joe Wyatt on January 3, 1981. Reelected in 1982 by defeating the man he replaced, Republican Joe Wyatt, and Libertarian Glenn Rasmussen. Unseated in the 1984 general election by Republican Mac Sweeney. Succeeded by Sweeney on January 3, 1985. Now resides in Austin.

JOHN WILLIAM WRIGHT PATMAN

Wright Patman

Born on August 6, 1893, near Hughes Springs in Cass County. Attended public schools and graduated from Hughes Springs High School in 1912 and Cumberland University law school in 1916. Farmed from 1913 until 1914. Admitted to the state bar in 1916. Baptist and Democrat. Practiced law in Hughes Springs for about six months, but this proved unprofitable and he moved to Linden. Served as Assistant Cass County Attorney in 1916 and 1917. Served in U.S. Army during World War I. Married Merle Connor in 1919 and they had four sons: Connor Wright, James Harold, William Neff (who was also a congressman from Texas), and Charles (who died in 1939). Practiced law in Linden with George T. Bartlett. Served two terms as state representative, District 2, from 1921 until 1924, and as district attorney, 5th Judicial District, from 1924 until 1928. Elected U.S. Representative, 1st District, by unseating incumbent Eugene Black in the July 1928 Democratic primary election and by defeating Republican Richard E. Stephens in the general election. Succeeded Black on March 4, 1929. Reelected in 1930 by defeating Republican Thomas A. Clark, in 1932 by defeating Republican A. O. Barker, in 1934 and 1936 by defeating Republican P. B. Gibbons, in 1938 by defeating Republican Joe C. Hailey, by running unopposed from 1940 through 1960, in 1962 by defeating Republican James Timberlake, in 1964 by defeating Republican Mrs. William E. Jones, by running unopposed in 1966 and 1968, and in 1970 by defeating Republican James Hogan, ran unopposed in 1972, in 1974 defeated Republican James W. Farris. On January 6, 1932, Patman introduced House Resolution 92 to impeach Secretary of the Treasury Andrew Mellon. Mellon was one of the country's wealthiest men, and Patman believed he could not execute his cabinet post without some personal interest being served. Mellon was appointed Ambassador to England a month later, and the impeachment proceedings were dropped. Wrote *Bankerteering, Bonuseering, and Melloneering* (1934) and *Patman's Appeal to Pay Veterans* (1934), both of which supported the concept of currency expansion and reform. Patman fought until 1936 for the passage of a "bonus" bill for World War I veterans. The resolution failed many times until it finally passed in 1936. Served on the Select Committee on Small Businesses (chairman from 1955 until 1963); also served on the Joint Economic; Coinage, Weights, and Measures; District of Columbia; War Claims; and Banking and Currency committees (He chaired the Currency Committe from 1963 to 1975). His wife Merle died in July 1967. The following year he married Pauline Tucker. Died while serving in office on March 7, 1976, in Bethesda, Maryland, and was buried at Hillcrest Cemetery in Texarkana. Succeeded by Sam Hall. (See also photo page 24.)

If the masses could only pierce the "Smoke screen of secrecy" and see what is actually going on behind closed doors in the financial world; could understand the plots and plans of these "money changers" in their efforts to fleece and flick an innocent and unsuspecting public; things would be changed in the twinkle of an eye.

—Wright Patman

NAT PATTON

Born on February 26, 1884, near Tadmor. Moved with his family to Brown County in 1886, but returned to Houston County in 1890. Attended local schools and Sam Houston Normal School. Taught school from 1899 to 1918 in Houston, Dickens, Fisher, and Trinity counties, and farmed. Married Mattie

Taylor in 1907 and they had four children: Bessie Louise, Weldon Taylor, Nat, and Bonnie Beatrice. Methodist Episcopalian, Mason, Knight of Pythias, and Democrat. Served two terms as state representative, District 24, from 1913 until 1917. Attended the University of Texas law school and was admitted to the state bar in 1918. Enlisted in the U.S. Army, but was not sworn in due to the impending armistice. Practiced law in Crockett. Served as Houston County Judge from 1918 to 1922, and served four terms as state senator, District 5, from 1929 to 1934. Candidate for U.S. representative, 7th District, in the June 1933 special election to fill the seat of the late Clay Stone Briggs, but was defeated by Clark Thompson. Elected U.S. representative, 7th District, in 1934 by defeating Republican Dudley B. Lawson. Succeeded Clark Thompson on January 3, 1935, who had served very briefly following the death of Clay Stone Briggs. Reelected in 1936 by defeating Republican O. J. Read, in 1938 by running unopposed, in 1940 by defeating Republican

Nat Patton

Dudley Lawson, and in 1942 by defeating Republican A. W. Orr. Patton was known for calling everyone by their first name preceded by "cousin." He even referred to Queen Elizabeth as "Cousin Elizabeth" and President Roosevelt as "Cousin Franklin." Roosevelt found it charming and frequently reciprocated with "Cousin Nat." Unseated in the 1944 Democratic primary election by Tom Pickett. Succeeded by Pickett on January 3, 1945. Returned to his law practice in Crockett. Died on July 27, 1957, in Crockett and was buried there at Evergreen Memorial Park.

> *If it hadn't been for Queen Victoria I wouldn't have been in Congress.*
>
> —Nat Patton Recounting the library of a local Englishman who received a scholarship from Queen Victoria and allowed the young Patton to use his library

Ron Paul

RONALD ERNEST "RON" PAUL

Born on August 20, 1935, in Pittsburgh, Pennsylvania. Received B.A. from Gettysburg College in 1957 and M.D. from Duke College of Medicine in 1961. Married Carol Wells in 1957 and they had five children: Ronnie, Lori Pyeatt, Rand, Robert and Joy LeBlanc. Served in the U.S. Air Force from 1963 until 1965 and the Air National Guard from 1965 until 1968. Received additional medical training at the University of Pittsburg from 1965 until 1968. Moved to Texas in 1968. Practicing obstetrician and gynecologist. Republican. Unsuccessful campaign against Bob Casey for 22nd District congressional seat in 1974. Elected U.S. representative, 22nd District, in a 1976 special election and runoff to fill the seat of Bob Casey by defeating Democrat Bob Gammage. Paul actually placed second in the pack of seven candidates, but he won a runoff election. He was unseated a few months later in the November 1976 general election by Democrat Bob Gammage. Served from April 3, 1976, until January 3, 1977, when he was succeeded by Gammage. Reelected in 1978 by unseating incumbent Bob Gammage. Succeeded Gammage on January 3, 1979. Reelected in 1980 by defeating Democrat Mike Andrews and in 1982 by running unopposed. Did not seek reelection to Congress in 1984 and returned to his medical practice. Succeeded by Tom DeLay on January 3, 1985. Was a candidate for the U.S. Senate in 1984, but was defeated by Gramm in the Republican primary. Published an investment newsletter and political report. Libertarian Party presidential candidate in 1988. Elected U.S. Representative, 14th District, in 1996 by defeating incumbent and now Republican Greg Laughlin in a runoff election. Succeeded Laughlin on January 3, 1997. Reelected in 1998 by defeating Democrat Loy Sneary and in 2000 by again defeating Sneary, in 2002 by defeating Democrat Corby Windham, and in 2004 by running unopposed, and in 2006 by defeating Democrat Shane Sklar. Serves on the House Committees on Financial Services and International Relations. Authored *Gold, Peace, and Prosperity: the Birth of a New Currency* (1981), *Challenge to Liberty, Ten Myths About Paper Money, The Case for Gold* (1982 and 2007), *A Republic, If You Can Keep It (2000), Mises and Austrian Economics: A Personal View* (1984), *Freedom Under Siege: The U.S. Constitution After 200 Years* (1987), *A Foreign Policy of Freedom* (2007).

GEORGE CASSIDY PENDLETON

George Pendleton

Born on April 23, 1845, near Viola, Tennessee. Moved to Ellis County, Texas in 1857, then moved to Belton. Attended local schools and Hannah High School. Democrat. Served in the Confederate States Army. Studied law in Waxahachie, but worked as a traveling salesman for twelve years following. Married Helen Embree in 1870 and they had five children. One of the Grange founders in Texas. Served three terms as state representative, District 56, from 1883 until 1889 and in his last session served as Speaker of the House, from 1887 to 1889. Elected lieutenant governor and served from 1891 until 1893 under Governor Hogg. Elected U.S. representative, 7th District, in 1892 by defeating People's Party candidate I. N. Barber. Succeeded William Crain on March 4, 1893. Reelected in 1895 by defeating now Populist candidate Barber. Did not seek reelection in 1896 and was succeeded by Robert Henry on

March 3, 1897. Moved to Temple and became a banker. While there, he finally was able to study law and was admitted to the bar in 1900. He practiced law until his death. He was appointed U.S. Postmaster of Temple, but died before he could take the position. He died on January 19, 1913, of a stroke in Temple and was buried there at City Cemetery.

THOMAS AUGUSTUS "TOM" PICKETT

Tom Pickett

Born on August 14, 1906, in Travis, Texas. Lived briefly in Iola and then moved to Palestine with his family in 1913. Attended public schools there and graduated from Palestine High School in 1923. Attended Conway's Business College and worked for one year in his father's law office. Attended the University of Texas from 1924 to 1928. While in his first year at the university, he was elected freshman class president. Admitted to the state bar and began practice in Palestine in 1929. Served as Anderson County Attorney from 1931 until 1935. Married Louise Watson in 1938 and they had two daughters: Helen Louise and Alice Melinda. Louise was Pickett's second wife; little is known about his prior marriage. Baptist until the late 1950s when he became an Episcopalian. Democrat. Served as district attorney, 3rd Judicial District, from 1935 to 1945. Unseated incumbent Nat Patton for U.S. representative, 7th

District, in the 1944 Democratic primary election and defeated Republican J. Perrin Willis in the general election. Succeeded Patton on January 3, 1945. Reelected in 1946, 1948, and 1950 by running unopposed. Served on the House Public Works, Veterans Affairs, and Administration committees. Resigned from office on June 30, 1952, did not run for reelection, and was succeeded by John Dowdy in September 1952. Served as vice-president of the National Coal Association from 1952 until 1961 and the Association of American Railroads from 1961 to 1968. Moved to Florida in 1968. Died on June 7, 1980, in Leesburg, Florida, and was cremated, and his ashes were buried at St. James Episcopal Church in Leesburg.

A political career is full of hazards. There is no stability in such a career since there is a no assurance of continuance in office.

—Tom Pickett

JAMES JARRELL "JAKE" PICKLE

Jake Pickle

Born on October 11, 1913, in Roscoe. Graduated from Big Spring High School. Graduated from the University of Texas in 1938. Employed by National Youth Administration (NYA) as area supervisor and later as area director. Married Ella Nora "Sugar" Critz in 1942 and they had one daughter: Peggy. Democrat. Served in the U.S. Navy during World War II. Worked in the radio business and then in advertising/public relations. His first wife, Sugar, died in 1952 from breast cancer. Served as executive director of State Democratic Executive Committee. Married Beryl Bolton McCarroll in 1960. She was a widow with two sons: Dick and Graham. Appointed by Governor Daniel to the Texas Employment Commission. Elected U.S. representative, 10th District, in a 1963 special election to fill the seat vacated by Homer Thornberry's resignation. Pickle defeated Republican Jim Dobbs and Democrat Jack Ritter in the special election and defeated Dobbs again in the runoff to get the majority, as required in Texas' special-election laws. Took office on December 21, 1963, as President Johnson had Pickle sworn in a few days early, which gave him a few days' seniority over his colleagues. Reelected in 1964 by defeating Republican Billie Pratt, in 1966 by defeating Republican Jane Sumner and Constitution Party candidate R. R. Richter, in 1968 by defeating Republican Ray Gabler, in 1970 by running unopposed, in 1972 by defeating Socialist Workers candidate Melissa Singler, in 1974 by defeating Republican Paul Weiss, in 1976 by defeating Republican Paul McClure, in 1978 by defeating Republican Emmett L. Hudspeth, in 1980 by defeating Republican John Biggar and Libertarian Michael Grossberg, in 1982 by defeating Libertarian William G. Kelsey and Citizens Party candidate Bradley Rockwell, in 1984 by defeating Hugh Wilson, in 1986 by defeating Republican Carol Rylander, in 1988 by defeating Libertarian Vincent J. May, in 1990 by defeating Republican David Beilharz and Libertarian Jeff Davis, and in 1992 by defeating Republican Herbert Spiro, Libertarian, Terry Blum, Independent Jeff Davis, and write-ins Stephen Hopkins and Robert Shaw. Served on the House Ways and Means Committee and the Social Security and Oversight subcommittees. Did not seek reelection in 1994 and retired from the Congress. Succeeded by Lloyd Doggett on January 3, 1995. Co-wrote *Jake* (1997) with his daughter Peggy. Retired to his home in Austin. The federal building on Eighth Street in Austin was renamed in his honor in 1999. Died on June 18, 2005, in Austin and was buried there at the State Cemetery.

Some men live to make money, drink, chase women, collect art, excel at a sport, or pursue other things that give them pleasure. The thing I got hooked on was helping people.

—Jake Pickle

TIMOTHY PILSBURY

Born on April 12, 1789, in Newburyport, Massachusetts. Attended local schools. Worked as a clerk at age twelve. Went to sea two years later and served on the boats *Romulus, Aurora, Hesper, Massachusetts*, and *Essex*, and, during the War of 1812, on the *Yankee*, which he eventually commanded. Off the Windwards Islands, the ship was captured by the British. Pilsbury fell ill in Barbados and was released by the British to return home. Pilsbury married the daughter of Ezekiel Prince and they had a number of children. He and his brother Wingate entered into a lucrative shipping business between Penobscot Bay and New York during the war. The business was sold, and Pilsbury returned to sea, commanding the *Harriet*. The boat sank near Madeira, and Pilsbury was sixteen months in returning home. He moved to Eastport, Maine, and

Timothy Pilsbury

returned to sea on the *Beaver*. He was elected and served as state representative in Maine in 1825 and 1826. He declared bankruptcy between the two elections and was not reelected in 1827. Was selected by the legislature as a member of Maine Governor Lincoln's executive council and served in this role from 1827 to 1836. He acquired a small schooner which he and his son sailed to New Orleans and sold. There he acquired three wrecked boats. This proved to be a ruinous venture, and they were all sold at a loss. He then acquired a small schooner that was sunk near what is now Belize. His son Edward was with him on this trip, and the boy fell quite ill. They were forty days on the island before being rescued. He returned to New Orleans and acquired another schooner that was nearly lost in a hurricane en route to Boston. Following his return, he ran again for Maine state representative in 1835 and was defeated by Frederic Hobbs. He again was chosen for the executive council of Maine Governor Dunlap. Candidate for U.S. representative from Maine in 1836, but was eventually defeated by Joseph Noyes following five ballots. Moved to Ohio, then New Orleans, and then to Brazoria County, Texas, in 1837. Worked as merchant and a farmer. Served as member of Texas Republic House of Representatives from Brazoria County from 1840 until 1841 and as state senator in the Texas Republic Senate from 1841 to 1842. He resigned this seat, but served again from 1844 to 1845. In the interim, he served as chief justice and judge of probate in Brazoria County. Nicknamed "Eyes and Nose" because of these prominent features he possessed. Mason and Calhoun Democrat. Following many years as a widower, he married Rebecca Carpenter, who was from Maine. Following Texas statehood, he was elected as the first U.S. representative from the 2nd District in a March 1846 special election by defeating Samuel M. Williams, William G. Cooke, John M. Lewis, Joseph C. Megginson, and Thomas J. Green. Took office on March 30, 1846. Reelected a few months later in the November 1846 general election by defeating William E. Jones, Samuel M. Williams, and R. E. Baylor. Unseated in 1849 by Volney E. Howard and was succeeded him on March 3, 1849. Died on November 23, 1858, in Henderson and was buried there at City Cemetery. His son Albert was an 1853 Maine gubernatorial candidate, and another son, Edward, was mayor of New Orleans during the 1870s.

Compare the history of revolution in Texas with that of any other revolution, and Texas stands unrivaled.

—Timothy Pilsbury

John McPherson Pinckney

Born on May 4, 1845, near Hempstead. Public and private education. Served in the Confederate States Army. Studied law and was admitted to the state bar in 1875. Practiced in Hempstead. Mason and Democrat. Served as district attorney, 23rd Judicial District, from 1890 until 1900 and Waller County Judge from 1900 until 1903. Elected U.S. representative, 8th District, in a November 1903 special election by running unopposed to fill the seat of Thomas Ball, who resigned the same month. Took office on November 17, 1903. Reelected in 1904 by defeating Republican H. F. McGregor. Served until he was assaulted and killed at a meeting of the Waller County Prohibition League in Hempstead on April 24, 1905. Pinckney never married, but lived with and supported his sister Sue, a widow, and her children. He was buried at City Cemetery in Hempstead. Succeeded in Congress by John Moore.

John Pinckney

I will not go back on my convictions for Congress or any other office.

—John M. Pinckney

William Robert "Bob" Poage

Born on December 28, 1899, in Waco. Moved briefly to Throckmorton County in 1901 with family. Graduated from Waco High School in 1918. Served in U.S. Navy during World War I. Attended the

University of Texas, the University of Colorado, and Baylor University. Received a B.A. from Baylor in 1921. Worked on a farm and taught geology at Baylor until 1924. Received L.L.B. from Baylor in 1924 and was admitted to the state bar. Taught at the law school while practicing in Waco until 1928. Presbyterian, Mason, and Democrat. Served two terms as state representative, District 97, from 1925 until 1929 and three terms as state senator, District 13, from 1931 (when he succeeded Edgar Witt, who became lieutenant governor) until 1937. Unsuccessful candidate for U.S. representative, 11th District, in the 1934 Democratic primary against Oliver H. Cross. Elected U.S. representative, 11th District, in 1936 by defeating Frank B. Tirey and C. A. Sherman in the primary and running unopposed in the general election.. Succeeded Cross on January 3, 1937. Married Frances Cotton in 1938; they had no children. Reelected in 1938 by defeating Republican D. E. Wooley. In 1940 O. H. Cross tried to regain his seat by running against Poage in the primary

Bob Poage

but lost. So in 1940 and 1942, Poage ran unopposed in the general election.. In 1944 defeated Republican Charles Nelson, in 1946 ran unopposed, in 1948 defeated Republican A. A. Warrington, from 1950 through 1962 was reelected without opposition, in 1964 defeated Republican Charles M. Isenhower, in 1966 and 1968 defeated Conservative Laurel N. Dunn, ran unopposed in 1970 and 1972, defeated Republican Don Clements and now Independent Laurel N. Dunn in 1974, and defeated Jack Burgess in 1976. Served on the House Agriculture Committee, which he chaired from 1967 to 1974. Delegate to the Democratic national conventions of 1956, 1960, and 1964. Resigned from office on December 31, 1978, did not seek reelection, and was succeeded by his former aide Marvin Leath on January 1, 1979. Father of the Poage-Aiken Act of 1965 which provided for the development of water and wastewater systems in small communities. The W. R. Poage Legislative Library for Graduate Studies and Research was dedicated at Baylor University in 1979. Author of *After the Pioneers* (1969), *Politics Texas Style* (1974), *McLennan County Before* 1980 (1981), *How We Lived* (1983), and *My First Eighty-Five Years* (1985). His wife Frances died in 1983. He died on January 3, 1987, in Temple and was buried at Oakwood Cemetery in Waco. (See also photo page 24.)

In local races, personal contacts are far more important than people seem to think. On the other hand, in national races, they are probably less important than the candidates seem to think

—Bob Poage

LLOYD THEODORE "TED" POE

Born October 13, 1948, in Temple. Received B.A. from Abilene Christian University in 1970 and J.D. from the University of Houston in 1973. Admitted to the state bar in 1973. Served in the Air Force from 1970 through 1976. Appointed and served as Felony Court Judge from 1981 through 2004. Served as a Trainer at the Federal Bureau of Investigations National Academy. Chief Felony Prosecutor, District Attorney, Harris County. Married Carol Poe and they had four children: Kim, Kara, Kurt, and Kellee. Elected U.S. Representative, 2nd District, in 2004 by unseating incumbent Democrat Nick Lampson whom he succeeded the following year. Serves on the House Committees for International Relations, Small Business, and Transportation and Infrastructure. Reelected in 2006 by defeating Democrat Gary E. Binderim and Libertarian Justo J. Perez. Serves on the House Committees for Foreign Affairs and Transportation and Infrastructure.

Ted Poe

JOE RICHARD POOL

Born on February 18, 1911, in Fort Worth. Attended Dallas public schools and graduated from Oak Cliff High School. Attended Texas Tech University from 1929 to 1933. Graduated from Southern Methodist University law school in 1937. Admitted to the state bar in 1937 and started practicing in Dallas. Married Elizabeth Chambliss in 1940 and they had four children: Richard Lee, Wesley James, John Kyle, and Joe Richards, Jr. Served in the U.S. Army Air Corps during World War II. Methodist and Democrat. Served three terms as state representative, District 51-5, from 1953 until 1959. Elected U.S. representative, At-Large District, in 1962 by defeating Republican Desmond A. Barry. Took office on January 3, 1963. Served on the House Un-American Activities and Postal Service committees. Reelected in 1964 by defeating Republican Bill Hayes and Constitution Party candidate W. A. "Bill" Johnson. The At-Large District ceased to exist with the creation of the 23rd Congressional District in 1966. Pool, however, was elected to the

Joe Pool

3rd District seat in 1966 by defeating Republican Jim Collins and served one term. Died while serving in office on July 14, 1968, of a heart attack in Houston and was buried at Laurel Land Memorial Park in Dallas. The Kiest-Polk postal station in Dallas was renamed in his honor in October 1968. Mrs. Joe Pool ran for her husband's unexpired seat in a special election during 1968, but was defeated by Jim Collins. Joe Pool Lake is named after him.

Keep Cool with Pool

—Joe Pool campaign slogan

ROBERT DALE "BOB" PRICE

Born on September 7, 1927, in Reading, Kansas. Attended local schools and graduated from Reading High School in 1945. Received a B.S. from Oklahoma State University in 1951. Served in the U.S. Air Force during the Korean War, flying F-86 fighters. Married Martha A. "Marty" White in 1951 and they had three children: Robert Grant, Benjamin Carl, and Janice Ann. Republican and rancher. Ran unsuccessfully for U.S. representative, 18th District, in 1964, and was defeated by incumbent Democrat Walter Rogers. Elected U.S. representative, 18th District, in 1966 by defeating Democrat Dee D. Miller. Succeeded Walter Rogers on January 3, 1967. Delegate to the Republican national convention in 1968. Served on the House Agriculture, Armed Services, and Science and Astronautics committees. Reelected in 1968 by defeating Democrat J. R. Brown, and in 1970 by running generally unopposed. Price was one of three Republican representatives from Texas at this time, and the Democratic-controlled state legislature did what it could

Bob Price

to remove him from office. Efforts included redistricting his 18th District seat, thus forcing him to run against incumbent Graham Purcell for the 13th District seat. Both were members of the House Agriculture Committee. Price unseated incumbent democrat Graham Purcell in the 13th District in 1972. This had been the second time Price's district was redistricted. Unseated by Democrat Jack Hightower in the 1974 general election and was succeeded by him on January 3, 1975. Was a candidate for his old 18th District seat in 1976, but was again defeated by Hightower. Elected state senator, District 31, on December 10, 1977, in a special election to succeed Max Sherman. Took office on January 18, 1978, and served part of two terms, from 1978 until 1981. Sought the Republican nomination for U.S. representative, 13th District, in 1988, but was defeated by Larry Milner. Retired to Pampa and operated a ranch with his son Carl. Died in Pampa on August 24, 2004, and was buried there at Fairview Cemetery.

The fear of crime is destroying some of the basic human freedoms which any society is supposed to safeguard—freedom of movement, freedom from harm, freedom from fear itself.

—Bob Price

GRAHAM BOYNTON PURCELL, JR.

Born on May 5, 1919, in Archer City. Attended local schools and graduated from Archer City High School in 1937. Attended Texas A&M University from 1937 to 1941. Served in the U.S. Army during World War II. Received a B.S. from Texas A&M University in 1946 and a J.D. from Baylor University in 1949. Married Betty Smith in 1942 and they had four children: Blaine, Kirk, Jannie, and Blake. Democrat. Admitted to the state bar in 1949 and began a law practice in Big Spring. Served as judge, 89th Judicial District, from 1955 until 1962. Elected U.S. representative, 13th District, by defeating Republican Joe Meissner and Democrats Jack Hightower, Vernon Stewart, and Jimmy P. Horany in the November 1961 special election and Meissner again in the January 1962 special election runoff to fill the seat of Frank Ikard who had resigned. Took office on January 27, 1962. Served on the House Agriculture and Post Office and Civil Service committees. Reelected in the November 1962 general election by again defeating Republican Meissner, in 1964

Graham Purcell

by defeating Republican George Corse, in 1966 by defeating Republican D. C. Norwood, in 1968 by defeating Republican Frank Crowley, and in 1970 by defeating Republican Joe Staley. In 1972 Purcell was unseated by Republican Bob Price, who succeeded him in 1973. Was a delegate to the Democratic national conventions of 1960, 1964, and 1968. Served as a lobbyist after leaving office and now lives in Wichita Falls.

Few of the ills of rural America can or will be cured without fair prices and equality of economic opportunity for farmers. Not without these can we assure the American people of the continual abundance we have come to expect as a matter of course.

—Graham Purcell

CHOICE BOSWELL RANDELL

Born on January 1, 1857, near Spring Place, Georgia. Nephew of Lucius Jeremiah Gartrell (1821–91) who was a U.S. representative from Georgia in the 1850s. Received public and private education. Attended North Georgia Agricultural College, but did not graduate and instead studied law, and was admitted to the Georgia state bar in 1878. Moved to Denison, Texas and married Anna Marschalk in 1879, and they had one son, Andrew. Served as Denison City Attorney from 1881 until 1882 and Grayson County Attorney from 1882 until 1888. Presbyterian, Mason, Odd Fellow, Knight of Pythias, Red Man, Woodman, and Democrat. Elected U.S. representative, 5th District, in 1900 by defeating Republican J. W. Thomas and Populist S. J. Hampton. Succeeded Joseph W. Bailey on March 4, 1901. Following some redistricting, Randell ran for the 4th District seat and was succeeded by Jack Beall in the 5th District. Elected U.S. representative, 4th District, in 1902 by defeating Republican C. A.

Choice B. Randell

Gray. Succeeded John L. Sheppard. Reelected in 1904 by defeating Republican R. E. Martin, in 1906 by defeating Republican W. C. McGinnis, in 1908 by defeating Republican R. H. Crabb and W. P. Beckley, and in 1910 by again defeating Republican C. A. Gray. Served on the House Ways and Means Committee. He did not seek reelection in 1912 and instead ran for U.S. senator in 1912, but was defeated by Morris Sheppard. Succeeded by Sam Rayburn on March 3, 1913. He was known for encouraging a study to look at dredging the Red River to make it navigable from Arkansas to Denison and wrote the Randell Anti-Graft Resolutions to keep members of Congress from receiving gifts from special interests. Died on October 14, 1945, in Sherman and was buried there at West Hill Cemetery.

SAMUEL TALIAFERRO "SAM" RAYBURN

Sam Rayburn

Born on January 6, 1882, near Kingston, Tennessee. Moved to near Windom in Fannin County, Texas, in 1887. Attended rural schools. Baptist, Mason, and Democrat. Received degree from Commerce at Mayo or East Texas Normal College (now East Texas State) in 1903. Taught school in Fanning County from 1903 to 1906. Served three terms as state representative, District 34, from 1907 until 1913. While in Austin, Rayburn studied law at the University of Texas and was admitted to the state bar in 1908. He served as Speaker of the Texas House in his last session in the legislature from 1911 until 1913. Elected U.S. representative, 4th District, in 1912 by defeating Republican C. E. Obenchain and Socialist candidate G. J. Barlow. Succeeded Choice B. Randell on March 4, 1913. Reelected in 1914 by defeating now Republican C. E. Obenchain and S. H. Dodson, in 1916 defeated Republican G. J. Barlow and Socialist W. J. Lennon, in 1918 ran unopposed, in 1920 defeated Republican A. W. Acheson, in 1922 and 1924 defeated Republican C. A. Gray, in 1926 defeated Republican Henry C. Barlow, in 1928, 1930, 1932, and 1934 defeated Republican Floyd Harry, in 1936 and 1938 defeated Republican Ross E. Johnson, in 1940, 1942, and 1944 ran unopposed, in 1946 defeated old foe Republican Floyd Harry, and in 1948, 1950, 1952, 1954, 1956, 1958, and 1960 ran unopposed for reelection. In 1917 he sponsored the War Risk Insurance Act. Was married for less than three months to Metze Jones—the young sister of his fellow congressman Marvin Jones—in late 1927. The breakup did not effect the friendship between Jones and Rayburn. They remained the best of friends. Served on the House Interstate and Foreign Commerce Committee which he chaired from 1931 to 1937. Served as majority leader from 1937 until 1939. Became Speaker of the House on September 16, 1940, to fill the seat of the late William Bankhead. Served as Speaker 1940–47, 1949–1953, and from 1955 until his death in 1961. During this time, he sponsored the "Board of Education," which included after-hours sessions in his office with fellow members of Congress. In the years when the Democrats were not in control of the House, he served as minority leader (1947–49, and 1953–55). Served as John Nance Garner's campaign manager in the 1940 race for the Democratic presidential nomination. Won the Collier's award in 1949 for distinguished service and used the award money to establish the Sam Rayburn Library, which was opened in 1957. Joined the Primitive Baptist Church in Tioga in 1956 following the death of his sister Lou. Authored the 1933 Truth in Securities Act and the Railroad Holding Company Bill. In 1934 he wrote the bill that created the Securities and Exchange Commission and the Federal Communications Commission. Co-authored the Rural Electrification Act of 1936. Chaired the Democratic national conventions in 1948, 1952, and 1956. Died on November 16, 1961, of pancreatic cancer, in Bonham and was buried there at Willow Wild Cemetery. His funeral was attended by all three living U.S. presidents: Truman, Eisenhower, and Kennedy. Rayburn was succeeded by Ray Roberts in his congressional seat in 1961. In 1977 the 65th Legislature established Sam Rayburn Day, which is celebrated every January 6. (See also photo page 29.)

> *The greatest ambition a man can have is to be a just man.*

—Sam Rayburn

JOHN HENNINGER REAGAN

John Reagan

Born on October 8, 1818, in Sevierville, Tennessee. Attended local schools. Served in the U.S. Army against the Cherokee Indians. Moved to Texas in 1839. Served as deputy surveyor of Public Lands from 1839 to 1843. Married Martha Music in 1844. A widow, she brought four children into the marriage: Sarah Marshall, William S., Henry J., and Joseph B., but Martha died just months later. Reagan studied law and farmed. Was admitted to the state bar in 1846 and became the first lawyer and, shortly thereafter, the first county judge of Henderson County. Served one term as state representative in the Second Legislature from 1847 until 1849 and was state judge from 1852 until 1857. Married Edwina Moss Nelms and moved to Palestine in 1853. They had six children including: John Edwin, Edwina, Elizabeth, and Diana Moss. Elected U.S. representative, 1st District, in 1857 by defeating American Party candidate Lemuel Dale Evans. Succeeded George W. Smyth in 1857. Reelected in 1859 by defeating Independent William B. Ochiltree. Served in this seat until 1861, when he resigned. He had seen the power of the secessionist movement, but did not agree with it. However, after Abraham Lincoln was elected, he recognized that the union would split. Served as delegate to Texas Secession Convention in 1861 and as delegate to the Confederate Provisional Congress in 1861. Served as Confederate postmaster general from 1861 until 1865. His wife Edwina died while they were in Richmond, Virginia in 1863. Reagan had no way to get her body home to Palestine. He had her embalmed and placed in a metal casket until she could be returned to Texas. The casket remained in their residence in Richmond until, through the efforts of slaves, Mrs. Reagan was returned to Texas for burial. Reagan married Molly Ford Taylor in 1865 and they would have five children: Mollie Walker, Jefferson Davis, Robert Lee, and two who died while very young (Bettie and Mills). Practiced law following the war. Served as delegate to state constitutional convention in 1875. Elected U.S. representative, 1st District, in 1874 by defeating Republican William Chambers. Succeeded William S. Herndon on March 4, 1875. Reelected in 1876 by defeating Republican L. W. Cooper, in 1878 by running unopposed, and in 1880 by defeating Greenbacker S. R. Withers. Following some redistricting, Reagan left his 1st District seat and elected U.S. representative, 2nd District, in 1882 by defeating B. F. Newman, M. H. Jackson, and Charles Stewart. The latter was most likely an incorrect vote for the man running in Reagan's old 1st District seat. Succeeded David Browning Culberson in the 2nd District seat in 1883. Reelected in 1884 by defeating Republican A. T. Monroe and in 1886 by defeating Opposition candidate John Collins. Served on the House Commerce Committee which he eventually chaired. Did not run for reelection to Congress in 1886, and was succeeded by William Harrison Martin in the 2nd District seat on March 3, 1887. Elected U.S. senator and took office on March 4, 1887. Followed Samuel B. Maxey in the Rusk succession of U.S. Senators from Texas. Served until June 10, 1891 and was succeeded by Horace Chilton. Appointed to the newly formed Railroad Commission in 1891 by Governor Hogg and served as its chair until 1903. Ran as a candidate for governor in 1894, but was defeated in the primary by Charles Culberson. Died on March 6, 1905, of pneumonia in Palestine and was buried there at East Hill Cemetery. Reagan County was named in his honor. (See also photo page 14.)

If this great Republic could be administered on the principles upon which it was founded by the fathers, it might continue to be an asylum for the most prosperous, the most enlightened, and for the freest, the happiest people on earth.

—John H. Reagan

KENNETH MILLS REGAN

Born on March 6, 1893, in Mount Morris, Illinois. Attended public schools and Vincinnes University.

Served as a signal corps aviator in World War I. Attended dental school briefly, but moved to Texas in 1920 to drill for oil. Married Roberta McGary in 1940. Democrat. Served as alderman and later mayor of Pecos from 1929 to 1932. Served two terms as state senator, District 29, from 1933 to 1937. Served two days as governor. Served as an intelligence officer in U.S. Army Air Corps during World War II. Returned to Midland after the war and worked in the oil business. Elected U.S. representative, 16th District, in 1947 special election by defeating L. J. Sulak, J. C. Trahan, George W. Hill, V. M. Stokes, Morris Schrieber, Ben H. Farber, Robert H. Abell, and George P. Barron to fill the seat of R. Ewing Thomason who had resigned. Regan took office on August 23, 1947. Served on the House Mines and Mining Committee. Reelected to his first full term in 1948 by defeating Progressive J. B. Chavez. Ran unopposed for reelection in 1950 and 1952. Unseated in Democratic primary election by J. T. Rutherford and was succeeded by him on

Ken Regan

January 3, 1955. Lobbied for the railroad industry in Washington in early 1959 and moved to Sante Fe, New Mexico, shortly before his death. Died on August 15, 1959, in Sante Fe and was buried at Resthaven Memorial Park in Midland.

> *When a fellow goes fishing, he comes home with a little string of fish to show off. It makes him feel very good to see what he's accomplished. Well, when I drive by Red Bluff Dam, I know it wouldn't have been there if I hadn't helped put it there. In a few years, no one will remember that I had anything to do with it, but I will. And that's my string of fish.*
>
> — Ken Regan, on why someone runs for Congress

SYLVESTRE "SILVER" REYES

Born on November 10, 1944, in Canutillo. Graduated from Canutillo High School in 1964. Received Associates Degree from El Paso Community College in 1976 and attended the University of Texas from 1964 until 1965 and Texas Western College in El Paso from 1965 to 1966. Served in U.S. Army, from 1966 to 1968, in Vietnam. Married Carolina Gaytan in 1968 and they had three children: Monica, Rebecca, and Silvestre, Jr. Democrat. Served with the Immigration and Naturalization Service and U.S. Border Patrol until retiring in 1995. Elected U.S. representative, 16th District, in 1996 by defeating Republican Rick Ledesma and Natural Law Party candidate Carl Proffer. Succeeded Ron Coleman on January 3, 1997. Reelected in 1998 by defeating Libertarian Stu Nance and Independent Lorenzo Morales and in 2000 by defeating Libertarian Dan Moser and Republican Daniel S. Power, in 2002 was unopposed, and in 2004 by defeating Republican David Brigham and Libertarian Brad Clardy, and in 2006 by defeating Libertarian Gordon R. Strickland. Serves on the House Committees on Armed Services and Intelligence.

Silver Reyes

HERBERT RAY ROBERTS

Born on March 28, 1913, near McKinney. Attended public schools and graduated from McKinney High School. Attended Texas A&M University, North Texas State University, and the University of Texas. Methodist and Democrat. Employed Lyndon Johnson in the National Youth Administration (NYA), beginning in 1935. Aide to Congressman Sam Rayburn from 1941 to 1942. Served in the U.S. Navy during World War II and was recalled during the Korean War. Served in the U.S. Naval Reserves until he retired at the rank of captain. Married Mary Juanita Duggan in 1938. They were divorced about 1945 and had no children. She was later Lyndon Johnson's secretary. Roberts married Elizabeth Ann Bush in 1945. It was her second marriage as well, and she brought a daughter, Kay Kelly, into the union. Businessman and farmer. Served four terms as state senator, District 9, from 1955 to 1961. Served as governor for a day on May 1, 1961. Elected U.S. representative, 4th District, in the December 1961 special election by defeating Democrats R. C. Slagle, David Brown, Jack Finney, and Roy Baker and Republican Conner Harrington to fill the seat of the late Sam Rayburn. However, Roberts and Slagle were forced into a special election runoff in January 1962. Took office on January 30, 1962. Served on the House Veterans Affairs Committee, which he chaired from 1975 to 1980, and the Public Works Committee. Elected to a full term later in 1962 by defeating Republican Conner Harrington, reelected in 1964 by defeating Fred Banfield, in 1966, 1968, and 1970 ran unopposed, in 1972 defeated James Russell, in 1974 defeated Dick LeTourneau, and in 1976 and 1978

Ray Roberts

defeated Frank S. Glenn. As any Texan is, Roberts was very interested in water, water rights, and water supplies. He wrote the 1977 Clean Water Act. Did not seek reelection in 1980 and was succeeded by Ralph M. Hall on January 3, 1981. Divorced from his second wife, Elizabeth, in 1980. Retired to Denton. Married Jean Massey in the 1980s. Died on April 13, 1992, and was buried at Roselawn Memorial Park in Denton. One of the lakes near Denton was renamed in his honor in 1980.

ORAN MILO ROBERTS

Born on July 9, 1815, in Laurens District, South Carolina, but moved to and grew up in Alabama. Graduated from the University of Alabama in 1832. Admitted to the Alabama state bar in 1837. Married Francis Edwards in 1837 and they had seven children: Peter, Oba Edwards, Maggie (Spain), Fannie (Jones), Robert Pinckney, Oran Milo, and an infant that died very young. Served as an Alabama state representative during the 1830s. Moved to San Augustine, Texas, in 1841. Took and passed the Texas bar the same year. His bar examiner was future governor J. Pinckney Henderson, who would soon appoint him to a post. Appointed by President Houston as district attorney in 1844. Appointed by Governor Henderson as district judge and served from 1846 to 1851. Served on the Texas Supreme Court from 1857 to 1866. Presided over the 1861 Secession Convention. Served briefly in the Confederate States Army. Appointed chief justice of State Supreme Court in 1864, and returned from the military to assume these duties, and served until he was removed by the military government on June 30, 1866. Served as a delegate to the state Constitutional Convention in 1866. Selected by the legislature for the U.S. senator post in the Rusk succession beginning on August 21, 1866. He had defeated Union Republican Benjamin H. Epperson. Roberts had reservations about the job because of his close work on the secession effort. Roberts reported with the other new members of Congress on the first day of the session on December 3 but was refused his seat. His papers informed senate leaders that he was present to serve the remainder of Louis T. Wigfall's term, which ran through March 30, 1869. He was never seated as a U.S. Senator. He returned to Gilmer to open a law school, but the school soon failed. Roberts returned to Tyler to reopen his legal practice. He was reappointed to the Supreme Court in 1874 and then elected to the position in 1878. Elected as governor and served from January 21, 1879, to January 16, 1883. During his time as governor, the University of Texas was founded and the contract for the capitol building was signed. Roberts served as a law professor from 1883 until 1893 at the new university and was nicknamed "Old Alcalde." Prior to this he had been nicknamed "Old Gray," as his hair had turned gray by the time he was thirty. His first wife, Francis, died in 1883, and he was

Oran M. Roberts

married Catherine E. Border in 1887. Moved to Marble Falls in 1893, but returned to Austin in 1895. He was key in forming the Texas State Historical Association, and he served as the organization's first president. Died on May 19, 1898, at home in Austin and was buried there at Oakwood Cemetery. Wrote *The Elements of Texas Pleading* (1890), "The Political, Legislative, and Judicial History of Texas for its Fifty Years of Statehood, 1845–1895" in the *Comprehensive History of Texas, 1685 to 1897* (1898), and the Texas sections in *Confederate Military History* by C. A. Evans (1899).

CIRO DAVIS RODRIGUEZ

Ciro Rodriguez

Born on December 9, 1946, in Piedras Negras, Mexico. Attended San Antonio College. Received B.A. in political science at St. Mary's University and M.A. from Our Lady of the Lake University. Democrat. Teacher at the Worden School of Social Work from 1987 to 1996. Married Carolina Pena and they had one daughter, Xochil Daria. Served as a board member of the Harlandale School District from 1975 to 1987. Served five terms as state representative, District 118, from 1987 to 1997. Elected U.S. representative, 28th District, in an April 1997 special election by defeating Democrats Juan F. Solis, III, Carlos I. Uresti, Lauro A. Bustamante, John A. "Drew" Traeger, Phil Ross, Mike G. Pacheco, Patrick A. Mason, and Michael Idrogo, and Republicans Mark Cude, John P. Kelly, Narciso V. Mendoza, Oliver Lowell Blair, Jose Julian De La Rocha, Independent Robert Cantu, and five write-in candidates to fill the seat of the late Frank Tejeda. Rodriguez won an April 12 runoff with Juan Solis. Sworn in on April 17, 1997. Reelected in 1998 by defeating Libertarian Dr. Ned Elmer and in 2000 by defeating Libertarian William A. "Bill" Stallknecht, and in 2002 by defeating Republican Gabriel Perales, Jr., and Libertarian William A. "Bill" Stallknecht. Served on the House National Security and Veterans Affairs Committees. Unseated in the 2004 Democratic Primary Election by Henry Cuellar and succeeded by him the following January. Ran unsuccessfully in the 2006 Democratic primary trying to regain his seat, but was unsuccessful against incumbent Henry Cuellar and Victor Morales. However, on June 28, 2006, the United States Supreme Court ruled that the Texas Legislature had violated the rights of Hispanic voters when it moved most of Laredo out of the neighboring 23rd District and replaced it with several heavily Republican San Antonio suburbs. It also ruled that the 25th District was not compact enough to be a replacement. The 25th District was nicknamed "the fajita strip" because of its shape. The ruling forced the redrawing of five districts between El Paso and San Antonio including the 23rd and a special election to select their representatives. This election was concurrent with the November general election. In this Special Election, Rodriguez ran with six others against incumbent Republican Henry Bonilla for the 23rd District seat. The race did not produce a clear winner and Bonilla and Rodriguez were forced into a runoff election on December 12, 2006. Rodriguez upset incumbent Bonilla in the election and succeeded him in Congress the following January. Serves on the House Appropriations Committee.

WALTER EDWARD ROGERS

Born on July 19, 1908 in Texarkana. Attended public schools in McKinney. Attended Austin College in 1926 and the University of Texas until 1935. Admitted to the state bar in 1935 and began his legal practice in Pampa. Married Catherine Regina Daly in 1936 and they had six children: John Edward, Walter Edward, Jr., Susan Daly (Healey), Thomas Kelly, Robert Joseph, and Mary Catherine (Cutter). Democrat. Served as Pampa City Attorney from 1938 until 1940 and District Attorney, 31st Judicial District, from 1943 until 1947. Ran unsuccessfully for the 1950 special election to fill the seat of Eugene Worley and was defeated by Republican Ben Guill as the large field of Democrats spread the vote so thin, none could keep the Republican from office. Elected U.S. Representative, 18th District, in 1950 by unseating incumbent Republican Ben Guill. Rogers had run four times for this post: in the May 1950 special election, the July 1950 Democratic primary, the August 1950 Democratic primary runoff, and the November 1950 general election. Took office on January 3, 1951. Reelected in 1952 by running unopposed, in 1954 by defeating Republican Leroy LeMaster, in 1956, 1958, and 1960 by running unopposed, in 1962 by defeating Republican Jack Seale, and in 1964 by defeating Republican Robert Price. Served on the House Interior and Insular Affairs and Interstate and Foreign Commerce Committees. Did not seek re-election in 1966 and was succeeded by Republican Bob Price on January 3, 1967. Returned to his law practice. Delegate to the Democratic National Conventions in 1952, 1956, 1960, and 1964. Served as the President of the Independent Natural Gas Association of America from 1969 until 1978. Retired to Florida. Died on May 31, 2001, in Naples, Florida.

Walter Rogers

THOMAS JEFFERSON RUSK

Born on December 5, 1803, in Pendleton District, South Carolina. Admitted to bar and began legal practice in 1825 in Georgia. Married Mary F. "Polly" Cleveland in 1827 and they had seven children: Thomas Jefferson, Jr., who died in infancy, Benjamin Livingston, John Cleveland, Cicero, Thomas David, Helena Argin, and another child who died in infancy. Moved to Texas in 1834 to pursue persons he had invested money with who had absconded with the investment. Appointed on December 10, 1835, along with James W. Fannin, as purchasing agent for the Texas army. Served as inspector general for the fledgling army from December 14 through February 26, 1836. Served as delegate from Nacogdoches to Texas Republic Constitutional Convention in 1836. Signer of the Texas Declaration of Independence in 1836. Commander-in-chief of the Republic's Army from May 4 through October 31, 1836. Served in Sam Houston's cabinet as secretary of war in 1836. Served as member of Texas Republic House of Representatives from 1837 to 1838. Ended Indian-Mexican rebellion led by Cordova in Nacogdoches

Thomas Rusk

in August 1838. Commanded regiment during the Cherokee War that led to the expulsion of the tribe from the state in 1839. Served as chief justice of Texas Republic Supreme Court from 1838 to 1840. Opened a law practice with James Pinckney Henderson in Nacogdoches and San Augustine in February 1841. Delegate from Nacogdoches to Texas state constitutional and annexation convention in 1845 and served as the convention's president. Elected by the first state legislature as the first U.S. senator from Texas in 1846. Served on and eventually chaired the Senate Post Offices and Post Roads Committee. Reelected in 1851. At the Baltimore convention in May of 1852, he was urged to allow his name to be submitted for the presidential or vice presidential nomination, but he refused. Served from February 21, 1846, until July 29, 1857. Succeeded by J. Pinckney Henderson on November 9, 1857. Rusk was reportedly offered the cabinet position of U.S. postmaster general by President Buchanan in 1857, but refused. Following his wife's death on April 23, 1856, Rusk fell into a deep depression. He died by his own hand on July 29, 1857, in Nacogdoches and was buried there at Oak Grove Cemetery. Rusk County and the town of Rusk in Cherokee County were named in his honor. He was a Mason and Democrat. In 1894, a monument was placed at his grave. It reads, "Patriot, Soldier, Statesman, Jurist ... He Lived for Texas."

I hope the day will come when an American citizen will look with a similar confidence to his Government; but, sir it pains me to say it, hitherto it has been far otherwise.

— Thomas Rusk on the loyalty of British subjects to his native country's institutions

GORDON JAMES RUSSELL

Gordon Russell

Born on December 22, 1859, in Huntsville, Alabama. Attended local schools, the Sam Bailey Institute in Griffin, and Crawford High School in Dalton. Graduated from the University of Georgia in 1877. Taught school and studied law. Admitted to the Georgia state bar in 1878. Practiced in Dalton until he moved to Van Zandt County, Texas, in 1879. Practiced law with W. B. "Buck" Wynne. Married Jennie Matthews in 1884. They were separated by her death or a divorce, and he then married Annie Ford. He had three daughters and one son, including Annie Laura, Mrs. Pline Lindsey, and Henry. Democrat. Served as Van Zandt County Judge from 1890 to 1892, as district attorney, 7th Judicial District, from 1892 to 1896, and district judge, 7th Judicial District, from 1896 to 1902. Elected U.S. Representative, 3rd District, in the November 1902 special election to fill the seat of the late Reese De Graffenreid.

There were actually two elections held this day: one to fill the balance of De Graffenreid's term for the December session of Congress, and another for a full term beginning in January 1903. Russell was unopposed in the special election and defeated Republicans L. L. Rhodes and J. W. Yates in the general election. He took office on November 4, 1902. Reelected in 1904 by defeating Republican C. T. White, in 1906 by defeating G. W. Smith and B. F. Bell, and in 1908 by defeating Republican J. A. Harper and Socialist Party candidate Reddin Andrews. Resigned from office on June 14, 1910, to accept a federal judgeship and was succeeded by Robert Lively. Served as judge, U.S. District Court, Eastern District of Texas, from 1910 until his death. Died on September 14, 1919, in Kerrville and was buried at Oakwood Cemetery in Tyler.

SAM MORRIS RUSSELL

Sam Russell

Born on August 9, 1889, near Stephenville. Attended rural schools and Tarleton College. Taught school in Erath County from 1918 until 1919. Married and was the father of two daughters: Laverna (Rummage) and Mary Louise Russell. Served in U.S. Army during World War I. Studied law and was admitted to the state bar in 1919. Practiced in Stephenville. Baptist and Democrat. Served as Erath County Attorney from 1919 to 1924, and as judge, 29th Judicial District, from 1928 to 1940. Elected U.S. representative, 17th District, in 1940 by unseating incumbent Clyde L. Garrett in the Democratic primary election, and running unopposed in the general election. Succeeded Garrett on January 3, 1941. Ran unopposed for reelection in 1942 and defeated Republican Clifton Woody in 1944. Served on the House District of Columbia, Claims, Invalid Pensions, Irrigation and Reclamation, and Elections committees. Did not seek reelection in 1946 and was succeeded by Omar Burleson on January 3, 1947. Resumed his law practice in Stephenville. Served as Democratic county chair from 1953 until 1955. Died on October 19, 1971, in Stephenville and was buried there at East Memorial Cemetery.

I believe that the matter of national unity could be settled overnight if it were possible to take some of the red blood that courses through the veins of Texans and transfuse it into some of the elements of this country that now are causing us so much concern.

—Sam Russell

J. T. "SLICK" RUTHERFORD

Born May 30, 1921, in Hot Springs, Arkansas. Attended public schools. Moved to Odessa, Texas in

1934 and attended Odessa High School. Served in the U.S. Marine Corps during World War II and transferred into the Marine Corps Reserves, where he remained until 1964. While in the marines, he was graduated from high school. Married Sara Jane Armstrong in 1948 and they had three children: Cleo Ann, Charles Lane, and Jane Ellen. Attended San Angelo College from 1946 to 1947, Sul Ross State College from 1947 to 1948, and Baylor University law school from 1948 to 1950. Democrat. Businessman. Served as the state Veterans of Foreign War (VFW) commander. Served two terms as state representative, District 88, from 1949 to 1953 and part of one session as state senator, District 29, from 1953 to September 27, 1954, when he resigned to run for Congress. Elected U.S. representative, 16th District, in 1954 by unseating incumbent Ken Regan in the Democratic primary election and by running unopposed in the November general election. Succeeded Regan on January 3, 1955.

Slick Rutherford

Served on the House Armed Services Committee. Reelected in 1956 by defeating Charles H. Gibson, ran unopposed in 1958, and in 1960 defeated Constitution Party candidate Dorothy Wyvell and Republican Ford Chapman. Unseated in the 1962 general election by Republican Ed Foreman. Succeeded by Foreman on January 3, 1963. Formed J. T. Rutherford & Associates upon leaving congress. Died in Arlington, Virginia on November 6, 2006. (See page photo 24.)

Where in the hell did you get this miss-mash?

— J. T. Rutherford (to author)

MORGAN GURLEY SANDERS

Born on July 14, 1878, near Ben Wheeler. Attended public schools and graduated from high school at Ben Wheeler in 1895. Graduated from the Alamo Institute. Taught in a public school while he studied law. Baptist, Mason, and Democrat. Married Jessie Irenie Cox in 1896 and they had one son, Gurley Holcott. Jessie died in 1898. Acquired Canton's *Free State Enterprise* newspaper in 1898. Edited the newspaper until 1901, when he was elected assistant journal clerk for the state senate. Admitted to the state bar in 1901 and shortly thereafter began a law partnership with Ben L. Cox in Austin. Served two terms as state representative, District 30, from 1903 to 1907. Married Noma Tull in 1905. Practiced law with Alex Collins until 1908 and then with W. J. Greer. Served as Van Zandt County Attorney from 1910 to 1914 and as District Attorney, 7th Judicial District, from 1915 to 1916. Practiced law with C. L. Stanford until 1920. Elected U.S. representative, 3rd District, in 1920 by defeating Republican J. A. Butler. Succeeded James

Morgan Sanders

Young on March 4, 1921. Reelected in 1922 by defeating Republican L. B. Cranford, in 1924 ran unopposed, in 1926 defeated Republican Enoch G. Fletcher, in 1928, 1930, 1932, and 1934 ran unopposed and in 1936 defeated Republican N. E. Hendrickson. Served on the House Ways and Means Committee. His second wife, Noma, died in 1932. Placed third in the Democratic primary for reelection in 1938 and failed to make the runoff and was succeeded by Lindley Beckworth on January 3, 1939. Returned to his law practice in Canton. Died on January 7, 1956, and was buried at Hillcrest Cemetery in Canton. (See page photo 29.)

MAX ALLEN SANDLIN, JR.

Born on September 29, 1952, in Texarkana, Arkansas. Graduated from Atlanta High School in Atlanta, Texas, in 1971. Received B.A. from Baylor University in 1975 and J.D. from Baylor in 1978.

Max Sandlin

Admitted to the state bar in 1978 and was board certified in family law. Baptist and Democrat. Married Leslie Howell in 1982 and they had four children: Hillary, Max, III, Emily, and Christian. Served as Harrison County Judge from 1986 to 1989 and as Harrison County court of law judge from 1989 to 1996. Partner in Sandlin and Buckner law firm from 1982 to 1996. Vice-president of Howell and Sandlin, Inc., from 1989 to 1996. President of East Texas Fuels from 1992 to 1996. Elected U.S. representative, 1st District, in 1996 by defeating Republican Ed Merritt and Natural Law Party candidate Margaret A. Palms. Succeeded Jim Chapman on January 3, 1997. Reelected in 1998 by defeating Republican Dennis Boerner and in 2000 by defeating Republican television actor Noble Willingham and Libertarian Ray Carr, and in 2002 by defeating Republican John Lawrence. Served on the House Transportation and Infrastructure and Banking and Financial Services Committees. Following extensive redistricting, Sandlin was unseated in 2004 by Republican Louie Gohmert. Joined Fleishman-Hillard Government Relations after leaving congress. Married South Dakota Congresswoman Stephanie Herseth in 2007.

WILLIAM C. "BILL" SARPALIUS

Bill Sarpalius

Born on January 10, 1948, in Los Angeles, California. His family was abandoned by their father, and from age twelve, grew up at Cal Farley's Boys Ranch. He graduated from Farley's. Presided over Texas Future Farmers of America Association from 1967 to 1968. Received an A.D. from Clarendon College in 1970, a B.S. from Texas Tech University in 1972, and an M.S. from West Texas State University in 1978. Married Donna Ritchie about 1970 and they had one son: David. Methodist and Democrat. Worked in the admissions department of Farley's Boys Ranch, near Amarillo, Texas, while in graduate school. Served as House Speaker Bill Clayton's district office Manager. Director at Center Plains Industries. Served four terms as state senator, District 31, from 1981 until 1989. Elected U.S. representative, 13th District, in 1988 by defeating Republican Larry Milner. Succeeded Beau Bolter on January 3, 1989. Served on the House Agriculture Committee. Divorced in 1988. Reelected in 1990 by defeating Republican Dick Waterfield and in 1992 by defeating Republican Beau Boulter. Unseated in 1994 by Republican William "Mac" Thornberry and was succeeded by him on January 3, 1995. Married Carol Fessler in 1994. Appointed by President Clinton to the U.S. Department of Agriculture Southwest area director and served during 1995. Remained in Washington and founded Advantage—a consulting and lobbying firm comprised of former members of Congress—where he is CEO and president.

JOSEPH DRAPER SAYERS

Born on September 23, 1841, in Grenada, Mississippi. Moved to Bastrop, Texas in 1851. Attended the Bastrop Military Institute until 1860. Democrat. Served in the Confederate States Army. Taught school, studied law, and was admitted to the state bar in 1866. Practiced law in Bastrop with George Washington Jones. Served one term as state senator, District 26, from 1873 to 1874. Chairman of State Democratic Executive Committee from 1875 to 1878. Served as lieutenant governor from 1878 to 1879. Married Orline Walton in 1879. Elected U.S. representative, 10th District, in 1884 by defeating Independent Republican J. B. Rector. Succeeded John Hancock on March 4, 1885. Reelected in 1886 by defeating Republican James P. Newcomb, in 1888 by defeating Republican Augustus Belknap, and in 1890 by defeating Republican W. G. Robinson. Following some redistricting, Sayers did not run for reelection to the 10th District seat and instead ran for the 9th District seat in 1892. Succeeded by Walter Gresham in the 10th District in 1893. Elected U.S. representative, 9th District, in 1892 by defeating Peoples and Republican Party candidate J. M. Horner, and succeeded Edwin LeRoy Antony in March 1893. Reelected in 1894 by defeating Populist W. O. Hutchison, and in 1896 by defeating Republican W. K. Makemson, Populist Reddin Andrews, and Republican J. T. Harris. Served on the House Naval Affairs and Appropriations committees. Did not seek reelection in 1898, resigned on January 16, 1899, and was succeeded in Congress by Albert S. Burleson on March 4, 1899. Served as governor from 1899 until 1903. Last Confederate soldier to serve as governor. Moved to San Antonio. Served as a University of Texas regent beginning in 1913. Served as a member and chair of the Industrial Accident Board (now the Texas Workers' Compensation Commission) from 1913 to 1915, was a member of the Board of Legal Examiners from 1922 until 1926, and served on the Board of Pardon Advisors from 1927 until his death. Died on May 15, 1929, in Austin and was buried at Fairview Cemetery in Bastrop. (See also photo page 14.)

Joseph D. Sayers

GUSTAV SCHLEICHER

Born on November 19, 1823, in Darmstadt, Hesse, Germany. Studied architecture and engineering at the University of Giessen. Employed as civil engineer building railroads in Europe. Immigrated to Texas and settled in a commune named Bettina in 1847. The communist enclave failed, and he remarked that life under that rule "would destroy the individual, intelligent, free and untrammeled production." Opened a shingle mill near New Braunfels. Moved to San Antonio in 1850 and began a bridge company. Received his U.S. citizenship in 1852. Democrat. Entrepreneur and businessman. Married Elizabeth Tinsley Howard in 1856 and they had seven children. Began publishing the *Texas Staats-Zeitung* newspaper with his brother in 1858, and co-founded the San Antonio Water Company in 1858, and co-founded Alamo College in 1860. Served one term as state representative, District 71, from 1853 until 1855, elected surveyor of the Bexar Land District, and one term as state senator, District 31, from 1859 to 1861. Many Central

Gustav Schleicher

Texas Germans were opposed to secession and the Confederacy, but Schleicher went along and eventually served in the Confederate States Army. Following the war, he and others began the Columbus, San Antonio, and Rio Grande Railroad. He also worked for the Gulf, Western Texas, and Pacific Railroad. Founded Cuero after making it a stop on the railroad and settled there himself in 1872. Elected as first U.S. representative from the newly created 6th District in 1874 by defeating Republican Jeremiah Galvan. Took office on March 4, 1875. Served on the House Indian Affairs, Railways and Canals (eventually chaired), and Foreign Affairs committees. Reelected in 1876 by defeating Republican James P. Newcomb and in 1878 by defeating Independent John Ireland. He died shortly thereafter while serving in office on January 10, 1879, in Washington, D.C., and was buried at the United States National Cemetery in San Antonio. Succeeded in Congress by Christopher Upson in 1879. Schleicher County is named in his honor.

Mr. Chairman, I have been accused of being a filibuster, of wanting to take Mexico, or part of it. Sir, I hesitate to say it, but I must say it: God forbids that this country should ever become bigger. It is far too large now for the minds and hearts of its legislators.

— Gustave Schliecher

RICHARDSON A. SCURRY

Born on November 11, 1811, in Gallatin, Tennessee. Brother of William R. Scurry (1821–64), a Confederate general and lawyer who was also active in politics at the time. Private education. Studied law and was admitted to the Tennessee state bar about 1830 and practiced in Covington. Moved to Clarksville, Texas, in 1836 and continued his law practice. Served in the Texas Army during War for Independence. Served at Battle of San Jacinto and resigned on October 4, 1836, at the rank of first lieutenant. Served as secretary of the Republic's first Senate. Appointed as district attorney, 1st Judicial District, in 1836. Served as judge, 6th Judicial District, from 1840 until 1841, when he resigned. Served as district attorney, 5th Judicial District, in the 1840s. Married Evantha Foster in 1843 and they had nine children; the four surviving were Kate, Richardson A., Jr., Tony, and Thomas. Served as Representative in Texas Republic House of Representatives from 1842 until 1844. Served as Speaker of the House in last session. Elected U.S. representative, 1st District, in 1851 by defeating William B. Ochiltree, B. R. Wallace, and N. H. Darnell. Succeeded David Kaufman on March 4, 1851. Served one term. Succeeded by George W. Smyth on March 3, 1853. Resumed law practice in Hempstead. Served as adjutant general on Albert Sidney Johnston's staff in the Confederate States Army. Accidentally shot himself in the foot while hunting in August 1854. The wound did not heal properly, and his leg was eventually amputated. He died as a result of the amputation on April 9, 1862, and was buried at Hempstead Cemetery in Hempstead.

SHELLY SEKULA-GIBBS

Born in Floresville, on June 22, 1953. Received a B.S. from Our Lady of the Lake University in 1975 and an M.D. from the University of Texas Medical Branch in 1979. Republican and Catholic. Married to Allen Greenberg and they had two children. Physician and Assistant Professor, Baylor College of Medicine in Houston. Greenberg was divorced and later drowned. Married to newscaster Sylvan Rodriquez until his death in 2000. Married Robert W. Gibbs, Jr., in June 2002. Served on Houston City Council from 2002 through 2006. Elected, U.S. Representative, 22nd District, in special election to fill the vacancy caused by the resignation of Tom DeLay. This election was to fill the seat for the unexpired term of Delay. She defeated Republicans Don Richardson, Steve Stockman, and Giannibicego Hoa Tran, and Libertarian M. Bob Smither. Served from November 13, 2006, until January 3, 2007. She was an unsuccessful write-in candidate for the 110th Congress in 2006. Succeeded by Nick Lampson.

Shelly Sekula-Gibbs

PETE ANDERSON SESSIONS

Born on March 22, 1955, in Dallas. Graduated from Churchill High School in San Antonio in 1973. Graduated from Southwestern University in 1978. Republican. Married Nita Sessions in 1984 and they had two children: Bill and Alex. Employed with Southwestern Bell and Bell Communications Research from 1978 to 1994. Vice-president for public policy at National Center for Policy Analysis from 1994 to 1995. Elected U.S. representative, 5th District, in 1996 by defeating John Pouland. The U.S. District Court redrew part of the boundary for this district, requiring Sessions to run in an open primary or special election in November 1996. This election coincided with the general election. Succeeded John Bryant on January 3, 1997. Reelected in 1998 by defeating Democrat Victor Morales and Libertarian Michael Needleman, and in 2000 by defeating Democrat Regina Montoya-Coggins and Libertarian

Pete Sessions

Ken Ashby. Served on the House Rules Committee. Did not seek re-election to the 5th District seat in 2002 and instead sought the newly created 32nd District. Elected U.S. Representative, 32nd District, in 2002 by defeating Democrat Pauline K. Dixon, Libertarian Steve Martin and Green Party candidate Carla Hubbell. Reelected following redistricting in 2004 by defeating Democrat Martin Frost and Libertarian Michael Needleman and in 2006 by defeating Democrat Will Pryor and, Libertarian John B. Hawley.

Too many in Washington still believe they can spend your money better than you can. I don't believe that.

—Pete Sessions

FRANKLIN BARLOW SEXTON

Franklin Sexton

Born on April 29, 1828, in New Harmony, Indiana. Moved to San Augustine, Texas with his family in 1838. Graduated from Wesleyan College in 1846. Worked in a print shop and studied law with Oran Roberts and James Henderson. These important friends ensured him a place in history, as they passed legislation allowing him to be admitted to the state bar before he was twenty-one. Episcopalian, Mason, and Democrat. Practiced law in San Augustine. Married Eliza Scott Richardson in 1852 and they had twelve children, but only four survived. One of those was Mamie. Elected state senator, District 15, in 1859 but had already joined the Confederate States Army and never took his seat. Presided over the state Democratic convention in April 1860. Elected representative, 4th District, to Confederate Congress, in November 1861 by defeating J. L. Hogg, J. N. Maxey, T. J. Wood, A. W. O. Hicks, and W. R. Poag. Served initially in the Confederate House Commerce, War Tax, Quartermaster's & Commissary Departments, and Military Transportation committees. In later sessions, he served on the Ways and Means, Post Office and Post Roads Committees. Reelected in 1863 by defeating James Anderson and served until 1865. Returned to San Augustine following the war. Moved to Marshall in 1872. Delegate to Democratic national convention in 1876. His wife Eliza died in May 1894, and he moved to El Paso to be near a daughter. Appointed and served on the State Supreme Court and as a U.S. Commissioner. Died on May 15, 1900, in El Paso and was buried in Mason.

JOHN LEVI SHEPPARD

John Levi Sheppard

Born on April 13, 1852, in Bluffton, Alabama. Moved to near Wheatville, Texas in 1858 with his family following his father's death. Attended local schools. Married Margaret Alice Eddins in 1873 and they had seven children, one of whom was John Morris Sheppard (1875–1941), a U.S. congressman and senator from Texas. Worked in a general store, studied law, and was admitted to the state bar in 1879. Practiced law in Daingerfield. Democrat. Served as district attorney, 5th Judicial District, from 1882 to 1888 and district judge from 1888 to 1896. Delegate to the Bimetallic Convention in 1893 and the Democratic national convention in 1896. Elected U.S. Representative, 4th District, in 1898 by defeating Populist J. L. Whittle. Succeeded John W. Cranford on March 4, 1899. Reelected in 1900 by defeating Republican J. C. Gibbons and Populist J. L. Darwin. Suffered from Bright's disease, a kidney ailment. Died while in office on October 11, 1902, in Eureka Springs, Arkansas, and was buried at Rose Hill Cemetery in Texarkana. His death occurred just before the 1902 general election. Redistricting had turned the 4th District seat into the 1st District, and John Sheppard was succeeded by his son Morris in a 1902 special election. Great-grandfather of Connie Mack (1940–) a U.S. representative and senator from Florida.

JOHN MORRIS SHEPPARD

Morris Sheppard

Born on May 28, 1875, in Pittsburg, Texas. Son of John Levi Sheppard (1852–1902), a U.S. congressman from Texas and grandfather of Connie Mack (1940–) U.S. representative and senator from Florida. Attended public and private schools of Daingerfield, Pittsburg, Cumby, Austin, and Linden. Received B.A. from the University of Texas in 1895 and law degree there in 1897, and master of laws from Yale University in 1898. Methodist, Woodman, and Democrat. Admitted to the state bar and began practice in Pittsburg. Moved to Texarkana in 1899. Served as first president of the Texas Fraternal Congress in 1901. Elected U.S. representative, 1st District, in the November 4, 1902, general election by defeating Republican John Hurley. Eleven days later, he won the special election to fill the remainder of his late father's 4th District congressional seat by defeating Republican Frank Lee. This special election was called to fill the late Morris' seat for the December session of Congress, and to further complicate this matter, redistricting had turned his father's old 4th District seat into the 1st District. The younger Sheppard took office on November 15, 1902, and began his first full term in January 1903. Reelected in 1904 by defeating Republican J. A. Armistead, in 1906 by defeating Republican Phil E. Baer, in 1908 by defeating Republican H. L. McQuiston, and in 1910 by defeating Republican Velmar Antle. Served on the House Committee on Public Buildings and Ground, which he eventually chaired. Married Lucile Sanderson in 1909 and they had three daughters: Janet (Arnold), Mrs. Cornelius McGillicuddy (also known as Connie Mack Jr.), and Lucille (Keyes). Did not run for reelection in 1912 and instead ran for U.S. senator. Was succeeded in Congress by Horace Vaughn in 1913. Elected U.S. senator by the legislature on January 29, 1913, in a very unique election. Governor Colquitt had appointed newspaper editor Rienzi Johnston of Houston to the remainder of Joseph W. Bailey's seat in the U.S. Senate. The legislature did not approve of Johnston, as he was a "wet" during the early stages of the groundswell for the prohibition movement. Sheppard had already won the November 1912 general election without opposition a few months earlier for the seat whose term would begin in March 1913. Sheppard and the legislature began a movement to encourage Johnston to resign. Johnston did resign his Senate seat on February 2, 1913, after only twenty-eight days in office. Sheppard took office on February 3, 1913, which gave him about one month's seniority over every other new U.S. senator scheduled to take office in March. Thus began Morris Sheppard's twenty-eight-year career in the U.S. Senate in the Houston succession of senators from Texas. Reelected in 1918 by defeating Republican J. W. Flanagan, in 1924 by defeating Fred W. Davis and John F. Maddox in the Democratic primary and Republican T. M. Kennerly in the general election, in 1930 by defeating Robert L. Henry and C. A. Mitchner in the primary and Republican Doran John Haesly in the general election, and in 1936 by defeating Joe H. Eagle and Guy B. Fisher in the primary and Republican Carlos G. Watson in the general election. Wrote *Fraternal and Other Addresses* (1914). As an ardent prohibitionist, he introduced legislation to ban the sale of alcohol in 1913 and 1914. In 1917 he made some progress toward prohibition by passing a law banning the sale of alcohol in the District of Columbia. Later in the year, his efforts on behalf of prohibition succeeded, and within two years, the Eighteenth Amendment to the U.S. Constitution was ratified by the required number of states. It became effective in 1920, and Sheppard thus became the father of prohibition in America. Co-sponsored the Sheppard-Towner Act of 1921 which provided health care for expectant mothers. Served as Democratic whip in the Senate beginning in 1929. Wrote Federal Credit Union Act. Supporter of the New Deal but disliked the repeal of Prohibition and the packing of the Supreme Court. Served as Chairman of the Senate Military Affairs and Census committees. Died while serving in office on April 9, 1941, of a brain hemorrhage and was buried at Hillcrest Cemetery in Texarkana. He was succeeded on April 21, 1941, by Andrew Jackson Houston who was appointed by Governor O'Daniel. Sheppard's widow eventually married an old friend and the other sitting senator from Texas at the time, Tom Connally. The U.S. Army airfield in Wichita Falls was named in his honor in 1941, and a Liberty transport ship, the *SS Sheppard*, was named in his honor in 1944.

> *The liquor traffic is a peril to society, because it undermines the health, the strength, and the integrity of man. It is a menace to the Republic, because a race of weaklings can not sustain or comprehend the institutions of liberty. It is a source of danger to posterity, because the alcoholic taint foredooms the unborn millions to degeneracy and to disease. I shall oppose this scourge from hell until my arm can strike no longer and my tongue can speak no more.*

—Morris Sheppard

JAMES LUTHER SLAYDEN

Born on June 1, 1853, in Mayfield, Kentucky. Moved to New Orleans in 1869 following the death of his father. Attended local schools. Attended Washington and Lee University during the early 1870s, but returned home. Moved to San Antonio, texas in 1876. Cotton merchant and rancher. Episcopalian, Mason, Elk, Odd Fellow, and Democrat. Married Ellen Maury in 1883 and they had no children. Served one term as state representative, District 89, from 1893 to 1895. Elected U.S. representative, 12th District, in 1896 by defeating incumbent Republican G. H. Noonan and Populist Taylor McRae. Succeeded Noonan on March 4, 1897. Reelected in 1898 by defeating G. H. Noonan and A. B. Surber and in 1900 by defeating Republican C. C. Drake, Social Democrat E. G. Cloar, and Socialist Labor candidate Frank J. Leitner. Did not run again for the 12th District seat and was succeeded there by Oscar Gillespie in 1903. A new district was created, and Slayden was elected as the first U.S. representative from the 14th District in 1902 by defeating Republican D. H. Meek and A. B. Surber. Reelected in 1904 by defeating Republican Alfred Vanderstucken, in 1906 by defeating Republican D. Doole, in 1908 by defeating Republican W. W. Buchanan and Socialist J. E. Elgin, in 1910 by defeating Socialist candidate J. M. Prier and Republican A. L. Horne, in 1912 by defeating Republican Julius Real and A. D. Zucht, in 1914 by defeating Socialist John A. Currie and Republican B. F. Kingsley, and in 1916 by defeating Republican D. F. Johnson. Served on the House Military Affairs Committee. Served as an envoy to the Mexican Centennial Celebration in September 1910. Trustee for the Carnegie Endowment for Peace and president of the American Peace Society. Did not seek reelection in 1918 and was succeeded by Carlos Bee on March 3, 1919. Retired to manage his orchard in Virginia, ranch in Texas, and mine in Mexico. Died on February 24, 1924, in San Antonio and was buried there at Mission Park Cemetery. His wife Ellen's journal was published in 1963 by her nephew's widow under the title Washington Wife: Journal of Ellen Maury Slayden from 1897-1919.

> *The Spanish-American War was not a great war. A large number of our troops took the hazard of watermelons in Georgia and Florida, and fought the malaria and mosquitoes, but very few Spanish. The Spanish-American War yielded comparatively little in heroics, [but] paid the most marvelous dividends in politics and in magazine articles of any war in the history of the country.*

—James L. Slayden

LAMAR SEELIGSON SMITH

Born on November 19, 1947, in San Antonio. Graduated from Texas Military Institute in San Antonio in 1965. Received B.A. from Yale University in 1969. Republican, lawyer, and Christian Scientist.. Management intern with Small Business Administration from 1969 to 1970. Business and financial writer for the *Christian Science Monitor* from 1970 to 1972. Received J.D. from Southern Methodist University School of Law in 1975 and was admitted to the state bar the same year. Practiced with Maebius and Duncan in San Antonio. Elected chair of Republican Party of Bexar County in 1978 and 1980. Elected state representative, District 57-F, in a November 1981 special election to fill the seat of Jim Nowlin, who

Lamar Smith

had resigned to accept a federal judgeship. Served from 1981 to 1982. Elected Bexar County Commissioner, Precinct 3, and served from 1982 to 1987. Partner in Lamar Seeligson Ranch in Jim Wells County. Elected U.S. representative, 21st District, in 1986 by defeating Democrat Pete Snelson and Libertarian James A. Robinson. Succeeded Tom Loeffler on January 3, 1987. Reelected in 1988 by defeating Libertarian James A. Robinson and in 1990 by defeating Democrat Kirby J. Roberts. Married Beth Schaefer in 1992 and they had two children: Nell Seeligson and Tobin Wells. Reelected in 1992 by defeating Democrat James D. Gaddy and Libertarian William E. Grisham, in 1994 by defeating Independent Kerry L. Lowry, in 1996 by defeating Democrat Gordon H. Wharton and Natural Law Party candidate Randy Rutenbeck, in 1998 by defeating Libertarian Jeffrey Blunt and Independent Gary Thurman, and in 2000 by defeating Democrat Jim Green and Libertarian C. W. "Jinx" Steinbrecher, in 2002 by defeating Democrat John Courage and Libertarian D. G. Roberts and in 2004 by defeating Democrat Rhett Smith and Libertarian Jason Pratt. On June 28, 2006, the United States Supreme Court ruled that the Texas Legislature had violated the rights of Hispanic voters when it moved most of Laredo out of the neighboring 23rd District and replaced it with several heavily Republican San Antonio suburbs. It also ruled that the 25th District was not compact enough to be a replacement. The 25th District was nicknamed "the fajita strip" because of its shape. The ruling forced the redrawing of five districts between El Paso and San Antonio including the 21st and a special election to select their representatives. This election was concurrent with the November general election. In 2006, Smith was reelected by defeating Independents Tommy Calvert, James Lyle Peterson, and Mark J. Rossano, Democrats John Courage and Gene Kelly, and Libertarian James Arthur Strohm. Serves on the House Budget and Judiciary committees. Smith's grandfather, Lamar Seeligson, ran unsuccessfully against Maury Maverick in the 1936 Democratic primary.

WILLIAM ROBERT SMITH

Born on August 18, 1863, near Tyler. Attended public schools. Graduated from Sam Houston Normal Institute in 1883. Studied law and was admitted to the state bar in 1885. Practiced in Tyler. Democrat. Moved to Colorado City in 1888. Married Francis Lipscomb Breedlove in 1890 and they had five children: Breedlove, Myron, Dorothy, Francis, and William Robert, Jr. Appointed judge, 32nd Judicial District, and served from 1897 until he resigned in 1903. Elected as the first U.S. representative from the newly created 16th District in 1902 by defeating Republican D. G. Hunt and D. H. Meeks. Took office on March 4, 1903. Reelected in 1904 by defeating Republican Logan McPherson, in 1906 by defeating Ben Vantuys and Socialist J. M. Ellis, in 1908 by defeating G. W. Boynton and Socialist candidate P. G. Zimmerman, in 1910 by defeating Socialist W. H. Harvey and Republican Robert A. Webb, and in 1912 and 1914 by running unopposed. Served on the House Elections, Interstate and Foreign Commerce, and Irrigation of Arid Lands committees. He eventually chaired the latter. Unseated by Thomas Blanton in the 1916 Democratic primary and was succeeded by him on March 3, 1917. Moved to El Paso. Appointed by President Wilson as U.S. District Court judge, Western District, and served from 1917 until his death. Died on August 16, 1924, in El Paso and was buried there at Evergreen Cemetery.

W. R. Smith

I sometimes walk past the White House, but have not done much sight seeing. Am ready to go home if I only could.

—W. R. Smith, in January 1905
letter to his wife

GEORGE WASHINGTON SMYTH, SR.

Born on May 16, 1803, in North Carolina. Lived in both Alabama and Tennessee. Worked in a dry-goods store in Fayetteville, Tennessee, from 1815 until 1818. Moved to join his father's family in Alabama in 1818. Removed to Maury County, Tennessee, about 1820. Moved to Bevil, Texas—where the present town of Jasper stands—in 1830. Worked as a surveyor. Graduated from Princeton College in 1831. Appointed surveyor by the Mexican government and was eventually made commissioner of titles and issued land grants to colonists. Married Frances M. Grigsby in 1834 and they had seven children, including George, Jr. Democrat. Signer of Texas Declaration of Independence in 1836. Served as delegate to Texas Republic constitutional convention in 1836. Appointed by Mirabeau B. Lamar to the boundary commission to set the U.S.-Texas border in 1839. Served as representative to Texas Republic House from 1844 to 1845 and as delegate to the state constitutional conventions in 1845 and 1866. Served as the second com-

George Washington Smyth

missioner of the General Land Office and from 1848 to 1852. Presidential elector for Franklin Piece in 1852. Elected U.S. representative, 1st District, in 1853 by defeating C. L. Mills and Benjamin H. Epperson. Succeeded Richardson Scurry on March 4, 1853. Did not run for reelection in 1855 and was succeeded by Lemuel Evans on March 3, 1855. Opposed to secession, but served in the Confederate States Army. Served as delegate to Constitutional Convention of 1866. Died while at state constitutional convention in Austin on February 21, 1866, and was buried there at the State Cemetery.

CHARLES LACY SOUTH

Born on July 22, 1892, near Damascus, Virginia. Moved with his parents to Callahan County, Texas, in 1898. Moved to Coleman in 1914. Attended local schools and Simmons University in Abilene from 1915 to 1916. Methodist, Mason, Lion, and Democrat. Married Etta Wireman and they had two sons: Carl and Robert. Taught school in Coleman County from 1914 to 1920 and served as Coleman County school superintendent from 1921 to 1925. Appointed by Annie Webb Blanton, then the state superintendent of public instruction, as a member of the State Board of Examination in 1919. Studied law and was admitted to the state bar in 1925. Served as Coleman County Judge from 1925 to 1931 and as district attorney, 35th Judicial District, from 1930 to 1934. Elected as the first U.S. representative to the newly created 21st District in 1934 by running unopposed. Took office on January 3, 1935. Reelected in 1936 and 1938 by defeating Republican Max J. Bierschwale and in 1940 by defeating Republican Ray Ridenhower. Unseated by O. C. Fisher in the 1942

Charles South

Democratic primary and was succeeded by him on January 3, 1943. Returned to Coleman to practice law. Served one term as state representative, District 125, from 1947 to 1949. Moved to Austin permanently in 1948. Died on December 20, 1965, in Austin and was buried at Coleman Cemetery in Coleman.

> *A public office is a public trust. If a public official will take care of the public, and the public interests, honestly and fairly, the public will take care of such official.*
>
> —Charles L. South

ALAN WATSON STEELMAN

Born on March 15, 1942, in Little Rock, Arkansas. Graduated from Arkadelphia High School in 1960 and moved to Texas to attend college. Married Carolyn Findley in 1962. They had five children: Robin Whitehead, Kim Cuban, Allison Carter, Alan, Jr. and Alex. Later divorced and married Susan Seligman Fuller. Step-father to Daniel and Elizabeth Fuller. Received B.A. from Baylor University in 1964 and M.L.A. from Southern Methodist University in 1971. Baptist and Republican. Served as executive director of the President's Advisory Council on Minority Business Enterprise from 1969 to 1972. Elected U.S. representative, 5th District, in 1972 by unseating incumbent Democrat Earle Cabell. Succeeded Cabell on January 3, 1973. Reelected in 1974 by defeating Democrat Mike McKool. Served two terms. Did not seek reelection in 1976 and was succeeded by Jim Mattox on January 3, 1977. Won the 1976 Republican nomination for U.S. senator, but was defeated by Lloyd Bentsen in the general election. Now a businessman, he lives in Dallas and is a senior principal with an international consulting firm.

Alan Steelman

We must . . . liberate our system from the big, impersonal special interests which dominate the high councils of government.

—Alan Steelman

CHARLES WALTER "CHARLIE" STENHOLM

Born on October 26, 1938, in Stamford. Attended public schools and graduated from Stamford High School in 1957. Attended Tarleton State Junior College in 1959. Received B.S. from Texas Tech University in 1961 and an M.S. from Texas Tech in 1962. Married Cynthia "Cindy" Ann Watson about 1966 and they had three children: Chris, Cary, and Courtney Ann. Lutheran and a boll weevil, now a blue dog, which is also known as a southern conservative Democrat. Former high school teacher. Farmer, executive director of the Rolling Plains Cotton Growers Association, and manager for the Stamford Electric Cooperative. Elected U.S. representative, 17th District, in 1978 by defeating Republican Billy Lee Fisher. Succeeded Omar Burleson on January 3, 1979. Served on the House Agriculture, Small Business, Veterans Affairs, and Budget committees. Reelected in 1980 without opposition, in 1982 by defeating Libertarian James A. Cooley, II, in 1984, 1986, 1988, and 1990 by running unopposed, in 1992 by defeating Republican Jeannie Sadowski, in

Charlie Stenholm

1994 by defeating Phil Boone, in 1996 by defeating Republican Rudy Izzard and Natural Law Party candidate Richard Caro, in 1998 by defeating Republican Rudy Izzard and Libertarian Gordon Mobley, and in 2000 by defeating Republican Darrell Clements, Reform Party candidate Pete Julia, and Libertarian Debra M. Monde, and in 2002 by defeating Republican Rob Beckham and Libertarian Fred Jones. Following extension redistricting, Stenholm ran unsuccessfully for the 19th District seat in 2004. He was succeeded by Republican Randy Neugebauer. Employed as a lobbyist after leaving congress.

In my first term in Congress everybody loved me. Some don't love me anymore. It came as quite a shock how anybody as clean and kind and good lookin' as I am wouldn't be loved.

—Charlie Stenholm

JOHN HALL STEPHENS

Born on November 22, 1847, in Shelby County. Attended public schools in Mansfield. Graduated from Mansfield College and received a law degree from Cumberland University in 1872. Admitted to the state bar in 1873 and practiced law in Montague. Presbyterian, Mason, and Democrat. Married Annie Chrisman in 1873 and they had seven children. Moved to Vernon in 1889. Served two terms as state senator, District 19, from 1889 to 1893. Continued his legal practice in Vernon. Elected U.S. representative, 13th District, in 1896 by defeating Republican H. L. Bentley. Succeeded James V. Cockrell on March 4, 1897. Reelected in 1898 by defeating Populist J. J. Eager, in 1900 by defeating Republican C. W. Johnson, in 1902 by defeating Republican R. O. Rector and Socialist Joseph Schmitt, in 1904 by defeating Republican James M. Kinred, in 1906 by defeating Republican E. E. Diggs and Socialist Joseph Schmitt, in 1908 by defeating Republican Jasper N. Haney and Socialist Party candidate W. R. Tramblade, in 1910 by defeating Republican T. S. Bugbee, Socialist John I. Green, and Prohibition candidate E. G. Cook, in 1912 by defeat-

John Stephens

ing Progressive Party candidate L. B. Lindsey and Republican H. H. Cooper, and in 1914 by defeating Republican C. T. Griffin. Served on the House Indian Affairs Committee. Unseated by John Marvin Jones in the 1916 Democratic primary and was succeeded by him on March 3, 1917. His first wife, Annie, died in 1906, and Stephens married Lizette Bristow Keenan in 1911. Moved to Monrovia, California, in 1917. Died on November 18, 1924, in Monrovia and was buried at East View Cemetery in Vernon, Texas.

CHARLES STEWART

Born on May 30, 1836, in Memphis, Tennessee. Moved to Galveston, Texas in 1845. Attended local schools. Studied law with James W. Henderson and was admitted to the state bar in 1854 a number of months before his eighteenth birthday. Moved to Marlin and practiced law. Mason and Democrat. Served as prosecuting attorney, 13th Judicial District, from 1856 to 1860. Married Rachel Barry in 1860 and they had one surviving child. Served as delegate to Texas Secession Convention in 1861. Served in the Confederate States Army. Moved to Houston in 1866 and continued his law practice with great success. Served as Houston City Attorney from 1874 to 1876. Served two terms as state senator, District 18 from 1879 to 1883. Elected U.S. representative, 1st District, in 1882 by defeating Republican William Chambers. Succeeded John H. Reagan on March 4, 1883. Reelected in 1884 by defeating Republicans John T. Brady and A. T. Monroe, in 1886 by defeating Republican H. D. Johnson, in 1888 by defeating Republican

Charles Stewart

Lock McDaniel and Independent Jack Davis, and in 1890 by defeating Republican E. L. Angler. Served on the House Rivers and Harbors Committee. Did not seek reelection in 1892, primarily because of his failing health, and was succeeded by Joseph C. Hutcheson on March 3, 1893. Returned to Houston and practiced law with his son, John. Died on September 21, 1895, in San Antonio and was buried at Glenwood Cemetery in Houston. (See also photo page 14.)

STEVEN ERNEST STOCKMAN

Born on November 14, 1956, in Bloomfield Hills, Michigan. Graduated from Dondero High School in Royal Oak, Michigan, in 1975. Moved to Madison, Wisconsin, in 1978. Moved to Fort Worth, Texas, in 1980. Received a B.S. from the University of Houston in 1990. Accountant. Married Patti Ferguson in 1988. Baptist and Republican. Sought Republican nomination for U.S. House, 9th District, in 1990 but lost primary runoff election to Maury Meyers. Won the primary in 1992, but lost to Democrat Jack Brooks in the general election. Elected U.S. representative, 9th District, in 1994 by defeating incumbent Democrat

Jack Brooks, Independent Bill Felton, and Libertarian Darla K. Beenau. Succeeded Brooks on January 3, 1995. The U.S. District Court redrew part of the boundary for Stockman's district, requiring him to run in an open primary or special election in November 1996. This election coincided with the general election. Stockman was unseated in this race by Democrat Nick Lampson after defeating him in close general election but finally losing to him in a December 1996 runoff. Succeeded by Lampson on January 3, 1997. Served as a consultant and Vice-President of Moody Bank. Unsuccessful candidate for the Republican nomination for Railroad Commission in 1998. Unsuccessful candidate for U.S. Representative, 22nd District, in 2006 to fill the seat of Tom Delay.

Steven Stockman

STERLING PRICE STRONG

Born on August 17, 1862, near Jefferson City, Missouri. Moved to Montague County, Texas, with parents in 1871. Attended rural schools. Graduated from Eastman's National Business College in New York in 1884. Democrat. Married Alice True in 1887 and they had three sons and two daughters: True, Jesse M., James W., Ruth, and Mrs. Raymond H. Newell. Served as Montague County Clerk from 1884 to 1888 and from 1896 to 1904. Elected and served as engrossing clerk for the 21st State Legislature in 1889 and as Hale County and District Clerk from 1889 to 1892. Employed as a salesman from 1892 to 1898. Served on State Democratic Executive Committee from 1900 to 1902. Moved to Dallas in 1908. Was employed as a bank cashier in Bowie from 1908 until 1911. Again worked as a traveling salesman from 1911 until 1932. Served as superintendent of the Anti-Saloon League of Texas. President of Garrison Coal and Oil Company. Unsuccessful candidate for lieutenant governor in 1930. Elected as one of three U.S. representatives for three at-large districts by defeating Republican John A. Simpson and Socialist P. L. Peterson in the 1932 general election. Took office on March 3, 1933. The at-large districts ceased to exist in 1935 when the 19th, 20th, and 21st districts came into being. Strong sought but did not receive a nomination for one of the new seats and left office on January 3, 1935. Died on March 28, 1936, in Dallas and was buried there at Old Oak Cliff Cemetery.

Sterling Strong

HATTON WILLIAM SUMNERS

Born on May 30, 1875, near Fayetteville, Tennessee. Moved to Dallas County, Texas with his parents in 1894. Graduated from Garland High School in 1894. Employed in general store and law office. He was unable to attend traditional university courses or law school and instead spent his time studying law in the offices of Dallas City Attorney A. P. Wozencraft. He was admitted to the state bar in 1897 and began his practice in Dallas. Methodist and Democrat. Elected as Dallas County Attorney in November 1900 on an anti-gambling platform, but was defeated for reelection in 1902. Reelected to the post in 1904, but did not seek reelection in 1906. Returned to private law practice and was employed by Frank Holland's *Farm and Ranch* magazine. He spent time in Europe during 1907 studying and reporting on agriculture and handling marketing for the magazine. Elected as U.S. representative in 1912, along with Daniel E. Garrett, to one of two at-large positions. Took office on March 4, 1913. He was the first freshmen congressman that session to get a bill through the house. He did not seek the at-large post in 1914 and instead was elected

Hatton Sumners

to the 5th District seat by defeating Socialist candidate J. S. Goode and Wade B. Leonard. Succeeded Jack Beall in 1915. Reelected in 1916 by defeating Republican B. F. Crews and Socialist W. G. Brewer, in 1918 ran unopposed, in 1920 defeated Republican J. O. Burleson, in 1922 defeated Republican Heber Page, in 1924 defeated Republican George G. Atkinson, in 1926 defeated Republican Clinton S. Bailey, in 1928 ran unopposed, in 1930 defeated Republican Clinton S. Bailey, in 1932 defeated Republican George J. McManus, in 1934 defeated Republican Aubrey J. Roberts, in 1936 defeated Republican D. C. Humphrey and Independent candidate J. W. Chandler, in 1938 by defeating Republican Heber Page and independent candidate H. T. Healey, in 1940 defeated Republican Floyd E. Boyer, in 1942 ran unopposed, and in 1944 defeated Republican Charles D. Turner. Served from 1919 to 1947 on the House Judiciary Committee which he chaired beginning in 1932. While in Congress, he oversaw the impeachment proceedings of Federal Judges George W. English, Harold Louderback, and Halstead L. Ritter. He was called "the best lawyer in Congress" by President Taft and took top honors in a 1939 *Life* magazine poll for integrity. He represented Congress before the Supreme Court on four occasions. Sumners broke with Franklin Roosevelt over the president's plan to "pack" the Supreme Court. Sumners backed a solution whereby the justices could retire at full pay at age seventy instead of automatic replacement as proposed by Roosevelt. Many thought he would be named to the Supreme Court, but the disagreement with Roosevelt naturally precluded this. Did not seek reelection in 1946 and retired to Dallas. Succeeded by J. Frank Wilson on January 3, 1947. Sumners moved into Lawyer's Inn on the Southern Methodist University Campus. There he was made a director of the Southwestern Legal Center in 1948. He created the Hatton W. Sumners Foundation in 1949 to fund educational opportunities. Wrote *The Private Citizen and His Democracy* (1959). Died on April 19, 1962, of a heart attack in Dallas and was buried at Knights of Pythias Cemetery in Garland. He never married. (See also photo page 29.)

If the people fail, democracy fails, because the people are the governors in a democracy. They are its last resort.

—Hatton Sumners

DAVID MCCANN "MAC" SWEENEY

Mac Sweeney

Born on September 15, 1955, in Wharton. Attended public schools and graduated from Wharton High School in 1974. Receive a B.A. in 1978 and a J.D. in 1990 from the University of Texas. Served as aide to U.S. Senator John Tower from 1977 to 1978 and to former Governor John Connally from 1979 to 1980 during his presidential campaign. Married Catherine Hellman in 1982, and they had four children: Walter, Stuart, Peter, and Jordan. Served as the White House director of administrative operations during the Reagan Administration from 1981 to 1983. Republican. Elected U.S. representative, 14th District, in 1984 by defeating incumbent Democrat Bill Patman. Succeeded Patman on January 3, 1985. Served on the House Armed Services Committee. Reelected in 1986 by defeating Democrat Greg Laughlin. Laughlin would return in 1988 to unseat him. Succeeded by Laughlin on January 3, 1989. After leaving Congress, worked with American General Life Insurance, finished his law degree, worked with a Wall Street law firm, with a Houston area port industry, in the insurance industry again, and had a private consulting practice. In the mid-1990s began working with a missionary organization in the Middle East and continues to do so.

OLIN EARL "TIGER" TEAGUE

Born April 6, 1910, in Woodward, Oklahoma. Attended elementary and high school in Mena, Arkansas. Earned the nickname "Tiger" from his basketball-playing days. Graduated from Texas A&M College in 1932. Married Freddie Dunman in 1932 and they had three children: John O., James M., and

Jill Ruth (Cochran). Employed by the U.S. Post Office in College Station until 1940, when he enlisted for active military service. He had been in the National Guard since 1939 and served during World War II. He was wounded three times. Baptist, Lion, and Democrat. Elected U.S. representative, 6th District, in the August 1946 special election to fill the seat of Luther A. Johnson, who had resigned. Took office on August 24, 1946. The day before, he had been a Lieutenant Colonel in Walter Reed Hospital. He was discharged and joined Congress. Reelected to his first full term in November 1946 by running unopposed, in 1948 by defeating Progressive candidate J. Hayden Moore, in 1950 by defeating Republican Mose Blumrosen, by running unopposed from 1952 to 1962, defeated Republican William Van Winkle in 1964, by running unopposed in 1966, 1968, and 1970, by defeating Carl Nigliazzo in 1972 and 1974, and by defeating Wesley Mowery and American Party candidate Harley L. Pinon in 1976. Wrote the Korean War Veterans

Tiger Teague

Act in 1950. Served on the House Veterans Affairs, Science and Astronautics, District of Columbia, and Standards of Official Conduct committees. Chaired the Veterans Affairs Committee from 1955 to 1972 and the Science and Astronautics Committee from 1973 to 1978. Served on the Board of Technology Assessment—later known as the Congressional Office of Technology Assessment—from 1972 to 1976. Did not run for reelection in 1978 because of failing health and was succeeded by Phil Gramm on January 3, 1979. However, Teague had endorsed Chet Edwards for the seat. Died on January 23, 1981, from complications from war wounds and heart failure at the Bethesda Naval Hospital in Maryland and was buried at Arlington National Cemetery in Virginia. The Teague Research Center at Texas A&M University and the Veteran's Administration hospital in Temple were named in his honor. (See also photo page 24.)

The country that controls science and technology will be the country that controls the world.

—Tiger Teague

FRANK MARIANO TEJEDA, JR.

Frank Tejeda

Born on October 2, 1945, in San Antonio. Attended St. Leo's Catholic School and Harlandale High School. Served in the U.S. Marine Corps from 1963 to 1967 and was a major in the Marine Corps Reserves. Received B.A. from St. Marys University in 1970, J.D. from University of California at Berkeley in 1974, M.P.A. from Harvard University, and L.L.M. from Yale law school in 1989. Married Cecelia Gaitan and they had three children: Marissa, Sonya, and Frank, III. Catholic and Democrat. Attorney. Admitted to the state bar in 1974. Served five terms as state representative, District 57-B and 118, from 1977 to 1987 and three terms as State Senator, District 19, from 1987 to 1993. Tejeda was laterdivorced. Elected as the first U.S. representative from the 28th Congressional District in 1992 by defeating Libertarian David C. Slatter. Took office on January 3, 1993. Reelected in 1994 by defeating Republican David C. Slatter and Libertarian Stephan "Steve" Rothstein and in 1996 by defeating Republican Mark L. Cude and Natural Law Party candidate Clifford Finley. Served on the House Armed Services and Veterans Affairs committees. Died on January 30, 1997, in San Antonio of complications from brain cancer and was buried in Ft. Sam Houston National Cemetery. Succeeded by Ciro Rodriguez in April 1997. The U.S. Post Office building on Barline Boulevard in San Antonio was renamed in his honor.

GEORGE BUTLER TERRELL

Born on December 5, 1862, in Linwood, near Alto, Texas. Attended public schools. Attended the Sam

Houston Normal Institute and received a teaching certificate and later a law degree from Baylor University. Married Allie Minchum Turney in 1896 and they had six children. Taught school in his native Cherokee County from 1896 to 1903. Served on the State Teachers Examining Board, Summer Normal Board, State Normal Board, and the State Textbook Commission around 1900. Democrat. Served a total of eight terms as state representative, District 28 from 1899 to 1903, District 16 from 1907 to 1913, District 26 from 1917 until he resigned in 1921, and finally in District 31 from 1931 until 1933. Served as agriculture commissioner from 1921 until 1931. Elected U.S. representative in 1932 in place one of three at-large districts by defeating Republican F. A. Blankenbeckler, Socialist H. M. Shelton, and Liberty Party candidate P. A. Spain. Took office on March 4, 1933. Served for one term until three new congressional districts (19th–21st) were created in 1934. He opposed most every New Deal effort. He did not seek reelection in 1934, partly because of poor health. Ran unsuccessfully for his old post of agricultural commissioner in 1936, losing the race to J. E. McDonald. Died on April 18, 1947, and was buried at Old Palestine Cemetery near Alto.

George Butler Terrell

ALBERT LANGSTON THOMAS

Born on April 12, 1898, in Nacogdoches. Attended public schools and graduated from Nacogdoches High School. Served in the U.S. Army during World War I. Following the war, he graduated from the Rice Institute (later Rice University) in 1920, then attended Harvard University law school in 1920 and 1921, but graduated from the University of Texas law school in 1926. Married Lera Millard in 1922 and they had three children: Anne (Lasater), Lera, and a son who died at age ten. Admitted to the state bar in 1927 and practiced in Nacogdoches. Served as Nacogdoches County Attorney from 1927 to 1930 and assistant U.S. district attorney, Southern District of Texas, from 1930 until 1936. Methodist and Democrat. Elected U.S. representative, 8th District, in 1936, by defeating Oscar Holcombe in the Democratic primary and by defeating Republican R. B. Nichols and A. C. Henderson in the general election. Succeeded Joe Eagle on January 3, 1937. Reelected in 1938 by defeating Republican John A. Deering, in 1940 by defeating

Albert Thomas

Republican M. U. S. Kjorlaud, in 1942 by defeating Republican M. U. S. Kjorlaud and Independent Vance Muse, in 1944 by defeating Republican Lester Robinson, in 1946 by defeating Republican Richard Burns, in 1948 by defeating Republican Joe Ingraham, in 1950 by defeating Republican B. F. Hanna, by running unopposed in 1952, in 1954 by defeating Republican W. B. Butler and Constitution Party candidate B. F. Hanna, in 1956 by defeating Republican C. A., Friloux Jr. and Constitution party candidate W. C. "Doc" Miller, in 1958 by defeating Republican Robert E. Nesmith, in 1960 by defeating Republican Anthony J. P. Farris and Constitution Party candidate Robert E. Nesmith, in 1962 by defeating Republican Farris again, and in 1964 by defeating Republican Bob Gilbert. Thomas rarely made speeches to the House, but preferred to work behind the scenes. He was instrumental in bringing NASA to Houston in 1961. Served on the House Irrigation and Reclamations, Pensions, Labor, Elections, Appropriations, and Atomic Energy committees. Died while serving in office on February 15, 1966, of cancer, in Washington, D.C., and was buried at the Veterans' Administration Cemetery in Houston. His wife, Lera Millard Thomas, succeeded him as representative from his district as the result of a special election. She was the first female U.S. representative from Texas. Houston's new convention center was named in Thomas's honor in 1967. (See also photo page 24.)

LERA MILLARD THOMAS

Born August 3, 1900, in Nacogdoches. Attended public schools and graduated from Nacogdoches High School about 1918. Attended Brenau College in Gainesville, Georgia, and the University of Alabama. Democrat. Married Albert Thomas in 1922 and they had three children: Anne (Lasater), Lera, and a son who died at age ten. Elected U.S. representative, 8th District, in a March 1966 special election in which she defeated Republican Louis Leman to succeed her late husband, Albert Thomas. She was the first woman elected to represent Texas in Congress, but did not seek reelection for a full term in November 1966. Served on the House Merchant Marine and Fisheries committee. She served from March 26, 1966, to January 3, 1967, when she was succeeded by Bob Eckhardt. Employed by the *Houston Chronicle* on assignments in Vietnam during the war. She returned to her hometown of Nacogdoches and operated a small farm and an antiques business. Her passion for historic preservation was realized by her founding in Nacogdoches of Millard Crossing, a collection of historic buildings including a country store, homes, log cabins, a school, and a church. She was appointed as a regent to Stephen F. Austin State University by Governor Briscoe. She died in Nacogdoches on July 23, 1993, and was buried there in Oak Grove Cemetery.

Lera Thomas

ROBERT EWING THOMASON

Born on May 30, 1879, in Rover, Tennessee. Moved to Era in Cooke County, Texas in 1880. Attended the public schools of Gainesville and Polytechnic College in Fort Worth. Graduated from Southwestern University in 1898 and received a law degree from the University of Texas in 1900. Admitted to the state bar in 1901 and practiced in Pauls Valley, Oklahoma, but returned to Era to recover from "the worst case of measles in all recorded history." Practiced law in Gainesville and was elected Cooke County Attorney and district attorney, a combined post, from 1902 until 1906. Married Belle Davis in 1905 and they had two children: William and Isabelle. Moved to El Paso in 1912 after having survived a bout of malaria. Presbyterian, Mason, and Democrat. Served two terms as state representative, District 119, from 1917 to 1921. His committee investigated Governor Jim Ferguson. They voted unanimously to condemn his actions, but not to impeach. Thomason

Ewing Thomason

was responsible for writing the committee's report. In his second and last term, he was elected without a contest as Speaker of the House and served from 1919 to 1921. He was the first and only man to be elected Speaker in his second term in the House and was the first to serve from west of the Pecos River. Ran for governor in 1920 but placed third behind Joseph Bailey and Pat Neff in the primary. His wife Belle died in 1921 following a very brief illness. Served as mayor of El Paso from 1927 to 1930. Married Abbie Mann Long in 1927. Elected U.S. representative, 16th District, in 1930 by defeating Republican Mitchell Waldrop. Succeeded the retiring Claude Hudspeth on March 4, 1931. Unopposed for reelection in 1932, 1934, 1936, 1938, 1940, 1942, 1944, and 1946. Fathered the Thomason Act of 1939, which provided military training for students. Served on the House Military Affairs and Armed Services committees. President Truman called early one morning and asked, "Ewing, how would you like to go back to a city where the sunshine spends the winter, for permanent resident?" Resigned from Congress on July 31, 1947, to accept a federal judgeship and was succeeded by Ken Regan in 1949. His workload as judge included approximately 36,000 civil and criminal cases and over 9,000 naturalization cases. Among these was the trial of Billie Sol Estes. Retired on June 1, 1963. Wrote *Thomason: The Autobiography of a Federal*

Judge (1971). Died on November 8, 1973, in El Paso and was buried at Restlawn Cemetery. Thomason General Hospital in El Paso was named in his honor in 1963.

> *The truth is that the only political ambition I ever had was to go to Congress. I thought I would love it and I did.*

—Ewing Thomason

CLARK WALLACE THOMPSON

Clark Thompson

Born on August 6, 1896, in La Crosse, Wisconsin. Grew up in Oregon. Attended the University of Oregon from 1915 to 1917. Moved to Galveston, Texas while serving in the Marine Corps during World War I. Married Libbie Moody in 1918 and they had two children: Clark Wallace, Jr. and Libbie (Marshall). Episcopal, Mason, Shriner, and Democrat. Worked as treasurer of the American National Insurance Company. Owned the Clark W. Thompson Company—a dry-goods firm—from 1920 to 1932. Elected U.S. representative, 7th District, in a 1933 special election by defeating fellow Democrats James D. Pickett, Nat Patton, Theodore B. Stubbs, R. E. Biggs, Jake B. Clegg, Julian Greer, and Nall Colson and Republican Thomas H. Dent to fill the seat of the late Clay Stone Briggs. Took office on June 24, 1933. Did not seek reelection in 1934 and was succeeded by Nat Patton on January 3, 1935. Served as an attorney for the Moody family from 1936 to 1947. He remained in the marine reserves and was called to active service during World War II. Elected U.S. representative, 9th District, in the August 1947 special election by defeating L. J. Sulak, J. C. Trahan, George W. Hill, V. M. Stokes, Morris Schrieber, Ben H. Farber, Robert H. Abell, and George P. Barron to fill the seat of the late Joseph J. Mansfield who had died while in office. Took office on August 23, 1947. Ran unopposed for reelection in 1948, 1950, 1952, 1954, 1956, and 1958, and in 1960 defeated Constitutional Party candidate P. D. Rogers, in 1962 and 1964 defeated Republican Dave Oakes. Served on the House Agricultural, Maritime and Fisheries, and Ways and Means committees. Did not seek reelection in 1966 and was succeeded by Jack Brooks on January 3, 1967. Remained in Washington following his departure from Congress and lobbied for Hill and Knowlton and Tenneco. Died on December 16, 1981, in Galveston and was buried there at Memorial Cemetery. (See also photo page 24.)

WILLIAM HOMER THORNBERRY

Homer Thornberry

Born on January 9, 1909, in Austin. He attended schools in Austin and graduated from Austin High School in 1927. Employed as a Travis County sheriff's deputy while in college. Received a B.B.A. in 1932 and an L.L.B. in 1936 from the University of Texas. Admitted to the state bar in 1936 and was in private practice with Powell, Wirtz, Rauhut, and Gideon from 1936 to 1941. Served two terms as state representative, District 82-2, from 1937 until 1941. Served as Travis County district attorney (53rd Judicial District) from 1941 to 1942. Served in the U.S. Navy during World War II. Following the war, he returned to private law practice with Herman Jones. Married Eloise Engle in 1945 and they had three children: Molly, David, and Kate. Methodist and Democrat. Served as Austin city councilman and mayor pro tempore from 1946 to 1948. Elected U.S. representative, 10th District, in 1948 by running unopposed. Succeeded Lyndon B. Johnson on January 3, 1949. Reelected in 1950, 1952, 1954, 1956, and 1958 by running unopposed, in 1960 by defeating Constitution Party candidate Roy R. Brown, and in 1962 by defeating Republican Jim Dobbs. Served on the House Rules Committee. Served as delegate at-large to the 1956 and 1960 Democratic national conventions. Served on the board of directors of Gallaudet University, the largest university for the deaf. Both of Thornberry's parents were deaf, and he actually learned to sign before he could speak. Resigned on December 20, 1963, to accept a federal judgeship following an appointment by President Kennedy. Succeeded by J. J. "Jake" Pickle in December 1963 as a result of a special election to fill his seat. Served as U.S. district judge, Western District of Texas, from 1963 to 1965 when he was appointed by President Johnson to the U.S. Court of Appeals, 5th Circuit, where he served from 1965 until his death. He became senior judge in 1978. In 1968, Thornberry was nominated to the Supreme Court by President Johnson. However, the man Thornberry was to replace—Abe Fortas—was unable to have his nomination as chief justice approved, so Thornberry's appointment stalled and he remained with the Court of Appeals. His first wife, Eloise, died in 1989. Married Marian Harris Gilliam in 1990. The Homer Thornberry Judicial Center on Ninth Street in Austin was renamed in his honor in 1993. Died on December 12, 1995, in Austin and was buried there at the state cemetery. (See also photo page 24.)

I wish my mother were alive to see this, I now have a good steady job.

—Homer Thornberry on his swearing in as a federal judge

Mac Thornberry

WILLIAM McCLELLAN "MAC" THORNBERRY

Born on July 15, 1958, in Clarendon. Graduated from Clarendon High School. Received B.A. from Texas Tech University in 1980 and J.D. from the University of Texas in 1983. Rancher and attorney. Republican. Admitted to the state bar in 1983. Aide to Congressman Tom Loeffler from 1983 to 1985 and chief of staff to Congressman Larry Combest from 1985 to 1988. Married Sally Adams in 1986 and they had two children: Will and Mary Kemp. Appointed and served as deputy assistant secretary of state for legislative affairs, Department of State, from 1988 until 1989. Elected U.S. representative, 13th District, in 1994 by defeating incumbent Democrat Bill Sarpalius. Succeeded Sarpalius on January 3, 1995. Reelected in 1996 by defeating Democrat Samuel Brown Silverman and Natural Law Party candidate Don Harkey, in 1998 by defeating Democrat Mark Harmon and Libertarian Georganne Baker Payne, and in 2000 by defeating Democrat Curtis Clinesmith and Libertarian Brad Clardy, in 2002 by defeating Democrat Zane Reese, and in 2004 by defeating Libertarian Marion J. "Smitty" Smith, and in 2006 by defeating Democrat Roger J. Waun and Libertarian Jim Thompson. Serves on the House Armed Services and Intelligence Committees, but previously served on Resources and Budget.

James Throckmorton

JAMES WEBB THROCKMORTON

Born on February 1, 1825, in Sparta, Tennessee. Moved to Arkansas in 1836. Moved to Texas in 1841 with his father and stepmother. Studied medicine in Kentucky. Democrat. Served in the U.S. Army during the Mexican War but was discharged for medical reasons. Married Annie Rattan in 1848 and they settled near McKinney and had ten children. Practiced medicine, business, and eventually law. Served three terms as State representative, District 25 and 7, from 1851 to 1857, and three terms as state senator, the first two terms in District 4, from 1857 to 1861 and the third in District 15, from 1863 to 1864. Ally of Governor Houston in trying to prevent secession. Voted against secession at the 1861 convention. He supported the state, however, and served in the Confederate States Army but again had to leave because of health reasons. Served as Confederate commissioner to the Indians. Delegate and chair of the State Constitutional Convention in 1866. His supporters there also supported him for governor, an office in which he served from August 9, 1866, until August 8, 1867. He was removed from office by the military government which barred him from holding any public office. Elected U.S. representative, 3rd District, in 1874 by defeating Republicans J. M. Valentine and F. W. Sumner. Succeeded DeWitt C. Giddings on March 4, 1875. Reelected in 1876 by defeating Republican J. C. Bigger. Did not run for reelection to Congress in 1878 and instead ran unsuccessfully for governor. Succeeded in Congress by Olin Wellborn on March 3, 1879. He returned to Congress, however, and was again elected U.S. representative, 5th District, in 1882 by defeating Greenback candidate John N. Dixon. Succeeded George Washington Jones on March 4, 1883. Unsuccessful candidate for U.S. Senator in 1881. Reelected in 1884 by defeating M. H. Eddy and H. C. Dillingham. His health again became an issue, and he chose not to run for reelection in 1886 and was succeeded by Silas Hare on March 3, 1887. He considered running again for governor in 1892. Delegate to the Democratic national convention in 1892. Died on April 21, 1894, and was buried at Pecan Grove Cemetery in McKinney. A statue of him in McKinney notes, "A Tennesseean by Birth, a Texan by Adoption."

JOHN GOODWIN TOWER

Born on September 29, 1925, in Houston. Attended public schools in Houston and Beaumont. Graduated from Beaumont High School in 1942. Attended Southwestern University briefly before serving in U.S. Navy during World War II. Received a B.A. from Southwestern University in 1948, attended the London School of Economics and Political Science from 1952 to 1953, and received an M.A. from Southern Methodist University in 1953. Worked as a radio announcer in Beaumont and Taylor, and sold insurance while in Dallas. Professor at Midwestern University in Wichita Falls from 1951 to 1960. A Democrat until 1951, when he joined the Republican Party. Married Lou Bullington in 1953 and they had three daughters: Penny, Marian, and Jeanne. Lou was the cousin of long-time Texas Republican Orville Bullington. Tower ran for state representative, District 81-1, in 1954, but was defeated by Vernon J. Stewart. Served as delegate to the Republican national convention in 1956, a role in which he would serve again in 1960, 1964, 1968, 1972, and 1980. Received Republican nomination for U.S. Senate in 1960, but was defeated by Lyndon Johnson who was also running for vice-president. In the special election to fill Johnson's seat in 1961, there were seventy-one candidates in the free-for-all open primary. William Blakley had been appointed by Governor Daniel to fill the seat until a senator could be elected. Blakley and Tower were the top two candidates, but neither received a majority as required by law in the first election to be declared the winner. In a special election runoff on May 27, Tower defeated Blakley and was sworn in on June 15, 1961. He was the first Republican senator the state had seen since Reconstruction in 1877. Reelected in 1966 by defeating Democrat Waggoner Carr and Constitution Party candidate James Barker Holland, in 1972 by defeating Democrat Barefoot Sanders, La Raza Unida Party candidate Flores N. Amaya, and Socialist Workers Party candidate Tom Leonard, in 1978 by defeating Democrat Bob Krueger, La Raza Unida party candidate Luis A. Diaz de Leon, and Socialist Workers Party candidate Miguel Pendas. Served on the Senate Labor and Public Welfare, Banking and Currency, and Armed Services committees (chaired Armed Services from 1981 to 1984), Defense Production and Republican Policy committees. He also chaired the Republican Policy Committee from 1973 until 1984. Served on the board of trustees of Southwestern University from 1968 to 1991. Tower was divorced from Lou in 1976 and married Lilla Burt Cummings in 1977, and they were divorced in 1987. Did not seek reelection to the Senate in 1984 and was succeeded by Phil Gramm on January 3, 1985. Appointed by President Reagan as chief negotiator at the Strategic Arms Reduction Talks (START) in Geneva from January 1985 to April 1986. Served as chairman of Towers, Eggers, and Greene Consulting in Dallas and Washington from 1986 to 1988. Served as chairman to the President's

John Tower

Special Review Board, also known as the "Tower Commission," to review the actions of employees of the National Security Council in the Iran-Contra affair in 1987. He remained in the naval reserves until 1989, when he retired at the rank of master chief boatswain's mate. Blocked by the Senate as President Bush's nominee for secretary of defense on March 9, 1989. Author and lecturer in retirement. *Wrote Consequences: A Personal and Political Memoir* (1991). Appointed by President Bush in 1990 to the President's Foreign Intelligence Advisory Board. Died on April 5, 1991, in a plane crash near New Brunswick, Georgia, with his daughter Marian and was buried at Sparkman Hillcrest Cemetery in Dallas.

> *It occurred to me at some point in time after I had completed a good part of my college education that the Republicans nationally more represented my views on things, my conservative, capitalist, particularist, oriented ideas.*

—John Tower

JAMES WILLIAM "JIM" TURNER

Jim Turner

Born on February 6, 1946, in Fort Lewis, Washington. Moved to Crockett, Texas, attended local schools, and graduated from Crockett High School in 1964. Received B.A. in 1968, M.A. in 1971, and L.L.B. in 1971 from the University of Texas. Served in U.S. Army. Married Ginny Ward in 1970 and they had two children: John and Susan. Baptist and Democrat. Served two terms as state representative, District 57-B, from 1981 to March 17, 1984, when he resigned. Served as special counsel for legislative affairs and executive assistant to Governor White from 1984 to 1985. Served as mayor of Crockett from 1989 to 1991. Served three terms as state senator, District 5, from 1991 to 1997. Elected U.S. representative, 2nd District, in 1996 by defeating Republican Brian Babin, Libertarian David Constant, Natural Law Party candidate Gary Hardy, and Independent Henry McCullough. Succeeded the retiring Charlie Wilson on January 3, 1997. Reelected in 1998 by defeating Republican Brian Babin and Libertarian Wendell Drye and in 2000 by defeating Libertarian Gary Lyndon Dye, in 2002 by defeating Republican Van Brookshire and Libertarian Peter Beach. Following redistricting and an impossible campaign, he did not seek re-election in 2004. Served on the House National Security and Government Reform and Oversight committees. Succeeded by Ted Poe. Joined Arnold & Porter as an attorney.

CHRISTOPHER COLUMBUS UPSON

Born on October 17, 1829, in Syracuse, New York. Attended local schools and Williams College in Massachusetts. Admitted to the state bar of Massachusetts in 1851. Democrat. Moved to Castroville, Texas in the early 1850s. Practiced law there and later in San Antonio. Served as a colonel in the Confederate States Army and during the war was appointed associate justice of Arizona. Returned to Texas following the war. Served as Democratic presidential elector in 1876. Elected U.S. representative, 6th District, in an April 1879 special election by defeating Greenback candidate Henry Maney to fill the seat of the late Gustave Schleicher in 1879. Took office on April 15, 1879. Reelected in 1880 by defeating Greenback candidate D. B. Robertson. Sought, but did not receive, the Democratic nomination for reelection in 1882. Succeeded by Olin Wellborn on March 3, 1883. Returned to San Antonio to continue the practice of law. Died on February 8, 1902, in San Antonio and was buried there at the Confederate Cemetery.

Christopher Upson

Tom Vandergriff

TOMMY JOE "TOM" VANDERGRIFF

Born on January 29, 1926, in Carrollton, Texas. Attended public schools in Carrollton and Arlington. Attended Northwestern University and Southern Methodist University. Received a B.A. from the University of Southern California in 1947. Automobile dealer. Married Anna Waynette Smith in 1949 and they had four children: Vanessa, Victor, Valerie, and Viveca. Served as mayor of Arlington from 1951 until 1973. Elected as the first U.S. representative for the newly created 26th District in 1982 by defeating Republican Jim Bradshaw. Unseated by Republican Dick Armey in the 1984 general election and was succeeded by him on January 3, 1985. Returned to his auto business. Originally a Democrat, but now a Republican. Served as Tarrant County Judge from 1991 until his retirement in 2006.

I should not pledge total agreement (or opposition) to any president, regardless of which party that president represents.

—Tom Vandergriff

HORACE WORTH VAUGHAN

Born December 2, 1867, near Jefferson. Grew up in Cass County. Attended public schools and studied law under the direction of his father. Admitted to the state bar in 1885. Moved the following year to Texarkana where he began practicing law in earnest. Married Pearl Lockett in 1888 and they had three children. Methodist, Mason, Odd Fellow, Woodman, and Democrat. Ran unsuccessfully for district attorney in 1888. Served as Texarkana city attorney from 1891 to 1898, Bowie county attorney from 1898 until 1906, and district attorney, 5th Judicial District, from 1906 to 1910. Served one full term as state senator, District 1, from 1911 to 1913. He had been reelected to the state senate, but resigned to accept his newly won congressional seat. Prohibitionist and member of the Anti-Saloon League of Texas. Elected U.S. representative, 1st District, in 1912 by defeating S. L. Willyard and Republican Josh Barker. Succeeded now Senator Morris Sheppard on March 4, 1913. Served one term and was unseated by Eugene Black in the 1914 Democratic primary. Succeeded by Black on March 3, 1915. Appointed by President Wilson as U.S. appointed district attorney in Hawaii and served from December 1915 to March 1916, and district judge from May 1916 to May 1922. Vaughan was distraught over the death of his only son and took his own life on November 10, 1922, in Honolulu, Hawaii, and was buried at Nuuanu Cemetery in Honolulu.

Horace Vaughn

MATTHIAS WARD

Born on October 13, 1805, in Elbert County, Georgia. Raised and educated in Madison County, Alabama. Attended college in Huntsville, Alabama. Taught school for two years and studied law. Moved to Bowie County, Texas, in 1836. Democrat. Served in Texas Republic House of Representatives from 1842 to 1844 and served one term as state senator, District 1, from 1849 to 1850. Ran unsuccessfully for lieutenant governor in 1851. Delegate to Democratic national convention in 1852

Matthias Ward

and 1856. Unsuccessful candidate for U.S. Congress in 1855. Presided over the state democratic convention of 1856. Elected U.S. senator by the legislature upon the death of James P. Henderson. Served from September 27, 1858, until December 5, 1859, and served in the Rusk succession of U.S. senators from Texas. Ward was not renominated by the Democrats and was succeeded by Louis T. Wigfall in 1859. Died on October 5, 1861, in Warm Springs, North Carolina, and was buried at Old City Cemetery in Nashville, Tennessee.

CRAIG ANTHONY WASHINGTON

Craig Washington

Born October 12, 1941, in Longview. Attended school in Galena Park and graduated from Fidelity Manor High School. Received B.A. from Prairie View A&M University in 1966 and law degree from Texas Southern University in 1969. Married Dorothy Marie Lampley and they had two children: Craig Anthony, II and Chival Antoinette. Practiced criminal defense law. Episcopal and Democrat. Served five terms as state representative, District 86, from 1973 to 1983, and three terms as state senator, District 13, from 1983 until 1989, when he resigned to accept his newly won congressional seat. Elected U.S. representative, 18th District, following the November 1989 special election and December 1989 special election runoff to fill the seat of the late Mickey Leland. Washington defeated fellow Democrats Anthony Hall, Ron Wilson, Al Edwards, Shirley Fobbs, Timothy J. Hattenback, and Lee A. Demas, Republicans Beverly A. Spencer, Manse R. Sharp, and Byron J. Johnson, and Libertarian Gary Johnson in the first election. However, Washington did not receive a clear majority, and he and Hall were forced into a runoff. Washington won the runoff and took office on January 23, 1990. Two days before his swearing-in ceremony, he served as governor for a day. Reelected in 1990 by defeating Republican Timothy J. Hattenbach, in 1992 defeated Republican Edward Blum, and was unseated in the 1994 Democratic primary by Sheila Jackson Lee. Succeeded by Lee on January 3, 1995. Divorced from his first wife, Dorothy, in 1993. Remarried and had three more children: Alexander, Cydney, and Christopher Alfred. Returned to Houston and resumed law practice with Washington, Lampley, Evans, and Branquet. Now practices law in Houston and Bastrop.

You can't limit yourself to doing what's popular.

—Craig Washington

THOMAS NEVILLE WAUL

Thomas Waul

Born on January 5, 1813, near Statesburg, South Carolina. Attended South Carolina College and taught school. Moved to Mississippi, studied law, and was admitted to the Mississippi state bar in 1835. Married America Simmons in 1837. Moved to Gonzales County, Texas in 1850. Practiced law. Candidate for U.S. representative, 2nd District, in 1859, but was defeated by Andrew J. Hamilton. Appointed by the secession convention to serve in the Confederate Provisional Congress from 1861 to 1862. Sought seat as Confederate senator in November 1861 but was defeated. Served as a general in the Confederate States Army. Delegate to the state Constitutional Convention of 1866. Lived in Galveston before retiring to Greenville. Died on July 28, 1903, near Greenville and was buried in Fort Worth.

OLIN WELLBORN

Born on June 18, 1843, in Cumming, Georgia. Attended local schools. Attended Emory College and the University of North Carolina, but quit his studies to join the Confederate States Army. After the war, he studied law and was admitted to the Georgia state bar in 1866. Practiced in Atlanta, Georgia. Moved to Dallas, Texas in 1871. Elected U.S. representative, 3rd District, in 1878 by defeating Greenback candidate E. M. Daggett and a handful of others. Succeeded James Throckmorton on March 4, 1879. Reelected in 1880 and 1882 by defeating Greenback candidate Jerome C. Kirby and in 1884 by defeating Republican J. C. Bigger. Following some redistricting, Wellborn's 6th District became the 3rd District in 1882. Served on and eventually chaired the House Indian Affairs Committee. Sought but did not receive his party's renomination in 1886 and was succeeded by Constantine Kilgore on March 3, 1887. Moved to San Diego and then Los Angeles, California. Appointed by President Cleveland as District Judge, Southern District of California, and served from 1895 to 1915. Retired. Died on December 6, 1921, in Los Angeles, California, and was buried there at Rosedale Cemetery.

Olin Wellborn

MILTON HORACE WEST

Born on June 30, 1888, near Gonzales. Attended public schools and graduated from the West Texas Military Academy in San Antonio in 1910. Served in the Texas Rangers until 1912. Studied law and was admitted to the state bar in 1915. Practiced law in Floresville and then Brownsville. Democrat. Married Temple Worley and they had one son. Elected and served as district attorney, 28th Judicial District, from 1922 to 1925. Served also as assistant district attorney, from 1927 to 1930. Served one full term as state representative, District 72, from 1931 to 1933. However, West resigned from the state House upon his election to the U.S. Congress. Elected U.S. representative, 15th District, in the April 1933 special election by defeating Republican Carlos Watson to fill the seat of John Nance Garner, who had resigned to become vice-president. Took office on April 22, 1933. Reelected in 1934 by defeating Republican G. C. Mann, in 1936 by defeating Republican John A. Simpson, in 1938 by running unopposed, in 1940 by defeating John

Milton West

A. Simpson again, and in 1942, 1944, and 1946 by running unopposed. Served on the House Ways and Means, Irrigation and Reclamation, Immigration and Naturalization, and Flood Control committees. Died prior to the 1948 general election on October 28, 1948, in Washington, D.C., and was buried at Buena Vista Cemetery in Brownsville. Succeeded in Congress by Lloyd M. Bentsen, Jr. in 1949.

RICHARD CRAWFORD WHITE

Born on April 29, 1923, in El Paso. Graduated from Dudley Primary School and El Paso High School. Married Katherine Huffman and they had three sons: Roderick James, Richard Whitman, and Raymond Edward. Attended the Citizen's Military Training Camp in San Antonio. Attended Texas Western College from 1940 to 1942. Served in the U.S. Marine Corps during World War II. Graduated from the University of Texas in 1946 and from its law school in 1949. Admitted to the state bar in 1949 and began practicing in El Paso. Democrat. Served two terms as state representative, District 105-3, from 1955 to 1959. Served as El Paso Democratic county chairman from 1963 to 1965. Elected U.S. representative, 16th District, in 1964 by unseating incumbent Republican Ed Foreman. Succeeded Foreman on January 3, 1965. Served on the House Interior Committee. Reelected in 1966 with no opposition, in

Richard White

1968 by defeating Republican Donald Slaughter, in 1970 by defeating Republican J. R. Provencio, in 1972 and 1974 by running unopposed, in 1976 by defeating Republican Vic Shackleford, in 1978 by defeating Republican Michael Giere, and in 1980 by defeating Libertarian Catherine McDivitt. Served on the House Committees for Armed Services, Interior, Post Office, Civil Service, Insular Affairs, and Science, Space, and Technology. His wife, Katherine, died in 1972. Married Kathleen Fitzgerald and had four children: Kenneth, Bonnie Kathleen, Sean, and Brian. Did not seek reelection in 1982. Succeeded by Ronald D. Coleman on January 3, 1983. Returned to El Paso and continued his legal practice. Died on February 18, 1998, in El Paso and was buried at Arlington National Cemetery. The federal building at 700 East San Antonio Street in El Paso was renamed in his honor in September 1999.

My view of a good Congressman is one who looks for good solutions for the benefit of the nation without strictly trying to get publicity. Too many look for publicity for publicity's sake.

—Richard C. White

GEORGE WASHINGTON WHITMORE

George Whitmore

Born on August 26, 1824, in McMinn County, Tennessee. Attended public schools. Moved to Harrison County, Texas, in 1848. Studied law, was admitted to the state bar in 1850 and practiced law in Tyler. Married Harriet Bell in 1851 and they adopted one child and raised three others. Originally a Whig supporter, he also was a member of the American (or Know-Nothing) Party and the Constitutional Union Party before finally becoming a Republican. Served two terms as state representative, District 15, from 1853 to 1855 and once again from 1859 to 1861. Resigned from the legislature because of his strong Union sentiment. Signed "The Address to the People of Texas," which condemned the secession movement. Moved to Smith County. Arrested and imprisoned by the Confederates without being charged with a crime for his outspoken support of the union. Appointed by Provisional Governor Hamilton as district attorney, 9th Judicial District, and served from 1866 to 1867. Appointed as a register for the Federal District Court at Tyler in 1867. Became a Republican. Served in the Constitutional Convention of 1868–69. Elected U.S. representative, 1st District, in 1869 by defeating Democrat James Armstrong and Horace Broughton. Took office on March 30, 1870. He was one of the first four Texas congressmen seated following the Civil War. Three of these were Republicans. He succeeded John H. Reagan, who left in 1861 upon secession. Served one term and was unseated by Democrat William S. Herndon in the 1871 general election. Succeeded by Herndon on March 3, 1871. Returned to Tyler to practice law. Died on October 14, 1876, in Tyler and was buried there at Oakwood Cemetery.

LOUIS TREZEVANT WIGFALL

Born on April 21, 1816, near Edgefield, South Carolina. Attended South Carolina College. Served in the U.S. Army during the Seminole War. Attended the University of Virginia and received a B.A. in 1837. Studied law and was admitted to the Virginia state bar in 1839. Moved to Marshall, Texas, in 1846. Married Charlotte Maria Cross and they had three children. Wigfall was wounded, wounded another man, and later killed a man in a duel. Moved to Galveston in 1848 and later to Nacogdoches. Democrat. Served one term as state representative, District 11, from 1849 to December 1850 and one term as state senator, District 8, from 1857 to 1859. Wigfall was undoubtedly the most radical states' rights advocate in Texas. Denounced Sam Houston at every opportunity and played a large part in his defeat for retaining the

Louis Wigfall

governor's seat in 1857. Elected U.S. senator by the state legislature on December 5, 1859 and served from December 5, 1859, until July 11, 1861, when he was expelled for being a supporter of the right of secession. Also running for the post were George W. Smyth, Albert H. Latimer, Matthias Ward, W. P. Hill, and others. Wigfall's term was scheduled to end on March 23, 1861. Succeeded Matthias Ward in the Rusk succession of Texas senators. Co-authored the "Southern Manifesto," which encouraged independence for the southern states. Served as general in Confederate States Army. Served as a delegate to the Confederate Provisional Congress from 1861 to 1862. Resigned from the army on February 18, 1862, to serve as senator to Confederate Congress following his election by the state legislature. Wigfall drew a four-year term and served from 1862 until the fall of the Confederacy in 1865. Chaired the Territories Committee and, during the last few months of the Confederacy, the Military Affairs Committee. During this time, he worked to undermine Confederate President Davis. Returned to Texas following the war and also spent some time in England. Moved to Baltimore in 1872 and back to Galveston in 1874, shortly before his death. Died on February 18, 1874, in Galveston and was buried there at Episcopal Cemetery.

JOHN ALLEN "JACK" WILCOX

Born on April 18, 1819, in Snow Hill, Greene County, North Carolina. Moved to Randolph, Tennessee as an infant. Grew up in Tipton. Educated in public schools and was self-educated in law. Moved to Aberdeen, Mississippi, about 1840. Married Mary E. Donelson in 1852 and they had two children. Served as Mississippi senate secretary in 1846. Served as colonel in the U.S. Army during the Mexican War. Democrat, but was also a Union Whig and a Know-Nothing Party member. Served as Mississippi state representative. Elected U.S. representative, District 2, from Mississippi by unseating incumbent Southern Rights Party candidate Winfield Scott "Old Swet" Featherston in the November 3–4, 1851, general election. Served from 1851 to 1853. Delegate to the Democratic national convention of 1852 in Baltimore. Unseated by Democrat William T. S. Barry in the November 7–8, 1853, general election. Moved to San Antonio, Texas in 1853. Served as Know-Nothing presidential elector for Millard Fillmore in 1856. Joined the Democratic Party. Served as a delegate to the State Secession Convention in 1861. Elected Representative, 1st District, to the Confederate Congress as a Whig in November 1861 by defeating Edward Hord and William Stewart. Reelected in 1863 by defeating J. W. Burton and served until his death. Served on the House Territories and Public Lands Committee, which he chaired, and the Military Affairs, Inauguration, and Enrolled Bills Committees. Died on February 7, 1864, of apoplexy in Richmond, Virginia, and was buried there at Hollywood Cemetery. Succeeded in the Confederate Congress by Stephen H. Darden.

My Democracy teaches me that the people are capable of self-government; that they are in fact the sovereignty, the state, and the impersonation of the law itself.

—John Allen Wilcox

Guinn Williams

GUINN TERRELL WILLIAMS

Born on April 22, 1871, near Beuela, Mississippi. Moved with family to near Nocona, Texas in 1876 and shortly thereafter to near Decatur, Texas. Attended public schools. Taught school. Studied business administration at Transylvania College in Kentucky in 1890. Married Minnie Leatherwood in 1893 and they had three daughters and one son. Pursued the livestock business and banking. Organized a bank—City National—in Decatur and served as its vice-president until 1926. Williams was involved in forming other banks in Mineral Wells, Perrin, Bridgeport, and Paradise, Texas, and in Artesia, New Mexico. Methodist, Mason, and Democrat. Served as Wise County Clerk from 1898 to 1902. Served part of one term as state senator, District 31, from 1921 until 1922, when he resigned for Congress. Elected U.S. representative, 13th

District, in a May 1922 special election to fill the seat of the late Lucian Parrish by defeating Democrats S. A. Morgan and Annie Blanton, Republican Orville Bullington, and W. S. Moore. Took office on May 13, 1922. Reelected later in the same year in the November general election by defeating Republican John Schmitz, in 1924 by defeating Republican C. W. Johnson, Jr., in 1926 by defeating Republican Mel E. Peters, in 1928 by defeating Republican Mrs. P. A. Welty, and in 1930 by defeating Republican W. C. Witcher. Served on the House Insular Affairs, Expenditures in the Executive Department, and Territories committees. Did not seek reelection in 1932. Succeeded by W. D. McFarlane on March 3, 1933. Returned to San Angelo. Managed the Regional Agricultural Credit Corporation. Presided over the Texas Production Credit Corporation, the Texas Goat Raisers Association, the Texas Wool and Mohair Company, and the 7th District Texas Bankers Association. Died on January 9, 1948, in San Angelo and was buried at Decatur Cemetery in Decatur. A street in Manila is named in his honor for his work on the Territories Committee. (See also photo page 29.)

ASA HOXIE WILLIE

Asa Willie

Born on October 11, 1829, in Washington, Georgia. Attended private schools and taught school. Moved to Texas in 1845 and lived with his uncle, Asa Hoxey, who had fought for Texas independence and had signed the Texas Declaration of Independence. Studied law and was admitted to the state bar in 1849. Served as district Attorney, 3rd Judicial District, from 1852 to 1854. Moved to Austin in 1857 with his brother James, who had become attorney general. Moved to Marshal in 1858 and began law practice. Married Bettie Johnson in 1859 and they had ten children, five of whom survived. Democrat. Served in the Confederate States Army. Served as a justice on the state supreme court from 1866 to 1867 but was removed by the military government. Moved to Galveston and practiced law. Elected U.S. representative for one of two at-large districts, along with Roger Q. Mills, in 1872 by defeating I. D. Evans and A. B. Norton. The two at-large districts ceased to exist in 1875 when the 5th and 6th congressional districts were formed and he did not seek election to one of those seats in 1874. Served as Galveston city attorney from 1875 to 1876. Appointed and served again on the Supreme Court as Chief Justice from 1882 until 1888. Returned to his law practice. Died on March 16, 1899, in Galveston and was buried there at Episcopal Cemetery.

CHARLES NESBIT "CHARLIE" WILSON

Born on June 1, 1933, in Trinity. Attended public schools and graduated from Trinity High School in 1950. Attended Lon Morris Junior College, Sam Houston State University from 1950 to 1951, and the University of Texas from 1951 to 1952. Graduated from the U.S. Naval Academy in 1956 and served in the U.S. Navy from 1956 to 1960. Married Jerry Carter in 1973 and they had no children. Lumber businessman in Lufkin. Methodist and Democrat. Served three terms as state representative, District 18 and 6, from 1961 to 1967 and three terms as state senator, District 3, from 1967 to 1973. Elected president pro tempore of the Senate during the 62nd Legislature, 1971–73, and served as governor for a day on December 2, 1972. Elected U.S. representative, 2nd District, in 1972 by defeating Republican Charles O. Brightwell. Succeeded John Dowdy on January 3, 1973. Reelected in 1974 by running unopposed, in 1976 by defeating American Party candidate James William Doyle, III, in 1978 by defeating Republican Jim "Matt" Dillon, in 1980 by defeating Republican F. H. Pannill, Sr. and Libertarian Martin Sorrels, in 1982 by defeating Libertarian Ed Richbourg, in 1984 by defeating Republican Louis Dugas, Jr., in 1986 by defeating Republican Julian Gordon and Independent Sam I. Paradice, in 1988 by defeating Libertarian Gary W. Nelson, in 1990 by defeating Republican Donna Peterson, in 1992 by defeating Republican Donna Peterson and Independent Roger Northen, and in 1994 by defeating Republican Peterson again. Served on the House Appropriations, Foreign Affairs, and Veteran Affairs committees. Divorced in 1983. Served as a Delegate to the Democratic national convention in 1984 and 1988. After campaigning sixteen times in thirty-two years, he chose not to seek reelection in 1996 and resigned his seat on October 8, 1996. About this time, he was fined $90,000 by the Federal Election Commission for failing to report an interest-free loan he had taken from his campaign funds. Succeeded by Jim Turner on January 3, 1997. Remained in Washington to lobby on behalf of Hooper, Hooper, Owen and Gould. Married Barbara Livshin Alberstadt Zavacky in 1999. Subject of a book by George Crile entitled *Charlie Wilson's War: The Extraordinary Story of the Largest Covert Operation in History* (2003). The book was also made into a movie starring Tom Hanks as Charlie Wilson.

Charlie Wilson

> *To friends, to life, to money, to power, to passion, to black lace. And to Texas, of course.*
> —Charlie Wilson's toast of his sixtieth birthday

JAMES CLIFTON WILSON

James C. Wilson

Born on June 21, 1874, in Palo Pinto. Attended public schools in Palo Pinto County, and Weatherford College. Married Esther English in 1905 and they had three children: James Jr., Horace E., and Emily Loving (Bird). Graduated from the law de,partment at the University of Texas in 1896. Admitted to the state bar in 1896 and practiced in Weatherford. Democrat. Served as Assistant Parker County prosecuting attorney from 1898 to 1900, was in private practice from 1900 to 1902, and was prosecuting attorney from 1902 to 1908. Moved to Fort Worth in 1912. Served as Tarrant County assistant district attorney from 1912 to 1913 and U.S. attorney, Northern District of Texas, from 1913 to 1919. Elected U.S. representative, 12th District, in 1916 by unseating incumbent Oscar Callaway in the Democratic primary and defeating Republican Henry Zweifel and Socialist Leland G. Baker in the general election. Succeeded Oscar Callaway on March 4, 1917. Ran unopposed for reelection in 1918. Received appointment for federal judgeship from President Wilson and resigned on March 3, 1919. Succeeded by Fritz Lanham in 1919. Served as U.S. district judge, Northern District of Texas, from 1919 until he retired in 1947. Died on August 3, 1951, and was buried at Rose Hill Cemetery in Fort Worth.

JOSEPH FRANKLIN WILSON

Born on March 18, 1901, in Corsicana. Moved to Memphis, Texas, in 1913. Attended public schools. Attended the Peacock Military Academy in San Antonio from 1917 to 1918 and the Tennessee Military Institute from 1918 to 1919. Graduated from Baylor University in 1923. Admitted to the state bar in 1923 and began law practice in Dallas. Married Ruby Lee Hopkins in 1926 and they had two children: J. Frank, Jr. and Marion Sue. Democrat. Dallas Lawyer. Delegate to the Democratic national convention in 1936. Chaired the Dallas County Democratic Executive Committee from 1942 to 1945. Served as district judge from 1943 to 1944 and 1955 to 1968. Elected U.S. Representative, 5th District, in 1946 by defeating Republican L. W. Stayart. Succeeded Hatton Sumners on January 3, 1947. Reelected in 1948 by defeating Progressive Joe Bailey Irwin and ran unopposed in 1950 and 1952. Did

Joseph Wilson

not seek reelection in 1954 and was succeeded by Republican Bruce Alger on January 3, 1955. Appointed judge, Criminal District Court No. 1, and served from 1955 until he retired 1968 due to failing health. Died on October 13, 1968, in Dallas and was buried there at Sparkman Hillcrest Cemetery.

DUDLEY GOODALL WOOTEN

Dudley Wooten

Born on June 19, 1860, near Springfield, Missouri. Family moved to Paris, Texas, during the Civil War. Graduated from Princeton College in 1875, attended Johns Hopkins University, and graduated from the law department of the University of Virginia in 1878. Admitted to the state bar in 1880, moved to Austin, and began to practice law. Served as Austin city attorney from 1884 to 1886. Married Ella R. Carter in 1883 and they had two children who both died in infancy. Ella died in 1886, and he later remarried. Baptist and Democrat. Moved to Dallas in 1888 and served as Dallas County judge from 1890 to 1892. Served one term as state representative, District 73, from 1899 to 1901. Wrote the two volume *Comprehensive History of Texas* (1898), which was eventually developed into *A Complete History of Texas* (1899). Served as the second president of the Texas State Historical Association, beginning in 1898.

Elected U.S. representative, 6th District, by defeating Philip Lindsey in the July 1901 special election to fill the seat of the late Robert Burke. Took office on July 13, 1901. Unseated by Scott Field in the 1902 Democratic primary and was succeeded by him on March 3, 1903. Moved to Seattle, Washington, and served on the Washington State Board of Higher Curricula. Taught law at Notre Dame University from 1924 to 1928. Died on February 7, 1929, while visiting Austin and was buried at Calvary Cemetery in Seattle, Washington.

FRANCIS EUGENE WORLEY

Eugene Worley

Born October 10, 1908, in Lone Wolf, Oklahoma. Moved to Shamrock, Texas, in 1922. Married Ann Spivey in 1937 and they had two children: Gene and Morgan. Attended public schools, Texas A&M College in 1927 and 1928, and the University of Texas law school from 1930 until 1935. Worked for a committee of the Texas legislature in 1932 while in school. Admitted to the state bar in 1935 and began law practice in Shamrock. Methodist, Mason, and Democrat. Served three terms as state representative, District 122, from 1935 to 1941. Served in the U.S. Navy during World War II. Elected U.S. representative, 18th District, in 1940 by defeating Republican J. V. Beveridge, and succeeded Marvin C. Jones on January 3, 1941. Reelected in 1942 by running unopposed, in 1944 by defeating Republican M. C. Bybee, in 1946 by defeating Republican Frank T. O'Brien, and in 1948 by defeating author and Republican J. Evetts Haley. Served on the House Agriculture Committee. Resigned on April 3, 1950, to accept a federal judgeship. Succeeded by Republican Ben H. Guill in May 1950. Served as U.S. Court of Customs and Patent Appeals judge from 1950 to 1959. Died on December 17, 1974, in Naples, Florida. His ashes were interred at Columbia Gardens Cemetery in Arlington, Virginia.

JAMES CLAUDE "JIM" WRIGHT, JR.

Born on December 22, 1922, in Fort Worth. Attended Fort Worth and Dallas public schools. Graduated from Adamson High School in Dallas in 1938. Attended Weatherford College from 1939 to 1940 and the University of Texas from 1940 to 1941. Married Mary Ethelyn "Mab" Lemons in 1942 and they had five children: James Claude, III, Virginia Sue "Ginger," Patricia Katherine, Alicia Marie, and Parker Stephen (who lived only eighteen months). Served in U.S. Army during World War II. Democrat.

Jim Wright

Served one term as state representative, District 103, from 1947 to 1949 and as mayor of Weatherford from 1950 to 1954. President of the League of Texas Municipalities in 1953. Elected U.S. representative, 12th District, in 1954 by unseating incumbent Wingate Lucas in the Democratic primary and by defeating Republican Tom S. Christopher in the general election. Succeeded Lucas on January 3, 1955. Reelected in 1956, 1958, and 1960 by running unopposed, in 1962 by defeating Republican Del Barron, in 1964 by defeating Republican Fred Dielman, and in 1966, 1968, 1970, and 1972 by running unopposed. Sought the U.S. Senate seat vacated by Lyndon Johnson in the 1961 special election, but placed third in the field of seventy-one candidates and did not make the runoff, which was won by Republican John Tower. Sought the U.S. Senate seat again briefly in 1966, but dropped out before the primary election. Divorced from his first wife in 1972. Married Betty Jean Hay later that year. Reelected in 1974 by defeating Republican James S. Garvey, in 1976 by defeating Republican W. R. Durham, in 1978 by defeating Republican Claude K. Brown, in 1980 by defeating Republican Jim Bradshaw and Libertarian Mrs. C. B. Maudlin, in 1982 by defeating Republican Jim Ryan and Libertarian Jim Ryan, in 1984 by running unopposed, in 1986 by defeating Republican Don McNiel, and in 1988 by defeating Independents Jim Ryan and Gary Johnson. Delegate to the Democratic national conventions in 1956, 1960, 1964, 1968, 1980, and 1984, and chaired the 1988 convention. Served as majority leader from 1977 through 1986. Served as Speaker of the U.S. House from 1987 to 1989. Resigned from Congress on June 30, 1989. Succeeded by Pete Geren in 1989. Authored *You and Your Congressman* (1965), *The Coming Water Famine* (1966), *Of Swords and Plowshares: A Collection of the Best Short Writings of Congressman Jim Wright* (1968), *Reflections of a Public Man* (1984), *Worth It All: My War for Peace* (1993), *Balance of Power* (1996), *Weatherford Days: A Time of Learnin'* (1996), and *The Flying Circus* (2005. Retired to Fort Worth.

> *What people really mean when they say "the system isn't working" is simply that they are not getting their way. The system assures that each of us may have his say. It does not guarantee that any of us will get his way.*
>
> —Jim Wright

WILLIAM BACON WRIGHT

Born on July 4, 1830, in Columbus, Georgia. Great-grandson of George Walton (1750–1804), who was a delegate to the Continental Congress from Georgia, from 1776 to 1777 and 1780 to 1781, and signer of the Declaration of Independence in 1776. Wright's obituaries reported that he graduated from Princeton University in 1847, but no records exist. He was also reported to have been a member of the state bar of Alabama and practiced law in Eufala. Married a Miss Greer in 1849 and they had four children. Moved to Texas in 1854 and practiced law. Elected representative, 6th District, to the Confederate Congress in November 1861 by defeating Benjamin H. Epperson, T. J. Rodgers, and R. H. Ward. Served on the House Patents, Claims, Enrolled Bills, and Indian Affairs committees. Unseated by Simpson Morgan in the 1863 general election. Served in Confederate States Army. Relocated to Clarksville following the war. His first wife died during the 1860s, and he married Pink Gates in 1868 and they had six children. Moved to Paris in 1873. Served as delegate to the State Constitutional Convention in 1875. Moved to San Antonio in

William Wright

1885 and entered the banking business. Died on August 10, 1895, in San Antonio, and was buried there at Dignowity Cemetery.

HARRY MCLEARY WURZBACH

Harry Wurzbach

Born on May 19, 1874, in San Antonio. Attended San Antonio public schools and graduated from Washington and Lee University in 1896. Studied law and was admitted to the state bar in 1896. Practiced law in San Antonio. Married Frances Darden Wagner in 1896. Republican. Served in the U.S. Army during the Spanish-American War. Following his time in the military, he moved to Seguin. Served as Guadalupe County prosecuting attorney from 1900 to 1902 and served four terms as Guadalupe County Judge from 1904 to 1910. Candidate for U.S. representative, 15th District, in 1916, but was defeated by incumbent Democrat John Nance Garner. Elected U.S. Representative, 14th District, in 1920 by unseating incumbent Democrat Carlos Bee in the general election. Succeeded Bee on March 4, 1921. Wurzbach was the first Texas-born Republican to be elected to Congress. Delegate to the Republican national convention in 1924. Reelected in 1922 by defeating Democrat Harry Hurtzburg, in 1924 by defeating Democrat D. S. Davenport, and in 1926 by defeating Democrat A. D. Rogers. In 1928 Wurzbach was unseated by Democrat Augustus McCloskey. Succeeded briefly by McCloskey on March 3, 1929. Wurzbach contested the November general election and eventually regained his seat on February 10, 1930, but only after McCloskey had served for almost one year. Reelected in 1930 by defeating Democrat Henry B. Dielman. Died while in office on November 6, 1931, in San Antonio and was buried there at the Military Cemetery. Succeeded in Congress by Richard M. Kleberg in November 1931. Wurzbach Road in San Antonio is named after his father Charles, (1835–92). Harry Wurzbach Road in San Antonio is named after the congressman. Wurzbach was the uncle of Texas congressman Robert Christian Eckhardt (1913–2001) (See also photo page 29.).

JOSEPH PEYTON WYATT JR.

Born on October 12, 1941, in Victoria. Attended Victoria public schools. Attended Victoria College in 1964. Received a B.A. in accounting from the University of Texas in 1968 and attended the University of Houston law school in 1970. Served in the U.S. Marine Corps Reserves from 1966 to 1970. Democrat, then a Republican. Married Mary Anne Wyatt. Served as aide to State Senator Bill Patman, U.S. Representative Clark Thompson, and Vice-president Lyndon Johnson. Delegate to the Democratic national convention in 1964. Employed as auditor with the Texas Alcoholic Beverage Commission. Served four terms as state representative, District 43 and 40, from 1971 to 1979. Elected U.S. representative, 14th District, in 1978 by unseating incumbent John Young in the Democratic primary and runoff and by defeating Republican Joy Yates in the November general election. Succeeded John Young on January 3, 1979. Young was under investigation at the time for sexual misconduct. Served on the House Ways and Means Committee. Served

Joe Wyatt

one term in Congress, until he himself was under investigation for sexual misconduct. Did not seek reelection in 1980 and was succeeded by Democrat Bill Patman on January 3, 1981. Joined the Republican Party about 1982. Ran unsuccessfully for his old congressional seat in the 1982 general election against Patman. Lives in Victoria.

RALPH WEBSTER YARBOROUGH

Born on June 8, 1903, in Chandler. Graduated from Tyler High School in 1919. Attended Sam Houston State Teachers College for one term and then received an appointment to the United States Military Academy at West Point in 1919. Attended West Point one year. Returned to Sam Houston State Teachers College in 1921. Taught school for three years in Delta and Martin Springs. Served in the Texas National Guard from 1923 to 1926. Spent one year working and studying in Germany at the Stendhal Academy. Employed by the American Chamber of Commerce in Berlin. Farm worker and oil tank builder. Graduated from the University of Texas law school in 1927. Baptist, Mason, Shriner, and Democrat. Admitted to the state bar and began practicing law in El Paso. Married Opal Warren in 1928 and they had one son, Richard. Hired by James Allred as assistant attorney general and served from 1931 to 1934. During this time, he was noted for defending the Permanent School Fund and winning cases against several oil companies, including the

Ralph Yarborough

Magnolia Petroleum Company. Served on the board of directors for the Lower Colorado River Authority from 1935 to 1936. Lectured on land law at the University of Texas in 1935. Appointed by now Governor Allred as judge, 53rd District, in Austin in 1936. Yarborough won the election for this post later in the year and served until 1941. Candidate for attorney general in 1938, but placed third behind Walter Woodul and Gerald Mann. Served in the U.S. Army during World War II. Served as a judge advocate in Germany and Japan. Returned to Austin to practice law following the war. Unsuccessful candidate for governor in 1952, 1954, and 1956, losing the Democratic primaries in those years to conservatives Allan Shivers and finally Price Daniel in the very close 1956 runoff election. Elected U.S. senator by defeating Democrat Martin Dies, Republican Thad Hutcheson, and others in the 1957 special election to fill the seat vacated by Price Daniel. Succeeded William Blakley in the Rusk succession of U.S. senators from Texas. One of five senators from the South to support the Civil Rights Act of 1957. Reelected to a full term in 1958 by defeating Blakley in the Democratic primary and Republican Roy Whittenburg in the general election, and in 1964 defeated Republican George H. W. Bush, but was unseated by Lloyd Bentsen in 1970 Democratic primary. Served as U.S. senator from April 29, 1957, to January 2, 1971. Served on the Senate Labor and Public Welfare Committee, which he chaired from 1969 to 1971. Wrote, sponsored, or co-sponsored the Elementary and Secondary Education Act of 1965, the Higher Education Act of 1965, the GI Bill of 1966, the Bilingual Education Act of 1967, and the Endangered Species Act of 1969. Supporter of civil rights, education, health and environmental legislation, and joined the handful of senators from the South in supporting Civil Rights Act of 1964 and the Voting Rights Act of 1965. His efforts in the Senate led to the preservation of the Texas-Padre Island National Seashore in 1962, Guadalupe Mountains National Park in 1966, and Big Thicket National Preserve in 1971, Fort Davis National Historic Site, and the Alibates Flint Quarries National Historic Monument. Wrote the introduction to *Three Men in Texas: Bedichek, Webb and Dobie* (1967) as Dobie was a close friend. Ran for John Tower's Senate seat in 1972, but was defeated in the Democratic primary by Barefoot Sanders. Resumed practice of law in Austin. Died on January 27, 1996, in Austin and was buried there at the State Cemetery. He was the last liberal to serve in national office from Texas. In 1995 the maintenance facility and visitor's center at the Big Thicket National Preserve was renamed the Ralph W. Yarborough Center in his honor. (See also photo page 24.)

Let's put the jam on the lower shelf so the little people can reach it.

—Ralph Yarborough

CHARLES HENDERSON YOAKUM

Born on July 10, 1849, near Tehuacana. Attended Larissa College and Cumberland College. Taught school and studied law. Admitted to the state bar in 1874 and practiced in Emory. Methodist Episcopal, Mason, Odd Fellow, and Democrat. Served as Rains County prosecuting attorney in 1876. Moved to Greenville in 1883 and continued to practice law. Elected district attorney, 8th Judicial District, and served from 1886 to 1890. Served one term as state senator, District 5, from 1893 to 1895, but resigned early to accept his congressional seat. Elected U.S. representative, 3rd District, in 1894 by defeating Populist J. M. Perdue and succeeded Constantine Kilgore on March 4, 1895. Did not seek reelection in 1896, due to poor health, and was succeeded by Reese De Graffenreid on March 3, 1897. Moved to Los Angeles, California. Returned to Texas and settled in Fort Worth in 1904 to take position as general attorney for the Frisco Rail System. Died on January 1, 1909, of a heart attack while at home in Fort Worth and was buried at Myrtle Cemetery in Ennis.

Charles Yoakum

JAMES YOUNG

Born July 18, 1866, in Henderson. Attended public schools. Graduated from the University of Texas law department in 1891. Admitted to the state bar and practiced in Kaufman. Married Allie Nash in 1892 and they had three children: Herbert, James, Jr., and Mrs T. L. Wynne. Democrat. Elected U.S. Representative, 3rd District, in 1910 by defeating R. B. Eldor. Succeeded Gordon J. Russell on March 4, 1911. Reelected 1912 by defeating B. F. Bryant, in 1914 by defeating Socialist E. T. Bryant, in 1916 by defeating Socialist J. L. Scoggin, and in 1918 by running unopposed. Did not seek reelection in 1920 and was succeeded by Morgan G. Sanders on March 3, 1921. Returned to Kaufman to practice law. Candidate for governor in 1930, but placed fifth in a field of seven candidates in the Democratic primary, well behind winner Miriam Ferguson. Moved to Henderson in 1931 and to Dallas six years later. Died on April 29, 1942, in Dallas and was buried at Kaufman Cemetery in Kaufman.

James Young

Failure to enforce any one law leads to infractions of another, and then another, until a state of mind is reached by which all laws will be disregarded.

—James Young

JOHN ANDREW YOUNG

Born November 10, 1916, in Corpus Christi. Attended Incarnate Word Academy and Corpus Christi College. Received B.A. from St. Edwards University in 1937 and L.L.B. from the University of Texas in 1940. Admitted to the state bar in 1940 and began his law practice. Served in the U.S. Navy during World War II. Married Jane F. Gallier in 1950 and they had five children: Catherine Gaffney, Nancy Rae, John, Jr., Robert Harold, and Mary Patricia. Democrat. Served as assistant Nueces County attorney in 1946, assistant Nueces County district attorney from 1947 to 1950, Nueces County attorney from 1951 to 1952, and Nueces County judge from 1953 to 1956. Elected U.S. representative, 14th District, in 1956 by defeating Republican Olive B. Stichter. Succeeded John J. Bell on January 3, 1957. Reelected in 1958 and 1960 by running unopposed, in 1962 by defeating Republican Lawrence E. Hoover, in

John Young

1964 by defeating Republican Billy Patton, in 1966, 1968, 1970, 1972, and 1974 by running unopposed, and in 1976 by defeating Republican L. Dean Holford. Served on the House Committee for Rules. Young received much negative publicity regarding an affair he had with an aide and the ensuing scandal. Unseated in the 1978 Democratic primary election by Joe Wyatt and was succeeded by him on January 3, 1979. Young remained in Washington, D.C., and lived in McLean, Virginia. Died on January 22, 2002, in Arlington, Virginia, and was buried in Arlington National Cemetery. (See also photo page 24.)

I don't see how anyone can be a member of Congress unless he is a lawyer.

—John Young

HISTORICAL DATA

CONTENTS

CHRONOLOGICAL LIST OF U.S. SENATORS BY SUCCESSION

The following is a list of the men and women who have represented Texas in the United States Senate. Each name is followed by the dates served in office. Each state is allowed two senators by the U.S. Constitution. These two lines or successions of Texas Senators carry the name of the first man to hold that office, either Thomas Rusk or Sam Houston. Only Horace Chilton and William A. Blakley have served in both lines. Of the four occasions, three followed appointments by the governor. Those noted with an asterisk were appointed by the governor. Oddly, none of those who have been appointed were ever reelected as a U.S. senator (Horace Chilton served non-consecutive terms in different successions). A gap in the list between 1860 and 1870 indicates the break in representation to the U.S. Senate during the Civil War. Louis T. Wigfall served as U.S. senator and as a Confederate senator. Representation to the Confederate Congress is shown elsewhere. Senators were selected by the state legislature, but with the passage of the Seventeenth Amendment to the U.S. Constitution in 1913, voters were given the ability to choose their senator directly. Following this, it was three years before a Texas senator's term expired. Charles A. Culberson was the first U.S. senator elected directly by the people of the state.

RUSK SUCCESSION

1. Thomas J. Rusk, February 21, 1846, to July 20, 1857
2. J. Pinckney Henderson, November 9, 1857, to June 4, 1858
3. Matthias Ward, September 27, 1858, to December 5, 1859
4. Louis T. Wigfall, December 5, 1859, to March 23, 1861
5. Oran M. Roberts, August 21, 1866

6. James W. Flanagan, March 30, 1870, to March 3, 1875
7. Samuel B. Maxey, March 4, 1875, to March 3, 1887
8. John H. Reagan, March 4, 1887, to June 10, 1891
9. Horace Chilton, June 10, 1891, to March 22, 1892 *
10. Roger Quarles Mills, March 29, 1892, to March 3, 1899
11. Charles A. Culberson, March 4, 1899, to March 3, 1923
12. Earle B. Mayfield, March 4, 1923, to March 3, 1929
13. Tom Connally, March 4, 1929, to January 3, 1953
14. Price Daniel, January 3, 1953, to January 14, 1957
15. William A. Blakley, January 15, 1957, to April 28, 1957 *
16. Ralph W. Yarborough, April 29, 1957, to January 2, 1971
17. Lloyd Bentsen, January 3, 1971, to January 20, 1993
18. Robert Krueger, January 21, 1993, to June 14, 1993 *
19. Kay Bailey Hutchison, June 14, 1993 to present

HOUSTON SUCCESSION

1. Sam Houston, February 21, 1846, to March 4, 1859
2. John Hemphill, March 4, 1859, to July 11, 1861
3. David Gouverneur Burnet, August 21, 1866

4. Morgan Calvin Hamilton, February 22, 1870, to March 3, 1877
5. Richard Coke, March 4, 1877, to March 3, 1895
6. Horace Chilton, March 4, 1895, to March 3, 1901
7. Joseph W. Bailey, March 4, 1901, to January 3, 1913
8. Rienzi Melville Johnston, January 4, 1913, to February 2, 1913
9. Morris Sheppard, Febuary 3, 1913, to April 9, 1941
10. Andrew Jackson Houston, April 21, 1941, to June 26, 1941 *
11. W. Lee O'Daniel, August 4, 1941, to January 3, 1949
12. Lyndon B. Johnson, January 3, 1949, to January 3, 1961
13. William A. Blakley, January 3, 1961, to June 14, 1961 *
14. John G. Tower, June 15, 1961, to January 3, 1985
15. William Philip Gramm, January 3, 1985, to December 2, 2002
16. John Cornyn, December 2, 2002, to present*

* Appointed by the governor

Chronological List Of U.S. Representatives By District

The following is a list of the men and women by congressional district who have represented Texas in the United States House of Representatives. The date the district was first represented is also noted. In the case of at-large districts, the time period that district existed is noted. A gap in the lists between 1860 and 1870 in the first two congressional districts is shown, indicating the break in representation to the U.S. Congress during the Civil War. Representation to the Confederate Congress is shown elsewhere.

1st Congressional District (first represented in 1846)

1. David Spangler Kaufman, 1846-1851
2. Richard A. Scurry, 1851-1853
3. George Washington Smyth, 1853-1855
4. Lemuel Dale Evans, 1855-1857
5. John H. Reagan, 1857-1861

6. George Washington Whitmore, 1870-1871
7. William Smith Herndon, 1871-1875
8. John H. Reagan, 1875-1883
9. Charles Stewart, 1883-1893
10. Joseph C. Hutcheson, 1893-1897
11. Thomas H. Ball, 1897-1903
12. Morris Sheppard, 1903-1913
13. Horace W. Vaughan, 1913-1915
14. Eugene Black, 1915-1929
15. Wright Patman, 1929-1977
16. Sam B. Hall, 1977-1985
17. Jim Chapman, 1985-1995
18. Max Sandlin, 1997-2005
19. Louie Gohmert, 2005-

2nd Congressional District (first represented in 1846)

1. Timothy Pilsbury, 1846-1849
2. Volney Erskine Howard, 1849-1853
3. Peter Hansborough Bell, 1853-1857
4. Guy Morrison Bryan, 1857-1859
5. Andrew Jackson Hamilton, 1859-1861

6. John Cogswell Conner, 1869-1873
7. William Pinckney McLean, 1873-1875
8. David Browning Culberson, 1875-1883
9. John H. Reagan, 1883-1887
10. William H. Martin, 1887-1891
11. John Benjamin Long, 1891-1893
12. Samuel Bronson Cooper, 1893-1905
13. Moses L. Broocks, 1905-1907
14. Samuel B. Cooper, 1907-1909
15. Martin Dies, 1909-1919
16. John C. Box, 1919-1931
17. Martin Dies, 1931-1945
18. Jesse M. Combs, 1945-1953
19. Jack Brooks, 1953-1967
20. John Dowdy, 1967-1973
21. Charles Wilson, 1973-1995
22. Jim Turner, 1997- 2005
23. Ted Poe, 2005-

3rd Congressional District (First Represented in 1869)

1. William Thomas Clark, 1869-1872
2. DeWitt Clinton Giddings, 1872-1875
3. James Webb Throckmorton, 1875-1879
4. Olin Wellborn, 1879-1883
5. James Henry Jones, 1883-1887
6. Constantine Buckley Kilgore, 1887-1895
7. Charles Henderson Yoakum, 1895-1897
8. Reese C. De Graffenreid, 1897-1903
9. Gordon J. Russell, 1903-1910
10. Robert Maclin Lively, 1910-1911
11. James Young, 1911-1921
12. Morgan G. Sanders, 1921-1939
13. Lindley Beckworth, 1939-1953
14. Brady Gentry, 1953-1955
15. Lindley Beckworth, 1955-1967
16. Joe Pool, 1967-1968
17. James M. Collins, 1968-1983
18. Steve Bartlett, 1983-1991
19. Sam Johnson, 1991-

4th Congressional District (First Represented in 1869)

1. Edward Degener, 1869-1871
2. John Hancock, 1871-1875
3. Roger Quarles Mills, 1875-1883
4. David Browning Culberson, 1883-1897
5. John W. Cranford, 1897-1899
6. John L. Sheppard, 1899-1902
7. Morris Sheppard, 1902-1903
8. Choice B. Randell, 1903-1913
9. Sam Rayburn, 1913-1961
10. Ray Roberts, 1961-1981
11. Ralph M. Hall, 1981-

Two At-Large Districts (1873-1875)

1. Roger Quarles Mills, 1873-1875
2. Asa Hoxie Willie, 1873-1875

5th Congressional District (First Represented in 1875)

1. John Hancock, 1875-1877
2. DeWitt Clinton Giddings, 1877-1879
3. George Washington Jones, 1879-1883
4. James Webb Throckmorton, 1883-1887
5. Silas Hare, 1887-1891
6. Joseph W. Bailey, 1891-1901
7. Choice B. Randell, 1901-1903
8. Jack Beall, 1903-1915
9. Hatton W. Sumners, 1915-1947
10. Frank Wilson, 1947-1955
11. Bruce Alger, 1955-1965
12. Earle Cabell, 1965-1973
13. Alan Steelman, 1973-1977
14. Jim Mattox, 1977-1983
15. John Bryant, 1983-1997
16. Pete Sessions, 1997-2003
17. Jeb Hensarling, 2003-

6th Congressional District (First Represented in 1875)

1. Gustave Schleicher, 1875-1879
2. Christopher Columbus Upson, 1879-1883
3. Olin Wellborn, 1883-1887
4. Jo Abbott, 1887-1897
5. Robert E. Burke, 1897-1901
6. Dudley Wooten, 1901-1903
7. Scott Field, 1903-1907
8. Rufus Hardy, 1907-1923
9. Luther A. Johnson, 1923-1947
10. Olin Teague, 1947-1979
11. Phil Gramm, 1979-1985
12. Joe Barton, 1985-

7th Congressional District (First Represented in 1883)

1. Thomas P. Ochiltree, 1883-1885
2. William Henry Crain, 1885-1893
3. George Cassety Pendleton, 1893-1897

4. Robert L. Henry, 1897-1903
5. Alexander W. Gregg, 1903-1919
6. Clay Stone Briggs, 1919-1933
7. Nat Patton, 1935-1945
8. Tom Pickett, 1945-1953
9. John Dowdy, 1953-1967
10. George Bush, 1967-1971
11. Bill Archer, 1971-2001
12. John Culberson, 2001-

8TH CONGRESSIONAL DISTRICT (FIRST REPRESENTED IN 1883)

1. James Francis Miller, 1883-1887
2. Littleton Wilde Moore, 1887-1893
3. Charles Keith Bell, 1893-1897
4. Samuel W. T. Lanham, 1897-1903
5. Thomas Ball, 1903-1903
6. John M. Pinckney, 1903-1905
7. John M. Moore, 1905-1913
8. Joe H. Eagle, 1913-1921
9. Daniel E. Garrett, 1921-1932
10. Joe H. Eagle, 1933-1937
11. Albert Thomas, 1937-1967
12. Bob Eckhardt, 1967-1981
13. Jack Fields, 1981-1997
14. Kevin Brady, 1997-

9TH CONGRESSIONAL DISTRICT (FIRST REPRESENTED IN 1883)

1. Roger Quarles Mills, 1883-1892
2. Edwin LeRoy Antony, 1892-1893
3. Joseph D. Sayers, 1893-1899
4. Albert S. Burleson, 1899-1903
5. George F. Burgess, 1903-1917
6. Joseph J. Mansfield, 1917-1949
7. Clark W. Thompson, 1949-1967
8. Jack Brooks, 1967-1995
9. Steve Stockman, 1995-1997
10. Nicholas V. Lampson, 1997-2005

11. Al Green, 2005-

10TH CONGRESSIONAL DISTRICT (FIRST REPRESENTED IN 1883)

1. John Hancock, 1883-1885
2. Joseph D. Sayers, 1885-1893
3. Walter Gresham, 1893-1895
4. Miles Crowley, 1895-1897
5. Robert B. Hawley, 1897-1901
6. George F. Burgess, 1901-1903
7. Albert S. Burleson, 1903-1913
8. James P. Buchanan, 1915-1937
9. Lyndon B. Johnson, 1937-1949
10. Homer Thornberry, 1949-1963
11. Jake Pickle, 1963-1995
12. Lloyd Doggett, 1995-2005
13. Mike McCaul, 2005-

11TH CONGRESSIONAL DISTRICT (FIRST REPRESENTED IN 1883)

1. S. W. T. Lanham, 1883-1893
2. William Henry Crain, 1893-1896
3. Rudolph Kleberg, 1896-1903
4. Robert L. Henry, 1903-1917
5. Tom Connally, 1917-1929
6. Oliver H. Cross, 1929-1937
7. W. R. Poage, 1937-1979
8. Marvin Leath, 1979-1991
9. Chet Edwards, 1991-2005
10. Michael Conaway, 2005-

12TH CONGRESSIONAL DISTRICT (FIRST REPRESENTED IN 1893)

1. Thomas Moore Paschal, 1893-1895
2. George Henry Noonan, 1895-1897
3. James L. Slayden, 1897-1903
4. Oscar W. Gillespie, 1903-1911
5. Oscar Callaway, 1911-1917
6. James C. Wilson, 1917-1921
7. Fritz G. Lanham, 1921-1947

8. Wingate H. Lucas, 1947-1955
9. Jim Wright, 1955-1989
10. Pete Geren, 1989-1997
11. Kay Granger, 1997-

13th Congressional District (First Represented in 1893)

1. James V. Cockrell, 1893-1897
2. John H. Stephens, 1897-1917
3. John Marvin Jones, 1917-1919
4. Lucian W. Parrish, 1919-1923
5. Guinn Williams, 1923-1933
6. William D. McFarlane, 1933-1939
7. Ed Gossett, 1939-1953
8. Frank Ikard, 1953-1963
9. Graham B. Purcell, 1963-1973
10. Bob Price, 1973-1975
11. Jack Hightower, 1975-1985
12. Beau Boulter, 1985-1989
13. Bill Sarpaulis, 1989-1995
14. William M. "Mac" Thornberry, 1995-

14th Congressional District (First Represented in 1903)

1. James L. Slayden, 1903-1919
2. Carlos Bee, 1919-1921
3. Harry M. Wurzbach, 1921-1929
4. Augustus McCloskey, 1929-1931
5. Harry M. Wurzbach, 1931
6. Richard M. Kleberg, 1931-1945
7. John E. Lyle, 1945-1955
8. John J. Bell, 1955-1957
9. John Young, 1957-1979
10. Joe Wyatt, 1979-1981
11. William N. Patman, 1981-1985
12. Mac Sweeney, 1985-1989
13. Greg H. Laughlin, 1989-1997
14. Ron Paul, 1997-

15th Congressional District (First Represented in 1903)

1. John N. Garner, 1903-1935
2. Milton H. West, 1935-1949
3. Lloyd M. Bentsen, Jr., 1949-1955
4. Joe Kilgore, 1955-1965
5. Eligio de la Garza, 1965-1997
6. Rubén Hinojosa, 1997-

16th Congressional District (First Represented in 1903)

1. William R. Smith, 1903-1917
2. Thomas L. Blanton, 1917-1919
3. Claude Hudspeth, 1919-1931
4. Ewing Thomason, 1931-1949
5. Ken Regan, 1949-1955
6. J. T. Rutherford, 1955-1963
7. Ed Foreman, 1963-1965
8. Richard C. White, 1965-1983
9. Ronald D. Coleman, 1983-1997
10. Silvestre Reyes, 1997-

Two At-Large Districts (1913-1919)

Daniel E. Garrett, 1913-1915
Hatton W. Summers, 1913-1915

James H. "Cyclone" Davis, 1915-1917
Atkins McLemore, 1915-1919

Daniel E. Garrett, 1917-1919

17th Congressional District (First Represented in 1919)

1. Thomas Blanton, 1919-1929
2. Robert Q. Lee, 1929-1931
3. Thomas Blanton, 1931-1937
4. Clyde L. Garrett, 1937-1941
5. Sam Russell, 1941-1947
6. Omar Burleson, 1947-1979
7. Charles W. Stenholm, 1979-2005

8. Chet Edwards, 2005-

18TH CONGRESSIONAL DISTRICT (FIRST REPRESENTED IN 1919)

1. Marvin Jones, 1919-1941
2. Eugene Worley, 1941-1951
3. Ben Guill, 1950-1951
4. Walter Rogers, 1951-1967
5. Bob Price, 1967-1973
6. Barbara Jordan, 1973-1979
7. Mickey Leland, 1979-1989
8. Craig Washington, 1991-1995
9. Sheila Jackson Lee, 1995-

THREE AT-LARGE DISTRICTS (1933-1935)

Three places were required to fill representative positions because the legislature failed to redistrict the state following the Census of 1930.

Place One
George B. Terrell

Place Two
Sterling P. Strong

Place Three
Joseph W. Bailey Jr.

19TH CONGRESSIONAL DISTRICT (FIRST REPRESENTED IN 1935)

1. George Mahon, 1935-1979
2. Kent Hance, 1979-1985
3. Larry Combest, 1985-2005
4. Randy Neugebauer, 2005-

20TH CONGRESSIONAL DISTRICT (FIRST REPRESENTED IN 1935)

1. Maury Maverick, 1935-1939
2. Paul Kilday, 1939-1961
3. Henry B. Gonzalez, 1961-1999
4. Charlie Gonzalez, 1999-

21ST CONGRESSIONAL DISTRICT (FIRST REPRESENTED IN 1935)

1. Charles L. South, 1935-1943
2. Ovie Clark Fisher, 1943-1975
3. Robert Krueger, 1975-1979
4. Tom Loeffler, 1979-1987
5. Lamar Smith, 1987-

ONE AT-LARGE DISTRICT (1953-1959)

Martin Dies, Jr., 1953-1959

22ND CONGRESSIONAL DISTRICT (FIRST REPRESENTED IN 1959)

1. Bob Casey, 1959-1976
2. Ron Paul, 1976-1977
3. Bob Gammage, 1977-1979
4. Ron Paul, 1979-1985
5. Thomas DeLay, 1985-2006
6. Shelley Sekula-Gibbs, 2006-2007
7. Nick Lampson, 2007-

ONE AT-LARGE DISTRICT (1963-1965)

Joe Pool, 1963-1965

23RD CONGRESSIONAL DISTRICT (FIRST REPRESENTED IN 1967)

1. Abraham Kazen, Jr., 1967-1985
2. Albert G. Bustamante, 1985-1993
3. Henry Bonilla, 1993-2007
4 Ciro Rodriguez, 2007-

24TH CONGRESSIONAL DISTRICT (FIRST REPRESENTED IN 1973)

1. Dale Milford, 1973-1979
2. Martin Frost, 1979-2005
3. Kenny Marchant, 2005-

25TH CONGRESSIONAL DISTRICT (FIRST REPRESENTED IN 1983)

1. Michael A. Andrews, 1983-1995
2. Ken Bentsen, 1995-2003
3. Chris Bell, 2003-2005

4. Lloyd Doggett, 2005-

26TH CONGRESSIONAL DISTRICT (FIRST REPRESENTED IN 1983)

1. Tom Vandergriff, 1983-1985
2. Dick Armey, 1985-2003
3. Mike Burgess, 2003-

27TH CONGRESSIONAL DISTRICT (FIRST REPRESENTED IN 1983)

1. Solomon P. Ortiz, 1983-

28TH CONGRESSIONAL DISTRICT (FIRST REPRESENTED IN 1993)

1. Frank Tejeda, 1993-1996
2. Ciro Rodriguez, 1997-2005
3. Henry Cueller, 2005-

29TH CONGRESSIONAL DISTRICT (FIRST REPRESENTED IN 1993)

1. Gene Green, 1993-

30TH CONGRESSIONAL DISTRICT (FIRST REPRESENTED IN 1993)

1. Eddie Bernice Johnson, 1993-

31ST CONGRESSIONAL DISTRICT (FIRST REPRESENTED IN 2002)

1. John Carter, 2002 -

32ND CONGRESSIONAL DISTRICT (FIRST REPRESENTED IN 2004)

1. Pete Sessions, 2004 -

Texas Representatives To The Confederate Congresses

The following is a list of the men who represented Texas in the Confederate Congress. The Confederate Congress was organized very similarly to the U.S. Congress. There were two senators, and Texas was allotted six congressional districts (allocation of districts because of the 1860 census would have given Texas a total of six districts in the U.S. Congress). A number of these men had also served in the U.S. Congress prior to the war. Only a handful would serve again in the U.S. Congress. The two senators drew a four-year and a six-year term and thus served for the duration of the war.

Delegates to the Confederate Provisional Congress, 1861-1862

John Hemphill
John Gregg
*William Beck Ochiltree
Williamson Simpson Oldham
John Henninger Reagan
Thomas Neville Waul
Louis Trezevant Wigfall

Senators in the Confederate Congress

Williamson Simpson Oldham, November 16, 1861, until fall of Confederacy
Louis Trezevant Wigfall, November 16, 1861, until fall of Confederacy

Representatives in the Confederate Congresses

First Confederate Congress, 1862-1864

1st District	John Allen Wilcox
2nd District	Caleb Claiborne Herbert
3rd District	Peter W. Gray
4th District	Franklin Barlow Sexton
5th District	Malcolm Daniel Graham
6th District	William Bacon Wright

Second Confederate Congress, 1864-1865

1st District	John Allen Wilcox (died in office, then)
	Stephen Heard Darden
2nd District	Caleb Claiborne Herbert
3rd District	Anthony Martin Branch
4th District	Franklin Barlow Sexton
5th District	John Robert Baylor
6th District	Simpson Harris Morgan

COMPOSITION OF CONFEDERATE CONGRESSIONAL DISTRICTS BY COUNTY

1ST DISTRICT

Anderson, Angelina, Chambers, Cherokee, Hardin, Houston, Jasper, Jefferson, Liberty, Nacogdoches, Newton, Orange, Panola, Polk, Sabine, San Augustine, Shelby, Trinity, Tyler

2ND DISTRICT

Atascosa, Bandera, Bee, Bexar, Blanco, Calhoun, Cameron, Comal, Concho, Dawson, DeWitt, Dimmit, Duval, Edwards, El Paso, Encinal (now part of Webb County), Frio, Gillespie, Goliad, Gonzales, Guadalupe, Hays, Hidalgo, Karnes, Kerr, Kimble, Kinney, La Salle, Live Oak, Llano, Mason, Maverick, McCulloch, McMullen, Medina, Menard, Nueces, Presidio, Refugio, San Patricio, San Saba, Starr, Uvalde, Victoria, Webb, Wilson, Zapata, Zavala,

3RD DISTRICT

Bosque, Brazos, Brown, Callahan, Coleman, Comanche, Coryell, Eastland, Ellis, Erath, Falls, Freestone, Galveston, Grimes, Hamilton, Harris, Hill, Johnson, Leon, Limestone, Madison, McLennan, Montgomery, Navarro, Robertson, Runnels, Taylor, Walker

4TH DISTRICT

Austin, Bastrop, Bell, Brazoria, Burleson, Burnet, Caldwell, Colorado, Fayette, Fort Bend, Jackson, Lampasas, Lavaca, Matagorda, Milam, Travis, Washington, Wharton, Williamson

5TH DISTRICT

Buchanan, Dallas, Harrison, Henderson, Jones, Kaufman, Palo Pinto, Parker, Rusk, Shackelford, Smith, Tarrant, Upshur, Van Zandt, Wood

6TH DISTRICT

Bowie, Cass, Clay, Collin, Cook, Denton, Fannin, Grayson, Greer, Hardeman, Haskell, Hopkins, Hunt, Jack, Lamar, Marion, Montague, Red River, Throckmorton, Titus, Wichita, Wilbarger, Wise, Young

Confederate Congress Session Dates

The first two sessions of the provisional congress were held in Montgomery, Alabama, but because of a severe shortage of space they moved to the Virginia State Capitol in Richmond.

CONGRESS	BEGINNING DATE	ENDING DATE
Provisional Congress		
First Session	February 4, 1861	March 16, 1861
Second Session	April 29, 1861	May 21, 1861
Third Session	July 20, 1861	August 31, 1861
Fourth Session	September 3, 1861	(one day only)
Fifth Session	November 18, 1861	February 17, 1862
First Congress		
First Session	February 18, 1862	April 21, 1862
Second Session	August 18, 1862	October 13, 1862
Third Session	January 12, 1863	May 1, 1863
Fourth Session	December 6, 1863	February 17, 1864
Second Congress		
First Session	May 2, 1864	June 14, 1864
Second Session	November 7, 1864	March 18, 1865

U.S. Congress Session Dates

Congress	Beginning Date	Ending Date
1st	March 4, 1789	March 3, 1791
2nd	October 24, 1791	March 2, 1793
3rd	December 2, 1793	March 3, 1795
4th	December 7, 1795	March 3, 1797
5th	May 15, 1797	March 3, 1799
6th	December 2, 1799	March 3, 1801
7th	December 7, 1801	March 3, 1803
8th	October 17, 1803	March 3, 1805
9th	December 2, 1805	March 3, 1807
10th	October 26, 1807	March 3, 1809
11th	May 22, 1809	March 3, 1811
12th	November 4, 1811	March 3, 1813
13th	May 24, 1813	March 3, 1815
14th	December 4, 1815	March 3, 1817
15th	December 1, 1817	March 3, 1819
16th	December 6, 1819	March 3, 1821
17th	December 3, 1821	March 3, 1823
18th	December 1, 1823	March 3, 1825
19th	December 5, 1825	March 3, 1827
20th	December 3, 1827	March 3, 1829
21st	December 7, 1829	March 3, 1831
22nd	December 5, 1831	March 2, 1833
23rd	December 2, 1833	March 3, 1835
24th	December 7, 1835	March 3, 1837

Texas Becomes an Independent Nation 1836

Congress	Beginning Date	Ending Date
25th	September 4, 1837	March 3, 1839
26th	December 2, 1839	March 3, 1841
27th	May 31, 1841	March 3, 1843
28th	December 4, 1843	March 3, 1845

Texas Admitted to the United States December 29, 1846

Congress	Beginning Date	Ending Date
29th	December 1, 1845	March 3, 1847
30th	December 6, 1847	March 3, 1849
31st	December 3, 1849	March 3, 1851
32nd	December 1, 1851	March 3, 1853
33rd	December 5, 1853	March 3, 1855
34th	December 3, 1855	March 3, 1857
35th	December 7, 1857	March 3, 1859
36th	December 5, 1859	March 3, 1861

Texas Secedes from the United States February 1, 1861

Congress	Beginning Date	Ending Date
37th	July 4, 1861	March 3, 1863
38th	December 7, 1863	March 3, 1865
39th	December 4, 1865	March 3, 1867
40th	March 4, 1867	March 3, 1869
41st	March 4, 1869	March 3, 1871

Texas Readmitted to the United States March 30, 1870

Congress	Beginning Date	Ending Date
42nd	March 4, 1871	March 3, 1873
43rd	December 1, 1873	March 3, 1875
44th	December 6, 1875	March 3, 1877

45th	October 15, 1877	March 3, 1879
46th	March 18, 1879	March 3, 1881
47th	December 5, 1881	March 3, 1883
48th	December 3, 1883	March 3, 1885
49th	December 7, 1885	March 3, 1887
50th	December 5, 1887	March 3, 1889
51st	December 2, 1889	March 3, 1891
52nd	December 7, 1891	March 3, 1893
53rd	August 7, 1893	March 3, 1895
54th	December 2, 1895	March 3, 1897
55th	March 15, 1897	March 3, 1899
56th	December 4, 1899	March 3, 1901
57th	December 2, 1901	March 3, 1903
58th	November 9, 1903	March 3, 1905
59th	December 4, 1905	March 3, 1907
60th	December 2, 1907	March 3, 1909
61st	March 15, 1909	March 3, 1911
62nd	April 4, 1911	March 3, 1913
63rd	April 7, 1913	March 3, 1915
64th	December 6, 1915	March 3, 1917
65th	April 2, 1917	March 3, 1919
66th	May 19, 1919	March 3, 1921
67th	April 11, 1921	March 3, 1923
68th	December 3, 1923	March 3, 1925
69th	December 7, 1925	March 3, 1927
70th	December 5, 1927	March 3, 1929
71st	April 15, 1929	March 3, 1931
72nd	December 7, 1931	March 3, 1933
73rd	March 9, 1933	June 18, 1934
74th	January 3, 1935	June 20, 1936
75th	January 5, 1937	June 16, 1938
76th	January 3, 1939	January 3, 1941
77th	January 3, 1941	December 16, 1942
78th	January 6, 1943	December 19, 1944
79th	January 3, 1945	August 2, 1946
80th	January 3, 1947	December 31, 1948
81st	January 3, 1949	January 2, 1951
82nd	January 3, 1951	July 7, 1952
83rd	January 3, 1953	December 2, 1954
84th	January 5, 1955	July 27, 1956
85th	January 3, 1957	August 24, 1958
86th	January 7, 1959	September 1, 1960
87th	January 3, 1961	October 13, 1962
88th	January 9, 1963	October 3, 1964
89th	January 4, 1965	October 22, 1966
90th	January 10, 1967	October 14, 1968
91st	January 3, 1969	January 2, 1971
92nd	January 21, 1971	October 18, 1972
93rd	January 3, 1973	December 20, 1974
94th	January 14, 1975	October 1, 1976
95th	January 4, 1977	October 15, 1978
96th	January 15, 1979	December 16, 1980
97th	January 25, 1981	December 23, 1982
98th	January 3, 1983	October 12, 1984
99th	January 3, 1985	October 18, 1986
100th	January 6, 1987	October 22, 1988
101st	January 3, 1989	October 28, 1990
102nd	January 3, 1991	October 9, 1992
103rd	January 5, 1993	December 1, 1994
104th	January 4, 1995	October 4, 1996
105th	January 3, 1997	December 19, 1998
106th	January 6, 1999	December 15, 2000
107th	January 3, 2001	November 22, 2002
108th	January 7, 2003	December 9, 2004
109th	January 4, 2005	

COMPOSITION OF U.S. CONGRESSIONAL DISTRICTS IN TEXAS BY COUNTY

The following is a list of Texas congressional districts by session of Congress, along with the counties that comprise the district. Some counties may contain several districts and are noted by "(part)." A small number of the counties noted no longer exist.

29TH THROUGH 31ST CONGRESSES (1845-1851)

1st District: Fanning, Red River, Bowie, Harrison, Shelby, Jefferson, Jasper, Rusk, Sabine, San Augustine, Liberty, Houston, Nacogdoches

2nd District: Robertson, Brazos, Montgomery, Harris, Galveston, Brazoria, Fort Bend, Matagorda, Jackson, Victoria, Austin, Colorado, Fayette, Gonzales, Travis, Bastrop, Washington, Bexar, Goliad, Refugio, San Patricio, Milam

32ND THROUGH 34TH CONGRESSES (1851-1859)

1st District: Anderson, Angelina, Bowie, Cass, Cherokee, Collin, Cooke, Dallas, Denton, Fannin, Grayson, Harrison, Henderson, Hopkins, Houston, Hunt, Jasper, Jefferson, Kaufman, Lamar, Liberty, Nacogdoches, Newton, Panola, Polk, Red River, Rusk, Sabine, San Augustine, Shelby, Smith, Titus, Tyler, Trinity, Upshur, Van Vandt, Wood

2nd District: Austin, Bastrop, Bell, Bexar, Brazoria, Brazos, Burleson, Caldwell, Calhoun, Cameron, Colorado, Comal, DeWitt, Ellis, El Paso, Falls, Fayette, Fort Bend, Galveston, Gillespie, Goliad, Gonzales, Grimes, Guadalupe, Hays, Harris, Jackson, Kinney, Lavaca, Leon, Limestone, Matagroda, McLennan, Medina, Milam, Montgomery, Navarro, Nueces, Presidio, Refugio, Robertson, San Patricio, Santa Fe, Starr, Tarrant, Travis, Victoria, Uvalde, Walker, Washington, Webb, Williamson, Wharton, Worth

36TH CONGRESS (1859-1861)

1st District: same as the previous

2nd District: Archer, Austin, Bastrop, Baylor, Bell, Bexar, Blanco, Brazoria, Brazos, Burleson, Caldwell, Calhoun, Callahan, Cameron, Colorado, Comal, Concho, Dawson, DeWitt, Dimmit, Duval, Eastland, Edwards, El Paso, Ellis, Falls, Fayette, Fort Bend, Frio, Galveston, Gillespie, Goliad, Gonzales, Grimes, Guadalupe, Hardeman, Hardin, Harris, Haskell, Hays, Jackson, Jones, Kimble, Kinney, Know, LaSalle, Lavaca, Leon, Limestone, Mason, Matagroda, Mclennan, McMullen, Medina, Menard, Milam, Montgomery, Navarro, Nueces, Presidio, Refugio, Robertson, Runnels, San Patricio, Santa Fe, Shackleford, Starr, Stephens, Tarrant, Taylor, Throckmorton, Travis, Uvalde, Victoria, Walker, Washington, Webb, Wharton, Wichita, Wilbarger, Williamson, Worth, Zapata, Zavala

37TH THROUGH 40TH CONGRESSES (1861-1869)

Texas had seceded from the United States and was a part of the Confederate States of America during this period.

41ST AND 42ND CONGRESSES (1869-1873)

1st District: Anderson, Angelina, Cherokee, Harrison, Henderson, Houston, Jasper, Jefferson, Liberty, Nacogdoches, Newton, Orange, Panola, Polk, Rusk, Sabine, San Augustine, Shelby, Smith, Trinity, Tyler, Hardin, Chambers, Van Zandt, Wood

2nd District: Archer, Bowie, Callahan, Clay, Collin, Cooke, Dallas, Davis, Denton, Eastland, Ellis, Erath, Fannin, Grayson, Hardeman, Haskell, Hood, Hopkins, Hunt, Jack, Johnson, Jones, Kaufman, Knox, Lamar, Marion, Montague, Palo Pinto, Parker, Red River, Shackleford, Stephens, Tarrant, Taylor, Throckmorton, Titus, Upshur, Wichita, Wilbarger, Wise, Young

3rd District: Austin, Bosque, Brazoria, Brazos, Burleson, Falls, Fort Bend, Freestone, Galveston, Grimes, Harris, Hill, Leon, Limestone, Madison, Matagorda, McLennan, Milam, Montgomery, Navarro, Robertson, Walker, Washington, Wharton

4th District: Atascosa, Bandera, Bastrop, Bee, Bell, Bexar, Blanco, Brown, Burnet, Caldwell, Calhoun, Cameron, Coleman, Colorado, Comal, Comanche, Concho, Coryell, Dawson, DeWitt, Dimmit, Duval, Edwards, El Paso, Encinal (now part of Webb County), Fayette, Frio, Gillespie, Goliad, Gonzales, Guadalupe, Hamilton, Hays, Hidalgo, Jackson, Karnes, Kendall, Kerr, Kinney, Lampasas, Lasalle, Lavaca, Live Oak, Llano, Mason, Maverick, McCulloch, McMullen, Medina, Nueces, Presidio, Refugio, Runnels, San Patricio, San Saba, Starr, Travis, Uvalde, Victoria, Webb, Williamson, Wilson, Zapata, Zavala

43RD CONGRESS (1873-1875)

1st, 2nd, 3rd, and 4th Districts: same as the previous Two At-Large Districts

44TH AND 45TH CONGRESSES (1875-1879)

1st District: Anderson, Angelina, Chambers, Cherokee, Hardin, Henderson, Houston, Jasper, Jefferson, Liberty, Nacogdoches, Newton, Orange, Panola, Polk, Rusk, Sabine, San Augustine, Shelby, Smith, Trinity, Tyler

2nd District: Bowie, Cass, Delta, Fannin, Gregg, Harrison, Hopkins, Hunt, Lamar, Marion, Rains, Red River, Titus, Upshur, Van Zandt, Wood

3rd District: Archer, Baylor, Callahan, Clay, Collin, Cooke, Dallas, Denton, Eastland, Ellis, Erath, Grayson, Hardeman, Haskell, Hill, Hood, Jack, Johnson, Jones, Kaufman, Knox, Montague, Palo Pinto, Parker, Rockwall, Shackleford, Stephens, Tarrant, Taylor, Throckmorton, Wichita, Wilbarger, Wise, Young

4th District: Bell, Bosque, Brazos, Comanche, Coryell, Falls, Waller, Fort Bend, Freestone, Grimes, Hamilton, Harris, Leon, Limestone, Madison, McLennan, Montgomery, Navarro, Robertson, San Jacinto, Walker

5th District: Austin, Bastrop, Brazoria, Brown, Burleson,

Burnet, Coleman, Colorado, Concho, Fayette, Galveston, Lampasas, Lavaca, Matagorda, McCulloch, Milam, Runnels, San Saba, Travis, Washington, Wharton, Williamson

6th District: Atascosa, Aransas, Bandera, Bee, Bexar, Blanco, Caldwell, Calhoun, Cameron, Comal, Dimmit, DeWitt, Duval, Edwards, El Paso, Encinal (now part of Webb County), Frio, Gillespie, Goliad, Gonzales, Guadalupe, Hays, Hidalgo, Jackson, Karnes, Kendall, Kerr, Kimball, Kinney, Llano, Mason, La Salle, Live Oak, Maverick, Medina, Menard, McMullen, Nueces, Pecos, Presidio, Refugio, San Patricio, Starr, Uvalde, Victoria, Webb, Wilson, Zapata, Zavalla

46TH AND 47TH CONGRESSES (1879-1883)

1st, 2nd, 4th, 5th, and 6th districts: same as the previous

3rd District: Archer, Baylor, Andrews, Armstrong, Bailey, Borden, Briscoe, Carson, Castro, Childress, Cochran, Collingsworth, Cottle, Crosby, Dallam, Deaf Smith, Dickens, Donley, Fisher, Floyd, Gaines, Garza, Gray, Hale, Hall, Hansford, Hartley, Hemphill, Hockley, Howard, Hutchinson, Kent, King, Lamb, Lipscomb, Lubbock, Lynn, Martin, Mitchell, Moore, Motley, Nolan, Ochiltree, Oldham, Parmer, Potter, Randall, Roberts, Scurry, Sherman, Stonewall, Swisher, Terry, Wheeler, Yoakum, Callahan, Clay, Collin, Cooke, Dallas, Denton, Eastland, Ellis, Erath, Grayson, Hardeman, Haskell, Hill, Hood, Jack, Johnson, Jones, Kaufman, Knox, Montague, Palo Pinto, Parker, Rockwall, Shackleford, Stephens, Tarrant, Taylor, Throckmorton, Wichita, Wilbarger, Wise, Young

48TH AND 49TH CONGRESSES (1883-1887)

1st District: Angelina, Brazos, Chambers, Grimes, Hardin, Harris, Jasper, Jefferson, Liberty, Madison, Montgomery, Newton, Orange, Polk, San Jacinto, Trinity, Tyler, Walker, Waller

2nd District: Anderson, Cherokee, Freestone, Henderson, Houston, Leon, Nacogdoches, Robertson, Sabine, San Augustine

3rd District: Camp, Gregg, Harrison, Hunt, Panola, Rains, Rusk, Shelby, Smith, Upshur, Van Zandt, Wood

4th District: Bowie, Cass, Delta, Fannin, Franklin, Hopkins, Lamar, Marion, Morris, Red River, Titus

5th District: Archer, Baylor, Clay, Collin, Cooke, Denton, Grayson, Montague, Rockwall, Wichita, Wise, Wilbarger

6th District: Bosque, Dallas, Ellis, Hill, Johnson, Kaufman, Tarrant

7th District: Aransas, Bee, Brazoria, Calhoun, Cameron, De Witt, Duval, Encinal (now part of Webb County), Fort Bend, Frio, Galveston, Goliad, Hidalgo, Jackson, La SalleDimmitt, Matagroda, Maverick, McMullen, Nueces, Refugio, San Patricio, Starr, Victoria, Webb, Wharton, Zapata, Zavala

8th District: Atascosa, Austin, Caldwell, Colorado, Fayette, Gonzales, Guadalupe, Hays, Karnes, Lavaca, Lee, Live Oak, Wilson

9th District: Bell, Burleson, Falls, Limestone, McLennan, Milam, Navarro, Washington

10th District: Bandera, Bastrop, Bexar, Blanco, Burnet, Coleman, Comal, Concho, Crockett, Edwards, Gillespie, Kendall, Kerr, Kimble, Kinney, Lampasas, Llano, Mason, McCulloch, Medina, Menard, Runnels, San Saba, Travis, Uvalde, Williamson

11th District: Andrews, Armstrong, Bailey, Borden, Briscoe, Brown, Callahan, Carson, Castro, Childress, Cochran, Collingsworth, Comanche, Coryell, Cottle, Crosby, Dallam, Dawson, Deaf Smith, Dickens, Donley, Eastland, El Paso, Erath, Fisher, Floyd, Gaines, Garza, Gray, Greer, Hale, Hall, Hamilton, Handford, Hardeman, Hartley, Haskell, Hemphill, Hockley, Howard, Hutchinson, Jack, Jones, Kent, King, Knox, Lamb, Lipscomb, Lubbock, Lynn, Martin, Mitchell, Moore, Motley, Nolan, Ochiltree, Oldham, Palo Pinto, Parker, Parmer,

Pecos, Potter, Presidio, Randall, Roberts, Scurry, Shackleford, Sherman, Somervell, Stephens, Stonewall, Swisher, Taylor, Terry, Throckmorton, Tom Green, Wheeler, Yoakum, Young

50TH CONGRESS (1887-1889)

1st, 2nd, 3rd, 4th, 5th, 6th, 7th, 8th, 9th, and 10th districts: same as the previous

11th District: Andrews, Armstrong, Bailey, Borden, Briscoe, Brown, Callahan, Carson, Castro, Childress, Cochran, Collingsworth, Comanche, Coryell, Cottle, Crosby, Dallam, Dawson, Deaf Smith, Dickens, Donley, Eastland, El Paso, Erath, Fisher, Floyd, Gaines, Garza, Gray, Greer, Hale, Hall, Hamilton, Handford, Hardeman, Hartley, Haskell, Hemphill, Hockley, Hood, Howard, Hutchinson, Jack, Jones, Kent, King, Knox, Lamb, Lipscomb, Lubbock, Lynn, Martin, Mitchell, Moore, Motley, Nolan, Ochiltree, Oldham, Palo Pinto, Parker, Parmer, Pecos, Potter, Presidio, Randall, Roberts, Scurry, Shackleford, Sherman, Somervell, Stephens, Stonewall, Swisher, Taylor, Terry, Throckmorton, Tom Green, Val Verde, Wheeler, Yoakum, Young

51ST AND 52ND CONGRESSES (1889-1893)

1st, 2nd, 3rd, 4th, 5th, 6th, 7th, 8th, 9th, and 10th districts: same as the previous

11th District: Andrews, Armstrong, Bailey, Borden, Briscoe, Brown, Callahan, Carson, Castro, Childress, Cochran, Collingsworth, Comanche, Coryell, Cottle, Crosby, Dallam, Dawson, Deaf Smith, Dickens, Donley, Eastland, El Paso, Erath, Fisher, Floyd, Gaines, Garza, Gray, Greer, Hale, Hall, Hamilton, Handford, Hardeman, Hartley, Haskell, Hemphill, Hockley, Hood, Howard, Hutchinson, Jack, Jones, Kent, King, Knox, Lamb, Lipscomb, Lubbock, Lynn, Martin, Mills, Mitchell, Moore, Motley, Nolan, Ochiltree, Oldham, Palo Pinto, Parker, Parmer, Pecos, Potter, Presidio, Randall, Roberts, Scurry, Shackleford, Sherman, Somervell, Stephens, Stonewall, Swisher, Taylor, Terry, Throckmorton, Tom Green, Val Verde, Wheeler, Yoakum, Young

53RD THROUGH 57TH CONGRESSES (1893-1903)

1st District: Chambers, Freestone, Grimes, Harris, Leon, Madison, Montgomery, Trinity, Walker, Waller

2nd District: Anderson, Angelina, Cherokee, Hardin, Harrison, Houston, Jasper, Jefferson, Liberty, Nacogdoches, Newton, Orange, Panola, Polk, Sabine, San Augustine, San Jacinto, Shelby, Tyler

3rd District: Gregg, Henderson, Hunt, Rains, Rockwall, Rusk, Smith, Upshur, Van Zandt, Wood

4th District: Bowie, Camp, Cass, Delta, Franklin, Hopkins, Lamar, Marion, Morris, Red River, Titus

5th District: Collin, Cooke, Denton, Fannin, Grayson, Montague

6th District: Bosque, Dallas, Ellis, Hill, Johnson, Kaufman, Navarro

7th District: Bell, Brazos, Falls, Limestone, McLennan, Milam, Robertson

8th District: Borwn, Coleman, Comanche, Coryell, Erath, Hamilton, Hood, Lampasas, Mills, Parker, Runnels, Somervell, Tarrant

9th District: Bastrop, Burleson, Burnet, Caldwell, Hays, Lee, Travis, Washington, Williamson

10th District: Ausitn, Brazoria, Colorado, Fayette, Fort Bend, Galveston, Gonzales, Lavaca, Matagorda

11th District: Aransas, Atascosa, Bee, Calhoun, Cameron, DeWitt, Duval, Encinal (now part of Webb County), Frio, Goliad, Guadalupe, Hidalgo, Jackson, Karnes, La Salle, Live Oak, McMullen, Nueces, Refugio, San Patricio, Simmitt, Starr, Uvalde, Victoria, Webb, Wharton, Wilson, Zapata, Zavala

12th District: Bandera, Bexar, Blanco, Brewster, Buchel, Coke, Comal, Concho, Crane, Crockett, Ector, Edwards, Foley, Gillespie, Glasscock, Irion, Jeff Davis, Kendall, Kerr, Kimble, Kinney, Llano, Mason, Maverick, McCulloch, Medina, Menard, Midland, Pecos, Presidio, San Saba, Schleicher, Sterling, Sutton, Tom Green, Upton, Val Verde

13th District: Andrews, Archer, Armstrong, Bailey, Baylor, Borden, Broscoe, Callahan, Carson, Castro, Childress, Clay, Cochran, Collingsworth, Cottle, Crosby, Dallam, Dawson, Deaf Smith, Dickens, Donley, Eastland, El Paso, Fisher, Floyd, Foard, Gaines, Garza, Gray, Greer, Hale, Hall, Hansford, Hardeman, Hartley, Haskell, Hemphill, Hockley, Howard, Hutchinson, Jack, Jones, Kent, King, Knox, Lamb, Lipscomb, Loving, Lubbock, Lynn, Martin, Mitchell, Moore, Motley, Nolan, Ochiltree, Oldham, Palo Pinto, Parmer, Potter, Randall, Reeves, Roberts, Scurry, Shackelford, Sherman, Stephens, Stonewall, Swisher, Taylor, Terry, Throckmorton, Ward, Wheeler, Wichita, Wilbarger, Winkler, Wise, Yoakum, Young

58TH THROUGH 61ST CONGRESSES (1903-1911)

1st District: Bowie, Camp, Cass, Delta, Franklin, Hopkins, Lamar, Marion, Morris, Red River, Titus

2nd District: Angelina, Cherokee, Hardin, Harrison, Jasper, Jefferson, Nacogdoches, Newton, Orange, Panola, Sabine, San Augustine, Shelby, Tyler

3rd District: Gregg, Henderson, Kaufman, Rusk, Smith, Upshur, Van Zandt, Wood

4th District: Collin, Fannin, Grayson, Hunt, Rains

5th District: Bosque, Dallas, Ellis, Hill, Rockwall

6th District: Brazos, Freestone, Limestone, Milam, Navarro, Robertson

7th District: Anderson, Chambers, Galveston, Houston, Liberty, Polk, San Jacinto, Trinity

8th District: Austin, Fort Bend, Grimes, Harris, Leon, Madison, Montgomery, Walker, Waller

9th District: Aransas, Bee, Brazoria, Calhoun, Colorado, DeWitt, Fayette, Goliad, Gonzales, Jackson, Karnes, Lavaca, Matagorda, Refugio, Victoria, Wharton

10th District: Bastrop, Burleson, Caldwell, Hays, Lee, Travis, Washington, Williamson

11th District: Bell, Coryell, Falls, Hamilton, McLennan

12th District: Comanche, Erath, Hood, Johnson, Parker, Somervell, Tarrant

13th District: Archer, Armstrong, Bailey, Baylor, Briscoe, Carson, Castro, Childress, Clay, Collingsworth, Cooke, Cottle, Dallam, Deaf Smtih, Denton, Dickens, Donley, Floyd, Foard, Gray, Hale, Hall, Hansford, Hardeman, Hartley, Hemphill, Hutchinson, Jack, Knox, Lamb, Lipscomb, Montague, Moore, Motley, Ochiltree, Oldham, Parmer, Potter, Randall, Roberts, Sherman, Swisher, Throckmorton, Wheeler, Wichita, Wilbarger, Wise, Young

14th District: Bandera, Bexar, Blanco, Brown, Burnet, Coleman, Comal, Gillespie, Kendall, Kerr, Lampasas, Llano, Mason, McCulloch, Mills, San Saba

15th District: Atascosa, Cameron, Dimmit, Duval, Frio, Guadalupe, Hidalgo, Kinney, LaSalle, Live Oak, Maverick, McMullen, Medina, Nuesves, San Patricio, Starr, Uvalde, Val Verde, Webb, Wilson, Zapata, Zavala

16th District: Andrews, Borden, Brewster, Callahan, Cochran, Coke, Concho, Crane, Crockett, Crosby, Dawson, Eastland, Ector, Edwards, El Paso, Fisher, Gaines, Garza, Glasscock, Haskell, Hockley, Howard, Irion, Jeff Davis, Jones, Kent, Kimble, King, Loving, Lubbock, Lynn, Martin, Menard, Midland, Mitchell, Nolan, Palo Pinto, Pecos, Presidio, Reeves, Runnels, Schackelford, Schleicher, Scurry, Stephens, Sterling, Stonewall, Sutton, Taylor, Terry, Tom Green, Upton, Ward, Winkler, Yoakum

62ND CONGRESS (1911-1913)

1st, 2nd, 3rd, 4th, 5th, 6th, 7th, 8th, 10th, 11th, 12th, 13th, 16th districts: same as the previous

9th District: Aransas, Brazoria, Calhoun, Colorado, DeWitt, Fayette, Goliad, Gonzales, Jackson, Karnes, Lavaca, Matagorda, Refugio, Victoria, Wharton

14th District: Bexar, Blanco, Brown, Burnet, Coleman, Comal, Gillespie, Kendall, Kerr, Lampasas, Llano, Mason, McCulloch, Mills, San Saba

15th District: Atascosa, Bandera, Bee, Cameron, Dimmit, Duval, Frio, Guadalupe, Hidalgo, Kinney, LaSalle, Live Oak, Maverick, McMullen, Medina, Nueces, San Patricio, Starr, Terrell, Uvalde, Val Verde, Webb, Wilson, Zapata, Zavala

63RD CONGRESS (1913-1915)

1st through 16th Districts: same as the previous
Two at-large districts

64TH AND 65TH CONGRESS (1915-1919)

1st through 15th districts: same as the previous

16th District: Andrews, Borden, Brewster, Callahan, Cochran, Coke, Concho, Crane, Crockett, Crosby, Dawson, Eastland, Ector, Edwards, El Paso, Fisher, Gaines, Garza, Glasscock, Haskell, Hockley, Howard, Irion, Jeff Davis, Jones, Kent, Kimble, King, Loving, Lubbock, Lynn, Martin, Menard, Midland, Mitchell, Nolan, Palo Pinto, Pecos, Presidio, Real, Reeves, Runnels, Schackelford, Schleicher, Scurry, Stephens, Sterling, Stonewall, Sutton, Taylor, Terry, Tom Green, Upton, Ward, Winkler, Yoakum,
Two at-large districts

66TH THROUGH 72ND CONGRESSES (1919-1933)

1st District: Bowie, Camp, Cass, Delta, Franklin, Hopkins, Lamar, Marion, Morris, Red River, Titus

2nd District: Angelina, Cherokee, Hardin, Harrison, Jasper, Jefferson, Nacogdoches, Newton, Orange, Panola, Sabine, San Augustine, Shelby, Tyler

3rd District: Gregg, Henderson, Kaufman, Rusk, Smith, Upshur, Van Zandt, Wood

4th District: Collin, Fannin, Grayson, Hunt, Rains

5th District: Dallas, Ellis, Rockwall

6th District: Brazos, Freestone, Hill, Leon, Limestone, Madison, Milam, Navarro, Robertson

7th District: Anderson, Chambers, Glaveston, Houston, Liberty, Montgomery, Polk, San Jacinto, Trinity, Walker

8th District: Fort Bend, Grimes, Harris, Waller

9th District: Brazoria, Calhoun, Colorado, DeWitt, Fayette, Goliad, Gonzales, Jackson, Lavaca, Matagorda, Refugio, Victoria, Wharton

10th District: Austin, Bastrop, Burleson, Caldwell, Hays, Lee, Travis, Washington, Williamson

11th District: Bell, Bosque, Coryell, Falls, Hamilton, McLennan

12th District: Erath, Hood, Johnson, Parker, Tarrant, Somervell

13th District: Archer, Baylor, Clay, Cooke, Denton, Jack, Montague, Throckmorton, Wichita, Wilbarger, Wise, Young

14th District: Aransas, Bee, Bexar, Blanco, Comal, Guadalupe, Karnes, Kendall, Nueces, San Patricio, Wilson

15th District: Atascosa, Brooks, Cameron, Dimmit, Duval, Frio, Hidalgo, Jim Hogg, Jim Wells, Kinney, Kleberg, LaSalle, Live Oak, Maverick, McMullen, Medina, Starr, Uvalde, Willacy, Zapata, Zavala

16th District: Andrews, Bandera, Brewster, Coke, Corckett, Crane, Culberson, Ector, Edwards, El Paso, Gillespie, Glasscock, Howard, Hudspeth, Irion, Jeff Davis, Kerr, Kimble, Loving, Martin, Mason, Menard, Midland, Mitchell, Pecos, Presidio, Reagan, Real, Reeves, Schleivher, Sterling, Sutton, Terrell, Tom Green, Upton, Val Verde, Ward, Winkler

17th District: Brown, Burnet, Callahan, Coleman, Comanche, Concho, Eastland, Jones, Lampasas, Llano, McCulloch, Mills, Nolan, Palo Pinto, Runnels, San Saba, Shackleford, Stephens, Taylor

18th District: Armstrong, Bailey, Borden, Broscoe, Carson, Castro, Childress, Cochran, Collingsworth, Cottle, Crosby, Dallam, Dawson, Deaf Smith, Dickens, Donley, Fisher, Floyd, Foard, Gaines, Garza, Gray, Hale, Hall, Hansford, Hardeman, Hartley, Haskell, Hemphill, Hockley, Hutchinson, Kent, King, Knox, Lamb, Lipscomb, Lubbock, Lynn, Moore, Motley, Ochiltree, Oldham, Palmer, Potter, Randall, Roberts, Scurry, Sherman, Stonewall, Swisher, Terry, Wheeler, Yoakum

73RD CONGRESS (1933-1934)

1st through 18th Districts: same as the previous
Three at-large districts

74TH THROUGH 82ND CONGRESS (1935-1952)

1st District: Bowie, Cass, Delta, Franklin, Harrison, Hopkins, Lamar, Marion, Morris, Red River, Titus

2nd District: Angelina, Hardin, Jasper, Jefferson, Liberty, Newton, Orange, Sabine, San Augustine, Shelby, Tyler

3rd District: Camp, Gregg, Ranola, Rusk, Smith, Upshur, Van Zandt, Wood

4th District: Collin, Fannin, Grayson, Hunt, Kaufman, Rains, Rockwall

5th District: Dallas

6th District: Brazos, Ellis, Freestone, Hill, Leon, Limestone, Navarro, Robertson

7th District: Anderson, Cherokee, Grimes, Henderson, Houston, Madison, Montgomery, Nacogdoches, Polk, San Jacinto, Trinity, Walker

8th District: Harris

9th District: Austin, Brazoria, Calhoun, Chambers, Colorado, Fayette, Fort Bend, Galveston, Goliad, Jackson, Lavaca, Matagorda, Victoria, Waller, Wharton

10th District: Bastrop, Blanco, Burleson, Burnet, Caldwell, Hays, Lee, Travis, Washington, Williamson

11th District: Bell, Bosque, Coryell, Falls, McLennan, Milam

12th District: Hood, Johnson, Parker, Somervell, Tarrant

13th District: Archer, Baylor, Clay, Cooke, Denton, Foard, Hardeman, Jack, Knox, Montague, Throckmorton, Wichita, Wilbarger, Wise, Young

14th District: Aransas, Atascosa, Bee, Brooks, Comal, DeWitt, Duval, Gonzales, Guadalupe, Jim Wells, Karnes, Kenedy, Kleberg, Live Oak, McMullen, Nueces, Refugio, San Patricio, Wilson

15th District: Cameron, Dimmit, Frio, Hidalgo, Jim Hogg, LaSalle, Maverick, Medina, Starr, Webb, Wilacy, Zapata, Zavala

16th District: Brewster, Crane, Crockett, Culberson, Ector, El Paso, Glasscock, Hudspeth, Jeff Davis, Loving, Midland, Pecos, Presidio, Reagan, Reeves, Terrell, Upton, Ward, Winkler

17th District: Callahan, Comanche, Eastland, Erath, Fisher, Hamilton, Jones, Nolan, Palo Pinto, Shackleford, Stephens, Taylor

18th District: Armstrong, Briscoe, Carson, Castro, Childress, CollingsworthParmer, Cottle, Dallas, Deaf Smith, Donley, Gray, Hall, Hansford, Hartley, Hemphill, Hutchinson, Lipscomb, Moore, Motley, Ochiltree, Oldham, Potter, Randall, Roberts, Sherman, Swisher, Wheeler

19th District: Andrews, Bailey, Borden, Cochran, Crosby, Dawson, Dickens, Floyd, Gaines, Garza, Hale, Haskell, Hockley, Howard, Kent, King, Lamb, Lubbock, Lynn, Martin, Mitchell, Scurry, Stonewall, Terry, Yoakum

20th District: Bexar

21st District: Bandara, Brown, Coke, Coleman, Concho, Edwards, Gillespie, Irion, Kendall, Kerr, Kimble, Kinney, Lampasas, Llano, Mason, McCulloch, Menard, Mills, Real, Runnels, San Saba, Schleicher, Sterling, Sutton, Tom Green, Uvalde, Val Verde

83RD THROUGH 85TH CONGRESSES (1953-1959)

1st through 21st Districts: same as the previous
One at-large district

86TH AND 87TH CONGRESSES (1959-1963)

1st District: Bowie, Cass, Delta, Franklin, Harrison, Hopkins, Lamar, Marion, Morris, Red River, Titus

2nd District: Hardin, Jasper, Jefferson, Liberty, Newton, Orange, Sabine, San Augustine, Tyler

3rd District: Camp, Gregg, Panola, Rusk, Shelby, Smith, Upshur, Van Zandt, Wood

4th District: Collin, Fannin, Grayson, Hunt, Kaufman, Rains, Rockwall

5th District: Dallas

6th District: Brazos, Ellis, Freestone, Hill, Hood, Johnson, Leon, Limestone, Navarro, Robertson, Somervell

7th District: Anderson, Angelina, Cherokee, Gimes, Henderson, Houston, Madison, Montgomery, Nacogdoches, Polk, San Jaconto, Trinity, Walker

8th District: Harris (part)

9th District: Austin, Brazoria, Calhoun, Chambers, Colorado, Fayette, Fort Bend, Galveston, Goliad, Jackson, Lavaca, Matagorda, Victoria, Waller, Wharton

10th District: Bastrop, Blanco, Burleson, Burnet, Caldwell, Hays, Lee, Travis, Washington, Williamson

11th District: Bell, Bosque, Coryell, Falls, McLennan, Milam

12th District: Tarrant

13th District: Archer, Baylor, Clay, Cooke, Denton, Foard, Hardeman, Haskell, Jack, Kent, King, Knox, Montague, Stonewall, Throckmorton, Wichita, Wilbarger, Wise, Young

14th District: Aransas, Atascosa, Bee, Brooks, Comal, DeWitt, Duval, Gonzales, Guadalupe, Jim Wells, Karnes, Kenedy, Kleberg, Live Oak, McMullen, Nueces, Refugio, San Patricio, Wilson

15th District: Cameron, Dimmit, Frio, Hidalgo, Jim Hogg, LaSalle, Maverick, Medina, Starr, Webb, Willacy, Zapata, Zavala

16th District: Brewster, Crane, Crockett, Culberson, Ector, El Paso, Glasscock, Hudspeth, Jeff Davis, Loving, Midland, Pecos, Presidio, Reagan, Reeves, Terrall, Upton, Ward, Winkler

17th District: Callahan, Comanche, Eastland, Erath, Fisher, Hamilton, Jones, Nolan, Palo Pinto, Parker, Scurry, Shackelford, Stephens, Taylor

18th District: Armstrong, Broscoe, Carson, Castro, Childress, Collingsworth, Cootle, Dallam, Deaf Smith, Donley, Gray, Hall, Hansford, Hartley, Hemphill, Hutchinson, Lipscomb, Moore, Motley, Ochiltree, Oldham, Parmer, Potter, Randall, Roberts, Sherman, Swisher, Wheeler

19th District: Andrews, Bailey, Borden, Cochran, Crosby, Dawson, Dickens, Floyd, Gaines, Garza, Hale, Hockley, Howard, Lynn, Lamb, Lubbock, Martin, Mitchell, Terry, Yoakum

20th District: Bexar

21st District: Bandera, Borwn, Coke, Coleman, Concho, Edwards, Gillespie, Irion, Kendall, Kerr, Kimble, Kinney, Lampasas, Llano, Mason, McCulloch, Menard, Mills, Real, Runnels, San Saba, Schleicher, Sterling, Sutton, Tom Green, Uvalde, Val Verde

22nd District: Harris (part)

88TH AND 89TH CONGRESSES (1963-1967)

1st through 22nd Districts: same as the previous
One at-large district

90TH CONGRESS (1967-1969)

1st District: Bowie, Camp, Cass, Cherokee, Delta, Franklin, Harrison, Hopkins, Lamar, Marion, Morris, Panola, Red River, Rusk, Shelby, Titus, Wood

2nd District: Anderson, Angelina, Hardin, Henderson, Houston, Jasper, Liberty, Montgomery, Nacogdoches, Newton, Orange, Polk, Sabine, San Augustine, San Jacinto, Trinity, Tyler, Walker

3rd District: Dallas (part)

4th District: Collin, Fannin, Grayson, Gregg, Hunt, Kaufman, Rains, Rockwall, Smith, Upshur, Van Zandt

5th District: Dallas (part)

6th District: Brazos, Dallas (part), Ellis, Freestone, Grimes, Hill, Johson, Leon, Madison, Navarro, Tarrant (part)

7th District: Harris (part)

8th District: Harris (part)

9th District: Brazoria (part), Chambers, Fort Bend, Galveston, Jefferson

10th District: Austin, Bastrop, Blanco, Burleson, Burnet, Caldwell, Colorado, Fayette, Hays, Lee, Travis, Waller, Washington, Williamson

11th District: Bell, Bosque, Coryell, Falls, Hood, Limestone, McLennan, Milam, Parker, Robertson, Somervell

12th District: Tarrant (part)

13th District: Archer, Baylor, Clay, Cooke, Dallas (part), Denton, Dickens, Foard, Hardeman, Jack, Kent, King, Knox, Montague, Stonewall, Wichita, Wilbarger, Wise, Young

14th District: Aransas, Brazoria (part), Calhoun, Goliad, Jackson, Live Oak, Matagorda, Nueces, Refugio, San Patricio, Victoria

15th District: Brooks, Cameron, Hidalgo, Jim Hogg, Kenedy, Kleberg, Starr, Willacy, Zapata

16th District: Brewster, Culberson, El Paso, Hudspeth, Jeff Davis, Loving, Pecos, Presidio, Reeves, Terrell, Ward, Winkler

17th District: Brown, Callahan, Coke, Coleman, Comanche, Concho, Eastland, Erath, Fisher, Glasscock, Hamilton, Haskell, Howard, Jones, Mills, Mitchell, Nolan, Palo Pinto, Runnels, Shackelford, Stephens, Sterling, Taylor, Throckmorton

18th District: Armstrong, Bailey, Briscoe, Carson, Castro, Childress, Collingsworth, Cottle, Dallam, Deaf Smith, Donley, Gray, Hall, Hansford, Hartley, Hemphill, Hutchnson, Lamb, Lipscomb, Moore, Motley, Ochiltree, Oldham, Parmer, Potter, Randall, Roberts, Shermanm, Swisher, Wheeler

19th District: Andrews, Borden, Cochran, Crosby, Dawson, Floyd, Gaines, Garza, Hale, Hockley, Lubbock, Lynn, Martin, Maidland, Scurry, Terry, Yoakum

20th District: Bexar (part)

21st District: Bandera, Bexar (part) Comal, Crane, Crockett, Ector, Edwards, Gillespie, Irion, Kendall, Kerr, Kimble, Kinney, Lampasas, Llano, McCulloch, Mason, Menard, Reagan, Real, San Saba, Schleicher, Sutton, Tom Green, Upton, Uvalde, Val Verde

22nd District: Harris (part)

23rd District: Atascosa, Bee, Bexar (part), DeWitt, Dimmit,

Duval, Frio, Gonzalez, Guadalupe, Jim Wells, Karnes, LaSalle, Lavaca, Maverick, McMullen, Medina, Webb, Wilson, Zavala

91ST AND 92ND CONGRESSES (1969-1972)

1st District: Bowie, Camp, Cass, Cherokee, Delta, Franklin, Harrison, Hopkins, Lamar, Marion, Morris, Panola, Red River, Rusk, Shelby, Titus, Upshur, Wood

2nd District: Anderson, Angelina, Hardin, Henderson, Houston, Jasper, Liberty, Montgomery, Nacogdoches, Newton, Orange, Polk, Sabine, San Augustine, San Jacinto, Trinity, Tyler, Walker

3rd District: Dallas (part)

4th District: Collin, Dallas (part), Fannin, Grayson, Gregg, Huint, Kaufman, Rains, Rockwall, Smith, Van Zandt

5th District: Dallas (part)

6th District: Austin, Brazos, Dallas (part), Ellis, Fort Bend, Freestone, Grimes, Hill, Johnson, Leons, Madison, Navarro, Tarrant (part), Waller, Washington

7th District: Harris (part)

8th District: Harris (part)

9th District: Chambers, Galveston, Jefferson

10th District: Bastrop, Blanco, Burleson, Caldwell, Colorado, Fayette, Hays, Jackson, Lee, Travis, Wharton, Williamson

11th District: Bell, Bosque, Coryell, Falls, Hood, Limestone, McLennan, Milam, Parker, Robertson, Somervell

12th District: Tarrant (part)

13th District: Archer, Baylor, Childress, Clay, Cooke, Cottle, Dallas (part), Denton, Dickens, Foard, Hardeman, Jack, Kent, King, Knox, Montague, Stonewall, Wichita, Wilbarger, Wise, Young

14th District: Aransas, Brazoria, Calhoun, Matagorda, Nueces, Refugio, San Patricio, Victoria

15th District: Brooks, Cameron, Hidalgo, Jim Hogg, Kenedy, Kleberg, Starr, Willacy, Zapata

16th District: Brewster, Culberson, El Paso, Hudspeth, Jeff Davis, Loving, Pecos, Presidio, Reeves, Terrell, Ward, Winkler

17th District: Brown, Burnett, Callahan, Coke, Coleman, COmanche, Concho, Eastland, Erath, Fisher, Glasscock, Hamilton, Haskell, Howard, Jones, Lampasas, Llano, Mason, McCulloch, Menard, Mills, Mitchell, Nolan, Palo Pinto, Runnels, San Saba, Shackelford, Stephens, Sterling, Taylor, Throckmorton

18th District: Armstrong, Bailey, Briscoe, Carson, Castro, Collingsworth, Dallam, Deaf Smith, Donley, Gray, Hale, Hall, Hansford, Hartley, Hemphill, Hutchison, Lamb, Lipscomb, Moore, Ochiltree, Oldham, Parmer, Potter, Randell, Roberts, Sherman, Swisher, Wheeler

19th District: Andrews, Borden, Cochran, Crosby, Dawson, Floyd, Gaines, Garza, Hockley, Lubbock, Lynn, Martin, Midland, Motley, Scurry, Terry, Yoakum

20th District: Bexar (part)

21st District: Bandera, Bexar (part), Comal, Crane, Crockett, Ector, Edwards, Gillsepie, Irion, Kendall, Kerr, Kimble, Kinney, Reagan, Real, Schleicher, Sutton, Tom Green, Upton, Uvalde, Val Verde

22nd District: Harris (part)

23rd District: Atascosa, Bee, Bexar (part), DeWitt, Dimmitt, Duval, Frio, Goliad, Gonzales, Guadalupe, Jim Wells, Karnes, LaSalle, Lavaca, Live Oak, Maverick, McMullen, Medina, Webb, Wilson, Zavala

93RD CONGRESS (1973-1975)

1st District: Bowie, Camp, Cass, Cherokee, Delta, Fannin, Franklin, Harrison, Henderson, Hopkins, Lamar, Marion, Morris, Panola, Red River, Rusk, San Augustine, Shelby, Titus, Upshur, Wood

2nd District: Anderson, Angelina, Freestone, Grimes, Hardin, Houston, Jasper, Leon, Liberty, Madison, Montgomery, Nacogdoches, Newton, Orange, Polk, Sabine, San Jacinto, Trinity, Tyler, Walker

3rd District: Dallas (part)

4th District: Collin, Dallas (part), Grayson, Gregg, Kaufman, Rains, Rockwall, Smith, Van Zandt

5th District: Dallas (part)

6th District: Brazos, Dallas (part), Ellis, Hill, Johnson, Limestone, Navarro, Robertson, Tarrant (part), Waller, Washington

7th District: Harris (part)

8th District: Harris (part)

9th District: Chambers, Galveston, Harris (part), Jefferson

10th District: Austin, Bastrop, Blanco, Burleson, Caldwell, Colorado, Fayette, Hays, Lee, Travis, Waller, Washington

11th District: Bell, Bosque, Burnet, Coryell, Falls, Hamilton, Hood, Lampasas, McLennan, Milam, Mills, Parker, Somervell, Williamson

12th District: Tarrant (part)

13th District: Archer, Baylor, Briscoe, Carson, Childress, Clay, Collingsworth, Cooke, Cottle, Dallam, Denton, Dickens, Donley, Foard, Gray, Hall, Hansford, Hardeman, Hartley, Hemphill, Hutchinson, Jack, Kent, King, Knox, Lipscomb, Montague, Moore, Motley, Ochiltree, Oldham, Potter, Randell, Roberts, Sherman, Stonewall, Swisher, Wheeler, Wichita, Wilbarger, Wise, Young

14th District: Aransas, Brazoria (part), Calhoun, Jackson, Matagorda, Nueces, Refugio, San Patricio, Victoria, Wharton

15th District: Brooks, Cameron, Duval, Hidalgo, Jim Hogg, Jim Wells, Kenedy, Kleberg, Live Oak, McMullen, Starr, Willacy, Zapata

16th District: Brewster, Culberson, Ector (part), El Paso, Hudspeth, Jeff Davis, Loving, Presidio, Reeves, Ward, Winkler

17th District: Borden, Brown, Callahan, Coleman, Comanche, Cooke, Crosby, Eastland, Erath, Fisher, Floyd, Garza, Haskell, Howard, Jack, Jones, Kent, McCulloch, Mitchell, Montague, Nolan, Palo Pinto, San Saba, Scurry, Shackelford, Stephens, Stonewall, Taylor, Throckmorton, Wise, Young

18th District: Harris (part)

19th District: Andrews, Bailey, Castro, Cochran, Dawson, Deaf Smith, Ector (part), Gaines, Hale, Hockley, Lamb, Lubbock, Lynn, Martin, Midland, Parmer, Terry, Yoakum

20th District: Bexar (part)

21st District: Bandera, Bexar (part), Coke, Comal, Concho, Crane, Crockett, Edwards, Gillsepie, Glasscock, Irion, Kendall,

★184★

Kerr, Kimble, Kinney, Llano, Mason, Menard, Pecos, Reagan, Real, Runnels, Schleicher, Sterling, Sutton, Terrell, Tom Green, Upton, Uvalde, Val Verde

22nd District: Brazoria (part), Fort Bend, Harris (part)

23rd District: Atascosa, Bee, Bexar (part), DeWitt, Dimmitt, Frio, Goliad, Gonzales, Guadalupe, Karnes, LaSalle, Lavaca, Maverick, Medina, Webb, Wilson, Zavala

24th District: Dallas (part), Denton, Tarrant (part)

94TH THROUGH 97TH CONGRESSES (1975-1983)

1st District: Bowie, Camp, Cass, Cherokee, Fannin, Franklin, Harrison, Henderson, Hopkins, Hunt (part), Lamar, Marion, Morris, Panola, Rains (part), Red River, Rusk, San Augustine, Shelby, Titus, Upshur, Wood

2nd District: Anderson, Angelina, Freestone (part), Grimes, Hardin, Houston, Jasper, Leon, Liberty, Madison, Montgomery, Nacogdoches, Newton, Orange, Polk, Sabine, San Jacinto, Trinity, Tyler, Walker

3rd District: Collin (part), Denton (part), Dallas (part)

4th District: Collin (part), Cooke (part), Grayson, Gregg, Hunt (part), Kaufman, Rains, (part), Rockwall, Smith, Van Zandt,

5th District: Dallas (part)

6th District: Brazos, Dallas (part), Ellis, Freestone (part), Hill, Johnson, Limestone, Navarro, Parker (part), Robertson, Tarrant (part)

7th District: Harris (part)

8th District: Harris (part)

9th District: Chambers, Galveston, Harris (part), Jefferson

10th District: Austin, Bastrop, Blanco, Burleson, Caldwell (part), Colorado (part), Fayette, Gonzales (part), Hays, Lavaca (part), Lee, Travis, Waller (part), Washington, Williamson (part)

11th District: Bell, Bosque, Brown, Coleman (part), Comanche (part), Coryell, Erath (part), Falls, Hamilton, Hood, Lampasas, McCulloch, McLennan, Milam, Mills, San Saba, Somervell, Williamson (part)

12th District: Tarrant (part)

13th District: Archer, Armstrong, Briscoe, Carson, Childress, Clay, Collingsworth, Cottle, Dallam, Dickens, Donley, Foard, Gray, Hall, Hansford, Hardeman, Hartley, Hemphill, Hutchison, King, Lipscomb, Moore, Motley, Ochiltree, Oldham, Potter, Randall, Roberts, Sherman, Swisher, Wheeler, Wichita, Wilbarger

14th District: Aransas, Calhoun, Colorado (part), Jackson, Lavaca (part), Matagorda, Nueces, Refugio, San Patricio, Victoria, Wharton

15th District: Bee (part), Brooks, Cameron, Duval, Hidalgo, Jim Hogg, Jim Wells, Karnes (part), Kenedy, Kleberg, Live Oak, McMullen, Starr, Willacy, Zapata

16th District: Culberson, Ector (part), El Paso, Hudspeth, Jeff Davis (part), Loving, Presidio, Reeves (part), Ward, Winkler

17th District: Baylor, Borden, Callahan, Coleman (part), Comanche (part), Cooke (part), Crosby, Dawson (part), Eastland, Erath (part), Fisher, Floyd, Garza, Haskell, Howard, Jack, Jones, Kent, Knox, Lynn, Mitchell, Montague, Nolan, Palo Pinto,

Parker (part)Scurry, Shackelford, Stephens, Stonewall, Taylor, Throckmorton, Wise, Young

18th District: Harris (part)

19th District: Andrews, Bailey, Castro, Cochran, Deaf Smith, Gaines, Hale, Hockley, Lamb, Lubbock, Martin, Midland, Parmer, Terry, Yoakum, Dawson (part), Ector (part)

20th District: Bexar (part)

21st District: Bandera, Bexar (part), Brewster, Coke, Comal, Concho, Crane, Crockett, Edwards, Gillespie, Glasscock, Irion, Jeff Davis (part), Kendall, Kerr, Kimble, Llano, Mason, Medina (part), Menard, Recos, Reagan, Runnels, Real, Reeves (part), Schleicher, Sterling, Sutton, Terrell, Tom Green, Upton, Val Verde

22nd District: Brazoria, Fort Bend, Harris (part), Waller (part)

23rd District: Atascosa, Bee (part), Bexar (part), Caldwell (part), DeWitt, Dimmit, Frio, Goliad, Gonzales (part), Guadalupe, Karnes (part), Kinney, LaSalle, Maverick, Medina (part), Uvalde, Webb, Wilson, Zavala

24th District: Dallas (part)

98TH THROUGH 102ND CONGRESSES (1983-1993)

1st District: Bowie, Camp, Cass, Cherokee, Delta, Franklin, Harrison, Henderson, Hopkins, Hunt (part), Lamar, Marion, Morris, Panola, Red River, Rusk, San Augustine, Shelby, Titus, Upshur

2nd District: Anderson, Angelina, Hardin, Houston, Jasper, Leon, Liberty, Montgomery (part), Nacogdoches, Newton, Orange, Polk, Sabine, San Jacinto, Trinity, Tyler, Walker

3rd District: Collin (part), Dallas (part)

4th District: Collin (part), Fannin, Grayson, Gregg, Hunt (part), Kaufman, Rains, Rockwall, Smith, Van Zandt, Wood

5th District: Dallas (part)

6th District: Brazos, Dallas (part), Ellis, Freestone, Grimes, Hill, Hood, Johnson, Leon, Limestone, Navarro, Madison, Montgomery (part), Navarro, Robertson,

7th District: Harris (part)

8th District: Harris (part), Montgomery (part)

9th District: Chambers, Galveston, Harris (part), Jefferson

10th District: Bastrop, Blanco, Burnet (part), Caldwell, Hays, Travis

11th District: Bell, Bosque, Brown, Burnet (part), Coryell, Falls, Hamilton, Lampasas, McLennan, Milam, Mills, San Saba, Williamson (part)

12th District: Tarrant (part)

13th District: Archer, Armstrong, Baylor, Briscoe, Carson, Childress, Clay, Collingsworth, Cottle, Dallam, Dickens, Donley, Floyd, Foard, Gray, Hall, Hansford, Hardeman, Hartley, Hemphill, Hutchison, Kent, King, Knox, Lipscomb, Moore, Motley, Ochiltree, Oldham, Potter, Randall, Roberts, Sherman, Swisher, Wheeler, Wichita, Wilbarger

14th District: Aransas, Austin, Bee, Brazoria (part), Burleson, Calhoun, Colorado, DeWitt, Fayette, Goliad, Gonzales (part), Guadalupe, Jackson, Lavaca, Lee, Matagorda, Refugio, Victoria, Waller, Washington, Wharton, Williamson (part)

15th District: Atascosa, Brooks, Duval, Frio, Gonzales (part),

Hidalgo, Jim Hogg, Jim Wells, Karnes (part), La Salle, Live Oak, McMullen, Nueces (part), San Particio, Starr, Wilson, Zapata

16th District: Culberson, El Paso, Hudspeth, Jeff Davis, Loving, Reeves, Ward, Winkler

17th District: Borden, Callahan, Coke, Coleman, Comanche, Concho, Cooke (part), Crosby, Eastland, Erath, Fisher, Garza, Glasscock, Haskell, Howard, Jack, Jones, Lynn, Martin, Mitchell, Montague, Nolan, Palo Pinto, Parker, Runnels, Scurry, Shackelford, Somervell, Stephens, Sterling, Stonewall, Taylor, Throckmorton, Wise, Young

18th District: Harris (part)

19th District: Andrews, Bailey, Castro, Cochran, Dawson, Deaf Smith, Ector, Gaines, Hale, Hockley, Lamb, Lubbock, Parmer, Terry, Yoakum

20th District: Bexar (part)

21st District: Bandera, Bexar (part), Brewster, Comal, Crane, Crockett, Edwards, Gillespie, Irion, Kendall, Kerr, Kimble, Llano, McCulloch, Mason, Menard, Midland, Pecos, Presidio, Reagan, Real, Schleicher, Sutton, Terrell, Tom Green, Upton, Val Verde

22nd District: Brazoria (part), Fort Bend, Harris (part)

23rd District: Bexar (part), Dimmit, Kinney, Maverick, Medina, Uvalde, Val Verde, Webb, Zavala

24th District: Dallas (part), Tarrant (part)

25th District: Harris (part)

26th District: Collin (part), Cooke (part), Denton, Tarrant (part)

27th District: Cameron, Kenedy, Kleberg, Nueces (part), Willacy

103RD THROUGH 106TH CONGRESSES (1993-2000)

1st District: Bowie, Camp, Cass, Delta, Franklin, Gregg, Harrison, Hopkins, Hunt, Lamar, Marion, Morris, Nacogdoches, Panola, Red River, Rusk, Smith, Titus, Upshur, Wood

2nd District: Angelina, Cherokee, Grimes, Hardin, Houston, Liberty, Montgomery (part), Nacogdoches (part), Newton, Orange, Polk, Sabine, San Augustine, San Jacinto, Shelby, Trinity, Tyler, Walker

3rd District: Dallas (part)

4th District: Collin (part), Cooke (part), Dallas (part), Denton (part), Grayson, Gregg (part), Hunt (part), Kaufman (part), Rains, Rockwall, Smith (part), Van Zandt

5th District: Anderson, Brazos (part), Dallas (part), Freestone, Henderson, Kaufman (part), Leon, Limestone, Madison, Robertson, Smith (part)

6th District: Dallas (part), Ellis (part), Johnson (part), Parker (part), Tarrant (part)

7th District: Harris (part)

8th District: Austin (part), Brazos (part), Harris, (part), Montgomery (part), Washington

9th District: Chambers, Galveston, Harris (part)

10th District: Travis (part),

11th District: Bell, Bosque, Coryell, Falls, Hamilton, Hill, Lampasas, McCulloch (part), McLennan, Milam, Mills, San Saba

12th District: Johnson (part), Parker (part), Tarrant (part)

13th District: Archer, Armstrong, Baylor, Briscoe, Carson, Castro, Childress, Clay, Collingsworth, Cottle, Crosby, Denton (part), Dickens, Donley, Floyd, Foard, Garza, Gray, Hale, Hall, Hardeman, Hemphill, Hutchinson, King, Knox, Lamb,

Lipscomb, Lubbock, Lynn, Montague, Motley, Potter, Wheeler, Roberts, Swisher, Wichita, Wilbarger

14th District: Aransas, Austin (part), Bastrop, Blanco, Brazoria (part), Burleson, Caldwell, Calhoun, Colorado, Fayette, Gonzales, Hays, Jackson, Lavaca, Lee, Matagorda, Refugio, Travis (part), Victoria, Waller (part), Wharton, Williamson (part)

15th District: Bee, Brooks, DeWitt, Goliad, Hidalgo, Jim Wells (part), Karnes, Kleberg (part), Live Oak, San Patricio, Willacy (part)

16th District: El Paso

17th District: Borden, Brown, Callahan, Coke, Coleman, Comanche, Concho, Dawson, Eastland, Erath, Fisher, Haskell, Hood, Howard, Jack, Jones, Kent, Martin, Mitchell, Nolan, Palo Pinto, Runnels, Scurry, Shackelford, Somervell, Stephens, Stonewall, Taylor, Throckmorton, Tom Green (part), Wise, Young

18th District: Harris County (part)

19th District: Andrews, Bailey, Cochran, Dallam, Deaf Smith, Ector (part), Gaines, Hansford, Hartley, Hockley, Lubbock (part), Midland (part), Moore, Ochiltree, Oldham, Parmer, Randall, Sherman, Terry, Yoakum

20th District: Bexar County (part)

21st District: Bandera, Bexar (part), Burnet, Comal, Gillespie, Glasscock, Guadalupe, Irion, Kendall, Kerr, Kimble, Llano, Mason, McCullough, (part), Menard, Midland (part), Real, Schleicher, Sterling, Tom Green (part), Williamson

22nd District: Brazoria, Fort Bend, Houston

23rd District: Bexar (part), Brewster, Crane, Crockett, Culberson, Dimmit, Ector (part), Edwards, El Paso (part), Hudspeth, Jeff Davis, Kinney, Loving, Maverick, Medina, Midland (part), Pecos, Presidio, Reagan, Reeves, Sutton, Terrell, Upton, Uvalde, Val Verde, Ward, Webb, Winkler, Zavala

24th District: Dallas (part), Ellis (part), Navarro, Tarrant (part)

25th District: Harris (part)

26th District: Collin (part), Dallas (part), Denton (part), Tarrant (part)

27th District: Cameron, Kenedy, Kleberg (part), Nueces (part), Willacy (part)

28th District: Atascosa, Bexar, Comal, Duval, Frio, Guadalupe, Jim Hogg, Jim Wells, La Salle, McMullen, Starr, Wilson, Zapata

29th District: Harris (part)

30th District: Dallas (part)

107TH CONGRESS (2001-2002)

1st District: Bowie, Camp, Cass, Delta, Franklin, Gregg, Harrison, Hopkins, Hunt, Lamar, Marion, Morris, Nacogdoches, Panola, Red River, Rusk, Smith, Titus, Upshur, Wood

2nd District: Angelina, Cherokee, Grimes, Hardin, Houston, Liberty, Montgomery (part), Nacogdoches (part), Newton, Orange, Polk, Sabine, San Augustine, San Jacinto, Shelby, Trinity, Tyler, Walker

3rd District: Dallas (part)

4th District: Collin, Cooke, Dallas (part), Denton (part), Fannin, Grayson, Gregg (part), Hunt (part), Kaufman (part), Rains, Rockwall, Smith (part), Van Zandt

5th District: Anderson, Brazos (part), Dallas (part), Freestone, Henderson, Kaufman (part), Leon, Limestone, Madison, Robertson, Smith (part)

6th District: Dallas (part), Ellis (part), Johnson (part), Parker (part), Tarrant (part)

7th District: Harris (part)

8th District: Austin (part), Brazos (part), Harris, (part), Montgomery (part), Washington

9th District: Chambers, Galveston, Harris (part), Jefferson

10th District: Travis (part)

11th District: Bell, Bosque, Coryell, Falls, Hamilton, Hill, Lampasas, McCulloch (part), McLennan, Milam, Mills, San Saba

12th District: Johnson (part), Parker (part), Tarrant (part)

13th District: Archer, Armstrong, Baylor, Briscoe, Carson, Castro, Childress, Clay, Collingsworth, Cook, Cottle, Crosby, Denton (part), Dickens, Donley, Floyd, Foard, Garza, Gray, Hale, Hall, Hardeman, Hemphill, Hutchinson, King, Knox, Lamb, Lipscomb, Lubbock (part), Lynn, Montague, Motley, Potter (part), Roberts, Swisher, Wheeler, Wichita, Wilbarger

14th District: Aransas, Austin (part), Bastrop, Blanco, Brazoria (part), Burleson, Caldwell, Calhoun, Colorado, Fayette, Gonzales, Hays, Jackson, Lavaca, Lee, Matagorda, Refugio, Travis (part), Victoria, Waller (part), Wharton, Williamson (part)

15th District: Bee, Brooks, DeWitt, Goliad, Hidalgo, Jim Wells (part), Karnes, Klegerg (part), Live Oak, San Patricio, and Willacy (part)

16th District: El Paso (part)

17th District: Borden, Brown, Callahan, Coke, Coleman, Comanche, Concho, Dawson, Eastland, Erath, Fisher, Haskell, Hood, Howard, Jack, Jones, Kent, Martin, Mitchell, Nolan, Palo Pinto, Runnels, Scurry, Shackelford, Somervell, Stephens, Stonewall, Taylor, Throckmorton, Tom Green (part), Wise, Young

18th District: Harris (part)

19th District: Andrews, Bailey, Cochran, Dallam, Deaf Smith, Ector (part), Gaines, Hansford, Hartley, Hockley, Lubbock (part), Midland (part), Moore, Ochiltree, Oldham, Parmer, Randall, Sherman, Terry, Yoakum

20th District: Bexar (part)

21st District: Bandera, Bexar (part), Burnet, Comal, Gillespie, Glasscock, Guadalupe, Irion, Kendall, Kerr, Kimble, Llano, Mason, McCullough, (part), Menard, Midland (part), Real, Schleicher, Sterling, Tom Green (part), Williamson

22nd District: Brazoria, Fort Bend, Harris (part)

23rd District: Bexar (part), Brewster, Crane, Crockett, Culberson, Dimmit, Ector, Edwards, El Paso (part), Hudspeth, Jeff Davis, Loving, Maverick, Medina, Midland (part), Pecos, Presidio, Reagan, Reeves, Sutton, Terrell, Uvalde, Val Verde, Webb, Winkler, Zavala

24th District: Dallas (part), Ellis (part), Navarro, Tarrant (part)

25th District: Harris (part)

26th District: Collin (part), Dallas (part), Denton (part), Tarrant (part)

27th District: Cameron, Kenedy, Kleberg (part), Nueces, Willacy (part)

28th District: Atascosa, Bexar, Comal, Duval, Frio, Guadalupe, Jim Hogg, Jim Wells, La Salle, McMullen, Starr, Wilson, Zapata

29th District: Harris (part)

30th District: Dallas (part)

108TH CONGRESS (2003-2004)

1st District: Bowie, Camp, Cass, Delta, Franklin, Harrison, Hopkins, Hunt (part), Lamar, Marion, Morris, Nacogdoches (part), Panola, Red River, Rusk, Shelby, Titus, Upshur, Wood

2nd District: Angelina, Cherokee, Grimes, Hardin, Houston, Jasper, Liberty, Montgomery (part), Nacogdoches (part), Newton, Orange, Polk, Sabine, San Augustine, San Jacinto, Trinity, Tyler, Walker

3rd District: Collin (part), Dallas (part)

4th District: Collin (part), Cooke, Fannin, Grayson, Gregg, Hunt, Kaufman (part), Rains, Rockwall, Smith, Van Zandt

5th District: Anderson, Dallas (part), Falls, Henderson, Kaufman (part), Leon, Limestone, Freestone, Madison, McLennan (part), Robertson

6th District: Ellis, Hill, Johnson, Navarro, Tarrant (part)

7th District: Harris (part)

8th District: Harris (part), Montgomery (part)

9th District: Chambers, Galveston, Harris (part), Jefferson

10th District: Travis (part)

11th District: Bell, Bosque, Coryell, Hamilton, Lampasas, McLennan, Milam, Mills, San Saba, Williamson (part)

12th District: Parker (part), Tarrant (part)

13th District: Archer, Armstrong, Baylor, Briscoe, Carson, Castro, Childress, Clay, Collingsworth, Cottle, Crosby, Dallam, Deaf Smith, Dickens, Donley, Floyd, Foard, Garza (part), Gray, Hale, Hansford, Hardeman, Hartley, Hemphill, Hutchinson, King, Knox, Lamb (part), Lipscomb, Montague, Moore, Motley, Ochiltree, Oldham, Potter, Randall, Roberts, Sherman, Swisher, Wheeler, Wichita, Wilbarger

14th District: Aransas, Bastrop (part), Brazoria (part), Caldwell, Calhoun, Colorado, DeWitt, Fayette, Gonzales, Guadalupe, Hays (part), Jackson, Karnes, Lavaca, Matagorda, Refugio, Victoria, Wharton, Wilson

15th District: Bee, Brooks, Goliad, Hidalgo (part), Kleberg (part), Live Oak, Nueces (part), San Patricio

16th District: El Paso (part)

17th District: Borden, Brown, Callahan, Coke, Coleman, Comanche, Concho, Dawson, Eastland, Erath, Fisher, Garza (part), Glasscock, Haskell, Hood, Irion, Jack, Jones, Kent, McCulloch, Mitchell, Nolan, Palo Pinto, Runnels, Schleicher, Scurry, Shackelford, Somervell, Stephens, Sterling, Stonewall, Taylor, Throckmorton, Tom Green, Wise, Young

18th District: Harris (part)

19th District: Andrews, Bailey, Cochran, Crane, Ector, Gaines, Hockley, Howard, Lamp (part), Loving, Lubbock, Lynn, Martin, Midland, Parmer, Terry, Ward, Winkler, Yoakum

20th District: Bexar (part)

21st District: Bandera, Bexar (part), Blanco, Burnet, Comal,

Gillespie, Hays (part), Kendall, Kerr, Kimble, Llano, Mason, Menard, Travis (part)

22nd District: Brazoria, Fort Bend Harris (part)

23rd District: Bexar, Brewster, Crockett, Culberson, Dimmit, Edwards, El Paso, Hudspeth, Jeff Davis, Kinney, Maverick, Medina, Pecos, Presidio, Reagan, Real, Reeves, Sutton, Terrell, Upton, Uvalde, Val Verde, Webb, Zavala

24th District: Dallas (part), Tarrant (part)

25th District: Harris (part), Fort Bend (part)

26th District: Collin (part), Denton, Tarrant (part), Wise (part)

27th District: Cameron, Kenedy (part), Kleberg (part), Nueces (part), Willacy

28th District: Atascosa, Bexar (part), Duval, Frio, Hidalgo (part), Jim Hogg, Jim Wells, La Salle, McMullen, Starr, Zapata

29th District: Harris (part)

30th District: Dallas (part)

31st District: Austin, Bastrop (part), Brazos (part), Burleson (part), Harris (part), Lee, Waller, Washington, Williamson (part)

32nd District: Dallas (part)

109TH CONGRESS (2005-2007)

1st District: Angelina (part), Cass (part), Gregg, Harrison, Marion, Nacogdoches, Panola, Rusk, Sabine, San Augustine, Shelby, Smith, Upshur

2nd District: Angelina (part), Cherokee, Grimes, Hardin, Houston, Jasper, Liberty, Montgomery (part), Nacogdoches (part), Newton, Orange, Polk, Sabine, San Augustine, San Jacinto, Trinity, Tyler, Walker

3rd District: Collin (part), Dallas (part)

4th District: Bowie, Camp, Cass, Collin, Delta, Fannin, Franklin, Grayson, Hopkins, Hunt, Lamar, Morris, Rains, Red River, Rockwall, Titus

5th District: Anderson, Cherokee, Dallas (part), Henderson, Kaufman, Van Zandt, Wood

6th District: Ellis, Freestone, Houston, Leon, Limestone, Navarro, Tarrant (part), Trinity

7th District: Harris (part)

8th District: Hardin, Jasper, Liberty (part), Montgomery, Newton, Orange, Polk, San Jacinto, Trinity (part), Tyler, Walker

9th District: Fort Bend (part), Harris (part)

10th District: Austin, Bastrop, Burleson, Harris, Lee, Travis, Waller, Washington

11th District: Andrews, Brown, Burnet, Coke, Coleman, Comanche, Concho, Crane, Dawson, Ector, Gillespie, Menard, Midland, Mills, Glasscock, Irion, Kimble, Lampasas, Llano, Loving, Martin, Mason, McCulloch, Sutton (part), Tom Green, Upton, Mitchell, Nolan (part), Reagan, Runnels, San Saba, Schleicher, Scurry, Sterling, Ward, Winkler

12th District: Parker, Tarrant (part), Wise

13th District: Archer (part), Armstrong, Baylor, Briscoe, Carson, Childress, Clay, Collingsworth, Cooke (part), Cottle, Crosby, Dallam, Dickens, Donley, Foard, Gray, Hall, Hansford, Hardeman, Hartley, Haskell, Hemphill, Hutchinson, Jack, Jones, King, Knox, Lipscomb, Montague, Moore, Motley, Ochiltree, Oldham, Palo Pinto, Potter, Randall, Roberts,

Sherman, Stonewall, Swisher, Throckmorton, Wheeler, Wichita, Wilbarger

14th District: Aransas, Brazoria (part), Calhoun, Chambers, Fort Bend (part), Galveston (part), Jackson, Matagorda, Victoria, Wharton

15th District: Bee, Brooks, Goliad, Hidalgo (part), Kleberg (part), Live Oak, Nueces (part), San Patricio (part)

16th District: El Paso (part)

17th District: Bosque, Brazos, Burleson (part), Grimes (part), Hill, Hood, Johnson, Limestone (part), Madison, McLennan, Robertson (part), Somervell

18th District: Harris County (part)

19th District: Archer, Bailey, Borden, Callahan, Castro, Cochran, Deaf Smith, Eastland, Fisher, Floyd, Gaines, Garza, Hale, Hockley, Howard, Kent, Lamb, Lubbock, Lynn, Nolan, Parmer, Shackelford, Stephens, Taylor, Terry, Yoakum, Young

20th District: Bexar (part)

21st District: Bexar (part), Blanco, Comal, Hays (part), Travis (part)

22nd District: Brazoria (part) Fort Bend (part) Galveston (part), Harris (part)

23rd District: Bandera, Bexar, Brewster, Crockett, Culberson, Dimmit, Edwards, El Paso, Hudspeth, Jeff Davis, Kerr, Kinney, Maverick, Medina, Pecos, Presidio, Real, Reeves, Sutton, Terrell, Uvalde, Val Verde, Webb, Zavala

24th District: Dallas (part), Tarrant (part)

25th District: Caldwell, Duval, Gonzales, Hidalgo (part), Jim Hogg, Karnes, Like Oak, Starr, Travis (part)

26th District: Cooke (part), Dallas (part), Denton (part), Tarrant (part)

27th District: Cameron (part), Kennedy, Kleberg, Nueces, San Patricio (part), Willacy

28th District: Atascosa, Bexar, Comal, Frio, Guadalupe, Hays, La Salle, McMullen, Webb, Wilson, Zapata

29th District: Harris (part)

30th District: Dallas (part)

31st District: Bell, Coryell, Erath, Falls, Hamilton, Milam, Robertson (part), Williamson

32nd District: Dallas (part)

LEGISLATIVE ELECTIONS FOR U.S. SENATOR BY SUCCESSION

Prior to 1913 and the ratification of the Seventeenth Amendment to the U.S. Constitution, state legislatures selected each of their U.S. senators to represent their state in Washington, D.C. Texas was no different, and beginning with the first two Senators—Thomas Rusk and Sam Houston—the state legislature chose every U.S. senator from 1846 until 1913, the only exception being those appointed for brief periods by the Governor. The first popular election for a U.S. senator was in 1912. This was followed closely by the last legislative election in 1913, which was unique and is described later in this section.

Typically, the state legislature—the house and the senate—met separately to nominate men, and voted on the men for the position of senator. The following day, a joint session was held with both halves of the legislature meeting to compare votes for each man. Usually, the house and the senate had cast votes in like percentages for each candidate. The joint session was simply a formality to confirm the selection. Once a candidate received a majority, he was declared the winner and was often given an opportunity to speak to the joint session of the legislature.

On July 25, 1866, legislation was passed that stated that on the second Tuesday after the first day of meeting, the state house of representatives and senate shall elect a U.S. senator. From 1865 until 1871, the two Senate offices were vacant because of Reconstruction following the Civil War. In 1870, the provisional legislature elected senators for the terms ending March 3, 1871, and March 3, 1875. However, the subsequent legislature determined that the provisional legislature did not have this authority.

CLASS 1—THE RUSK SUCCESSION

1846 LEGISLATIVE ELECTION (FEBRUARY 20)

	Senate Votes	House Votes	Total
Sam Houston	19	50	69
James Love	2	2	4
James B. Miller	0	1	1
Thomas Rusk	19	51	70
H. G. Runnels	0	1	1

A single election was held to select both U.S. senators. Sam Houston and Thomas Rusk received the most votes and they were declared the two senators. This election was for the term ending in March 1851. The house and senate nominations, joint session, and voting occurred on February 20, 1846. Thomas Rusk was elected as Texas' first U.S. senator. He served until his death in 1857.

1850 LEGISLATIVE ELECTION (AUGUST 26)

	Senate Votes	House Votes	Total
Thomas Rusk	18		
Louis T. Wigfall	1		
"Blank"	1		

This election was held to fill the seat for the term beginning March 4, 1851, and ending March 3, 1857. An unnamed candidate referred to as "Blank" was among the candidates voted upon. There is no record of who this candidate was. It may simply have been a protest vote. Thomas Rusk was reelected for another six-year term.

1857 LEGISLATIVE ELECTION (NOVEMBER 9)

	Senate Votes	House Votes	Total
J. Pinckney Henderson	28	79	107
George W. Smyth	0	3	3

The legislature elected two senators on this day. This election was for the balance of

Thomas Rusk's term. J. Pinckney Henderson was elected but died in office in June 1858 after serving less than seven months.

1860 LEGISLATIVE ELECTION (JANUARY 20)

1st Ballot	Senate Votes	House Votes	Total
W. P. Hill	0	6	6
Matthias Ward	3	4	7
Louis T. Wigfall	16	43	59
Oran M. Roberts	0	6	6
George W. Smyth	5	20	25
W. J. Sparks	0	1	1
H. Latimer	5	10	15
—— Jarvis	0	0	0
—— Graham	2	0	2

2nd Ballot	Senate Votes	House Votes	Total
W. P. Hill	0	6	6
Matthias Ward	2	3	5
Louis T. Wigfall	16	43	59
Oran M. Roberts	0	5	5
George W. Smyth	6	17	23
W. J. Sparks	0	0	0
H. Latimer	5	15	20
—— Jarvis	0	1	1
—— Graham	1	0	1
Simpson H. Morgan	1	0	1

3rd Ballot	Senate Votes	House Votes	Total
W. P. Hill	0	4	4
Matthias Ward	0	1	1
Louis T. Wigfall	17	43	60
Oran M. Roberts	4	8	12
George W. Smyth	4	9	13
W. J. Sparks	0	0	0
H. Latimer	5	21	26
—— Jarvis	0	0	0
—— Graham	0	1	1
Simpson H. Morgan	1	0	1

This election was held on January 20, 1860, for the balance of J. Pinckney Henderson's term. Louis T. Wigfall was elected.

1861 LEGISLATIVE ELECTION (NOVEMBER 16)

	Senate Votes	House Votes	Total
Louis T. Wigfall	30	82	112

This election was held to select a senator to serve in the Confederate Congress. Louis T. Wigfall was selected. He was already serving as one of the United States senators from Texas.

1866 LEGISLATIVE ELECTION (AUGUST 21-24)

August 21—1st Ballot	Senate Votes	House Votes	Total
W. B. Ochiltree	3	10	13
Oran M. Roberts	7	32	39
Benjamin H. Epperson	8	25	33
William Steadman	3	8	11
A. M. Branch	3	0	3
C. H. Latimer	2	7	9
—— Barrett	0	3	3
D. B. Culberson	0	4	4

August 22—2nd Ballot	Senate Votes	House Votes	Total
W. B. Ochiltree	4	7	11
Oran M. Roberts	6	24	30
Benjamin H. Epperson	10	33	43

	Senate Votes	House Votes	Total
William Steadman	3	11	14
A. M. Branch	2	4	6
D. B. Culberson	4	0	4
E. M. Pease	1	4	5

August 22—3rd Ballot

	Senate Votes	House Votes	Total
W. B. Ochiltree	6	8	14
Oran M. Roberts	9	27	36
Benjamin H. Epperson	10	33	43
William Steadman	2	9	11
A. M. Branch	2	4	6
E. M. Pease	1	3	4

August 22—4th Ballot

	Senate Votes	House Votes	Total
W. B. Ochiltree	6	8	14
Oran M. Roberts	8	30	38
Benjamin H. Epperson	10	32	42
William Steadman	5	13	18
E. M. Pease	1	3	4

August 23—5th Ballot

	Senate Votes	House Votes	Total
W. B. Ochiltree	6	7	13
Oran M. Roberts	10	30	40
Benjamin H. Epperson	8	34	42
William Steadman	4	9	13
E. M. Pease	0	1	1

August 23—6th Ballot

	Senate Votes	House Votes	Total
W. B. Ochiltree	4	7	11
Oran M. Roberts	10	26	36

	Senate Votes	House Votes	Total
Benjamin H. Epperson	8	31	39
William Steadman	3	9	12
D. B. Culberson	3	7	10
E. M. Pease	0	1	1

August 23—7th Ballot

	Senate Votes	House Votes	Total
W. B. Ochiltree	3	4	7
Oran M. Roberts	11	27	38
Benjamin H. Epperson	8	31	39
William Steadman	3	9	12
D. B. Culberson	3	9	12
E. M. Pease	0	1	1

August 23—8th Ballot

	Senate Votes	House Votes	Total
Oran M. Roberts	10	29	39
Benjamin H. Epperson	8	31	39
William Steadman	2	0	2
D. B. Culberson	4	9	13
W. P. Hill	4	11	15
E. M. Pease	0	1	1

August 24—9th Ballot

	Senate Votes	House Votes	Total
Oran M. Roberts	12	26	38
Benjamin H. Epperson	5	25	30
William Steadman	1	11	12
D. B. Culberson	4	6	10
W. P. Hill	4	8	12
C. L. Cleveland	0	9	9

August 24—10th Ballot

	Senate Votes	House Votes	Total

	Senate Votes	House Votes	Total
Oran M. Roberts	12	24	36
Benjamin H. Epperson	5	27	32
William Steadman	3	9	12
D. B. Culberson	6	6	12
W. P. Hill	3	8	11
C. L. Cleveland	1	8	9

August 24—11th Ballot

	Senate Votes	House Votes	Total
Oran M. Roberts	10	24	34
Benjamin H. Epperson	6	32	38
D. B. Culberson	6	9	15
W. P. Hill	3	8	11
C. L. Cleveland	1	10	11

August 24—12th Ballot

	Senate Votes	House Votes	Total
Oran M. Roberts	12	28	40
Benjamin H. Epperson	8	35	43
D. B. Culberson	5	11	16
C. L. Cleveland	2	7	9

August 24—13th Ballot

	Senate Votes	House Votes	Total
Oran M. Roberts	14	36	50
Benjamin H. Epperson	9	33	42
D. B. Culberson	4	12	16

August 24—14th Ballot

	Senate Votes	House Votes	Total
Oran M. Roberts	17	44	61
Benjamin H. Epperson	10	39	49

This election was held to fill the unexpired term of Louis Wigfall that ended March 4, 1869. The house and senate nominations in joint session occurred over the course of four days. Oran Roberts was eventually elected U.S. senator but was rebuked upon his arrival in Washington and was never seated as a U.S. Senator. Another senator was chosen several years later in the 1870 election.

1870 LEGISLATIVE ELECTION (FEBRUARY 23)

	Senate Votes	House Votes	Total
James W. Flanagan	18	56	74
Nelson Plato	9	23	32
L. D. Evans	1	0	1
A. B. Norton	0	1	1
S. D. Wood	0	3	3

This was one of three legislative elections for U.S. senator on this day. This election was for a U.S. senator to serve from Texas' readmission to the U.S. until March 1875. The house and senate nominations occurred on February 21, 1870, and final election occurred in joint session two days later. James W. Flanagan, a Republican, was elected U.S. senator. He succeeded Oran Roberts, who was never seated.

1874 LEGISLATIVE ELECTION (JANUARY 29)

	Senate Votes	House Votes	Total
James W. Throckmorton	9	31	40
Edward T. Randle	2	11	13
John H. Reagan	1	0	1
Samuel B. Maxey	13	46	59
Dan McGary	1	0	1

This election was for the six-year term beginning on March 4, 1875, to succeed J. W. Flanagan. The house and senate nominations and voting occurred on January 28, and the joint session and election were held the following day. Samuel Bell Maxey was elected U.S. senator.

1881 LEGISLATIVE ELECTION (JANUARY 26)

	Senate Votes	House Votes	Total
Samuel Bell Maxey	22	51	73
James W. Throckmorton	8	34	42
Edmund J. Davis	1	5	6

John H. Reagan | 0 | 1 | 1

This election was for the six-year term beginning on March 4, 1881, and ending on March 3, 1887. The house and senate nominations and voting occurred on January 25, 1881, and the joint session and election were held the following day. Samuel B. Maxey was reelected U.S. senator.

1887 LEGISLATIVE ELECTION (FEBRUARY 2)

1st Ballot	Senate Votes	House Votes	Total
Samuel Bell Maxey	34	15	49
John H. Reagan	7	42	49
A. W. Terrell	9	27	36
O. M. Roberts	0	2	2

2nd Ballot	Senate Votes	House Votes	Total
Samuel Bell Maxey	15	33	48
John H. Reagan	7	42	49
A. W. Terrell	8	28	36
O. M. Roberts	1	2	3

3rd Ballot	Senate Votes	House Votes	Total
Samuel Bell Maxey	15	32	47
John H. Reagan	5	43	48
A. W. Terrell	10	28	38
O. M. Roberts	1	2	3

4th Ballot	Senate Votes	House Votes	Total
Samuel Bell Maxey	14	32	46
John H. Reagan	6	46	52
A. W. Terrell	9	29	38
O. M. Roberts	2	2	4

5th Ballot	Senate Votes	House Votes	Total
Samuel Bell Maxey	14	32	46
John H. Reagan	7	45	52
A. W. Terrell	9	26	35
O. M. Roberts	1	2	3

6th Ballot	Senate Votes	House Votes	Total
Samuel Bell Maxey	13	33	46
John H. Reagan	11	48	59
A. W. Terrell	7	24	31
O. M. Roberts	0	0	0

7th Ballot	Senate Votes	House Votes	Total
Samuel Bell Maxey	12	13	25
John H. Reagan	16	85	101
A. W. Terrell	0	1	1
O. M. Roberts	2	2	4
John Ireland	1	4	5

John Ireland was not considered until the seventh and final balloting. A.W. Terrell's name was withdrawn in the final ballot, but he still received one vote in the house. This election was for the six-year term beginning on March 4, 1887, and ending on March 3, 1893. The house and senate nominations and voting occurred on February 1, 1887, and the joint session and election were held the following day. Following seven ballots, John H. Reagan was elected U.S. senator, thus unseating incumbent Samuel Bell Maxey.

1892 LEGISLATIVE ELECTION (MARCH 23)

	Senate Votes	House Votes	Total
Horace Chilton	0	3	3
Joseph D. Sayers	1	0	1
George W. Jones	1	0	1
Joseph W. Bailey	0	4	4
Roger Q. Mills	29	94	123
Barnett Gibbs	0	2	2

| David B. Culberson | 0 | 1 | 1 |

This election was called to fill the balance of the term of John H. Reagan, who had resigned. The house and senate nominations and voting occurred on March 22, 1892, and the joint session and election were held the following day. Roger Q. Mills was elected U.S. senator.

1893 Legislative Election (January 25)

	Senate Votes	House Votes	Total
Roger Q. Mills	29	115	144
Thomas L. Nugent	1	8	9
N. W. Cuney	0	1	1

This election was for the six-year term beginning on March 4, 1893, and ending on March 3, 1899. The house and senate nominations and voting occurred on January 24, 1893, and the joint session and election were held the following day. Roger Q. Mills was reelected U.S. senator for his first full term.

1899 Legislative Election (January 25)

	Senate Votes	House Votes	Total
Charles A. Culberson	26	118	144
Tom McNeil	0	0	1
E. H. R. Green	0	0	1
C. H. Jenkins	0	0	1

This election was for the six-year term beginning on March 4, 1899, and ending on March 3, 1905. The house and senate nominations and voting occurred on January 24, 1899, and the joint session and election were held the following day. Charles A. Culberson was elected U.S. senator.

1905 Legislative Election (January 25)

	Senate Votes	House Votes	Total
Charles A. Culberson	26	99	125

This election was for the six-year term beginning on March 4, 1905, and ending on March 3, 1911. The house and senate nominations and voting occurred on January 24, 1905, and the joint session and election were held the following day. Charles A. Culberson was reelected U.S. senator.

1911 Legislative Election (January 25)

	Senate Votes	House Votes	Total
Charles A. Culberson	31	119	150

This election was for the six-year term beginning on March 4, 1911. The house and senate nominations and voting occurred on January 24, 1911, and the joint session and election were held the following day. Charles A. Culberson was reelected U.S. senator. This was the second-to-the-last legislative election for U.S. senator in Texas and the last for the Rusk succession. The next election for this succession was in 1916 and was a popular election.

Class 2—The Houston Succession

1846 Legislative Election (February 20)

	Senate Votes	House Votes	Total
Sam Houston	19	50	69
James Love	2	2	4
James B. Miller	0	1	1
Thomas Rusk	19	51	70
H. G. Runnels	0	1	1

A single election was held to select both U.S. senators. Sam Houston and Thomas Rusk received the most votes and they were declared the two U.S. senators. Houston received the second highest number of votes and thus the shorter term ending in March 1848. The house and senate nominations, joint session, and voting occurred on February 20, 1846. Sam Houston was elected as one of Texas' first U.S. Senators. He served until 1859.

1847 Legislative Election (December 15)

	Senate Votes	House Votes	Total
Sam Houston	15	54	69
Antonio Navarro	1	0	1
James Webb	1	0	1
Timothy Pilsbury	1	0	1
J. P. Henderson	1	0	1
Gen. Burleson	1	0	1
John C. Hays	1	0	1

This election was for the six-year term beginning on March 4, 1847. The votes for the other candidates were expressions of appreciation. Sam Houston was reelected U.S. senator.

1853 LEGISLATIVE ELECTION (JANUARY 15)

	Senate Votes	House Votes	Total
Sam Houston	19	46	65
John Hemphill	2	12	14
George W. Smyth	1	0	1

This election was for the six-year term beginning on March 4, 1853. The house and senate nominations, voting, and joint session were held on January 15, 1853. Sam Houston was reelected U.S. senator.

1857 LEGISLATIVE ELECTION (NOVEMBER 9)

	Senate Votes	House Votes	Total
John Hemphill	28	82	110

The legislature elected two senators on this day. This election was for the six-year term beginning on March 4, 1859, and ending on March 3, 1865. Sam Houston had served in this seat, but because of his stance on secession, few sought his return to the Senate. John Hemphill was elected U.S. senator. Hemphill was eventually expelled from the U.S. Senate on July 11, 1861, because of Texas' joining in the Confederacy.

1861 LEGISLATIVE ELECTION (NOVEMBER 16)

1st Ballot	Senate Votes	House Votes	Total
W. S. Oldham	12	42	54
John Hemphill	13	22	25
Thomas N. Waul	5	22	27
—— Stockdale	1	0	1
G. W. Kendall	0	1	1
W. B. Ochiltree	0	1	1

2nd Ballot	Senate Votes	House Votes	Total
W. S. Oldham	14	44	58
John Hemphill	12	22	34
Thomas N. Waul	5	21	26

3rd Ballot	Senate Votes	House Votes	Total
W. S. Oldham	17	46	61
John Hemphill	14	23	37
Thomas N. Waul	3	18	21

This election was held to select a senator to serve in the Confederate Congress. Stockdale, Kendall, and Ochiltree withdrew after the first ballot. Williamson Oldham was elected Confederate States Senator after three ballots. He served until the end of the Civil War.

1866 LEGISLATIVE ELECTION (AUGUST 22)

	Senate Votes	House Votes	Total
David G. Burnet	18	47	65
Elisha M. Pease	1	6	7
John Hancock	11	32	43

This election was held to fill the unexpired term ending March 4, 1871. House and senate elections were held on August 21 and the votes were compared and made final in a joint session the following day. David G. Burnet was elected U.S. senator but was rebuked upon his arrival in Washington and was never seated as a U.S. senator. Another senator was chosen several years later in the 1870 election.

1870 LEGISLATIVE ELECTION (FEBRUARY 23)

	Senate Votes	House Votes	Total
Morgan C. Hamilton	17	52	69
A. H. Latimer	11	24	35
H. B. Saunders	0	1	1
J. J. Jarvis	0	4	4
Nelson Plato	0	1	1
J. W. Glenn	0	1	1

This was one of three legislative elections for U.S. senator on this day. This election was for a U.S. senator to serve from Texas' readmission to the United States (March 30, 1870) until March 4, 1871. The house and senate nominations occurred on February 21, 1870, and final election occurred in joint session two days later. Republican Morgan C. Hamilton was elected U.S. senator. He succeeded David G. Burnet, who had been elected but was never seated.

1870 Legislative Election (February 23)

	Senate Votes	House Votes	Total
Morgan C. Hamilton	17	54	71
Horace Boughton	11	28	39
A. B. Norton	0	1	1

This was one of three legislative elections for U.S. senator on this day. This election was for the term beginning on March 4, 1871, and ending on March 4, 1877. The house and senate nominations occurred on February 21, 1870, and final election occurred in joint session two days later. Morgan C. Hamilton also won this election.

1871 Legislative Election (January 25)

	Senate Votes	House Votes	Total
Gen. Joseph J. Reynolds	16	48	64
E. B. Pickett	8	22	30
Judge Shutze	1	0	1
Charles Demoss	1	0	1
J. W. Throckmorton	1	0	1
Morgan C. Hamilton	0	8	8
Others	0	6	6

This election was an attempt to unseat the rightfully elected Morgan C. Hamilton from office because of his split from the Radical Republicans. Hamilton split because he believed the legislators had violated the party's pledges to the people on issues relating to the militia, state police, etc. The state house and senate attempted to replace him as the newly elected U.S. senator with Gen. Joseph J. Reynolds. Reynolds commanded the Department of Texas in Galveston beginning in September 1867 and was a leader in the state Republican Party. Reynolds was supported by the moderate Republicans under A. J. Hamilton and then the radicals under E. J. Davis for the U.S. Senate seat. Reynolds was ending his military command of Texas and greatly wanted the senatorship. He was considered before the election in 1870, but due to heavy criticism, especially in the press, he withdrew his name from consideration. However, in 1871, he was more successful. The legislature said the election in 1870 was invalid because Texas was not yet a state. Reynolds went to Washington in February 1871 expecting President Grant to validate his position. However, the U.S. Senate agreed that Hamilton was the legitimate Senator from Texas. Hamilton returned to his seat in the U.S. Senate.

1876 Legislative Election (May 3-5)

May 3—1st Ballot	Senate Votes	House Votes	Total
Richard Coke	15	34	49
John Ireland	7	32	39
John Hancock	8	21	29
F. S. Stockdale	1	4	5

May 4—2nd Ballot	Senate Votes	House Votes	Total
Richard Coke	16	36	52
John Ireland	7	29	36
John Hancock	6	22	28
F. S. Stockdale	2	2	4

May 5—3rd Ballot	Senate Votes	House Votes	Total
Richard Coke	19	49	59
John Ireland	10	39	49
John Hancock	*withdrew, 1	1	2
F. S. Stockdale	withdrew	0	0
J. G. Tracy	1	1	2

*Hancock's nomination had been withdrawn by the third ballot, but he still received one vote in the house and the senate.

This election was for the six-year term beginning on March 4, 1877, and ending on March 3, 1883. The house and senate election process took three days to complete. Richard Coke, the sitting governor of Texas, was elected U.S. Senator. Upon his election as senator, he resigned the governorship and served as senator from March 4, 1877, until March 3, 1895.

1883 Legislative Election (January 24)

	Senate Votes	House Votes	Total
Richard Coke	29	99	128

This election was for the six-year term beginning on March 4, 1883, and ending on March 3, 1889. The house and senate nominations and voting occurred on January 23, 1883, and the joint session and election were held the following day. Richard Coke was reelected U.S. senator.

1889 Legislative Election (January 23)

	Senate Votes	House Votes	Total
Richard Coke	30	100	130

This election was for the six-year term beginning on March 4, 1889, and ending on March 3, 1895. The house and senate nominations and voting occurred on January 22, 1889, and the joint session and election were held the following day. Richard Coke was reelected U.S. senator.

1895 Legislative Election (January 23)

	Senate Votes	House Votes	Total
Horace Chilton	27	101	128
Thomas L. Nugent	2	21	23
T. S. Smith	1	0	1

This election was for the six-year term beginning on March 4, 1895, and ending on March 3, 1901. The house and senate nominations and voting occurred on January 22, 1895, and the joint session and election were held the following day. Horace Chilton was elected U.S. Senator.

1901 Legislative Election (January 23)

	Senate Votes	House Votes	Total
Joseph W. Bailey	27	110	137
Horace Chilton	0	2	0
M. M. Crane	0	1	1
John H. Reagan	0	1	1
Travis C. Henderson	0	1	1
E. A. Atlee	2	0	2

This election was for the six-year term beginning on March 4, 1901, and ending on March 3, 1907. The house and senate nominations and voting occurred on January 22, 1901, and the joint session and election were held the following day. Joseph W. Bailey was elected U.S. senator, defeating the incumbent Horace Chilton.

1907 Legislative Election (January 23)

	Senate Votes	House Votes	Total
Joseph W. Bailey	19	89	108
A. W. Terrell	1	0	1
W. L. Cabell	1	0	1
Horace Chilton	1	0	1
W. L. Bostick	0	1	1
Cecil A. Lyon	0	2	2
Robert L. Cole	0	2	2
Sam L. Green	0	1	1
J. Felton Lane	0	1	1
George T. Jester	0	1	1
June Kimble	0	1	1
J. R. Wiley	0	1	1
J. F. Onion	0	1	1
J. W. Logan	0	2	2
Tom Connally	0	1	1
E. H. Rogan	0	1	1
J. F. Peek	0	1	1
P. F. Dunn	0	1	1
T. M. Campbell	0	3	3
Perry Ray	0	1	1
J. E. Yantis	0	2	2
W. J. McDowell	0	1	1
W. F. Brown	0	1	1
James B. Kimball	0	1	1
Guy S. McFarland	0	1	1
S. P. Wilson	0	1	1
Tom M. Drew	0	1	1
R. N. Stafford	0	1	1
C. K. Bell	0	1	1
Hamp Cook	0	1	1

C. F. Clint	0	1	1
W. J. McManus	0	1	1
T. J. Brown	0	1	1
R. R. Gaines	0	1	1

This election was for the six-year term beginning on March 4, 1907, and ending on March 3, 1913. The house and senate nominations and voting occurred on January 22, 1901, and the joint session and election were held the following day. Joseph W. Bailey was reelected U.S. senator.

1913 Legislative Election (January 29)

	Senate Votes	House Votes	Total
Morris Sheppard	87	17	104
Choice B. Randell	1	0	1
Reinzi M. Johnston	54	12	66

This election was held to fill the seat of Joseph W. Bailey for the balance of his term, ending March 3, 1913. See the next election for more details on this series of events.

1913 Legislative Election (January 29)

	Senate Votes	House Votes	Total
Morris Sheppard	142	30	172

This election was held to fill the seat of Joseph W. Bailey for the term beginning March 4, 1913. The 1913 legislative election was the last for a U.S. senator and was quite unique. Governor Colquitt had appointed newspaper editor Rienzi Johnston of Houston to the remainder of Joseph W. Bailey's seat in the U.S. Senate. The legislature did not approve of Johnston, as he was a "wet" during the early stages of the groundswell for the prohibition movement. Sheppard had already won the November 1912 general election a few months earlier for the seat whose term would begin in March 1913. Sheppard and the legislature began a movement to encourage Johnston to resign. Johnston did resign his senate seat on February 2, 1913, after only twenty-eight days in office. Sheppard took office on February 3, 1913, giving him about one month seniority over every other new U.S. Senator scheduled to take office in March. Thus began Morris Sheppard's twenty-eight-year career in the U.S. Senate.

U.S. Senator Election Returns By Succession

U.S. Senators were chosen by the state legislatures prior 1913. Following the Seventeenth Amendment to the U.S. Constitution, their selection was made by direct election by the people. The first Texas candidate this affected was Morris Sheppard, a year earlier in 1912. The two successions, lines, or classes of U.S. senators from the state are referred to by the man who first held the office—either Rusk or Houston.

Class 1—The Rusk Succession

1916 Democratic Primary Election (July 22)

Charles A. Culberson	19.7	78,641
Samuel Palmer Brooks	16.5	65,721
Oscar B. Colquitt	21.9	87,421
Thomas M. Campbell	30.0	119,598
John Davis	2.5	9,924
Robert Lee Henry	9.5	37,726

Second Democratic Primary Election (August 26)

Charles A. Culberson	63.7	155,410
Oscar B. Colquitt	36.3	88,435

General Election (November 7)

Charles A. Culberson, Democrat	81.3	303,035
Alex W. Atcheson, Republican	13.1	48,788
F. A. Hickey, Socialist	5.0	18,616
F. H. Combeau, Prohibition	0.6	2,319

1922 Democratic Primary Election (July 22)

Earle B. Mayfield	26.8	153,538
James E. Ferguson	22.2	127,071
Charles A. Culberson	17.4	99,635
Cullen F. Thomas	15.4	88,026
Clarence N. Ousley	10.9	62,451
Robert Lee Henry	7.3	41,567
Sterling P. Strong		1,085

The election was close enough that a runoff election was held on August 26, 1922.

Democratic Runoff Election (August 26)

Earle B. Mayfield	54.4	273,308
James E. Ferguson	45.6	228,701

General Election (November 7)

Earle B. Mayfield, Democrat	66.9	264,201
George E. B. Peddy, Republican	33.1	130,731

1928 Democratic Primary Election (July 28)

Earle B. Mayfield	29.7	200,246
Tom Connally	26.4	178,091
Alvin M. Owsley	19.5	131,755
Thomas L. Blanton	18.8	126,758
Minnie Fisher Cunningham	4.3	28,944
Jeff McLemore	1.4	9,244

The election was close enough that a runoff election was held on August 25, 1928.

DEMOCRATIC RUNOFF ELECTION (AUGUST 25)

	%	Votes
Tom Connally	55.4	320,071
Earle B. Mayfield	44.6	257,747

GENERAL ELECTION (NOVEMBER 6)

	%	Votes
Tom Connally, Democrat	81.2	566,139
T. M. Kennerly, Republican	18.6	129,910
David Curran, Socialist	0.1	690
John Rust, Communist	0.0	114

1934 DEMOCRATIC PRIMARY ELECTION (JULY 28)

	%	Votes
Tom Connally	59.9	567,139
Joseph W. Bailey, Jr.	37.6	355,963
Guy B. Fisher	4.4	41,421

REPUBLICAN PRIMARY ELECTION (JULY 28)

	%	Votes
U. S. Goen	100.0	1,148

General Election (November 6)

	%	Votes
Tom Connally, Democrat	96.7	439375
U. S. Goen, Republican	2.8	12,895
W. B. Starr, Socialist	0.4	1,828
L. C. Keel, Communist	0.1	310

1940 DEMOCRATIC PRIMARY ELECTION (JULY 27)

	%	Votes
Tom Connally	84.8	923,219
Guy B. Fisher	9.0	98,125
A. P. Belcher	6.2	66,962

GENERAL ELECTION (NOVEMBER 5)

	%	Votes
Tom Connally, Democrat	94.2	978,095
George I. Shannon, Republican	5.7	59,340
Homer Brooks, Communist	0.0	408

1946 DEMOCRATIC PRIMARY ELECTION (JULY 27)

	%	Votes
Tom Connally	75.4	823,818
Floyd E. Ryan	7.8	85,292
Arlon B. Davis	6.8	74,252
Terrell Sledge	6.1	66,947
Laverne Somerville	3.9	42290

GENERAL ELECTION (NOVEMBER 5)

	%	Votes
Tom Connally, Democrat	88.5	336,931
Murray C. Sells, Republican	11.5	43,569
write-ins	0.0	5

1952 DEMOCRATIC PRIMARY ELECTION (JULY 26)

	%	Votes
Price Daniel	72.6	940,770
Lindley Beckworth	22.0	285,842
E. W. Napier	5.4	70,132

GENERAL ELECTION (NOVEMBER 4)

	Votes
Price Daniel, Democrat	1,425,007
Price Daniel, Republican	469,594
Price Daniel, no party	591
	1,895,192

1957 SPECIAL ELECTION (APRIL 2)

	%	Votes
Ralph Yarborough, Democrat	38.1	364,605
Martin Dies, Democrat	30.4	290,803
Thad Hutcheson, Republican	22.9	219,591
Searcy Bracewell, Democrat	3.5	33,384
James P. Hart, Democrat	2.1	19,739
John C. White, Democrat	1.2	11,876
Ralph W. Hammonds, Democrat	0.3	2,372
Elmer Adams, Democrat	0.2	2,228
M. T. Banks, Democrat	0.2	2,153

Candidate	%	Votes
Frank G. Cortez, Democrat	0.1	1,350
Charles W. Hill, Democrat	0.1	1,025
Jacob Bergolofsky, Democrat	0.1	890
J. Cal Courtney, Democrat	0.1	879
Hugh Wilson, Democrat	0.1	851
J. Perrin Willis, Democrat	0.1	817
Charles Otto Foerster, Jr., Democrat	0.1	776
Curtis Ford, Democrat	0.1	767
R. Waire Currin, Democrat	0.1	646
John C. Burns, Democrat	0.1	600
H. J. Antoine, Sr., Republican	0.1	576
H. Frank Connally, Democrat	0.1	514
Walter S. McNutt, Democrat	0.1	500
Clyde R. Orms, Democrat	0.0	356

This special election was held to fill the seat of Price Daniel, who had resigned to become the governor of Texas. Under a state law passed after this 1957 special election, candidates in special elections for the Senate would all run together regardless of party affiliation. If none received a majority, a runoff would be called between the top two contenders.

1958 Democratic Primary Election (July 26)

Ralph Yarborough	58.7	761,511
William A. Blakley	41.3	535,418

Republican Primary Election (July 26)

Roy Whittenburg	100.0

General Election (November 4)

Ralph Yarborough, Democrat	74.6	587,030
Roy Whittenburg, Republican	23.6	185,926
Bard A. Logan, Constitution	1.8	14,172

1964 Democratic Primary Election (May 2)

Ralph Yarborough	57.4	904,811
Gordon McLendon	42.6	672,573

Republican Primary Election (May 2)

George Bush	44.1	62,985
Jack Cox	31.9	45,561
Robert Morris	19.8	28,279
Milton V. Davis	4.2	6,067

The election was close enough that a runoff election was held on June 6, 1964.

Republican Primary Runoff Election (June 6)

George Bush	62.1	49,751
Jack Cox	37.9	30,333

General Election (November 3)

Ralph Yarborough, Democrat	56.2	1,463,958
George Bush, Republican	43.6	1,134,337
Jack Carswell, Constitution	0.2	5,542

1970 Democratic Primary Election (May 2)

Lloyd Bentsen	53.0	816,641
Ralph Yarborough	47.0	724,122

Republican Primary Election (May 2)

George Bush	87.6	96,806
Robert Morris	12.4	13,654

General Election (November 3)

Lloyd Bentsen, Democrat	53.6	1,194,069
George Bush, Republican	46.5	1,035,794
Others	0.0	1,808

1976 Democratic Primary Election (May 1)

Lloyd Bentsen	63.5	970,983
Phil Gramm	28.0	427,597

Hugh Wilson — 7.2 — 10,715

REPUBLICAN PRIMARY ELECTION (MAY 1)

	%	Votes
Alan Steelman	70.5	251,252
Hugh Sweeney	18.1	64,404
Louis Leman	11.4	40,651

GENERAL ELECTION (NOVEMBER 2)

	%	Votes
Lloyd Bentsen, Democrat	56.8	2,199,956
Alan Steelman, Republican	42.2	1,636,370
Marjorie P. Gallion, American	0.5	17,355
Pedro Velasquez, Socialist Workers	0.5	20,549

1982 DEMOCRATIC PRIMARY ELECTION (MAY 1)

	%	Votes
Lloyd Bentsen	78.1	987,153
Joe Sullivan	21.9	276,314

REPUBLICAN PRIMARY ELECTION (MAY 1)

	%	Votes
James M. Collins	58.0	152,469
Walter H. Mengden	34.9	91,780
Don L. Richardson	7.1	18,616

GENERAL ELECTION (NOVEMBER 2)

	%	Votes
Lloyd Bentsen, Democrat	58.6	1,818,223
James M. Collins, Reublican	40.5	1,256,759
John E. Ford, Libertarian	0.7	23,494
Lineaus Hooer Lorette, Citizens	0.2	4,564
Write-ins (including Darryl Anderson)	0.0	127

1988 DEMOCRATIC PRIMARY ELECTION (MARCH 8)

	%	Votes
Lloyd Bentsen	84.9	1,342,189
Joe Sullivan	15.1	239,622

REPUBLICAN PRIMARY ELECTION (MARCH 8)

	%	Votes
Beau Boulter	30.5	228,519
Milton Fox	18.4	137,863
Wesley Gilbreath	36.6	274,493
Ned Snead	14.6	109,462

The election was close enough that a runoff election was held on April 12, 1988.

REPUBLICAN PRIMARY RUNOFF ELECTION (APRIL 12)

	%	Votes
Beau Boulter	60.5	111,683
Wesley Gilbreath	40.0	74,029

GENERAL ELECTION (NOVEMBER 8)

	%	Votes
Lloyd Bentsen, Democrat	59.2	3,149,806
Beau Boulter, Republican	40.0	2,129,228
Jeff Daiell, Libertarian	0.8	43,989
Write-ins	0.0	583

1993 SPECIAL ELECTION (MAY 13)

	%	Votes
Kay Bailey Hutchison, Republican	29.0	593,338
Robert Krueger, Democrat	29.0	593,239
Joe Barton, Republican	13.9	284,135
Jack Fields, Republican	13.6	277,560
Richard Fisher, Democrat	8.1	165,564
Jose Angel Gutierrez, Democrat	2.5	52,103
Stephen Hopkins, Republican	0.7	14,753
Gene Kelly, Democrat	0.6	11,331
C. "Sonny" Payne, Democrat	0.3	6,782
Don Richardson, Independent	0.3	6,209
Rick Draheim, Libertarian	0.3	5,677
Clymer Wright, Republican	0.2	5,111
Herbert Spiro, Republican	0.2	4,459
Charles Ben Howell, Republican	0.2	3,866
Roger Henson, Independent	0.2	3,092
Chuck Sibley, Republican	0.1	2,406
Rose Floyd, Socialist	0.1	2,301

Thomas D. Spink, Republican — 0.1 — 2,281
Lottie Bolling Hancock, Independent — 0.1 — 2,242
Lou Zaeske, Independent — 0.1 — 2,191
Billy Brown, Prohibition — 0.1 — 2,187
James Vallaster, Republican — 0.1 — 2,124
Louis C. Davis, Independent — 0.1 — 1,548
Maco Stewart, Independent — 0.1 — 1,260

This special election was held to fill the seat of Lloyd Bentsen, who resigned to accept an appointment by President Clinton as secretary of the treasury. No candidate received a majority in this special election, so a runoff was held on June 2 between the top two candidates. Under a state law passed after the 1957 special election, candidates in special elections for the Senate would all run together regardless of party affiliation. If none received a majority, a runoff would be called between the top two contenders. The election was close enough that a runoff election was held on June 9, 1993.

1993 Special Election Runoff (June 9)

Kay Bailey Hutchison, Republican — 67.3 — 1,188,716
Robert Krueger, Democrat — 32.7 — 576,538

This special election runoff was held to fill the seat of Lloyd Bentsen as no candidate received a majority in the special election held the month before.

1994 Democratic Primary Election (March 8)

Michael A. Andrews — 15.6 — 159,828
Richard Fisher — 37.8 — 387,989
Evelyn K. Lantz — 6.2 — 63,517
Jim Mattox — 40.5 — 416,342

The election was close enough that a runoff election was held on April 12, 1994.

Republican Primary Election (March 8)

Kay Bailey Hutchison — 84.3 — 467,975
M. Troy Mata — 1.6 — 8,632
Ernest J. Schmidt — 1.6 — 8,690
Tom Spink — 1.0 — 5,692
James C. Currey — 2.8 — 15,625
Roger Henson — 2.5 — 14,021
Stephen Hopkins — 6.2 — 34,703

Democratic Primary Runoff Election (April 12)

Richard Fisher — 53.6 — 400,227
Jim Mattox — 46.4 — 346,414

General Election (November 8)

Kay Bailey Hutchison, Republican — 60.8 — 2,604,218
Richard Fisher, Democrat — 38.3 — 1,639,615
Pierre Blondeau, Libertarian — 0.8 — 36,107

2000 Republican Primary Election (March 14)

Kay Bailey Hutchison — 100.0 — 955,033

Democratic Primary Election (March 14)

H. Gerald Bintliff — 5.5 — 34,137
Don Clark — 22.6 — 141,150
Charles Gandy — 22.7 — 141,618
Gene Kelly — 35.8 — 223,392
Bobby Wightman-Cervantes — 13.5 — 84,335

The election was close enough that a runoff election was held on April 11, 2000.

Democratic Primary Runoff Election (April 11)

Charles Gandy — 41.5 — 102,315
Gene Kelly — 58.5 — 143,970

General Election (November 7)

Kay Bailey Hutchison, Republican — 65.0 — 4,082,091
Gene Kelly, Democrat — 32.3 — 2,030,315
Doug S. Sandage, Green Party — 1.5 — 91,448
Mary J. Ruwart, Libertarian — 1.2 — 72,798

2006 Republican Primary Election (March 7)

Kay Bailey Hutchison — 100.0 — 627,163

DEMOCRATIC PRIMARY ELECTION (MARCH 7)

Darrel Reece Hunter	18.7	93,609
Gene Kelly	38.2	191,400
Barbara Ann Radnofsky	43.1	215,776

The election was close enough that a runoff election was held on April 11, 2006.

DEMOCRATIC PRIMARY RUNOFF ELECTION (APRIL 11)

Gene Kelly	39.8	82,589
Barbara Ann Radnofsky	60.2	124,663

GENERAL ELECTION (NOVEMBER 7)

Kay Bailey Hutchison, Republican	61.7	2,661,789
Barbara Ann Radnofsky	36.0	1,555,202
Scott Lanier Jameson, Libertarian	2.26	97,672

CLASS 2—THE HOUSTON SUCCESSION

1912 DEMOCRATIC PRIMARY ELECTION (JULY 26)

Morris Sheppard	48.9	182,907
Jake Wolters	39.1	146,214
Choice B. Randell	10.9	40,693
Matthew Zollner	1.1	3,960

GENERAL ELECTION (NOVEMBER 1)

Morris Sheppard, Democrat	100.0	unopposed

1918 DEMOCRATIC PRIMARY ELECTION (JULY 27)

Morris Sheppard	99.7	649,876
W. F. Heller	0.3	1,760

GENERAL ELECTION (NOVEMBER 5)

Morris Sheppard, Democrat	86.7	155,178
J. W. Flanagan, Republican	12.4	22,214
M. A. Smith, Socialist	0.9	1608

1924 DEMOCRATIC PRIMARY ELECTION (JULY 26)

Morris Sheppard	64.8	440,511
Fred W. Davis	23.5	159,663
John F. Maddox	11.8	80,070

GENERAL ELECTION (NOVEMBER 4)

Morris Sheppard, Democrat	85.4	591,913
T. M. Kennerly, Republican	14.6	101,208

1930 DEMOCRATIC PRIMARY ELECTION (JULY 26)

Morris Sheppard	71.1	526,293
Robert Lee Henry	23.5	174,260
C. A. Mitchner	5.4	40,130

REPUBLICAN PRIMARY ELECTION (JULY 26)

Doran John Haesly	40.5	3,645
C. O. Harris	31.0	2,784
Harve H. Haines	28.5	2,568

GENERAL ELECTION (NOVEMBER 4)

Morris Sheppard, Democrat	86.4	266,559
Doran John Haesly, Republican	13.2	39,055
Guy L. Smith, Socialist	0.3	808

This election was the first direct election by the voters of Texas for a U.S. senator and was for the term beginning in March 1913. The general election was closely followed by the 1913 legislative election. Governor Colquitt had appointed newspaper editor Rienzi Johnston of Houston to the remainder of Joseph W. Bailey's seat in the U.S. Senate. The legislature did not approve of Johnston, as he was a "wet" during the early stages of the groundswell for the prohibition movement. Sheppard had already won the November 1912 general election for the seat whose term would begin in March 1913. Sheppard and the legislature began a movement to encourage Johnston to resign. Johnston did resign his senate seat on February 2, 1913, after only twenty-eight days in office. Sheppard took office on February 3, 1913, giving him about one month seniority over every other new U.S. Senator scheduled to take office in March. Thus began Morris Sheppard's twenty-eight-year career in the U.S. Senate.

W. A. Berry, Communist — 0.1 — 296

1936 DEMOCRATIC PRIMARY ELECTION (JULY 25)

Candidate	%	Votes
Morris Sheppard	64.6	616,293
Joe H. Eagle	14.3	136,718
Guy B. Fisher	9.3	89,215
Joseph H. Price	4.8	45,919
Richard C. Bush	4.0	37,842
J. Edward Glenn	3.0	28,641

GENERAL ELECTION (NOVEMBER 3)

Candidate	%	Votes
Morris Sheppard, Democrat	92.6	775,022
Carlos G. Watson, Republican	7.1	59,491
Gertrude Wilson, Union	0.2	1,836
W. B. Starr, Socialist	0.1	958

1941 SPECIAL ELECTION (JUNE 28)

Candidate	%	Votes
W. Lee O'Daniel, Democrat	30.5	175,590
Lyndon B. Johnson, Democrat	30.3	174,299
Gerald C. Mann, Democrat	24.5	140,807
Martin Dies, Democrat	14.0	80,551
Sam Morris, Democrat	0.3	1,654
24 Others	0.3	1,866

Joseph C. Bean, Dr. John R. Brinkley, Homer Brooks, E. A. Calvin, Arlon B. Davis, Polite Elvins, Guy B. Fisher, Enoch Fletcher, W. E. Gilliland, A. B. Harding, Commodore Basil Muse Hatfield, Robert Grammer Head, O. P. Heath, Sr., Bubba Hicks, W. R. Jones, W. W. King, Starl Newsome, Floyd E. Ryan, Walter A. Schultz, C. L. Somerville, Joe Thompson, Edwin Waller, W. C. Welch, Johne Williams

This special election was held to fill the seat of the late Andrew Jackson Houston. Houston had been picked by Governor O'Daniel to fill the seat of the late Morris Sheppard, but Houston only lived a brief time after his swearing-in. There were 25 Democrats, 2 Republicans, 1 Independent, and 1 Communist running in this open primary.

1942 DEMOCRATIC PRIMARY ELECTION (JULY 25)

Candidate	%	Votes
W. Lee O'Daniel	48.3	475,541
James V. Allred	32.3	317,501
Dan Moody	18.1	178,471
Floyd E. Ryan	1.2	12,213

The election was close enough that a runoff election was held on August 22, 1942.

DEMOCRATIC PRIMARY RUNOFF ELECTION (AUGUST 22)

Candidate	%	Votes
W. Lee O'Daniel	51.0	451,359
James Allred	49.0	433,203

GENERAL ELECTION (NOVEMBER 3)

Candidate	%	Votes
W. Lee O'Daniel, Democrat	94.9	260,629
Dudley Lawson, Republican	4.4	12,064
Charles L. Somerville, People's Unity	0.7	1,934

1948 DEMOCRATIC PRIMARY ELECTION (JULY 24)

Candidate	%	Votes
Coke R. Stevenson	39.7	477,077
Lyndon B. Johnson	33.7	405,617
George E. B. Peddy	19.7	237,195
Otis C. Myers	1.3	15,330
F. B. Clark	0.6	7,420
Roscoe H. Collier	1.0	12,327
Arlon B. Davis	0.9	10,871
Frank G. Cortez	1.1	13,344
Jesse C. Saunders	0.6	7,401
Terrell Sledge	0.6	6,692
James F. Alford	0.8	9,117
Write-in	0.0	1

The election was close enough that a runoff election was held on August 28, 1948.

DEMOCRATIC PRIMARY RUNOFF ELECTION (AUGUST 28)

Candidate	%	Votes
Lyndon B. Johnson	50.0	494,191
Coke R. Stevenson	50.0	494,104

GENERAL ELECTION (NOVEMBER 2)

Lyndon B. Johnson, Democrat	66.2	702,985
Jack Porter, Republican	32.9	349,665
Sam Morris, Prohibition	0.9	8,913

1954 DEMOCRATIC PRIMARY ELECTION (JULY 24)

Lyndon B. Johnson	71.4	883,264
Dudley T. Dougherty	28.6	354,188

REPUBLICAN PRIMARY ELECTION (JULY 24)

Carlos G. Watson	100.0	9,206

GENERAL ELECTION (NOVEMBER 2)

Lyndon B. Johnson, Democrat	84.6	538,417
Carlos G. Watson, Republican	14.9	95,033
Fred T. Spangler, Constitution	0.5	3,025

1960 DEMOCRATIC PRIMARY ELECTION (MAY 7)

Lyndon B. Johnson	100.0	

GENERAL ELECTION (NOVEMBER 8)

Lyndon B. Johnson, Democrat	58.0	1,306,605
John G. Tower, Republican	41.1	926,653
Bard A. Logan, Constitution	0.9	20,506

1961 SPECIAL ELECTION (APRIL 4)

John G. Tower, Republican	30.9	327,308
William A. Blakley, Democrat	18.1	190,818
Jim Wright, Democrat	16.2	171,328
Will Wilson, Democrat	11.5	121,961
Maury Maverick, Jr., Democrat	9.9	104,992
Henry B. Gonzalez, Democrat	9.2	97,659
Eristus Sams	0.4	4,490
Hugh Wilson	0.3	2,997
Delbert C. Grandstaff	0.3	2,959
Hoyt G. Wilson	0.2	2,165
W. L. Burleson	0.2	1,695
Arthur Glover	0.1	1,528
Martha Tredway	0.1	1,227
Steve Nemecek	0.1	1,017
57 Others	2.5	25,938

Dr. G. H. Allen, Jim Amos, Dale Baker, Dr. Mali Jean Rauch Barraco, Tom E. Barton, R. G. Becker, Jacob Bergolofsky, Dr. Ted Bisland, G. E. Blewett, Lawrence S. Bosworth, Jr., Joyce J. Bradshaw, Chester D. Brooks, Ronald J. Byers, Joseph M. Carter, George A. Davisson, Jr., Mrs. Winnie K. Derrick, Harry R. Diehl, Harvill O. Eaton, Rev. Jonnie Mae Eckman, Paul F. Eix, Ben H. Faber, Dr. H. E. Fanning, Charles Otto Foerster, Jr., Harold Franklin, George N. Gallagher, Jr., Richard J. Gay, Van T. George, Jr., Arthur Glover, Curtis E. Hill, Willard Park Holland, John N. Hopkins, Ben M. Johnson, Guy Johnson, Morgan H. Johnson, C. B. Kennedy, H. Springer Knoblauch, Hugh O. Lea, V. C. Logan, Frank A. Matera, Brown McCallum, James E. McKee, George E. Noyes, Cecil D. Perkins, William H. Posey, George Red, Wesley Roberts, D. T. Sampson, A. Dale Savage, Carl A. Schrade, Albert Roy Smith, Homer Hyrim Stalarow, Frank Stanford, John B. Sypert, Mrs Martha Tredway, S. S. Vela, Bill Whitten, Marcos Zertuche

This special election was held to fill the seat of Lyndon Johnson, who had resigned from the U.S. Senate to become vice-president. None of the seventy-one candidates received a clear majority, so the top two candidates—Tower and Blakley—competed in a special runoff election on May 27. Under a state law passed after the 1957 special election, candidates in special elections for the Senate would all run together regardless of party affiliation. If none received a majority, a runoff would be called between the top two contenders. The election was close enough that a runoff election was held on May 27, 1961.

1961 SPECIAL RUNOFF ELECTION (MAY 27)

John G. Tower, Republican	50.6	448,217
William A. Blakley, Democrat	49.4	437,874

1966 REPUBLICAN PRIMARY ELECTION (MAY 7)

John Tower	100.0	

DEMOCRATIC PRIMARY ELECTION (MAY 7)

Waggoner Carr	79.9	899,523
John R. Willoughby	20.1	226,598

General Election (November 8)

John Tower, Republican	56.4	842,501
Waggoner Carr, Democrat	43.1	643,855
James Barker Holland, Constitution	0.5	6,778
Others	0.0	45

1972 Republican Primary Election (May 6)

John Tower	100.0	

Democratic Primary Election (May 6)

Ralph Yarborough	50.0	1,032,606
Harold Barefoot Sanders	38.1	787,504
Hugh Wilson	6.1	125,460
Thomas M. Cartlidge		

The election was close enough that a runoff election was held on June 3, 1972.

Democratic Primary Runoff Election (June 3)

Harold Barefoot Sanders	52.1	1,008,499
Ralph Yarborough	47.9	928,132

General Election (Novemebr 7)

John Tower, Republican	53.4	1,882,877
Harold Barefoot Sanders, Democrat	44.3	1,511,985
Flores N. Amaya, La Raza Unida	1.8	63,543
Tom Leonard, Socialist Workers	0.4	14,464
Write-ins	0.0	1,034

1978 Republican Primary Election (May 6)

John Tower	100.0	

Democratic Primary Election (May 6)

Robert Krueger	54.7	853,460
Joe Christie	45.3	707,738

General Election (November 7)

John Tower, Republican	49.8	1,151,376
Robert Krueger, Democrat	49.3	1,139,149
Luis A. Diaz de Leon, La Raza	0.8	17,869
Miguel Pendas, Socialist Workers	0.2	4,018
Other	0.0	128

1984 Republican Primary Election (May 5)

Phil Gramm	73.2	246,716
Ron Paul	16.5	55,431
Rob Mosbacher	7.5	26,279
Henry Grover	2.5	8388

Democratic Primary Election (May 5)

Kent Hance	31.2	456,446
Lloyd Doggett	31.2	456,173
Robert Krueger	31.1	454,886
Harley Schlanger	1.0	14149
Robert Sullivan	2.4	34733
David Young	3.2	47062

The election was close enough that a runoff election was held on June 2, 1984.

Democratic Primary Runoff Election (June 2)

Lloyd Doggett	50.0	489,932
Kent Hance	50.0	489,834

The election was close enough that a recount was called.

Democratic Primary Runoff Recount

Lloyd Doggett	50.1	491,251
Kent Hance	50.0	489,906

General Election (November 6)

Phil Gramm, Republican	58.5	3,111,348
Lloyd Doggett, Democrat	41.5	2,202,557
Others	0.0	273

1990 Republican Primary Election (March 13)

Phil Gramm	100.0	

Democratic Primary Election (March 13)

Hugh Parmer	75.4	766,284
Harley Schlanger	24.6	249,445

General Election (November 6)

Phil Gramm, Republican	60.2	2,302,357
Hugh Parmer, Democrat	37.4	1,429,986
Gary Johnson, Libertarian	2.3	89,089
Ira Calkins, Independent	0.0	725

1996 Republican Primary Election (March 12)

Phil Gramm	85.0	838,339
Henry C. "Hank" Grover	7.3	72,400
David Young	7.7	75,463

Democratic Primary Election (March 12)

John Bryant	30.0	267,545
Jim Chapman	26.9	239,427
Victor M. Morales	36.2	322,218
John Will Odam	6.9	61,433

Democratic Primary Runoff Election (April 9)

John Bryant	48.8	235,281
Victor M. Morales	51.2	246,614

General Election (November 5)

Phil Gramm, Republican	54.8	3,027,680
Victor M. Morales, Democrat	43.9	2,428,776
Michael Bird, Libertarian	0.9	51,516
John Huff, Natural Law	0.4	19,469

2002 Republican Primary Election (March 12)

John Cornyn	77.3	478,825
Lawrence Cranberg	2.9	17,757
Douglas G. Deffenbaugh	7.0	46,907
Bruce Rusty Lang	7.6	46,907
Dudley F. Mooney	5.2	32,202

The election was close enough that a runoff election was held on April 9, 1996.

U.S. Representative Election Returns

The section includes election returns for the U.S. representative posts for Texas from 1846 to 2000. The information for general elections is complete. The information for primary elections is not complete. The first primary election for U.S. representatives in Texas was held by the Democratic Party in 1906. Republican Party primary elections have been held every two years since 1962. Before that, they were held only in 1926, 1930, 1934, 1954, and 1958.

Election data has been compiled from a variety of sources. The secretary of state in Austin is the official keeper of Texas election data. They have excellent records for general elections, as does the clerk of the U.S. House of Representatives. Unfortunately and quite surprisingly, much of the primary election data has been lost to history. The State Library and Archives also has little primary election data. As primary elections are more a function of the party than the state, parties were turned to for this information. Neither party has good records on primary elections. From 1906 to 1960, no official returns of primaries were required except to party officials. In 1960, each party's county executive committee had to canvass the primary elections votes and file the results with the county clerk. The Texas Almanac turns out to be the best source of primary election data for post-1940 elections, and unfortunately, much of that information is incomplete. Unfortunately, the Dallas Morning News, which publishes the Almanac, reports not to have any other data that which was printed at the time. Newspapers of the day present (1) who ran in the primary and (2) the vote count at the time of printing. However, rarely would a newspaper dedicate space to final primary election tabulations of the canvass by party officials. Data is included for primary elections as it could be found and is mostly complete for the second half of the twentieth century.

Generally, election data is from:

★ General election returns and primary election returns (1956-1970) are from the Texas Election Register, the Clerk of the U.S. House of Representatives, Dubin (1998), and the State Library and Archives

★ Primary and general election returns (1992-date) are from the Texas secretary of state

★ Primary elections returns (1940-1990) from Texas Almanac (various) and newspapers (various)

The year and type of election is followed by the date of the election in parentheses. Candidates and returns are sorted by congressional district. Candidates are listed in no particular order within the district. The candidate's party affiliation follows his name. The number of votes is followed by a value that represents the percentage of the total vote count in that race. Any at-large representative posts are listed last. Any notes or commentary about the election follow the election data. If only part of a name is present, that is all that is known. For at-large posts a "W" next to a candidate's returns indicates that they won the election and were one of several congressmen serving at-large. Candidates that were unopposed in a primary election or for reelection may not have vote tallies. In some cases, they are simply noted as "unopposed" and their percentage of the vote listed as "100.0" percent. If no candidate sought the office, "(none)" is found where the candidate's name would usually appear. If you can supply any missing names or information, please contact the Poage Library at Baylor University: poage_library@baylor.edu.

1846 Special Election (March 30)

	Candidate	Votes	%
1	David Kaufman, Democrat	1,559	53.9
	William R. Scurry	761	26.3
	William B. Ochiltree	573	19.8
2	Timothy Pilsbury, Calhoun Democrat	1,150	30.1
	Samuel M. Williams	1,070	28.0
	William G. Cooke	912	23.9
	John M. Lewis	362	9.5
	Joseph C. Megginson	207	5.4
	Thomas J. Green	91	2.4
	Other	27	0.7

1846 General Election (November 2)

	Candidate	Votes	%
1	David Kaufman, Democrat	901	98.2
	Other	17	1.8
2	Timothy Pilsbury, Calhoun Democrat	2,223	57.5
	William E. Jones	454	11.7
	Samuel M. Williams	794	20.5
	R. E. B. Baylor	395	10.2

1849 General Election (August 6)

	Candidate	Votes	%
1	David Kaufman, Democrat	8,944	96.0
	—— Fitzpatrick	307	3.3
	Other	66	0.7
2	Volney E. Howard, Democrat	4,417	41.9
	Robert M. Williamson	3,053	28.9
	Timothy Pilsbury, Democrat	2,170	20.6
	Hugh McLeod	908	8.6

1851 General Election (August 4)

	Candidate	Votes	%
1	Richardson A. Scurry, Democrat	7,460	55.2
	William B. Ochiltree	4,354	32.2
	B. Rush Wallace	1,148	8.5
	N. H. Darnell	564	4.2
2	Volney Howard, Democrat	6,853	49.5
	Gideon K. Lewis	2,615	18.9
	Hugh McLeod	2,935	21.2
	Henry N. Potter	1,231	8.9
	William Menifee	207	1.5

1853 General Election (August 1)

	Candidate	Votes	%
1	George M. Smyth, Democrat	15,015	98.9
	C. L. Mills	147	1.0
	Benjamin H. Epperson	21	0.1
2	Peter H. Bell, Democrat	7,629	42.0
	William R. Scurry, Democrat	3,885	21.4
	Gideon K. Lewis, Democrat	2,914	16.0
	B. F. Carouthers, Whig	2,326	12.8
	Thomas W. Blake, Democrat	1,422	7.8

1855 General Election (August 6)

	Candidate	Votes	%
1	Lemuel Evans, American	10,352	50.1
	Matthias Ward, Democrat	10,311	49.9
2	Peter H. Bell, Democrat	14,599	60.8
	John Hancock, American	9,427	39.2

1857 General Election (August 3)

	Candidate	Votes	%
1	John H. Reagan, Democrat	15,341	60.7
	Lemuel Dale Evans, American	9,929	39.3
2	Guy M. Bryan, Democrat	20,341	81.9
	William E. Howth, American	4,505	18.2

1861 Legislative Election (February 2 or 3) for Delegates to Provisional Congress

Nat M. Burford
Robert C. Campbell
T.C. Chambers
—— Chilton
George W. Crawford

Delegates / Candidates

Name	Selected
John Dancy	
Thomas J. Devine	
George M. Flournoy	
—— Foscue	
—— Graham	
Peter W. Gray	W
John Gregg	W
John Hemphill	
A. W. O. Hicks	
James S. Hogg	
Albert C. Horton	
Sam Houston	
Francis R. Lubbock	
—— Maverick	
Hugh McLeod	
John T. Mills	
W. B. Ochiltree	W
Williamson S. Oldham	W
Wm H Parsons	
—— Pope	
—— Rainey	
John H. Reagan	W
T. R. Rogers	
H. R. Runnels	
—— Scott	
W. R. Scurry	
F. B. Sexton	
Fletcher S. Stockdale	
Matthias Ward	
Thomas Waul	W
John A. Wharton	
—— Wheeler	
Louis T. Wigfall	W
John A. Wilcox	
P. Wiley	

1859 GENERAL ELECTION (AUGUST 1)

District	Candidate	Votes	%
1	John H. Reagan, Democrat	23,620	89.1
	William B. Ochiltree, Independent	2,858	10.9
2	Andrew J. Hamilton, Independent Democrat	16,316	51.2
	Thomas N. Waul, Democrat	15,565	48.9

1861 GENERAL ELECTION (NOVEMBER 6)

District	Candidate	Votes	%
1	John A. Wilcox, Whig	3,448	47.1
	Edward R. Hord	2,470	33.7
	William Stewart	1,403	19.2
2	Caleb C. Herbert, Democrat	2,479	38.1
	Fred Tate	2,034	31.2
	A. M. Lewis	1,367	21.0
	E. W. Chandler	633	9.7
3	Peter W. Gray, Democrat	4,952	74.5
	A. P. Wiley	1,673	25.2
	W. R. Reagan	21	0.3
	Other	5	0.0
4	Franklin B. Sexton, Democrat	1,644	32.0
	Joseph Lewis Hogg	1,062	20.7
	J. N. Maxey	1,053	20.5
	T. J. Wood	926	18.0
	A. W. O. Hicks	350	6.8
	W. R. Poag	100	1.9
5	Malcom D. Graham, Democrat	2,946	52.3
	R. B. Hubbard	2,686	47.7
6	William B. Wright, Democrat	3,444	49.1
	Benjamin H. Epperson	2,777	39.6
	T. J. Rodgers	537	7.7
	R. H. Ward	256	3.6

This election was held by the state legislature to select delegates for the first provisional Confederate Congress in Montgomery, Alabama.

This was the first congressional election for the Confederate Congress.

	Candidate	Votes	%
	—— Hill	125	3.2
	Other	22	0.6
3	Anthony M. Branch	1,204	42.5
	R. A. Mills	797	28.1
	—— Bassett	578	20.4
	—— Greeley	210	7.4
4	Caleb C. Herbert	1,448	45.9
	I. W. Henderson	747	23.7
	—— Finley	621	19.7
	—— Darden	272	8.6
	Other	67	2.1

All the southern states which had seceeded to form the Confederacy held elections about this time. However, representatives selected in these elections were rejected by the U.S. Congress. The only exception was the delegation from Tennessee. Of the four, Herbert and Branch had served in the Confederate Congress. Only Branch would eventually serve in the U.S. Congress.

1869 GENERAL ELECTION (NOVEMBER 30-DECEMBER 3)

	Candidate	Votes	%
1	George W. Whitmore, Republican	8,456	52.0
	James Armstrong, Democrat	7,406	45.6
	Horace Broughton	381	2.4
2	John C. Conner, Democrat	6,378	41.9
	B. F. Grafton, Republican	4,355	28.6
	J. F. Johnson, Republican	3,540	23.2
	R. H. Taylor, Republican	944	6.2
3	William T. Clark, Republican	16,582	65.9
	Jacob Elliot, Democrat	8,564	34.0
4	Edward Degener, Republican	9,312	47.7
	John L. Haynes, Democrat	9,240	47.3
	W. M. Varnell, Republican	949	4.9

This was the first recognized election held following the end of the Civil War. Texas had now grown to require four seats in the U.S. House. Three of the four elected were Republicans, and only Clark was considered a carpetbagger. These men did not serve a full two-year term, but were seated after the beginning of the first session of Congress. They were admitted on March 30, 1870, only after President Johnson signed the legislation allowing Texas' representatives to be seated.

1863 GENERAL ELECTION (AUGUST 3)

	Candidate	Votes	%
1	John A. Wilcox, Whig	2,853	61.8
	J. W. Bunton	1,762	38.2
2	Caleb C. Herbert, Democrat	3,294	57.9
	Eggleston D. Townes	2,396	42.1
3	Anthony M. Branch	3,706	63.1
	Peter W. Gray	2,166	36.9
4	Franklin B. Sexton, Democrat	2,065	51.8
	James M. Anderson	1,920	48.2
5	John R. Baylor	2,494	50.6
	Malcolm D. Graham	2,396	48.6
	—— Crosely	39	0.8
6	Simpson H. Morgan	2,585	53.4
	William B. Wright	2,061	42.5
	J. W. Mosley	198	4.1

This election was held to select representatives to the second Confederate Congress. All the incumbents sought reelection. However, only half (three) were returned to office. John Wilcox died shortly after being elected and a special election was called in 1864 to fill his seat.

1864 SPECIAL ELECTION (AUGUST)

	Candidate	Votes	%
1	Stephen H. Darden		
	J. W. Davis		

This special election was held to fill the seat of the John A. Wilcox, who died on February 7, 1864, while serving in Richmond, Virginia, at the Confederate Congress. Darden was selected to fill the balance of Wilcox's term.

1866 GENERAL ELECTION (OCTOBER 15)

	Candidate	Votes	%
1	George W. Chilton	1,818	43.2
	I. M. Burroughs	747	17.8
	I. M. Camp	463	11.0
	A. B. Norton	431	10.3
	A. T. Rainey	254	6.0
	Y. G. Word	246	5.85
	William B. Ochiltree	139	3.3
	Others	106	2.5
2	Benjamin H. Epperson	2,466	62.7
	Amzi Bradshaw	1,318	33.5

1871 GENERAL ELECTION (OCTOBER 3-6)

1	William S. Herndon, Democrat	14,521	58.7
	George W. Whitmore, Republican	10,209	41.3
2	John C. Connor, Democrat	15,900	79.9
	Anthony M. Bryant, Republican	4,002	20.1
3	William T. Clark, Republican	18,407	51.3
	DeWitt C. Giddings, Democrat	17,082	47.6
	Louis W. Stevenson, Independent	407	1.1
4	John Hancock, Democrat	15,022	57.4
	Edward Degener, Republican	11,153	42.6

This was the second election following the Civil War. Texans and Democrats had fought and regained control of most of the state from the Radical Republicans. All three of the Republicans elected in 1869 were unseated. One reason for this was because the conservative Republicans were beginning to side with the Democrats instead of with their radical brethren. However, many voting irregularities were found. In the race for the 3rd District seat, William Clark was declared the winner over DeWitt C. Giddings, although Giddings had received more votes. Giddings protested to the governor. Governor Davis agreed with the seating of Clark. Giddings protested to the Congressional Committee on Elections and they agreed with him. Clark was removed from his seat on May 31, 1872, after serving less than one year. The vote count was revised to Giddings 25,391 and Clark 19,460. Texas was slowly returning to its Democratic roots.

1872 GENERAL ELECTION (NOVEMBER 5)

1	William S. Herndon, Democrat	11,252	51.2
	Robert K. Smith, Republican	9,150	42.1
	William Chambers, Liberal Republican	1,287	5.9
2	William McLean, Democrat	15,784	72.9
	F. W. Minor, Rupublican	5,882	27.2
3	DeWitt C. Giddings, Democrat	22,173	51.6
	A. J. Evans, Republican	19,759	48.4
4	John Hancock, Democrat	19,584	54.3
	W. O. Hutchinson, Republican	16,468	45.7
At-Large	Asa H. Willie, Democrat	69,078 W	59.5
	Roger Q. Mills, Democrat	68,836 W	59.3
	I. D. Evans, Republican	47,096	40.6
	A. B. Norton, Republican	47,125	40.6

1874 GENERAL ELECTION (NOVEMBER 3)

1	John H. Reagan, Democrat	7,103	70.7
	William Chambers, Republican	2,939	29.3
2	David B. Culberson, Democrat	4,256	100.0
3	James Throckmorton, Democrat	6,000	94.5
	J. M. Valentine, Republican	280	4.4
	F. W. Sumner, Republican	70	1.1
4	Roger Mills, Democrat	9,449	70.7
	Pleasant M. Yell, Republican	3,906	29.3
5	John Hancock, Democrat	5,050	95.8
	Other	220	4.2
6	Gustave Schleicher, Democrat	6,510	69.2
	Jeremiah Galvan, Republican	2,900	30.8

1876 GENERAL ELECTION (NOVEMBER 7)

1	John H. Reagan, Democrat	13,097	67.1
	L. W. Cooper, Republican	6,415	32.9
2	David Culberson, Democrat	17,326	65.5
	Stilwell H. Russell, Republican	9,130	34.5
3	James Throckmorton, Democrat	24,138	91.4
	J. C. Bigger, Republican	2,283	8.6
4	Roger Q. Mills, Democrat	20,731	70.1
	J. P. Osterhaut, Republican	8,839	29.9
5	DeWitt C. Giddings, Democrat	15,286	53.5
	George W. Jones, Independent Republican	13,277	46.5
6	Gustave Schleicher, Democrat	11,954	81.5
	James P. Newcomb, Republican	2,711	18.5

1878 GENERAL ELECTION (NOVEMBER 5)

1	John H. Reagan, Democrat	19,338	98.9
	Other	225	1.1
2	David Culberson, Democrat	19,728	63.1
	Henry F. O'Neal, Greenback	9,617	30.8
	R. H. Taylor, Democrat	1,918	6.1
3	Olin Wellborn, Democrat	40,848	80.5

			%
	E. M. Daggett, Greenback	9,718	19.2
	Other	158	0.3
4	Roger Q. Mills, Democrat	30,535	75.7
	A. N. Smith, Greenback	9,039	22.4
	James Mitchell	745	1.9
5	George W. Jones, Greenback & Democrat	21,101	51.7
	John Hancock, Democrat	19,721	48.3
6	Gustave Schleicher, Democrat	19,199*	55.1
	John Ireland, Independent Democrat	15,671	44.9

*Gustave Schleicher died on January 10, 1879, and did not serve in the 46th Congress.

1879 SPECIAL ELECTION (APRIL 15)

			%
6	Christopher Upson, Democrat	9,520	71.7
	Henry Maney, Greenback	3,756	28.3

This special election was held to fill the seat of the late Gustave Schleicher.

1880 GENERAL ELECTION (NOVEMBER 2)

			%
1	John H. Reagan, Democrat	21,227	77.7
	S. R. Withers, Greenback	6,095	22.3
	Other	1	0.0
2	David B. Culberson, Democrat	26,624	68.6
	Henry F. O'Neal, Greenback	12,194	31.4
3	Olin Wellborn, Democrat	48,005	78.7
	Jerome C. Kirby, Greenback	13,014	21.3
	Other	19	0.0
4	Roger Q. Mills, Democrat	30,087	62.6
	John T. Brady, Greenback	17,977	37.4
	Other	7	0.0
5	George W. Jones, Greenback	22,941	50.3
	Seth Shepard, Democrat	22,708	49.7
6	Christopher Upson, Democrat	27,521	97.3
	D. B. Robertson, Greenback	653	2.3
	Other	117	0.4

The election of 1880 saw the first strong showing by the Greenback Party.

1882 GENERAL ELECTION (NOVEMBER 7)

			%
1	Charles Stewart, Democrat	14,882	62.7
	William Chambers, Republican	8,850	37.3
2	John H. Reagan, Democrat	12,035	82.6
	B. F. Newman	2,354	16.2
	M. H. Jackson	157	1.1
	Charles Stewart	27	0.2
3	James H. Jones, Democrat	14,045	58.0
	S. H. Russell, Republican	9,492	39.1
	H. W. Wade, Independent	699	2.9
4	David B. Culberson, Democrat	13,487	63.4
	E. L. Dehoney, Greenback	7,785	36.6
5	James W. Throckmorton, Democrat	16,163	72.0
	John N. Dixon, Greenback	6,280	28.0
6	Olin Wellborn, Democrat	17,510	71.6
	Jerome C. Kirby, Greenback	6,949	28.4
7	Thomas P. Ochiltree, Independent	12,457	55.8
	George P. Finlay, Democrat	9,851	44.1
8	James F. Miller, Democrat	12,297	59.0
	Robert Zapp, Greenback	6,528	31.3
	Joseph O'Connor, Independent	1,774	8.5
	Other	231	1.1
9	Roger Q. Mills, Democrat	14,730	63.9
	J. D. Rankin, Greenback	8,329	35.1
10	John Hancock, Democrat	16,098	62.2
	Edmund J. Davis, Republican	9,783	37.8
11	Samuel W. T. Lanham, Democrat	10,493	51.0
	J. W. Barnett, Greenback	4,744	23.1
	J. H. Davenport, Independent Democrat	3,807	18.5
	S. C. Buck, Independent Democrat	1,532	7.4

1884 GENERAL ELECTION (NOVEMBER 4)

			%
1	Charles Stewart, Democrat	24,145	99.9
	John T. Brady, Republican	12	0.0
	A. T. Monroe, Republican	3	0.0
2	John H. Reagan, Democrat	16,840	67.1

District	Candidate	Votes	%
	A. T. Monroe, Republican	8,276	33.0
3	James H. Jones, Democrat	23,504	97.2
	G. F. Conley, Republican	529	2.2
	John O'Brien	149	0.6
4	David Culberson, Democrat	23,165	100.0
5	James W. Throckmorton, Democrat	29,462	98.9
	M. H. Eddy	171	0.6
	H. C. Dillingham	159	0.5
6	Olin Wellborn, Democrat	27,804	85.5
	J. C. Bigger, Republican	4,721	14.5
7	William H. Crain, Democrat	15,471	59.2
	R. B. Renfro, Republican	9,586	36.7
	Richard Nelson, Republican	1,084	4.2
8	James F. Miller, Democrat	17,143	66.9
	W. P. Burns, Republican	8,473	33.1
9	Roger Q. Mills, Democrat	22,333	69.0
	J. P. Osterhaut, Republican	9,049	31.0
10	Joseph D. Sayers, Democrat	21,523	63.7
	J. B. Rector, Independent Republican	12,253	36.3
11	Samuel W. T. Lanham, Democrat	29,738	99.4
	W. A. Saylor, Republican	184	0.6

1886 GENERAL ELECTION (NOVEMBER 2)

District	Candidate	Votes	%
1	Charles Stewart, Democrat	16,844	62.0
	H. D. Johnson, Republican	10,344	38.0
2	*John H. Reagan, Democrat	16,413	96.0
	John Collins, Opposition	680	4.0
3	Constantine B. Kilgore, Democrat	16,695	69.4
	W. E. Farmer, Opposition	7,359	30.6
4	David B. Culberson, Democrat	17,234	78.5
	James T. Fleming, Opposition	4,701	21.4
5	Silas Hare, Democrat	11,774	41.8
	G. B. Pickett, Independent Democrat	8,315	29.5
	H. C. Mack, Opposition	8,065	28.6
6	Jo Abbott, Democrat	19,185	59.9
	Jerome C. Kearby, Independent	11,756	36.7
	A. B. Norton, Republican	1,069	3.3
7	William H. Crain, Democrat	18,511	89.1
	J. L. Haynes, Republican	1,293	6.2
	N. W. Cuney, Republican	960	4.6
8	Littleton W. Moore, Democrat	22,908	92.3
	W. O. Hutchinson, Republican	1,912	7.7
9	Roger Q. Mills, Democrat	17,168	60.2
	J. D. Rankin, Population-Labor	11,337	39.8
10	Joseph D. Sayers, Democrat	26,809	78.2
	J. P. Newcomb, Republican	7,492	21.8
11	Samuel W. T. Lanham, Democrat	21,980	74.0
	J. W. Barnett, Independent	7,744	26.1

*John H. Reagan resigned on March 4, 1887, following his election as U.S. senator and did not serve in the 50th Congress as a U.S. representative.

1887 SPECIAL ELECTION (APRIL 5)

District	Candidate	Votes	%
2	William H. Martin, Democrat	unopposed	100.0

This special election was held to fill the seat of John H. Reagan, who had resigned to accept a U.S. Senate seat. No record could be found of Martin having any opponent in this election.

1888 GENERAL ELECTION (NOVEMBER 6)

District	Candidate	Votes	%
1	Charles Stewart, Democrat	14,813	51.4
	Lock McDaniel, Republican	9,817	34.1
	Jack Davis, Independent	4,166	14.5
2	William H. Martin, Democrat	16,210	70.9
	R. M. Humphrey, Union Labor	6,656	29.1
3	Constantine Kilgore, Democrat	20,579	68.0
	W. E. Farmer, Labor-Republican	9,697	32.0
4	David Culberson, Democrat	24,300	100.0
5	Silas Hare, Democrat	27,006	85.0
	I. W. Thomas, Republican	4,482	14.1
	Other	280	0.9
6	Jo Abbott, Democrat	26,815	68.9
	Samuel Evans, Labor	12,126	31.1

District	Candidate	Votes	%
7	William H. Crain, Democrat	15,610	56.4
	Calvin G. Brewster, Republican	12,063	43.6
8	Littleton Moore, Democrat	21,022	69.3
	T. C. Cook, Republican	8,460	27.9
	R. G. Sledge, Union Labor	849	2.8
9	Roger Q. Mills, Democrat	20,701	57.5
	E. A. Jones, Independent Democratic Republican & Prohibition	15,316	42.5
10	Joseph D. Sayers, Democrat	24,094	66.3
	Augustus Belknap, Republican	12,266	33.7
11	Samuel W. T. Lanham, Independent Democrat	28,561	87.4
	D. M. Rumph, Independent	3,130	9.6
	David Redfield, Republican	975	3.0

1890 General Election (November 4)

District	Candidate	Votes	%
1	Charles Stewart, Democrat	19,356	63.1
	*E. L. Angier, Republican	11,292	36.8
2	John B. Long, Democrat	12,973	99.6
3	Constantine B. Kilgore, Democrat	19,038	71.3
	L. B. Fish, Republican	7,340	27.5
	John O. Byrne, Prohibition	325	1.2
4	David B. Culberson, Democrat	17,290	74.9
	J. C. Gibbons, Republican	5,279	22.8
	Patrick B. Clark, Independent	532	2.3
5	Joseph W. Bailey, Democrat	26,791	81.9
	A. W. Achison, Republican	4,252	13.0
	W. R. Lamb, Independent	1,683	5.1
6	Jo Abbott, Democrat	29,982	85.7
	Isaac Darter, Republican	4,430	12.7
	H. W. Barclay, Republican	571	1.6
7	William H. Crain, Democrat	18,550	67.2
	J. V. Spohn, Republican	9,069	32.8
8	Littleton W. Moore, Democrat	20,739	71.3
	William Greene, Republican	8,368	28.8
9	Roger Q. Mills, Democrat	21,847	79.6
	D. W. Roberts, Republican	5,600	20.4
10	Joseph D. Sayers, Democrat	32,479	92.4
	W. G. Robinson, Republican	2,537	7.2
	Other	147	0.4
11	Samuel W. T. Lanham, Democrat	38,348	97.8
	C. W. Johnson, Republican	859	2.2

* Name also found as "Angier" in some references.

1892 Special Election (June 14)

District	Candidate	Votes	%
9	Edwin L. Anthony, Democrat	13,639	55.8
	I. N. Barber, People's	10,804	44.2

This special election was held to fill the seat of Roger Mills, who resigned on March 28, 1892, to accept his post as U.S. senator.

1892 General Election (November 8)

District	Candidate	Votes	%
1	Joseph C. Hutcheson, Democrat	14,439	59.7
	J. B. Stephenson, People's	6,081	25.1
	Daniel Taylor, Republican	3,703	15.3
2	Samuel B. Cooper, Democrat	19,894	61.5
	T. A. Wilson, People's	10,275	31.7
	T. A. Skillern, Republican	1,508	4.7
	W. C. Averill, Republican	698	2.2
3	Constantine B. Kilgore, Democrat	16,335	57.3
	J. M. Perdue, People's Progressive	12,177	42.7
4	David B. Culberson, Democrat	16,521	52.3
	Patrick B. Clark, People's Progressive	10,371	32.8
	J. A. Hurley, Republican	4,709	14.9
5	Joseph W. Bailey, Democrat	24,983	66.2
	R. B. Bell, Lily White Republican	8,170	21.7
	John Grant, Republican	4,563	12.1
6	Jo Abbott, Democrat	24,913	59.3
	J. C. Kearby, People's & Republican	17,078	40.6
7	George C. Pendleton, Democrat	19,937	56.1
	I. N. Barber, People's Progressive	15,587	43.8
8	Charles K. Bell, Democrat	17,997	54.5
	Evan Jones, People's Progressive	12,937	39.2
	C. C. Drake, Republican	2,009	6.1

	Votes	%
Other	98	
9 Joseph D. Sayers, Democrat	19,763	61.5
J. M. Horner, People's & Republican	12,384	38.5
10 Walter Gresham, Democrat	13,017	48.6
A. J. Rosenthal, Republican	9,452	35.3
E. O. Meitzn, People's Progressive	4,297	16.1
11 William H. Crain, Democrat	15,257	52.4
Calvin G. Brewster, Republican	8,055	27.7
Ben Terrell, People's Progressive	5,765	19.8
12 Thomas M. Paschal, Democrat	13,930	50.1
Henry Terrell, Republican	7,290	26.2
T. J. McMinn, People's Progressive	6,574	23.6
13 Jeremiah V. Cockrell, Democrat	21,922	65.6
W. J. Maltby, People's Progressive	9,825	29.4
A. G. Malloy, Republican	1,659	5.0

The election of 1892 saw the emergence of the Lily White Republicans.

1894 GENERAL ELECTION (NOVEMBER 6)

District / Candidate	Votes	%
1 Joseph C. Hutcheson, Democrat	14,920	55.3
J. J. Burroughs, Populist	10,037	37.0
L. E. Dunn, Republican	2,164	8.0
2 Samuel B. Cooper, Democrat	23,323	59.3
B. A. Calhoun, Populist	16,025	40.7
3 Charles H. Yoakum, Democrat	15,461	55.5
J. M. Perdue, Populist	12,411	44.5
4 David B. Culberson, Democrat	15,872	49.2
J. H. Davis, Populist	14,604	45.3
H. S. Sanderson, Republican	1,728	5.4
5 Joseph W. Bailey, Democrat	19,722	56.7
N. W. Browder, Populist	13,540	38.9
W. S. Farmer, Republican	1,517	4.4
6 Jo Abbott, Democrat	19,965	49.2
J. C. Kearby, Populist	19,621	48.4
B. O. James, Republican	968	2.4
7 George W. Pendleton, Democrat	18,822	52.4
I. N. Barber, Populist	17,092	47.6
8 Charles K. Bell, Democrat	16,480	50.6
C. H. Jenkins, Populist	16,104	49.4
9 Joseph D. Sayers, Democrat	18,460	52.7
W. O. Hutchison, Populist	16,591	47.3
10 Miles Crowley, Democrat	12,177	39.4
A. J. Rosenthal, Republican	10,874	35.2
J. C. McBride, Populist	7,847	25.4
11 William H. Crain, Democrat	17,946	52.7
V. Weldon, Populist	16,089	47.3
12 George H. Noonan, Republican	11,958	43.4
A. W. Houston, Democrat	11,045	40.1
A. V. Gates, Populist	4,545	16.5
13 Jeremiah V. Cockrell, Democrat	13,687	39.8
D. B. Gilliland, Populist	13,321	38.8
J. M. Dean, Independent Democrat	5,780	16.8
B. B. Kenyon, Republican	1,588	4.6

Populists becoming active and some were supported by Republicans. In the 12th District, Gates was listed on returns as "E.V.," "R.V.," and "E.G." These are assumed to be the same individual.

1896 SPECIAL ELECTION (APRIL 7)

District / Candidate	Votes	%
11 Rudolph Kleberg, Democrat	12,431	54.0
Calvin G. Brewster, Republican	5,572	24.2
Luther A. Lawhon, Populist	5,037	21.9

This special election was held to fill the seat of William Crain, who died on February 10, 1896.

1896 GENERAL ELECTION (NOVEMBER 3)

District / Candidate	Votes	%
1 Thomas H. Ball, Democrat	19,161	55.5
Joe H. Eagle, Populist & Republican	15,189	44.0
A. C. Tompkins, Republican	153	0.4
2 Samuel B. Cooper, Democrat	25,158	57.0
B. A. Calhoun, Populist	12,822	29.0
J. M. Claiborne, Republican	6,188	14.0
3 Reese C. De Graffenreid, Democrat	21,208	56.5
W. E. Farmer, Populist	16,351	43.5
4 John W. Cranford, Democrat	20,187	54.0
J. H. Davis, Populist	13,703	36.7

District	Candidate	Votes	%
	M. W. Johnson, National Democrat	3,468	9.3
5	Joseph W. Bailey, Democrat	28,416	61.2
	W. D. Gordon, Republican	13,242	28.5
	R. C. Foster, National Democrat	4,747	10.2
6	Robert E. Burke, Democrat	33,144	56.8
	Barnett Gibbs, Populist	25,230	43.2
7	Robert L. Henry, Democrat	26,151	55.2
	W. F. Douthitt, Populist	11,632	24.5
	T. A. Pope, Republican	9,634	20.3
8	Samuel W. T. Lanham, Democrat	20,935	53.4
	C. H. Jenkins, Populist	17,510	44.7
	J. P. Smith, Republican	747	1.9
9	Joseph D. Sayers, Democrat	20,381	51.4
	W. K. Makemson, Republican	11,495	29.0
	Reddin Andrews, Populist	6,787	17.1
	J. T. Harris, Republican	955	2.4
10	Robert B. Hawley, Republican	17,936	45.7
	J. H. Shelburne, Democrat	15,757	40.2
	Noah Allen, Populist	5,476	14.0
11	Rudolph Kleberg, Democrat	19,059	45.6
	*H. Gras, Republican	18,449	44.1
	J. M. Smith, Populist	4,074	9.8
	Other	210	0.5
12	James L. Slayden, Democrat	14,744	46.0
	G. H. Noonan, Republican	13,558	42.3
	Taylor McRae, Populist	3,730	11.6
13	John H. Stephens, Democrat	22,988	61.0
	H. L. Bentley, Republican	14,219	37.8
	Other	453	1.2

* Name also found as "Gress" in some references.

1898 General Election (November 8)

District	Candidate	Votes	%
1	Thomas H. Ball, Democrat	18,544	67.2
	O. A. Blackwell, Republican	5,751	20.8
	Joe H. Eagle, Populist	3,289	11.9
2	Samuel B. Cooper, Democrat	22,086	68.9

District	Candidate	Votes	%
	T. J. Russell, Populist	7,781	24.3
	John A. McAyeal, Republican	2,093	6.5
	Robert B. Hawley	91	0.3
3	Reese C. De Graffenreid, Democrat	17,996	66.3
	H. D. Wood, Populist	9,169	33.8
4	John L. Sheppard, Democrat	18,190	62.9
	J. L. Whittle, Populist	10,709	37.1
5	Joseph W. Bailey, Democrat	16,978	74.1
	W. S. Holt, Populist	4,345	19.0
	A. W. Atchison, Republican	1,487	6.5
	J. W. Thomas, Independent	119	0.5
6	Robert E. Burke, Democrat	25,116	65.8
	*T. B. Gore, Populist	9,677	25.4
	Andrew J. Houston, Republican	3,375	8.8
7	Robert L. Henry, Democrat	22,203	68.7
	A. W. Cunningham, Populist	7,928	24.5
	Russell Kingsbury, Republican	2,197	6.8
8	Samuel W. T. Lanham, Democrat	18,580	58.1
	**W. J. Shands, Populist	11,138	34.9
	Arthur Springer, Republican	2,239	7.0
9	Albert S. Burleson, Democrat	20,378	61.7
	G. W. Jones, Populist	12,632	38.3
10	Robert B. Hawley, Republican	17,757	48.0
	W. S. Robson, Democrat	16,462	44.5
	J. W. Baird, Populist	2,604	7.0
	Frank Gary	186	0.5
11	Rudolph Kleberg, Democrat	18,319	55.5
	B. L Crouch, Republican	14,687	44.5
12	James L. Slayden, Democrat	16,363	56.1
	G. H. Noonan, Republican	10,472	35.9
	A. B. Surber	2,110	7.2
	Frank Leitner, Socialist Labor	212	0.7
13	John H. Stephens, Democrat	24,876	73.7
	J. J Eager, Populist	8,887	26.3

* Name also found as "Goren" in some references.

** First name also found as "N. J." in some references.

1900 General Election (November 6)

1	Thomas H. Ball, Democrat	11,887	65.7
	S. E. Tracy, Republican	5,391	29.8
	S. E. Traylor, Prohibition	815	4.5
2	Samuel B. Cooper, Democrat	31,774	98.5
	J. B. Wallace, Republican	470	1.5
3	Reese C. De Graffenreid, Democrat	19,091	61.0
	C. G. White, Republican	12,230	39.1
4	John L. Sheppard, Democrat	17,647	57.6
	J. C. Gibbons, Republican	9,818	32.1
	J. L. Darwin, Populist	3,154	10.3
5	Choice B. Randell, Democrat	28,074	90.4
	J. W. Thomas, Republican	1,790	5.8
	S. J. Hampton, Populist	1,185	3.8
6	Robert E. Burke, Democrat	33,320	77.7
	S. H. Lumpkin, Populist	7,432	17.4
	O. F. Dornbhager, Republican	1,524	3.6
	A. N. Cochran	581	1.4
7	Robert L. Henry, Democrat	27,243	92.1
	W. L. Harrison, Populist	1,287	4.4
	J. E. Boynton, Republican	1,044	3.5
8	Samuel W. T. Lanham, Democrat	24,093	68.2
	J. S. Daley, Populist	6,465	18.3
	N. A. Dodge, Republican	4,760	13.5
9	Albert S. Burleson, Democrat	25,494	91.3
	Nat Q. Henderson, Republican	2,419	8.7
10	George F. Burgess, Democrat	18,203	59.5
	Walter C. Jones, Republican	12,255	40.1
	C. K. Walter, People's	115	0.4
11	Rudolph Kleberg, Democrat	21,329	59.2
	B. L. Crouch, Republican	14,706	40.8
12	James L. Slayden, Democrat	18,321	60.8
	C. C. Drake, Republican	11,530	38.1
	E. G. Cloar, Social Democrat	241	0.8
	Frank J. Leitner, Socialist Labor	96	0.3
13	John H. Stephens, Democrat	30,726	85.1
	C. W. Johnson, Republican	5,354	14.8

1901 Special Election (July 13)

6	Dudley G. Wooten, Democrat	11,174	84.1
	Philip Lindsey	2,063	15.5
	Other	57	0.4

This special election was held to fill the seat of Robert Burke, who died on june 5, 1901, before the 57th Congress.

1902 Special Election (November 4)

3	Gordon Russell, Democrat	13,710	100.0

This special election was held to fill the seat of Reese De Graffenreid, who died on August 29, 1902, for the December session of Congress. This special election was held concurrent with the 1902 general election that Russell also won to succeed De Graffenreid for a full term in Congress.

1902 General Election (November 4)

1	Morris Sheppard, Democrat	19,214	83.2
	John Hurley, Republican	3,875	16.8
2	Samuel B. Cooper, Democrat	17,165	86.7
	Warren McDaniel, Republican	2,632	13.3
3	Gordon J. Russell, Democrat	16,628	95.0
	L. L. Rhodes, Republican	561	3.2
	J. W. Yates, Republican	281	1.6
4	Choice B. Randell, Democrat	17,464	85.1
	C. A. Gray, Republican	3,063	14.9
5	Jack Beall, Democrat	16,310	88.4
	S. H. Lumpkin, Republican	1,633	8.9
	A. F. Dornblaser, Populist	358	1.9
	M. C. Scott, Socialist	151	0.8
6	Scott Field, Democrat	16,753	100.0
7	Alexander W. Gregg, Democrat	13,162	100.0
8	Thomas H. Ball, Democrat	14,301	68.0
	Lock McDaniel, Republican	6,431	30.6
	M. H. Kimpton	267	1.3
	Sam Bogio	35	0.2
9	George F. Burgess, Democrat	18,316	61.3
	B. R. Burrow, Republican	11,574	38.7
10	Albert S. Burleson, Democrat	20,539	87.2

District	Candidate	Votes	%
	Charles Schenken, Republican	2,990	12.7
11	Robert L. Henry, Democrat	14,548	94.2
	A. Wurts, Republican	690	4.5
	G. B. Harris	149	1.0
	G. A. Boynton	41	0.3
12	Oscar W. Gillespie, Democrat	16,220	82.6
	S. A. Greenwell, Republican	3,424	17.4
13	John A. Stephens, Democrat	24,027	91.8
	R. O. Rector, Republican	2,034	7.8
	Joseph Schmitt, Socialist	123	0.5
14	James L. Slayden, Democrat	19,889	78.4
	D. H. Meek, Republican	4,915	19.4
	A. B. Surber	344	1.36
15	John N. Garner, Democrat	16,542	60.6
	John C. Scott, Republican	10,707	39.2
	D. C. Crider	51	0.2
16	William R. Smith, Democrat	22,118	88.1
	D. G. Hunt, Republican	2,911	11.6
	D. H. Meeks	87	0.4

1902 SPECIAL ELECTION (NOVEMBER 15)

District	Candidate	Votes	%
4	Morris Sheppard, Democrat	8,972	86.1
	Frank Lee, Republican	1,426	13.7

This special election was held to fill the seat of John Sheppard, who died on October 11, 1902, for the December session of Congress. John Sheppard's son Morris, won the election for his seat to fill in for the balance of his father's term and he had won the general election eleven days earlier to fill the full term beginning in January 1903.

1903 SPECIAL ELECTION (NOVEMBER 17)

District	Candidate	Votes	%
8	John M. Pinckney, Democrat	4,986	100.0

This special election was held to fill the seat of Thomas Ball, who resigned on November 16, 1903.

1904 GENERAL ELECTION (NOVEMBER 8)

District	Candidate	Votes	%
1	Morris Sheppard, Democrat	12,473	72.1
	J. A. Armistead, Republican	4,838	28.0
2	Moses L. Broocks, Democrat	13,119	76.2
	Andrew Jackson Houston, Republican	4,099	23.8
3	Gordon J. Russell, Democrat	12,473	73.7
	C. T. White, Republican	4,441	26.3
4	Choice B. Randell, Democrat	14,435	90.4
	R. E. Martin, Republican	1,537	9.6
5	Jack Beall, Democrat	14,292	86.0
	J. J. Cypert, Republican	2,327	14.0
6	Scott Field, Democrat	9,438	100.0
7	Alexander W. Gregg, Democrat	8,040	100.0
8	John M. Pinckney, Democrat	9,804	69.1
	H. F. McGregor, Republican	4,384	30.9
9	George F. Burgess, Democrat	14,316	72.3
	B. L. Osgood, Republican	5,484	27.7
10	Albert S. Burleson, Democrat	11,761	100.0
11	Robert L. Henry, Democrat	10,305	84.4
	Joe E. Williams, Republican	1,912	15.7
12	Oscar W. Gillespie, Democrat	12,480	74.4
	Frank B. Stanley, Republican	2,357	14.1
	J. M. Mallett, People's	1,933	11.5
13	John H. Stephens, Democrat	18,604	89.6
	James M. Kindred, Republican	2,157	10.4
14	James L. Slayden, Democrat	15,097	98.3
	Alfred Vanderstucken, Republican	259	1.7
15	John N. Garner, Democrat	10,647	64.9
	J. S. Morin, Republican	5,767	35.1
16	William R. Smith, Democrat	17,488	83.1
	Logan McPherson, Republican	3,562	16.9

1905 SPECIAL ELECTION (JUNE 6)

District	Candidate	Votes	%
8	John M. Moore, Democrat	4,202	81.3
	Max Urwitz, Republican	964	18.7

This special election was held to fill the seat of John M. Pinckney, who died on April 24, 1905, before the 59th Congress.

1906 DEMOCRATIC PRIMARY ELECTION (JULY 28)

		Votes	%
1	Morris Sheppard	unopposed	100.0
2*	Samuel B. Cooper		
	Moses L. Broocks		
3	Gordon J. Russell	unopposed	100.0
4*	Choice B. Randell	11,576	51.1
	Alva Pearl Barrett	11,072	48.9
5	Jack Beall	unopposed	100.0
6*	Rufus Hardy	4,711	30.9
	T. S. Henderson	6,075	39.8
	Richard Mays	4,472	29.3
7	Alexander W. Gregg	unopposed	100.0
8	John M. Moore	unopposed	100.0
9	George F. Burgess	unopposed	100.0
10	Albert S. Burleson	unopposed	100.0
11	Robert L. Henry	unopposed	100.0
12	Oscar W. Gillespie	unopposed	100.0
	T. J. Powell		
	James W. Swayne		
13	John H. Stephens	unopposed	100.0
14	James L. Slayden	unopposed	100.0
15	John N. Garner	unopposed	100.0
16	William R. Smith	unopposed	100.0
	J. F. Cunningham		

Clearly, this post-primary convention was not a good idea, and the state legislature immediately began to revise the Terrell Election Law to fix the problem. It was not until 1918 that a runoff or second primary was held. Since the primary of 1918, candidates have been required to receive a majority of votes.

1906 GENERAL ELECTION (NOVEMBER 6)

		Votes	%
1	Morris Sheppard, Democrat	9,479	90.6
	Phil E. Baer, Ecopole	886	8.5
	J. T. Thompson, Socialist	102	1.0
2	Samuel B. Cooper, Democrat	9,593	93.0
	J. H. Kurth, Republican	622	6.0
	Charles E. Second	99	1.0
3	Gordon J. Russell, Democrat	8,522	89.3
	G. W. Smith, Republican	753	7.9
	B. F. Bell	266	2.8
4	Choice B. Randell, Democrat	11,508	87.3
	W. G. McGinnis, Republican	1,678	12.7
5	Jack Beall, Democrat	9,060	91.9
	A. M. Cochran, Republican	525	5.3
	M. T. Connor, Reorganized Republican	206	2.1
	Virgil Pittman, Socialist	63	0.6
6	Rufus Hardy, Democrat	5,536	92.1
	T. S. Henderson, Prohibition	188	3.1
	Jonathan T. Atkisson	170	2.8
	Richard Mays	116	1.9
7	Alexander W. Gregg, Democrat	6,590	100.0
8	John M. Moore, Democrat	8,536	84.3
	W. A. Matthai, Republican	1,593	15.7
9	George F. Burgess, Democrat	10,257	75.6
	A. M. Waugh, Republican	3,043	22.4
	J. B. Gay, Socialist	251	1.9
10	Albert S. Burleson, Democrat	8,103	88.6
	Carl Beck, Republican	1,041	11.4
11	Robert L. Henry, Democrat	7,183	100.0
12	Oscar W. Gillespie, Democrat	9,790	95.6
	Laura B. Payne, Socialist	456	4.5
13	John H. Stephens, Democrat	14,120	90.2
	E. E. Diggs, Republican	1,295	8.3

This was the first primary election held for members of the U.S. Congress in Texas. From 1906 until 1918 the candidate receiving the most votes won the election, but not necessarily the nomination. Conventions were still used to canvas the popular votes and validate a candidate's nomination. If a candidate failed to receive a majority in the election, a Congressional District Convention was held to decide the party's candidate in the general election. In this election there were three conventions held: one in the 2nd, 4th, and 6th congressional districts (noted with * above). These were held on August 25. At the 2nd District Convention held in Nacogdoches, Cooper easily won the nomination. At the 4th District Convention held in Greenville, Barrett withdrew from the race and Randell was named the nominee. At the 6th District Convention held in Wooten Wells, the delegates voted to reconvene at Groesbeck three days later before any voting was done on the candidates. So, on Tuesday August 28, in Groesbeck the top popular vote-getter Henderson tried to withdraw from the race. However, the convention did not accept his withdrawal. Hardy had received the second highest number of popular votes and delegate votes. Henderson's withdrawal eliminated the Mays movement and Hardy was declared the nominee.

(continued from previous page)

District	Candidate	Votes	%
	Joseph Schmitt, Socialist	245	1.6
14	James L. Slayden, Democrat	12,294	82.0
	D. Doole, Republican	2,692	18.0
15	John N. Garner, Democrat	9,284	63.7
	Dr. T. W. Moore, Republican	5,281	36.3
16	William R. Smith, Democrat	13,030	92.0
	Ben Van Tuys, Republican	744	5.3
	J. M. Ellis, Socialist	390	2.8

1908 General Election (November 3)

District	Candidate	Votes	%
1	Morris Sheppard, Democrat	14,775	84.7
	H. L. McQuiston, Republican	2,304	13.2
	J. C. Thompson, Socialist	370	2.1
2	Martin Dies, Democrat	14,559	81.9
	C. E. Smith, Republican	2,719	15.3
	John Johnson, Socialist	498	2.8
3	Gordon J. Russell, Democrat	11,651	74.3
	J. A. Harper, Republican	3,289	21.0
	Reddin Andrews, Socialist	751	4.8
4	Choice B. Randell, Democrat	16,017	80.6
	R. H. Crabb, Republican	3,205	16.1
	W. P. Beckley	659	3.3
5	Jack Beall, Democrat	17,840	84.4
	Marion T. Connor, Republican	3,177	15.0
	John Kerrigan, Socialist	190	0.6
6	Rufus Hardy, Democrat	10,350	84.4
	C. L. McCoy, Republican	1,919	15.6
7	Alexander W. Gregg, Democrat	8,625	97.6
	J. W. Boynton, Republican	212	2.4
8	John M. Moore, Democrat	12,285	77.6
	T. M. Kennerly, Republican	3,482	22.0
	Laura B. Payne, Socialist	60	0.4
9	George F. Burgess, Democrat	13,191	67.6
	O. S. York, Republican	5,897	30.2
	Frank Hubbel, Socialist	416	2.1
10	Albert S. Burleson, Democrat	13,314	80.7
	Joseph W. Burke, Republican	3,185	19.3
11	Robert L. Henry, Democrat	10,114	100.0
12	Oscar W. Gillespie, Democrat	17,778	81.6
	W. A. Dodge, Republican	3,095	14.2
	G. V. Stratton, Socialist	905	4.2
13	John H. Stephens, Democrat	24,705	84.3
	Jasper W. Haney, Republican	3,715	12.7
	W. R. Tramblade, Socialist	886	3.0
14	James L. Slayden, Democrat	16,801	99.5
	W. W. Buchanan, Republican	79	0.5

1908 Democratic Primary Election (July 25)

District	Candidate	Votes	%
1	Morris Sheppard	unopposed	100.0
2	Martin Dies		
	S. B. Cooper		
3	Gordon J. Russell	unopposed	100.0
4	Choice B. Randell	unopposed	100.0
	Alva Pearl Barrett		
5	Jack Beall		
	W. G. Sterett		
6	Rufus Hardy	unopposed	100.0
7	Alexander W. Gregg	unopposed	100.0
8	John M. Moore	unopposed	100.0
	Stone		
9	George F. Burgess	unopposed	100.0
10	Albert S. Burleson	unopposed	100.0
11	Robert L. Henry		
	W. W. Hair		
12	Oscar W. Gillespie		
	Oscar Callaway		
	J. M. Pressler		
13	John H. Stephens	unopposed	100.0
14	James L. Slayden	unopposed	100.0
15	John N. Garner		
	Denman		
16	William R. Smith		
	J. F. Cunningham		

J. E. Elgin, Socialist	10	0.1
15 John N. Garner, Democrat	11,682	61.7
W. T. Moore, Republican	7,179	37.9
C. C. Heath, Socialist	67	0.4
16 William R. Smith, Democrat	22,159	88.7
G. W. Boynton, Republican	2,544	10.2
P. G. Zimmerman, Socialist	285	1.1

1910 SPECIAL ELECTION (JULY 23)

3 Robert M. Lively, Democrat	12,357	100.0

This special election was held to fill the seat of Gordon Russell, who resigned on June 14, 1910.

1910 DEMOCRATIC PRIMARY ELECTION (JULY 23)

1 Morris Sheppard	unopposed	100.0
2 Martin Dies	unopposed	100.0
3 James Young		
—— Geddie		
—— Andrews		
—— Beavers		
4 Choice B. Randell		
B. Q. Evans		
5 Jack Beall		
Dwight J. Lewelling		
6 Rufus Hardy	unopposed	100.0
7 Alexander W. Gregg		
C. C. Stokes		
8 John M. Moore	unopposed	100.0
9 George F. Burgess	unopposed	100.0
10 Albert S. Burleson	unopposed	100.0
11 Robert L. Henry	unopposed	100.0
12 Oscar Callaway		
Oscar Gillespie		
D. M. Alexander		
13 John H. Stephens		
—— Veale		

14 James L. Slayden	unopposed	100.0
15 John N. Garner	unopposed	100.0
16 William R. Smith	unopposed	100.0

1910 GENERAL ELECTION (NOVEMBER 5)

1 Morris Sheppard, Democrat	10,707	87.4
Velmar Antle, Republican	1,148	9.4
W. H. Hicks, Socialist	392	3.2
2 Martin Dies, Democrat	10,898	94.4
W. J. Collier, Republican	549	4.8
George W. Eason, Republican	97	0.9
3 James Young, Democrat	9,450	98.9
R. B. Eldor	109	1.1
4 Choice B. Randell, Democrat	9,719	88.9
C. A. Gray, Republican	1,208	11.1
5 Jack Beall, Democrat	10,939	95.0
C. G. Schwartz, Socialist	292	2.5
M. T. Connor, Republican	190	1.7
Z. Gilder, Socialist's Labor	99	0.9
6 Rufus Hardy, Democrat	7,826	97.9
W. H. Wilson, Socialist	165	2.1
7 Alexander W. Gregg, Democrat	6,566	88.2
Willis Kendall, Republican	843	11.4
8 John M. Moore, Democrat	11,654	90.4
A. M. Lawson, Republican	1,112	8.6
James M. Lairson, Republican	120	0.9
9 George F. Burgess, Democrat	10,244	78.0
E. C. Webster, Republican	2,108	16.1
Frank Hubbell, Independent	498	3.8
G. W. Dunn, Socialist	281	2.1
10 Albert S. Burleson, Democrat	10,118	100.0
11 Robert L. Henry, Democrat	7,384	98.6
E. J. Vesey, Republican	105	1.4
12 Oscar Callaway, Democrat	10,525	82.0
Robert G. Martin, Socialist	1,270	9.9
C. C. Littleton, Republican	836	6.5

Dist	Candidate	Votes	%
	N. C. Pile, Prohibition	206	1.6
13	John H. Stephens, Democrat	19,543	83.4
	T. S. Bugbee, Republican	2,039	8.7
	Jonathan I. Green, Socialist	1,488	6.4
	E. G. Cook, Prohibition	358	1.5
14	James L. Slayden, Democrat	14,256	94.8
	J. M. Prier, Socialist	544	3.6
	A. L. Horne, Republican	234	1.6
15	John N. Garner, Democrat	14,300	71.7
	Noah Allen, Republican	5,287	26.5
	Oscar Krohn, Socialist	355	1.8
16	William R. Smith, Democrat	18,058	85.4
	W. H. Harvey, Socialist	1,749	8.2
	Robert A. Webb, Republican	1,384	6.5

Dist	Candidate	Votes	%
6	Rufus Hardy	unopposed	100.0
7	Alexander W. Gregg	unopposed	100.0
8	—— Kittrell		
	Joe H. Eagle	unopposed	100.0
9	George F. Burgess	unopposed	100.0
10	Albert S. Burleson	unopposed	100.0
11	Robert L. Henry		
12	Oscar Callaway		
	Oscar Gillespie		
	Lindey M. Brown		
	A. H. Yeager		
13	John H. Stephens	unopposed	100.0
14	James L. Slayden	unopposed	100.0
15	John N. Garner	unopposed	100.0
16	William R. Smith	unopposed	100.0
At-Large	Daniel E. Garrett	78,276 W	13.6
	Hatton W. Summers	61,797 W	10.7
	Jeff McLemore	46,743	8.1
	C. M. Cureton	49,759	8.6
	Method Pazdral	29,276	5.1
	E. W. Bounds	16,107	2.8
	James K. Browning	31,758	5.5
	George A. Harmon	17,192	3.0
	W. B. Featherstone	11,539	2.0
	Alexander S. Garrett	unknown	
	V. W. Grubbs	21,325	3.7
	S. C. Harris	13,679	2.4
	E. L. Kellie	14,205	2.5
	Joe E. Lancaster	26,286	4.6
	W. T. Loudermilk	29,831	5.2
	Sebe Newman	10,574	1.8
	Frederick Opp	24,353	4.2
	Frank T. Roche	20,168	3.5
	R. R. Smith	12,711	2.2
	J. K. Steet	17,574	3.1
	R. E. Yantis	19,587	3.4

1912 Democratic Primary Election (July 27)

Dist	Candidate	Votes	%
1	Horace W. Vaughan		
	H. Bascom Thomas		
	Fred Dudley		
	R. B. Sturgeon		
2	Martin Dies		
	George B. Terrell		
	John H. Brooks		
	V. A. Collins		
	John E. Little		
3	James Young		
	R. M. Lively		
4	Sam Rayburn	4,983	23.4
	Tom Perkins	4,493	21.1
	B. L. Jones	4,365	20.4
	W. J. Gibson	3,790	17.9
	Tom Wells	1,961	9.2
	M. M. Morrison	798	3.7
	J. B. Erwin	656	3.1
	R. A. Lovelace	290	1.4
5	Jack Beall	unopposed	100.0

		Votes	%
	W. A. Harris	13,531	2.4
	— Kennedy	unknown	
	R. H. Harrison	9,041	1.6

Vote total includes all but four counties.

1912 GENERAL ELECTION (NOVEMBER 5)

District	Candidate	Votes	%
1	Horace W. Vaughan, Democrat	13,228	85.9
	S. L. Willyard	1,646	10.6
	Josh Barker, Republican	530	3.4
2	Martin Dies, Democrat	14,116	80.3
	J. A. Freeland	2,415	13.7
	Howard M. Smith, Republican	610	3.5
	E. G. Christian, Progressive	442	2.5
3	James Young, Democrat	12,158	96.6
	B. F. Bryant	427	3.4
4	Sam Rayburn, Democrat	13,900	89.6
	C. E. Obenchain, Republican	1,340	8.6
	G. J. Barlow, Socialist	282	1.8
5	Jack Beall, Democrat	16,915	97.8
	M. C. Scott	390	2.3
6	Rufus Hardy, Democrat	9,743	96.0
	W. H. Wilson, Socialist	409	4.0
7	Alexander W. Gregg, Democrat	9,132	100.0
8	Joe H. Eagle, Democrat	13,762	83.3
	Jeff N. Miller, Republican	1,658	10.0
	J. E. Curd	1,111	6.7
9	George F. Burgess, Democrat	13,738	99.7
10	Albert S. Burleson, Democrat	12,383	100.0
11	Robert L. Henry, Democrat	11,429	98.1
	C. G. Davidson, Socialist	216	1.9
12	Oscar Callaway, Democrat	17,283	97.6
	Clarence Nugent, Socialist	422	2.4
13	John H. Stephens, Democrat	25,630	89.0
	L. B. Lindsey, Progressive	1,656	5.8
	H. H. Cooper, Republican	1,465	5.1
14	James L. Slayden, Democrat	17,675	97.5
	Julius Real, Republican	239	1.3
	A. D. Zucht	218	1.2
15	John N. Garner, Democrat	17,231	99.9
16	William R. Smith, Democrat	23,763	99.9
At-Large			
	Daniel E. Garrett, Democrat	235,065 W	78.6
	Hatton W. Sumners, Democrat	234,591 W	78.5
	D. D. Richardson, Socialist	24,466	8.2
	J. M. Haggard, Socialist	24,400	8.2
	R. B. Harrison, Republican	22,795	7.6
	J. E. Elgin, Republican	22,656	7.6
	Z. T. White, Progressive	16,422	5.5
	F. M. Etheridge, Progressive	16,408	5.5
	R. B. Harrison, Prohibition	1,195	0.4

1913 SPECIAL ELECTION (APRIL 5)

District	Candidate	Votes	%
10	James P. Buchanan, Democrat	11,256	57.5
	George Calhoun, Democrat	8,337	45.6

This special election was held to fill the seat of Albert Sidney Burleson, who resigned on March 6, 1913, to become postmaster general.

1914 DEMOCRATIC PRIMARY ELECTION (JULY 25)

District	Candidate	Votes	%
1	Eugene Black		
	Horace Vaughan		
2	Martin Dies	unopposed	100.0
3	James Young		
	R. W. Simpson		
4	Sam Rayburn	17,416	
	Tom W. Perkins	8,324	
5	Hatton Sumners		
	Tom R. Ridgell		
	J. K. Street		
6	Rufus Hardy	unopposed	100.0
7	Alexander W. Gregg	unopposed	100.0
8	Louis H. Bailey	8,090	
	Joe H. Eagle	17,555	
9	George F. Burgess	unopposed	100.0

Dist.	Candidate	Votes	%
10	James Buchanan	unopposed	100.0
	Robert L. Henry		
	Sam R. Scott		
12	Oscar Callaway		
	James W. Swayne		
	Sam J. Hunter		
	Robert F. Milam		
13	John H. Stephens		
	W. E. Prescott		
14	James L. Slayden		
	M. B. Slator or M. D. Slater		
15	John N. Garner		
	——— Mason		
	——— Maney		
16	William R. Smith		
	Thomas Blanton		
At-Large			
	James H. "Cyclone" Davis	W	
	Atkins Jeff. McLemore	W	
	——— Porter		
	——— Harris		
	Daniel Edward Garrett		
	——— Sheild		
	——— Lowry		
	——— Lane		
	——— O'Donnell		
	——— Davis		
	——— Kone		

1914 GENERAL ELECTION (NOVEMBER 3)

Dist.	Candidate	Votes	%
1	Eugene Black, Democrat	10,711	87.7
	J. C. Thompson, Socialist	1,498	12.3
2	Martin Dies, Democrat	11,425	84.0
	A. Lingan, Socialist	2,132	15.7
	Charles A. Chaison, Progressive	42	0.3
3	James Young, Democrat	11,584	75.2
	E. T. Bryant, Socialist	3,818	24.8
4	Sam Rayburn, Democrat	9,762	85.0
	C. E. Obenchain, Socialist	1,449	12.6
	S. H. Dodson	278	2.4
5	Hatton Summers, Democrat	10,430	94.9
	J. S. Goode, Socialist	428	3.9
	Wade B. Leonard	128	1.2
6	Rufus Hardy, Democrat	7,772	86.4
	W. H. Wilson, Republican	1,229	13.7
7	Alexander W. Gregg, Democrat	7,001	100.0
8	Joe H. Eagle, Democrat	10,078	84.7
	E. B. Miller, Socialist	1,090	9.2
	S. L. Hain, Republican	725	6.1
9	George F. Burgess, Democrat	11,083	88.5
	B. F. Wright, Socialist	1,169	9.3
	Irvin Kibbe	272	2.2
10	James Buchanan, Democrat	8,348	100.0
11	Robert L. Henry, Democrat	6,677	92.9
	Duncan Carrick, Republican	484	6.7
12	Oscar Callaway, Democrat	11,997	85.4
	S. J. Browson, Republican	2,043	14.5
13	John H. Stephens, Democrat	15,680	87.0
	C. T. Griffin, Republican	2,335	13.0
14	James L. Slayden, Democrat	13,896	90.7
	John A. Currie, Socialist	921	6.0
	B. F. Kingsley, Republican	487	3.2
15	John N. Garner, Democrat	15,678	100.0
16	William R. Smith, Democrat	15,181	100.0
At-Large			
	James H. "Cyclone" Davis, Democrat	172,533 W	82.5
	Atkins Jeff. McLemore, Democrat	173,177 W	82.8
	Nat B. Hunt, Socialist	24,180	11.6
	Reddin Andrews, Socialist	24,276	11.6
	Charles A. Warnken, Republican	10,605	5.1
	E. E. Diggs, Republican	10,492	5.0
	J. E. Williams, Progressive	1,581	0.8
	H. L. McCuistion or McCuiston, Progressive	1,537	0.7

1916 Democratic Primary Election (July 22)

District	Candidate	Votes	%
1	Eugene Black		
	Charles S. Todd		
2	Martin Dies		
	C. W. Howth		
3	James Young		
4	Sam Rayburn	13,116	54.7
	Andrew Randell	9,572	39.9
	Dr. T. W. Wiley	1,280	5.3
5	Hatton Sumners	unopposed	100.0
6	Rufus Hardy		
	W. A. Bedford		
	James L. Adams		
7	Alexander W. Gregg		
	Lewis Fisher		
	John W. Campbell		
8	J. Fred Cook		
	Joe H. Eagle		
	L. H. Bailey		
9	Joseph Mansfield		
	George Scheleicher		
10	W. R. Smith		
11	R. N. Gresham		
At-Large	Atkins Jeff McLemore		W
	Daniel E. Garrett		W
	J. H. "Cyclone" Davis		
	H. Nugent Fitzgerald		
	R. L. Darwin		
	Roger Byrne		
	S. C. Paddleford		
	H. G. Cooley		
	J. E. Porter		
	Rufus J. Lackland		
	Arthur E. Firmin		
	W. R. Cox		
	John J. Harrington		

This was the last primary election before the passage in 1917 of the Terrell Election Law, which required a candidate to receive a majority of votes to be considered their party's nominee. If a majority was not received in the first primary, a second primary was held.

1916 General Election (November 7)

District	Candidate	Votes	%
1	Eugene Black, Democrat	16,525	83.3
	David H. Morris, Republican	2,182	11.0
	J. C. Thompson, Socialist	1,122	5.7
2	Martin Dies, Democrat	16,956	86.1
	J. B. Truitt, Socialist	1,462	7.4
	A. E. Sweatland, Republican	1,266	6.4
3	James Young, Democrat	15,169	88.3
	J. L. Scroggin, Socialist	2,014	11.7
4	Sam Rayburn, Democrat	17,785	83.5
	G. J. Barlow, Republican	2,043	9.6
	W. J. Lennon, Socialist	1,460	6.9
5	Hatton Sumners, Democrat	24,949	88.2
	B. F. Crews, Republican	2,879	10.2
	W. G. Brewer, Socialist	444	1.6
6	Rufus Hardy, Democrat	12,046	95.3
	W. H. Wilson, Socialist	590	4.7

Dist.	Candidate	Votes	%
7	Alexander W. Gregg, Democrat	10,921	79.4
	Theodore F. Heiger, Republican	1,561	11.4
	W. C. Kendall, Republican	703	5.1
	T. E. Foster, Socialist	568	4.1
8	Joe H. Eagle, Democrat	18,980	82.2
	Ira P. Jones, Republican	3,276	14.2
	John W. Connor, Socialist	842	3.7
9	Joseph Mansfield, Democrat	16,453	76.4
	C. M. Hughes, Republican	4,149	19.2
	B. F. Wright, Socialist	946	4.4
10	James Buchanan, Democrat	15,740	86.8
	Robert A. Brooks, Republican	2,405	13.2
11	Tom Connally, Democrat	14,695	87.7
	John L. Vaughn, Republican	1,443	8.6
	T. M. De Loach, Socialist	620	3.7
12	James C. Wilson, Democrat	20,175	85.7
	Henry Zweifel, Republican	1,843	7.8
	Leland G. Baker, Socialist	1,517	6.5
13	Marvin Jones, Democrat	33,942	85.8
	J. L. Van Natta, Republican	3,125	7.9
	J. A. Pressly, Socialist	2,489	6.3
14	James L. Slayden, Democrat	22,435	79.4
	D. F. Johnson, Republican	5,815	20.6
15	John N. Garner, Democrat	16,906	73.4
	Harry M. Wurzbach, Republican	5,561	24.1
	J. E. Grer, Socialist	572	2.5
16	Thomas L. Blanton, Democrat	30,194	85.0
	T. B. Holiday, Socialist	2,286	8.0
	C. O. Harris, Republican	2,509	7.1
At-Large	Atkins Jeff. McLemore, Democrat	300,302 W	82.0
	Daniel E. Garrett, Democrat	298,966 W	81.6
	Charles A. Warnken, Republican	46,914	12.8
	M. A. Taylor, Republican	46,467	12.7
	Arch Lingan, Socialist	18,583	5.1
	W. D. Simpson, Socialist	18,192	5.0
	I. E. Teague, Prohibition	1,525	0.4
	E. G. Cook, Prohibition	1,457	0.4

1918 Democratic Primary Election (July 27)

Dist.	Candidate	Votes	%
1	Eugene Black	unopposed	100.0
2	John C. Box		
	V. A. Collins		
	——— O'Brien		
	——— Kings		
	——— Ricks		
3	James Young	unopposed	100.0
4	Sam Rayburn	26,025	
	Robert Lovelace	6,110	
5	Hatton Sumners	unopposed	100.0
6	Rufus Hardy		
	——— Dechard		
7	Clay S. Briggs		
	——— Hill		
	——— McLemore		
8	Joe H. Eagle		
	Daniel E. Garrett		
9	Joseph Mansfield	unopposed	100.0
10	James Buchanan	unopposed	100.0
11	Tom Connally	unopposed	100.0
12	James C. Wilson		
	James W. Swayne		
13	Lucian W. Parrish		
	Charles F. Spencer		
	——— Haney		
14	Carlos Bee		
	Alva Pearl Barrett		
15	John N. Garner	unopposed	100.0
16	Claude Hudspeth		
	Zach Cobb		
17	Thomas L. Blanton	32,034	65.6
	Joe Adkins	9,816	20.1
	William G. Blackmon	3,651	7.5

District	Candidate	Votes	%
	Oscar Callaway	3,355	6.9
	Hugh E. Exum	513	4.7
18	Marvin Jones		
	Lackey		

This was the first primary election after the passage in 1917 of the Terrell Election Law, which required a candidate to receive a majority of votes to be considered their party's nominee. If a majority was not received in the first primary, a second primary was held. The elections were close enough in the races for the 2nd and 13th district seats that runoff elections were held on August 26, 1918.

1919 Special Election (April 19)

District	Candidate	Votes	%
12	Fritz Lanham	1,442	100.0
	Other	8	0.0

This special election was called to fill the seat of James Wilson, who had resigned on March 13, 1919, to accept a federal judgeship before the 66th Congress.

1920 Democratic Primary Election (July 24)

District	Candidate	Votes	%
1	Eugene Black	unopposed	100.0
2	John C. Box	unopposed	100.0
3	Morgan Sanders		
	Thomas R. Bond		
	Will D. Suiter		
	Robert E. Yantis		
4	Sam Rayburn	16,526	
	Ed Westbrook	11,042	
5	Hatton Sumners	unopposed	100.0
6	Rufus Hardy	unopposed	100.0
7	Clay S. Briggs	unopposed	100.0
8	Daniel E. Garrett		
	Harry V. Fisher		
9	Joseph Mansfield	unopposed	100.0
10	James Buchanan		
	A. T. McKean		
	Victor Marcellin Machet		
11	Tom Connally	unopposed	100.0
12	Fritz Lanham	unopposed	100.0
13	Lucian W. Parrish	unopposed	100.0
14	Carlos Bee		
	Luther Slayden		
15	John N. Garner	unopposed	100.0
16	Claude Hudspeth	unopposed	100.0
17	Thomas L. Blanton		
	R. N. Grisham		
18	Marvin Jones	unopposed	100.0

1918 Democratic Primary Runoff Election (August 24)

District	Candidate
2	John C. Box
	V. A. Collins
13	Lucian W. Parrish
	Charles F. Spencer

1918 General Election (November 5)

District	Candidate	Votes	%
1	Eugene Black, Democrat	9,460	100.0
2	John C. Box, Democrat	10,474	100.0
3	James Young, Democrat	10,183	100.0
4	Sam Rayburn, Democrat	9,755	100.0
5	Hatton Sumners, Democrat	6,946	100.0
6	Rufus Hardy, Democrat	10,496	86.9
	Charles W. Beck, Republican	1,577	13.1
7	Clay S. Briggs, Democrat	6,671	100.0
8	Joe H. Eagle, Democrat	7,557	96.1
	M. H. Broyles	306	3.9
9	Joseph Mansfield, Democrat	7,672	100.0
10	James Buchanan, Democrat	8,576	100.0
11	Tom Connally, Democrat	9,304	100.0
12	James C. Wilson, Democrat	9,307	100.0
13	Lucian W. Parrish, Democrat	9,700	100.0
14	Carlos Bee, Democrat	8,038	68.4
	John D. Hartman, Republican	3,717	31.6
15	John N. Garner, Democrat	6,814	100.0
16	Claude Hudspeth, Democrat	6,211	100.0
17	Thomas L. Blanton, Democrat	11,194	100.0
18	Marvin Jones, Democrat	10,497	95.3

1920 General Election (November 2)

District	Candidate	Votes	%
1	Eugene Black, Democrat	17,814	92.3
	G. T. Bartlett, Republican	1,497	7.8
2	John C. Box, Democrat	21,692	92.8
	G. E. Meyer, American	1,671	7.2
3	Morgan Sanders, Democrat	15,575	83.2
	J. A. Butler, Republican	3,149	16.8
4	Sam Rayburn, Democrat	17,795	77.6
	A. W. Acheson, Republican	5,124	22.4
5	Hatton Sumners, Democrat	19,785	80.2
	J. O. Burleson, Republican	4,883	19.8
6	Rufus Hardy, Democrat	17,555	72.5
	Clyde Essex, American	3,668	15.2
	D. H. Merrill, Republican	2,512	10.4
7	Clay S. Briggs, Democrat	12,656	96.6
8	Daniel E. Garrett, Democrat	18,474	55.7
	E. B. Barden, Republican	7,001	21.1
	M. H. Broyles, Black & Tan Republican	5,750	17.4
	J. M. Gibson, American	1,918	5.8
9	Joseph Mansfield, Democrat	12,311	58.7
	James W. Rugeley, Republican	8,667	41.3
10	James Buchanan, Democrat	14,411	65.5
	B. G. Neighbors, American	7,597	34.5
11	Tom Connally, Democrat	15,621	79.1
	W. D. Lewis, American	4,124	20.9
12	Fritz Lanham, Democrat	20,925	80.5
	Sam Davidson, Republican	4,203	16.2
	S. T. Green, Republican	871	3.3
13	Lucian W. Parrish, Democrat	18,951	88.4
	C. W. Johnson, Republican	2,483	11.6
14	Harry M. Wurzbach, Republican	17,265	55.6
	Carlos Bee, Democrat	13,771	44.4
15	John N. Garner, Democrat	10,265	99.9
16	Claude Hudspeth, Democrat	15,658	69.7
	William Easterling, Republican	6,796	30.3
17	Thomas L. Blanton, Democrat	22,311	83.8
	W. D. Cowan, American	4,298	16.2
18	Marvin Jones, Democrat	25,996	97.0
	L. P. Loomis, Republican	796	3.0

1922 Special Election (May 22)

District	Candidate	Votes	%
13	Guinn Williams, Democrat	11,435	49.8
	S. A. Morgan, Democrat	6,735	29.3
	Annie W. Blanton, Democrat	3,008	13.1
	Orville Bullington, Republican	1,765	7.7
	W. S. Moore	35	0.2

This special election was held to fill the seat of Lucian Parrish, who died on March 27, 1922. Williams took his seat on May 13.

1922 Democratic Primary Election (July 22)

District	Candidate	Votes	%
1	Eugene Black	18,474	55.7
	Cyclone Davis	7,001	21.1
2	John C. Box	5,750	17.4
	—— Burns	1,918	5.8
	—— Fairchild	12,311	58.7
	—— Oliver	8,667	41.3
3	Morgan Sanders	unopposed	100.0
4	Sam Rayburn	18,148	65.5
	Ed Westbrook	16,970	34.5
5	Hatton Sumners	15,621	79.1
	—— Ballowe	4,124	20.9
6	Luther Johnson	unopposed	80.5
7	Clay S. Briggs	unopposed	16.2
8	Daniel E. Garrett	871	3.3
	—— Murphy	18,951	88.4
	—— Maddox	2,483	11.6
9	Joseph Mansfield	17,265	55.6
	—— Fly	13,771	44.4
	—— Schleicher	10,265	99.9
	—— Griffen	15,658	69.7
	—— Holman	6,796	30.3
	—— Hughes	22,311	83.8

1922 Democratic Primary Election (continued)

District	Candidate	Votes	Percent
10	James Buchanan	unopposed	100.0
11	Tom Connally		
	Lewis		
12	Fritz Lanham	unopposed	100.0
13	Guinn Williams		
	Williams		
	Bell		
	Moore		
14	Harry Hertzberg		
	J. F. Cunningham		
	Carlos Bee		
	Harley		
	Hopkins		
	Glover		
15	John N. Garner		
	Briscoe		
16	Claude Hudspeth	unopposed	100.0
17	Thomas L. Blanton	24,895	49.9
	Oscar Callaway	10,447	20.9
	J. F. Cunningham	9,382	18.8
	Joseph P. Dibrell	5,151	10.3
	N. S. Holland	unknown	
	Ernest G. Allbright	unknown	
18	Marvin Jones	unopposed	100.0

1922 DEMOCRATIC PRIMARY RUNOFF ELECTION (AUGUST 26)

District	Candidate	Votes	Percent
2	John C. Box		
	Burns		
17	Thomas L. Blanton	18,861	62.5
	Oscar Callaway	11,481	37.5

1922 GENERAL ELECTION (NOVEMBER 7)

District	Candidate	Votes	Percent
1	Eugene Black, Democrat	15,697	93.5
	G. T. Bartlett, Republican	1,087	6.5
2	John C. Box, Democrat	21,216	94.8
	C. A. Lord, Republican	1,171	5.2
3	Morgan Sanders, Democrat	16,323	91.7
	L. B. Cranford, Republican	1,478	8.3
4	Sam Rayburn, Democrat	21,327	91.1
	C. A. Gray, Republican	2,079	8.9
5	Hatton Sumners, Democrat	23,051	88.3
	Heber Page, Republican	3,046	11.7
6	Luther Johnson, Democrat	18,938	94.0
	D. H. Merrill, Republican	1,208	6.0
7	Clay S. Briggs, Democrat	12,171	93.3
	Frank Sneed Camper, Republican	880	6.7
8	Daniel E. Garrett, Democrat	20,058	85.3
	E. B. Barden, Republican	3,454	14.7
9	Joseph Mansfield, Democrat	17,479	64.7
	Willett Wilson, Republican	9,954	35.3
10	James Buchanan, Democrat	18,590	81.0
	W. J. Kveton, Republican	4,374	19.1
11	Tom Connally, Democrat	16,092	90.8
	R. A. Hanrick, Republican	1,630	9.2
12	Fritz Lanham, Democrat	20,014	91.9
	Joe Kingsberry, Jr., Republican	1,772	8.1
13	Guinn Williams, Democrat	21,187	93.2
	John B. Schmitz, Republican	1,538	6.8
14	Harry M. Wurzbach, Republican	19,083	54.8
	Harry Hertzberg, Democrat	15,760	45.2
15	John N. Garner, Democrat	14,319	100.0
16	Claude Hudspeth, Democrat	18,164	81.0
	John A. Simpson, Republican	4,257	19.0
17	Thomas L. Blanton, Democrat	24,576	91.6
	W. D. Girand, Republican	2,266	8.4
18	Marvin Jones, Democrat	24,515	93.7
	H. O. Ward, Republican	1,649	6.3

1924 DEMOCRATIC PRIMARY ELECTION (JULY 26)

District	Candidate	Votes	Percent
1	Eugene Black		
	J. J. Murray		
	B. B. Sturgeon		

District	Candidate	Votes	%
2	John C. Box		
	W. R. Cousins		
3	Morgan Sanders		
	J. H. Beavers		
4	Sam Rayburn	24,105	
	M. M. Morrison	15,032	
5	Hatton Sumners		
	D. P. McCalib		
	—— Field		
6	Luther Johnson	unopposed	100.0
7	Clay S. Briggs		
	H. L. Nelson		
8	Daniel E. Garrett		
	Joe H. Eagle		
9	Joseph Mansfield	unopposed	100.0
10	James Buchanan	unopposed	100.0
11	Tom Connally	unopposed	100.0
12	Fritz Lanham		
13	C. E. Farmer		
14	Guinn Williams	unopposed	100.0
15	D. S. Davenport	unopposed	100.0
16	John N. Garner	unopposed	100.0
17	Claude Hudspeth	unopposed	100.0
18	Thomas L. Blanton	unopposed	100.0
	Marvin Jones	unopposed	100.0

1924 GENERAL ELECTION (NOVEMBER 4)

District	Candidate	Votes	%
1	Eugene Black, Democrat	28,218	90.9
	R. B. Johnson, Republican	2,826	9.1
2	John C. Box, Democrat	41,188	89.9
	A. E. Sweatland, Republican	4,625	10.1
3	Morgan Sanders, Democrat	30,618	100.0
4	Sam Rayburn, Democrat	31,825	91.1
	C. A. Gray, Republican	3,111	8.9
5	Hatton Sumners, Democrat	43,781	87.6
	George S. Atkinson, Republican	6,193	12.4
6	Luther Johnson, Democrat	33,169	93.2
	Tyler Haswell, Republican	2,440	6.9
7	Clay S. Briggs, Democrat	23,947	89.1
	John T. Wheeler, Republican	2,941	10.9
8	Daniel E. Garrett, Democrat	35,189	86.0
	Clarence A. Miller, Republican	5,712	14.0
9	Joseph Mansfield, Democrat	31,444	82.3
	Ed Franz, Republican	6,742	17.7
10	James Buchanan, Democrat	36,681	90.5
	Otto Stolley, Republican	3,850	9.5
11	Tom Connally, Democrat	29,247	88.2
	C. C. Baker, Republican	3,918	11.8
12	Fritz Lanham, Democrat	33,186	100.0
13	Guinn Williams, Democrat	32,721	88.6
	C. W. Johnson, Jr., Republican	4,197	11.4
14	Harry M. Wurzbach, Republican	31,784	62.4
	D. S. Davenport, Democrat	19,165	37.6
15	John N. Garner, Democrat	22,776	99.9
16	Claude Hudspeth, Democrat	27,506	88.5
	Vernon L. Sullivan, Republican	3567	11.5
17	Thomas L. Blanton, Democrat	44,377	100.0
18	Marvin Jones, Democrat	42,399	89.7
	A. B. Spencer, Republican	4,887	10.3

1926 DEMOCRATIC PRIMARY ELECTION (JULY 24)

District	Candidate	Votes	%
1	Eugene Black	unopposed	100.0
2	John C. Box	37,133	71.7
	W. W. King	14,678	28.3
3	Morgan Sanders	unopposed	100.0
4	Sam Rayburn	unopposed	100.0
5	Hatton Sumners	37,280	87.0
	W. P. McCalib	5,595	13.0
6	Luther Johnson	unopposed	100.0
7	Clay S. Briggs	unopposed	100.0
8	Daniel E. Garrett	31,271	79.3
	H. C. Gerlach	8,177	20.7
9	Joseph Mansfield	unopposed	100.0

10	James Buchanan	21,630	50.4
	James R. Hamilton	21,274	49.6
11	Tom Connally	30,627	84.4
	Lowesco Braun	5,681	15.6
12	Fritz Lanham	33,162	77.4
	C. E. Farmer	9,702	22.6
13	Guinn Williams	24,785	56.1
	Ben D. Sartin	19,416	43.9
14	A. D. Rogers	16,749	50.9
	R. E. Chrone	5,643	17.1
	John R. Pfeiffer	10,542	32.0
15	John N. Garner	18,546	71.8
	Sid Hardin	7,287	28.2
16	Claude Hudspeth	unopposed	100.0
17	Thomas L. Blanton	41,937	74.2
	J. R. Smith	14,577	25.8
18	Marvin Jones	unopposed	100.0

1926 Republican Primary Election (July 24)

1 O. F. Wimmer
2 William C. Hall
   Lord
3 Enoch G. Fletcher
4 Henry C. Barlow
5 Clinton S. Bailey
6 John A. Newsom
7 Sam R. Halstead
   Kendall
8 J. M. Gibson
9 E. F. Glaze
10 W. H. Matthai
11 W. H. Black
12 David Sutton
13 Mel E. Peters
14 Harry M. Wurzbach
   Fred M. Knetsch
15 Hardie H. Jefferies
16 A. N. Norcup
17 H. B. Tanner
18 S. E. Fish

This was the first Republican Party Primary Election held in Texas. Until 1962, the only other Republican Party primary elections for U.S. Representative were in 1930, 1934, 1954, and 1958.

1926 General Election (November 2)

1	Eugene Black, Democrat	9,828	94.4
	O. F. Wimmer, Republican	579	5.6
2	John C. Box, Democrat	11,955	95.6
	William C. Hall, Republican	546	4.4
3	Morgan Sanders, Democrat	11,336	91.2
	Enoch G. Fletcher, Republican	1,098	8.8
4	Sam Rayburn, Democrat	13,499	89.9
	Henry C. Barlow, Republican	1,524	10.1
5	Hatton Sumners, Democrat	29,687	96.5
	Clinton S. Bailey, Republican	1,087	3.5
6	Luther Johnson, Democrat	10,162	96.1
	John A. Newsom, Republican	409	3.9
7	Clay S. Briggs, Democrat	7,678	94.1
	Sam R. Halstead, Republican	478	5.9
8	Daniel E. Garrett, Democrat	8,459	91.0
	J. M. Gibson, Republican	842	9.1
9	Joseph Mansfield, Democrat	10,577	82.6
	E. F. Glaze, Republican	2,228	17.4
10	James Buchanan, Democrat	12,051	93.2
	W. H. Matthai, Republican	886	6.9
11	Tom Connally, Democrat	8,481	94.2
	W. H. Black, Republican	526	5.8
12	Fritz Lanham, Democrat	10,466	94.4
	David Sutton, Republican	620	5.6
13	Guinn Williams, Democrat	12,406	94.0
	Mel E. Peters, Republican	797	6.0
14	Harry M. Wurzbach, Republican	14,224	57.2
	A. D. Rogers, Democrat	10,633	42.8

#	Candidate	Votes	%
15	John N. Garner, Democrat	13,551	82.8
	Hardie H. Jefferies, Republican	2,825	17.3
16	Claude Hudspeth, Democrat	15,732	86.1
	A. N. Norcup, Republican	2,542	13.9
17	Thomas L. Blanton, Democrat	15,935	93.7
	H. B. Tanner, Republican	1,065	6.3
18	Marvin Jones, Democrat	18,027	93.6
	S. E. Fish, Republican	1,237	6.4

1928 DEMOCRATIC PRIMARY ELECTION (JULY 28)

#	Candidate	Votes	%
1	Wright Patman	20,606	
	Eugene Black	17,755	
2	John C. Box		
	—— King		
	—— Sanders		
3	Morgan Sanders	16,730	
4	Sam Rayburn	7,685	
	Wallace Hughston	2,716	
	John L. Andrews	2,258	
	B. L. Sherley		
5	Hatton Sumners		
	—— Ray		
	—— McCalib		
6	Luther Johnson		
7	Clay S. Briggs		
	—— Holbrook		
8	Daniel E. Garrett		
9	Joseph Mansfield	unopposed	100.0
10	James Buchanan		
11	Oliver H. Cross		
	—— Jones		
	—— Maxwell		
12	Fritz Lanham	unopposed	100.0
13	Guinn Williams		
14	Augustus McCloskey		
	—— Rogers		
15	John N. Garner		
	—— Hardin		
16	Claude Hudspeth		
	Reid		
17	Robert Q. Lee		
	Oscar Callaway		
	T. P. Perkins		
	—— Grisham		
	—— Shanks		
18	Marvin Jones		
	—— Bell		

No Republican Primary Election was held in 1928.

1928 GENERAL ELECTION (NOVEMBER 6)

#	Candidate	Votes	%
1	Wright Patman, Democrat	24,267	87.9
	Richard F. Stephens, Republican	3,349	12.1
2	John C. Box, Democrat	38,901	100.0
3	Morgan Sanders, Democrat	22,194	100.0
4	Sam Rayburn, Democrat	23,847	84.2
	Floyd Harry, Republican	4,488	15.8
5	Hatton Sumners, Democrat	42,482	100.0
6	Luther Johnson, Democrat	26,412	90.7
	H. Lee Monroe, Republican	2,714	9.3
7	Clay S. Briggs, Democrat	21,461	88.4
	A. J. Long, Republican	2,827	11.6
8	Daniel E. Garrett, Democrat	43,891	81.8
	George E. Kepple, Republican	9,739	18.2
9	Joseph Mansfield, Democrat	24,742	86.9
	Louis B. Allen, Republican	3,718	13.1
10	James Buchanan, Democrat	27,890	91.9
	David H. Morris, Republican	2,457	8.1
11	Oliver H. Cross, Democrat	21,484	90.9
	R. C. Bush, Republican	2,141	9.1
12	Fritz Lanham, Democrat	30,905	79.6
	David Sutton, Republican	7,921	20.4
13	Guinn Williams, Democrat	30,926	88.5
	Mrs. P.-A. Welty, Republican	4,026	11.5

District	Candidate	Votes	%
14	Augustus McCloskey, Democrat	29,085	50.3*
	Harry M. Wurzbach, Republican	28,766	49.7
15	John N. Garner, Democrat	28,417	100.0
	J. L. Burd	1	0.0
16	Claude Hudspeth, Democrat	31,132	100.0
17	Robert Q. Lee, Democrat	41,727	100.0
18	Marvin Jones, Democrat	58,667	86.5
	V. C. Nelson, Republican	9,137	13.5

*McCloskey took office, but Wurzbach contested the election and won. McCloskey served less than one year before Wurzbach returned to his former seat.

1930 SPECIAL ELECTION (MAY 20)

District	Candidate	Votes	%
17	Thomas Blanton, Democrat	10,225	56.1
	Mrs. Robert Q. Lee, Democrat	8,012	43.9

This special election was held to fill the seat of Robert Q. Lee, who died on April 18, 1930.

1930 DEMOCRATIC PRIMARY ELECTION (JULY 26)

District	Candidate	Votes	%
1	Wright Patman	unopposed	100.0
2	Martin Dies		
	John C. Box		
3	Morgan Sanders	unopposed	100.0
4	Sam Rayburn	15,744	51.3
	Choice B. Randell	11,237	36.6
	B. L. Sherley	3,716	12.1
5	Hatton Summers		
	—— Moore		
	Walter J. Reid		
6	Luther Johnson	unopposed	100.0
7	Clay S. Briggs	unopposed	100.0
8	Daniel E. Garrett		
	—— Bailey		
	—— Murphy		
	John M. Snell		
9	Joseph Mansfield		
	Leo C. Buckley		
	George Seydler, Sr.	unopposed	100.0
10	James Buchanan	unopposed	100.0
	—— Hornsby		
	—— Human		
	—— Nolan		
11	Oliver H. Cross		
12	Fritz Lanham		
13	Guinn Williams		
	W. D. McFarlane		
	Ben D. Sartin		
	—— Smith		
	—— Williams		
14	Henry B. Dielman		
15	John N. Garner		
16	R. Ewing Thomason		
	E. E. "Pat" Murphy		
	Marvin L. Birkhead		
	—— Pipe		
	—— Waldrip		
17	Thomas Blanton		
	Venus Earl Earp		
18	Marvin Jones	unopposed	100.0

1930 REPUBLICAN PRIMARY ELECTION (JULY 26)

District	Candidate
1	Thomas A. Clarke
2	(none)
3	(none)
4	Floyd Harry
5	Clinton S. Bailey
6	(none)
7	(none)
8	(none)
9	(none)
10	(none)
11	(none)
12	(none)

1930 GENERAL ELECTION (NOVEMBER 4)

1. Wright Patman, Democrat — 9,160 — 94.7
   - Thomas A. Clarke, Republican — 515 — 5.3
2. Martin Dies, Democrat — 14,236 — 100.0
3. Morgan Sanders, Democrat — 8,162 — 100.0
4. Sam Rayburn, Democrat — 9,385 — 88.8
   - Floyd Harry, Republican — 1,189 — 11.2
5. Hatton Sumners, Democrat — 9,924 — 88.1
   - Clinton S. Bailey, Republican — 1,344 — 11.9
6. Luther Johnson, Democrat — 12,396 — 100.0
7. Clay S. Briggs, Democrat — 9,357 — 100.0
8. Daniel E. Garrett, Democrat — 12,877 — 100.0
9. Joseph Mansfield, Democrat — 14,855 — 86.9
   - George Seydler, Sr., Republican — 2,239 — 13.1
10. James Buchanan, Democrat — 12,780 — 100.0
11. Oliver H. Cross, Democrat — 10,381 — 100.0
12. Fritz Lanham, Democrat — 9,846 — 100.0
13. Guinn Williams, Democrat — 12,840 — 91.1
    - W. C. Witcher, Republican — 1,257 — 8.9
14. Harry M. Wurzbach, Republican — 27,206 — 59.3
    - Henry B. Dielman, Democrat — 18,707 — 40.7
15. John N. Garner, Democrat — 20,733 — 77.5
    - Carlos G. Watson, Republican — 6,016 — 22.5
16. R. Ewing Thomason, Democrat — 18,915 — 84.1
    - Mitchell Waldrop, Republican — 3,581 — 15.9
17. Thomas Blanton, Democrat — 17,199 — 100.0
18. Marvin Jones, Democrat — 26,697 — 93.2
    - S. E. Fish, Republican — 1,934 — 6.8

1931 SPECIAL ELECTION (NOVEMBER 24)

14. Richard M. Kleberg, Democrat — 19,038 — 47.1
    - Carl W. Johnson — 13,945 — 34.5
    - Charles W. Anderson — 5,759 — 14.2
    - Tom B. Smiley, Republican — 1,715 — 4.2

This special election was held to fill the seat of Harry Wurzbach, who died on November 27, 1930, before the 72nd Congress.

1932 DEMOCRATIC PRIMARY ELECTION (JULY 23)

1. Wright Patman
2. Martin Dies
3. Morgan Sanders
4. Sam Rayburn — 18,177 — 51.0
   - Jess Morris — 10,438 — 29.3
   - Choice B Randell — 7,028 — 19.7
5. Hatton Sumners
   - —— Gallagher
   - Walter J. Reid
   - —— Rogers
6. Luther Johnson
7. Clay S. Briggs
   - —— Cook
8. Daniel E. Garrett
   - —— Eagle
   - —— Lewis
9. Joseph Mansfield
   - —— Kuwalik
10. James Buchanan
    - Merton L. Harris
11. Oliver H. Cross
12. Fritz Lanham
    - Albert G. Baskin
13. W. D. McFarlane
    - W. C. Witcher
14. Harry M. Wurzbach
    - Jese A. Chase
15. —— Booher
    - —— Simpson
    - Carlos G. Watson
16. Mitchell Waldrop
17. (none)
18. S. E. Fish

District / Place	Candidate	Votes	%
	George W. Backus		
	Dillard Henson		
14	Richard Kleberg		
	— Barrett		
	— Britt		
	— Maloney		
15	John N. Garner		
16	R. Ewing Thomason		
	Dan M. Jackson		
17	Thomas Blanton		
	Joe H. Jones		
18	Marvin Jones		
At-Large—Place 1			
	Mrs. Alex W. Adams	46,633	6.1
	Ernest C. "Ozro" Cox	66,523	8.7
	Ida M. Darden	44,724	5.8
	R. B. Hood	56,171	7.4
	Chesley W. Jurney	37,909	5.0
	Sherman Nelson	24,251	3.2
	Pink Parrish	99,026	13.0
	W. Seldon Reed	32,082	4.2
	George J. Schleicher	29,996	3.9
	E. G. Senter	43,655	5.7
	George B. Terrell	124,133	16.3
	Lawrence Westbrook	69,765	9.1
	W. Erskine Williams	87,789	11.5
At-Large—Place 2			
	Joseph W. Bailey, Jr.	199,131	25.3
	J. H. "Cyclone" Davis	122,905	15.6
	P. L. Downs	57,612	7.3
	G. B. Fisher	33,081	4.2
	Lamar Gill	27,525	3.5
	W. H. Hawkins	45,472	5.8
	Oscar Holcombe	108,322	13.7
	W. E. Myres	29,390	3.7
	D. B. Sartain	63,195	8.0
	L. J. Sulak	37,696	4.8
	Phoebe K. Warner	64,290	8.1
At-Large—Place 3			
	J. E. Boog-Scott	52,717	7.0
	Joe Burkett	97,250	13.0
	W. I. Cargile	17,282	2.3
	Ben F. Harigel	47,945	6.4
	Julien C. Hyer	72,219	9.6
	A. H. King	44,103	5.9
	W. E. Lea	37,434	5.0
	Douglas W. McGregor	89,979	8.0
	John L. Meany	15,605	2.0
	C. A. Mitchener	9,985	1.3
	Mrs. Fred Real	35,408	4.7
	Alfred William Sasse	29,040	3.9
	Sterling P. Strong	170,996	22.9
	Monte Warner	27,831	3.7

The elections were close enough in the at-large seat races that runoff elections were held on August 27, 1932.

No Republican Primary Election was held in 1932.

1932 DEMOCRATIC PRIMARY RUNOFF (AUGUST 27)

Place	Candidate	Votes	%
At-Large—Place 1			
	Pink Parrish	387,255	44.6
	George B. Terrell	481,374	55.4
At-Large—Place 2			
	Joseph W. Bailey, Jr.	519,393	59.0
	J. H. "Cyclone" Davis	361,485	41.0
At-Large—Place 3			
	Joe Burkett	397,402	46.0
	Sterling P. Strong	467,393	54.0

1932 GENERAL ELECTION (NOVEMBER 8)

District	Candidate	Votes	%
1	Wright Patman, Democrat	30,854	98.0
	A. O. Barker, Republican	776	2.0
2	Martin Dies, Democrat	51,999	95.4
	J. H. Buchanan, Republican	2,522	4.6

District	Candidate	Votes	%
	John W. Conner, Liberty	3	0.0
3	Morgan Sanders, Democrat	36,507	100.0
4	Sam Rayburn, Democrat	23,404	95.2
	Floyd Harry, Republican	1,171	4.8
5	Hatton Sumners, Democrat	52,598	92.1
	George J. McManus, Republican	4,539	7.9
6	Luther Johnson, Democrat	32,966	100.0
7	Clay S. Briggs, Democrat	28,490	95.3
	Arthur J. Long, Republican	1,421	4.8
8	*Daniel E. Garrett, Democrat	57,882	92.0*
	William E. Lang, Republican	5,015	8.0
	J. W. McDonald, Liberty	5	0.0
9	Joseph Mansfield, Democrat	33,366	97.5
	Lewis Allen, Republican	1,240	
10	James Buchanan, Democrat	33,232	100.0
11	Oliver H. Cross, Democrat	35,186	96.6
	C. C. Baker, Republican	1,247	
12	Fritz Lanham, Democrat	41,151	93.3
	George Calvert, Republican	2,968	6.7
13	W. D. McFarlane, Democrat	33,023	100.0
14	Richard Kleberg, Democrat	69,471	91.5
	Frank B. Vaughn, Republican	6,456	8.5
15	John N. Garner, Democrat	44,300	88.4
	Carlos G. Watson, Republican	5,785	11.6
16	R. Ewing Thomason, Democrat	49,068	99.7
17	Thomas Blanton, Democrat	43,959	100.0
18	Marvin Jones, Democrat	76,918	96.1
	S. E. Fish, Republican	3,245	
At-Large—Place 1			
	George B. Terrell, Democrat	794,520	92.6
	F. A. Blankenbeckler, Republican	60,360	7.0
	H. M. Shelton, Socialist	2,534	0.3
	P. A. Spain, Liberty	188	0.0
At-Large—Place 2			
	Joseph W. Bailey, Jr., Democrat	790,024	92.3
	Enoch Fletcher, Republican	62,957	7.4
	Ben O. Miller, Socialist	2,424	0.3
	H. G. Eastridge, Liberty	172	0.0
	John L. Andrews, Jacksonian Democrat	97	0.0
At-Large—Place 3			
	Sterling P. Strong, Democrat	794,333	92.8
	John A. Simpson, Republican	59,390	6.9
	P. L. Petersen, Socialist	2,530	0.3

*Daniel Garrett died just weeks after the 1932 general election. A special election was held on January 28, 1933, to fill his seat. Three at-large seats were created due to the inability of the legislature to create three districts following the dicennial census of 1930.

1933 SPECIAL ELECTION (JANUARY 28)

District	Candidate	Votes	%
8	Joe Eagle, Democrat	24,722	55.0
	Chester H. Bryan, Democrat	6,807	15.2
	Robert J. Cole, Democrat	6,012	13.4
	Charles Murphy, Democrat	1,834	4.1
	Allen V. Peden, Democrat	1,313	2.9
	Mrs. W. Ray Scruggs, Democrat	618	1.4
	Clarence A. Miller, Republican	550	1.2
	J. Dixie Smith, Democrat	508	1.1
	E. A. Dunman, Democrat	402	0.9
	Ellis G. Binford, Democrat	382	0.9
	Edgar Soule, Democrat	285	0.6
	C. D. Little, Democrat	249	0.6
	W. W. Jackson, Democrat	207	0.5
	A. Judson Henderson, Democrat	138	0.3
	John Nissing, Democrat	95	0.2
	V. C. Porter, Democrat	84	0.2
	T. E. Barlow, Democrat	84	0.2
	Carlton Moore, Democrat	82	0.2
	William M. Rudersdorf, Democrat	81	0.2
	J. E. Gibson, Democrat	72	0.2
	J. P. Gillen, Democrat	69	0.2
	Thomas C. Turnley, Democrat	55	0.1
	Robert W. Castleberry, Democrat	50	0.1
	8 Other Candidates	214	0.3

This special election was held to fill the seat of Daniel Garrett. It was held conincidental with the next election. The two elections are explained below.

1933 SPECIAL ELECTION (JANUARY 28)

8	Joe Eagle, Democrat	23,831	53.6
	Chester H. Bryan, Democrat	7,023	15.8
	Robert J. Cole, Democrat	5,915	13.3
	Charles Murphy, Democrat	1,845	4.2
	Allen V. Peden, Democrat	1,258	2.8
	Mrs. W. Ray Scruggs, Democrat	639	1.4
	J. Dixie Smith, Democrat	531	1.2
	Clarence A. Miller, Republican	488	1.1
	Ellis G. Binford, Democrat	487	1.1
	E. A. Dunman, Democrat	384	0.9
	Edgar Soule, Democrat	273	0.6
	J. E. Gibson, Democrat	233	0.5
	C. D. Little, Democrat	232	0.5
	W. W. Jackson, Democrat	175	0.4
	A. Judson Henderson, Democrat	121	0.3
	Franklin P. Davis, Democrat	109	0.3
	John Nissing, Democrat	105	0.2
	William M. Rudersdorf, Democrat	100	0.2
	Carlton Moore, Democrat	97	0.2
	Rob R. Nichols, Democrat	75	0.2
	Chester Rogers, Democrat	73	0.2
	T. E. Barlow, Democrat	72	0.6
	V. E. Arnold, Democrat	69	0.2
	J. P. Gillen, Democrat	66	0.2
	Robert W. Castleberry, Democrat	65	0.2
	Thomas C. Turnley, Democrat	53	0.1
	7 Other Candidates	165	0.4

1933 SPECIAL ELECTION (APRIL 22)

15	Milton West, Democrat	13,546	91.2
	Carlos G. Watson, Republican	1,302	8.8

This special election was held to fill the seat of John Nance Garner who had resigned from Congress on March 3, 1933, to become vice-president.

1933 SPECIAL ELECTION (JUNE 24)

7	Clark Thompson, Democrat	3,798	24.2
	James D. Pickett, Democrat	2,756	17.5
	Nat Patton, Democrat	2,638	16.8
	Theodore B. Stubbs, Democrat	2,334	14.9
	R. E. Biggs, Democrat	1,372	8.8
	Jake B. Clegg, Democrat	1,148	7.3
	Julian Greer, Democrat	774	4.9
	Thomas H. Dent, Republican	710	4.5
	Nall Colson, Democrat	183	1.2

This special election was held to fill the seat of Clay Stone Briggs, who died on April 29, 1933.

1934 DEMOCRATIC PRIMARY ELECTION (JULY 28)

1	Wright Patman	unopposed	100.0
2	Martin Dies	unopposed	100.0
3	Morgan Sanders		
	A. V. Grant		
	Herman V. Puckett		
	Garland A. Farmer		
4	Sam Rayburn	25,887	58.8
	Jess Morris	18,166	41.2
5	Hatton Sumners		
	Sterling P. Strong		
6	Luther Johnson		
	Tom White		
	E. B. Creech		
7	Nat Patton		
	Roger Davis		
	Bonner Frizzell		

There were two special elections held simultaneously to fill the seat of Daniel Garrett, who died on December 13, 1932, before the 73rd Congress. The first was to fill the balance of Garrett's unexpired term in the standing Congress, and the second was for Garrett's full term. This occurred prior to the Twentieth Amendment to the Constitution, which was ratified five days before this election. This Amendment sets the term dates for members of Congress and the president. It notes that the terms of Senators and Representatives shall begin and end at noon on the third day of January and that the terms of their successors shall also begin at that time. Prior to this, Congress held what was called the "lame duck" session each December following the November general election.

—— Justice
—— Fulgham
—— Thompson

District	Candidate		%
8	Joe H. Eagle		
	W. Everett Dupuy		
	Frank Putnam		
	—— Nissing		
	—— Weldon		
	—— Simms		
9	Joseph Mansfield	unopposed	100.0
10	James Buchanan	unopposed	100.0
11	Oliver H. Cross		
	Robert Pogue		
12	Fritz Lanham		
	Fred J. Berry		
	Theo Koenig		
13	W. D. McFarlane		
	Sam B. Spence		
	George W. Backus		
14	Richard Kleberg	unopposed	100.0
15	Milton West		
	Gordon Griffin		
16	R. Ewing Thomason	unopposed	100.0
17	Thomas Blanton		
	Carl Hamlin		
	Oscar F. Chastain		
18	Marvin Jones	unopposed	100.0
19	George Mahon		
	Clark M. Mullican		
	Homer L. Pharr		
	Arthur P. Duggan		
	Fred C. Haile		
	Joe H. Thompson		
	Taylor White		
	J. A. "Swede" Johnson		
20	Maury Maverick		
	C. K. Quin		
	John K. Weber		
	—— Barrett		
	—— Cullen		
21	Charles L. South		
	Carl Runge		
	E. E. "Pat" Murphy		
	Culberson Deal		

The elections were close enough in the races for the 7th, 13th, 19th, 20th, and 21st district seats that runoff elections were held on August 25, 1934.

1934 REPUBLICAN PRIMARY ELECTION (JULY 28)

District	Candidate		%
1	P. B. Gibbons		
2	(none)		
3	(none)		
4	Floyd Harry		
5	Aubrey J. Roberts		
6	(none)		
7	Dudley B. Lawson		
8	P. Loreng Petersen		
9	(none)	unopposed	100.0
10	(none)		
11	(none)		
12	Joe Ingraham		
13	(none)	unopposed	100.0
14	(none)		
15	G. C. Mann		
16	(none)	unopposed	100.0
17	(none)		
18	James M. Kernan		
19	(none)		
20	H. M. Shelton		
21	(none)		

1934 DEMOCRATIC PRIMARY RUNOFF (AUGUST 25)

District	Candidate	Votes	%
7	Nat Patton	24,832	52.8
	Roger Davis	22,170	47.2

District	Candidate	Votes	%
13	W. D. McFarlane	31,919	54.2
	Sam B. Spence	27,002	45.8
19	George Mahon	35,400	64.4
	Clark M. Mullican	19,591	35.6
20	Maury Maverick	20,462	54.3
	C. K. Quin	17,230	45.7
21	Charles L. South	28,068	54.2
	Carl Runge	23,711	45.8

1934 GENERAL ELECTION (NOVEMBER 6)

District	Candidate	Votes	%
1	Wright Patman, Democrat	18,608	98.3
	P. B. Gibbons, Republican	325	1.7
2	Martin Dies, Democrat	16,628	100.0
3	Morgan Sanders, Democrat	14,790	100.0
4	Sam Rayburn, Democrat	16,684	96.8
	Floyd Harry, Republican	544	3.2
5	Hatton Sumners, Democrat	27,302	96.9
	Aubrey J. Roberts, Republican	871	3.1
6	Luther Johnson, Democrat	16,294	100.0
7	Nat Patton, Democrat	18,063	99.1
	Dudley B. Lawson, Republican	168	0.9
8	Joe H. Eagle, Democrat	40,400	99.5
	P. Loreng Petersen, Republican	124	0.3
	E. J. Hicks	97	0.2
9	Joseph Mansfield, Democrat	23,257	100.0
10	James Buchanan, Democrat	19,306	100.0
11	Oliver H. Cross, Democrat	20,383	100.0
12	Fritz Lanham, Democrat	24,984	98.4
	Joe Ingraham, Republican	404	1.6
13	W. D. McFarlane, Democrat	21,005	100.0
14	Richard Kleberg, Democrat	26,276	100.0
15	Milton West, Democrat	20,102	88.0
	G. C. Mann, Republican	2,739	12.0
16	R. Ewing Thomason, Democrat	11,063	100.0
17	Thomas Blanton, Democrat	17,266	100.0
18	Marvin Jones, Democrat	23,202	97.0
	James M. Kernan, Republican	576	2.4
	R. D. Tomlinson	133	0.6
19	George Mahon, Democrat	20,169	100.0
20	Maury Maverick, Democrat	17,810	98.8
	H. M. Shelton, Republican	217	1.2
21	Charles L. South, Democrat	26,093	100.0

1936 DEMOCRATIC PRIMARY ELECTION (JULY 25)

District	Candidate	Votes	%
1	Wright Patman	48,179	100.0
2	Martin Dies	34,876	66.1
	Clyde Smith	17,872	33.9
3	Morgan Sanders	24,357	52.7
	Alvin Grant	21,876	47.3
4	Sam Rayburn	31,166	65.4
	Jess Morris	12,845	27.0
	Will A. Harris	3,618	7.6
5	Hatton Sumners	22,122	51.6
	Leslie Jackson	6,027	14.4
	Claud C. Westerfeld	8,728	20.4
	King S. Williamson	5,960	13.9
6	Luther Johnson	27,278	57.6
	James O. Burleson	3,460	9.0
	George B. Butler	6,964	18.0
	Noble Cook	4,484	11.6
	T. White	1,464	3.8
7	Nat Patton	22,473	48.8
	Emerson Stone **	13,383	29.0
	Bonner Frizzell	10,222	22.2
8	Albert Thomas	22,948	36.1
	Oscar Holcombe	23,097	36.4
	John R. Cox	749	1.2
	G. W. Dixon	166	0.3
	R. C. Duff	861	1.4
	George L. Glass	1,037	1.6
	Earl Jacoby	427	0.7
	B. A. Mitchner	114	0.2

District	Candidate	Votes	%
	J. B. Simons	118	0.2
	John Snell	9,097	14.3
	C. A. Teagle	3,907	6.2
	Lytton Wells	767	1.2
	Bates F. Wilson	142	0.2
	C. A. Vallade	59	0.1
9	Joseph Mansfield	32,507	74.6
	C. C. Calloway	11,030	25.4
10	James Buchanan	33,509	73.4
	Ayres K. Ross	12,158	26.6
11	W. R. Poage	26,860	55.6
	C. A. Sherman	3,531	7.3
	Frank B. Tirey	17,932	37.1
12	Fritz Lanham	22,711	45.1
	Dr. F. E. Harrison	1,630	3.2
	Jerome C. Martin	5,786	11.5
	W.E. Myres	5,207	10.3
	*Julien C. Hyer	15,044	29.9
13	W. D. McFarlane	21,305	34.9
	Ed Gossett	11,158	18.3
	Grady Woodruff	9,873	16.2
	Ben G. Oneal	8,890	14.6
	B. D. Sartin	7,307	12.0
	T. H. McKee	669	1.1
	George W. Backus	1,785	2.9
14	Richard Kleberg	33,940	69.8
	Adolph Seidemann	14,693	30.2
15	Milton West	24,989	69.8
	Noble Cofer	10,836	30.2
16	R. Ewing Thomason	31,079	100.0
17	Clyde L. Garrett	24,495	54.9
	Thomas Blanton	20,088	45.1
18	Marvin Jones	38,428	71.5
	John B. Miller	15,316	28.5
19	George Mahon	40,093	73.4
	E. B. Speck	14,557	26.6
20	Maury Maverick	21,703	49.7
	Lamar Seeligson	14,378	32.9
	James O. Rail	24	0.1
	R. S. Menefee	7,606	17.4
21	Charles L. South	36,955	72.3
	Dr. H. F. Miller	14,159	27.7

There was no Republican Primary Election held in 1936.

The elections were close enough in the races for the 8th, 12th, 13th, and 17th District seats that runoff elections were held on August 22, 1936.

* Julien Hyer won the right to a runoff election, but he withdrew from the race and Lanham was declared the nominee.

** Emerson Stone won the right to a runoff election, but he withdrew from the race and Patton was declared the nominee.

1936 DEMOCRATIC PRIMARY RUNOFF ELECTION (AUGUST 22)

District	Candidate	Votes	%
8	Albert Thomas	34,213	57.5
	Oscar Holcombe	25,240	42.5
12	Fritz Lanham	31,465	86.6
	Fred Cook (write-in) *	4,870	13.4
13	W. D. McFarlane	28,746	52.5
	Ed Gossett	26,068	47.6
17	Clyde L. Garrett		
	Thomas Blanton		

* Lanham's opposition in the first primary withdrew from the race and did not compete in the second primary. Between the two primaries, Cook announced his candidacy and mounted a write-in campaign.

1936 GENERAL ELECTION (NOVEMBER 3)

District	Candidate	Votes	%
1	Wright Patman, Democrat	29,351	97.6
	P. B. Gibbons, Republican	727	2.4
2	Martin Dies, Democrat	39,484	100.0
	A. E. Sweatland	2	0.0
	Sam Lipscomb	1	0.0
3	Morgan Sanders, Democrat	29,482	96.3
	N. E. Hendrickson, Republican	1,146	3.7
4	Sam Rayburn, Democrat	33,355	97.5
	Ross E. Johnson, Republican	855	2.5
5	Hatton Sumners, Democrat	43,954	88.5

District	Candidate	Votes	%
	Dee C. Humphrey, Republican	5,579	11.2
	J. W. Chandler	114	0.2
6	Luther Johnson, Democrat	29,574	97.3
	C. David Thompson, Republican	834	2.7
7	Nat Patton, Democrat	29,011	97.6
	O. J. Read, Republican	702	2.4
8	Albert Thomas, Democrat	61,616	91.8
	Roy B. Nichols, Republican	5,456	8.1
	A. C. Henderson	68	0.1
9	Joseph Mansfield, Democrat	36,968	93.2
	F. W. Dusek, Republican	2,700	6.8
	Lewis Allen	1	0.0
10	James Buchanan, Democrat	33,631	99.5
	David Lyons,	181	0.5
	E. J. Enoch	1	0.0
	O. L. Ulrich	1	0.0
11	W. R. Poage, Democrat	31,227	100.0
	T. V. Freeman	2	0.0
	C. A. Sherman	1	0.0
12	Fritz Lanham, Democrat	39,708	93.3
	Arnold Davis, Republican	2,845	6.7
	Julian C. Hyer	1	0.0
	Nat Patton	1	0.0
13	W. D. McFarlane, Democrat	40,935	95.2
	R. L. Ratliff, Republican	2,051	4.8
14	Richard Kleberg, Democrat	39,576	92.1
	Howell Ward, Republican	3,408	7.9
	Adolph Seideman	8	0.2
	Ed Lyons	1	0.0
15	Milton West, Democrat	29,598	82.6
	John A. Simpson, Republican	6,244	17.4
16	R. Ewing Thomason, Democrat	26,353	100.0
	U. S. Goen	3	0.0
	J. Johnson	1	0.0
	Lytton Taylor	1	0.0
17	Clyde L. Garrett, Democrat	35,386	100.0
	W. F. Nelson	9	0.0
18	Marvin Jones, Democrat	44,652	94.1
	S. E. Fish, Republican	2,526	5.3
	Theodore Conrad, Union	262	0.6
19	George Mahon, Democrat	39,059	100.0
20	Maury Maverick, Democrat	34,478	71.6
	Ernest W. Clements, Republican	12,056	25.0
	James O. Rail, Independent	1,649	3.4
21	Charles L. South, Democrat	37,964	88.6
	Max J. Bierschwale, Republican	4,891	11.4

1937 Special Election (April 10)

District	Candidate	Votes	%
10	Lyndon B. Johnson, Democrat	8,280	27.7
	Morton Harris, Democrat	5,111	17.1
	Polk Shelton, Democrat	4,420	14.8
	Sam V. Stone, Democrat	4,048	13.5
	C. N. Avery, Democrat	3,951	13.2
	Houghton Brownell, Democrat	3,019	10.1
	Ayers K. Ross, Democrat	1,088	3.6
	Other	30	0.1

This special election was held to fill the seat of James Buchanan, who died on February 22, 1937. The seat was filled by Lyndon B. Johnson.

1938 Democratic Primary Election (July 23)

District	Candidate	Votes	%
1	Wright Patman		
	Blackburn		
2	Martin Dies		
	Hendricks		
3	Lindley Beckworth	14,107	24.8
	Brady P. Gentry	13,449	23.7
	Morgan G. Sanders	13,193	23.2
	Alton V. Grant	7,631	13.4
	Walter G. Russell	8,399	14.8
4	Sam Rayburn		100.0
5	Hatton Sumners	21,232	
	Leslie Jackson	11,277	
	Thomas B. Love	2,861	

District	Candidate	Votes	%
6	Luther Johnson		
	——— Cook		
	——— Kirby		
7	Nat Patton		
	——— Howe		
8	Albert Thomas		100.0
9	Joseph Mansfield		100.0
10	Lyndon Johnson		100.0
11	W. R. Poage		100.0
12	Fritz Lanham		
	Alvin E. Amos		
	B. F. Barnes		
	J. J. Connolly		
	Dr. F. E. Harrison		
	Curtis McBroom		
	A. H. Wheeler		
13	Ed Gossett	30,219	48.5
	W. D. McFarlane	27,555	44.2
	C. L. Somerville	790	1.3
	K. C. Spell	3,693	5.9
14	Richard Kleberg, Democrat	23,438	100.0
	——— Bird		
	Thurman Barrett		
15	Milton West		
16	R. Ewing Thomason		100.0
17	Clyde L. Garrett		100.0
18	Marvin Jones		
	James O. Cade		
19	George Mahon		
20	Maury Maverick	24,287	49.6
	Paul Kilday	24,835	50.6
21	Charles L. South		

1938 Democratic Primary Runoff Election (August 27)

District	Candidate	Votes	%
3	Lindley Beckworth	29,274	52.8
	Brady P. Gentry	26,137	47.2
13	Ed Gossett	29,782	52.0
	W. D. McFarlane	27,444	48.0

1938 General Election (November 8)

District	Candidate	Votes	%
1	Wright Patman, Democrat	14,833	98.7
	Joe C. Hailey, Republican	201	1.2
2	Martin Dies, Democrat	12,816	100.0
	Other	8	0.0
3	Lindley Beckworth, Democrat	17,115	100.0
	Other	3	0.0
4	Sam Rayburn, Democrat	16,523	97.9
	Ross E. Johnson, Republican	349	2.1
	Other	5	0.0
5	Hatton Summers, Democrat	10,344	95.0
	Heber Page, Republican	508	4.7
	H. T. Healey	37	0.3
6	Luther Johnson, Democrat	15,619	100.0
	Other	1	0.0
7	Nat Patton, Democrat	16,467	100.0
	Other	11	0.0
8	Albert Thomas, Democrat	36,989	98.3
	John A. Deering, Republican	631	1.7
9	Joseph Mansfield, Democrat	16,680	100.0
	Other	7	0.0
10	Lyndon Johnson, Democrat	14,476	100.0
	Other	2	0.0
11	W. R. Poage, Democrat	14,664	98.6
	D. E. Wooley, Republican	207	1.4
	Other	3	0.0
12	Fritz Lanham, Democrat	12,972	100.0
13	Ed Gossett, Democrat	20,620	98.6
	Adolph Lohman, Republican	298	1.4
	Other	2	0.0

No Republican Primary Election was held in 1938.

The elections were close enough in the races for the 3rd and 13th district seats that runoff elections were held on August 27, 1938.

District	Candidate	Votes	%
14	Richard Kleberg, Democrat	23,438	100.0
15	Milton West, Democrat	18,995	100.0
	Other	2	0.0
16	R. Ewing Thomason, Democrat	9,237	100.0
	Other	2	0.0
17	Clyde L. Garrett, Democrat	17,107	100.0
18	Marvin Jones, Democrat	19,048	100.0
19	George Mahon, Democrat	16,372	100.0
20	Paul J. Kilday, Democrat	16,703	100.0
21	Charles L. South, Democrat	21,671	93.0
	Max J. Bierschwale, Republican	1,621	7.0

1940 Democratic Primary Election (July 27)

District	Candidate	Votes	%
1	Wright Patman	37,507	63.8
	Howard Smith	13,570	23.1
	K. G. Waters	7,702	13.1
2	Martin Dies	55,173	88.4
	W. F. Hill	4,176	6.7
	James L. Latimer	3,070	4.9
3	Lindley Beckworth	46,272	77.3
	Frank Bezoni	13,601	22.7
	—— Bruce	unknown	
4	Sam Rayburn	43,634	84.8
	B. R. Galbraith	7,789	15.1
	Henry Zoller	22	0.0
5	Hatton Summers	unopposed	100.0
6	Luther Johnson	unopposed	100.0
7	Nat Patton	unopposed	100.0
8	Albert Thomas	53,614	75.1
	Joe H. Eagle	17,816	24.9
9	Joseph Mansfield	35,218	62.6
	C. O. Forester, Jr.	5,728	10.2
	L. J. Sulak	15,334	27.2
10	Lyndon Johnson	unopposed	100.0
11	W. R. Poage	35,520	65.8
	O. H. Cross	18,492	34.2
12	Fritz Lanham	36,613	67.7
	Jack Langdon	17,480	32.2
13	Ed Gossett	35,508	54.9
	W. D. McFarlane	27,777	42.9
	Charles H. Ripley	1,429	2.2
14	Richard Kleberg	34,936	60.6
	Gabe Garrett	8,959	15.6
	Wesley Seale	13,709	23.8
15	Milton West	unopposed	100.0
16	R. Ewing Thomason	unopposed	100.0
17	Sam Russell	16,733	29.5
	Clyde Garrett	20,481	36.1
	Thomas L. Blanton	9,041	15.9
	Otin Mills	9,069	15.9
18	Joe H. Sheppard	1,407	2.5
	James O. Cade	1,489	2.5
	Henry S. Bishop	2,921	4.8
	R. V. Converse	2,584	4.3
	Tom V. Ellzey	3,428	5.7
	Lewis P. Fields	3,868	6.4
	Lewis Goodrich	4,355	7.2
	Allen Harp	5,060	8.4
	Lee McConnell	1,153	1.9
	E. T. "Dusty" Miller	8,692	14.4
	Deskin Wells	15,820	26.2
	Eugene Worley	9,597	15.9
	Dennis Zimmerman	1,333	2.2
19	George Mahon	50,206	75.7
	C. L. Harris	9,784	14.7
	M. D. Ramsey	6,352	9.6
20	Paul J. Kilday	40,861	81.7
	Francis Haskell Edmondson	9,165	18.3
21	Charles L. South	100.0	

No Republican Primary Election was held in 1940. The elections were close enough in the races for the 17th and 18th district seats that runoff elections were held on August 24, 1940.

1940 DEMOCRATIC PRIMARY RUNOFF ELECTION (AUGUST 24)

No.	Candidate	Votes	%
17	Sam Russell	27,715	53.2
	Clyde Garrett	24,424	46.8
18	Deskin Wells	23,014	43.0
	Eugene Worley	30,565	57.0

1940 GENERAL ELECTION (NOVEMBER 5)

No.	Candidate	Votes	%
1	Wright Patman, Democrat	27,030	100.0
2	Martin Dies, Democrat	43,597	100.0
3	Lindley Beckworth, Democrat	47,292	100.0
4	Sam Rayburn, Democrat	46,333	100.0
5	Hatton Sumners, Democrat	57,789	87.5
	Floyd E. Boyer, Republican	8,273	12.5
6	Luther Johnson, Democrat	33,546	100.0
7	Nat Patton, Democrat	30,384	98.2
	Dudley B. Lawson, Republican	565	1.8
8	Albert Thomas, Democrat	89,796	94.8
	M. U. S. Kjorlaug, Republican	4,925	5.2
9	Joseph Mansfield, Democrat	52,754	100.0
10	Lyndon Johnson, Democrat	48,442	100.0
11	W. R. Poage, Democrat	37,227	99.9
12	Fritz Lanham, Democrat	54,108	100.0
13	Ed Gossett, Democrat	50,076	96.4
	Louis N. Gould, Republican	1,894	3.6
14	Richard Kleberg, Democrat	59,016	100.0
15	Milton West, Democrat	32,300	92.5
	John A. Simpson, Republican	2,628	7.5
16	R. Ewing Thomason, Democrat	34,515	99.9
17	Sam Russell, Democrat	45,456	100.0
18	Eugene Worley, Democrat	51,660	96.5
	John W. Beveridge, Republican	1,858	3.5
19	George Mahon, Democrat	56,343	100.0
20	Paul J. Kilday, Democrat	47,075	83.4
	Harry Hotchkin, Republican	9,296	16.5
	Emma Tenoyuca, Comm	76	0.1
21	Charles L. South, Democrat	49,468	7.2

1942 DEMOCRATIC PRIMARY ELECTION (JULY 25)

No.	Candidate	Votes	%
	Ray Ridenhour, Republican	3,832	7.2
1	Wright Patman	47,066	100.0
2	Martin Dies	52,575	100.0
3	Lindley Beckworth	27,969	43.7
	Ernest S. Goens	21,721	43.7
4	Sam Rayburn	35,433	77.5
	George T. Balch	10,265	22.5
5	Hatton Sumners	25,425	69.3
	Harry Hines	11,287	30.7
6	Luther Johnson	33,474	84.1
	W. E. Reid	6,333	15.9
7	Nat Patton	46,773	100.0
8	Albert Thomas	52,312	87.2
	George H. Loenberger	7,676	12.8
9	Joseph Mansfield	34,898	70.5
	J. A. Clements	14,609	29.5
10	Lyndon Johnson	44,656	100.0
11	W. R. Poage	41,216	100.0
12	Fritz Lanham	31,704	84.9
	B. Y. Cummings	5,628	15.1
	F. E. Harrington		
13	Ed Gossett	60,663	100.0
14	Richard Kleberg	53,613	100.0
15	Milton West	33,628	100.0
16	R. Ewing Thomason	23,442	88.1
	Louis A. Fail	3,156	11.9
17	Sam Russell	50,960	100.0
18	Eugene Worley	40,578	89.5
	Lynn Miller	4,778	10.5
19	George Mahon	59,187	100.0
20	Paul J. Kilday	15,691	100.0
21	*O. C. Fisher	24,167	45.8
	Harry Knox	7,062	13.4
	Charles South	21,495	40.8

No Republican Primary Election was held in 1942.

*O.C. Fisher and Charles South were scheduled for a runoff election on August 22, 1942. However, South, the incumbent, withdrew from the race and Fisher was declared the nominee.

1942 GENERAL ELECTION (NOVEMBER 3)

#	Candidate	Votes	%
1	Wright Patman, Democrat	9,502	100.0
2	Martin Dies, Democrat	10,128	100.0
3	Lindley Beckworth, Democrat	10,929	100.0
4	Sam Rayburn, Democrat	11,768	100.0
5	Hatton Sumners, Democrat	10,568	100.0
6	Luther Johnson, Democrat	10,726	100.0
7	Nat Patton, Democrat	11,043	99.1
	A. W. Orr, Republican	96	0.9
8	Albert Thomas, Democrat	31,038	96.9
	M. U. S. Kjorlaug, Republican	622	1.9
	Vance Muse, Independent	369	1.2
9	Joseph Mansfield, Democrat	13,852	100.0
10	Lyndon Johnson, Democrat	12,799	100.0
11	W. R. Poage, Democrat	7,554	99.9
12	Fritz Lanham, Democrat	25,894	100.0
13	Ed Gossett, Democrat	12,677	98.1
	Louis H. Gould, Republican	251	1.9
14	Richard Kleberg, Democrat	16,212	100.0
15	Milton West, Democrat	12,169	100.0
16	R. Ewing Thomason, Democrat	6,612	100.0
17	Sam Russell, Democrat	13,261	100.0
18	Eugene Worley, Democrat	10,739	100.0
19	George Mahon, Democrat	12,216	100.0
20	Paul J. Kilday, Democrat	8,860	81.7
	William A. Turner, Republican	1,980	18.3
21	O. C. Fisher, Democrat	16,554	100.0

1944 DEMOCRATIC PRIMARY ELECTION (JULY 22)

#	Candidate	Votes	%
1	Wright Patman		
2	Jesse M. Combs		
3	Lindley Beckworth		
	Martin		
	Meredith		
4	Sam Rayburn	24,306	55.4
	G. C. Morris	18,672	42.5
	George Balch	933	2.1
5	Hatton Sumners		
6	Luther Johnson		
	North		
7	Tom Pickett		
	Nat Patton		
	Brannen		
8	Albert Thomas		
9	Joseph Mansfield		
	Barron		
	Ben H. Faber		
	Chalres L. Krueger		
	L. J. Sulak		
10	Lyndon Johnson		
11	W. R. Poage	25912	70.6
	A. Judson Henderson	4440	12.1
	Walter D. Hardin	6349	17.3
12	Fritz Lanham		
	O. A. Cole		
	Clory Cole		
	Virgil Goodman		
	F. E. Harrington		
	John J. Connolly		
	F. E. Corey		
13	Ed Gossett		
	George Moffett		
14	John E. Lyle		
15	Milton West		
16	R. Ewing Thomason	unopposed	100.0
17	Sam Russell		
	Clyde Garrett		
	Fitzgerald		

District	Candidate	Votes	%
18	Eugene Worley		
19	George Mahon		
20	Paul J. Kilday		
21	O. C. Fisher		

No Republican Primary Election was held in 1944.

The elections were close enough in the races for the 7th, 9th, and 17th district seats that runoff elections were held on August 26, 1944.

1944 DEMOCRATIC PRIMARY RUNOFF ELECTION (JULY 22)

District	Candidate	Votes
7	Tom Pickett	20433
	Nat Patton	16050
9	Joseph Mansfield	15031
	L. J. Sulak	13862
17	Sam Russell	17660
	Clyde Garrett	13881

1944 GENERAL ELECTION (NOVEMBER 7)

District	Candidate	Votes	%
1	Wright Patman, Democrat	39,404	100.0
	Other	3	0.0
2	Jesse M. Combs, Democrat	54,258	94.0
	Lamar Cecil, Republican	3,442	6.0
	Other	9	0.0
3	Lindley Beckworth, Democrat	36,954	93.3
	O. P. Stephens, Republican	2,668	6.7
4	Sam Rayburn, Democrat	40,039	100.0
	Other	4	0.0
5	Hatton Sumners, Democrat	62,459	71.4
	Charles D. Turner, Republican	25,027	28.6
6	Luther Johnson, Democrat	36,884	100.0
	Charles W. Beck, Republican (deceased)	7	0.0
	Other	7	0.0
7	Tom Pickett, Democrat	32,850	96.1
	J. Perrin Willis, Republican	1,328	3.9
	Other	1	0.0
8	Albert Thomas, Democrat	90,963	92.3
	—— Wagstaff	7,555	7.7
	Lester B. Robinson, Republican		
9	Joseph Mansfield, Democrat	56,194	93.4
	Lewis Allen, Republican	3,967	6.6
	Other	23	0.0
10	Lyndon Johnson, Democrat	44,602	92.9
	Arthur H. Bartel, Republican	3,423	7.1
	Other	2	0.0
11	W. R. Poage, Democrat	39,866	95.3
	Charles R. Nelson, Republican	1,968	4.8
	Other	4	0.0
12	Fritz Lanham, Democrat	59,119	100.0
13	Ed Gossett, Democrat	53,503	95.4
	L. C. Harper, Republican	2,586	4.6
	Other	10	0.0
14	John E. Lyle, Democrat	53,756	100.0
	Other	10	0.0
15	Milton West, Democrat	35,862	100.0
	Other	5	0.0
16	R. Ewing Thomason, Democrat	31,658	100.0
	Other	8	0.0
17	Sam Russell, Democrat	43,785	96.8
	Clifton Woody, Republican	1,468	3.2
	Other	7	0.0
18	Eugene Worley, Democrat	47,638	93.3
	McD. C. Bybee, Republican	3,435	6.7
	Other	4	0.0
19	George Mahon, Democrat	53,326	100.0
	Other	5	0.0
20	Paul J. Kilday, Democrat	39,394	100.0
21	O. C. Fisher, Democrat	47,796	88.1
	Maurice J. Lehman, Republican	6,474	11.9

1946 SPECIAL ELECTION (AUGUST 24)

District	Candidate	Votes	%
6	Olin Teague, Democrat	36,365	100.0
	Tom Tyson	1	0.0

This special election was held to fill the seat of Luther Johnson, who resigned on July 17, 1946, to accept a federal judgeship.

1946 DEMOCRATIC PRIMARY ELECTION (JULY 27)

District	Candidate	Votes	%
1	Wright Patman	39,818	74.0
	Henry L. Ray	13,954	26.0
2	Jesse M. Combs	45,031	70.9
	G. M. Stephens	7,774	12.2
	Hugh A. Wilson	10,683	16.8
	H. G. Hendrick	2	0.0
	—— Gresham	6	0.0
	W. Tom Keene	1	0.0
3	Lindley Beckworth	29,519	50.3
	D. S. Meredith	12,859	21.9
	Earl Roberts	16,282	27.8
4	Sam Rayburn	48,929	100.0
5	J. Frank Wilson	18,512	32.6
	William Burrow	9,492	16.7
	W. C. Graves	6,674	11.8
	Sarah T. Hughes	19,820	35.0
	Preston Pope Reynolds	2,172	3.8
6	Olin Teague	10,872	22.2
	Joe Crowley	7,315	14.9
	Lynn B. Griffith	10,517	21.4
	H. Fountain Kirby	7,172	14.6
	Tom Tyson	13,198	26.9
7	Tom Pickett	54,092	100.0
8	Albert Thomas	54,511	68.1
	Bert Horne	25,502	31.9
9	Joseph Mansfield	20,601	33.6
	C. E. Forester, Jr.	1,800	2.9
	Clyde B. Kennelly	3,586	5.8
	Clark W. Thompson	16,364	26.7
	Ben H. Faber	1,553	2.5
	L. J. Sulak	17,435	23.5
10	Lyndon Johnson	42,980	68.0
	Hardy Hollers	17,782	28.1
	Charles E. King	2,468	3.9
11	W. R. Poage	50,378	100.0
12	Wingate Lucas	14,645	22.2
	H. C. Allison	2,575	3.9
	Lindsey M. Brown	1,467	2.2
	Byron Buckeridge	3,567	5.4
	Clory F. Cole	7,450	11.3
	Goldman S. Drury	5,309	8.1
	Ernest O. Gillam	7,020	10.7
	A. E. Harding	1,026	1.6
	Penn J. Jackson	13,743	20.9
	Ernest May	7,089	10.8
	Curtis McBroom	989	1.5
13	Walter A. Nelson	1,032	1.6
	Ed Gossett	36,557	60.2
	John R. Good	3,551	5.9
	Houston McMurray	12,992	21.4
	Mack Taylor	7,477	12.3
14	John E. Lyle	67,197	100.0
15	Richard Kleberg	1	0.0
	Milton West	21,156	50.0
	J. T. Ellis, Jr.	13,819	32.7
	William Henry Yaeger, Jr.	7,325	17.3
16	R. Ewing Thomason	23,948	73.6
	Pat Hargrove	8,599	26.4
17	Omar Burleson	9,450	17.3
	William W. Blanton	10,213	18.7
	Byron B. Bradbury	6,926	12.7
	Gilbert Sandefer	4,901	9.0
	R. M. Wagstaff	5,372	9.8
	Robert B. Herring	7,905	14.4
	Nina J. Hendrick	2,661	4.9
	Ted Moles	7,316	13.4
18	Eugene Worley	57,006	100.0
	Torchie Mitchell	2	0.0
19	George Mahon	44,508	62.3
	Hop Halsey	2,688	37.7
20	Paul J. Kilday	24,762	65.1

	Jack Davis	13,246	34.9
21	O. C. Fisher	56,476	100.0

No Republican Primary Election was held in 1946. The elections were close enough in the races for the 5th, 9th, 12th, 15th, and 17th district seats that runoff elections were held on August 24, 1946.

1946 DEMOCRATIC PRIMARY RUNOFF ELECTION (AUGUST 24)

5	J. Frank Wilson	37,206	61.2
	Sarah T. Hughes	23,590	38.8
9	Joseph Mansfield	29,942	53.1
	L. J. Sulak	26,438	46.9
12	Wingate Lucas	30,312	51.1
	Penn J. Jackson	29,044	48.9
15	Milton West	22,044	50.8
	J. T. Ellis, Jr.	21,355	49.2
17	Omar Burleson	27,022	56.4
	William W. Blanton	20,856	43.6

1946 GENERAL ELECTION (NOVEMBER 5)

1	Wright Patman, Democrat	11,929	100.0
2	Jesse M. Combs, Democrat	19,909	96.2
	Don Parker, Republican	793	3.8
	Other	2	0.0
3	Lindley Beckworth, Democrat	10,686	100.0
	Other	2	0.0
4	Sam Rayburn, Democrat	11,957	93.7
	Floyd Harry, Republican	800	6.3
	Other	4	0.0
5	J. Frank Wilson, Democrat	12,267	75.8
	Lewis W. Stayart, Republican	3,921	24.2
6	Olin Teague, Democrat	9,221	100.0
7	Tom Pickett, Democrat	14,810	100.0
	Other	1	0.0
8	Albert Thomas, Democrat	42,163	90.8
	Richard F. Burns, Republican	4,253	9.2
9	Joseph Mansfield, Democrat	16,712	100.0

	Other	7	0.0
10	Lyndon Johnson, Democrat	16,947	100.0
11	W. R. Poage, Democrat	9,178	100.0
12	Wingate Lucas, Democrat	15,266	87.7
	Elton M. Hyder, Republican	2,146	12.3
13	Ed Gossett, Democrat	17,714	100.0
	Other	4	0.0
14	John E. Lyle, Democrat	30,064	100.0
	Other	6	0.0
15	Milton West, Democrat	16,674	100.0
	Other	3	0.0
16	R. Ewing Thomason, Democrat	8,114	100.0
17	Omar Burleson, Democrat	14,874	100.0
18	Eugene Worley, Democrat	11,869	74.1
	Frank T. O'Brien, Republican	4,180	25.9
19	George Mahon, Democrat	15,821	94.6
	Mohler D. Temple, Republican	905	5.4
20	Paul J. Kilday, Democrat	10,543	100.0
21	O. C. Fisher, Democrat	15,943	100.0

1947 SPECIAL ELECTION (AUGUST 23)

9	Clark Thompson, Democrat	15,495	45.8
	L. J. Sulak, Democrat	11,124	32.9
	J. C. Trahan, Democrat	4,397	13.0
	George W. Hill	1,960	5.8
	V. M. Stokes	315	0.9
	Morris Schrieber	287	0.9
	Ben H. Farber	144	0.4
	Robert H. Abell	84	0.3
	George P. Barron	41	0.1
	Donald Markle	1	0.0
	Ed Kissling	1	0.0
	J. I. Toothaker	1	0.0
	Jack Dentin	1	0.0
16	Ken Regan, Democrat	6,932	43.5
	Woodrow W. Bean, Democrat	6,109	38.3

Victor B. Gilbert, Democrat — 1,350 — 8.5
Ord Gary, Democrat — 1,015 — 6.4
Louis A. Fail, Democrat — 322 — 2.0
James W. Metcalf, Democrat — 122 — 0.8
Pat Hargrove, Democrat — 87 — 0.6

This special election was held to fill the seat of Joe Mansfield, who died on July 12, 1947, and Ewing Thomason, who resigned on July 31, 1947, to accept a federal judgeship.

1948 Democratic Primary Election (July 24)

Dist.	Candidate	Votes	%
1	Wright Patman	37,614	63.3
	Goebel Templeton	7,891	13.4
	Ben Woodall	12,181	20.7
	F. G. Cloninger	496	0.8
	Isom P. Hydrick, Jr.	1,003	1.7
2	Jesse M. Combs	48,475	72.4
	Hugh Wilson	8,831	13.2
	G. M. Stephens	9,587	14.3
	W. R. Beaumier	85	0.1
3	Lindley Beckworth	55,255	100.0
4	Sam Rayburn	31,677	63.0
	G. C. Morris	12,292	24.4
	David Brown	6,310	12.5
5	J. Frank Wilson	42,336	67.6
	William O. Cooper	20,246	32.4
6	Olin Teague	unopposed	100.0
7	Tom Pickett	23,537	45.7
	Burke T. Summers	5,915	11.5
	Nat Patton	22,088	42.9
8	Albert Thomas	68,706	70.2
	Charles Murphy	29,228	29.8
9	Clark Thompson	58,797	100.0
10	Homer Thornberry	23,256	39.1
	Creekmore Fath	11,063	18.6
	Magnesse L. Foster	375	0.6
	W. K. McClain	10,804	18.1
	James A. Stanford	8,655	14.5
	O. P. Lockhart	5,386	9.0
11	W. R. Poage	50,260	100.0
12	Wingate Lucas	37,841	61.1
	John H. Elkins	3,115	5.0
	W. O. Asch	2,021	3.3
	Ernest O. Gillam	18,912	30.6
13	Ed Gossett	44,987	77.3
	Mrs. Edith Wilmans	13,239	22.7
14	John E. Lyle	51,651	79.7
	Morris Knight	13,183	20.3
15	Lloyd Bentsen, Jr.	18,913	34.8
	Augustine Celaya	7,787	14.3
	J. T. Ellis, Jr.	11,586	12.9
	Philip A. Kazen	16,042	29.5
16	Ken Regan	27,540	59.8
	Woodrow Wilson Bean	18,484	40.2
17	Omar Burleson	51,954	100.0
18	Eugene Worley	60,459	99.9
	other	68	0.1
19	George Mahon	70,752	100.0
20	Paul J. Kilday	32,701	63.2
	Woodville J. Rogers	19,037	36.8
21	O. C. Fisher	33,919	58.0
	Howell E. Cobb	11,195	19.1
	Charles L. South	13,362	22.9

No Republican Primary Election was held in 1948.

The elections were close enough in the races for the 7th, 10th, and 15th district seats that runoff elections were held on August 28, 1948.

1948 Democratic Primary Runoff Election (August 28)

Dist.	Candidate	Votes	%
7	Tom Pickett	25,807	55.7
	Nat Patton	20,556	44.3
10	Homer Thornberry	33,318	59.9
	W. K. McClain	22,318	40.1
15	Lloyd Bentsen, Jr.	31,801	59.6
	Philip A. Kazen	21,533	40.0

1948 GENERAL ELECTION (NOVEMBER 2)

1	Wright Patman, Democrat	40,162	100.0
2	Jesse M. Combs, Democrat	55,072	93.3
	Don Parker, Republican	3,978	6.7
3	Lindley Beckworth, Democrat	36,361	88.7
	R. E. Kennedy, Republican	4,642	11.3
4	Sam Rayburn, Democrat	38,211	100.0
5	J. Frank Wilson, Democrat	66,484	98.4
	Joe Bailey Irwin, Progressive	1,060	1.6
6	Olin Teague, Democrat	18,731	99.8
	J. Hayden Moore, Sr., Progressive	33	0.2
7	Tom Pickett, Democrat	27,945	100.0
8	Albert Thomas, Democrat	100,721	85.5
	Joe Ingraham, Republican	17,124	14.5
9	Clark Thompson, Democrat	55,606	100.0
10	Homer Thornberry, Democrat	45,007	100.0
11	W. R. Poage, Democrat	40,795	96.3
	A. A. Warrington, Republican	1,558	3.7
12	Wingate Lucas, Democrat	61,206	89.1
	Eldon M. Hyder, Republican	7,480	10.9
13	Ed Gossett, Democrat	44,274	100.0
14	John E. Lyle, Democrat	59,163	88.9
	James M. Swafford, Republican	7,262	10.9
	Tom Neal, Progressive	158	0.2
15	Lloyd Bentsen, Jr., Democrat	27,402	100.0
16	Ken Regan, Democrat	37,173	99.5
	J. B. Chavez, Progressive	198	0.5
17	Omar Burleson, Democrat	34,078	100.0
18	Eugene Worley, Democrat	48,985	88.7
	J. Everts Haley, Republican	6,266	11.3
19	George Mahon, Democrat	58,585	95.6
	Mohler D. Temple, Republican	2,724	4.4
20	Paul J. Kilday, Democrat	43,709	75.3
	J. P. Ledvina, Republican	14,376	24.8
21	O. C. Fisher, Democrat	45,274	100.0

1948 SPECIAL ELECTION (DECEMBER 4)

15	Lloyd Bentsen, Jr., Democrat	2,396	100.0
	Charles McNelly (write-in)	1	0.0

This special election was held to fill the seat of the late Milton West, who had died just before the November general election. Bentsen was elected to fill the remainder of the late Milton West's seat for the December session of Congress.

1950 SPECIAL ELECTION (MAY 6)

18	Ben H. Guill, Republican	7,717	23.2
	Mrs. Altavene Clark, Democrat	5,702	17.1
	J. Blake Timmons, Democrat	5,083	15.3
	Walter Rogers, Democrat	4,979	14.9
	LeRoy "Pete" LeMaster, Democrat	3,288	9.9
	Ronald Davis, Democrat	2,539	7.6
	E. T. Burk, Democrat	2,192	6.6
	Talma Smith, Democrat	1,080	3.2
	Ben Pickel, Democrat	447	1.3
	W. W. Montgomery, Democrat	195	0.6
	Hule H. Bice, Democrat	98	0.3

This Special Election was held to fill the seat of Eugene Worley, who resigned from Congress on April 3, 1950. Guill received 7,717 votes, winning plurality over the field of eleven candidates. He was the first Republican congressman elected from Texas in twenty-four years.

1950 DEMOCRATIC PRIMARY ELECTION (JULY 22)

1	Wright Patman	31,803	68.6
	Abe M. Mays	14,567	31.4
2	Jesse M. Combs	39,829	62.8
	Price Rodgers	39,829	28.5
	Hugh Wilson	5,507	8.7
3	Lindley Beckworth	40,434	81.5
	E. A. Martin	9,151	18.5
4	Sam Rayburn	40,007	100.0
5	J. Frank Wilson	29,120	65.8
	James J. Jeffries	15,135	34.2
6	Olin Teague	16,249	100.0
7	Tom Pickett	31,441	63.9
	Roger A. Knight	4,581	9.3

District	Candidate	Votes	%
	J. S. Holleman	13,151	26.7
8	Albert Thomas	83,610	100.0
9	Clark Thompson	46,523	81.2
	Dan M. Kimbrough	10,754	18.8
10	Homer Thornberry	40,165	90.6
	Magnesse L. Foster	4,167	9.4
11	W. R. Poage	29,789	66.0
	Mrs. Tom E. Travis	4,956	11.0
	Richard C. Bush	5,386	11.9
	John L. Bates	5,009	11.1
12	Wingate Lucas	31,458	64.9
	F. M. Lanham	6,238	12.9
	John B. "Roscoe" Pierce	10,786	22.2
13	Ed Gossett	46,424	85.4
	Mrs. Edith Wilmans	7,966	14.6
14	John E. Lyle	73,956	100.0
15	Lloyd Bentsen, Jr.	54,901	100.0
16	Ken Regan	22,244	45.2
	Fred Hervey	8,971	18.2
	Paul Moss	18,034	36.6
17	Omar Burleson	45,866	100.0
18	Mrs. Altavene Clark	15,924	30.1
	Blake Timmons	10,373	19.6
	Walter Rogers	13,712	28.9
	LeRoy "Pete" LeMaster	12,956	24.5
19	George Mahon	54,979	89.2
	Anton Mike Phipps	6,681	10.8
20	Paul J. Kilday	37,327	100.0
21	O. C. Fisher	53,898	100.0

No Republican Primary Election was held in 1950.
The elections were close enough in the races for the 16th and 18th district seats that runoff elections were held on August 26, 1950.

1950 DEMOCRATIC PRIMARY RUNOFF (AUGUST 26)

District	Candidate	Votes	%
16	Ken Regan	21,167	55.0
	Paul Moss	17,303	45.0
18	Mrs. Altavene Clark	14,895	40.8
	Walter Rogers	21,653	59.2

1950 GENERAL ELECTION (NOVEMBER 7)

District	Candidate	Votes	%
1	Wright Patman, Democrat	12,444	100.0
2	Jesse M. Combs, Democrat	16,900	100.0
3	Lindley Beckworth, Democrat	11,784	91.1
	R. E. Kennedy, Republican	1,145	8.9
4	Sam Rayburn, Democrat	11,546	100.0
5	J. Frank Wilson, Democrat	23,568	100.0
6	Olin Teague, Democrat	8,118	98.1
	Mose R. Blumrosen, Republican	159	1.9
7	Tom Pickett, Democrat	12,537	100.0
8	Albert Thomas, Democrat	19,068	77.8
	B. F. Hanna, Republican	5,427	22.2
9	Clark Thompson, Democrat	20,200	100.0
10	Homer Thornberry, Democrat	13,703	100.0
11	W. R. Poage, Democrat	10,573	100.0
12	Wingate Lucas, Democrat	13,179	80.7
	Harold G. Neely, Republican	3,162	19.4
13	Ed Gossett, Democrat	14,761	100.0
14	John E. Lyle, Democrat	31,201	100.0
15	Lloyd Bentsen, Jr., Democrat	18,524	100.0
16	Ken Regan, Democrat	8,828	100.0
17	Omar Burleson, Democrat	10,228	100.0
18	Walter Rogers, Democrat	25,666	52.5
	Ben H. Guill, Republican	23,259	47.5
19	George Mahon, Democrat	17,828	93.9
	Mohler D. Temple, Republican	1,162	6.1
20	Paul J. Kilday, Democrat	9,138	100.0
21	O. C. Fisher, Democrat	16,334	100.0

1951 SPECIAL ELECTION (SEPTEMBER 8)

District	Candidate	Votes	%
13	Frank Ikard, Democrat	8,970	31.0
	Walter Jenkins, Democrat	5,363	18.5
	Joe Jackson, Republican	5,101	17.6
	Wayne W. Wagonseller, Democrat	4,225	14.6

William D. McFarlane, Democrat	2,786	9.6
Doug Crouch	2,423	8.4
Edith E. Wilmans, Democrat	60	0.2
James A. Stephens, Democrat	41	0.1

This special election was held to fill the seat of Ed Gossett, who resigned on June 30, 1952. Ikard received 8,970 votes, winning plurality of the field of six candidates.

1952 DEMOCRATIC PRIMARY ELECTION (JULY 26)

1	Wright Patman	41,174	67.0
	Joe McCasland	20,288	33.0
2	Joe H. Tonahill	20,954	25.6
	Jack Brooks	15,826	19.3
	M. T. Banks, Sr.	2,138	2.6
	Walter M. Casey	9,430	11.5
	Julian P. Green	4,872	6.0
	Benjamin M. Harrison	6,193	7.6
	De Witt Kinard	8,166	10.0
	Jack Neil	12,612	15.4
	G. M. Stephens	1,663	2.0
3	Brady Gentry	30,560	50.0
	J. O. Duncan, Jr.	5,216	8.5
	Fred Whitaker	9,102	14.9
	R. L. Whitehead	9,121	14.9
	Alton D. Wood	7,153	11.7
4	Sam Rayburn	29,844	66.0
	Reagan Brown	15,360	34.0
5	J. Frank Wilson	unopposed	100.0
6	Olin Teague	unopposed	100.0
7	John Dowdy	14,274	28.8
	Joe Griggs	10,122	20.4
	Roger Knight	2,841	5.7
	Jim Norton	10,674	21.5
	William J. Robison, Jr.	1,225	2.5
	Jack Wisener	10,468	21.1
8	Albert Thomas	unopposed	100.0
9	Clark Thompson	31,183	40.3
	T. W. "Buckshot" Lane	29,321	37.9

	James B. Pattison	16,897	21.8
	Homer Thornberry	unopposed	100.0
10	W. R. Poage	37,776	77.4
11	Mrs. Tom Travis	11,058	22.6
12	Wingate Lucas	50,036	68.6
	Jim C. Mason	22,861	31.4
13	Frank Ikard	unopposed	100.0
14	John E. Lyle	52,582	72.7
	Joe C. Blacknall, Jr.	19,697	27.3
15	Lloyd Bentsen, Jr.	30,057	50.4
	Jack Cox	29,622	49.6
	Write-in	1	0.0
16	Ken Regan	unopposed	100.0
17	Omar Burleson	unopposed	100.0
18	Walter Rogers	57,433	100.0
	Write-in	2	0.0
19	George Mahon	unopposed	100.0
20	Paul J. Kilday	29,216	100.0
	Write-ins	4	0.0
21	O. C. Fisher	38,822	65.3
	Ira Gallaway	20,591	34.7
At-Large	*Martin Dies	612,840	49.9
	Charles M. Dickson	86,282	0.7
	Phil Hamburger	104,913	8.5
	Edwin O. Nimitz	65,595	5.3
	Herb Petry, Jr.	97,149	7.9
	Roy Selman	42,904	3.5
	John Lee Smith	217,784	17.7

No Republican Primary Election was held in 1952.

* John Lee Smith won the right to a runoff election with Martin Dies but withdrew from the race and no runoff was held.

The elections were close enough in the races for the 2nd, 3rd, 7th, and 9th district seats that runoff elections were held on August 23, 1952.

1952 DEMOCRATIC PRIMARY RUNOFF (AUGUST 23)

2	Joe H. Tonahill	28,572	49.6

1952 Democratic Primary Election (continued)

District	Candidate	Votes	%
	Jack Brooks	28,986	50.4
3	Brady Gentry	31,992	80.3
	R. L. Whitehead	7,859	19.7
7	John Dowdy	20,376	57.7
	Jim Norton	14,925	42.3
9	Clark Thompson	29,908	50.2
	T. W. "Buckshot" Lane	29,690	49.8
At-Large	Martin Dies	600,494	100.0

1952 SPECIAL ELECTION (SEPTEMBER 23)

District	Candidate	Votes	%
7	John Dowdy, Democrat	4,646	88.5
	Jack Weisener	366	7.0
	Jim Norton	237	4.5
	Joe Griggs	1	0.0

This special election was held to fill the seat of Tom Pickett, who resigned on July 31, 1952. Dowdy was elected after the end of the 82nd Congress. He was elected in November 1952 for the 83rd Congress.

1952 GENERAL ELECTION (NOVEMBER 4)

District	Candidate	Votes	%
1	Wright Patman, Democrat	56,491	100.0
2	Jack Brooks, Democrat	83,267	79.0
	Randolph C. Reed, Republican	22,108	21.0
3	Brady Gentry, Democrat	57,033	100.0
4	Sam Rayburn, Democrat	47,888	100.0
5	J. Frank Wilson, Democrat	172,539	100.0
6	Olin Teague, Democrat	49,461	100.0
7	John Dowdy, Democrat	52,410	100.0
8	Albert Thomas, Democrat	200,608	100.0
9	Clark Thompson, Democrat	96,214	100.0
10	Homer Thornberry, Democrat	65,944	100.0
11	W. R. Poage, Democrat	59,088	100.0
12	Wingate Lucas, Democrat	101,964	100.0
13	Frank Ikard, Democrat	72,373	100.0
14	John E. Lyle, Democrat	94,866	100.0
15	Lloyd Bentsen, Jr., Democrat	63,723	100.0
16	Ken Regan, Democrat	67,782	100.0
17	Omar Burleson, Democrat	59,386	100.0
18	Walter Rogers, Democrat	77,661	100.0
19	George Mahon, Democrat	87,894	100.0
20	Paul J. Kilday, Democrat	64,841	100.0
21	O. C. Fisher, Democrat	65,762	100.0
At-Large	Martin Dies, Democrat	1,514,796	76.5
	Martin Dies, Republican	464,472	23.5
	Martin Dies, no party	621	0.0

1954 DEMOCRATIC PRIMARY ELECTION (JULY 24)

District	Candidate	Votes	%
1	Wright Patman	32,243	24.7
	Kenneth W. Simmons	22,870	17.5
	Douglas E. Wright	4,013	3.1
2	Jack Brooks	unopposed	100.0
	Jack Niel	unknown, may have withdrawn	
3	Brady Gentry	32,067	51.1
	Lindley Beckworth	30,721	48.9
4	Sam Rayburn	30,818	75.3
	A. G. McRae	10,124	24.7
5	Wallace Savage	25,768	42.4
	Leslie Hacker	13,365	22.0
	Dick Connolly	10,712	17.6
	Lamar Holley	5,567	9.2
	Leslie Jackson	5,333	8.7
6	Olin Teague	unopposed	100.0
7	John Dowdy	unopposed	100.0
8	Albert Thomas	unopposed	100.0
9	Clark Thompson	49,780	66.4
	Clyde B. Kennelly	25,146	33.6
10	Homer Thornberry	unopposed	100.0
11	W. R. Poage	unopposed	100.0
12	Jim Wright	44,738	59.4
	Wingate Lucas	30,579	40.6
13	Frank Ikard	unopposed	100.0

District	Candidate	Votes	%
14	John J. Bell	31,057	39.9
	William H. Shireman	23,936	30.7
	Gabe Garrett	16,457	21.1
	Roy A. Scott	6,291	8.1
	D. C. DeWitt	134	0.2
15	Joe M. Kilgore	30,009	52.7
	Hubert R. Hudson	26,939	47.3
16	J. T. Rutherford	25,213	50.1
	Ken Regan	25,064	49.9
	Write-in	1	0.0
17	Omar Burleson	unopposed	100.0
18	Walter Rogers	48,665	85.5
	Michael M. Kemp	4,574	8.0
	George W. Crawford	3,690	6.5
	Write-ins	17	0.0
19	George Mahon	unopposed	100.0
20	Paul J. Kilday	unopposed	100.0
21	O. C. Fisher	37,600	67.0
	Sam Connally	18,518	33.0
At-Large	Martin Dies	1,161,201	100.0
	Write-in	1	0.0

1954 REPUBLICAN PRIMARY ELECTION (JULY 24)

District	Candidate	Votes	%
1	(none)		
2	(none)		
3	(none)		
4	(none)		
5	Bruce Alger	unopposed	100.0
6	(none)		
7	(none)		
8	William B. Butler		
	Jerry McAfee		
9	(none)		
10	(none)		
11	(none)		
12	Tom S. Christopher		
13	(none)		
14	D. C. DeWitt		
15	(none)		
16	(none)		
17	(none)		
18	Leroy LeMaster	unopposed	
19	(none)		
20	(none)		
21	(none)		
At-Large	Tom Nolan	9,238	100.0

The elections were close enough in the races for the 5th and 14th district seats that runoff elections were held on August 24, 1954.

1954 DEMOCRATIC PRIMARY RUNOFF ELECTION (AUGUST 24)

District	Candidate	Votes	%
5	Wallace Savage	52,442	56.1
	Leslie Hacker	41,110	43.9
14	John J. Bell	44,506	54.9
	William H. Shireman	36,501	45.1

1954 GENERAL ELECTION (NOVEMBER 2)

District	Candidate	Votes	%
1	Wright Patman, Democrat	18,104	100.0
2	Jack Brooks, Democrat	25,008	100.0
3	Brady Gentry, Democrat	20,767	100.0
4	Sam Rayburn, Democrat	15,177	100.0
5	Bruce Alger, Republican	27,982	52.9
	Wallace Savage, Democrat	24,904	47.1
6	Olin Teague, Democrat	15,161	100.0
7	John Dowdy, Democrat	18,361	100.0
8	Albert Thomas, Democrat	60,374	62.1
	William B. Butler, Republican	36,405	37.4
	B. F. Hanna, Constitution	481	0.5
9	Clark Thompson, Democrat	29,952	100.0
10	Homer Thornberry, Democrat	23,752	100.0
11	W. R. Poage, Democrat	17,739	100.0
12	Jim Wright, Democrat	35,611	98.8

District	Candidate	Votes	%
	Tom S. Christopher, Republican	420	1.2
13	Frank Ikard, Democrat	25,085	100.0
14	John J. Bell, Democrat	36,284	93.8
	D. C. DeWitt, Republican	2,384	6.2
15	Joe M. Kilgore, Democrat	29,113	100.0
16	J. T. Rutherford, Democrat	25,122	100.0
17	Omar Burleson, Democrat	18,484	100.0
18	Walter Rogers, Democrat	25,430	64.9
	Leroy LeMaster, Republican	13,756	35.1
19	George Mahon, Democrat	26,829	100.0
20	Paul J. Kilday, Democrat	23,533	100.0
21	O. C. Fisher, Democrat	25,381	100.0
At-Large	Martin Dies, Democrat/Republican	555,446	88.0
	Tom Nolan, Republican	75,472	12.0

1956 Democratic Primary Election (July 28)

District	Candidate	Votes	%
1	Kenneth W. Simmons	24,594	37.5
	Wright Patman	41,077	62.5
2	Melvin Combs	34,926	36.9
	Jack Brooks	59,643	63.1
3	Lindley Beckworth	37,578	58.6
	R. E. "Peppy" Blount	26,570	41.4
4	Sam Rayburn	43,394	100.0
5	Henry Wade	66,291	100.0
6	Olin Teague	43,566	100.0
7	Gilbert Spring	17,911	34.3
	John Dowdy	34,362	65.7
8	Albert Thomas	82,317	100.0
9	Jerome L. Korenek	15,342	18.9
	Clark Thompson	65,844	81.1
10	Homer Thornberry	68,257	100.0
11	W. R. Poage	101,896	100.0
12	Jim Wright	83,406	100.0
13	Frank Ikard	59,826	100.0
14	John J. Bell	32,488	38.1
	John Young	52,774	61.9
15	Joe M. Kilgore	60,298	100.0
16	William W. Blanton	18,340	31.1
	J. T. Rutherford	40,696	68.9
17	Dan Kralis	14,915	27.6
	Omar Burleson	39,126	72.4
18	Walter Rogers	54,207	100.0
19	George Mahon	74,754	100.0
20	Paul J. Kilday	53,387	100.0
21	O. C. Fisher	56,591	100.0
At-Large	Martin Dies	905,685	67.4
	Bill Elkins	438,684	32.6

There was no Republican Primary Election held in 1956.

1956 General Election (November 6)

District	Candidate	Votes	%
1	Wright Patman, Democrat	54,837	100.0
2	Jack Brooks, Democrat	81,343	100.0
3	Lindley Beckworth, Democrat	47,570	83.5
	R. E. Kennedy, Republican	9,402	16.5
4	Sam Rayburn, Democrat	41,867	100.0
5	Bruce Alger, Republican	102,380	55.6
	Henry Wade, Democrat	81,705	44.4
6	Olin Teague, Democrat	42,383	100.0
7	John Dowdy, Democrat	44,456	100.0
8	Albert Thomas, Democrat	137,950	60.5
	C. Anthony Friloux, Jr., Republican	86,640	38.0
	W. C. "Doc" Miller, Constitution	3,619	1.6
9	Clark Thompson, Democrat	88,467	100.0
10	Homer Thornberry, Democrat	68,697	100.0
11	W. R. Poage, Democrat	56,990	100.0
12	Jim Wright, Democrat	110,196	100.0
13	Frank Ikard, Democrat	66,108	100.0
14	John Young, Democrat	85,922	87.3
	Olive B. Stichter, Republican	12,517	12.7
15	Joe M. Kilgore, Democrat	64,011	100.0
16	J. T. Rutherford, Democrat	50,704	64.6

District	Candidate	Votes	Percent
	Charles H. Gibson, Republican	27,821	35.4
17	Omar Burleson, Democrat	53,003	100.0
18	Walter Rogers, Democrat	75,243	100.0
19	George Mahon, Democrat	85,566	100.0
20	Paul J. Kilday, Democrat	67,707	100.0
21	O. C. Fisher, Democrat	60,344	100.0
22	Bob Casey	39,313	63.0
	Rolland Bradley	3,043	4.9
	George W. Eddy	13,074	20.9
	Roy B. Oakes	6,994	11.2
At-Large	Martin Dies, Democrat/Republican	1,436,830	98.5
	Fred T. Spangler, Constitution	21,868	1.5

1958 DEMOCRATIC PRIMARY ELECTION (JULY 26)

District	Candidate	Votes	Percent
1	Wright Patman		100.0
2	Jack Brooks		100.0
3	Lindley Beckworth	35,551	60.5
	Fred Hudson	23,246	39.5
4	Sam Rayburn		100.0
5	Barefoot Sanders	46,422	53.7
	Joe Pool	35,668	41.3
	James M. Shepard	4,298	5.0
6	Olin Teague		100.0
7	John Dowdy	30,457	71.5
	E. A. Stanfield	12,138	28.5
8	Albert Thomas		100.0
9	Clark Thompson		100.0
10	Homer Thornberry		100.0
11	W. R. Poage		100.0
12	Jim Wright	55,812	100.0
13	Frank Ikard		100.0
14	John Young		100.0
15	Joe M. Kilgore		100.0
16	J. T. Rutherford		100.0
17	Omar Burleson		100.0
18	Walter Rogers		100.0
19	George Mahon		100.0
20	Paul J. Kilday		100.0
21	O. C. Fisher		100.0

1958 REPUBLICAN PRIMARY ELECTION (JULY 26)

District	Candidate	Votes	Percent
1	(none)		
2	(none)		
3	(none)		
4	(none)		
5	Bruce Alger	9,299	98.9
	Grover Cantrell	101	1.1
6	(none)		
7	Joseph E. A. Ross		
8	(none)		
9	(none)		
10	(none)		
11	(none)		
12	(none)		
13	(none)		
14	(none)		
15	(none)		
16	(none)		
17	(none)		
18	(none)		
19	(none)		
20	(none)		
21	(none)		
22	T. Everton Kennerly		

1958 GENERAL ELECTION (NOVEMBER 4)

District	Candidate	Votes	Percent
1	Wright Patman, Democrat	19,203	100.0
2	Jack Brooks, Democrat	47,092	100.0
3	Lindley Beckworth, Democrat	22,751	100.0
4	Sam Rayburn, Democrat	15,942	100.0
5	Bruce Alger, Republican	62,722	52.6

District	Candidate	Votes	%
	Barefoot Sanders, Democrat	56,566	47.4
6	Olin Teague, Democrat	25,827	100.0
7	John Dowdy, Democrat	22,733	96.7
	Joseph E. A. Ross, Republican	771	3.3
8	Albert Thomas, Democrat	33,393	88.2
	R. E. Nesmith, Republican	4,477	11.8
9	Clark Thompson, Democrat	36,012	100.0
10	Homer Thornberry, Democrat	28,990	100.0
11	W. R. Poage, Democrat	21,898	100.0
12	Jim Wright, Democrat	38,180	100.0
13	Frank Ikard, Democrat	27,671	100.0
14	John Young, Democrat	37,861	100.0
15	Joe M. Kilgore, Democrat	28,404	100.0
16	J. T. Rutherford, Democrat	28,744	100.0
17	Omar Burleson, Democrat	25,123	100.0
18	Walter Rogers, Democrat	34,617	100.0
19	George Mahon, Democrat	29,068	100.0
20	Paul J. Kilday, Democrat	23,539	100.0
21	O. C. Fisher, Democrat	26,497	100.0
22	Bob Casey, Democrat	43,660	61.7
	T. Everton Kennerly, Republican	23,317	33.0
	Jack Gardner, Constitution	3,789	5.4

1960 DEMOCRATIC PRIMARY ELECTION (MAY 7)

District	Candidate	Votes	%
1	Wright Patman	unopposed	100.0
2	Jack Brooks	unopposed	100.0
3	Lindley Beckworth	unopposed	100.0
4	Sam Rayburn	unopposed	100.0
5	Joe Pool	unopposed	100.0
6	W. T. Moore	18,722	33.5
	Olin Teague	37,192	66.5
7	William H. "Bill" Crook	32,724	46.3
	John Dowdy	37,988	53.7
8	Albert Thomas	unopposed	100.0
9	Clark Thompson	unopposed	100.0
10	Homer Thornberry	unopposed	100.0
11	W. R. Poage	unopposed	100.0
12	Jim Wright	unopposed	100.0
13	Frank Ikard	unopposed	100.0
14	Dudley Dougherty	34,798	38.0
	John Young	56,896	62.0
15	John M. Westburg	11,926	19.2
	Joe M. Kilgore	50,117	80.8
16	J. T. Rutherford	unopposed	100.0
17	R. M. Wagstaff	14,509	21.9
	Roy Skaggs	9,403	14.2
	Omar Burleson	42,322	63.9
18	Arthur J. Glover	18,705	26.6
	Walter Rogers	51,692	73.4
19	George Mahon	unopposed	100.0
20	Paul J. Kilday	unopposed	100.0
21	O. C. Fisher	unopposed	100.0
22	Bob Casey	unopposed	100.0

No Republican Primary Election was held in 1960.

1960 GENERAL ELECTION (NOVEMBER 8)

District	Candidate	Votes	%
1	Wright Patman, Democrat	58,674	100.0
2	Jack Brooks, Democrat	75,657	69.7
	Fred S. Neumann, Republican	32,473	29.9
	Robert E. Allen, Constitution	393	0.4
3	Lindley Beckworth, Democrat	59,386	100.0
4	Sam Rayburn, Democrat	44,902	100.0
5	Bruce Alger, Republican	129,886	57.3
	Joe Pool, Democrat	96,709	42.7
6	Olin Teague, Democrat	56,603	100.0
7	John Dowdy, Democrat	61,586	100.0
8	Albert Thomas, Democrat	76,767	68.6
	Anthony J.P. Farris, Republican	24,486	21.9
	Robert E. Nesmith, Constitution	10,684	9.5
9	Clark Thompson, Democrat	95,586	94.3
	Paul D. Rogers, Constitution	5,981	5.7
10	Homer Thornberry, Democrat	75,165	98.1

This special election was held to fill the seat of Frank Ikard, who resigned December 15, 1961. This was in fact an open primary, where a majority was required by a candidate to be declared the winner. Since no candidate received a majority, a runoff was held January 27, 1962.

1961 SPECIAL ELECTION (DECEMBER 23)

4	Ray Roberts, Democrat	8,154	36.9
	R. C. Slagle, Democrat	5,945	26.9
	David Brown, Democrat	2,393	10.8
	Conner Harrington, Republican	2,353	10.6
	Jack Finney, Democrat	2,211	10.0
	Roy Baker, Democrat	1,066	4.8

This special election was held to fill the seat of the Sam Rayburn, who died on November 16, 1961. As in the previous special election, this was an open primary and no clear majority was received by any candidate, so the top two candidates, Roberts and Slagle, ran again in a runoff on January 30, 1962.

1962 SPECIAL ELECTION RUNOFF (JANUARY 27)

| 13 | Graham B. Purcell, Jr., Democrat | 23,905 | 62.9 |
| | Joe Meissner, Republican | 14,098 | 37.1 |

This was the runoff election required since no candidate received a majority in the December 16, 1961, special election to fill the seat of Frank Ikard.

1962 SPECIAL ELECTION RUNOFF (JANUARY 30)

| 4 | Ray Roberts, Democrat | 16,109 | 54.3 |
| | R. C. Slagle, Democrat | 13,572 | 45.7 |

This was the runoff election required since no candidate received a majority in the December 23, 1961, special election to fill the seat of Sam Rayburn.

1962 DEMOCRATIC PRIMARY ELECTION (MAY 5)

1	Wright Patman	34,944	61.4
	Sam B. Hall, Jr.	21,930	38.6
2	Jack Brooks	43,701	58.7
	W. S. Martin, Jr.	21,564	30.0
	Earl B. Stover	9,139	12.3
3	Lindley Beckworth	unopposed	100.0
4	Ray Roberts	unopposed	100.0

	Roy R. Brown, Constitution	1,468	1.9
11	W. R. Poage, Democrat	64,351	100.0
12	Jim Wright, Democrat	115,797	100.0
13	Frank Ikard, Democrat	75,972	100.0
14	John Young, Democrat	105,792	100.0
15	Joe M. Kilgore, Democrat	76,421	100.0
16	J. T. Rutherford, Democrat	63,634	58.9
	Dorothy Wyvell, Constitution	24,996	23.1
	Ford Chapman, Republican	19,491	18.0
17	Omar Burleson, Democrat	60,401	77.6
	Max V. Mossholder, Republican	17,400	22.4
18	Walter Rogers, Democrat	79,675	100.0
19	George Mahon, Democrat	77,415	85.7
	John Richard Anderson, Constitution	12,953	14.3
20	Paul J. Kilday, Democrat	84,487	100.0
21	O. C. Fisher, Democrat	63,277	100.0
22	Bob Casey, Democrat	109,418	58.3
	James Carter Noonan, Republican	73,503	39.2
	D. F. Vancleve, Constitution	4,749	2.5

1961 SPECIAL ELECTION (NOVEMBER 4)

20	Henry B. Gonzalez, Democrat	52,696	54.6
	John Goode, Republican	42,511	44.0
	Ernest T. Cude	818	0.9
	G. H. Allen	300	0.3
	Norman Brock	209	0.2

This special election was held to fill the seat of Paul Kilday, who resigned on September 24, 1961.

1961 SPECIAL ELECTION (NOVEMBER 16)

13	Graham Purcell, Jr., Democrat	8,960	33.6
	Joe Meissner, Republican	6,740	25.3
	Jack Hightower, Democrat	6,157	23.1
	Vernon Stewart, Democrat	2,706	10.2
	Jimmy P. Horany, Democrat	2,076	7.8

Dist.	Candidate	Votes	%
5	Bill Jones	41,216	
	Baxton Bryant	40,946	
	Robert K. Sutton		
6	Olin Teague	unopposed	100.0
7	John Dowdy	31,230	50.0
	Benton Musselwhite	31,189	50.0
8	Albert Thomas	unopposed	100.0
9	Clark Thompson	44,650	55.4
	Austen H. Forse	17,397	21.6
	Jim Simpson	14,032	17.4
	Bronko Popovich	4,471	5.6
10	Homer Thornberry		
	Paul W. Stimson		
11	W. R. Poage	unopposed	100.0
12	Jim Wright	unopposed	100.0
13	Graham Purcell	unopposed	100.0
14	John Young	unopposed	100.0
15	Joe M. Kilgore	unopposed	100.0
16	J. T. Rutherford	28,902	51.7
	Robert Frias	6,880	12.3
	Dr. W. D. Kelley	8,167	14.6
	Tom Diamond	11,949	21.4
17	Omar Burleson	unopposed	100.0
18	Walter Rogers	unopposed	100.0
19	George Mahon	unopposed	100.0
20	Henry B. Gonzalez	unopposed	100.0
21	O. C. Fisher	unopposed	100.0
22	Bob Casey	58,096	68.5
	Claude E. Hooten, Jr.	26,698	31.5
At-Large	Joe Pool	226,515	19.2
	Woodrow W. Bean	249,847	21.1
	Manley Head	161,521	13.7
	Warren G. Moore	187,109	15.8
	Charles H. Stevenson, Jr.	204,315	17.3
	Russell K. Van Kueren	68,126	5.8
	Phil Willis	84,204	7.1
	Write-ins	6	0.0

The election was close enough in the race for the at-large seat that a runoff election was held on June 2, 1962.

1962 Republican Primary Election (May 5)

Dist.	Candidate	Votes	%
1	James A. Timberlake		
2	Roy James, Jr.		
3	William M. Steger		
	M. J. Harvey, Jr.		
4	Conner Harrington		
5	Bruce Alger		
	Paul Eix		
	John D. Ferris		
6	(none)		
7	Raymond Ramage		
8	Anthony J.P. Farris		
9	Dave Oakes		
10	Jim Dobbs		
	Hal Hendrix		
11	(none)		
12	Del Barron		
13	Joe Meissner		
14	Lawrence E. Hoover		
15	(none)		
16	Ed Foreman		
17	(none)		
18	Jack Seale		
19	Dennis D. Taylor		
20	(none)		
21	Edwin S. Mayer, Jr.		
22	Ross G. Baker		
	Joe Poindexter		
	Julia Mae Anderson Barnhart		
At-Large	Desmond A. Barry	55,706	50.1
	Joe B. Phillips	25,058	22.5
	Giles Miller	30,517	27.4

Republican Party primary elections for U.S. Representative were held every two years from this point forward. Prior to this, they were held only in 1926, 1930, 1954, and 1958 for the U.S. representative's seat.

1962 DEMOCRATIC PRIMARY RUNOFF ELECTION (JUNE 2)

At-Large

Joe Pool	571,246	55.9
Woodrow Wilson Bean	450,135	44.1

1962 GENERAL ELECTION (NOVEMBER 6)

1	Wright Patman, Democrat	26,669	67.3
	James Timberlake, Republican	12,938	32.7
2	Jack Brooks, Democrat	47,037	68.8
	Roy James, Jr., Republican	21,385	31.2
3	Lindley Beckworth, Democrat	26,915	52.0
	William Steger, Republican	24,803	48.0
4	Ray Roberts, Democrat	23,573	72.0
	Conner Harrington, Republican	9,165	28.0
5	Bruce Alger, Republican	89,938	56.3
	Bill Jones, Democrat	69,813	43.7
6	Olin Teague, Democrat	33,617	100.0
7	John Dowdy, Democrat	37,756	88.2
	Raymond Ramage, Republican	5,045	11.8
8	Albert Thomas, Democrat	51,285	71.5
	Anthony J.P. Farris, Republican	20,475	28.5
9	Clark Thompson, Democrat	56,179	66.3
	Dave Oakes, Republican	28,594	33.7
10	Homer Thornberry, Democrat	43,396	63.3
	Jim Dobbs, Republican	25,165	36.7
11	W. R. Poage, Democrat	41,698	100.0
12	Jim Wright, Democrat	53,705	60.6
	Del Barron, Republican	34,879	39.4
13	Graham Purcell, Democrat	37,941	67.1
	Joe Meissner, Republican	18,578	32.9
14	John Young, Democrat	60,803	70.4
	Lawrence E. Hoover, Republican	25,623	29.7
15	Joe M. Kilgore, Democrat	53,552	100.0
16	Ed Foreman, Republican	44,095	53.8
	J. T. Rutherford, Democrat	37,821	46.2
17	Omar Burleson, Democrat	46,895	100.0
18	Walter Rogers, Democrat	43,389	58.8
	Jack Seale, Republican	30,393	41.2
19	George Mahon, Democrat	46,925	67.1
	Dennis Taylor, Republican	23,022	32.9
20	Henry B. Gonzalez, Democrat	62,776	100.0
21	O. C. Fisher, Democrat	39,261	76.1
	E.S. Mayer, Jr., Republican	12,310	23.9
22	Bob Casey, Democrat	73,141	53.6
	Ross Baker, Republican	63,452	46.5

At-Large

Joe Pool, Democrat	870,860	56.1
Desmond A. Barry, Republican	680,569	43.9

1963 SPECIAL ELECTION (NOVEMBER 5)

10	J. J. Pickle, Democrat	14,496	35.3
	Jim Dobbs, Republican	13,702	33.3
	Jack Ritter, Democrat	13,027	31.4

This special election was held to fill the seat of Homer Thornberry, who resigned December 20, 1963. This was in fact an open primary, where a majority was required by a candidate to be declared the winner. Since no candidate received a majority, a runoff was held December 21, 1963.

1963 SPECIAL ELECTION RUNOFF (DECEMBER 21)

10	J.-J. Pickle, Democrat	27,228	62.9
	Jim Dobbs, Republican	16,052	37.1

This was the runoff election required since no candidate received a majority in the November 5, 1963, special election to fill the seat of Homer Thornberry.

1964 DEMOCRATIC PRIMARY ELECTION (MAY 2)

1	Wright Patman	56,297	100.0
	Write-ins	4	0.0
2	Jack Brooks	80,232	100.0
	Write-ins	55	0.0

District	Candidate	Votes	%
3	Lindley Beckworth	39,396	60.4
	L. E. Page	19,283	29.6
	Charlie Langfort	6,510	10.0
4	Ray Roberts	46,627	100.0
5	Earle Cabell	73,959	65.8
	Baxton Bryant	38,441	34.2
6	Olin Teague	37,653	73.7
	Jack Zubik	13,417	26.3
7	John Dowdy	46,286	56.8
	Benton Musselwhite	35,274	43.2
8	Albert Thomas	32,240	100.0
9	Clark Thompson	89,488	100.0
	Write-ins	3	0.0
10	J. J. Pickle	72,859	100.0
11	W. R. Poage	43,107	78.2
	Godfrey Sullivan	245	0.4
	Joe F. McAllister	11,791	21.4
12	Jim Wright	70,450	91.3
	Tommy Thompson	6,719	8.7
13	Graham Purcell	67,653	100.0
	Write-ins	8	0.0
14	John Young	90,023	100.0
	Write-in	1	0.0
15	Eligio de la Garza	30,494	44.1
	Gene McCullough	17,882	25.8
	Lindsay Rodriguez	20,814	30.1
	Write-ins	2	0.0
16	Richard C. White	30,161	48.2
	Malcolm McGregor	25,027	40.0
	Betty Dooley	7,417	11.8
	Write-in	1	0.0
17	Omar Burleson	45,006	69.4
	Max Carriker	19,882	30.6
18	Walter Rogers	57,854	100.0
19	George Mahon	75,578	100.0
20	Henry B. Gonzalez	57,745	100.0
21	O. C. Fisher	55,981	100.0
	Write-ins	3	0.0
22	Bob Casey	53,905	100.0
At-Large	Joe Pool	678,584	48.4
	Bill Elkins	95,942	6.8
	Robert W. Baker	311,411	22.2
	Bob Looney	104,783	7.5
	Dan Sullivan	210,169	15.0
	Write-ins	2	0.0

The elections were close enough in the races for the 15th, 16th, and at-large district seats that runoff elections were held on June 6, 1964.

1964 REPUBLICAN PRIMARY ELECTION (MAY 2)

District	Candidate	Votes	%
1	Mrs. William E. Jones	889	100.0
2	John Greco	2,169	100.0
	Write-ins	6	0.0
3	James Warren	3,788	100.0
	Write-in	1	0.0
4	Fred Banfield	1,036	100.0
5	Bruce Alger	25,367	100.0
6	William Van Winkle	999	100.0
7	James W. Orr	434	97.5
	Write-ins	11	2.5
8	Robert Gilbert	3,136	100.0
9	Dave Oakes	4,582	100.0
10	Billie J. Pratt	3,628	100.0
	Write-ins	2	0.0
11	Charles M. Isenhower	1,612	100.0
12	Fred Dielman	10,379	100.0
13	George Corse	2,877	100.0
	Write-in	1	0.0
14	W. F. "Billy" Patton	4,690	100.0
15	Joseph B. Coulter	3,037	100.0
	Write-ins	2	0.0
16	Ed Foreman	12,056	100.0
	Write-in	1	0.0
17	Phil M. Bridges	1,284	51.5

District	Candidate	Votes	%
	Clyde Morgan	1,207	48.5
18	Robert Price	8,141	79.9
	Frank Hinkson	2,044	20.1
	Write-in	1	0.0
19	Joe B. Phillips	4,801	100.0
	Write-ins	2	0.0
20	John M. O'Connell	00.0	0.0
21	Harry Claypool	2,565	99.7
	Write-ins	7	0.3
22	Desmond Barry	20,702	100.0
At-Large			
	Bill Hayes	123,363	100.0
	Write-ins	17	0.0

1964 DEMOCRATIC PRIMARY RUNOFF ELECTION (JUNE 6)

District	Candidate	Votes	%
15	Eligio de la Garza	34,127	64.2
	Lindsay Rodriguez	18,994	35.8
16	Richard C. White	19,328	53.3
	Malcolm McGregor	16,935	46.7
At-Large			
	Joe Pool	358,885	57.2
	Robert W. Baker	268,087	42.8

1964 GENERAL ELECTION (NOVEMBER 3)

District	Candidate	Votes	%
1	Wright Patman, Democrat	52,698	74.6
	Mrs. William E. Jones, Republican	17,967	25.4
2	Jack Brooks, Democrat	75,226	62.7
	John Greco, Republican	44,772	37.3
3	Lindley Beckworth, Democrat	53,331	59.3
	James Warren, Republican	36,566	40.7
4	Ray Roberts, Democrat	46,782	81.4
	Fred Banfield, Republican	10,707	18.6
5	Earle Cabell, Democrat	172,287	57.5
	Bruce Alger, Republican	127,568	42.5
6	Olin Teague, Democrat	55,155	82.2
	William Van Winkle, Republican	11,967	17.8
7	John Dowdy, Democrat	64,456	83.6
	James W. Orr, Republican	12,606	16.4
8	Albert Thomas, Democrat	103,595	76.8
	Bob Gilbert, Republican	31,351	23.2
9	Clark Thompson, Democrat	105,631	75.3
	Dave Oakes, Republican	34,692	24.7
10	J. J. Pickle, Democrat	80,045	75.8
	Billie Pratt, Republican	25,594	24.2
11	W. R. Poage, Democrat	62,175	81.5
	Charles M. Isenhower, Republican	14,094	18.5
12	Jim Wright, Democrat	107,896	68.5
	Fred Dielman, Republican	49,633	31.5
13	Graham Purcell, Democrat	67,947	75.2
	George Corse, Republican	22,429	24.8
14	John Young, Democrat	105,352	77.5
	W. F. "Billy" Patton, Republican	30,522	22.5
15	Eligio de la Garza, Democrat	66,897	69.4
	Joe B. Coulter, Republican	29,551	30.6
16	Richard C. White, Democrat	70,262	55.7
	Ed Foreman, Republican	55,951	44.3
17	Omar Burleson, Democrat	59,769	76.4
	Phil M. Bridges, Republican	18,440	23.6
18	Walter Rogers, Democrat	58,701	55.0
	Robert Price, Republican	48,054	45.0
19	George Mahon, Democrat	87,555	77.6
	Joe B. Phillips, Republican	25,243	22.4
20	Henry B. Gonzalez, Democrat	103,464	64.6
	John M. O'Connell, Republican	56,601	35.4
21	O. C. Fisher, Democrat	61,785	78.1
	Harry Claypool, Republican	17,295	21.9
22	Bob Casey, Democrat	136,289	58.1
	Desmond Barry, Republican	98,287	41.9
At-Large			
	Joe Pool, Democrat	1,690,674	66.9
	Bill Hayes, Republican	826,991	32.7
	W. A. "Bill" Johnson, Constitution	9,190	0.4

1966 Special Election (March 26)

		Votes	%
8	Lera Thomas, Democrat	6,120	74.0
	Louis Leman, Republican	2,147	26.0

This special election was held to fill the seat of Albert Thomas, who died on February 15, 1966. This was in fact an open primary, where a majority was required by a candidate to be declared the winner. Thomas' wife Lera won the election and was the first woman elected to the U.S. House from Texas.

1966 DEMOCRATIC PRIMARY ELECTION (MAY 2)

		Votes	%
1	Wright Patman	66,369	100.0
	write-ins	5	0.0
2	John Dowdy	47,063	51.9
	Martin Dies, Jr.	43,569	48.1
	write-in	1	0.0
3	Joe Pool	17,707	
	James M. Sheppard		
4	Ray Roberts	37,262	56.2
	Lindley Beckworth	29,076	43.8
5	Earle Cabell	18,975	100.0
6	Olin Teague	48,422	100.0
7	Frank Briscoe	31,045	
	John Wildenthal, Jr.	13,377	
	David Van Orsdale		
8	Bob Eckhardt	20,475	41.4
	Albert Thomas (deceased)	20,457	41.4
	Larry McKastle	8,521	17.2
9	Jack Brooks	43,509	100.0
	Write-in	1	0.0
10	J. J. Pickle	76,649	100.0
11	W. R. Poage	47,114	100.0
	Write-ins	5	0.0
12	Jim Wright	31,920	100.0
13	Graham Purcell	50,389	100.0
	Write-in	1	0.0
14	John Young	56,303	100.0
15	Eligio de la Garza	4,090	100.0
16	Richard C. White	33,143	100.0
17	Omar Burleson	41,268	63.3
	Eldon Mahon	23,968	36.7
	Dee D. Miller		
19	George Mahon	48,320	100.0
20	Henry B. Gonzalez	39,675	100.0
21	O. C. Fisher	61,788	100.0
	Write-ins	2	0.0
22	Bob Casey	29,331	54.6
	Bill Kilgarlin	24,403	45.4
23	Abraham Kazen, Jr.	38,043	56.7
	Randolph A. Sherwood	7,399	11.0
	Roy Martin	21,620	32.2
	Write-ins	3	0.0

1966 REPUBLICAN PRIMARY ELECTION (MAY 2)

1	(none)
2	(none)
3	James M. Collins
4	(none)
5	Duke Burgess
6	(none)
7	George Bush
8	E. A. Rose
9	(none)
10	Miss Jane Sumners
11	(none)
12	(none)
13	D. C. Norwood
14	(none)
15	(none)
16	(none)
17	(none)
18	Robert Price
19	(none)
20	(none)

21	(none)		
22	(none)		
23	(none		

1966 General Election (November 8)

Dist.	Candidate	Votes	%
1	Wright Patman, Democrat	50,072	100.0
	Other	1	0.0
2	John Dowdy, Democrat	55,134	99.9
	Other	35	0.1
3	Joe Pool, Democrat	35,081	53.4
	James M. Collins, Republican	30,588	46.5
	Other	2	0.0
4	Ray Roberts, Democrat	51,895	100.0
	Other	1	0.0
5	Earle Cabell, Democrat	39,977	61.0
	Duke Burgess, Republican	25,563	39.0
	Other	3	0.0
6	Olin Teague, Democrat	42,017	100.0
7	George Bush, Republican	53,756	57.1
	Frank Briscoe, Democrat	39,958	42.4
	Bob Gray, Constitution	488	0.5
8	Bob Eckhardt, Democrat	38,497	92.3
	W. D. Spayne, Constitution	3,207	7.7
9	Jack Brooks, Democrat	47,604	100.0
	Other	13	0.0
10	J. J. Pickle, Democrat	55,424	74.3
	Jane Sumner, Republican	18,343	24.6
	R. R. Richter, Constitution	849	1.1
11	W. R. Poage, Democrat	39,410	94.9
	Laurel N. Dunn, Conservative	2,102	5.1
	Other	17	0.0
12	Jim Wright, Democrat	27,070	100.0
13	Graham Purcell, Democrat	43,820	57.1
	D. C. Norwood, Republican	32,960	42.9
14	John Young, Democrat	52,861	100.0
15	Eligio de la Garza, Democrat	33,129	100.0
16	Richard C. White, Democrat	33,179	100.0
	Other	4	0.0
17	Omar Burleson, Democrat	52,169	100.0
	Other	4	0.0
18	Robert Price, Republican	45,209	59.5
	Dee D. Miller, Democrat	30,822	40.5
	Other	1	0.0
19	George Mahon, Democrat	56,792	100.0
20	Henry B Gonzalez, Democrat	41,067	87.1
	Robert C. Moore, Conservative	3,671	7.8
	Bert Ellis, Constitution	2,390	5.1
21	O. C. Fisher, Democrat	60,497	100.0
	Other	1	0.0
22	Bob Casey, Democrat	60,817	100.0
	Other	1	0.0
23	Abraham Kazen, Jr., Democrat	50,322	96.4
	Richard K. Troxell, Constitution	1,898	3.6
	Other	4	0.0

1968 Democratic Primary Election (May 4)

Dist.	Candidate	Votes	%
1	Wright Patman	unopposed	100.0
2	Dempsie Henley	39,063	38.3
	John Dowdy	62,864	61.7
3	*Joe Pool	33,037	74.6
	David M. Ivy	11,249	25.4
4	Ray Roberts	unopposed	100.0
5	Earle Cabell	unopposed	100.0
6	Olin Teague	unopposed	100.0
7	(none)		
8	Bob Eckhardt	unopposed	100.0
9	Jack Brooks	unopposed	100.0
10	Fagan Dickson	13,997	16.5
	J. J. Pickle	70,577	83.5
11	W. R. Poage	unopposed	100.0
12	Jim Wright	unopposed	100.0
13	Graham Purcell	unopposed	100.0
14	Hubert Letts	11,297	17.6

#		Votes	%
	John Young	53,050	82.4
15	Eligio de la Garza	unopposed	100.0
16	Richard C. White	unopposed	100.0
17	Omar Burleson	unopposed	100.0
18	J. R. Brown	unopposed	100.0
19	George Mahon	unopposed	100.0
20	Henry B. Gonzalez	unopposed	100.0
21	Gordon F. Johnson	12,225	18.0
	O. C. Fisher	55,808	82.0
22	Clyde Doyal	23,915	34.6
	Bob Casey	45,126	65.4
23	Abraham Kazen, Jr.	unopposed	100.0

* Joe Pool died after this primary election but before the 1968 general election.

1968 REPUBLICAN PRIMARY ELECTION (MAY 4)

#	
1	(none)
2	(none)
3	James M. Collins
4	(none)
5	Roy Wagoner
6	(none)
7	George Bush
8	Joe Stevens
9	Henry Pressler
10	Ray Gabler
11	Laurel N. Dunn
12	(none)
13	Frank Crowley
14	(none)
15	(none)
16	Donald Slaughter
17	(none)
18	Robert Price
19	(none)
20	Robert A. Schneider
21	W. J. Alexander
22	Walter Blaney
23	(none)

1968 SPECIAL ELECTION (AUGUST 24)

#		Votes	%
3	James M. Collins, Republican	13,828	61.0
	Elizabeth (Mrs. Joe) Pool, Democrat	9,209	39.5

The special election was held to fill the seat of Joe Pool, who died on July 14, 1968.

1968 GENERAL ELECTION (NOVEMBER 5)

#		Votes	%
1	Wright Patman, Democrat	87,038	100.0
2	John Dowdy, Democrat	87,565	100.0
3	James M. Collins, Republican	81,696	59.4
	Robert H. Hughes, Democrat	55,939	46.0
4	Ray Roberts, Democrat	95,413	100.0
5	Earle Cabell, Democrat	79,317	61.4
	Roy Wagoner, Republican	49,821	38.6
6	Olin Teague, Democrat	90,889	100.0
7	George Bush, Republican	110,455	100.0
8	Bob Eckhardt, Democrat	63,256	70.6
	Joe Stevens, Republican	26,402	29.5
9	Jack Brooks, Democrat	71,937	60.6
	Henry Pressler, Republican	46,829	39.4
10	J. J. Pickle, Democrat	85,037	62.1
	Ray Gabler, Republican	51,933	37.9
11	W. R. Poage, Democrat	78,127	96.5
	Laurel N. Dunn, Republican	2,807	3.5
12	Jim Wright, Democrat	86,069	100.0
13	Graham Purcell, Democrat	83,839	55.8
	Frank Crowley, Republican	66,477	44.2
14	John Young, Democrat	89,868	100.0
15	Eligio de la Garza, Democrat	57,618	100.0
16	Richard C. White, Democrat	62,491	73.5
	Donald Slaughter, Republican	22,510	26.5
17	Omar Burleson, Democrat	90,856	100.0
18	Robert Price, Republican	81,715	65.2
	J. R. Brown, Democrat	43,568	34.8

District	Candidate	Votes	Percent
19	George Mahon, Democrat	79,161	100.0
20	Henry B. Gonzalez, Democrat	64,112	81.5
	Robert A. Schneider, Republican	14,569	18.5
21	O. C. Fisher, Democrat	91,784	60.8
	W. J. Alexander, Republican	59,082	39.2
22	Bob Casey, Democrat	101,498	62.4
	Walter Blaney, Republican	61,278	37.7
23	Abraham Kazen, Jr., Democrat	75,026	100.0

1970 DEMOCRATIC PRIMARY ELECTION (MAY 2)

District	Candidate	Votes	Percent
1	Wright Patman	59,479	76.9
	Bill Russell	17,845	23.1
2	John Dowdy	66,058	100.0
3	John Mead	32,446	86.4
	Mrs. Dorothy Bach	5,117	13.6
4	Ray Roberts	55,471	100.0
5	Earle Cabell	29,787	53.6
	Mike McKool	25,742	46.4
6	Olin Teague	55,395	100.0
7	Jim Greenwood	23,749	48.4
	W. Kendall Baker	12,820	26.1
	Jim Brady	12,473	25.4
8	Bob Eckhardt	31,279	76.9
	Bobby A. Carley	3,999	23.1
9	Jack Brooks	37,546	100.0
10	J. J. Pickle	66,948	100.0
11	W. R. Poage	49,763	100.0
12	Jim Wright	40,049	100.0
13	Graham Purcell	58,825	100.0
14	John Young	55,860	100.0
15	Eligio de la Garza	49,925	100.0
16	Richard C. White	41,142	67.7
	Raymond Telles	19,664	32.3
17	Omar Burleson	60,019	100.0
18	(none)		
19	George Mahon	42,216	100.0
20	Henry B. Gonzalez	34,873	100.0
21	O. C. Fisher	58,756	100.0
22	Bob Casey	39,679	69.4
	Paul B. Haring	17,530	30.6
23	Abraham Kazen, Jr.	54,284	100.0

The election was close enough in the race for the 7th District seat that a runoff election was held on June 6, 1970.

1970 REPUBLICAN PRIMARY ELECTION (MAY 2)

District	Candidate	Votes	Percent
1	James Hogan	unopposed	100.0
2	(none)		
3	James M. Collins	unopposed	100.0
4	(none)		
5	Frank Crowley	unopposed	100.0
6	(none)		
7	Bill Archer	13,331	53.7
	Ross Baker	6,119	24.6
	Dudley Sharp Jr.	5,381	21.7
8	(none)		
9	Henry Pressler	1,925	60.3
	William McAnich	1,266	39.7
10	(none)		
11	(none)		
12	(none)		
13	Joe H. Staley Jr.	unopposed	100.0
14	(none)		
15	Ben A. Martinez	unopposed	100.0
16	J. R. Provencio	1,536	58.3
	John Karr	1,099	41.7
17	(none)		
18	Robert Price	unopposed	100.0
19	(none)		
20	(none)		
21	Richardson B. Gill	unopposed	100.0
22	Arthur W. Busch, Republican	58,598	44.4
23	(none)		

1970 Democratic Primary Runoff Election (June 6)

District	Candidate	Votes	%
7	Jim Greenwood	8,426	69.2
	W. Kendall Baker	3,744	30.8

1970 General Election (November 3)

District	Candidate	Votes	%
1	Wright Patman, Democrat	67,883	78.9
	James Hogan, Republican	18,614	21.6
	Other	7	0.0
2	John Dowdy, Democrat	52,634	73.6
	Eugene Hoyt, Independent	11,987	17.2
	Joe Runnels, Independent	4,693	6.8
	Other	389	0.1
3	James M. Collins, Republican	63,690	60.6
	John Mead, Democrat	41,425	39.4
	Other	1	0.0
4	Ray Roberts, Democrat	70,103	100.0
	Other	3	0.0
5	Earle Cabell, Democrat	57,058	59.7
	Frank Crowley, Republican	38,481	40.3
	Other	5	0.0
6	Olin Teague, Democrat	74,038	100.0
	Other	29	0.0
7	Bill Archer, Republican	93,457	64.8
	Jim Greenwood, Democrat	50,750	35.2
8	Bob Eckhardt, Democrat	26,294	100.0
9	Jack Brooks, Democrat	57,180	64.5
	Henry Pressler, Republican	31,483	35.5
	Other	4	0.0
10	J. J. Pickle, Democrat	78,872	100.0
	Other	26	0.0
11	W. R. Poage, Democrat	59,641	99.9
	Other	39	0.0
12	Jim Wright, Democrat	62,057	100.0
13	Graham Purcell, Democrat	80,070	64.9
	Joe H. Staley, Jr., Republican	43,319	35.1
	Other	13	0.0
14	John Young, Democrat	62,560	100.0
	Other	24	0.0
15	Eligio de la Garza, Democrat	54,498	76.2
	Ben A. Martinez, Republican	17,049	23.8
	Other	1	0.0
16	Richard C. White, Democrat	54,617	82.7
	J. R. Provencio, Republican	11,420	17.3
	Other	13	0.0
17	Omar Burleson, Democrat	70,040	100.0
	Other	33	0.0
18	Robert Price, Republican	52,845	99.9
	Other	79	0.0
19	George Mahon, Democrat	59,996	100.0
	Other	24	0.0
20	Henry B. Gonzalez, Democrat	48,710	100.0
	Other	1	0.0
21	O. C. Fisher, Democrat	76,004	61.4
	Richardson B. Gill, Republican	47,868	38.6
	Other	12	0.0
22	Bob Casey, Democrat	73,514	55.7
	Arthur W. Busch, Republican	58,598	44.4
	Other	5	0.0
23	Abraham Kazen, Jr., Democrat	61,068	100.0
	Other	6	0.0

1972 Democratic Primary Election (May 6)

District	Candidate	Votes	%
1	Wright Patman	69,579	56.6
	Fred Hudson, Jr.	53,255	43.4
2	Charles Wilson	85,517	63.6
	J. D Dowdy	23,808	17.7
	Norman T. Birdwell	13,398	10.0
	Louis V. McIntire	9,863	7.3
	Thomas W. Porter	1,919	1.4
3	George A. Hughes	24,265	59.9
	James M. Sheppard	16,266	40.1
4	Ray Roberts	65,194	100.0
5	Earle Cabell	39,485	76.4
	Mrs. Emily Cathey	12,179	23.6

Democratic Primary (continued)

District	Candidate	Votes	%
6	Olin Teague	66,500	100.0
7	Jim Brady	45,239	76.3
	Sam W. Bostick	14,045	23.7
	C. L. Crider	0	0.0
8	Bob Eckhardt	37,109	77.1
	David L. Shall	11,022	22.9
9	Jack Brooks	52,289	100.0
10	J. J. Pickle	81,104	100.0
11	W. R. Poage	62,410	60.5
	Murray Watson	40,761	39.5
12	Jim Wright	48,461	100.0
13	Graham Purcell	63,456	100.0
14	John Young	61,118	66.0
	Yancy White	31,374	34.0
15	Eligio de la Garza	73,101	83.8
	Ben A. Martinez	14,177	16.2
16	Richard C. White	55,380	100.0
17	Omar Burleson	82,887	100.0
18	Barbara Jordan	47,713	80.6
	B. T. Bonner II	1,777	3.0
	Curtis M. Graves	8,106	13.7
	Milton King	1,573	2.7
	Walter M. Ladnier	0	0.0
19	George Mahon	63,918	100.0
20	Henry B. Gonzalez	47,257	100.0
21	O. C. Fisher	71,657	100.0
22	Bob Casey	51,040	68.2
	Ben G. Levy	4,282	5.7
	Johnny Nelms	19,532	26.1
23	Abraham Kazen, Jr.	57,156	78.7
	Frank Boone	15,514	21.3
24	Dale Milford	21,992	31.8
	Jesse A. Coffey	5,570	8.1
	Mike McKool	25,655	37.1
	Lee Goodman	5,248	7.6
	Jesse Price	6,646	9.6
	Dorothy Bach	934	1.3
	Lon Williams	1,620	2.3
	Jim Hilley	1,474	2.1

The election was close enough in the race for the 24th District seat that a runoff election was held on June 3, 1972.

1972 Republican Primary Election (May 6)

District	Candidate	Votes	%
1	(none)		
2	Charles O. Brightwell	781	64.1
	Maurice C. Elsberry	437	35.9
3	James M. Collins	13,367	67.8
	Tom Crouch	6,362	32.2
4	James Russell	2,653	100.0
5	Alan Steelman	2,803	41.9
	Robert E. Lyle	2,058	30.7
	Gaylord E. Marshall	1,578	23.6
	Ken Sikorski	256	3.8
6	Carl A. Nigliazzo	3,275	100.0
7	Bill Archer	18,577	100.0
8	Lewis Emerich	1,440	100.0
9	Randolph C. Reed	1,626	100.0
10	(none)		
11	(none)		
12	(none)		
13	Bob Price	3,654	100.0
14	(none)		
15	(none)		
16	(none)		
17	(none)		
18	Paul Merritt	1,283	100.0
19	(none)		
20	(none)		
21	Douglas S. Harlan	3,637	59.9
	J. P. "Pete" Williams, Jr.	2,437	40.1
22	James Griffin	3,076	72.5
	Elsworth Tonn	1,168	27.5
23	(none)		
24	Courtney G. Roberts	1,775	43.7

Dist.	Candidate	Votes	%
	George Arias	293	7.2
	James Bond	561	13.8
	Don Reeves	1,021	25.1
	Ross Vernon	414	10.2

The elections were close enough in the races for the 5th and 24th district seats that runoff elections were held on June 3, 1972.

1972 Democratic Primary Runoff Election (June 3)

Dist.	Candidate	Votes	%
24	Dale Milford	37,287	50.5
	Mike McKool	31,595	49.5

1972 Republican Primary Runoff Election (June 3)

Dist.	Candidate	Votes	%
5	Alan Steelman	2,782	63.2
	Robert E. Lyle	1,619	36.8
24	Courtney G. Roberts	1,492	72.7
	Don Reeves	560	27.3

1972 General Election (November 7)

Dist.	Candidate	Votes	%
1	Wright Patman, Democrat	93,891	100.0
2	Charles Wilson, Democrat	100,345	83.8
	Charles O. Brightwell, Republican	35,600	26.2
3	James M. Collins, Republican	122,984	73.3
	George A. Hughes, Democrat	44,708	26.7
4	Ray Roberts, Democrat	95,674	70.2
	James Russell, Republican	40,548	29.8
5	Alan Steelman, Republican	74,932	55.7
	Earle Cabell, Democrat	59,601	44.3
6	Olin Teague, Democrat	100,917	72.6
	Carl A. Nigliazzo, Republican	38,086	27.4
7	Bill Archer, Republican	171,127	82.3
	Jim Brady, Democrat	36,899	17.7
8	Bob Eckhardt, Democrat	73,909	64.6
	Lewis Emerich, Republican	39,686	34.7
	Susan Ellis, Socialist Workers	847	0.8
9	Jack Brooks, Democrat	89,113	66.2

Dist.	Candidate	Votes	%
	Randolph C. Reed, Republican	45,462	33.8
10	J.J. Pickle, Democrat	130,973	91.2
	Melissa Singler, Socialist Workers	12,682	9.8
11	W. R. Poage, Democrat	88,861	100.0
12	Jim Wright, Democrat	84,356	100.0
13	Bob Price, Republican	87,084	54.8
	Graham Purcell, Democrat	71,730	45.2
14	John Young, Democrat	89,725	100.0
15	Eligio de la Garza, Democrat	73,994	100.0
16	Richard C. White, Democrat	81,347	100.0
17	Omar Burleson, Democrat	95,122	100.0
18	Barbara Jordan, Democrat	85,672	80.6
	Paul Merritt, Republican	19,355	18.2
	Emmanuel "Tank" Barrera, Socialist Workers	1,287	1.2
19	George Mahon, Democrat	97,084	100.0
20	Henry B. Gonzalez, Democrat	81,443	96.9
	Steve Wattenmaker, Socialist Workers	2,596	3.1
21	O. C. Fisher, Democrat	91,180	56.8
	Douglas S. Harlan, Republican	69,374	43.2
22	Bob Casey, Democrat	101,786	70.2
	James Griffin, Republican	42,094	29.0
	Frank Peto, Independent	1,169	0.8
23	Abraham Kazen, Jr, Democrat	72,799	100.0
24	Dale Milford, Democrat	91,054	65.1
	Courtney Roberts, Republican	48,853	34.9

1974 Democratic Primary Election (May 4)

Dist.	Candidate	Votes	%
1	Fred Hudson	28,106	26.5
	Glen Jones	20,167	19.0
	Wright Patman	57,609	54.4
2	Charles Wilson	73,686	100.0
3	Jim Wilson	13,998	42.8
	Harold Collum	18,736	57.2
4	Ray Roberts	52,151	100.0
5	Earl Luna	9,219	28.7
	John Sartain	5,993	18.7

District	Candidate	Votes	Percent
	Mike McKool	16,901	52.6
6	Olin Teague	48,268	100.0
7	Don H. Shepler	6,068	22.4
	Jim Brady	20,984	77.6
8	David L. Shall	5,929	23.2
	Bob Eckhardt	19,671	76.8
9	Jack Brooks	36,504	100.0
10	E. H. Meadows	3,938	3.9
	Larry Bales	29,034	28.8
	Jake Pickle	67,794	67.3
11	Connie Lawson	12,053	19.2
	W. R. Poage	50,692	80.8
12	Jim Wright	32,923	100.0
13	Ray Ruffin	14,627	21.0
	Louis A. Finney	9,598	13.8
	Jack Hightower	45,378	65.2
14	John Young	43,895	100.0
15	Eligio de la Garza	51,435	100.0
16	Richard C. White	26,996	100.0
17	Omar Burleson	68,691	100.0
18	Barbara Jordan	20,269	100.0
19	George Mahon	51,887	100.0
20	Henry B. Gonzalez	34,102	100.0
21	Nelson W. Wolff	32,877	40.1
	John H. Poerner	14,742	18.0
	Allen Moore	3,031	3.7
	Joe Sullivan	3,166	3.9
	Patrick M. Ainsworth	1,827	2.2
	Bob Krueger	26,361	32.1
22	J. Kent Hackleman	16,411	33.5
	Bob Casey	32,524	66.5
23	Jon Roland	10,376	16.7
	Jake Johnson	7,669	12.3
	Abraham Kazen, Jr.	44,070	70.9
24	Martin Frost	14,989	42.1
	Dale Milford	20,643	57.9

The election was close enough in the race for the 21st District seat that a runoff election was held on June 1, 1974.

1974 Republican Primary Election (May 4)

District	Candidate	Votes	Percent
1	James W. Farris	415	100.0
2	(none)		
3	Jim White	2,596	17.9
	James M. Collins	11,891	82.1
4	Dick LeTourneau	1,476	100.0
5	Alan Steelman	2,418	100.0
6	Carl A. Nigliazzo	1,971	100.0
7	Bill Archer	11,035	100.0
8	Donald D. Whitefield	614	100.0
9	Coleman R. Ferguson	1,098	100.0
10	Paul A. Weiss	1,918	100.0
11	Don Clements	882	100.0
12	James S. Garvey	2,069	100.0
13	Bob Price	3,724	100.0
14	(none)		
15	(none)		
16	(none)		
17	(none)		
18	Robbins Mitchell	374	100.0
19	(none)		
20	(none)		
21	Van Archer	1,998	29.4
	Simon T. Garza	317	4.7
	Bobby A. Locke	266	3.9
	Douglas S. Harlan	4,215	62.0
22	Ron Paul	1,681	100.0
23	(none)		
24	Joseph Beaman, Jr.	2,228	100.0

1974 Democratic Primary Runoff Election (June 1)

District	Candidate	Votes	Percent
21	Nelson W. Wolff	27,515	48.4
	Robert Krueger	29,332	51.6

1974 General Election (November 5)

District	Candidate	Votes	%
1	Wright Patman, Democrat	49,426	68.6
	James W. Farris, Republican	22,619	31.4
2	Charles Wilson, Democrat	57,096	100.0
3	James M. Collins, Republican	63,489	64.7
	Harold Collum, Democrat	34,623	35.3
4	Ray Roberts, Democrat	48,209	74.9
	Dick LeTourneau, Republican	16,113	25.1
5	Alan Steelman, Republican	28,446	52.1
	Mike McKool, Democrat	26,190	47.9
6	Olin Teague, Democrat	53,345	83.0
	Carl A. Nigliazzo, Republican	10,908	17.0
7	Bill Archer, Republican	70,363	79.2
	Jim Brady, Democrat	18,524	20.8
8	Bob Eckhardt, Democrat	30,158	72.2
	Donald D. Whitefield, Republican	11,605	27.8
9	Jack Brooks, Democrat	37,275	61.9
	Coleman R. Ferguson, Republican	22,935	38.1
10	Jake Pickle, Democrat	76,240	80.4
	Paul A. Weiss, Republican	18,560	19.6
11	W.R. Poage, Democrat	46,828	81.6
	Don Clements, Republican	9,883	17.2
	Laurel N. Dunn, Independent	650	1.1
12	Jim Wright, Democrat	42,632	78.7
	James S. Garvey, Republican	11,543	21.3
13	Jack Hightower, Democrat	53,094	57.6
	Bob Price, Republican	39,087	42.4
14	John Young, Democrat	41,066	100.0
15	Eligio de la Garza, Democrat	42,567	100.0
16	Richard C. White, Democrat	42,880	100.0
17	Omar Burleson, Democrat	64,595	100.0
18	Barbara Jordan, Democrat	36,597	84.8
	Robbins Mitchell, Republican	6,053	14.0
	Kris Vasquez, Socialist Workers	518	1.2
19	George Mahon, Democrat	49,619	100.0
20	Henry B. Gonzalez, Democrat	49,358	100.0
21	Bob Krueger, Democrat	53,543	52.6
	Douglas S. Harlan, Republican	45,959	45.2
	Ed Gallion, American Party	2,254	2.2
22	Bob Casey, Democrat	47,783	69.5
	Ron Paul, Republican	19,483	28.4
	Jill Fein, Socialist Workers	602	0.9
	James T. Smith, American Party	847	1.2
23	Abraham Kazen, Jr., Democrat	47,249	100.0
24	Dale Milford, Democrat	36,085	75.8
	Joseph Beaman, Jr., Republican	9,698	20.4
	Earl W. Armstrong, American Party	1,653	3.9

1976 Special Election (February 28)

District	Candidate	Votes	%
22	Bob Gammage, Democrat	15,287	42.1
	Ron Paul, Republican	14,386	39.6
	John S. Brunson, Democrat	3,670	10.1
	Roy Ybarra, Democrat	1,456	4.0
	J. Charles Whitfield	776	2.1
	Joe W. Jones	568	1.6
	Erich J. Brann	197	0.5

This special election was held to fill the seat of Bob Casey, who resigned on January 22, 1976. The race failed to yield a majority, so a runoff election was held on April 3, 1976.

1976 Special Election Runoff (April 3)

District	Candidate	Votes	%
22	Ron Paul, Republican	39,041	56.2
	Bob Gammage, Democrat	30,483	43.8

This runoff election was held to select a replacement for Bob Casey. No candidate received a majority in the first special election.

1976 Democratic Primary Election (May 1)

District	Candidate	Votes	%
1	Kenneth V. Burkhalter, Jr.	999	0.8
	Sam B. Hall, Jr.	27,787	22.1
	Fred Hudson, Jr.	18,448	14.7
	Glen Jones	24,929	19.8
	Jess Nickerson	3,294	2.6
	Shelby Parish	23,126	18.4
	George L. Preston	16,182	12.9

District	Candidate	Votes	%
	Sam Taylor	1,472	1.2
	John E. Wade	2,758	2.2
	James Allison	6,768	5.4
2	Richard Brown	27,327	23.4
	Charles Wilson	89,349	76.6
3	Clarence M. Lambright	7,432	27.6
	Les E. Shackelford, Jr.	19,458	72.4
4	David H. Brown	20,950	26.0
	Ben Henry Zollner	7,309	9.1
	Ray Roberts	52,232	64.9
5	B. D. Howard, Jr.	1,628	5.1
	Wes Wise	10,757	34.0
	Jim Mattox	19,289	60.9
6	Ron Godbey	33,884	45.7
	Olin Teague	40,181	54.3
7	(none)		
8	Bob Eckhardt	18,690	81.4
	Perry Roach	4,279	18.6
9	Jack Brooks	unopposed	100.0
10	J. J. Pickle	88,949	82.8
	E. H. Meadows	18,528	17.2
11	Steve S. Alexander	21,947	27.0
	W. R. Poage	59,481	73.0
12	Jim Wright	unopposed	100.0
13	Jack Hightower	unopposed	100.0
14	John Young	unopposed	100.0
15	Angel Noe Gonzales	20,740	22.9
	Eligio de la Garza	69,987	77.1
16	Jack Gregory	923	1.4
	Edgar Griggs	4,867	7.2
	George A. McAlmon	23,583	34.8
	Richard C. White	38,468	56.7
17	Omar Burleson	unopposed	100.0
18	Barbara Jordan	unopposed	100.0
19	George Mahon	unopposed	100.0
20	Henry B. Gonzalez	unopposed	100.0
21	Joe Sullivan	10,323	13.0
	Bob Krueger	64,478	86.2
22	John S. Brunson	11,062	23.1
	J. Charles Whitfield	4,634	9.7
	Bob Gammage	32,276	67.3
23	Abraham Kazen, Jr.	unopposed	100.0
24	Dale Milford	18,232	69.8
	James Ross	7,900	30.2

The election was close enough in the race for the 1st District seat that a runoff election was held on June 5, 1976.

1976 REPUBLICAN PRIMARY ELECTION (MAY 1)

District	Candidate	Votes	%
1	Jessalyn Davis	1,758	31.2
	James Hogan	3,868	68.8
2	(none)		
3	James M. Collins	42,126	73.7
	Roger Chafin	15,006	23.3
4	Frank S. Glenn	unopposed	100.0
5	Nancy Judy	unopposed	100.0
6	Wes Mowery	11,816	86.2
	Carl Nigliazzo	1,897	13.8
7	Bill Archer	unopposed	100.0
8	Nick Gearhart	unopposed	100.0
9	(none)		
10	Paul McClure	7,152	56.6
	Bill Murray	5,487	43.4
11	Jack Burgess	unopposed	100.0
12	W.R. Durham	unopposed	100.0
13	Bob Price	unopposed	100.0
14	L. Dean Holford	unopposed	100.0
15	R. L. "Lendy" McDonald	unopposed	100.0
16	Vic Shackleford	unopposed	100.0
17	(none)		
18	Sam H. Wright	unopposed	100.0
19	Jim Reese	unopposed	100.0
20	(none)		
21	Bobby A. Locke	14,056	53.5
	C. J. Calnan	12,199	46.5

District	Candidate	Votes	%
22	Ron Paul	19,119	93.4
	Joe W. Jones	1,341	6.6
23	(none)		
24	Leo Berman	7,536	57.5
	Lowry Davison	5,569	42.5

1976 DEMOCRATIC PRIMARY RUNOFF ELECTION (JUNE 5)

District	Candidate	Votes	%
1	Sam G. Hall, Jr.	50,082	52.2
	Glen Jones	45,836	47.8

1976 SPECIAL ELECTION (JUNE 19)

District	Candidate	Votes	%
1	Sam B. Hall, Democrat	20,556	72.2
	Glen Jones, Democrat	6,327	22.0
	James Hogan, Republican	1,395	4.9
	Fred Hudson, Democrat	271	0.9

This special election was held to fill the seat of Wright Patman, who died on March 7, 1976.

1976 GENERAL ELECTION (NOVEMBER 2)

District	Candidate	Votes	%
1	Sam B. Hall, Jr., Democrat	135,384	83.7
	James Hogan, Republican	26,334	16.3
2	Charles Wilson, Democrat	133,910	95.0
	James William Doyle, III, American	6,992	5.0
3	James M. Collins, Republican	171,343	74.0
	Les E. Shackleford, Jr., Democrat	60,070	26.0
4	Ray Roberts, Democrat	105,394	62.7
	Frank S. Glenn, Republican	62,641	37.3
5	Jim Mattox, Democrat	67,871	54.0
	Nancy Judy, Republican	56,056	44.6
	Sam McDonnell, American	1,841	1.5
6	Olin Teague, Democrat	119,025	65.9
	Wes Mowery, Republican	60,316	33.4
	Harley L. Pinon, American	1,193	0.7
7	Bill Archer, Republican	193,127	100.0
8	Bob Eckhardt, Democrat	84,404	60.7
	Nick Gearhart, Republican	54,566	39.2
	Gene Lantz, Socialist Workers	193	0.1
9	Jack Brooks, Democrat	112,945	99.9
10	Jake Pickle, Democrat	160,683	76.8
	Paul McClure, Republican	48,482	23.2
11	W. R. Poage, Democrat	92,142	57.4
	Jack Burgess, Republican	68,373	42.6
12	Jim Wright, Democrat	101,814	75.8
	W. R. Durham, Republican	31,941	23.8
	Larry Kutchinski, American	504	0.4
13	Jack Hightower, Democrat	101,798	59.3
	Bob Price, Republican	69,328	40.4
	William K. Hathcock, American	547	0.3
14	John Young, Democrat	93,589	61.4
	L. Dean Holford, Republican	58,788	38.6
15	Eligio de la Garza, Democrat	102,837	74.4
	R. L. "Lendy" McDonald, Republican	35,446	25.6
16	Richard C. White, Democrat	71,876	57.8
	Vic Shackleford, Republican	52,499	42.2
17	Omar Burleson, Democrat	127,613	99.9
18	Barbara Jordan, Democrat	93,953	85.5
	Sam H. Wright, Republican	15,381	14.0
	Sylvia Zapata, Socialist Workers	542	0.5
19	George Mahon, Democrat	87,908	54.6
	Jim Reese, Republican	72,991	45.4
20	Henry B. Gonzalez, Democrat	90,173	100.0
21	Bob Krueger, Democrat	149,395	71.0
	Bobby A. Locke, Republican	56,211	26.7
	Ramon E. Carrillo, La Raza Unida	2,515	1.2
	Ed Gallion, American	2,179	1.0
22	Bob Gammage, Democrat	96,535	50.1
	Ron Paul, Republican	96,267	49.9
23	Abraham Kazen, Jr., Democrat	96,481	100.0
24	Dale Milford, Democrat	82,743	63.4
	Leo Berman, Republican	47,075	36.1
	Earl Armstrong, American	704	0.5

1978 DEMOCRATIC PRIMARY ELECTION (MAY 6)

District	Candidate	Votes	%
1	Sam B. Hall, Jr.	unopposed	100.0
2	Charles Wilson	unopposed	100.0
3	(none)		
4	James R. Dockray	14,190	17.9
	Barbara V. Montgomery	11,420	14.4
	Ray Roberts	53,540	67.6
5	Jim Mattox	unopposed	100.0
6	Thomas C. Edwards	22,157	27.2
	Ron Godbey	23,521	28.9
	Kay Jones	2,922	3.6
	Don R. McNiel	10,389	12.8
	Phil Gramm	22,342	27.5
7	Robert Lawrence Hutchings	unopposed	100.0
8	Bob Eckhardt	unopposed	100.0
9	Alan Verret	17,178	30.3
	Jack Brooks	39,470	69.7
10	Jake Pickle	unopposed	100.0
11	Steve S. Alexander	1,208	1.2
	Lane Denton	38,984	39.5
	Perry Ellis	6,015	6.1
	Lyndon Olson, Jr.	22,929	23.2
	J. Marvin Leath	29,523	29.9
12	Jim Wright	unopposed	100.0
13	Jack Hightower	unopposed	100.0
14	Jason Luby	16,383	20.0
	John Young	30,871	37.6
	Joe Wyatt	34,812	42.4
15	Eligio de la Garza	unopposed	100.0
16	Bert Williams	12,185	20.1
	Richard C. White	48,493	79.9
17	Jim Baum	16,622	16.4
	Fike Godfrey	6,089	6.0
	Crews McCulloch	3,892	3.8
	A. L. Rhodes	34,172	33.7
	James B. Sharp, Jr.	1,994	2.0
	Jim Snowden	2,116	2.1
	Charles W. Stenholm	36,527	36.0
18	Mickey Leland	unopposed	100.0
19	Morris Sheats	25,791	35.7
	Kent Hance	46,505	64.3
20	Henry B. Gonzalez	unopposed	100.0
21	Steve Clark	4,139	4.3
	Paul Dahlgren	2,008	2.1
	Woodrow "Woody" Glasscock	28,942	30.2
	Joe Sullivan	11,512	12.0
	Nelson William Wolff	49,172	51.3
22	Gerald Liedtke	3,027	4.9
	Mike Richards	21,588	34.9
	George Stewart	2,698	4.4
	Bob Gammage	34,599	55.9
23	Martin P. Ross	15,597	19.6
	Abraham Kazen, Jr.	63,847	80.4
24	Martin Frost	22,791	55.1
	Dale Milford	18,595	44.9

The elections were close enough in the races for the 6th, 11th, 14th, and 17th district seats that runoff elections were held on June 3, 1978.

1978 REPUBLICAN PRIMARY ELECTION (MAY 6)

District	Candidate	Votes	%
1	Fred Hudson	unopposed	100.0
2	Jim "Matt" Dillon	unopposed	100.0
3	James M. Collins	unopposed	100.0
4	Frank S. Glenn	unopposed	100.0
5	Thomas W. Pauken	unopposed	100.0
6	Carl H. Krohn	793	14.6
	Wesley H. Mowery	4,630	85.4
7	Bill Archer	unopposed	100.0
8	Nick Gearhart	unopposed	100.0
9	Ed Falk	1,180	47.7
	Randy Evans	1,295	52.3
10	Emmett L. Hudspeth	2,700	62.2
	Rex Repass	1,638	37.8

District	Candidate	Votes	%
11	Jack Burgess	unopposed	100.0
12	Claude K. Brown	unopposed	100.0
13	Clifford A. Jones	2,944	51.7
	Larry Kelly	2,746	48.3
14	Joy Yates	unopposed	100.0
15	Robert L. McDonald	unopposed	100.0
16	Michael Giere	unopposed	100.0
17	Billy Lee Fisher	unopposed	100.0
18	(none)		
19	George W. Bush	6,296	47.5
	Jim Reese	5,498	41.5
	Joe Hickox	1,455	11.0
20	(none)		
21	Neil Calnan	2,007	13.6
	Wallace R. Larson	2,558	17.3
	Bobby Locke	1,433	9.7
	Thomas G. Loeffler	8,779	59.4
22	Ron Paul	unopposed	100.0
23	(none)		
24	Leo Berman	4,685	82.8
	Ben Franklin Bruce	970	17.2

The election was close enough in the race for the 19th District seat that a runoff election was held on June 3, 1978.

1978 DEMOCRATIC PRIMARY RUNOFF ELECTION (JUNE 3)

District	Candidate	Votes	%
6	Phil Gramm	23,762	52.9
	Ron Godbey	21,169	47.1
11	Marvin Leath	40,261	54.9
	Lane Denton	33,029	45.1
14	Joe Wyatt	36,409	55.7
	John Young	28,905	44.3
17	Charlie Stenholm	46,559	67.1
	A. L. Rhodes	22,865	32.9

1978 REPUBLICAN PRIMARY RUNOFF ELECTION (JUNE 3)

District	Candidate	Votes	%
19	George Bush	6,802	55.8
	Jim Reese	5,395	44.2

1978 GENERAL ELECTION (NOVEMBER 7)

District	Candidate	Votes	%
1	Sam B. Hall, Jr., Democrat	73,708	78.1
	Fred Hudson, Republican	20,700	21.9
2	Charles Wilson, Democrat	66,986	70.1
	Jim "Matt" Dillon, Republican	28,584	29.9
3	James M. Collins, Republican	96,406	100.0
4	Ray Roberts, Democrat	58,336	61.5
	Frank S. Glenn, Republican	36,582	38.5
5	Jim Mattox, Democrat	35,524	50.3
	Thomas W. Pauken, Republican	34,672	49.1
	James Michael White, Socialist Workers	397	0.6
6	Phil Gramm, Democrat	66,025	65.1
	Wesley H. Mowery, Republican	35,393	34.9
7	Bill Archer, Republican	128,214	85.1
	Robert Lawrence Hutchings, Democrat	22,415	14.9
8	Bob Eckhardt, Democrat	39,429	61.5
	Nick Gearhart, Republican	24,673	38.5
9	Jack Brooks, Democrat	50,792	63.3
	Randy Evans, Republican	29,473	36.7
10	J. J. Pickle, Democrat	94,529	76.3
	Emmett L. Hudspeth, Republican	29,328	23.7
11	J. Marvin Leath, Democrat	53,354	51.6
	Jack Burgess, Republican	49,965	48.4
12	Jim Wright, Democrat	46,456	68.5
	Claude K. Brown, Republican	21,364	31.5
13	Jack Hightower, Democrat	75,271	74.9
	Clifford A. Jones, Republican	25,275	25.1
14	Joe Wyatt, Democrat	63,953	72.4
	Joy Yates, Republican	24,325	27.6
15	Eligio de la Garza, Democrat	54,560	66.2
	Robert L. McDonald, Republican	27,853	33.8
16	Richard C. White, Democrat	53,090	70.0
	Michael Giere, Republican	22,743	30.0
17	Charles W. Stenholm, Democrat	69,030	68.1

Dist.	Candidate	Votes	%
	Billy Lee Fisher, Republican	32,302	31.9
18	Mickey Leland, Democrat	36,783	96.8
	Deborah Vernier, Socialist Workers	1,235	3.3
19	Kent Hance, Democrat	54,729	53.2
	George W. Bush, Republican	48,070	46.8
20	Henry B. Gonzalez, Democrat	51,584	100.0
21	Thomas G. Loeffler, Republican	84,336	57.0
	Nelson William Wolff, Democrat	63,501	43.0
22	Ron Paul, Republican	54,643	50.6
	Bob Gammage, Democrat	53,443	49.4
23	Abraham Kazen, Jr., Democrat	62,649	89.7
	Augustin Mata, La Raza Unida	7,185	10.3
24	Martin Frost, Democrat	39,201	54.1
	Leo Berman, Republican	33,314	45.9

1980 DEMOCRATIC PRIMARY ELECTION (MAY 3)

Dist.	Candidate	Votes	%
1	Sam B. Hall, Jr.	unopposed	100.0
2	Charles Wilson	88,557	77.8
	Allen Sumners	25,338	22.2
3	Earle Stephen Porter	unopposed	100.0
4	Ralph M. Hall	36,874	57.4
	Gary Jerdy	27,341	42.6
5	Jim Mattox	unopposed	100.0
6	Phil Gramm	unopposed	100.0
7	Robert Lawrence Hutchings	unopposed	100.0
8	Bob Eckhardt	unopposed	100.0
9	Jack Brooks	26,343	50.5
	W. L. "Bubba" Pate	22,188	42.6
	Jack Brookshire	3,600	6.9
10	J. J. Pickle	65,409	75.5
	Greg Stallings	21,271	24.5
11	J. Marvin Leath	unopposed	100.0
12	Jim Wright	unopposed	100.0
13	Jack Hightower	unopposed	100.0
14	William N. Patman	32,258	35.3
	Robert N. Barnes	28,660	31.3
	Jason Luby	8,600	9.4
	Joe Salem	21,974	24.0
15	Eligio de la Garza	unopposed	100.0
16	Richard C. White	unopposed	100.0
17	Charles W. Stenholm	unopposed	100.0
18	Mickey Leland	unopposed	100.0
19	Kent Hance	unopposed	100.0
20	Henry B. Gonzalez	unopposed	100.0
21	Joe Sullivan	36,151	60.0
	Marilyn Jones	24,143	40.0
22	Mike Andrews	17,986	38.8
	Bob Gammage	21,208	45.7
	Joe Pentony	7,209	15.5
23	Abraham Kazen, Jr.	59,210	76.4
	Paul Rich	18,275	23.6
24	Martin Frost	unopposed	100.0

The elections were close enough in the races for the 14th and 22nd district seats that runoff elections were held on June 7, 1980.

1980 REPUBLICAN PRIMARY ELECTION (MAY 3)

Dist.	Candidate	Votes	%
1	(none)		
2	F. H. Pannill, Sr.	unopposed	100.0
3	James M. Collins	unopposed	100.0
4	John H. Wright	8,836	52.5
	J. L. Gulley	7,988	47.5
5	Thomas W. Pauken	unopposed	100.0
6	Dave "Buster" Haskins	9,252	53.1
	Darla H. Mortensen	8,171	46.9
7	Bill Archer	unopposed	100.0
8	Jack Fields	unopposed	100.0
9	(none)		
10	John Biggar	8,308	48.7
	Jack Bower	7,151	42.0
	Radcliffe J. Finley	1,585	9.3
11	(none)		
12	Jim Bradshaw	14,102	82.0
	——— Ryan	3,105	18.0

District	Candidate	Votes	%
13	Ron Slover	unopposed	100.0
14	Charles L. Concklin	5,312	58.6
	Russ Baird	2,340	25.8
	Gerald D'Unger	1,415	15.6
15	Robert L. McDonald	unopposed	100.0
16	(none)		
17	(none)		
18	C. L. Kennedy	unopposed	100.0
19	(none)		
20	Merle W. Nash	unopposed	100.0
21	Thomas G. Loeffler	unopposed	100.0
22	Ron Paul	unopposed	100.0
23	Bobby Locke	4,099	53.7
	Martin P. Ross	3,535	46.3
24	Clay Smothers	unopposed	100.0

The election was close enough in the race for the 10th District seat that a runoff election was held on June 7, 1980.

1980 Democratic Primary Runoff Election (June 7)

District	Candidate	Votes	%
14	William N. Patman	25,480	51.6
	Robert N. Barnes	23,923	48.4
22	Mike Andrews	14,259	56.5
	Bob Gammage	10,983	43.5

1980 Republican Primary Runoff Election (June 7)

District	Candidate	Votes	%
10	John Biggar	2,365	72.3
	Jack Bower	907	27.7

1980 General Election (November 4)

District	Candidate	Votes	%
1	Sam B. Hall, Jr., Democrat	137,665	100.0
2	Charles Wilson, Democrat	142,496	69.3
	F. H. Pannill, Sr., Republican	60,742	29.5
	Martin Sorrels, Libertarian	2,530	1.2
3	James M. Collins, Republican	218,228	79.3
	Earle Stephen Porter, Democrat	49,667	18.0
	William Stephen Briggs, Libertarian	7,339	2.7
4	Ralph M. Hall, Democrat	102,787	52.3
	John H. Wright, Republican	93,915	47.7
5	Jim Mattox, Democrat	70,892	51.0
	Thomas W. Pauken, Republican	67,848	48.8
	Write-ins	295	0.2
6	Phil Gramm, Democrat	144,816	70.9
	Dave "Buster" Haskins, Republican	59,503	29.1
7	Bill Archer, Republican	242,810	82.1
	Robert Lawrence Hutchings, Democrat	48,594	16.4
	William Ware, Libertarian	4,278	1.5
	Write-ins	2	0.0
8	Jack Fields, Republican	72,856	51.8
	Bob Eckhardt, Democrat	67,921	48.2
9	Jack Brooks, Democrat	103,225	99.6
	Dean Allen I	349	0.4
10	Jake Pickle, Democrat	135,618	59.1
	John Biggar, Republican	88,940	38.8
	Michael Grossberg, Libertarian	4,866	2.1
11	J. Marvin Leath, Democrat	128,520	100.0
12	Jim Wright, Democrat	99,104	59.9
	Jim Bradshaw, Republican	65,005	39.3
	Mrs. C. B. Maudlin, Libertarian	1,281	0.8
13	Jack Hightower, Democrat	98,779	55.0
	Ron Slover, Republican	80,819	45.0
14	William N. Patman, Democrat	93,884	56.8
	Charles L. Concklin, Republican	71,495	43.2
15	Eligio de la Garza, Democrat	105,325	70.0
	Robert L. McDonald, Republican	45,090	30.0
16	Richard C. White, Democrat	107,734	84.6
	Catherine McDivitt, Libert	19,010	15.4
17	Charles W. Stenholm, Democrat	130,465	100.0
18	Mickey Leland, Democrat	71,985	79.9
	C. L. Kennedy, Republican	16,128	17.9
	William Fraser, Libertarian	1,983	2.2
19	Kent Hance, Democrat	126,632	93.5
	J. D. Webster, Libert	8,792	6.5

District	Candidate	Votes	%
20	Henry B. Gonzalez, Democrat	84,113	81.9
	Merle W. Nash, Republican	17,725	17.3
	Tom Burnham, Libertarian	846	0.8
	Write-in	1	0.0
21	Thomas G. Loeffler, Republican	196,424	76.5
	Joe Sullivan, Democrat	58,425	22.8
	William Rice, Libertarian	1,895	0.7
22	Ron Paul, Republican	106,797	51.0
	Mike Andrews, Democrat	101,094	48.3
	Vaudie V. Nance, Independent	1,360	0.7
23	Abraham Kazen, Jr, Democrat	104,595	69.8
	Bobby Locke, Republican	45,139	30.1
	Write-ins	46	0.0
24	Martin Frost, Democrat	93,960	61.3
	Clay Smothers, Republican	59,172	38.7

1982 Democratic Primary Election (May 1)

District	Candidate	Votes	%
1	Sam B. Hall, Jr.	82,384	86.0
	Jim Zorn	13,364	14.0
2	Charles Wilson	66,492	74.1
	William B. Duncan	23,286	25.9
3	James L. McNees, Jr.	6,164	59.9
	Nita K. O. H. Smith	4,135	40.1
4	Ralph M. Hall	unopposed	100.0
5	John Bryant	14,571	66.5
	Bill Blackburn	4,756	21.7
	J. B. Jackson	2,584	11.8
6	Phil Gramm	41,150	61.6
	John Olin "Jack" Teague	18,923	28.3
	Rex Carey	2,700	4.0
	Wayne Sadberry	3,987	6.0
7	Dennis G. Scoggins	unopposed	100.0
8	Henry E. Allee	unopposed	100.0
9	Jack Brooks	37,264	53.4
	W. L. "Bubba" Pate	15,230	21.8
	Thomas B. Combs	7,812	11.2
	E. Douglas McLeod	8,573	12.3
	Bob Ener	929	1.3
10	J. J. Pickle	unopposed	100.0
11	J. Marvin Leath	52,029	82.0
	Jay P. Larsen	11,383	18.0
12	Jim Wright	unopposed	100.0
13	Jack Hightower	unopposed	100.0
14	William N. Patman	unopposed	100.0
15	Eligio de la Garza	unopposed	100.0
16	Ronald Coleman	14,668	33.0
	T. Udell Moore	10,335	23.3
	Jim Scherr	6,100	13.7
	Danny Anchondo	9,294	20.9
	Ronald P. McCluskey	4,002	9.0
17	Charles W. Stenholm	unopposed	100.0
18	Mickey Leland	22,119	84.3
	Harrel Tillman	4,117	15.7
19	Kent Hance	unopposed	100.0
20	Henry B. Gonzalez	unopposed	100.0
21	Charles S. Strough	unopposed	100.0
22	(none)		
23	Abraham Kazen, Jr.	unopposed	100.0
24	Martin Frost	unopposed	100.0
25	Mike Andrews	10,541	42.8
	John Ray Harrison	7,500	30.5
	Tom Bass	6,582	26.7
26	Tom Vandergriff	unopposed	100.0
27	Solomon P. Ortiz	19,497	25.7
	Joe Salem	18,984	25.0
	Jorge Rangel	14,008	18.5
	Arnold Gonzales	13,072	17.2
	Ruben M. Torres	10,302	13.6

The elections were close enough in the races for the 16th, 25th, and 27th district seats that runoff elections were held on June 5, 1982.

1982 Republican Primary Election (May 1)

District	Candidate	Votes	%
1	(none)		

District	Candidate	Votes	%
2	(none)		
3	Steve Bartlett	12,170	28.1
	Kay Bailey Hutchison	15,820	36.5
	Jim Jackson	9,494	21.9
	Dee Travis	4,154	9.6
	Dede Casad	1,698	3.9
4	Peter J. Collumb	unopposed	100.0
5	Joe Devany	unopposed	100.0
6	Kayte Kowierschke	unopposed	100.0
7	Bill Archer	unopposed	100.0
8	Jack Fields	unopposed	100.0
9	John W. Lewis	2,244	44.7
	Frank Urbanic	1,563	31.1
	John Taylor	1,215	24.2
10	(none)		
11	(none)		
12	Jim Ryan	unopposed	100.0
13	Ron Slover	5,338	54.9
	Beau Boulter	4,380	45.1
14	Joe Wyatt, Jr.	3,699	61.7
	Tom Newton	2,298	38.3
15	(none)		
16	Pat B. Haggerty	5,046	67.8
	Hadley Robinson	2,392	32.2
17	(none)		
18	C. Leon Pickett	unopposed	100.0
19	E. L. Hicks	unopposed	100.0
20	(none)		
21	Thomas G. Loeffler	unopposed	100.0
22	Ron Paul	14,676	87.5
	Jerry Ford	2,094	12.5
23	Jeff Wentworth	5,177	81.7
	Bobby Locke	1,160	18.3
24	Lucy P. Patterson	unopposed	100.0
25	Mike Faubion		
	J. C. Helms		
	5 others		
26	Jim Bradshaw	14,062	64.7
	Morris Sheats	7,664	35.3
27	Jason Luby	2,186	55.3
	Thomas M. McRee	1,768	44.7

The elections were close enough in the races for the 3rd, 9th, and 25th district seats that runoff elections were held on June 5, 1982.

1982 DEMOCRATIC PRIMARY RUNOFF ELECTION (JUNE 5)

District	Candidate	Votes	%
16	Ronald Coleman	20,537	54.7
	T. Udell Moore	17,003	45.3
25	Mike Andrews	11,011	57.8
	John Ray Harrison	8,029	42.2
27	Solomon P. Ortiz	24,539	51.5
	Joe Salem	23,082	48.5

1982 REPUBLICAN PRIMARY RUNOFF ELECTION (JUNE 5)

District	Candidate	Votes	%
3	Steve Bartlett	18,159	57.0
	Kay Bailey Hutchison	13,715	43.0
9	John L. Lewis	1,435	64.7
	Frank Urbanic	783	34.3
25	Mike Faubion		
	J. C. Helms		

1982 GENERAL ELECTION (NOVEMBER 2)

District	Candidate	Votes	%
1	Sam B. Hall, Jr., Democrat	100,685	97.5
	John Traylor, Libertarian	2,598	2.5
2	Charles Wilson, Democrat	91,762	94.3
	Ed Richbourg, Libertarian	5,584	5.7
3	Steve Bartlett, Republican	99,852	77.1
	James L. McNees, Jr., Democrat	28,223	21.8
	Jerry R. Williamson, Libertarian	1,453	1.1
4	Ralph M. Hall, Democrat	94,134	73.8
	Peter J. Collumb, Republican	32,221	25.3
	Bruce Iiams, Libertarian	1,141	0.9
5	John Bryant, Democrat	52,214	64.8

District	Candidate	Votes	%
	Joe Devany, Republican	27,121	33.7
	John Richard Bridges, Citizens	459	0.6
	Richard Squire, Libertarian	732	0.9
	Write-ins	4	0.0
6	Phil Gramm, Democrat	91,546	94.5
	Ron Hard, Libertarian	5,288	5.5
7	Bill Archer, Republican	108,718	85.0
	Dennis G. Scoggins, Democrat	17,866	14.0
	William Ware, Libertarian	1,338	1.1
8	Jack Fields, Republican	50,630	56.7
	Henry E. Allee, Democrat	38,041	42.6
	Mike Angwin, Libertarian	547	0.6
9	Jack Brooks, Democrat	78,965	67.6
	John W. Lewis, Republican	35,422	30.3
	Dean Allen, Libertarian	2,510	2.2
10	Jake Pickle, Democrat	121,030	90.1
	William G. Kelsey, Libertarian	8,735	6.5
	Bradley Louis Rockwell, Citizens	4,511	3.4
11	J. Marvin Leath, Democrat	83,236	96.3
	Thomas B. Kilbride, Libertarian	3,136	3.6
	Write-ins	23	0.0
12	Jim Wright, Democrat	78,913	68.9
	Jim Ryan, Republican	34,879	30.5
	Edward Olson, Libertarian	743	0.7
13	Jack Hightower, Democrat	86,376	63.6
	Ron Slover, Republican	47,877	35.3
	Rod Collier, Libertarian	1,567	1.2
14	William N. Patman, Democrat	76,851	60.7
	Joe Wyatt, Jr., Republican	48,942	38.6
	Glenn Rasmussen, Libertarian	919	0.7
15	Eligio de la Garza, Democrat	76,544	95.7
	Frank L. Jones III, Libertarian	3,458	4.3
16	Ronald Coleman, Democrat	44,024	53.9
	Pat B. Haggerty, Republican	36,064	44.2
	Catherine A. McDivitt, Libertarian	1,583	1.9
17	Charles W. Stenholm, Democrat	109,359	97.1
	James A. Cooley II, Libertarian	3,271	2.9
18	Mickey Leland, Democrat	68,014	82.6
	C. Leon Pickett, Republican	12,104	14.7
	Thomas P. Bernhardt, Libertarian	2,215	2.7
	Write-in	2	0.0
19	Kent Hance, Democrat	89,702	81.6
	E. L. Hicks, Republican	19,062	17.3
	Mike Read, Libertarian	1,206	1.1
20	Henry B. Gonzalez, Democrat	68,544	91.5
	Roger V. Gary, Libertarian	4,163	5.6
	Benedict D. LaRosa, Independent	2,213	3.0
	Write-in	4	0.0
21	Thomas G. Loeffler, Republican	106,515	74.6
	Charles S. Stough, Democrat	35,112	24.6
	Jeffrey J. Brown, Libertarian	1,243	0.9
	Write-in	2	0.0
22	Ron Paul, Republican	66,536	98.6
	Nick Benton, Independent	943	1.4
23	Abraham Kazen, Jr., Democrat	51,690	55.3
	Jeff Wentworth, Republican	41,363	44.2
	Parker Abell, Libertarian	475	0.5
24	Martin Frost, Democrat	63,857	72.9
	Lucy P. Patterson, Republican	22,798	26.0
	David Guier, Libertarian	998	1.1
25	Mike Andrews, Democrat	63,974	60.4
	Mike Faubion, Republican	40,112	37.9
	Jeff Calvert, Libertarian	864	0.8
	Barbara Coldiron, Citizens	963	0.9
	Write-in	1	0.0
26	Tom Vandergriff, Democrat	69,782	50.1
	Jim Bradshaw, Republican	69,438	49.9
27	Solomon P. Ortiz, Democrat	66,604	64.0
	Jason Luby, Republican	35,209	33.8
	Steven R. Roberts, Libertarian	2,231	2.1

1983 SPECIAL ELECTION (FEBRUARY 12)

District	Candidate	Votes	%
6	Phil Gramm, Republican	46,371	55.3

	Candidate	Votes	%
	Dan Kubiak, Democrat	33,201	39.6
	John Henry Faulk, Democrat	3,070	3.7
	Bill Powers, Democrat	318	0.4
	Rex Carey, Democrat	268	0.3
	H. Martin Gibson, Libertarian	223	0.3
	George W. Chamberlain, Democrat	153	0.2
	3 Others	223	0.3

This special election was called following Phil Gramm's resignation from the Democratic Party and Congress. He was reelected as a Republican.

1984 DEMOCRATIC PRIMARY ELECTION (MAY 5)

	Candidate	Votes	%
1	Sam B. Hall, Jr.	unopposed	100.0
2	Charles Wilson	61,684	55.2
	Lloyd Dickens	9,045	8.1
	William Duncan	4,373	3.9
	Mitchell Hickman	4,245	3.8
	Jerry Johnson	32,438	29.0
3	James Westbrook	6,889	58.3
	James McNees	4,928	41.7
4	Ralph M. Hall	unopposed	100.0
5	John Bryant	unopposed	100.0
6	Dan Kubiak	38,143	54.3
	Jesse M. Van Winkle	5,279	7.5
	Hugh Parmer	26,770	38.1
7	Billy Willibey	unopposed	100.0
8	Donald Buford	11,083	51.1
	Jay Hill	10,621	48.9
9	Jack Brooks	unopposed	100.0
10	Jake Pickle	unopposed	100.0
11	J. Marvin Leath	unopposed	100.0
12	Jim Wright	unopposed	100.0
13	Jack Hightower	unopposed	100.0
14	William N. Patman	unopposed	100.0
15	Eligio de la Garza	unopposed	100.0
16	Ronald Coleman	unopposed	100.0
17	Charles W. Stenholm	81,312	88.2
	Noel Cowling	10,867	11.8
18	Mickey Leland	33,072	90.6
	Frank Saulsberry	3,421	9.4
19	Don R. Richards	18,411	31.0
	Gary D. Condra	4,779	8.0
	Delwin Jones	7,987	13.4
	Thomas Richards	17,481	29.4
	John Selby	10,808	18.2
20	Henry B. Gonzalez	unopposed	100.0
21	Joe Sullivan	24,431	56.8
	Bobby Locke	18,582	43.2
22	Douglas Williams	10,256	47.4
	Nick Benton	4,873	22.5
	Jim Mooney	6,507	30.1
23	Albert Bustamante	40,855	58.6
	Stanley Green	3,286	4.7
	Abraham Kazen	25,588	36.7
24	Martin Frost	25,248	92.0
	Dan Leach	2,185	8.0
25	Mike Andrews	28,513	94.3
	Bruce Director	1,737	5.7
26	Tom Vandergriff	unopposed	100.0

The elections were close enough in the races for the 19th and 22nd district seats that runoff elections were held on June 2, 1984.

1984 REPUBLICAN PRIMARY ELECTION (MAY 5)

	Candidate	Votes	%
1	(none)		
2	Louis Dugas, Jr.	unopposed	100.0
3	Steve Bartlett	unopposed	100.0
4	Thomas Blow	unopposed	100.0
5	(none)		
6	Joe L. Barton	7,563	42.0
	Bob Harris	2,857	15.9
	Max Hoyt	5,590	31.0
	Pat Friedrichs	2,014	11.2
7	Bill Archer	unopposed	100.0
8	Jack Fields	unopposed	100.0
9	Jim Mahan	4,227	53.5

10	Lisa Duperier	3,675	46.5
11	(none)		
12	(none)		
13	Beau Boulter	unopposed	100.0
14	Mac Sweeney	4,455	49.7
	Chris Mealy	3,346	37.3
	Wayne Pryor	1,167	13.0
15	(none)		
16	Jack Hammond	unopposed	100.0
17	(none)		
18	Glen E. Beaman	unopposed	100.0
19	Larry Combest	5,562	48.4
	Ron Fleming	3,881	33.8
	Tom Schaefer	1,624	14.1
	Richard Wilder	421	3.7
20	(none)		
21	Thomas G. Loeffler	unopposed	100.0
22	Tom DeLay	11,580	53.3
	Joe Agris	279	1.3
	Gary Engebretson	1,006	4.6
	Ellen Heath	2,135	9.8
	J.C. Helms	5,711	26.3
	Don Richardson	1,029	4.7
23	(none)		
24	Bob Burk	5,570	60.8
	Jack Bower	3,598	39.2
25	Jerry Patterson	unopposed	100.0
26	Dick Armey	unopposed	100.0

The elections were close enough in the races for the 6th, 14th, and 19th district seats that runoff elections were held on June 2, 1984.

1984 Democratic Primary Runoff Election (June 2)

19	Don R. Richards	29,144	50.6
	Thomas Richards	28,429	49.4
22	Douglas Williams	8,717	61.8
	Jim Mooney	5,398	38.2

1984 Republican Primary Runoff Election (June 2)

6	Joe L. Barton	4,632	50.1
	Max Hoyt	4,622	49.9
14	Mac Sweeney	2,887	59.8
	Chris Mealy	1,944	40.2
19	Larry Combest	4,255	57.5
	Ron Fleming	3,143	42.5

1984 General Election (November 6)

1	Sam B. Hall, Jr., Democrat	139,829	100.0
2	Charles Wilson, Democrat	113,225	59.3
	Louis Dugas, Jr., Republican	77,842	40.7
3	Steve Bartlett, Republican	228,819	83.0
	Jim Westbrook, Democrat	46,890	17.0
4	Ralph M. Hall, Democrat	120,749	58.0
	Thomas Blow, Republican	87,553	42.0
	Other	39	0.0
5	John Bryant, Democrat	94,391	100.0
6	Joe L. Barton, Republican	131,482	56.6
	Dan Kubiak, Democrat	100,799	43.4
7	Bill Archer, Republican	213,480	86.7
	Billy Willibey, Democrat	32,835	13.3
8	Jack Fields, Republican	113,031	64.6
	Don Buford, Democrat	62,072	35.4
9	Jack Brooks, Democrat	120,559	58.9
	Jim Mahan, Republican	84,306	41.2
10	Jake Pickle, Democrat	186,447	99.8
	Hugh Wilson	338	0.2
11	J. Marvin Leath, Democrat	112,940	100.0
12	Jim Wright, Democrat	106,299	100.0
	Other	3	0.0
13	Beau Boulter, Republican	107,600	53.0
	Jack Hightower, Democrat	95,367	47.0
14	Mac Sweeney, Republican	104,181	51.3
	William N. Patman, Democrat	98,885	48.7
15	Eligio de la Garza, Democrat	104,863	100.0

District	Candidate	Votes	%
16	Ronald Coleman, Democrat	76,375	57.4
	Jack Hammond, Republican	56,589	42.6
17	Charles W. Stenholm, Democrat	143,012	100.0
18	Mickey Leland, Democrat	109,626	78.8
	Glen E. Beaman, Republican	26,400	19.0
	Jose Alvarado, Independent	3,064	2.2
	Other	20	0.0
19	Larry Combest, Republican	102,805	58.1
	Don R. Richards, Democrat	74,044	41.9
20	Henry B. Gonzalez, Democrat	100,443	100.0
21	Thomas G. Loeffler, Republican	199,909	80.6
	Joe Sullivan, Democrat	48,039	19.4
	Other	32	0.0
22	Tom DeLay, Republican	125,225	65.3
	Doug Williams, Democrat	66,495	34.7
	Other	31	0.0
23	Albert Bustamante, Democrat	95,721	100.0
24	Martin Frost, Democrat	105,210	59.5
	Bob Burk, Republican	71,703	40.5
	Other	5	0.0
25	Mike Andrews, Democrat	113,945	64.0
	Jerry Patterson, Republican	63,974	36.0
26	Dick Armey, Republican	126,641	51.3
	Tom Vandergriff, Democrat	120,451	48.7
	Other	2	0.0
27	Solomon P. Ortiz, Democrat	105,516	63.6
	Richard Moore, Republican	60,283	36.4

1985 SPECIAL ELECTION (JUNE 29)

District	Candidate	Votes	%
1	Edd Hargett, Republican	29,720	42.0
	Jim Chapman, Democrat	21,382	30.2
	Sam W. Russell, Democrat	13,099	18.6
	Jim McWilliams, Democrat	3,410	4.8
	Billy W. Flanagan, Democrat	2,270	3.2
	Carl Brown, Democrat	416	0.6
	Warren G. Harding, Democrat	305	0.4
	Fred J. Wieder, Christian Contenders	130	0.2

This special election was held to fill the seat of Sam Hall, who resigned on May 27, 1985, to accept a federal judgeship. The first special election failed to yield a majority, so a runoff election was called.

1985 SPECIAL ELECTION RUNOFF (AUGUST 3)

District	Candidate	Votes	%
1	Jim Chapman, Democrat	52,665	50.9
	Edd Hargett, Republican	50,741	49.1

This special election runoff was held to fill the seat of Sam Hall. The first special election failed to yield a majority.

1986 DEMOCRATIC PRIMARY ELECTION (MAY 3)

District	Candidate	Votes	%
1	Jim Chapman	56,004	100.0
2	Charles Wilson	53,856	100.0
3	(none)		
4	Ralph M. Hall	32,441	100.0
5	John Bryant	12,715	93.3
	Gregory A. Witherspoon	912	6.7
6	Pete Geren	33,849	84.5
	Leonard Rinaldo	6,200	15.5
7	Harry Kniffen	unopposed	100.0
8	Blaine Mann	6,509	73.4
	Harley Schlanger	2,357	26.6
9	Jack Brooks	32,758	100.0
10	Jake Pickle	49,101	81.0
	Nina Butts	11,502	19.0
11	J. Marvin Leath	42,486	100.0
12	Jim Wright	18,135	90.7
	Elizabeth Arnold	1,869	9.3
13	Doug Seal	23,126	57.2
	Don Stribling	17,293	42.8
14	Greg H. Laughlin	unopposed	100.0
15	Eligio de la Garza	52,358	100.0
16	Ronald Coleman	26,722	100.0
17	Charles W. Stenholm	44,490	100.0
18	Mickey Leland	17,895	91.3
	Dorothy Stephans	1,706	8.7

District	Candidate	Votes	Percent
19	Gerald McCathern	18,719	62.8
	Mary Nell Mathis	11,110	37.2
20	Henry B. Gonzalez	26,936	100.0
21	Pete Snelson	18,211	57.3
	David Hunsicker	6,102	19.2
	Terry M. Lowry	2,368	7.5
	Joe Sullivan	5,076	16.0
22	Susan Director	unopposed	100.0
23	Albert Bustamante	40,170	100.0
24	Martin Frost	19,701	93.2
	Gardell A. Morehead	1,438	6.8
25	Mike Andrews	16,678	94.4
	Curtis Perry, II	990	5.6
26	George Richardson	6,311	63.5
	David Smith	3,355	34.7
27	Solomon P. Ortiz	44,709	84.8
	Ken Rich	8,013	15.2

1986 REPUBLICAN PRIMARY ELECTION (MAY 3)

District	Candidate	Votes	Percent
1	(none)		
2	Julian Gordon	2,882	58.3
	Louis Dugas	2,058	41.7
3	Steve Bartlett	42,668	100.0
4	Thomas Blow	unopposed	100.0
5	Tom Carter	unopposed	100.0
6	Joe Barton	17,890	100.0
7	Bill Archer	24,362	100.0
8	Jack Fields	9,635	100.0
9	Lisa D. Duperier	unopposed	100.0
10	Carole K. Rylander	unopposed	100.0
11	(none)		
12	Don McNeil	9,279	69.4
	Clint Young	4,089	30.6
13	Beau Boulter	17,488	100.0
14	Mac Sweeney	13,733	100.0
15	(none)		
16	Roy Gillia	unopposed	100.0
17	(none)		
18	(none)		
19	Larry Combest	26,735	100.0
20	(none)		
21	Lamar Smith	18,390	31.1
	Van Archer	14,616	24.7
	Jeff Wentworth	11,781	19.9
	G.Thane Akins	8,103	13.7
	Henry Gandy	5,809	9.8
	Lowell "Duke" Embs	376	0.6
22	Tom DeLay	17,524	100.0
23	(none)		
24	Bob Burk	8,646	57.9
	Scot E. Kurth	6,280	42.1
25	(none)		
26	Dick Armey	26,245	85.2
	Bill Friday	2,917	9.5
	Clyde Riddle, Jr.	1,656	8.4
27	(none)		

The election was close enough in the race for the 21st District seat that a runoff election was held on June 7, 1986.

1986 REPUBLICAN PRIMARY RUNOFF ELECTION (JUNE 7)

District	Candidate	Votes	Percent
21	Lamar Smith	18,140	53.6
	Van Archer	15,714	46.4

1986 GENERAL ELECTION (NOVEMBER 4)

District	Candidate	Votes	Percent
1	Jim Chapman, Democrat	84,445	100.0
2	Charles Wilson, Democrat	78,529	56.7
	Julian Gordon, Republican	55,986	40.5
	Sam I. Paradice, Independent	3,838	2.8
3	Steve Bartlett, Republican	143,381	94.1
	Brent Barnes, Independent	6,268	4.1
	Dou Gough, Libertarian	2,736	1.8
4	Ralph M. Hall, Democrat	97,540	71.7

District	Candidate	Votes	%
	Thomas Blow, Republican	38,578	28.3
5	John Bryant, Democrat	57,410	58.5
	Tom Carter, Republican	39,945	40.7
	Robert Brewer, Libertarian	749	0.8
6	Joe Barton, Republican	86,190	55.8
	Pete Geren, Democrat	68,270	44.2
7	Bill Archer, Republican	129,673	87.4
	Harry Kniffen, Democrat	17,635	11.9
	Roger Phail, Libertarian	1,087	0.7
8	Jack Fields, Republican	66,280	68.4
	Blaine Mann, Democrat	30,617	31.6
	Write-ins	6	0.0
9	Jack Brooks, Democrat	73,285	61.5
	Lisa D. Duperier, Republican	48,834	38.5
10	Jake Pickle, Democrat	135,863	72.3
	Carole K. Rylander, Republican	52,000	27.7
11	J. Marvin Leath, Democrat	84,201	100.0
12	Jim Wright, Democrat	84,831	68.7
	Don McNeil, Republican	38,620	31.3
13	Beau Boulter, Republican	84,980	64.9
	Doug Seal, Democrat	45,907	35.7
14	Mac Sweeney, Republican	74,471	52.3
	Greg H. Laughlin, Democrat	67,852	47.7
15	Eligio de la Garza, Democrat	70,777	100.0
16	Ronald Coleman, Democrat	50,590	65.7
	Roy Gillia, Republican	26,421	34.3
17	Charles W. Stenholm, Democrat	97,791	100.0
18	Mickey Leland, Democrat	63,335	90.2
	Joanne Kuniansky, Independent	6,884	9.8
19	Larry Combest, Republican	68,695	62.0
	Gerald McCathern, Democrat	42,129	38.0
20	Henry B. Gonzalez, Democrat	55,363	100.0
21	Lamar Smith, Republican	100,346	60.6
	Pete Snelson, Democrat	63,779	38.5
	James A. Robinson, Libertarian	1,432	0.9
	Write-ins	10	0.0
22	Tom DeLay, Republican	76,459	71.8
	Susan Director, Democrat	30,079	28.2
23	Albert Bustamante, Democrat	68,131	90.7
	Ken Hendrix, Libertarian	7,001	9.3
24	Martin Frost, Democrat	69,368	67.2
	Bob Burk, Republican	33,819	32.8
	Write-ins	4	0.0
25	Mike Andrews, Democrat	67,435	100.0
26	Dick Armey, Republican	101,735	68.1
	George Richardson, Democrat	47,651	31.9
27	Solomon P. Ortiz, Democrat	64,165	100.0

1988 Democratic Primary Election (March 8)

District	Candidate	Votes	%
1	Jim Chapman	unopposed	100.0
2	Charles Wilson	unopposed	100.0
3	Blake Cowden	unopposed	100.0
4	Ralph M. Hall	unopposed	100.0
5	John Bryant	unopposed	100.0
6	N. P. "Pat" Kendrick	21,245	36.5
	Alton Parish	16,651	28.6
	John E. Welch	20,275	34.9
7	Diane Richards	unopposed	100.0
8	(none)		
9	Jack Brooks	unopposed	100.0
10	Jake Pickle	unopposed	100.0
11	J. Marvin Leath	unopposed	100.0
12	Jim Wright	unopposed	100.0
13	Bill Sarpalius	37,745	55.4
	Randy Hollums	10,755	15.8
	Ed Lehman	19,629	28.8
14	Greg H. Laughlin	59,213	72.2
	Michael L. Herzik	22,770	27.8
15	Eligio de la Garza	unopposed	100.0
16	Ronald Coleman	unopposed	100.0
17	Charles W. Stenholm	unopposed	100.0
18	Mickey Leland	38,963	82.4
	Elizabeth Spates	8,321	17.6

(continued)

District	Candidate	Votes	Percent
19	Gerald McCathern	unopposed	100.0
20	Henry B. Gonzalez	unopposed	100.0
21	(none)		
22	Wayne Walker	12,049	42.2
	Richard Konrad	8,775	30.7
	Ray Lemmon	7,715	27.0
23	Albert Bustamante	unopposed	100.0
24	Martin Frost	unopposed	100.0
25	Mike Andrews	unopposed	100.0
26	Jo Ann Reyes	unopposed	100.0
27	Solomon P. Ortiz	unopposed	100.0

The elections were close enough in the races for the 6th and 22nd district seats that runoff elections were held on April 12, 1988.

1988 REPUBLICAN PRIMARY ELECTION (MARCH 8)

District	Candidate	Votes	Percent
1	Horace McQueen	unopposed	100.0
2	(none)		
3	Steve Bartlett	unopposed	100.0
4	Randy Sutton	unopposed	100.0
5	Lon Williams	17,356	72.8
	Kay Cohlmia	6,482	27.2
6	Joe Barton	unopposed	100.0
7	Bill Archer	unopposed	100.0
8	Jack Fields	unopposed	100.0
9	(none)		
10	(none)		
11	(none)		
12	(none)		
13	Larry S. Milner	10,129	24.6
	Jim Brandon	7,830	19.0
	Ron Buffum	5,031	12.2
	Alan Pickering	3,737	9.1
	Bob Price	7,953	19.3
	Chip Staniswalis	6,464	15.7
14	Mac Sweeney	unopposed	100.0
15	(none)		
16	(none)		
17	(none)		
18	(none)		
19	Larry Combest	unopposed	100.0
20	Lee Trevino	6,399	54.3
	Terry Peters	5,389	45.7
21	Lamar Smith	unopposed	100.0
22	Tom DeLay	unopposed	100.0
23	Jerome L. Gonzales	unopposed	100.0
24	(none)		
25	George H. Loeffler, Jr.	13,066	76.8
	Lon Peyton Arnett	3,936	23.2
26	Dick Armey	unopposed	100.0
27	(none)		

The election was close enough in the race for the 13th District seat that a runoff election was held on April 12, 1988.

1988 DEMOCRATIC PRIMARY RUNOFF ELECTION (APRIL 12)

District	Candidate	Votes	Percent
6	N. P. "Pat" Kendrick	12,209	50.8
	John E. Welch	11,838	49.2
22	Wayne Walker	3,757	50.6
	Richard Konrad	3,667	49.4

1988 REPUBLICAN PRIMARY RUNOFF ELECTION (APRIL 12)

District	Candidate	Votes	Percent
13	Larry S. Milner	12,013	56.3
	Bob Price	9,322	43.7

1988 GENERAL ELECTION (NOVEMBER 8)

District	Candidate	Votes	Percent
1	Jim Chapman, Democrat	122,566	62.2
	Horace McQueen, Republican	74,357	37.8
2	Charles Wilson, Democrat	145,614	87.7
	Gary W. Nelson, Libertarian	20,475	12.3
3	Steve Bartlett, Republican	227,882	81.8
	Blake Cowden, Democrat	50,627	18.2
4	Ralph M. Hall, Democrat	139,379	66.4
	Randy Sutton, Republican	67,337	32.1

District	Candidate	Votes	%
	Melanie A. Dunn, Libertarian	3,152	1.5
5	John Bryant, Democrat	95,376	60.7
	Lon Williams, Republican	59,877	38.1
	Ken Ashby, Libertarian	1,786	1.1
6	Joe Barton, Republican	164,692	67.6
	N. P. "Pat" Kendrick, Democrat	78,786	32.4
7	Bill Archer, Republican	185,203	79.1
	Leo Sadovy, Libertarian	48,824	20.9
8	Jack Fields, Republican	90,503	100.0
9	Jack Brooks, Democrat	137,270	100.0
10	Jake Pickle, Democrat	232,213	93.4
	Vincent J. May, Libertarian	16,281	6.6
11	J. Marvin Leath, Democrat	134,207	95.4
	Frederick M. King, Libertarian	6,533	4.6
12	Jim Wright, Democrat	135,459	99.3
	Jim Ryan, I	767	0.6
	Gary Johnson, I	230	0.2
13	Bill Sarpalius, Democrat	98,345	52.5
	Larry S. Milner, Republican	89,105	47.5
14	Greg H. Laughlin, Democrat	111,395	53.2
	Mac Sweeney, Republican	96,042	45.9
	Don Kelly, Libertarian	1,779	0.9
15	Eligio de la Garza, Democrat	93,672	93.9
	Gloria Joyce Hendrix, Libertarian	6,133	6.1
16	Ronald Coleman, Democrat	104,514	100.0
17	Charles W. Stenholm, Democrat	149,064	100.0
18	Mickey Leland, Democrat	94,408	92.9
	J. Alejandro Snead, Libertarian	7,235	7.1
19	Larry Combest, Republican	113,068	67.7
	Gerald McCathern, Democrat	53,932	32.3
20	Henry B. Gonzalez, Democrat	94,527	70.7
	Lee Trevino, Republican	36,801	27.5
	Theresa S. Doyle, Libertarian	2,368	1.8
21	Lamar Smith, Republican	203,989	93.2
	James A. Robinson, Libertarian	14,801	6.8
22	Tom DeLay, Republican	125,733	67.4
	Wayne Walker, Democrat	58,471	31.4
	George Harper, Libertarian	2,276	1.2
	Write-ins	4	0.0
23	Albert Bustamante, Democrat	116,423	64.5
	Jerome L. Gonzales, Republican	60,559	33.6
	Tony R. Garza, Libertarian	3,448	1.9
24	Martin Frost, Democrat	135,794	92.6
	Leo Sadovy, Libertarian	10,841	7.4
25	Mike Andrews, Democrat	113,499	71.4
	George H. Loeffler, Jr., Republican	44,043	27.7
	Kevin Southwick, Libertarian	1,494	0.9
26	Dick Armey, Republican	194,944	69.3
	Jo Ann Reyes, Democrat	86,490	30.7
	Write-ins	12	0.0
27	Solomon P. Ortiz, Democrat	105,085	100.0

1989 SPECIAL ELECTION (AUGUST 12)

District	Candidate	Votes	%
12	Robert Lanier, Republican	21,978	39.4
	Pete Geren, Democrat	17,751	31.8
	Jim Lane, Democrat	12,308	22.1
	Laraine Bethke, Republican	1,313	2.4
	Bill Turner, Democrat	854	1.5
	Jim Hunter, Liber	475	0.9
	George J. Petrovich, Democrat	217	0.4
	Other	78	0.1

This special election was held to fill the seat of Jim Wright, who resigned on June 29, 1989. The race failed to yield a majority, so a runoff election was held on September 12, 1989, between the top two candidates.

1989 SPECIAL ELECTION RUNOFF (SEPTEMBER 12)

District	Candidate	Votes	%
12	Pete Geren, Democrat	40,210	51.0
	Robert Lanier, Republican	38,590	49.0

This runoff election was held to select a replacement for Jim Wright. No candidate received a majority in the first special election.

1989 SPECIAL ELECTION (NOVEMBER 7)

District	Candidate	Votes	%
18	Craig Washington, Democrat	27,367	41.3

Anthony Hall, Democrat — 22,797 — 34.4
Ron Wilson, Democrat — 4,948 — 7.8
Al Edwards, Democrat — 3,095 — 4.7
Beverly A. Spencer, Republican — 2,123 — 3.2
Shirley Fobbs, Democrat — 1,315 — 2.0
Timothy J. Hattenback, Democrat — 1,267 — 1.9
Manse R. Sharp, Republican — 1,079 — 1.6
Byron J. Johnson, Republican — 1,058 — 1.6
Gary Johnson, Libertarian — 829 — 1.3
Lee A. Demas, Democrat — 342 — 0.5

This special election was held to fill the seat of Mickey Leland, who died in a plane crash in Ethiopia on August 7, 1989. The race failed to yield a majority, so a runoff election was held on December 9, 1989.

1989 SPECIAL ELECTION RUNOFF (DECEMBER 9)

District	Candidate	Votes	%
18	Craig Washington, Democrat	24,140	56.6
	Anthony Hall, Democrat	18,484	43.4

This runoff election was held to select a replacement for Mickey Leland. No candidate received a majority in the first special election.

1990 DEMOCRATIC PRIMARY ELECTION (MARCH 13)

District	Candidate	Votes	%
1	Jim Chapman	unopposed	100.0
2	Charles Wilson	unopposed	100.0
3	(none)		
4	Ralph M. Hall	unopposed	100.0
5	John Bryant	unopposed	100.0
6	John E. Welch	unopposed	100.0
7	(none)		
8	(none)		
9	Jack Brooks	44,781	72.2
	Jack Brookshire	17,268	27.8
10	Jake Pickle	83,989	88.7
	John Longsworth	4,589	4.8
	Robin Mills	6,116	6.5
11	Chet Edwards	unopposed	100.0
12	Pete Geren	unopposed	100.0
13	Bill Sarpalius	unopposed	100.0
14	Greg H. Laughlin	unopposed	100.0
15	Eligio de la Garza	unopposed	100.0
16	Ronald Coleman	unopposed	100.0
17	Charles W. Stenholm	unopposed	100.0
18	Craig Washington	unopposed	100.0
19	(none)		
20	Henry B. Gonzalez	unopposed	100.0
21	Kirby J. Roberts	unopposed	100.0
22	Bruce Director	unopposed	100.0
23	Albert Bustamante	unopposed	100.0
24	Martin Frost	unopposed	100.0
25	Mike Andrews	unopposed	100.0
26	John Wayne Caton	17,051	64.9
	Craig Hotzclaw	9,208	35.1
27	Solomon P. Ortiz	unopposed	100.0

1990 REPUBLICAN PRIMARY ELECTION (MARCH 13)

District	Candidate	Votes	%
1	Hamp Hodges	unopposed	100.0
2	Donna Peterson	unopposed	100.0
3	Steve Bartlett	unopposed	100.0
4	(none)		
5	Jerry Rucker	unopposed	100.0
6	Joe Barton	unopposed	100.0
7	Bill Archer	unopposed	100.0
8	Jack Fields	unopposed	100.0
9	Maury Meyers	7,383	44.5
	Steve Clifford	2,435	14.7
	Steve Stockman	6,755	40.8
10	David Beilharz	15,870	52.9
	Matt Harnest	14,130	47.1
11	Hugh D. Shine	11,852	42.2
	Jim Mathis	8,239	29.3
	David Sibley	8,017	28.5
12	Mike McGinn	unopposed	100.0
13	Dick Waterfield	21,11/	69.4
	Bob Price	9,324	30.6

District	Candidate	Votes	%
14	Joe Dial	unopposed	100.0
15	(none)		
16	(none)		
17	(none)		
18	Timothy J. Hattenbach	unopposed	100.0
19	Larry Combest	unopposed	100.0
20	(none)		
21	Lamar Smith	unopposed	100.0
22	Tom DeLay	unopposed	100.0
23	Jerome L. Gonzales	unopposed	100.0
24	(none)		
25	(none)		
26	Dick Armey	unopposed	100.0
27	(none)		

The elections were close enough in the races for the 9th and 11th district seats that runoff elections were held on April 10, 1990.

1990 REPUBLICAN PRIMARY RUNOFF ELECTION (APRIL 10)

District	Candidate	Votes	%
9	Maury Meyers	5,907	61.0
	Steve Stockman	3,777	39.0
11	Hugh D. Shine	6,504	39.4
	Jim Mathis	10,018	60.6

1990 GENERAL ELECTION (NOVEMBER 6)

District	Candidate	Votes	%
1	Jim Chapman, Democrat	89,241	61.0
	Hamp Hodges, Republican	56,954	39.0
2	Charles Wilson, Democrat	76,974	55.6
	Donna Peterson, Republican	61,555	44.4
3	Steve Bartlett, Republican	153,857	99.6
	Noel Kopala, Write-in	617	0.4
4	Ralph M. Hall, Democrat	108,300	99.6
	Tim J. McCord, Write-in	394	0.4
5	John Bryant, Democrat	65,228	59.6
	Jerry Rucker, Republican	41,307	37.7
	Kenneth Ashby, Libertarian	2,939	2.7
6	Joe Barton, Republican	125,049	66.5
	John E. Welch, Democrat	62,344	33.1
	Michael Worsham, Write-in	737	0.4
7	Bill Archer, Republican	114,254	100.0
8	Jack Fields, Republican	60,603	100.0
9	Jack Brooks, Democrat	79,786	57.7
	Maury Meyers, Republican	58,339	42.3
10	Jake Pickle, Democrat	152,784	64.9
	David Beilharz, Republican	73,766	31.3
	Jeff Davis, Libertarian	8,905	3.8
	Write-ins	41	0.0
11	Chet Edwards, Democrat	73,810	53.5
	Hugh D. Shine, Republican	64,269	46.5
12	Pete Geren, Democrat	98,026	71.3
	Mike McGinn, Republican	39,438	28.7
13	Bill Sarpalius, Democrat	81,815	56.5
	Dick Waterfield, Republican	63,045	43.5
14	Greg H. Laughlin, Democrat	89,251	54.3
	Joe Dial, Republican	75,098	45.7
15	Eligio de la Garza, Democrat	72,461	100.0
16	Ronald Coleman, Democrat	62,455	95.6
	William Burgett, Independent	2,854	4.4
17	Charles W. Stenholm, Democrat	104,100	100.0
18	Craig Washington, Democrat	54,477	99.6
	Timothy J. Hattenbach, Republican	166	0.3
	Other	77	0.1
19	Larry Combest, Republican	83,795	100.0
20	Henry B. Gonzalez, Democrat	56,318	100.0
21	Lamar Smith, Republican	144,570	74.8
	Kirby J. Roberts, Democrat	48,585	25.2
22	Tom DeLay, Republican	93,425	71.2
	Bruce Director, Democrat	37,721	28.8
23	Albert Bustamante, Democrat	71,052	63.5
	Jerome L. Gonzales, Republican	40,856	36.5
24	Martin Frost, Democrat	86,297	100.0
25	Mike Andrews, Democrat	67,427	100.0
26	Dick Armey, Republican	147,856	70.4
	John Wayne Caton, Democrat	62,158	29.6

27 Solomon P. Ortiz, Democrat — 62,822 — 100.0

1991 Special Election (May 4)

District	Candidate	Votes	%
3	Tom Pauken, Republican	15,018	27.5
	Sam Johnson, Republican	10,855	19.9
	William Hammond, Republican	6,756	12.4
	Paul Z. Pilzer, Republican	5,909	10.8
	Dan Branch, Republican	5,484	10.0
	Pete Sessions, Republican	5,156	9.4
	Wayne E. Putnam, Democrat	2324	4.3
	Farrell Ray, Republican	1,139	2.1
	Robert E. Lyle, Republican	806	1.5
	Mel Richardson, Independent	802	1.5
	Rufus Higginbotham, Independent	238	0.4
	David Corlet, Republican	168	0.3

This special election was held to fill the seat of Steve Bartlett, who resigned on March 11, 1991, to run for mayor of Dallas. The race failed to yield a majority, so a runoff election was held on May 18.

1991 Special Election Runoff (May 18)

District	Candidate	Votes	%
3	Sam Johnson, Republican	24,004	52.6
	Tom Pauken, Republican	21,647	47.4

This runoff election was held to select a replacement for Steve Bartlett. No candidate received a majority in the first special election.

1992 Democratic Primary Election (March 10)

District	Candidate	Votes	%
1	Jim Chapman	81,080	100.0
2	Edgar J. "Bubba" Groce	13,912	13.2
	Stuart Williamson	16,938	16.0
	Charles Wilson	74,674	70.8
3	(none)		
4	Ralph M. Hall	36,837	66.2
	Roger Sanders	18,833	33.8
5	John Bryant	38,783	100.0
6	John Dietrich	11,603	53.8
	Frank F. Smith	9,977	46.2
8	Donald Murphy Guillory	6,774	38.8
	Charles Robinson	10,687	61.2
9	Jack Brooks	44,236	100.0
10	John Longsworth	12,034	17.8
	J. J. Pickle	55,703	82.2
11	Chet Edwards	50,389	100.0
12	Pete Geren	37,722	100.0
13	Bill Sarpalius	56,064	100.0
14	Greg Laughlin	62,440	100.0
15	Eligio de la Garza	48,908	100.0
16	Jorge Artalejo	1,856	4.3
	Ronald Coleman	27,562	63.8
	R. K. Jones	2,704	6.3
	Charles Ponzio, Jr.	11,104	25.7
17	Charles W. Stenholm	75,719	100.0
18	Craig A. Washington	32,365	100.0
19	Terry Lee Moser	24,129	100.0
20	Henry B. Gonzalez	23,363	100.0
21	James M. Gaddy	26,394	100.0
22	Richard Konrad	15,884	100.0
23	Albert G. Bustamante	44,856	68.2
	Clayton H. Mulvaney, Jr.	20,934	31.8
24	Martin Frost	27,112	100.0
25	Mike Andrews	25,291	82.5
	Mary Robb Whipple	5,371	17.5
26	John Wayne Caton	9,584	100.0
27	Solomon P. Ortiz	45,602	100.0
28	Frank Tejeda	42,011	100.0
29	Andrew C. Burks, Jr.	804	2.6
	Sylvia R. Garcia	6,487	20.9
	Gene Green	8,533	27.5
	Albert 'Al' Luna, III	4,661	15.0
	Ben Reyes	10,504	33.9
	Adolph Hauntz	3,794	8.4
30	Eddie Bernice Johnson	41,587	91.6

The election was close enough in the race for the 29th District seat that a runoff election was held on April 14, 1992.

1992 REPUBLICAN PRIMARY ELECTION (MARCH 10)

District	Candidate	Votes	%
1	Robert E. "Swede" Lee	9,164	100.0
2	D. J. Fillippa, Jr.	1,866	19.1
	Donna Peterson	7,916	80.9
3	David Corley	9,107	16.9
	Sam Johnson	44,920	83.1
4	David L. Bridges	13,661	58.8
	Tim McCord	9,583	41.2
5	Farrell Ray	5,592	45.2
	Richard Stokley	6,784	54.8
6	Joe Barton	34,366	79.1
	Mike McGinn	9,089	20.9
7	Bill Archer	34,527	100.0
8	Jack M. Fields, Jr.	35,968	100.0
9	Steve Stockman	11,871	100.0
10	Herbert Spiro	18,902	100.0
11	James W. Broyles	11,643	100.0
12	Terry Lee Hicks	4,575	22.8
	David Hobbs	15,452	77.2
13	Beau Boulter	13,285	57.9
	Ernie Houdashell	3,692	16.1
	Ray Powell	1,438	6.3
	Bob Price	4,532	19.7
14	Humberto J. "Bert" Garza	10,878	100.0
15	Tom Haughey	3,992	16.0
	Pat O'Rourke	5,001	33.3
	Chip Taberski	6,795	45.3
	Michael G. "Mike" White	2,605	17.3
	W. E. "Walt" Woelper	610	4.1
17	Jeannie Sadowski	12,398	100.0
18	Edward Blum	7,214	74.1
	C. L. Kennedy	2,518	25.9
19	Larry Combest	41,824	100.0
21	Lamar Smith	54,634	100.0
22	Tom DeLay	31,122	100.0
23	Henry Bonilla	9,013	63.3
	Dick Bowen	5,216	36.7
24	Phillip Bielamowicz	3,674	21.7
	Reby Cary	3,090	18.3
	Steve Masterson	7,056	41.8
	Duane McGuffey	3,080	18.2
25	Dolly Madison McKenna	10,402	54.9
	Esther Lee Yao	8,532	45.1
26	Dick Armey	32,826	100.0
27	Jay Kimbrough	8,019	70.8
	Henry Kosling	3,305	29.2
29	Clark Kent Ervin	3,614	55.0
	Freddy Rios	2,952	45.0
30	Lucy Cain	4,758	52.1
	Kelvin Malone	4,382	47.9

The elections were close enough in the races for the 16th and 24th district seats that runoff elections were held on April 14, 1992.

1992 DEMOCRATIC PRIMARY RUNOFF (APRIL 14)

District	Candidate	Votes	%
29	Gene Green	15,844	50.3
	Ben Reyes	15,664	49.7

1992 REPUBLICAN PRIMARY RUNOFF (APRIL 14)

District	Candidate	Votes	%
16	Pat O'Rourke	2,231	23.6
	Chip Taberski	7,229	76.4
24	Phillip Bielamowicz	1,634	41.9
	Steve Masterson	2,268	58.1

1992 GENERAL ELECTION (NOVEMBER 3)

District	Candidate	Votes	%
1	Jim Chapman, Democrat	152,209	100.0
2	Charles Wilson, Democrat	118,625	56.1
	Donna Peterson, Republican	92,176	43.6
	Roger Northen, Independent	549	0.3
3	Sam Johnson, Republican	201,569	86.1
	Noel Kopala, Libertarian	32,570	13.9
4	Ralph M. Hall, Democrat	128,008	58.1
	David L. Bridges, Republican	83,875	38.1

District	Candidate	Votes	%
5	John Bryant, Democrat	98,567	58.9
	Steven Rothacker, Libertarian	8,450	3.8
	Richard Stokley, Republican	62,419	37.3
	William H. Walker, Libertarian	6,344	3.8
6	John Dietrich, Democrat	73,933	28.1
	Joe Barton, Republican	189,140	71.9
7	Bill Archer, Republican	169,407	100.0
8	Charles Robinson, Democrat	53,473	23.0
	Jack M. Fields, Jr., Republican	179,349	77.0
9	Jack Brooks, Democrat	118,690	53.6
	Steve Stockman, Republican	96,270	43.5
	Billy Joe Crawford, Libertarian	6,401	2.9
10	J. J. Pickle, Democrat	177,233	67.7
	Herbert Spiro, Republican	68,646	26.2
	Terry Blum, Libertarian	6,353	2.4
	Jeff Davis, Independent	6,056	2.3
	Stephen Hopkins, write-in	3,510	1.3
	Robert L. Shaw, write-in	94	0.0
11	Chet Edwards, Democrat	119,999	67.4
	James W. Broyles, Republican	58,033	32.6
12	Pete Geren, Democrat	125,492	62.8
	David Hobbs, Republican	74,432	37.2
13	Bill Sarpalius, Democrat	117,892	60.3
	Beau Boulter, Republican	77,514	39.7
14	Greg Laughlin, Democrat	135,930	68.1
	Humberto J. "Bert" Garza, Republican	54,412	27.3
	Vic Vreeland, Independent	9,329	4.7
15	Eligio de la Garza, Democrat	86,351	60.4
	Tom Haughey, Republican	56,549	39.6
16	Ronald Coleman, Democrat	66,731	51.9
	Chip Taberski, Republican	61,870	48.1
17	Charles W. Stenholm, Democrat	136,213	66.1
	Jeannie Sadowski, Republican	69,958	33.9
18	Craig A. Washington, Democrat	111,422	64.7
	Edward Blum, Republican	56,080	32.6
	Gregg Lassen, Libertarian	4,706	2.8
19	Terry Lee Moser, Democrat	47,325	22.6
	Larry Combest, Republican	162,057	77.4
20	Henry B. Gonzalez, Democrat	103,755	100.0
21	James M. Gaddy, Democrat	62,827	23.7
	Lamar Smith, Republican	190,979	72.2
	William E. Grisham, Libertarian	10,847	4.1
22	Richard Konrad, Democrat	67,812	31.1
	Tom DeLay, Republican	150,221	68.9
23	Albert G. Bustamante, Democrat	63,797	38.4
	Henry Bonilla, Republican	98,259	59.1
	David Alter, Libertarian	4,291	2.6
24	Martin Frost, Democrat	104,174	59.8
	Steve Masterson, Republican	70,042	40.2
25	Mike Andrews, Democrat	98,975	56.0
	Dolly Madison McKenna, Republican	73,192	41.4
	Richard Mauk, Libertarian	4,710	2.7
26	John Wayne Caton, Democrat	55,237	26.9
	Dick Armey, Republican	150,209	73.1
	Steve Love, write-in	85	0.0
27	Solomon P. Ortiz, Democrat	87,022	55.5
	Jay Kimbrough, Republican	66,853	42.6
	Charles Henry Schoonover, Libertarian	2,969	1.9
28	Frank Tejeda, Democrat	122,457	87.1
	David C. Slatter, Libertarian	18,128	12.9
29	Gene Green, Democrat	64,064	64.9
	Clark Kent Ervin, Republican	34,609	35.1
30	Eddie Bernice Johnson, Democrat	107,831	71.5
	Lucy Cain, Republican	37,853	25.1
	Ken Ashby, Libertarian	5,063	3.4

1994 Republican Primary Election (March 8)

District	Candidate	Votes	%
1	Mike Blankenship	6,301	65.3
	Dennis Boerner	3,353	34.7
2	Donna Peterson	5,335	67.5
	John E. Thomas	2,567	32.5
3	David Corley	2,063	6.2
	Sam Johnson	29,546	88.8

District	Candidate	Votes	%
	Dave Schum	1,680	5.0
4	David L. Bridges	13,250	67.0
	Tim McCord	6,534	33.0
5	Pete Sessions	5,786	56.4
	Richard Stokley	4,478	43.6
6	Joe Barton	23,063	89.5
	Jerry Goode	2,707	10.5
7	Bill Archer	29,997	100.0
8	Jack Fields	32,244	100.0
9	John LeCour	2,468	20.7
	James C. Milburn	802	6.7
	Steve Stockman	8,644	72.6
10	A. Jo Baylor	7,945	49.8
	Bryce Goodman	5,747	36.0
	Herbert Spiro	2,255	14.1
11	Jim Broyles	7,840	100.0
12	Ernest J. Anderson, Jr.	8,398	100.0
13	Wayne Collins	2,147	13.9
	Flavious Smith	1,714	11.1
	William M. "Mac" Thornberry	11,568	75.0
14	Ed Baker	5,048	42.3
	Jim Deats	6,880	57.7
15	Bonnie Abbott	1,563	23.9
	Tom Haughey	3,397	51.9
	Lister H. Reeves, Jr.	1,579	24.1
16	Dick Bowen	3,069	34.0
	Rick Ledesma	2,895	32.1
	Bobby Ortiz	3,055	33.9
17	Phil Boone	10,631	71.1
	Roy Emerson Falls	1,336	8.9
	Don Schmidt, Jr.	2,977	19.9
18	Jerry Burley	4,950	100.0
19	Larry Combest	37,092	100.0
20	Carl Bill Colyer	6,111	100.0
21	Scott Campbell	10,050	18.4
	Lamar Smith	44,600	81.6
22	Tom DeLay	25,731	100.0
23	Henry Bonilla	9,931	100.0
24	Ed Harrison	7,301	69.2
	Ken Scarborough	3,243	30.8
25	Gene Fontenot	8,726	56.0
	Dolly Madison McKenna	6,866	44.0
26	Dick Armey	20,905	100.0
27	Erol A. Stone	6,559	100.0
28	David C. Slatter	5,260	100.0
29	Harold "Oilman" Eide	2,321	100.0
30	Lucy Cain	4,474	100.0

The elections were close enough in the races for the 10th and 16th district seats that runoff elections were held on April 12, 1994.

1994 DEMOCRATIC PRIMARY ELECTION (MARCH 8)

District	Candidate	Votes	%
1	Jim Chapman	57,454	100.0
2	Edgar J. "Bubba" Groce	26,635	32.4
	Charles Wilson	55,676	67.6
4	Doug Dudley	7,250	21.1
	Ralph M. Hall	27,081	78.9
5	John Bryant	26,559	100.0
6	Terry Jesmore	6,899	100.0
9	Jack Brooks	37,648	71.1
	Geraldine Sam	15,340	28.9
10	Lloyd Doggett	33,682	82.5
	John Longsworth	7,130	17.5
11	Chet Edwards	35,564	100.0
12	Pete Geren	16,782	100.0
13	Bill Sarpalius	30,988	100.0
14	Greg Laughlin	45,753	100.0
15	Eligio de la Garza	40,513	60.5
	Rigo Martinez	8,998	13.4
	Eli Ochoa	17,481	26.1
16	Ronald Coleman	20,990	62.0
	Mike Crowley	12,871	38.0
17	Charles W. Stenholm	40,421	100.0
18	Sheila Jackson Lee	26,672	63.4
	Craig A. Washington	15,381	36.6

District	Candidate	Votes	%
20	Henry B. Gonzalez	15,702	100.0
22	Philip Butcher	4,576	36.5
	Scott Douglas Cunningham	7,978	63.5
23	Rolando L. Rios	37,473	100.0
24	Martin Frost	13,687	100.0
25	Ken Bentsen	6,778	26.1
	Beverley Clark	9,614	37.1
	Paul Colbert	5,914	22.8
	Joel F. Dejean	266	1.0
	Carrin Patman	3,373	13.0
26	Le Earl Ann Bryant	3,674	59.9
	Jerry L. Coker	2,464	40.1
27	Solomon P. Ortiz	37,405	100.0
28	Frank Tejeda	32,836	100.0
29	Gene Green	16,934	55.1
	Ben T. Reyes	13,795	44.9
30	Eddie Bernice Johnson	15,613	100.0

The election was close enough in the race for the 25th District seat that a runoff election was held on April 12, 1994.

1994 REPUBLICAN PRIMARY RUNOFF ELECTION (APRIL 12)

District	Candidate	Votes	%
10	A. Jo Baylor	5,545	76.9
	Bryce Goodman	1,669	23.1
16	Dick Bowen	1,846	35.2
	Bobby Ortiz	3,402	64.8

1994 DEMOCRATIC PRIMARY RUNOFF ELECTION (APRIL 12)

District	Candidate	Votes	%
25	Ken Bentsen	11,812	63.9
	Beverley Clark	6,684	36.1

1994 GENERAL ELECTION (NOVEMBER 8)

District	Candidate	Votes	%
1	Jim Chapman, Democrat	86,480	55.3
	Mike Blankenship, Republican	63,911	40.9
	Thomas "Jefferson" Mosser, Independent	6,001	3.8
2	Charles Wilson, Democrat	87,709	57.0
	Donna Peterson, Republican	66,071	42.9
3	Sam Johnson, Republican	157,011	90.9
	Tom Donahue, Libertarian	15,611	9.0
4	Ralph M. Hall, Democrat	99,303	58.8
	David L. Bridges, Republican	67,267	39.8
	Steven Rothacker, Libertarian	2,377	1.4
5	John Bryant, Democrat	61,877	50.1
	Pete Sessions, Republican	58,521	47.3
	Noel Kopala, Libertarian	876	0.7
	Regina Arashvand, Independent	627	0.5
	Barbara Morgan, Independent	1,715	1.4
6	Terry Jesmore, Democrat	44,286	22.0
	Joe Barton, Republican	152,038	75.6
	Bill Baird, Libertarian	4,688	2.3
7	Bill Archer, Republican	116,873	100.0
8	Jack Fields, Republican	148,473	92.0
	Russ Klecka, Independent	12,831	8.0
9	Jack Brooks, Democrat	71,643	45.7
	Steve Stockman, Republican	81,353	51.9
	Darla K. Beenau, Libertarian	1,656	1.1
	Bill Felton, Independent	2,145	1.4
10	Lloyd Doggett, Democrat	113,738	56.3
	A. Jo Baylor, Republican	80,382	39.8
	Jeff Hill, Libertarian	2,953	1.5
	Michael L. Brandes, Independent	2,579	1.3
	Jeff Davis, Independent	2,334	1.2
11	Chet Edwards, Democrat	76,667	59.2
	Jim Broyles, Republican	52,876	40.8
12	Pete Geren, Democrat	96,372	68.7
	Ernest J. Anderson, Jr., Republican	43,959	31.3
13	Bill Sarpalius, Democrat	63,923	44.6
	William M. "Mac" Thornberry, Republican	79,466	55.4
14	Greg Laughlin, Democrat	86,175	55.6
	Jim Deats, Republican	68,793	44.4
15	Eligio de la Garza, Democrat	61,527	59.0
	Tom Haughey, Republican	41,119	39.4
	John C. C. Hamilton, Independent	1,720	1.6

1996 Republican Primary Election (March 12)

District	Candidate	Votes	%
1	Dennis Boerner	6,386	29.5
	Hamp Hodges	5,150	23.8
	Ed Merritt	10,133	46.8
2	Brian Babin	7,094	31.0
	Ben Bius	2,986	13.1
	Bob Currie	2,348	10.3
	Jim Hughes	2,401	10.5
	Donna Peterson	8,047	35.2
3	Sam Johnson	42,882	100.0
4	Jerry Ray Hall	20,024	53.8
	Jon Newton	17,169	46.2
5	Glenn Box	8,259	41.9
	Pete Sessions	11,464	58.1
6	Joe Barton	49,172	100.0
7	Bill Archer	40,364	100.0
8	Kevin Brady	14,769	22.1
	Gene Fontenot	24,204	36.2
	Don Henderson	10,599	15.8
	Daniel D. New	2,772	4.1
	Betty Reinbeck	4,800	7.2
	Fred D. Thornberry	9,786	14.7
9	Steve Stockman	19,647	100.0
10	Teresa Doggett	29,479	100.0
11	Jim Broyles	4,459	15.8
	Dave Jenkins	1,197	4.2
	Jay Mathis	12,981	46.0
	Brian Pardo	9,587	34.0
12	Ernest J. Anderson, Jr.	6,355	20.2
	Bill Burch	3,355	10.7
	Kay Granger	21,774	69.2
13	Mac Thornberry	27,184	100.0
14	Ted Bozarth	398	1.1
	Jim Deats	8,466	24.4
	Greg Laughlin	14,777	42.5
	Ron Paul	11,112	32.0
15	Jose Aliseda	3,453	31.0

District	Candidate	Votes	%
16	Ronald Coleman, Democrat	49,815	57.1
17	Bobby Ortiz, Republican	37,409	42.9
	Charles W. Stenholm, Democrat	83,497	53.7
	Phil Boone, Republican	72,108	46.3
18	Sheila Jackson Lee, Democrat	84,790	73.5
	Jerry Burley, Republican	28,153	24.4
	George M. Hollenbeck, Libertarian	1,169	1.0
	J. Larry Snellings, Independent	1,278	1.1
19	Larry Combest, Republican	120,641	100.0
20	Henry B. Gonzalez, Democrat	60,114	62.5
	Carl Bill Colyer, Republican	36,035	37.5
21	Lamar Smith, Republican	165,595	90.0
	Kerry L. Lowry, Independent	18,480	10.0
22	Scott Douglas Cunningham, Democrat	38,826	23.8
	Tom DeLay, Republican	120,302	73.7
	Gregory D. Pepper, Independent	4,016	2.5
23	Rolando L. Rios, Democrat	44,101	37.4
	Henry Bonilla, Republican	73,815	62.6
24	Martin Frost, Democrat	65,019	52.8
	Ed Harrison, Republican	58,062	47.2
25	Ken Bentsen, Democrat	61,959	52.3
	Gene Fontenot, Republican	53,321	45.0
	Robert F. Lockhart, Libertarian	1,189	1.0
	Sarah Klein-Tower, Independent	2,060	1.7
26	Le Earl Ann Bryant, Democrat	39,763	22.4
	Dick Armey, Republican	135,398	76.4
	Alfred Adask, Libertarian	2,030	1.1
27	Solomon P. Ortiz, Democrat	65,325	59.4
	Erol A. Stone, Republican	44,693	40.6
28	Frank Tejeda, Democrat	73,986	70.9
	David C. Slatter, Republican	28,777	27.6
	Stephan "Steve" Rothstein, Libertarian	1,612	1.5
29	Gene Green, Democrat	44,102	73.4
	Harold "Oilman" Eide, Republican	15,952	26.6
30	Eddie Bernice Johnson, Democrat	73,166	72.6
	Lucy Cain, Republican	25,848	25.7
	Ken Ashby, Libertarian	1,728	1.7

District	Candidate	Votes	%
	Tom Haughey	7,697	69.0
16	Dick Bowen	5,225	38.5
	Rick Ledesma	8,329	61.5
17	Rudy Izzard	20,454	100.0
18	Larry White	6,296	100.0
19	Larry Combest	52,286	100.0
20	Kirk K. Colyer	4,771	30.0
	John Shull	4,872	30.6
	James Walker	6,274	39.4
21	Lamar Smith	77,143	100.0
22	Tom DeLay	41,874	80.0
	Greg Pepper	10,464	20.0
23	Henry Bonilla	21,619	100.0
24	Olivia Coggin Eudaly	5,305	24.8
	Ed Harrison	16,078	76.0
25	Bill Brock	5,796	34.3
	Brent Perry	11,093	65.7
26	Dick Armey	43,012	100.0
27	Joe Gardner	13,043	100.0
28	Mark L. Cude	10,328	100.0
29	Jack Rodriguez	3,605	100.0
30	John Hendry	5,743	100.0

The elections were close enough in the races for the 1st, 2nd, 8th, 11th, 14th, and 20th district seats that runoff elections were held on April 9, 1996.

1996 Democratic Primary Election (March 12)

District	Candidate	Votes	%
1	Jo Ann Howard	28,962	34.1
	Tommy Kessler	19,948	23.5
	Max Sandlin	36,142	42.5
2	Edgar J. "Bubba" Groce	15,171	19.8
	Fred Hudson	16,068	21.0
	Jim Turner	45,453	60.0
4	Ralph M. Hall	23,743	100.0
5	William A. Foster, III	11,510	36.4
	John Pouland	20,150	63.6
6	Terry Jesmore	1,480	17.1
	Janet Carroll Richardson	7,193	82.9
8	Robert W. Musemeche	3,083	38.0
	C. J. Newman	5,026	62.0
9	Rusty Isaac Bertrand	1,766	3.8
	Jack Cherry	6,741	14.5
	Nick Lampson	32,161	69.0
	Mat Safran	815	1.7
	Geraldine Sam	5,147	11.0
10	Lloyd Doggett	34,640	100.0
11	Chet Edwards	33,837	100.0
12	Hugh Parmer	17,625	100.0
13	Aaron Alejandro	16,732	48.3
	Samuel Brown Silverman	17,931	51.7
14	Charles "Lefty" Morris	36,388	100.0
15	Reynaldo Balli, Jr.	1,877	3.0
	Renato Cuellar	13,832	21.8
	Tony Dominguez	5,008	7.9
	Ruben Hinojosa	21,726	34.2
	Jim Selman	21,138	33.2
16	Dolores Briones	11,583	22.2
	Robert A. (Bob) Levy	610	1.2
	Tom Petersen	3,095	5.9
	Silvestre Reyes	22,119	42.5
	Jose Luis Sanchez	14,698	28.2
17	Charles W. Stenholm	44,528	100.0
18	Sheila Jackson Lee	22,475	100.0
19	Michael G. Clennan	3,798	30.1
	John W. Sawyer	8,833	69.9
20	Henry B. Gonzalez	17,167	100.0
21	Gordon H. Wharton	15,876	100.0
22	Scott Douglas Cunningham	8,132	100.0
23	Charles P. Jones	17,837	39.9
	Allen Rindfuss	5,811	13.0
	Joseph P. "Joe" Sullivan	21,085	47.1
24	Martin Frost	16,479	100.0
25	Ken Bentsen	13,984	100.0
26	Jerry Frankel	4,190	100.0
27	Mary Helen Berlanga	16,097	30.1

District	Candidate	Votes	%
	John Davis, Libertarian	5,045	2.6
	Bernice Johnson, write-in	1	0.0
	James P. Hebert, write-in	1	0.0
5	Pete Sessions, Republican	80,196	53.1
	John Pouland, Democrat	70,922	46.9
	Jesus Christ, write-in	1	0.00
6	Joe Barton, Republican	160,800	77.1
	Janet Carroll "Skeet" Richardson, Independent	26,713	12.8
	Catherine A. Anderson, Libertarian	14,456	6.9
	Doug Williams, U.S. Taxpayers	6,547	3.1
7	Bill Archer, Republican	152,024	81.4
	Al J. K. Siegmund, Democrat	28,187	15.1
	Gene Hsiao, Independent	3,896	2.1
	Robert R. "Randy" Sims, Jr., Independent	2,724	1.5
8	Kevin Brady, Republican	80,325	41.5
	Gene Fontenot, Republican	75,399	38.9
	Cynthia (CJ) Newman, Democrat	26,246	13.6
	Robert Musemeche, Democrat	11,689	6.0
9	Steve Stockman, Republican	88,171	46.4
	Nick Lampson, Democrat	83,782	44.1
	Geraldine Sam, Democrat	17,887	9.4
18	Sheila Jackson Lee, Democrat	106,111	77.1
	Larry White, Republican	13,956	10.1
	Jerry Burley, Republican	7,877	5.7
	George A. Young, Republican	5,332	3.9
	Mike Lamson, Democrat	4,412	3.2
22	Tom DeLay, Republican	126,056	68.1
	Scott Douglas Cunningham, Democrat	59,030	31.9
24	Martin Frost, Democrat	77,847	55.7
	Ed Harrison, Republican	54,551	39.1
	Marion Jacob, Democrat	4,656	3.3
	Dale Mouton, Independent	2,574	1.8
	Fred Hank, write-in	1	0.0
	Martin Frost, write-in	8	0.0
25	Ken Bentsen, Democrat	43,701	34.0
	Beverley Clark, Democrat	21,699	16.9
	Dolly Madison McKenna, Republican	21,898	17.1
	Solomon P. Ortiz	37,434	69.9
28	Frank Tejeda	36,257	100.0
29	Felix Fraga	7,680	36.5
	Gene Green	13,352	63.5
30	Eddie Bernice Johnson	17,238	100.0

The elections were close enough in the races for the 1st, 15th, 16th, and 23rd district seats that runoff elections were held on April 9, 1996.

1996 Republican Primary Runoff Election (April 9)

District	Candidate	Votes	%
1	Dennis Boerner	3,644	45.3
	Ed Merritt	4,403	54.7
2	Brian Babin	7,405	66.8
	Donna Peterson	3,675	33.2
8	Kevin Brady	18,583	53.4
	Gene Fontenot	16,244	46.6
11	Jay Mathis	10,655	70.2
	Brian Pardo	4,520	29.8
14	Ron Paul	11,244	54.1
	Greg Laughlin	9,555	45.9
20	John Shull	2,649	43.6
	James Walker	3,432	56.4

1996 Democratic Primary Runoff Election (April 9)

District	Candidate	Votes	%
1	Jo Ann Howard	25,063	44.2
	Max Sandlin	31,659	55.8
15	Ruben Hinojosa	24,940	52.0
	Jim Selman	22,983	48.0
16	Silvestre Reyes	21,161	51.2
	Jose Luis Sanchez	20,157	48.8
23	Charles P. Jones	9,384	50.7
	Joseph P. "Joe" Sullivan	9,131	49.3

1996 Special Election (November 5)

District	Candidate	Votes	%
3	Sam Johnson, Republican	142,325	73.0
	Lee Cole, Democrat	47,654	24.4

November 12, 1996, the governor would canvass the results of the special election and order a runoff if necessary; and that on December 10, 1996, a special election runoff, would be held, if necessary. See Bush v. Vera (Sup. Ct. Doc. No. 94-09805); Vera v. Bush, Civil No. H-0994-09277 (S.D. Tex, filed August 6, 1996.). The elections were close enough in the races for the 8th, 9th, and 25th district seats that runoff elections were held on December 10, 1996.

1996 GENERAL ELECTION (NOVEMBER 5)

District	Candidate	Votes	%
1	Max Sandlin, Democrat	102,697	51.6
	Ed Merritt, Republican	93,105	46.7
	Margaret A. Palms, Natural Law	3,368	1.7
2	Jim Turner, Democrat	102,908	52.2
	Brian Babin, Republican	89,838	45.6
	Henry McCullough, Independent	2,390	1.2
	David Constant, Libertarian	1,240	0.6
	Gary Hardy, Natural Law	595	0.3
4	Ralph M. Hall, Democrat	132,126	63.8
	Jerry Ray Hall, Republican	71,065	34.3
	Steven Rothacker, Libertarian	3,172	1.5
	Enos M. Denham, Jr., Natural Law	814	0.4
10	Lloyd Doggett, Democrat	132,066	56.2
	Teresa Doggett, Republican	97,204	41.4
	Gary Johnson, Libertarian	3,950	1.7
	Steve Klayman, Natural Law	1,771	0.8
11	Chet Edwards, Democrat	99,990	56.8
	Jay Mathis, Republican	74,549	42.4
	Ken Hardin, Natural Law	1,396	0.8
12	Kay Granger, Republican	98,349	57.8
	Hugh Parmer, Democrat	69,859	41.0
	Heather Proffer, Natural Law	1,996	1.2
13	Mac Thornberry, Republican	116,098	66.9
	Samuel Brown Silverman, Democrat	56,066	32.3
	Don Harkey, Natural Law	1,463	0.8
14	Ron Paul, Republican	99,961	51.1
	Charles (Lefty) Morris, Democrat	93,200	47.6
	Ed Fasanella, Natural Law	2,538	1.3
15	Ruben Hinojosa, Democrat	86,347	62.3
	Tom Haughey, Republican	50,914	36.7
	Rob Wofford, Natural Law	1,333	1.0
	Brent Perry, Republican	16,737	13.0
	John Devine, Republican	9,070	7.1
	John M. Sanchez, Republican	8,984	7.0
	Dotty Quinn Collins, Republican	561	0.4
	Jerry Freiwirth, Socialist Workers	270	0.2
	Ken G. Mathis, Republican	3,649	2.8
	Ron "RC" Meinke, Republican	997	0.8
	Lloyd W. Oliver, Republican	827	0.6
26	Dick Armey, Republican	163,708	73.6
	Jerry Frankel, Democrat	58,623	26.4
	Martin Frost, write-in	2	0.0
	Ron Paul, write-in	2	0.0
	Dick Amrey, write-in	1	0.0
	Loren Wienstein, write-in	1	0.0
	Chester Hollis, write-in	1	0.0
	Erich Von Colberg, write-in	1	0.0
	Ray Anderson, write-in	1	0.0
	Kenny Marchant, write-in	1	0.0
	Robert McCluky, write-in	1	0.0
29	Gene Green, Democrat	61,751	67.5
	Jack Rodriguez, Republican	28,381	31.0
	Jack W. Klinger, U.S. Taxpayers	1,340	1.5
30	Eddie Bernice Johnson, Democrat	61,723	54.6
	John Hendry, Republican	20,664	18.3
	James L. Sweatt, Democrat	9,909	8.8
	Marvin E. Crenshaw, Democrat	7,765	6.9
	Lisa Kitterman, Republican	7,761	6.9
	Lisa Hembry, Independent	3,501	3.2
	Ada Granado, Independent	1,278	1.1
	Stevan A. Hammond, Independent	468	0.4
	John Hendry, write-in	1	0.0
	Edith B Johnson, write-in	1	0.0
	E. Johnson, write-in	1	0.0

A three-judge court of the U.S. District Court for the Southern District of Texas redrew the boundaries of districts 18, 29, and 30, and redrew portions of districts 3, 5, 6, 7, 8, 9, 22, 24, 25, and 26. The district court further ordered that the candidates in these districts who had filed by August 30, 1996, and been certified by September 5, 1996, would compete in an open primary (special election) on November 5, 1996, concurrent with the general election; that on

District	Candidate	Votes	Percentage
16	Silvestre Reyes, Democrat	90,260	70.6
	Rick Ledesma, Republican	35,271	27.6
	Carl Proffer, Natural Law	2,253	1.8
17	Charles W. Stenholm, Democrat	99,678	51.6
	Rudy Izzard, Republican	91,429	47.4
	Richard Caro, Natural Law	1,887	1.0
19	Larry Combest, Republican	156,910	80.4
	John W. Sawyer, Democrat	38,316	19.6
20	Henry B. Gonzalez, Democrat	88,190	63.7
	James Walker, Republican	47,616	34.4
	Alejandro (Alex) DePena, Libertarian	2,156	1.6
	Lyndon Felps, Natural Law	447	0.3
21	Lamar Smith, Republican	205,830	76.4
	Gordon H. Wharton, Democrat	60,338	22.4
	Randy Rutenbeck, Natural Law	3,139	1.2
23	Henry Bonilla, Republican	101,332	61.8
	Charles P. Jones, Democrat	59,596	36.4
	Linda J. Caswell, Natural Law	2,911	1.8
27	Solomon P. Ortiz, Democrat	97,350	64.6
	Joe Gardner, Republican	50,964	33.8
	Kevin G. Richardson, Natural Law	2,286	1.5
28	Frank Tejeda, Democrat	110,148	75.4
	Mark L. Cude, Republican	34,191	23.4
	Clifford Finley, Natural Law	1,796	1.2

1996 SPECIAL ELECTION RUNOFF (DECEMBER 10)

District	Candidate	Votes	Percentage
8	Kevin Brady, Republican	30,366	59.1
	Gene Fontenot, Republican	21,004	40.9
9	Nick Lampson, Democrat	59,225	52.8
	Steve Stockman, Republican	52,870	47.2
25	Ken Bentsen, Democrat	29,396	57.3
	Dolly Madison McKenna, Republican	21,892	42.7

1997 SPECIAL ELECTION (MARCH 15)

District	Candidate	Votes	Percentage
28	Ciro D. Rodriguez, Democrat	14,018	46.1
	Juan F. Solis III, Democrat	8,056	26.5
	Mark Cude, Republican	2,452	8.0
	Carlos I. Uresti, Democrat	1,345	4.4
	John P. Kelly, Republican	1,229	4.0
	Lauro A. Bustamante, Democrat	818	2.7
	John A. (Drew) Traeger, Democrat	718	2.4
	Narciso V. Mendoza, Republican	621	2.0
	Phil Ross, Democrat	376	1.2
	Mike G. Pacheco, Democrat	231	0.8
	Oliver Lowell Blair, Republican	168	0.6
	Patrick A. Mason, Democrat	158	0.5
	Robert Cantu, Independent	82	0.3
	Michael Idrogo, Democrat	64	0.2
	Jose Julian De La Rocha, Republican	53	0.2
	Steven Finch, write-in	1	0.0
	Joyce Wageck, write-in	1	0.0
	Lauro Bustamante, write-in	1	0.0
	Jerome Gonzales, write-in	1	0.0
	Frances Gasch, write-in	1	0.0

This special election was held to fill the seat of Frank Tejeda, who died on January 30, 1997. The election was close enough that a runoff was held on April 12, 1997.

1997 SPECIAL ELECTION RUNOFF (APRIL 12)

District	Candidate	Votes	Percentage
28	Ciro D. Rodriguez, Democrat	19,992	66.7
	Juan F. Solis III, Democrat	9,990	33.3

No candidate received a majority in the special election, so a runoff was held with the top two candidates from the special election.

1998 REPUBLICAN PRIMARY ELECTION (MARCH 10)

District	Candidate	Votes	Percentage
1	Dennis Boerner	9,416	100.0
2	Brian Babin	8,717	100.0
3	Sam Johnson	14,621	100.0
4	Jim Lohmeyer	19,205	68.8
	Ray Hall	6,258	22.4
	Douglas Jones	1,457	5.2
	Geoffrey Fielding Walsh	975	3.5
5	Pete Sessions	11,266	100.0

District	Candidate	Votes	%
6	Joe Barton	21,480	72.9
	Greg Mullanax	7,965	27.1
7	Bill Archer	28,625	96.8
	Gene Hsiao	961	3.2
8	Kevin Brady	34,841	88.7
	Andre' Dean	4,452	11.3
9	Tom Cottar	5,451	45.2
	Adonn Slone	2,617	21.7
	Onzelo Markum	2,048	17.0
	Don Beagle	1,944	16.1
12	Kay Granger	12,952	100.0
13	Mac Thornberry	19,827	93.6
	Richard Amon	1,345	6.4
14	Ron Paul	19,883	100.0
15	Tom Haughey	4,551	100.0
17	Rudy Izzard	20,527	100.0
19	Larry Combest	41,939	100.0
20	James Walker	5,729	62.9
	John Shull	3,384	37.1
21	Lamar Smith	48,664	100.0
22	Tom DeLay	24,849	100.0
23	Henry Bonilla	10,909	100.0
24	Shawn Terry	6,723	71.2
	Stan C. Penn	2,715	28.8
25	John M. Sanchez	6,673	47.5
	Beverley Clark	5,027	35.7
	Bill Brock	2,362	16.8
26	Dick Armey	25,523	100.0
27	Erol A. Stone	5,743	100.0
30	Carrie Kelleher	2,361	100.0

The elections were close enough in the races for the 9th and 25th district seats that runoff elections were held on April 15, 1998.

1998 DEMOCRATIC PRIMARY ELECTION (MARCH 10)

District	Candidate	Votes	%
1	Max Sandlin	45,774	100.0
2	Jim Turner	53,821	100.0
4	Ralph M. Hall	14,388	100.0
5	Victor M. Morales	17,907	69.2
	William A. Foster, III	7,968	30.8
6	Ben B. Boothe	3,648	100.0
9	Nick Lampson	30,284	100.0
10	Lloyd Doggett	25,275	100.0
11	Chet Edwards	19,956	100.0
12	Tom Hall	7,309	100.0
13	Mark Harmon	17,162	68.1
	Ed True	8,051	31.9
14	Loy Sneary	18,149	40.1
	Tom Reed	12,123	26.8
	Margaret Dunn	11,056	24.4
	Roger M. Elliott	3,912	8.6
15	Ruben Hinojosa	39,522	100.0
16	Silvestre Reyes	30,264	100.0
17	Charlie Stenholm	32,399	100.0
18	Sheila Jackson Lee	10,147	100.0
19	Sidney Blankenship	9,377	100.0
20	Charlie Gonzalez	9,482	44.0
	Maria Antonietta Berriozabal	4,809	22.3
	Christine Hernandez	2,731	12.7
	Walter Martinez	2,109	9.8
	Armando Falcon	1,572	7.3
	Steve Walker	529	2.5
	Richard Garcia	344	1.6
22	Hill Kemp	5,222	100.0
23	Charlie Urbina Jones	20,838	45.2
	Joseph P. "Joe" Sullivan	19,961	43.3
	Allen Rindfuss	5,334	11.6
24	Martin Frost	9,202	100.0
25	Ken Bentsen	6,260	100.0
27	Solomon P. Ortiz	32,908	100.0
28	Ciro D. Rodriguez	28,420	75.9
	Lauro A. Bustamante	4,780	12.8
	Oscar H. Flores	4,227	11.3
29	Gene Green	5,004	100.0
30	Eddie Bernice Johnson	6,769	100.0

The elections were close enough in the races for the 14th, 20th, and 23rd district seats that runoff elections were held on April 15, 1998.

1998 REPUBLICAN PRIMARY RUNOFF (APRIL 15)

District	Candidate	Votes	%
9	Tom Cottar	2,646	56.3
	Adonn Slone	2,057	43.7
25	John M. Sanchez	6,056	60.5
	Beverley Clark	3,953	39.5

1998 DEMOCRATIC PRIMARY RUNOFF (APRIL 15)

District	Candidate	Votes	%
14	Loy Sneary	15,734	52.3
	Tom Reed	14,338	47.7
20	Charlie Gonzalez	13,439	62.1
	Maria Antonietta Berriozabal	8,188	37.9
23	Charlie Urbina Jones	9,167	52.7
	Joseph P. "Joe" Sullivan	8,235	47.3

1998 GENERAL ELECTION (NOVEMBER 3)

District	Candidate	Votes	%
1	Max Sandlin, Democrat	80,788	59.4
	Dennis Boerner, Republican	55,191	40.6
2	Jim Turner, Democrat	81,556	58.4
	Brian Babin, Republican	56,891	40.8
	Wendell Drye, Libertarian	1,142	0.8
3	Sam Johnson, Republican	106,690	91.2
	Ken Ashby, Libertarian	10,288	8.8
4	Ralph Hall, Democrat	82,989	57.6
	Jim Lohmeyer, Republican	58,954	40.9
	Jim Simon, Libertarian	2,137	1.5
5	Pete Sessions, Republican	61,714	55.8
	Victor Morales, Democrat	48,073	43.4
	Michael Needleman, Libertarian	880	0.8
6	Joe Barton, Republican	112,957	73.0
	Ben Boothe, Democrat	40,112	25.9
	Richard Bandlow, Libertarian	1,817	1.2
7	Bill Archer, Republican	110,010	93.4
	Drew Parks, Libertarian	7,889	6.6
8	John R. Skone-Palmer, Independent	47	0
	Kevin Brady, Republican	123,372	92.8
	Don Richards, Libertarian	9,576	7.2
9	Nick Lampson, Democrat	86,055	63.7
	Tom Cottar, Republican	49,107	36.3
10	Lloyd Doggett, Democrat	116,127	85.2
	Ken Eckel, Jr., Libertarian	20,155	14.8
11	Chet Edwards, Democrat	71,142	82.5
	Vince Hanke, Libertarian	15,161	17.5
12	Kay Granger, Republican	66,740	61.9
	Tom Hall, Democrat	39,084	36.3
	Paul Barthel, Libertarian	1,917	1.8
13	Mac Thornberry, Republican	81,141	68.0
	Mark Harmon, Democrat	37,027	31.0
	Georganne Baker Payne, Libertarian	1,298	1.1
14	Ron Paul, Republican	84,459	55.3
	Loy Sneary, Democrat	68,014	44.5
	Cynthia Newman, write-in	390	0.3
15	Rubén Hinojosa, Democrat	47,957	58.4
	Tom Haughey, Republican	34,221	41.6
16	Silvestre Reyes, Democrat	67,486	87.9
	Stu Nance, Libertarian	5,329	6.9
	Lorenzo Morales, Independent	3,952	5.1
17	Charlie Stenholm, Democrat	75367	53.6
	Dr. Rudy Izzard, Republican	63700	45.3
	Gordon Mobley, Libertarian	1,618	1.2
18	Sheila Jackson Lee, Democrat	82,091	89.9
	James Galvan, Libertarian	9,176	10.1
19	Larry Cornbest, Republican	108,266	83.7
	Sidney Blankenship, Democrat	21,162	16.4
20	Charlie Gonzalez, Democrat	50,356	63.2
	James Walker, Republican	28,347	35.6
	Alejandro "Alex" DePeña, Libertarian	1010	1.3
	Steve Mendoza, Independent		
21	Lamar Smith, Republican	165,047	91.4
	Jeffrey Charles Blunt, Libertarian	15,561	8.6

District	Candidate	Votes	%
	Gary Thurman, Independent		
22	Tom DeLay, Republican	87,840	65.2
	Hill Kemp, Democrat	45,386	33.7
	Steve Grupe, Libertarian	1,494	1.1
23	Henry Bonilla, Republican	73,177	63.8
	Charlie Urbina Jones, Democrat	40,281	35.1
	Bill Stallknecht, Libertarian	1,262	1.1
24	Martin Frost, Democrat	56,321	57.5
	Shawn Terry, Republican	40,105	40.9
	David A. Stover, Libertarian	736	0.8
	George Arias, Independent	830	0.8
25	Ken Bentsen, Democrat	58,591	57.9
	John Sanchez, Republican	41,848	41.3
	Eric Atkisson, Libertarian	830	0.8
26	Dick Armey, Republican	120,332	88.1
	Joe Turner, Libertarian	16,182	11.9
	William Kenneth Cheek, Independent		
27	Solomon Ortiz, Democrat	61,638	63.3
	Erol Stone, Republican	34,284	35.2
	Mark G. Pretz, Libertarian	1,476	1.5
28	Ciro Rodriguez, Democrat	71,849	90.5
	Dr. Ned (or Edward) Elmer, Libertarian	7,504	9.5
29	Gene Green, Democrat	44,179	92.8
	James P. Chudleigh, Libertarian	1,439	3.0
	Lea Sherman, Independent	2,013	4.2
30	Eddie Bernice Johnson, Democrat	57,603	72.2
	Carrie Kelleher, Republican	21,338	26.8
	Barbara L. Robinson, Libertarian	811	1.0

2000 Democratic Primary Election (March 14)

District	Candidate	Votes	%
1	B. D. Blount	9,834	15.2
	Max Sandlin	54,730	84.8
2	Jim Turner	65,446	100.0
3	Billy Wayne Zachary	6,031	100.0
4	Ralph M. Hall	16,403	100.0
5	Regina Montoya Coggins	18,368	68.1
	Gary L. Harrison	8,619	31.9
6	(none)		
7	Jeff Sell	3,828	100.0
8	(none)		
9	Nick Lampson	27,457	100.0
10	Lloyd Doggett	31,638	100.0
11	Chet Edwards	28,053	100.0
12	Prentiss Bryant Davis	2,964	23.8
	Mark Greene	9,495	76.2
13	Curtis Clinesmith	18,805	100.0
14	Loy Sneary	28,318	100.0
15	Mel Buentello Hawkins	3,984	6.2
	Ruben Hinojosa	46,890	73.5
	Diana Rivera-Martinez	12,896	20.2
16	Sylvestre Reyes	20,169	100.0
17	Charles W. Stenholm	36,753	100.0
18	Shiela Jackson Lee	16,067	100.0
19	(none)		
20	Charlie A. Gonzalez	22,213	100.0
21	Jim Green	12,381	100.0
22	Jo Ann Matranga	4,833	51.3
	Virginia "Ginny" Stogner	4,590	48.7
23	Isidro Garza, Jr.	43,424	69.6
	Joseph P. "Joe" Sullivan	18,938	30.4
24	Martin Frost	18,892	100.0
25	Ken Bentsen	9,455	100.0
26	Steve Love	6,128	100.0
27	Solomon P. Ortiz	36,569	100.0
28	Ciro D. Rodriguez	37,110	100.0
29	Gene Green	9,673	100.0
30	Eddie Bernice Johnson	20,119	100.0

2000 Republican Primary Election (March 14)

District	Candidate	Votes	%
1	John Lawrence	10,951	42.7
	Noble Willingham	14,702	57.3
2	(none)		

District	Candidate	Votes	%
3	Sam Johnson	40,802	93.5
	J. A. Gonnell	2,843	6.5
4	Jon Newton	22,898	54.2
	Mark D. Peterman	19,351	45.8
5	Pete Sessions	26,179	100.0
6	Joe Barton	51,664	100.0
7	Mark Brewer	4,862	7.7
	John Culberson	23,872	37.7
	Wallace Henley	4,647	7.3
	Gene Hsiao	1,061	1.7
	Ron Kapche	3,105	4.9
	Susan Malfer	410	0.6
	Catherine McConn	8,480	13.4
	Peter Wareing	16,814	26.6
8	Kevin Brady	61,252	100.0
9	Paul Williams	19,886	100.0
10	Ronnie "Reeferseed" Gjemre	2,759	8.2
	Jerry J. Mikus, Jr.	11,002	32.7
	Charles Moritz	19,889	59.1
11	Rob Curnock	7,107	19.8
	Ramsey Farley	14,220	39.6
	Rodney Geer	14,555	40.6
12	Kay Granger	32,382	100.0
13	David G. Morris	3,363	9.4
	Mac Thornberry	32,585	90.6
14	Ron Paul	37,892	100.0
15	(none)		
16	(none)		
17	Darrell Clements	15,149	51.6
	Shane Hunt	14,230	48.4
18	Bob Levy	5,230	54.1
	Elmer L. Zoch	4,435	45.9
19	Larry Combest	64,433	100.0
21	Lamar Smith	90,924	100.0
22	Tom DeLay	42,016	83.3
	Michael "Fjet" Fjetland	8,415	16.7
23	Henry Bonilla	25,231	100.0
24	Cynthia Newman	3,883	22.6
	Bill Payne	4,571	26.6
	Mac Warren	3,173	18.4
	James "Bryndan" Wright	5,577	32.4
25	Tom Reiser	11,028	48.7
	Phil Sudan	11,630	51.3
26	Dick Armey	62,199	87.1
	Larry K. Thompson	9,201	12.9
27	Pat Ahumada	13,652	100.0
28	(none)		
29	Allen H. Goforth	3,683	48.2
	Joe Vu	3,958	51.8
30	(none)		

The elections were close enough in the races for the 7th, 11th, and 24th district seats that runoff elections were held on April 11, 2000.

2000 REPUBLICAN PRIMARY RUNOFF ELECTION (APRIL 11)

District	Candidate	Votes	%
7	John Culberson	29,968	60.0
	Peter Wareing	20,015	40.0
11	Ramsey Farley	6,710	55.8
	Rodney Geer	5,314	44.2
24	Bill Payne	1,371	38.0
	James "Bryndan" Wright	2,240	62.0

2000 GENERAL ELECTION (NOVEMBER 7)

District	Candidate	Votes	%
1	Max Sandlin, Democrat	118,157	55.8
	Noble Willingham, Republican	91,912	43.4
	Ray Carr, Libertarian	1,779	0.8
2	Jim Turner, Democrat	162,891	91.1
	Gary Lyndon Dye, Libertarian	15,939	8.9
3	Sam Johnson, Republican	187,486	71.6
	Billy Wayne Zachary, Democrat	67,233	25.7
	Lance Flores, Libertarian	7,178	2.7
4	Ralph Hall, Democrat	145,887	60.3
	Jon Newton, Republican	91,574	37.9
	Joe Turner, Libertarian	4,417	1.8

District	Candidate	Votes	%
5	Pete Sessions, Republican	100,487	54.0
	Regina Montoya Coggins, Democrat	82,629	44.4
	Ken Ashby, Libertarian	2,842	1.5
6	Joe Barton, Republican	222,685	88.1
	Frank Brady, Libertarian	30,056	11.9
7	John Culberson, Republican	183,712	73.9
	Jeff Sell, Democrat	60,694	24.4
	Drew Parks, Libertarian	4,182	1.7
	John Richard Skone-Palmer, Independent	5	0.0
8	Kevin Brady, Republican	233,848	91.6
	Gil Guillory, Libertarian	21,368	8.4
9	Nick Lampson, Democrat	130,143	59.2
	Paul Williams, Republican	87,165	39.7
	Chuck Kuipp, Libertarian	2,508	1.1
10	Lloyd Doggett, Democrat	203,628	84.6
	Michael Davis, Libertarian	37,203	15.4
11	Chet Edwards, Democrat	105,782	54.8
	Ramsey Farley, Republican	85,546	44.3
	Mark Swanstrom, Libertarian	1,590	0.8
12	Kay Granger, Republican	117,739	62.7
	Mark Greene, Democrat	67,612	36.0
	Rick Clay, Libertarian	2,565	1.4
13	Mac Thornberry, Republican	117,995	67.6
	Curtis Clinesmith, Democrat	54,343	31.2
	Brad Clardy, Libertarian	2,137	1.2
14	Ron Paul, Republican	137,370	59.7
	Loy Sneary, Democrat	92,689	40.3
15	Rubén Hinojosa, Democrat	106,570	88.5
	Frank Jones III, Libertarian	13,167	10.9
	Israel Cantu, write-in	711	0.6
16	Silvestre Reyes, Democrat	92,649	68.3
	Dan Moser, Libertarian	2,080	1.5
	Daniel Power, Republican	40,921	30.2
17	Charlie Stenholm, Democrat	120,670	59.0
	Darrell Clements, Republican	72,535	35.5
	Pete Julia, Reform	45	0.0
	Debra M. Monde, Libertarian	11,180	5.5
18	Sheila Jackson Lee, Democrat	131,857	76.5
	Bob Levy, Republican	38,191	22.2
	Colin E. Nankervis, Libertarian	2,330	1.4
19	Larry Combest, Republican	170,319	91.6
	Dr. John A. Turnbow, Libertarian	15,579	8.4
20	Charlie Gonzalez, Democrat	107,487	87.7
	Alejandro "Alex" de Pena, Libertarian	15,087	12.3
21	Lamar Smith, Republican	251,049	75.9
	Jim Green, Democrat	73,326	22.2
	C.W. "Jinx" Steinbrecher, Libertarian	6,503	2.0
22	Tom DeLay, Republican	154,662	60.4
	Jo Ann Matranga, Democrat	92,645	36.2
	Kent J. Probst, Libertarian	3,383	1.3
	Robert A. Schneider, Independent	5,577	2.2
23	Henry Bonilla, Republican	119,679	59.3
	Isidro Garza, Jr., Democrat	78,274	38.8
	Jeffrey C. Blunt, Libertarian	3,801	1.9
24	Martin Frost, Democrat	103,152	61.8
	James "Bryndan" Wright, Republican	61,235	36.7
	Robert "Bob" Worthington, Libertarian	2,561	1.5
25	Ken Bentsen, Democrat	106,112	60.1
	Phil Sudan, Republican	68,010	38.5
	Clifford Lee Messina, Libertarian	2,400	1.4
26	Dick Armey, Republican	214,025	72.5
	Steve Love, Democrat	75,601	25.6
	Fred E. Badagnani, Libertarian	5,646	1.9
27	Solomon Ortiz, Democrat	102,088	63.4
	Pat Ahumada, Republican	54,660	33.9
	William Bunch, Libertarian	4,324	2.7
28	Ciro Rodriguez, Democrat	123,104	89.0
	William A. "Bill" Stallknecht, Libertarian	15,156	11.0
29	Gene Green, Democrat	84,665	73.3
	Joe Vu, Republican	29,606	25.6
	Ray Dittmar, Libertarian	1,204	1.0
30	Eddie Bernice Johnson, Democrat	109,163	91.8
	Kelly Rush, Libertarian	9,798	8.2

2002 Democratic Primary Election (March 12)

District	Candidate	Votes	%
1	Max Sandlin	51,009	100.0
2	Jim Turner	50,387	100.0
3	Manny Molera	5,363	100.0
4	Ralph M. Hall	17,404	100.0
5	Bill Bernstein	5,902	22.8
	Ron Chapman	18,298	70.8
	Wayne Gordon Raasch	1,635	6.3
6	Felix Alvarado	13,604	100.0
7	(none)		
8	(none)		
9	Nick Lampson	32,700	100.0
10	Lloyd Doggett	33,083	90.3
	Jennifer Gale	3,554	9.7
11	Chet Edwards	17,191	100.0
12	(none)		
13	Zane Reese	15,564	100.0
14	Sergio Martinez	16,207	43.2
	Corby Windham	21,335	56.8
15	Ruben Hinojosa	46,688	86.7
	Mel "El Tejano" Hawkins	7,138	13.3
16	Sylvestre Reyes	33,904	100.0
17	Charles W. Stenholm	30,426	100.0
18	Shiela Jackson Lee	31,563	94.4
	Lenwood Johnson	1,871	5.6
19	(none)		
20	Charlie A. Gonzalez	25,645	100.0
21	John Courage	16,654	100.0
22	Frank "Chip" Briscoe	4,316	48.4
	Tim Riley	4,606	51.6
23	Henry Cuellar	51,495	100.0
24	Martin Frost	17,963	100.0
25	Chris Bell	7,443	36.1
	Paul Colbert	4,307	20.9
	Stephen King	3,274	15.9
	Carroll G. Robinson	5,597	27.1
26	Paul William LeBon	5,182	100.0
27	Solomon P. Ortiz	41,574	100.0
28	Ciro D. Rodriguez	41,152	100.0
29	Gene Green	11,891	100.0
30	Eddie Bernice Johnson	27,670	100.0
31	David Bagley	11,741	100.0
32	Pauline K. Dixon	9,384	72.4
	Walter W. Hofheinz	3,572	27.6

The election was close enough in the race for the 25th and District seats that runoff elections were held on April 9, 2002.

2002 Republican Primary Election (March 12)

District	Candidate	Votes	%
1	John Lawrence	13,875	100.0
2	Van Brookshire	10,962	100.0
3	Sam Johnson	17,153	84.3
	Tom Caiazzo	3,184	15.7
4	Edward G. Conger	9,627	30.7
	John Graves	21,781	69.3
5	Mike Armour	3,247	16.6
	Dan Hagood	3,628	18.6
	Jeb Hensarling	10,475	53.6
	Phil Sudan	1,632	8.3
	Fred A. Wood	574	2.9
6	Joe Barton	23,758	100.0
7	John Culberson	17,843	100.0
8	Kevin Brady	31,116	100.0
9	Paul Williams	10,782	100.0
10	(none)		
11	Rob Curnock	5,792	21.3
	Ramsey Farley	17,985	66.1
	James "Dub" Maines	3,452	12.7
12	Kay Granger	20,769	87.1
	Philip Hillery	3,067	12.9
13	Mac Thornberry	35,367	100.0
14	Ron Paul	22,715	100.0
15	(none)		
16	(none)		

District	Candidate	Votes	%
17	Rob Beckham	21,662	100.0
18	Phillip J. Abbott	4,252	100.0
19	Larry Combest	30,440	100.0
20	(none)		
21	Lamar Smith	49,752	100.0
22	Tom DeLay	22,379	79.9
	Mike Fjetland	5,645	20.1
23	Henry Bonilla	25,231	100.0
24	Mike Rivera Ortega	5,770	100.0
25	Tom Reiser	10,995	100.0
26	Scott Armey	11,493	45.4
	Michael C. Burgess	5,703	22.5
	David Gulling	204	0.8
	Dave Kovatch	675	2.7
	Keith A. Self	5,610	22.2
	Roger Sessions	1,630	6.4
27	Pat Ahumada	9,614	100.0
28	Gabriel Perales, Jr.	4,422	100.0
29	(none)		
30	Ron Bush	3,958	75.3
	Zach Rader	1,296	24.7
31	Flynn Adcock	1,117	3.2
	Brad Barton	5,751	16.4
	John R. Carter	9,144	26.0
	C. Patrick Meece	3,653	10.4
	Roy Streckfuss	898	2.6
	Terry S. Ward	600	1.7
	Peter Wareing	12,987	36.9
	Eric Whitfield	1,014	2.9
32	Pete Sessions	19,973	93.5
	Danny Davis	1,391	6.5

The elections were close enough in the races for the 26th and 31st District seats that runoff elections were held on April 9, 2002.

2002 Democratic Primary Runoff Election (April 9)

District	Candidate	Votes	%
25	Chris Bell	9,752	54.3
	Carroll G. Robinson	8,056	45.7

2002 Republican Primary Runoff Election (April 9)

District	Candidate	Votes	%
26	Scott Armey	8,737	45.4
	Michael C. Burgess	10,522	54.6
31	John R. Carter	13,150	56.8
	Peter Wareing	9,986	43.2

2002 General Election (November 5)

District	Candidate	Votes	%
1	Max Sandlin, Democrat	86,384	56.4
	John Lawrence, Republican	66,654	43.6
2	Jim Turner, Democrat	85,492	60.8
	Van Brookshire, Republican	53,656	38.2
	Peter Beach, Libertarian	1,353	<1.0
3	Sam Johnson, Republican	113,974	73.9
	Manny Molera, Democrat	37,503	24.3
	John Davis, Libertarian	2,656	1.7
4	Ralph Hall, Democrat	97,304	57.8
	John Graves, Republican	67,939	40.4
	Barbara Robinson, Libertarian	3,042	1.8
5	Jeb Hensarling, Republican	81,439	58.2
	Ron Chapman, Democrat	56,330	40.3
	Dan Michalski, Libertarian	1,283	0.9
	Thomas J. Kemper, Green	856	0.6
6	Joe Barton, Republican	115,396	70.3
	Felix Alvarado, Democrat	45,404	27.7
	Frank Brady, Libertarian	1,992	1.2
	B. J. Armstrong, Green	1,245	0.8
7	John Culberson, Republican	96,795	89.2
	Drew Parks, Libertarian	11,674	10.8
	John R. Skone-Palmer, Independent	58	<0.1
8	Kevin Brady, Republican	140,575	93.1
	Gil Guillory, Libertarian	10,351	6.9
9	Nick Lampson, Democrat	86,710	58.6
	Paul Williams, Republican	59,635	40.3
	Dean L. Tucker, Libertarian	1,613	1.1

Dist.	Candidate	Votes	%
10	Lloyd Doggett, Democrat	114,428	84.4
	Michele Messina, Libertarian	21,196	15.6
11	Chet Edwards, Democrat	74,678	51.6
	Ramsey Farley, Republican	68,236	47.1
	Andrew Paul Farris, Libertarian	1,943	1.3
12	Kay Granger, Republican	121,208	91.9
	Edward A. Hanson, Libertarian	10,723	8.1
13	Mac Thornberry, Republican	119,401	79.3
	Zane Reese, Democrat	31,218	20.7
14	Ron Paul, Republican	102,905	68.1
	Corby Windham, Democrat	48,224	31.9
15	Rubén Hinojosa, Democrat	66,311	100.0
16	Silvestre Reyes, Democrat	72,383	100.0
17	Charlie Stenholm, Democrat	84,136	51.4
	Rob Beckham, Republican	77,622	47.4
	Fred Jones, Libertarian	2,046	1.2
18	Sheila Jackson Lee, Democrat	99,161	76.9
	Phillip J. Abbott, Republican	27,980	21.7
	Brent Sullivan, Libertarian	1,785	1.4
19	Larry Combest, Republican	117,092	91.6
	Larry Johnson, Libertarian	10,684	8.4
20	Charlie A. Gonzalez, Democrat	68,685	100.0
21	Lamar Smith, Republican	161,836	72.9
	John Courage, Democrat	56,206	25.3
	DG Roberts, Libertarian	4,051	1.8
22	Tom DeLay, Republican	100,499	63.2
	Gerald W. "Jerry" LaFleur, Libertarian	1,612	1.0
	Tom Riley, Democrat	55,716	35.0
	Joel West, Green	1,257	0.8
23	Henry Bonilla, Republican	77,573	51.5
	Henry Cuellar, Democrat	71,067	47.2
	Jeffrey C. Blunt, Libertarian	1,106	0.7
	Ed Scharf, Green	806	0.5
24	Martin Frost, Democrat	73,002	64.7
	Mike Rivera Ortega, Republican	38,332	34.0
	Ken Ashby, Libertarian	1,560	1.4
25	Chris Bell, Democrat	63,590	54.8
	Tom Reiser, Republican	50,041	43.1
	Guy McLendon, Libertarian	1,096	0.9
	George Reiter, Green	1,399	1.2
26	Michael C. Burgess, Republican	123,195	74.8
	Paul William LeBon, Democrat	37,485	22.8
	David Wallace Croft, Libertarian	2,367	1.4
	Gary R. Page, Green	1,631	<1.0
27	Solomon Ortiz, Democrat	68,559	61.1
	Pat Ahumada, Republican	41,004	36.5
	Christopher J. Claytor, Libertarian	2,646	2.4
28	Ciro Rodriguez, Democrat	71,393	71.1
	Gabriel Perales, Jr., Republican	26,973	26.9
	William A. "Bill" Stallknecht, Libertarian	2,054	2.0
29	Gene Green, Democrat	55,760	95.2
	Paul Hansen, Libertarian	2,833	4.8
30	Eddie Bernice Johnson, Democrat	28,981	24.2
	Ron Bush, Republican	88,980	74.3
	Lance Flores, Libertarian	1,856	1.5
31	David Bagley, Democrat	44,183	27.4
	John R. Carter, Republican	111,556	69.1
	Clark Simmons, Libertarian	2,037	1.3
	John S. Petersen, Green	1,992	1.2
	R.C. Crawford, Independent	1,716	1.1
32	Pauline K. Dixon, Democrat	44,886	30.3
	Pete Sessions, Republican	100,226	67.8
	Steve Martin, Libertarian	1,582	1.1
	Carla Hubbell, Green	1,208	0.8

2003 Special Election (May 3)

Dist.	Candidate	Votes	%
19	Randy Neugebauer, Republican	13,091	22.4
	Stace Williams, Republican	2,609	4.5
	Richard Bartlett, Republican	1,046	1.8
	Mike Conaway, Republican	12,270	21.0
	Donald May, Republican	629	1.1
	David R. Langston, Republican	8,053	13.8
	Carl H. Isett, Republican	11,015	18.9

2003 Special Election (continued)

Candidate	Votes	%
Jerri Simmons-Asmussen, Democrat	898	1.5
Jamie Berryhill, Republican	1,907	3.3
William M. (Bill) Christian, Republican	1,029	1.8
Richard "Chip" Peterson, Libertarian	159	0.3
John D. Bell, Republican	1,883	3.2
Vickie Sutton, Republican	1,987	3.4
E.L. "Ed" Hicks, Independent	81	0.1
Kaye Gaddy, Democrat	1,396	2.4
Julia Penelope, Green Party	223	0.4
Thomas Flournoy, Constitution Party	93	0.2

This special election was held to fill the seat of Larry Combest who retired on XX 2003. The election was close enough that a runoff was held on June 7, 2003, between Republicans Randy Neugebauer of Lubbock and Mike Conaway of Midland.

2003 Special Election Runoff (June 3)

District	Candidate	Votes	%
19	Randy Neugebauer, Republican	28,546	50.5
	Mike Conaway, Republican	27,959	49.5

2004 Democratic Primary Election (March 9)

District	Candidate	Votes	%
1	Max Sandlin	26,400	100.0
2	Nick Lampson	27,284	100.0
3	(none)		
4	Jerry D. Ashford, Jr.	12,513	34.1
	Jim Nickerson	24,141	65.9
5	Bill Bernstein	14,012	100.0
6	Morris Meyer	13,564	100.0
7	John Martinez	10,372	100.0
8	James "Jim" Wright	32,535	100.0
9	Chris Bell	8,492	31.3
	Al Green	18,034	66.5
	Beverly A. Spencer	607	2.2
10	(none)		
11	Wayne Raasch	13,948	100.0
12	Felix Alvarado	10,452	100.0
13	(none)		
14	(none)		
15	Ruben Hinojosa	44,427	100.0
16	Silvestre Reyes	27,469	100.0
17	Chet Edwards	17,754	100.0
18	Sheila Jackson Lee	19,565	100.0
19	Charles W. Stenholm	16,576	100.0
20	Charles A. Gonzalez	16,804	100.0
21	Rhett R. Smith	26,297	100.0
22	Richard R. Morrison	7,303	71.4
	Erik Saenz	2,920	28.6
23	Joe Sullivan	29,061	63.8
	Virgil W. Yanta	16,523	36.2
24	Gary R. Page	6,572	100.0
25	Lloyd Doggett	40,306	64.4
	Leticia Hinojosa	22,305	35.6
26	Lico Reyes	10,880	100.0
27	Solomon P. Ortiz	44,849	100.0
28	Henry Cuellar	24,651	50.2
	Ciro D. Rodriguez	24,448	49.8
29	Gene Green	9,337	100.0
30	Eddie Bernice Johnson	25,719	100.0
31	Jon Porter	14,909	100.0
32	Martin Frost	9,943	100.0

2004 Republican Primary Election (March 9)

District	Candidate	Votes	%
1	Wayne Christian	6,854	14.7
	Louis Gohmert	19,421	41.7
	John Graves	13,933	29.9
	Emily Mathews	1,266	2.7
	Larry Thornton	457	1.0
	Lyle Thorstenson	4,604	9.9
	Andrew J. Bolton	246	1.0
2	George Fastuca	3,668	15.0
	Mark Henry	2,423	9.9
	Clint Moore	2,868	11.7
	John Nickell	285	1.2
	Ted Poe	14,932	61.1

District	Candidate	Votes	%
3	Sam Johnson	12,429	84.0
	Brian Rubarts	2,357	15.9
4	Ralph Hall	22,484	77.2
	Mike Mosher	3,122	10.7
	Mike Murphy	3,524	12.1
5	Jeb Hensarling	18,756	100.0
6	Joe Barton	13,486	100.0
7	John Culberson	26,561	92.2
	Sam Texas	2,245	7.8
8	Kevin Brady	26,445	100.0
9	A.R. Hassan	1,132	19.0
	Arlette Molina	4,836	81.0
10	John Devine	7,096	21.3
	Teresa Doggett Taylor	1,494	4.50
	Pat Elliott	1,245	3.7
	John Kelley	952	2.9
	Michael T. McCaul	7,953	23.9
	Dave Phillips	4,460	13.4
	Ben Streusand	9,364	28.2
	Brad Tashenberg	695	2.1
11	Mike Conaway	38,792	74.5
	Bill Lester	13,255	25.5
12	Kay Granger	17,964	100.0
13	Mac Thornberry	40,801	100.0
14	Ron Paul	21,095	100.0
15	Alexander Hamilton	3,795	41.5
	Paul B. Haring	1,954	21.4
	Michael D. Thamm	3,398	37.1
16	David Brigham	4,127	53.2
	Bobby Ortiz	3,626	46.8
17	Dave McIntyre	10,681	28.2
	Dot Snyder	11,568	30.5
	Arlene Wohlgemuth	15,627	41.3
19	Randy Neugebauer	24,712	100.0
20	Roger Scott	4,832	100.0
21	Lamar Smith	28,144	100.0
22	Tom DeLay	15,490	100.0
23	Henry Bonilla	21,299	100.0
24	Bill Dunn	1,096	8.9
	Kenny Marchant	9,073	73.5
	Cynthia Newman	1,103	8.9
	Terry Waldrum	1,074	8.7
25	Regner A. Capener	1,788	32.7
	Rebecca Armendariz Klein	3,679	67.3
26	Michael C. Burgess	17,184	100.0
27	Jesus A. Caquias	2,401	30.1
	William (Willie) Vaden	5,582	69.9
28	Chris Bellamy	1,478	14.9
	Francisco "Quico" Canseco	2,115	21.4
	James (Jim) F. Hopson	4,856	49.1
	Gabriel (Gabe) Perales, Jr.	1,445	14.6
31	Dirk Armbrust	2,868	7.9
	John R. Carter	25,293	69.5
	Wes Riddle	8,215	22.6
32	Pete Sessions	11,819	100.0

The elections were close enough in the races for the 1st, 10th, 15th, 17th, and 28th District seats that runoff elections were held on April 13, 2004.

2004 REPUBLICAN PRIMARY RUNOFF ELECTION (APRIL 13)

District	Candidate	Votes	%
1	Louis Gohmert	16,549	57.4
	John Graves	12,290	42.6
10	Michael T. McCaul	15,081	63.2
	Ben Streusand	8,800	36.9
15	Alexander Hamilton	1,822	39.2
	Michael D. Thamm	2,829	60.8
17	Dot Snyder	14,494	46.0
	Arlene Wohlgemuth	17,010	54.0
28	Francisco "Quico" Canseco	1,035	35.5
	James (Jim) F. Hopson	1,884	64.5

2004 GENERAL ELECTION (NOVEMBER 2)

District	Candidate	Votes	%
1	Max Sandlin, Democrat	96,281	37.7
	Louie Gohmert, Republican	157,068	61.5

District	Candidate	Votes	%
	Dean Tucker, Libertarian	2,158	0.8
2	Nick Lampson, Democrat	108,156	42.9
	Ted Poe, Republican	139,951	55.5
	Sandra Leigh Saulsbury, Libertarian	3,931	1.6
3	Sam Johnson, Republican	180,099	85.6
	Paul Jenkins, Independent	16,966	8.1
	James Vessels, Libertarian	13,287	6.3
4	Ralph Hall, Republican	182,866	68.2
	Jim Nickerson, Democrat	81,585	30.4
	Kevin D. Anderson, Libertarian	3,491	1.3
5	Jeb Hensarling, Republican	148,816	64.5
	Bill Bernstein, Democrat	75,911	32.9
	John Gonzalez, Libertarian	6,118	2.7
6	Joe Barton, Republican	168,767	66.0
	Morris Meyer, Democrat	83,609	32.7
	Stephen Schrader, Libertarian	3,251	1.3
7	John Culberson, Republican	175,440	64.1
	John Martinez, Democrat	91,126	33.3
	Drew Parks, Libertarian	3,372	1.2
	Paul Staton, Independent	3,713	1.4
8	Kevin Brady, Republican	179,599	68.9
	James Wright, Democrat	77,324	29.7
	Paul Hansen, Libertarian	3,705	1.4
9	Al Green, Democrat	114,462	72.2
	Arlette Molina, Republican	42,132	26.6
	Stacey Lynn Bourland, Libertarian	1,972	1.2
10	Mike McCaul, Republican	182,113	78.6
	Lorenzo Sadun, Write-in	13,961	6.0
	Robert Frittie, Libertarian	35,569	15.4
11	Wayne Raasch, Democrat	50,339	21.8
	Mike Conaway, Republican	177,291	76.8
	Jeffrey Blunt, Libertarian	3,347	1.4
12	Kay Granger, Republican	173,222	72.3
	Felix Alvarado, Democrat	66,316	27.7
13	Mac Thornberry, Republican	189,448	92.3
	Marion J. "Smitty" Smith, Libertarian	15,793	7.7
14	Ron Paul, Republican	173,668	100.0
15	Ruben Hinojosa, Democrat	96,089	57.8
	Michael D. Thamm, Republican	67,917	40.8
	William R. Cady, Libertarian	2,352	1.4
16	Silvestre Reyes, Democrat	108,577	67.5
	David Brigham, Republican	49,972	31.1
	Brad Clardy, Libertarian	2,224	1.4
17	Chet Edwards, Democrat	125,309	51.2
	Arlene Wohlgemuth, Republican	116,049	47.4
	Clyde L. Garland, Libertarian	3,390	1.4
18	Sheila Jackson Lee, Democrat	136,018	88.9
	Brent Sullivan, Libertarian	7,183	4.7
	Tom Bazán, Independent	9,787	6.4
19	Randy Neugebauer, Republican	136,459	58.4
	Charlie Stenholm, Democrat	93,531	40.1
	Richard "Chip" Peterson, Libertarian	3,524	1.5
20	Charlie Gonzalez, Democrat	112,480	65.5
	Roger Scott, Republican	54,976	32.0
	Jessie Bouley, Libertarian	2,377	1.4
	Michael Idrogo, Independent	1,971	1.1
21	Lamar Smith, Republican	209,774	61.5
	Rhett Smith, Democrat	121,129	35.5
	Jason Pratt, Libertarian	10,216	3.0
22	Tom DeLay, Republican	150,386	55.2
	Richard R. Morrison, Democrat	112,034	41.1
	Thomas Morrison, Libertarian	4,886	1.8
	Michael Fjetland, Independent	5,314	1.9
23	Henry Bonilla, Republican	170,716	69.3
	Joe Sullivan, Democrat	72,480	29.4
	Nazirite Ruben "Conrade" Perez, Libertarian	3,307	1.3
24	Gary R. Page, Democrat	82,599	34.2
	Kenny Marchant, Republican	154,435	64.0
	James H. Lawrence, Libertarian	4,340	1.8
25	Lloyd Doggett, Democrat	108,309	67.6
	Becky Armendariz Klein, Republican	49,252	30.7
	James Werner, Libertarian	2,656	1.7

General Election (continued)

District	Candidate	Votes	%
26	Michael C. Burgess, Republican	180,519	65.8
	Lico Reyes, Democrat	89,809	32.7
	James Gholston, Libertarian	4,211	1.5
27	Solomon P. Ortiz, Democrat	112,081	63.1
	William "Willie" Vaden, Republican	61,955	34.9
	Christopher J. Claytor, Libertarian	3,500	2.0
28	James (Jim) F. Hopson, Republican	69,538	38.6
	Henry Cuellar, Democrat	106,323	59.0
	Ken Ashby, Libertarian	4,305	2.4
29	Gene Green, Democrat	78,256	94.1
	Clifford L. Messina, Libertarian	4,868	5.9
30	Eddie Bernice Johnson, Democrat	144,513	93.0
	James Davis, Libertarian	10,821	7.0
31	John Carter, Republican	160,247	64.8
	Jon Porter, Democrat	80,292	32.5
	Celeste Adams, Libertarian	6,888	2.8
32	Pete Sessions, Republican	109,859	54.3
	Martin Frost, Democrat	89,030	44.0
	Michael David Needleman, Libertarian	3,347	1.7

2006 DEMOCRATIC PRIMARY ELECTION (MARCH 7)

District	Candidate	Votes	%
1	Roger L. Owen	10,121	53.3
	Duane Shaw	8,851	46.7
2	Gary E. Binderim	18,491	100.0
3	Dan Dodd	2,478	100.0
4	Glenn Melancon	15,696	100.0
5	Charlie Thompson	7,516	100.0
6	David T. Harris	8,538	100.0
7	Jim Henley	3,950	67.5
	David Murff	1,902	32.5
8	James "Jim" Wright	19,881	100.0
9	Al Green	10,549	100.0
10	Ted Ankrum	3,703	36.7
	Paul Foreman	3,610	35.8
	Pat Mynatt	1,291	12.8
	Sid Smith	1,475	14.6
11	(none)		
12	John R. Morris	4,846	100.0
13	Roger J. Waun	10,651	100.0
14	Shane Sklar	13,244	100.0
15	Rubén Hinojosa	39,094	100.0
16	Jorge Artalejo	0	0.0
	Silvestre Reyes	28,931	100.0
17	Chet Edwards	11,913	100.0
18	Sheila Jackson Lee	9,512	100.0
19	Robert Ricketts	9,656	100.0
20	Charles A. Gonzalez	16,398	100.0
21	John Courage	11,264	100.0
22	Nick Lampson	7,993	100.0
23	Rick Bolanos	30,164	100.0
24	Gary R. Page	3,089	100.0
25	Lloyd Doggett	29,119	100.0
26	Tim Barnwell	5,157	100.0
27	Solomon P. Ortiz	31,563	100.0
28	Henry Cuellar	24,256	53.1
	Victor Morales	2,943	6.4
	Ciro D. Rodriguez	18,484	40.5
29	Gene Green	4,538	100.0
30	Eddie Bernice Johnson	17,490	100.0
31	Mary Beth Harrell	7,023	100.0
32	Will Pryor	3,622	100.0

The race was close enough in the 10th District seat race that a special runoff election was held on April 11, 2006.

2006 REPUBLICAN PRIMARY ELECTION (MARCH 7)

District	Candidate	Votes	%
1	Louie Gohmert	35,267	100.0
2	Ted Poe	16,723	100.0
3	Bob Johnson	2,292	14.7
	Sam Johnson	13,348	85.3
4	Ralph M. Hall	24,409	100.0
5	Jeb Hensarling	24,793	100.0
6	Joe L. Barton	23,222	100.0
7	John Culberson	27,788	100.0

District	Candidate	Votes	%
8	Kevin Brady	24,727	100.0
9	(none)		
10	Michael T. McCaul	22,901	100.0
11	Mike Conaway	37,391	100.0
12	Kay Granger	20,426	100.0
13	Mac Thornberry	36,477	100.0
14	Ron Paul	24,086	77.6
	Cynthia Sinatra	6,935	22.4
15	Paul B. Haring	5,552	70.9
	Eddie Zamora	2,278	29.1
16	(none)		
17	Tucker Anderson	14,712	46.0
	Van Taylor	17,291	54.0
18	Ahmad R. Hassan	2,753	100.0
19	Randy Neugebauer	37,038	100.0
21	Lamar Smith	27,166	100.0
22	Pat Baig	1,115	3.4
	Tom Campbell	9,941	30.0
	Tom DeLay	20,563	62.00
	Mike Fjetland	1,550	4.7
23	Henry Bonilla	17,929	100.0
24	Kenny E. Marchant	9,716	100.0
25	(none)		
26	Michael C. Burgess	17,964	100.0
27	William "Willie" Vaden	7,207	100.0
28	(none)		
29	Eric Story	2,113	100.0
30	Wilson Aurbach	1,614	44.5
	Amir Omar	1,308	36.1
	Fred A. Wood	704	19.4
31	John R. Carter	23,438	100.0
32	Pete Sessions	13,210	100.0

The race was close enough in the 30th District seat race that a special runoff election was held on April 11, 2006.

2006 DEMOCRATIC PRIMARY RUNOFF ELECTION (APRIL 11)

2006 REPUBLICAN PRIMARY RUNOFF ELECTION (APRIL 11)

District	Candidate	Votes	%
10	Ted Ankrum	2,611	70.8
	Paul Foreman	1,078	29.2
30	Wilson Aurbach	1,129	60.8
	Amir Omar	727	39.2

2006 GENERAL ELECTION (NOVEMBER 7)

District	Candidate	Votes	%
1	Louie Gohmert, Republican	104,099	68.0
	Roger L. Owen, Democrat	46,303	30.2
	Donald Perkison, Libertarian	2,668	1.7
2	Ted Poe, Republican	90,490	65.6
	Gary E. Binderim, Democrat	45,080	32.7
	Justo J. Perez, Libertarian	2,295	1.7
3	Sam Johnson, Republican	88,690	62.5
	Dan Dodd, Democrat	49,529	34.9
	Christopher J. Claytor, Libertarian	3,662	2.6
4	Ralph M. Hall, Republican	106,495	64.4
	Glenn Melancon, Democrat	55,278	33.4
	Kurt G. Helm, Libertarian	3,496	2.1
5	Jeb Hensarling, Republican	88,478	61.8
	Charlie Thompson, Democrat	50,983	35.6
	Mike Nelson, Libertarian	3,791	2.6
6	Joe L. Barton, Republican	91,927	60.5
	David T. Harris, Democrat	56,369	37.1
	Carl Nulsen, Libertarian	3,740	2.5
7	John Culberson, Republican	99,318	59.2
	Jim Henley, Democrat	64,514	38.5
	Drew Parks, Libertarian	3,953	2.4
8	Kevin Brady, Republican	105,665	67.3
	James "Jim" Wright, Democrat	51,393	32.7
9	Al Green, Democrat	60,253	100.0
10	Michael T. McCaul, Republican	97,726	55.3
	Ted Ankrum, Democrat	71,415	40.4
	Michael Badnarik, Libertarian	7,614	4.3
11	Mike Conaway, Republican	107,268	100.0

District	Candidate	Votes	%
12	Kay Granger, Republican	98,371	66.9
	John R. Morris, Democrat	45,676	31.1
	Gardner Osborne , Libertarian	2,888	2.0
13	Mac Thornberry, Republican	108,107	74.4
	Roger J. Waun, Democrat	33,460	23.0
	Jim Thompson, Libertarian	3,829	2.6
14	Ron Paul, Republican	94,380	60.2
	Shane Sklar, Democrat	62,429	39.8
15	(see special election below)		
16	Silvestre Reyes, Republican	61,116	78.7
	Gordon R. Strickland, Libertarian	16,572	21.3
17	Van Taylor, Republican	64,142	40.3
	Chet Edwards, Democrat	92,478	58.1
	Guillermo Acosta, Libertarian	2,504	1.6
18	Ahmad Hassan, Republican	16,448	19.1
	Sheila Jackson Lee, Democrat	65,936	76.6
	Patrick Warren, Libertarian	3,667	4.3
19	Randy Neugebauer, Republican	94,785	67.7
	Robert Ricketts, Democrat	41,676	29.8
	Fred C. Jones, Libertarian	3,349	2.4
	Mike Sadler, write-in	197	0.1
20	Charles A. Gonzalez, Democrat	68,348	87.4
	Michael Idrogo, Libertarian	9,897	12.6
21	(see special election below)		
22	Nick Lampson, Democrat	76,775	51.8
	Bob Smither, Libertarian	9,009	6.1
	Joe Reasbeck, write-in	89	0.1
	Don Richardson, write-in	428	0.3
	Shelley Sekula Gibbs, write-in	61,938	41.8
23	(see special election below)		
24	Kenny E. Marchant, Republican	83,835	59.8
	Gary R. Page, Democrat	52,075	37.2
	Mark Frohman, Libertarian	4,228	3.0
25	(see special election below)		
26	Michael C. Burgess, Republican	94,219	60.2
	Tim Barnwell, Democrat	58,271	37.2
	Rich Haas, Libertarian	3,993	2.6
27	William "Willie" Vaden , Republican	42,538	38.9
	Solomon P. Ortiz, Republican	62,058	56.8
	Robert Powell, Libertarian	4,718	4.3
28	(see special election below)		
29	Eric Story, Republican	12,347	24.4
	Gene Green, Democrat	37,174	73.5
	Clifford Lee Messina, Libertarian	1,029	2.0
30	Wilson Aurbach, Republican	17,850	17.6
	Eddie Bernice Johnson, Democrat	81,348	80.2
	Ken Ashby, Libertarian	2,250	2.2
31	John R. Carter, Republican	90,869	58.5
	Mary Beth Harrell, Democrat	60,293	38.8
	Matt McAdoo, Libertarian	4,221	2.7
32	Pete Sessions, Republican	71,461	56.4
	Will Pryor, Democrat	52,269	41.3
	John B. Hawley, Libertarian	2,922	2.3

2006 Special Election (November 7)

District	Candidate	Votes	%
15	Paul B. Haring, Republican	16,601	23.7
	Rubén Hinojosa, Democrat	43,236	61.8
	Eddie Zamora, Republican	10,150	14.5
21	Tommy Calvert, Independent	5,280	2.6
	John Courage, Democrat	49,957	24.5
	Gene Kelly, Democrat	18,355	9.0
	James Lyle Peterson, Independent	2,189	1.1
	Mark J. Rossano, Independent	1,439	0.7
	Lamar Smith, Republican	122,486	60.1
	James Arthur Strohm, Libertarian	4,076	2.0
22	(Unexpired term)		
	Don Richardson, Republican	7,405	6.0
	Shelley Sekula-Gibbs, Republican	76,924	62.1
	M. Bob Smither, Libertarian	23,425	18.9
	Steve Stockman, Republican	13,600	11.0
23	Giannibicego Hoa Tran, Republican	2,568	2.1
	August G. "Augie" Beltran, Democrat	2,647	2.1
	Rick Bolanos, Democrat	2,564	2.1

★315★

	Henry Bonilla, Republican	60,175	48.6
	Adrian DeLeon, Democrat	2,198	1.8
	Lukin Gilliland, Democrat	13,728	11.1
	Ciro D. Rodriguez, Democrat	24,594	19.9
	Craig T. Stephens, Independent	3,341	2.7
	Albert Uresti, Democrat	14,552	11.8
25	Barbara Cunningham, Libertarian	6,942	4.2
	Lloyd Doggett, Democrat	109,911	67.3
	Brian Parrett, Independent	3,596	2.2
	Grant Rostig, Republican	42,975	26.3
28	Ron Avery, Conservative	9,383	12.1
	Henry Cuellar, Democrat	52,574	67.6
	Frank Enriquez, Democrat	15,798	20.3

On June 28, 2006, the United States Supreme Court ruled that the Texas Legislature had violated the rights of Hispanic voters when it moved most of Laredo out of the neighboring 23rd District and replaced it with several heavily Republican San Antonio suburbs. It also ruled that the 25th District was not compact enough to be a replacement. The 25th District was nicknamed "the fajita strip" because of its shape. The ruling forced the redrawing of five districts between El Paso and San Antonio and a special election to select their representatives. This election was coincidental with the November general election. The races were close enough in the 23rd District seat race that a runoff election was held on December 12, 2006.

2006 GENERAL ELECTION RUNOFF (DECEMBER 12, 2006)

23	Henry Bonilla, Republican	32,217	45.7
	Ciro D. Rodriguez, Democrat	38,256	54.3

ALPHABETICAL LIST OF TEXAS CONGRESSMEN

Member Name	Birth-Death	Position	Party	Congress	Years Served
ABBOTT, Jo (Joseph)	1840-1908	Representative	Democrat	50 – 54	1887 - 1896
ALGER, Bruce Reynolds	1918-	Representative	Republican	84 – 88	1955 - 1964
ANDREWS, Michael Allen	1944-	Representative	Democrat	98 – 103	1983 - 1994
ANTONY, Edwin Le Roy	1852-1913	Representative	Democrat	52	1891 - 1892
ARCHER, William Reynolds, Jr.	1928-	Representative	Republican	92 –106	1971 - 2000
ARMEY, Richard Keith	1940-	Representative	Republican	99 –107	1985 - 2002
BAILEY, Joseph Weldon	1862-1929	Representative	Democrat	52 – 56	1891 - 1900
BAILEY, Joseph Weldon	1862-1929	Senator	Democrat	57 – 62	1901 - 1912
BAILEY, Joseph Weldon, Jr.	1892-1943	Representative	Democrat	73	1933 - 1934
BALL, Thomas Henry	1859-1944	Representative	Democrat	55 – 58	1897 - 1904
BARTLETT, Harry Stephen (Steve)	1947-	Representative	Republican	98 – 102	1983 - 1992
BARTON, Joe Linus	1949-	Representative	Republican	99 –110	1985 - 2008
BEALL, James Andrew (Jack)	1866-1929	Representative	Democrat	58 – 63	1903 - 1914
BECKWORTH, Lindley Garrison, Sr.	1913-1984	Representative	Democrat	76 – 89	1939 - 1966
BEE, Carlos	1867-1932	Representative	Democrat	66	1919 - 1920
BELL, Charles Keith	1853-1913	Representative	Democrat	53 – 54	1893 - 1896
BELL, Chris	1959-	Representative	Democrat	108	2003 - 2004
BELL, John Junior	1910-1963	Representative	Democrat	84	1955 - 1956
BELL, Peter Hansbrough	1812-1898	Representative	Democrat	33 – 34	1853 - 1856
BENTSEN, Kenneth E., Jr.	1959-	Representative	Democrat	104 –107	1995 - 2002
BENTSEN, Lloyd Millard, Jr.	1921-2006	Representative	Democrat	80 – 83	1947 - 1954
BENTSEN, Lloyd Millard, Jr.	1921-2006	Senator	Democrat	92 – 103	1971 - 1994
BLACK, Eugene	1879-1975	Representative	Democrat	64 – 70	1915 - 1928
BLAKLEY, William Arvis	1898-1976	Senator	Democrat	85 – 87	1957 - 1962
BLANTON, Thomas Lindsay	1872-1957	Representative	Democrat	65 –74	1917 - 1936
BONILLA, Henry	1954-	Representative	Republican	103 – 109	1993 - 2006
BOULTER, Eldon Beau	1942-	Representative	Republican	99 – 100	1985 - 1988
BOX, John Calvin	1871-1941	Representative	Democrat	66 – 71	1919 - 1930
BRADY, Kevin Patrick	1955-	Representative	Republican	105 –110	1997 - 2008
BRIGGS, Clay Stone	1876-1933	Representative	Democrat	66 – 73	1919 - 1934
BROOOCKS, Moses Lycurgus	1864-1908	Representative	Democrat	59	1905 - 1906
BROOKS, Jack Bascom	1922-	Representative	Democrat	83 - 103	1953 - 1994

★317★

Member Name	Birth-Death	Position	Party	Congress	Years Served
BRYAN, Guy Morrison	1821-1901	Representative	Democrat	35	1857 - 1858
BRYANT, John Wiley	1947-	Representative	Democrat	98 - 104	1983 - 1996
BUCHANAN, James Paul	1867-1937	Representative	Democrat	63 - 75	1913 - 1938
BURGESS, George Farmer	1861-1919	Representative	Democrat	57 - 64	1901 - 1916
BURGESS, Michael C.	1950-	Representative	Republican	108 - 110	2003 - 2004
BURKE, Robert Emmet	1847-1901	Representative	Democrat	55 - 57	1897 - 1902
BURLESON, Albert Sidney	1863-1937	Representative	Democrat	56 - 63	1899 - 1914
BURLESON, Omar Truman	1906-1991	Representative	Democrat	80 - 95	1947 - 1978
BUSH, George Herbert Walker	1924-	Representative	Republican	90 - 91	1967 - 1968
BUSTAMANTE, Albert Garza	1935-	Representative	Democrat	99 - 102	1985 - 1992
CABELL, Earle	1906-1975	Representative	Democrat	89 - 92	1965 - 1972
CALLAWAY, Oscar	1872-1947	Representative	Democrat	62 - 64	1911 - 1916
CARTER, John R.	1941-	Representative	Republican	108 - 110	2003 - 2008
CASEY, Robert Randolph	1915-1986	Representative	Democrat	86 - 94	1959 - 1976
CHAPMAN, Jim	1945-	Representative	Democrat	99 - 104	1985 - 1996
CHILTON, Horace	1853-1932	Senator	Democrat	52 - 56	1891 - 1900
CLARK, William Thomas	1831-1905	Representative	Republican	41 - 42	1869 - 1872
COCKRELL, Jeremiah Vardaman	1832-1915	Representative	Democrat	53 - 54	1893 - 1896
COKE, Richard	1829-1897	Senator	Democrat	45 - 53	1877 - 1894
COLEMAN, Ronald D'Emory	1941-	Representative	Democrat	98 - 104	1983 - 1996
COLLINS, James Mitchell	1916-1989	Representative	Republican	90 - 97	1967 - 1982
COMBEST, Larry Ed	1945-	Representative	Republican	99 - 108	1985 - 2004
COMBS, Jesse Martin	1889-1953	Representative	Democrat	79 - 82	1945 - 1952
CONAWAY, K. Michael	1948-	Representative	Republican	109 - 110	2005 - 2008
CONNALLY, Thomas Terry (Tom)	1877-1963	Representative	Democrat	65 - 70	1917 - 1928
CONNALLY, Thomas Terry (Tom)	1877-1963	Senator	Democrat	71 - 82	1929 - 1952
CONNER, John Coggswell	1842-1873	Representative	Democrat	41 - 42	1869 - 1872
COOPER, Samuel Bronson	1850-1918	Representative	Democrat	53 - 60	1893 - 1908
CORNYN, John	1952-	Senator	Republican	107 - 110	2001 - 2008
CRAIN, William Henry	1848-1896	Representative	Democrat	49 - 54	1885 - 1896
CRANFORD, John Walter	1862-1899	Representative	Democrat	55	1897 - 1898
CROSS, Oliver Harlan	1868-1960	Representative	Democrat	71 - 74	1929 - 1936
CROWLEY, Miles	1859-1921	Representative	Democrat	54	1895 - 1896
CUELLAR, Henry	1955-	Representative	Democrat	109 - 110	2005 - 2008
CULBERSON, Charles Allen	1855-1925	Senator	Democrat	56 - 67	1899 - 1922
CULBERSON, David Browning	1830-1900	Representative	Democrat	44 - 54	1875 - 1896
CULBERSON, John	1956-	Representative	Republican	107 - 110	2001 - 2008
DANIEL, Marion Price	1910-1988	Senator	Democrat	83 - 85	1953 - 1958

Member Name	Birth-Death	Position	Party	Congress	Years Served
DAVIS, James Harvey (Cyclone)	1853-1940	Representative	Democrat	64	1915 - 1916
DE GRAFFENREID, Reese Calhoun	1859-1902	Representative	Democrat	55 - 57	1897 - 1902
de la GARZA, Eligio, II (Kika)	1927-	Representative	Democrat	89 - 104	1965 - 1996
DEGENER, Edward	1809-1890	Representative	Republican	41	1869 - 1870
DeLAY, Thomas Dale	1947-	Representative	Republican	99 - 109	1985 - 2006
DIES, Martin	1870-1922	Representative	Democrat	61 - 65	1909 - 1918
DIES, Martin, Jr.	1900-1972	Representative	Democrat	72 - 85	1931 - 1958
DOGGETT, Lloyd Alton, II	1946-	Representative	Democrat	104 - 110	1995 - 2008
DOWDY, John Vernard	1912-1995	Representative	Democrat	82 - 92	1951 - 1972
EAGLE, Joe Henry	1870-1963	Representative	Democrat	63 - 74	1913 - 1936
ECKHARDT, Robert Christian	1913-2001	Representative	Democrat	90 - 96	1967 - 1980
EDWARDS, Thomas Chester (Chet)	1951-	Representative	Democrat	102 - 110	1991 - 2008
EVANS, Lemuel Dale	1810-1877	Representative	American	34	1855 - 1856
FIELD, Scott	1847-1931	Representative	Democrat	58 - 59	1903 - 1904
FIELDS, Jack Milton, Jr.	1952-	Representative	Republican	97 - 104	1981 - 1996
FISHER, Ovie Clark	1903-1994	Representative	Democrat	78 - 93	1943 - 1974
FLANAGAN, James Winright	1805-1887	Senator	Republican	41 - 43	1869 - 1874
FOREMAN, Edgar Franklin	1933-	Representative	Republican	88	1963 - 1964
FROST, Jonas Martin	1942-	Representative	Democrat	96 - 108	1979 - 2004
GAMMAGE, Robert Alton	1938-	Representative	Democrat	95	1977 - 1978
GARNER, John Nance	1868-1967	Representative	Democrat	58 - 73	1903 - 1934
GARRETT, Clyde Leonard	1885-1959	Representative	Democrat	75 - 76	1937 - 1940
GARRETT, Daniel Edward	1869-1932	Representative	Democrat	63 - 72	1913 - 1932
GENTRY, Brady Preston	1896-1966	Representative	Democrat	83 - 84	1953 - 1956
GEREN, Preston M. (Pete)	1952-	Representative	Democrat	101 - 104	1989 - 1996
GIDDINGS, De Witt Clinton	1827-1903	Representative	Democrat	42 - 45	1871 - 1878
GILLESPIE, Oscar William	1858-1927	Representative	Democrat	58 - 61	1903 - 1910
GOHMERT, Louie	1953-	Representative	Republican	109 - 110	2005 - 2008
GONZALEZ, Charles A.	1945-	Representative	Democrat	106 - 110	1999 - 2008
GONZÁLEZ, Henry Barbosa	1916-2000	Representative	Democrat	87 - 105	1960 - 1998
GOSSETT, Ed Lee	1902-1990	Representative	Democrat	76 - 82	1939 - 1952
GRAMM, William Philip (Phil)	1942-	Representative	Democrat/Republican	96 - 98	1979 - 1984
GRAMM, William Philip (Phil)	1942-	Senator	Republican	99 - 107	1985 - 2002
GRANGER, Kay	1943-	Representative	Republican	105 - 110	1997 - 2008
GREEN, Al	1947-	Representative	Democrat	109 - 110	2005 - 2008
GREEN, Raymond Eugene (Gene)	1947-	Representative	Democrat	103 - 110	1993 - 2008
GREGG, Alexander White	1855-1919	Representative	Democrat	58 - 65	1903 - 1918
GRESHAM, Walter	1841-1920	Representative	Democrat	53	1893 - 1894

Member Name	Birth-Death	Position	Party	Congress	Years Served
GUILL, Ben Hugh	1909-1994	Representative	Republican	81	1949 - 1950
HALL, Ralph Moody	1923-	Representative	Democrat/Republican	97 - 110	1981 - 2008
HALL, Sam Blakeley, Jr.	1924-1994	Representative	Democrat	94 - 99	1975 - 1986
HAMILTON, Andrew Jackson	1815-1875	Representative	Independent/Democrat	36	1859 - 1860
HAMILTON, Morgan Calvin	1809-1893	Senator	Republican/Liberal Republican	41 - 44	1869 - 1876
HANCE, Kent Ronald	1942-	Representative	Democrat	96 - 98	1979 - 1984
HANCOCK, John	1824-1893	Representative	Democrat	42 - 48	1871 - 1884
HARDY, Rufus	1855-1943	Representative	Democrat	60 - 67	1907 - 1922
HARE, Silas	1827-1907	Representative	Democrat	50 - 51	1887 - 1890
HAWLEY, Robert Bradley	1849-1921	Representative	Republican	55 - 56	1897 - 1900
HEMPHILL, John	1803-1862	Senator	Democrat	36 - 37	1859 - 1862
HENDERSON, James Pinckney	1808-1858	Senator	Democrat	35	1857 - 1858
HENRY, Robert Lee	1864-1931	Representative	Democrat	55 - 64	1897 - 1916
HENSARLING, Jeb	1957-	Representative	Republican	108 - 110	2003 - 2008
HERNDON, William Smith	1835-1903	Representative	Democrat	42 - 43	1871 - 1874
HIGHTOWER, Jack English	1926-	Representative	Democrat	94 - 98	1975 - 1984
HINOJOSA, Rubén	1940-	Representative	Democrat	105 - 110	1997 - 2008
HOUSTON, Andrew Jackson	1854-1941	Senator	Democrat	77	1941 - 1942
HOUSTON, Samuel	1793-1863	Senator	Democrat/American(Know-Nothing)	29 - 35	1845 - 1858
HOWARD, Volney Erskine	1809-1889	Representative	Democrat	31 - 32	1849 - 1852
HUDSPETH, Claude Benton	1877-1941	Representative	Democrat	66 - 71	1919 - 1930
HUTCHESON, Joseph Chappell	1842-1924	Representative	Democrat	53 - 54	1893 - 1896
HUTCHISON, Kathryn Ann Bailey (Kay)	1943-	Senator	Republican	103 - 110	1993 - 2008
IKARD, Frank Neville	1913-1991	Representative	Democrat	82 - 87	1951 - 1962
JACKSON-LEE, Sheila	1950-	Representative	Democrat	104 - 110	1995 - 2008
JOHNSON, Eddie Bernice	1935-	Representative	Democrat	103 - 100	1993 - 2008
JOHNSON, Luther Alexander	1875-1965	Representative	Democrat	68 - 79	1923 - 1946
JOHNSON, Lyndon Baines	1908-1973	Representative	Democrat	75 - 80	1937 - 1948
JOHNSON, Lyndon Baines	1908-1973	Senator	Democrat	81 - 86	1949 - 1960
JOHNSON, Sam	1930-	Representative	Republican	102 - 110	1991 - 2008
JOHNSTON, Rienzi Melville	1849-1926	Senator	Democrat	62	1911 - 1912
JONES, George Washington	1828-1903	Representative	National	46 - 48	1879 - 1882
JONES, James Henry	1830-1904	Representative	Democrat	48 - 49	1883 - 1886
JONES, John Marvin	1886-1976	Representative	Democrat	65 - 76	1879 - 1940
JORDAN, Barbara Charline	1936-1996	Representative	Democrat	93 - 95	1973 - 1978
KAUFMAN, David Spangler	1813-1851	Representative	Democrat	29 - 31	1845 - 1850
KAZEN, Abraham, Jr.	1919-1987	Representative	Democrat	90 - 98	1967 - 1984
KILDAY, Paul Joseph	1900-1968	Representative	Democrat	76 - 87	1939 - 1962

Member Name	Birth-Death	Position	Party	Congress	Years Served
KILGORE, Constantine Buckley	1835-1897	Representative	Democrat	50 - 53	1887 - 1894
KILGORE, Joe Madison	1918-1999	Representative	Democrat	84 - 88	1955 - 1964
KLEBERG, Richard Mifflin, Sr.	1887-1955	Representative	Democrat	72 - 78	1931 - 1944
KLEBERG, Rudolph	1847-1924	Representative	Democrat	54 - 57	1895 - 1902
KRUEGER, Robert Charles	1935-	Representative	Democrat	94 - 95	1975 - 1978
KRUEGER, Robert Charles	1935-	Senator	Democrat	103	1993 - 1994
LAMPSON, Nicholas V.	1945-	Representative	Democrat	105 - 110	1997 - 2008
LANHAM, Fritz Garland	1880-1965	Representative	Democrat	66 - 79	1919 - 1946
LANHAM, Samuel Willis Tucker	1846-1908	Representative	Democrat	48 - 57	1883 - 1902
LAUGHLIN, Gregory H.	1942-	Representative	Democrat/Republican	101 - 104	1989 - 196
LEATH, James Marvin	1931-2000	Representative	Democrat	96 - 101	1979 - 1990
LEE, Robert Quincy	1869-1930	Representative	Democrat	71	1929 - 1930
LELAND, George Thomas (Mickey)	1944-1989	Representative	Democrat	96 - 101	1979 - 1990
LIVELY, Robert Maclin	1855-1929	Representative	Democrat	61	1909 - 1910
LOEFFLER, Thomas Gilbert	1946-	Representative	Republican	96 - 99	1979 - 1986
LONG, John Benjamin	1843-1924	Representative	Democrat	52	1891 - 1892
LUCAS, Wingate Hezekiah	1908-1989	Representative	Democrat	80 - 83	1947 - 1954
LYLE, John Emmett, Jr.	1910-2003	Representative	Democrat	79 - 83	1945 - 1954
MAHON, George Herman	1900-1985	Representative	Democrat	74 - 95	1935 - 1978
MANSFIELD, Joseph Jefferson	1861-1947	Representative	Democrat	65 - 80	1917 - 1948
MARCHANT, Kenny	1951-	Representative	Republican	109 - 110	2005 - 2008
MARTIN, William Harrison	1823-1898	Representative	Democrat	50 - 51	1887 - 1890
MATTOX, James Albon	1943-	Representative	Democrat	95 - 97	1977 - 1982
MAVERICK, Fontaine Maury	1895-1954	Representative	Democrat	74 - 75	1935 - 1938
MAXEY, Samuel Bell	1825-1895	Senator	Democrat	44 - 49	1875 - 1886
MAYFIELD, Earle Bradford	1881-1964	Senator	Democrat	68 - 70	1923 - 1928
McCAUL, Michael T.	1962-	Representative	Republican	109 - 110	2005 - 2008
McCLOSKEY, Augustus	1878-1950	Representative	Democrat	71	1929 - 1930
McFARLANE, William Doddridge	1894-1980	Representative	Democrat	73 - 75	1933 - 1938
McLEAN, William Pinkney	1836-1925	Representative	Democrat	43	1873 - 1874
McLEMORE, Atkins Jefferson	1857-1929	Representative	Democrat	64 - 65	1915 - 1918
MILFORD, Dale	1926-1997	Representative	Democrat	93 - 95	1973 - 1978
MILLER, James Francis	1830-1902	Representative	Democrat	48 - 49	1883 - 1886
MILLS, Roger Quarles	1832-1911	Representative	Democrat	43 - 51	1873 - 1890
MILLS, Roger Quarles	1832-1911	Senator	Democrat	52 - 55	1891 - 1898
MOORE, John Matthew	1862-1940	Representative	Democrat	59 - 62	1905 - 1912
MOORE, Littleton Wilde	1835-1911	Representative	Democrat	50 - 52	1887 - 1892
NEUGEBAUER, Randy	1949-	Representative	Republican	108 - 110	2003 - 2008

Member Name	Birth-Death	Position	Party	Congress	Years Served
NOONAN, George Henry	1828-1907	Representative	Republican	54	1895 - 1896
O'DANIEL, Wilbert Lee (Pappy)	1890-1969	Senator	Democrat	77 - 80	1941 - 1948
OCHILTREE, Thomas Peck	1837-1902	Representative	Independent	48	1883 - 1884
ORTIZ, Solomon Porfirio	1938-	Representative	Democrat	98 - 110	1983 - 2008
PARRISH, Lucian Walton	1878-1922	Representative	Democrat	66 - 67	1919 - 1922
PASCHAL, Thomas Moore	1845-1919	Representative	Democrat	53	1893 - 1894
PATMAN, John William Wright	1893-1976	Representative	Democrat	71 - 94	1929 - 1976
PATMAN, William Neff	1927-	Representative	Democrat	97 - 98	1981 - 1984
PATTON, Nat	1884-1957	Representative	Democrat	74 - 78	1935 - 1944
PAUL, Ronald Ernest	1935-	Representative	Republican	94 - 110	1975 - 2008
PENDLETON, George Cassety	1845-1913	Representative	Democrat	53 - 54	1893 - 1896
PICKETT, Thomas Augustus	1906-1980	Representative	Democrat	79 - 82	1945 - 1952
PICKLE, James Jarrell (Jake)	1913-2005	Representative	Democrat	88 - 103	1963 - 1994
PILSBURY, Timothy	1789-1858	Representative	Democrat	29 - 30	1845 - 1848
PINCKNEY, John McPherson	1845-1905	Representative	Democrat	58 - 59	1903 - 1906
POAGE, William Robert	1899-1987	Representative	Democrat	75 - 95	1937 - 1978
POE, Ted	1948-	Representative	Republican	109 - 110	2005 - 2008
POOL, Joe Richard	1911-1968	Representative	Democrat	88 - 90	1963 - 1968
PRICE, Robert Dale	1927-2004	Representative	Republican	90 - 93	1967 - 1974
PURCELL, Graham Boynton, Jr.	1919-	Representative	Democrat	87 - 92	1961 - 1972
RANDELL, Choice Boswell	1857-1945	Representative	Democrat	57 - 62	1901 - 1912
RAYBURN, Samuel Taliaferro	1882-1961	Representative	Democrat	63 - 87	1913 - 1962
REAGAN, John Henninger	1818-1905	Representative	Democrat	35 - 49	1857 - 1886
REAGAN, John Henninger	1818-1905	Senator	Democrat	50 - 52	1887 - 1892
REGAN, Kenneth Mills	1893-1959	Representative	Democrat	80 - 83	1947 - 1954
REYES, Silvestre	1944-	Representative	Democrat	105 - 110	1997 - 2008
ROBERTS, Herbert Ray	1913-1992	Representative	Democrat	87 - 96	1961 - 1980
RODRIGUEZ, Ciro D.	1946-	Representative	Democrat	105 - 110	1997 - 2008
ROGERS, Walter Edward	1908-2001	Representative	Democrat	82 - 89	1951 - 1966
RUSK, Thomas Jefferson	1803-1857	Senator	Democrat	29 - 35	1845 - 1858
RUSSELL, Gordon James	1859-1919	Representative	Democrat	57 - 61	1901 - 1910
RUSSELL, Sam Morris	1889-1971	Representative	Democrat	77 - 79	1941 - 1946
RUTHERFORD, J. T.	1921-2006	Representative	Democrat	84 - 87	1955 - 1962
SANDERS, Morgan Gurley	1878-1956	Representative	Democrat	67 - 75	1921 - 1938
SANDLIN, Max A.	1952-	Representative	Democrat	105 - 108	1997 - 2004
SARPALIUS, William	1948-	Representative	Democrat	101 - 103	1989 - 1994
SAYERS, Joseph Draper	1841-1929	Representative	Democrat	49 - 55	1885 - 1898
SCHLEICHER, Gustave	1823-1879	Representative	Democrat	44 - 45	1875 - 1878

Member Name	Birth-Death	Position	Party	Congress	Years Served
SCURRY, Richardson	1811-1862	Representative	Democrat	32	1851 - 1852
SEKULA GIBBS, Shelley	1953-	Representative	Republican	109	2005 - 2006
SESSIONS, Pete	1955-	Representative	Republican	105 - 110	1997 - 2008
SHEPPARD, John Levi	1852-1902	Representative	Democrat	56 – 57	1899 - 1902
SHEPPARD, Morris	1875-1941	Representative	Democrat	57 - 62	1901 - 1912
SHEPPARD, Morris	1875-1941	Senator	Democrat	62 - 77	1912 - 1942
SLAYDEN, James Luther	1853-1924	Representative	Democrat	55 - 64	1897 - 1918
SMITH, Lamar Seeligson	1947-	Representative	Republican	100 - 110	1987 - 2008
SMITH, William Robert	1863-1924	Representative	Democrat	58 - 64	1903 - 1916
SMYTH, George Washington	1803-1866	Representative	Democrat	33	1853 - 1854
SOUTH, Charles Lacy	1892-1965	Representative	Democrat	74 - 77	1935 - 1942
STEELMAN, Alan Watson	1942-	Representative	Republican	93 - 94	1973 - 1976
STENHOLM, Charles Walter	1938-	Representative	Democrat	96 - 108	1979 - 2004
STEPHENS, John Hall	1847-1924	Representative	Democrat	55 - 64	1897 - 1916
STEWART, Charles	1836-1895	Representative	Democrat	48 - 52	1883 - 1892
STOCKMAN, Steve	1956-	Representative	Republican	104	1995 - 1996
STRONG, Sterling Price	1862-1936	Representative	Democrat	73	1933 - 1934
SUMNERS, Hatton William	1875-1962	Representative	Democrat	63 - 79	1913 - 1946
SWEENEY, David McCann (Mac)	1955-	Representative	Republican	99 - 100	1985 - 1988
TEAGUE, Olin Earl	1910-1981	Representative	Democrat	79 - 95	1945 - 1978
TEJEDA, Frank Mariano	1945-1997	Representative	Democrat	103 - 105	1993 - 1998
TERRELL, George Butler	1862-1947	Representative	Democrat	73	1933 - 1934
THOMAS, Albert	1898-1966	Representative	Democrat	75 - 89	1937 - 1966
THOMAS, Lera Millard	1900-1993	Representative	Democrat	89	1965 - 1966
THOMASON, Robert Ewing	1879-1973	Representative	Democrat	72 - 80	1931 - 1948
THOMPSON, Clark Wallace	1896-1981	Representative	Democrat	73 - 89	1933 - 1966
THORNBERRY, William Homer	1909-1995	Representative	Democrat	81 - 88	1949 - 1964
THORNBERRY, William McClellan (Mac)	1958-	Representative	Republican	104 - 110	1995 - 2008
THROCKMORTON, James Webb	1825-1894	Representative	Democrat	44 - 49	1875 - 1886
TOWER, John Goodwin	1925-1991	Senator	Republican	87 - 98	1961 - 1984
TURNER, Jim	1946-	Representative	Democrat	105 - 108	1997 - 2004
UPSON, Christopher Columbus	1829-1902	Representative	Democrat	46 - 47	1879 - 1882
VANDERGRIFF, Tommy (Tom) Joe	1926-	Representative	Democrat	98	1983 - 1984
VAUGHAN, Horace Worth	1867-1922	Representative	Democrat	63	1913 - 1914
WARD, Matthias	1805-1861	Senator	Democrat	35 - 36	1857 - 1860
WASHINGTON, Craig Anthony	1941-	Representative	Democrat	101 - 103	1989 - 1994
WELLBORN, Olin	1843-1921	Representative	Democrat	46 - 49	1879 - 1886
WEST, Milton Horace	1888-1948	Representative	Democrat	73 - 80	1933 - 1948

Member Name	Birth-Death	Position	Party	Congress	Years Served
WHITE, Richard Crawford	1923-1998	Representative	Democrat	89 - 97	1965 - 1982
WHITMORE, George Washington	1824-1876	Representative	Republican	41	1869 - 1870
WIGFALL, Louis Trezevant	1816-1874	Senator	Democrat	36 - 37	1859 - 1860
WILLIAMS, Guinn	1871-1948	Representative	Democrat	67 - 72	1921 - 1932
WILLIE, Asa Hoxie	1829-1899	Representative	Democrat	43	1873 - 1874
WILSON, Charles	1933-	Representative	Democrat	93 - 104	1973 - 1974
WILSON, James Clifton	1874-1951	Representative	Democrat	65 - 66	1917 - 1920
WILSON, Joseph Franklin	1901-1968	Representative	Democrat	80 - 83	1947 - 1954
WOOTEN, Dudley Goodall	1860-1929	Representative	Democrat	57	1901 - 1902
WORLEY, Francis Eugene	1908-1974	Representative	Democrat	77 - 81	1941 - 1942
WRIGHT, James Claude, Jr.	1922-	Representative	Democrat	84 - 101	1955 - 1990
WURZBACH, Harry McLeary	1874-1931	Representative	Republican	67 - 72	1921 - 1932
WYATT, Joseph Peyton, Jr.	1941-	Representative	Democrat	96	1979 - 1980
YARBOROUGH, Ralph Webster	1903-1996	Senator	Democrat	85 - 91	1957 - 1970
YOAKUM, Charles Henderson	1849-1909	Representative	Democrat	54	1895 - 1896
YOUNG, James	1866-1942	Representative	Democrat	62 - 66	1911 - 1920
YOUNG, John Andrew	1916-2002	Representative	Democrat	85 - 95	1957 - 1978

BIBLIOGRAPHY

Abilene Reporter-News. "Tribute From a Grateful Constituency to a Worthy United States Congressman." Wednesday and Thursday, May 4 and 5, 1966. Appreciation Edition. (Omar Burleson).

Abilene Reporter-News. August 12, 1957. (Blanton Obituary).

Acheson, Sam Hanna. Joe Bailey: The Last Democrat. New York, New York: MacMillan, 1932.

Adair, A. Garland. Texas Heritage. Volume 1, Number 1. November 1959.

Adams, Frank Carter. Texas Democracy. A Centennial History of Politics and Personalities of the Democratic Party, 1836-1936. Austin, Texas: Democratic Historical Association. 4 Volumes. 1936-1937.

Adams, Mark, and Creekmore Fath. Yarborough, Portrait of a People's Senator: A Political Profile. Austin, Texas: Chaparral Press, 1957.

Alcalde. March 1937. (Buchanan Obituary).

Allen, Edward. Sam Rayburn: Leading the Lawmakers. Chicago, Illinois: Encyclopaedia Britannica Press, 1963.

Anderson, Adrian. "President Wilson's Politician: Albert Sidney Burleson of Texas." Southwestern Historical Quarterly 77, January 1974.

Anderson, Adrian. Albert Sidney Burleson: A Southern Politician in the Progressive Era. Ph.D. Dissertation. Texas Technological College. Lubbock, Texas. 1967.

Andrews, Mike. Papers. Congressional History Collection. The Center for American History. University of Texas. Austin, Texas.

Austin American-Statesman, April 15, 1934. (Buchanan Obituary.)

Austin American-Statesman. August 12, 15, 1989. (Leland Obituary.)

Austin American-Statesman. February 11, 1999. (Joe Kilgore Obituary.)

Austin American-Statesman. January 24, 1991. (Teague Obituary.)

Austin American-Statesman. January 28, 1996. (Yarborough Obituary.)

Austin American-Statesman. June 7, 1965. (Luther Johnson Obituary.)

Austin American-Statesman. May 16, 1991. (Omar Burleson Obituary.)

Austin American-Statesman. May 9, 1955. (Richard Kleberg Obituary.)

Austin American-Statesman. November 13, 1972. (Dies Obituary.)

Austin American-Statesman. November 25, 1937. (Albert Burleson Obituary.)

Austin American. October 29, 1948. (West Obituary.)

Avillo, Philip J., Jr. "Phantom Radicals: Texas Republicans in Congress, 1870-1873." Southwestern Historical Quarterly 77, April 1974.

Bailey, Lelia. The Life and Public Career of O. M. Roberts, 1815-1883. Ph.D. Dissertation. University of Texas. Austin, Texas. 1932.

Bailey, Richard Ray. Morris Sheppard of Texas: Southern Progressive and Prohibitionist. Ph.D. Dissertation. Texas Christian University. 1980.

Bailey, Richard. "Morris Sheppard." In Profiles in Power: Twentieth-Century Texans in Washington, edited by Kenneth E. Hendrickson, Jr., and Michael L. Collins. Arlington Heights, Il: Harlan Davidson, 1993.

Bailey, Richard. "Troubles in Texas: Senator Morris Sheppard of Texas, 1913-1919." Red River Valley Historical Review 7, summer 1982.

Barnes, Charles Merritt. Combats and Conquests of Immortal Heroes, Sung in Song and Told in Story. San Antonio, Texas: Guessaz & Ferlet Company, 1910.

Barr, C. Alwyn. "The Making of a Secessionist: The Antebellum Career of Roger Q. Mills." Southwestern Historical Quarterly 79. October 1975.

Barr, C. Alwyn. "John Nance Garner's First Campaign for Congress." West Texas Historical Association Yearbook 48, 1972.

Barr, C. Alwyn. Reconstruction to Reform: Texas Politics, 1876-1906. Austin, Texas: University of Texas Press. 1971.

Bartlett, Steve. Papers. Congressional History Collection. The Center for American History. University of Texas. Austin, Texas.

Beaumont Enterprise. August 22, 1953. (Combs Obituary.)

Bentsen, Lloyd. Papers. Congressional History Collection. The Center for American History. University of Texas. Austin, Texas.

Berke, Richard L. "Tough Texas Phil Gramm." New York Times Magazine, February 19, 1995.

Biographical Directory of the Texan Conventions and Congresses, 1832-1845. Austin, Texas: Book Exchange, 1941. Reprinted 1986 by Sons of the Republic of Texas.

Biographical Directory of the United States Congress, 1774-1989. Washington, D.C.: Government Printing Office, 1989.

Biographical Encyclopedia of Texas. New York: Southern, 1880.

Biographical Gazetteer of Texas.

Blount, Lois Foster. "A Brief Study of Thomas J. Rusk Based on His Letters to His Brother, David, 1835-1856." Southwestern Historical Quarterly 34. January 1931 and April 1931.

Braider, Donald. Solitary Star: A Biography of Sam Houston. New York: Putnam. 1974.

Brown, D. Clayton. "Sam Rayburn and the Development of Public Power in the Southwest." Southwestern Historical Quarterly 78, October 1974.

Brown, George R. The Leadership of Congress. Indianapolis: Bobbs-Merrill. 1922.

————. The Speaker of the House: The Romantic Story of John N. Garner. New York, New York: Putnam's. 1932.

Brown, John Henry. Indian Wars and Pioneers of Texas. Austin, Texas: L.E. Daniel, 1890.

Brown, Norman D. Hood, Bonnet, and Little Brown Jug: Texas Politics, 1921-1928. College Station: Texas A&M University Press, 1984.

Brownsville Herald. October 31, 1948. (West Obituary.)

Bryan Eagle. February 2, 1937. (Buchanan Obituary.)

Bryan, Guy Morrison. Papers. Congressional History Collection. The Center for American History. University of Texas. Austin, Texas.

Bryant, Ira B. Barbara Charline Jordan: From the Ghetto to the Capitol. Houston, Texas: D. Armstrong Co., 1977.

Buchanan, James Paul. Papers. Congressional History Collection. The Center for American History. University of Texas. Austin, Texas.

Burka, Paul. "Last of the Line." Texas Monthly, February 1993. (Lloyd Bentsen)

Burleson, Albert Sidney. Papers. Congressional History Collection. University of Texas. The Center for American History. Austin, Texas.

Cabell, Earle. Papers. Southern Methodist University. Dallas, Texas.

Campbell, Randolph B. "George W. Whitmore: East Texas Unionist." East Texas Historical Journal 28, Spring 1990.

Campbell, Randolph B. "The Whig Party of Texas in the Elections of 1848 and 1852." Southwestern Historical Quarterly 73, July 1969.

Campbell, Randolph B. Sam Houston and the American Southwest. New York: Harper Collins, 1993.

Carney, Carolyn. Paper. "Born on the Right: Bruce Alger and Texas Republican Politics, 1954-1965." 1998.

Caro, Robert. The Years Of Lyndon Johnson: Means Of Ascent. New York: Alfred A. Knopf, 1990.

Caro, Robert. The Years Of Lyndon Johnson: The Path To Power. New York: Alfred A. Knopf, 1982.

Casdorph, Paul. A History of the Republican Party in Texas, 1865-1965. Austin, Texas: Pemberton Press, 1965.

Cattleman. April 1941. (Hudspeth)

Cattleman. March 1927. (Hudspeth)

Cattleman. March 1940. (Moore)

Champagne, Anthony. "Sam Rayburn: Achieving Party Leadership." Southwestern Historical Quarterly 90, April 1987.

Champagne, Anthony. Congressman Sam Rayburn. New Brunswick, N.J.: Rutgers University Press, 1984.

Champagne, Anthony. Sam Rayburn: A Bio-Bibliography. New York: Greenwood Press, 1988.

Chilton, Horace. Papers. Congressional History Collection. The Center for American History. University of Texas. Austin.

Clarke, Mary (Whatley). Thomas J. Rusk: Soldier, Statesman, Jurist. Austin: Jenkins Publishing Co., 1971.

Clarke, Mary Whatley. David G. Burnet. Austin. Texas: Pemberton Press, 1969.

Clarke, Mary Whatley. Thomas J. Rusk: Soldier, Statesman, Jurist. Austin, Texas: Jenkins Publishing, 1971.

Collier, Everett. "Rayburn for President? A Footnote to the 1952 Election." Texas Quarterly 9, Winter 1966.

Colorado Citizen. July 17, 1947. (Mansfield Obituary.)

Confederate Veteran Magazine III, p. 380. (Waul.)

Congress A to Z. Washington, D.C.: Congressional Quarterly, Inc.

Connally, Tom. My Name Is Tom Connally. New York: Thomas Y. Crowell, 1954.

Cotner, Robert C. James Stephen Hogg: A Biography. Austin, Texas: University of Texas Press, 1959.

Cox, Patrick L. "Put the Jam on the Lower Shelf": The Early Career of U.S. Senator Ralph Webster Yarborough. Ph.D. Dissertation. University of Texas. Austin, Texas. 1996.

Cross, O. H. Congressional, After Dinner and Other Speeches. 1937.

Curtis, Rosalee Morris. John Hemphill. First Chief Justice of the State of Texas. Austin, Texas: Jenkins Publishing, 1971.

Dallas Morning News. "The Politics of Good Family Life." August 5, 1986.

Dallas Morning News. April 15, 1992. (Ray Roberts Obituary.)

Dallas Morning News. April 15, 1995. (Dowdy Obituary.)

Dallas Morning News. April 30, 1933. (Briggs Obituary.)

Dallas Morning News. August 23, 1953. (Combs Obituary.)

Dallas Morning News. August 26, 1988. (Price Daniel Obituary.)

Dallas Morning News. August 30, 1902. (De Graffenreid Obituary.)

Dallas Morning News. December 1, 1987. (Kazen Obituary.)

Dallas Morning News. December 10, 1994. (Fisher Obituary.)

Dallas Morning News. December 14, 1932. (Garrett Obituary.)

Dallas Morning News. February 13, 1929. (Beall Obituary.)

Dallas Morning News. February 6, 7, May 30, 1934, April 19, 20, 1947. (Terrell Obituary.)

Dallas Morning News. January 10, 1948. (Guinn Williams Obituary.)

Dallas Morning News. January 17, 1913. (Antony Obituary.)

Dallas Morning News. January 2, 1909. (Yoakum Obituary.)

Dallas Morning News. January 20, 1913. (Pendleton Obituary.)

Dallas Morning News. January 24, 1981. (Teague Obituary.)

Dallas Morning News. January 31 and February 1, 1997. (Tejeda Obituary.)

Dallas Morning News. January 8, 1956. (Sanders Obituary.)

Dallas Morning News. July 15, 1968. (Pool Obituary.)
Dallas Morning News. July 29, 1933. (Waul Obituary.)
Dallas Morning News. March 14, 1925. (McLean Obituary.)
Dallas Morning News. March 29 and 31, 1936. (Strong Obituary.)
Dallas Morning News. May 15, 1956. (Luther Johnson Obituary.)
Dallas Morning News. May 16 and May 18, 1991. (Omar Burleson Obituary.)
Dallas Morning News. May 2, 1991. (Ikard Obituary.)
Dallas Morning News. May 28, 1989. (Lucas Obituary.)
Dallas Morning News. November 8, 1990. (Gossett Obituary.)
Dallas Morning News. October 22, 1945. (Randell Obituary.)
Dallas Times Herald. June 8, 1980. (Pickett Obituary.)
Dallas Times Herald. May 16, 1991. (Omar Burleson Obituary.)
Dallas Times Herald. November 9, 1990. (Gossett Obituary.)
Dallek, Robert. Lone Star Rising: Lyndon Johnson and His Times, 1908-1960. New York and Oxford: Oxford University Press, 1991.
Daniel, Edward Oda. "Sam Rayburn: Trials of a Party Man." Ph.D. Dissertation. North Texas State University. Denton, Texas. 1979.
Daniel, Price. Papers. Sam Houston Regional Library and Research Center. Liberty, Texas.
Daniell, L. E. Personnel of the Texas State Government, with Sketches of Representative Men of Texas. San Antonio, Texas: Maverick Printing House, 1892.
Daniell, Lewis E. Personnel of the Texas State Government with Sketches of Distinguished Texans, Embracing the Executive and Staff, Heads of the Departments, United States Senators and Representatives, Members of the 20th Legislature. Austin, Texas: Press of the City Printing Co., 1887.
Davis, Cyclone. Memoir. Sherman, Texas: Courier Press, 1935.
De Bruhl, Marshall. Sword of San Jacinto: A Life of Sam Houston. New York: Random House. 1993.
Dies, Martin. Martin Dies' Story. New York, New York: Bookmailer. 1963.
Dies, Martin. Papers. Texas State Library. Liberty, Texas.
Dies, Martin. The Trojan Horse in America. New York, New York: Dodd, Mead. 1940. New York: Arno Press, 1977.
Dixon, Ford. "Oran Milo Roberts" in Ten More Texans in Gray. Hillsboro, Texas: Hill Junior College Press, 1980.
Dodd, Lawrence C., and Donald C. Bacon. Rayburn: A Biography. Austin: Texas Monthly Press, 1987.
Dorough, C. Dwight. Mr. Sam. New York: Random House, 1962.
Douglas, C. L., and Francis Miller. The Life Story of W. Lee O'Daniel. Dallas, Texas: Regional Press, 1939.
Dowdy, John V., Sr. Papers. Baylor Collection of Political Materials. Baylor University. Waco, Texas.
Doyle, Judith Kaaz. An Ironic Crusade: Maury Maverick, San Antonio Politics, and the Black Political Machine, 1938-1941. M.A. Report. University of Texas. Austin, Texas. 1982.
Dies, Martin. Out of Step: Maury Maverick and the Politics of the Depression and the New Deal. Ph.D. Dissertation. University of Texas. Austin, Texas. 1989.
Draper, Robert. "Senator Spite." Texas Monthly, February 1993. (Gramm.)
Dubin, Michael J. United States Congressional Elections, 1788-1997. Jefferson, North Carolina: McFarland & Company, 1998.
Duke, Escal F. The Life and Political Career of Fritz G. Lanham. M.A. Thesis. University of Texas. Austin, Texas. 1941.
Duke, Escal F. The Political Career of Morris Sheppard, 1875-1941. Ph.D. Dissertation. University of Texas. Austin, Texas. 1958.
Dulaney, H.G., and Edward Hake Phillips, eds. Impressions of Mr. Sam: A Cartoon Profile. Preface by MacPhelan Reese. Bonham, Tex.: Sam Rayburn Foundation, 1987.
Dulaney, H.G., and MacPhelan Reese, eds. "Speak, Mr. Speaker." Bonham, Tex.: Sam Rayburn Foundation, 1978.
Duncan, Merle Mears. "The Death of Senator Coke." Southwestern Historical Quarterly 63, January 1960.
Eckhardt, Robert. The Tides of Power: Conversations on the American Constitution between Bob Eckhardt, Member of Congress from Texas and Charles L. Black. New Haven, Connecticut: Yale University Press, 1976.
Elliott, Claude. Leathercoat: The Life History of a Texas Patriot. San Antonio, Texas, 1938. (Throckmorton.)
Emswiler, Marilyn. "Mr. Speaker: Sam Rayburn." Texas Historian 33, March 1973.
Essin, Emmett M., III. The Democratic Senatorial Primary in Texas: Yarborough versus Blakley. Master's thesis. Texas Christian University. Fort Worth, Texas. 1965.
Estill, Mary Sexton, ed. "Diary of a Confederate Congressman." Southwestern Historical Quarterly 38 and 39. April and July 1935. (Sexton.)
Evans, Wanda Webb. One Honest Man: George Mahon—A Story of Power, Politics and Poetry. Canyon, Texas: Staked Plains Press, 1978.
Fields, Dorothy Louise. "David Gouverneur Burnet." Southwestern Historical Quarterly 49, October 1945.
Fisher, Kevin. "Judge William Homer Thornberry. A Profile of the life and career of Judge William Homer Thornberry." Fifth Circuit Reporter, January 1996.
Fisher, O. C. Cactus Jack. Waco, Texas: Texian Press, 1978.
Fisher, O. C. From New Deal to Watergate. Waco, Texas: Texian Press, 1980.
Fisher, O. C. Papers. Baylor Collection of Political Materials. Baylor University. Waco, Texas.
Fleischer, Mary Beth, ed. "Dudley G. Wooten's Comment on Texas Histories and Historians of the Nineteenth Century." Southwestern Historical Quarterly 73, October 1969.

Fontaine, Edward. "Honorable William S. Oldham." De Bow's Revie,. Article 8, Volume 37.

Fort Worth Record. January 2, 1909. (Yoakum Obituary.)

Fort Worth Record. June 6, 1901. (Burke Obituary.)

Fort Worth Star-Telegram. August 2, 1965. (Fritz Lanham Obituary.)

Fort Worth Star-Telegram. May 12, 1969. (O'Daniel Obituary.)

Friend, Llerena B. Sam Houston: The Great Designer. Austin, Texas: University of Texas Press, 1969.

Fulmore, Zachary T. "General Volney Erskine Howard." Quarterly of the Texas State Historical Association 14, October 1910.

Gaines, Reuben Reid. "John Hemphill, 1803-1862." Great American Lawyers, ed. William Draper Louis, ed. Philadelphia, Pennsylvania: Winston, 1907-1909.

Gaines, Rueben Reid. "John Hemphill." Great American Lawyers. William Draper Lewis, ed. Philadelphia, Pennsylvania: John C. Winston Co., 1908.

Galloway, George B. History of the House of Representatives. New York: Crowell, 1976.

Galveston News. November 29, 1921. (Hawley Obituary.)

Galveston News. September 23, 1921. (Crowley Obituary.)

Gamble, Stephen Grady. "James Pinckney Henderson in Europe: The Diplomacy of the Republic of Texas, 1837-1840." Ph.D. dissertation. Texas Tech University. Lubbock, Texas. 1976.

Garner, John Nance. Papers. Congressional History Collection. The Center for American History. University of Texas. Austin, Texas.

Garner, W.-F. The Primaries in Texas. M.A. thesis. University of Texas. Austin, Texas. 1920.

Garrison, George P. "Guy Morrison Bryan." Quarterly of the Texas State Historical Association 5, October 1901.

Geiser, S. W. "David Gouverneur Burnet, Satirist." Southwestern Historical Quarterly 48, July 1944.

Gellerman, William. Martin Dies. New York: Day, 1944. (Also: New York: De Capo, 1972.)

Gossett, Ed Lee. Papers. Baylor Collection of Political Materials. Baylor University. Waco, Texas.

Gould, Lewis L. Progressives and Prohibitionists: Texas Democrats in the Wilson Era. Austin, Texas: University of Texas Press, 1973. (Also: Austin, Texas: Texas State Historical Association, 1992.)

Grant, P. A. "East Texas Congressmen during the New Deal." East Texas Historical Journal 11, Fall 1973.

Green, George N. The Establishment in Texas Politics. Westport, Connecticut: Greenwood. 1979.

Gregory, Jack, and Rennard Strickland. Sam Houston with the Cherokees, 1829-1833. Austin, Texas: University of Texas Press, 1976.

Guide to U.S. Elections. Washington, D.C.: Congressional Quarterly, Inc. Various years.

Hairgrove, Kenneth D. "Sam Rayburn: Congressional Leader, 1940-1952." Ph.D. dissertation. Texas Tech University. Lubbock, Texas. 1974.

Hall, Claude H. "The Fabulous Tom Ochiltree." Southwestern Historical Quarterly 71, January 1968.

Hall, Sam B. Jr. Papers. Baylor Collection of Political Materials. Baylor University. Waco, Texas.

Hamilton, Andrew Jackson. Papers. Congressional History Collection. The Center for American History. University of Texas. Austin, Texas.

Hardeman, D. B. "Sam Rayburn and the House of Representatives." The Presidency and the Congress: A Shifting Balance of Power, 226-252. William S. Livingston, ed.

Hart, James P. "John Hemphill, Chief Justice of Texas." Southwestern Law Journal, Fall 1949.

Haskins, James. Barbara Jordan. New York: Dial Press, 1977.

Heard, Alexander and Don Stuart Strong. Southern Primaries and Elections, 1920-1949. Tuscaloosa, Alabama: University of Alabama Press, 1950.

Heard, Robert. Miracle of the Killer Bees: Twelve Senators Who Changed Texas Politics. Austin: Honey Hill, 1981.

Hemphill, John. "Eulogy of the Life and Character of the Honorable Thomas J. Rusk, Late U.S. Senator from Texas." Austin, Texas: John Marshall & Co., 1857.

Hemphill, John. "Texas Letter from John Hemphill to his Brother, James, in Tennessee." Southwestern Historical Quarterly 57. October 1953.

Henderson, Richard B. Maury Maverick: A Political Biography. Austin: University of Texas Press, 1970.

Hendrickson, Kenneth E., and Michael L. Collins, eds. Profiles in Power: Twentieth-Century Texans in Washington. Arlington Heights, Illinois: Harlan Davidson, 1993.

Herring, Charles, Jr., and Walter Richter. Don't Throw Feathers at Chickens. A Collection of Texas Political Humor. Plano, Texas: Wordware Publishing, 1992.

Hightower, Jack English. Papers. Baylor Collection of Political Materials. Baylor University. Waco, Texas.

Hinga, Don. "Sam Rayburn: Texas Squire." Southwest Review 29, Summer 1944.

Hogg, Kerek Darren. Wash Jones: The Life of George Washington Jones, Economic Radical and Political Dissenter. M.A. thesis. Texas Tech University. Lubbock, Texas. 1993.

Holcomb, Bob Charles. "Senator Joe Bailey, Two Decades of Controversy." Ph.D. dissertation. Texas Technological College. Lubbock, Texas. 1968.

Hopewell, Clifford. Sam Houston: Man of Destiny. Austin, Texas: Eakin Press, 1987.

Horton, Louise. Samuel Bell Maxey: A Biography. Austin, Texas: University of Texas Press, 1974.

Houston Daily Post. August 20, 1903. (Giddings Obituary.)

Houston Post-Dispatch. March 1, 1926. (Rienzi Johnston Obituary.)

Houston Post. December 14 and 15, 1932. (Daniel Garrett Obituary.)

Houston Post. May 27, 1924. (Hutcheson Obituary.)

Houston Post. November 10, 1966. (Gentry Obituary.)

Houston, Andrew Jackson. Texas Independence. Houston: Anson Jones Press, 1938.

Houston, Sam. Papers. Congressional History Collection. The Center for American History. University of Texas. Austin, Texas.

Howard, Richard Winston. The Works of Albert Sidney Burleson as Postmaster General. M.A. thesis. University of Texas. Austin, Texas. 1938.

Huckaby, George P. Oscar Branch Colquitt: A Political Biography. Ph.D. dissertation. University of Texas. Austin, Texas. 1946.

Hughes, Pollyanna B., and Elizabeth B. Harrison. "Charles A. Culberson: Not a Shadow of Hogg." East Texas Historical Journal 11, Fall 1973.

Hunt, Lenoir. "My Master": The Inside Story of Sam Houston and His Time. Jeff Hamilton as told to Lenoir Hunt. Dallas, Texas: Manfred Van Nort, 1940.

Huston, Cleburne. Towering Texan: A Biography of Thomas J. Rusk. Waco, Texas: Texian Press, 1971.

Ide, Arthur Frederick. From Stardom to Scandal: The Rise and Fall of Kay Bailey Hutchison. Las Colinas, Texas: Monument Press, 1994.

Ikard, Frank. Papers. Congressional History Collection. The Center for American History. University of Texas. Austin, Texas.

Irvin, William V. Interview from Folkway, the WPA Life History Project, with O.H. Cross. File No. 240. Feb. 11, 1941.

James, Marquis. Mr. Garner of Texas. Indianapolis: Bobbs-Merrill. 1939.

James, Marquis. The Raven: A Biography of Sam Houston. Indianapolis, Indiana: Bobbs-Merrill, 1929.

Jarboe, Jan. "The Eternal Challenger." Texas Monthly. October 1992. (Henry B. Gonzalez)

Jarboe, Jan. "The Other Henry." Texas Monthly. December 1993. (Bonilla)

Jaynes, R.T. Thomas Jefferson Rusk. Walhalla, South Carolina. 1944. A compilation of articles originally published in the Keowee (South Carolina) Courier.

Jennings, Gary Lee. Finding Guide and Index to the Hatton W. Sumners Papers. Master's Project. University of Texas at Arlington. Arlington, Texas. 1980.

Johnson, Frank W. A History of Texas and Texans. Chicago and New York: American Historical Society, 1914. Reprinted 1916. 5 volumes.

Johnson, Lady Bird. A White House Diary. New York: Holt, Rinehart and Winston, 1970.

Johnson, Sam Houston. My Brother Lyndon. New York: Cowles, 1970.

Johnson, Sidney Smith. Texans Who Wore the Gray. Tyler, Texas, 1907.

Jones, Charles. Every Second Year. Washington, D.C.: Brookings Institute, 1967.

Jones, Marvin. Marvin Jones Memoirs. El Paso, Texas: Texas Western Press, 1973.

Jones, Marvin. Papers. Irvin M. May Collection. Texas A&M University Archives. College Station, Texas.

Jordan, Barbara, and Shelby Hearon. Barbara Jordan: A Self Portrait. Garden City, New York: Doubleday, 1979.

Kemper, Billie Bundick. Lindley Beckworth: Grassroots Congressman. M.A. Thesis. Stephen F. Austin State University. Nacogdoches, Texas. 1980.

Key, V.-O. Southern Politics in State and Nation. New York: Knopf, 1955.

Keyes, Lucile Sheppard. Morris Sheppard. Manuscript. Barker Texas History Center, University of Texas. Austin, Texas. 1950.

Kilby, William Henry. Eastport and Passamaquoddy. 1888. Reprinted 1982. (Pilsbury.)

Kilday, Paul. Papers. Congressional History Collection. The Center for American History. University of Texas. Austin, Texas.

Kilgore, Joe. Papers. Congressional History Collection. The Center for American History. University of Texas. Austin, Texas.

King, Alma Dexta. "The Political Career of Williamson Simpson Oldham." Southwestern Historical Quarterly 33, October 1929.

King, Alvy L. Louis T. Wigfall: Southern Fire-Eater. Baton Rouge, Louisiana: Louisiana State University Press, 1970.

Kittrell, Norman G. Governors Who Have Been and Other Public Men of Texas. Houston, Texas: Dealy-Adey-Elgin, 1921.

Knights Templars Masonic Order. History of the Grand Commandery, Knights Templar of Texas. 1899.

Krueger, Robert. Papers. Congressional History Collection. The Center for American History. University of Texas. Austin, Texas.

Lanham, Fritz G. Papers. Congressional History Collection. The Center for American History. University of Texas. Austin.

Lanham, Samuel W. T. Papers. Congressional History Collection. The Center for American History. University of Texas. Austin, Texas.

Law, Ron C. Congressman Hatton W. Sumners of Dallas: His Life and Congressional Career, 1875-1937. Ph.D. thesis. Texas Christian University. Fort Worth, Texas. 1990.

Lea, Tom. "Portrait of a Statesman." Dallas Morning News. July 19, 1953. (Thomason.)

Leath, Marvin. Papers. Baylor Collection of Political Materials. Baylor University. Waco, Texas.

Ledbetter, Billy D. "The Election of Louis T. Wigfall." Southwestern Historical Quarterly 77, October 1973.

Lemons, J. Stanley. "The Sheppard-Towner Act: Progressivism in the 1920s." Journal of American History 55, March 1969.

Lester, C. Edwards. Sam Houston and His Republic. New York: Burgess, Stringer, 1846. (Also: New York: Books for Libraries Press, 1972.)

Liberty Vindicator. August 28, 1988. (Price Daniel Obituary.)

Liles, Maurine Walpole. Sam and the Speaker's Chair. Austin, Texas: Eakin Press, 1994.

Little, Dwayne Lee. "The Political Leadership of Speaker Sam Rayburn, 1940-1961." Ph.D. dissertation. University of Cincinnati. Cincinnati, Ohio. 1970.

Loe, Victoria. "The Making of a Congressman." Texas Monthly, January 1983. (Andrews.)

Lord, Clyde W. Ante-Bellum Career of Louis Trezevant Wigfall. M.A. thesis. University of Texas. Austin, Texas. 1925.

Madden, James William. Charles Allen Culberson: His Life, Character and Public Service. Austin, Texas: Gammel's Book Store, 1929.

Mahon, George. Archives and oral history. Texas Tech University. Lubbock, Texas.

Mahon, George. Oral history. Lyndon B. Johnson Library. Austin, Texas.

Mahon, George. Papers. Southwest Collection. Texas Tech University. Lubbock, Texas.

Marburger, Harold J. Texas Elections, 1918-1954. Austin, Texas: Texas State Library, 1956.

Martin, Roscoe C. The People's Party in Texas. Austin, Texas: University of Texas, 1933. (Also: University of Texas Press, 1970.)

Martis, Kenneth. The Historical Atlas of the Congresses of the Confederate States of America, 1861-1865. New York: Simon & Schuster, 1994.

Martis, Kenneth. The Historical Atlas of United States Congressional Districts, 1789-1983. New York: Free Press, 1983.

Mason, Alan. Bruce Alger: An Oral History Interview. East Texas State University Oral History Program. Commerce, Texas. 1983.

Maverick, Maury, Sr. Papers. Congressional History Collection. The Center for American History. University of Texas. Austin, Texas.

Maverick, Maury. A Maverick American. New York: Covici-Friede, 1937.

Maxey, Samuel Bell. Papers. Congressional History Collection. The Center for American History. University of Texas. Austin, Texas.

May, Irvin M. Marvin Jones, the Public Life and Agrarian Advocate. College Station: Texas A&M University Press, 1980.

Mayfield, John S. "Eugene O'Neill and the Senator from Texas." New Haven, Yale University Library Gazette, Vol. 35, No. 2, October 1960.

McDaniel, Dennis Kay. The First Congressman Martin Dies of Texas. Southwestern Historical Quarterly, October 1998.

McDaniel, Dennis Kay. Martin Dies of Un-American Activities: His Life and Times. Ph.D. Dissertation. University of Houston. Houston, Texas. 1988.

McFarlane, William D. Papers. Congressional History Collection. The Center for American History. University of Texas. Austin, Texas.

McKay, Seth Sheppard. Texas Politics 1906-1944. Lubbock, Texas: Texas Tech Press. 1952.

McKay, Seth Sheppard. W. Lee O'Daniel and Texas Politics, 1938-1942. Lubbock, Texas: Texas Tech Press, 1944.

McLemore, Atkins Jefferson. Papers. Congressional History Collection. The Center for American History. University of Texas. Austin.

McNutt, Walter Scott. Benjamin H. Epperson and the House of the Seasons He Built in Texas. Jefferson, Texas: Four States Publishing House, 1957.

Miller, Hope Ridings. "In Memoriam: Mr. Sam." Diplomat 12, December 1961.

Miller, Thomas L. "Oscar Callaway and Preparedness." West Texas Historical Association Year Book 43, 1967.

Miller, William "Fishbait." Fishbait: The Memoirs of the Congressional Doorkeeper. Englewood Cliffs, New Jersey: Prentice-Hall, 1977.

Mills, Roger Q. Papers. Congressional History Collection. The Center for American History. University of Texas. Austin, Texas.

Moley, Raymond, and Celeste Jodel. "The Gentleman Who Does Not Yield." Saturday Evening Post, May 10, 1941. (Sumners.)

Moneyhon, Carl H. Republicanism in Reconstruction Texas. Austin, Texas: University of Texas Press, 1980.

Monroe, Mary Catherine. A Day in July: Hatton W. Sumners and the Court Reorganization Plan of 1937. M.A. thesis. University of Texas at Arlington. Arlington, Texas. 1973.

Mooney, Booth. Roosevelt and Rayburn: A Political Partnership. Philadelphia, Pennsylvania: Lippincott, 1971.

Morris, Elizabeth Yates. James Pinckney Henderson. M.A. thesis. University of Texas. Austin, Texas, 1931.

Murph, David Rupert. "Price Daniel: The Life of a Public Man, 1910-1956." Ph.D. dissertation. Texas Christian University. Fort Worth, Texas. 1975.

Naples (Florida) Monitor. March 30, 1928. (Black Obituary.)

Nash, Walter C. Sam Rayburn: The Congressman of the Fourth District. M.A. thesis. East Texas State Teachers College. Commerce, Texas. 1950.

Navarro County Bar Association. Proceedings from Meeting Held at Carnegie Library, Corsicana, Sunday, September 24, 1911, in memory of Col. Roger Q. Mills. Corsicana, Texas: Corsicana Printing Company, 1911.

Neu, C. T. "The Giddings-Clark Election Contest, 1871-1872." Bulletin of the East Texas State Teachers College 14. Commerce, Texas, June 1931.

New York Times. May 13, 1944; May 14, 1947; May 18, 1950; and August 23, 1953. (Combs)

New Yorks Times Magazine. "A Texas vs. Big Oil," October 12, 1980. (Eckhardt.)

Nunn, William C. Texas Under the Carpetbaggers. Austin, Texas: University of Texas Press, 1962.

O'Quinn, Trueman. Manual for Texas Elections and Conventions of Political Parties. State Democratic Executive Committee of Texas.

Obadale-Starks, Ernest M.B. "Ralph Yarborough of Texas and the Road to Civil Rights." East Texas Historical Association Journal 24, 1994.

Ogden, August Raymond. The Dies Committee. Washington, D.C.: Catholic University of America Press, 1945. (Revised: Westport, Connecticut: Greenwood, 1984.)

Ollen, Roger M. From Token to Triumph: The Texas Republicans Since 1920. Dallas, Texas: SMU Press, 1982.

Ornish, Natalie. Pioneer Jewish Texans. Dallas, Texas: Texas Heritage Press, 1989.

Patenaude, Lionel V. Texans, Politics and the New Deal. New York: Garland, 1983.

Patman, Wright. Papers. Lyndon Baines Johnson Library. Austin, Texas.

Pearson, Alec Philmore. Olin E. Teague and the Veterans' Administration. Ph.D. dissertation. Texas A&M University. College Station, Texas, 1977.

Phillips, Michael. Paper for the Citadel Symposium on Southern Politics in Charleson, South Carolina. "Party Realignment, Race, and the Career of Congressman Bruce Alger, 1954-1964." March 5, 1998.

Phillips, William C. Yarborough of Texas. Washington, D.C.: Acropolis Books, 1969.

Phipps, Joe. Summer Stock: Behind the Scenes with LBJ in '48. Fort Worth, Texas: TCU Press, 1992.

Pickett, Thomas A. Papers. Baylor Collection of Political Materials. Baylor University. Waco, Texas.

Pickle, J. J. "Jake," Thomas M. Reavley, and Sam Sparks. "In Memoriam: William Homer Thornberry." Texas Law Review, April 1996.

Pickle, J. J., and Peggy Pickle. Jake. Austin, Texas: University of Texas Press. 1997.

Poage, W. R. Papers. Baylor Collection of Political Materials. Baylor University. Waco, Texas.

Porter, David. "The Battle of the Texas Giants: Hatton Sumners, Sam Rayburn, and the Logan-Walter Bill of 1939." Texana 12, 1973.

Procter, Ben H. Not Without Honor: The Life of John H. Reagan. Austin, Texas: University of Texas Press, 1962.

Provost, Norma Matlock. Issues in the Texas Gubernatorial Race of 1954: Shivers versus Yarborough. Master's thesis. Lamar University. Beaumont, Texas. 1981.

Purifoy, Russell A., Jr. Statesman from Texas: Roger Q. Mills. M.A. thesis. North Texas State University. Denton, Texas. 1954.

Rainey, Homer P. The Tower and the Dome: A Free University Versus Political Control. Boulder, Colorado: Pruett, 1971.

Ralph Yarborough at 80: A Gathering of Tributes from Several of His Book-Loving Friends. Austin, Texas: Privately printed, 1984.

Ramsdell, Charles W. Reconstruction in Texas. New York: Columbia University Press, 1910. (Also: Austin, Texas: Texas State Historical Association. 1970.)

Rankin, Daniel F., Jr. "Thomas J. Rusk and the Convention of 1845." Master's thesis. Stephen F. Austin State University. Nacogdoches, Texas. 1988.

Rayburn, Sam. Guide to the Microfilm Edition of the Sam Rayburn Papers. Bonham, Texas: Sam Rayburn Library. 1972.

Rayburn, Sam. Papers. Congressional History Collection. The Center for American History. University of Texas. Austin, Texas.

Rayburn, Sam. "A Teacher Who Seized Time by the Forelock." National Education Association Journal 49. March 1960.

Reagan, John H. Memoirs. New York: Neale Publishing. 1906. (Also: Austin, Texas: Pemberton Press. 1968).

Reagan, John H. Papers. Congressional History Collection. The Center for American History. University of Texas. Austin, Texas.

Roberts, Madge Thornall. Star of Destiny: The Private Life of Sam and Margaret Houston. Denton, Texas: University of North Texas Press, 1993.

Roberts, Myrtle. Roger Quarles Mills. M.A. thesis. University of Texas. Austin, Texas. 1929.

Roberts, Naurice. Barbara Jordan, the Great Lady from Texas. Chicago, Illinois: Children's Press, 1984.

Robinson, Chandler. The Collected Speeches of Judge Rufus Hardy. Self-published, 1969.

Robinson, Chandler. Judge Rufus Hardy, Pioneer Texan. Self-published, 1970.

Rogers, Mary Beth. Barbara Jordan American Hero. New York, New York: Bantam Books. 1998.

Romano, Michael J. The Emergence of John Nance Garner as a Figure in American National Politics, 1924-1941. Ph.D. Dissertation. New York, New York: St. John's University. 1974.

Rusk, Thomas Jefferson. Papers. Congressional History Collection. The Center for American History. University of Texas. Austin, Texas.

San Antonio Express. April 24, 1932. (Kleberg Obituary.)

San Antonio Express. March 5, 1929. (McLemore Obituary.)

San Antonio Express-News. November 29, 2000. (Henry B. Gonzalez Obituary.)

Sayers, Joseph D. Papers. Congressional History Collection. The Center for American History. University of Texas. Austin, Texas.

Schmelzer, Janet Louise. The Early Life and Early Congressional Career of Wright Patman, 1893-1941. Ph.D. dissertation. Texas Christian University. Fort Worth, Texas. 1978.

Schoonover, Thomas, ed. "Documents Concerning Lemuel Dale Evans' Plan to Keep Texas in the Union in 1861." East Texas Historical Journal 12, Spring 1974.

Schott, Christine. "Gustavus Schleicher: A Representative of the Early German Emigrants in Texas." West Texas Historical Association Year Book 28, 1952.

Schwartz, Jordan A. "John Nance Garner and the Sales Tax Rebellion of 1932." Journal of Southern History, May 1964.

Scoma, Anthony. Paper. "You are Known by Your Political Enemies: Bruce Alger and Sam Rayburn, 1954-1964." 1995.

Seale, William. Sam Houston's Wife: A Biography of Margaret Lea Houston. Norman, Oklahoma: University of Oklahoma Press, 1970.

Sexton, F. B. "J. Pinckney Henderson." Quarterly of the Texas State Historical Association 1, January 1898.

Shanks, Alexander Graham. "Sam Rayburn and the Democratic Convention of 1932." Texana, Winter 1965.

Shanks, Alexander Graham. "Sam Rayburn and the New Deal, 1933-1936." Ph.D. Dissertation. Chapel Hill, North Carolina: University of North Carolina. 1965.

Shanks, Alexander Graham. "Sam Rayburn in the Wilson Administration, 1913-1921." East Texas Historical Journal 6, March 1968.

Shanks, Alexander Graham. "Sam Rayburn: The Texas Politician as New Dealer." East Texas Historical Journal 5, March 1967.

Sheppard, Morris. Papers. Congressional History Collection. The Center for American History. University of Texas. Austin, Texas.

Sheppard, Morris. Fraternal and Other Addresses. Omaha: Beacon Press, 1910.

Sholars, Fannie B. Life and Services of Guy M. Bryan. M.A. thesis. University of Texas. Austin, Texas. 1930.

Shook, Robert W. "The Texas 'Election Outrage' of 1886." East Texas Historical Journal 10, 1972.

Slater, John Thomas, ed. The American Politician. Chapel Hill, North Carolina: University of North Carolina Press, 1938.

Slayden, Ellen Maury. Washington Wife: Journal of Ellen Maury Slayden from 1897-1919. 1963.

Smallwood, James. "Sam Rayburn and the Rules Committee Change of 1961." East Texas Historical Journal 11, Spring 1973.

Smith, W. R. Papers. Authors collection. Fort Worth, Texas.

Smyrl, Frank H. "Unionism in Texas, 1856-1861." Southwestern Historical Quarterly 68, October 1964.

Smythe, George W. "The Autobiography of George W. Smyth." Southwestern Historical Quarterly 36, January 1933.

Smyth, George Washington, Papers. Congressional History Collection. University of Texas. The Center for American History. Austin, Texas.

Sons of the South, Alamo Encampment. Eulogy upon the Life and Character of Hon. John A. Wilcox, Pronoucned by Hon C. Upson, at San Antonio, March 12th, 1864. San Antonio. 1864.

Speer, Ocie. Texas Jurists. Austin, Texas, 1936.

State of Texas. Members of the Texas Congress, 1846-1992. Austin, Texas: Senate Engrossing and Enrolling and Senate Reproduction, 1992.

Stayton, R.W. Address on Thomas J. Rusk before the Texas Bar Association. Texas Law Review, October 1925.

Stayton, Robert W. "Thomas J. Rusk." Texas Law Review 44, October 1925.

Steelman, Alan. Papers. Baylor Collection of Political Materials. Baylor University. Waco, Texas.

Steinberg, Alfred. Sam Johnson's Boy. New York: Macmillan, 1968.

Steinberg, Alfred. Sam Rayburn: A Biography. New York, New York: Hawthorn Books, 1975.

Sterrett, Carrie Belle. The Life of Thomas J. Rusk. M.A. Thesis. University of Texas. Austin, Texas. 1922.

Sumners, Hatton W. Papers. Dallas Historical Society Research Center. Dallas, Texas.

Sumners, Hatton W. The Private Citizen and His Democracy. Dallas, Texas: The Hatton W. Sumners Foundation. 1959.

Sussman, Robert, and Robert Cochran. Ralph Nader Congress Project. Citizens Look at Congress. Wright Patman, Democratic Representative from Texas. Washington, D.C.: Grossman, 1972.

Teague, Olin E. Papers. University Archives, Texas A&M University. College Station, Texas.

Terry, J. W. Terry on Crowley. Massachusetts' gift to Texas. Political and criminal record of Miles Crowley, alias Miles Morris candidate for Congress. Galveston, Texas. About 1894. 84 p.

Texans and Their State: A Newspaper Reference Work. Houston, Texas: Texas Biographical Association, 1918.

Texas House of Representatives. Biographical Directory of the Texan Conventions and Congresses, 1832-1845. Austin, Texas: Book Exchange, 1941.

Texas Legislative Council. Presiding Officers of the Texas Legislature, 1846-1982. Austin, Texas: Texas House of Representatives, 1982.

Texas Observer. December 29, 1989. (Leland Obituary.)

Texas State Directory. Austin: Texas State Directory, Inc. Various years.

Texas State Historical Association. The New Handbook of Texas. 1996.

Texas State Library. Governors' Messages: Coke to Ross, 1874-1891. Austin, Texas: Archives and History Department. 1916.

Texas Supreme Court. Memorial Service for the Honorable Price Daniel, May 22, 1989. Austin, Texas. 1989.

Thomason, Ewing. Thomason: The Autobiography of a Federal Judge. El Paso, Texas: Texas Western Press, 1971.

Timmons, Bascom N. Garner of Texas: A Personal History. New York: Harper. 1948.

Timmons, Bascom N. Papers. University Archives, Texas A&M University. College Station, Texas

Tower, John G. Consequences A Personal and Political Memoir. Boston, Massachusetts. Little, Brown & Co. 1991.

Tower, John G. Oral History Interview. August 8, 1971, by Joe B. Frantz. LBJ Presidential Library.

Tower, John G. A Program For Conservatives: A Leading Conservative Offers Some Bold New Thoughts On American Policy At Home and Abroad. New York: Macfaddon, 1962

Turner, Martha Anne, ed. "Four Letters from J. Pinckney Henderson." Texana 5, Winter 1967, p. 359-365.

Tyler Courier-Times-Telegraph. March 11, 1984. (Beckworth Obituary.)

United States Congress. House Committee on Banking and Currency. Reception and ceremony commemorating the commencement of the 40th year of service in the Congress of the United States by the Honorable Wright Patman. March 5, 1968. Washington, D.C.: U.S. Government Printing Office, 1968.

United States Congress. Memorial Addresses on the Life and Character of Gustave Schleicher Delivered in the House of Representatives and in the Senate. Washington, D.C.: Government Printing Office, 1880.

United States Congress. Memorial Addresses on the Life and Character of John Levi Sheppard. Washington, D.C.: U.S. Government Printing Office, 1903.

United States Congress. Memorial Addresses on the Life and Character of Robert E. Burke Delivered in the House of Representatives and in the Senate. Washington, D.C.: Government Printing Office, 1902.

United States Congress. Memorial Addresses on the Life and Character of William H. Crain Delivered in the House of Representatives and Senate. Washington, D.C.: Government Printing Office, 1897.

United States Congress. Memorial Services Held in the House of Representatives and Senate of the United States, Together with Remarks Presented in Eulogy of Albert Thomas, Late a Representative from Texas. Washington, D.C.: U.S. Government Printing Office, 1966.

United States Congress. Memorial Services Held in the House of Representatives and Senate of the United States Together with

Remarks Presented in Eulogy of Andrew Jackson Houston, Late a Senator from Texas. Washington, D.C.: Government Printing Office, 1944.

United States Congress. Memorial Services Held in the House of Representatives of the United States, Together with Remarks Presented in Eulogy of James Paul Buchanan, Late a Representative from Texas. Washington, D.C.: Government Printing Office, 1938.

United States Congress. Memorial Services Held in the House of Representatives and Senate of the United States, Together with Remarks Presented in Eulogy of Morris Sheppard, Late a Senator from Texas. Washington, D.C.: Government Printing Office, 1943.

United States Congress. Memorial Services Held in the House of Representatives of the United States, Together with Remarks Presented in Eulogy of Robert Q. Lee, Late a Representative from Texas. Washington, D.C.: U.S. Government Printing Office. 1930.

United States Congress. Memorial Services Held in the House of Representatives and Senate of the United States, Together with Remarks Presented in Eulogy of Sam Rayburn, Late a Representative of Texas. Washington, D.C.: U.S. Government Printing Office. 1962.

United States Congress. Memorial Tribute Held in the House of Representatives of the United States, Together with Tributes Presented in Eulogy of Frank M. Tejeda, Late a Representative from Texas. Washington, D.C.: U.S. Government Printing Office, 1997.

United States Congress. Memorial Tribute: John Goodwin Tower, 1925-1991, Late a Senator from Texas. Washington, D.C.: U.S. Government Printing Office, 1994.

United States Congress. Mr. Speaker: Excerpts from the Congressional Record . . . in Tribute to the Honorable Sam Rayburn, of Bonham, Texas. Washington, D.C.: U.S. Government Printing Office, 1952.

United States Congress. Obituary services on the death of Hon. David S. Kaufman of Texas. Washington, D.C.: J.T. Towers, 1851.

United States Congress. Tributes to the Honorable Ralph Yarborough of Texas in the United States Senate: Upon the Occasion of His Retirement from the Senate. Washington, D.C.: Government Printing Office. 1971.

United States Constitution. As amended.

United States House of Representatives. The Leadership of Sam Rayburn: Collected Tributes of His Congressional Colleagues. Washington, D.C.: U.S. Government Printing Office. 1961.

United States House of Representatives, Office of Clerk. Statistics of the Congressional Elections. Various years: 1920-date.

United States House of Representatives. Proceedings at the Dedication of the Sam Rayburn Statue, Rayburn House Office Building, Washington, D.C., January 6, 1965. Washington, D.C.: U.S. Government Printing Office. 1965.

United States Senate. Committee on Banking and Currency. Rayburn Medal. Washington, D.C.: U.S. Government Printing Office, 1962.

Uvalde Leader-News. June 21, 1956. (Luther Johnson Obituary.)

Waco Tribune-Herald. December 10, 2000. (Leath Obituary.)

Wakelyn, Jon L. Biographical Dictionary of the Confederacy. Westport, Connecticut: Greenwood, 1977.

Warner, Ezra J., and W. Buck Yearns. Biographical Register of the Confederate Congress. Baton Rouge, Louisiana: Louisiana State University Press, 1975.

Washington Post. May 27, 1975. (Black Obituary.)

The Washingtonian. October 1968. "The Day Congress Read the D--ty Words." (Blanton.)

Weeks, O. Douglas. "The Texas Direct Primary System." Southwest Social Science Quarterly, Volume 13, No 2. September 1932, pp. 95-120.

Welch, June Rayfield. Texas Governors. Dallas, Texas: GLA Press, 1977.

Welch, June Rayfield. Texas Senators. Dallas, Texas: GLA Press, 1978.

Wheeler, Henry G. History of Congress. New York: Harper & Brothers Publishers, 1848. (Pilsbury.)

Wigfall Family Papers. U.S. Library of Congress. Washington, D.C.

Wigfall, Louis T. Papers. Congressional History Collection. The Center for American History. University of Texas. Austin, Texas.

Williams Amelia W. and Eugene C. Barker, eds. The Writings of Sam Houston, 1813-1863. 8 volumes. Austin, Texas: University of Texas Press, 1938-1943. (Also: Austin and New York: Pemberton Press, 1970.)

Williams, John Hoyt. Sam Houston: A Biography of the Father of Texas. New York: Simon and Schuster, 1993.

Wilson, Charles. Papers. Stephen F. Austin State University; East Texas Research Center. Nacogdoches, Texas.

Winchester, Robert Glenn. James Pinckney Henderson. San Antonio, Texas: Naylor, 1971.

Winkler, E. W. Platforms of Political Parties in Texas. Austin, Texas: University of Texas. 1916.

Winkler, E. W, ed. "The Bryan-Hayes Correspondence." Southwestern Historical Quarterly 25, October 1921-April 1922.

Wisehart, Marion Karl. Sam Houston. Washington, D.C: Luce, 1962.

Wooley, Bryan. "One-Man Army." Dallas Life Magazine, June 2, 1991. (Armey.)

Wooster, Ralph A. "Early Texas Politics: The Henderson Administration." Southwestern Historical Quarterly 73, October 1969.

Wooster, Ralph A. "An Analysis of the Membership of the Texas Secession Convention." Southwestern Historical Quarterly 62. January 1959.

Wooster, Ralph A. "Ben H. Epperson: East Texas Lawyer, Legislator, and Civic Leader." East Texas Historical Journal 5. March 1967.

Wooten, Dudley G. A Comprehensive History Of Texas, 1685-1897. Dallas, Texas: W. G. Carff. 1898.

Wright, Jim. Balance of Power: Presidents & Congress from the Era of McCarthy to the Age of Gingrich. Atlanta, Georgia: Turner, 1996.

Wright, Jim. The Coming Water Famine. New York, New York: Coward-McCann, 1966.

Wright, Jim. Congressional papers and correspondence. Texas Christian University. Mary Couts Burnet Library. Fort Worth, Texas.

Wright, Jim. "Legislation and the Will of God." In Congress and Conscience, edited by John B. Anderson, pp. 21-50. New York: J. B. Lippincott, 1970.

Wright, Jim. Of Swords and Plowshares: A Collection of the Best Short Writings of Congressman Jim Wright. Fort Worth, Texas: Stafford-Lowdon, 1968.

Wright, Jim. Oral History: June 30, 1969. Lyndon B. Johnson Library. Austin, Texas.

Wright, Jim. Reflections of a Public Man. Fort Worth, Texas: Madison Publishing, 1984.

Wright, Jim. Worth It All: My War for Peace. Washington, D.C.: Brassey's, 1993.

Wright, Jim. You and Your Congressman. New York, New York: Coward-McCann, 1965.

Wurzbach, Harry M. Papers. Congressional History Collection. The Center for American History. University of Texas. Austin, Texas.

Wyatt, Joe. Papers. Special Collections/Archives. Victoria College, Victoria, Texas.

Yarborough, Ralph W. Papers. Congressional History Collection. The Center for American History. University of Texas. Austin, Texas.

Yarborough, Ralph W. Frank Dobie: Man and Friend. Washington: Potomac Corral, The Westerners, 1967.

Yearns, Wilfred Buck. The Confederate Congress. Athens, Georgia: University of Georgia. 1960.

Young, Nancy Beck. Wright Patman: Congressman to the Nation, 1893-1953. Dallas, Texas: Southern Methodist University Press. 2000.

Yarborough, Ralph W. Wright Patman: Congressman to the Nation, 1893-1953. Ph. D. thesis. University of Texas at Austin. 1995.

Young, Valton Joseph. The Speaker's Agent. New York: Vantage Press. 1956.

PHOTO CREDITS

In most cases, the photos used in this book were public domain photos available from members of Congress, former members of Congress, the Library of Congress, or the U.S. Government Printing Office. Many of the photos were from the author's collection of Texas political memorabilia.

The following people or organizations provided the photographs noted. Some generous organizations or individuals donated photos at no cost with no strings attached. They are thanked greatly for their courteous nature. Other organizations provided photos at great cost with numerous strings attached. They are thanked for having the photos available. Most photo sources were in between these two extremes. Their provision of photos is also worthy of thanks.

- *The Texas Observer*, Austin, Texas
    Bruce Alger, George Bush, Kika de la Garza, Bob Eckhardt, Ed Foreman, Bob Gammage, Sam Hall, Jack Hightower, Barbara Jordan, Abraham Kazen, Marvin Leath, Jim Mattox, Bill Patman, Jake Pickle, Bob Price, Bill Sarpalius, Charlie Stenholm, Frank Tejeda, Tom Vandergriff, Richard C. White, Charlie Wilson
- Lynda Welch, June Welch Papers, Waxahachie, Texas
    Peter H. Bell, David G. Burnet, George W. Chilton, Richard Coke, Charles A. Culberson, Andrew J. Hamilton, John Hemphill, James P. Henderson, Rienzi Johnston, Samuel B. Maxey, Earle B. Mayfield, Williamson S. Oldham, Oran M. Roberts, Thomas Rusk, Joseph D. Sayers, Morris Sheppard, Matthias Ward, Louis Wigfall
- Georgetown University, Washington, D.C.
    William T. Clarke, De Witt C. Giddings, Morgan C. Hamilton, John Hancock, Gustave Schleicher, James W. Throckmorton, George W. Whitmore, Asa Willie
- Bob Poage Papers, Baylor Collection of Political Materials, Baylor University, Waco, Texas
    Beau Boulter, John Bryant, Earle Cabell, Martin Dies, Jr., Clyde Garrett, Brady Gentry, Ben Guill, Wingate Lucas, John Lyle, Craig Washington, Milton West, and Joe F. Wilson
- University of Texas at Arlington, Arlington, Texas
    Joe Eagle, Oscar Gillespie, James H. Jones, James F. Miller, John M. Moore, George H. Noonan, Sam Russell, Christopher C. Upson, Eugene Worley
- Library of Congress, Washington, D.C.
    Oscar Callaway, John C. Conner, Edward Degener, James W. Flanagan, Thomas P. Ochiltree, Lucian Parrish, 1887 Group Photo
- Texas State Library and Archives Commission, Austin, Texas
    Carlos Bee and Alexander Gregg
- Institute of Texan Cultures, San Antonio, Texas
    Augustus McCloskey and William B. Wright
- King Ranch Inc., Kingsville, Texas
    Richard Kleberg and Rudolph Kleberg
- Harold B. Simpson Hill College Museum and Research Center, Hillsboro, Texas
    Anthony M. Branch and Caleb C. Herbert
- Center for American History, University of Texas, Austin, Texas
    Martin Dies and 1928-era Group Photo
- Speaker Jim Wright Collection, Texas Christian University, Fort Worth, Texas
    1960 Group Photo
- Texas Collection, Baylor University, Waco, Texas
    Robert L. Henry
- Rosenberg Library, Galveston, Texas
    Robert Hawley

1989861

Made in the USA